Multicultural Issues in Counseling
New Approaches to Diversity

Third Edition

Edited by
Courtland C. Lee

AMERICAN COUNSELING ASSOCIATION
5999 Stevenson Avenue
Alexandria, VA 22304
www.counseling.org

Multicultural Issues in Counseling
New Approaches to Diversity

Third Edition

10   9   8   7   6   5   4   3   2

American Counseling Association
5999 Stevenson Avenue
Alexandria, VA 22304

Director of Publications
Carolyn C. Baker

Production Manager
Bonny E. Gaston

Copy Editor
Sharon Sites

Cover design by Michael J. Comlish

Cover photograph by Garry R. Waltz

Library of Congress Cataloging-in-Publication Data
Multicultural issues in counseling: new approaches to diversity/Courtland C. Lee, editor—3rd ed.
  p. cm.
  ISBN 1-55620-189-3 (alk. paper)
  ISBN 13: 978-1-55620-189-9
  1. Cross-cultural counseling—United States.   I.   Lee, Courtland, C.

BF637.C6M84   2005
158´.3´08—dc22   2005001828

To My Parents, Two of the Greatest of the "Greatest Generation"

Table of Contents

Preface ix
About the Editor xv
About the Contributors xvii

Part I ■ Introduction

1 Multicultural Counseling: A New Paradigm for a New Century 3
Courtland C. Lee and Cara J. Ramsey

2 Entering the *Cross-Cultural Zone:* Meeting the Challenge of Culturally Responsive Counseling 13
Courtland C. Lee

Part II ■ Direction for Culturally Responsive Counseling

The Native American Experience 23

3 When Eagle Speaks: Counseling Native Americans 25
Michael Tlanusta Garrett

The African American Experience 55

4 A Cultural Framework for Counseling African Americans 57
C. Emmanuel Ahia

5 Counseling High-Achieving African Americans 63
Donna Y. Ford and H. Richard Milner

6 Counseling African American Women and Girls 79
Carla Adkison-Bradley and Jo-Ann Lipford Sanders

Table of Contents

7 Counseling African American Male Youth and Men   93
Courtland C. Lee and Deryl F. Bailey

8 Developing Effective Partnerships in Order to Utilize and
Maximize the Resources of the African American Church:
Strategies and Tools for Counseling Professionals   113
Bernard L. Richardson and Lee N. June

The Asian American Experience   125

9 Counseling Strategies for Chinese Americans   127
David Sue

10 Counseling Japanese Americans: From Internment to Reparation   139
Satsuki Ina

11 Counseling Americans of Southeast Asian Descent: The Impact
of the Refugee Experience   151
Rita Chi-Ying Chung and Fred Bemak

12 Counseling Korean Americans   171
Catherine Y. Chang

The Latino American Experience   185

13 Counseling Latinas: Culturally Responsive Interventions   187
Sandra I. Lopez-Baez

14 Counseling Cuban Americans Using the Framework for
Embracing Cultural Diversity   195
Silvia Echevarria-Doan and Martha Gonzalez Marquez

15 Counseling Mexican American College Students   207
*Madonna G. Constantine, Alberta M. Gloria, and
Augustine Barón*

16 Puerto Ricans in the Counseling Process: The Dynamics of
Ethnicity and Race in Social Context   223
Jesse M. Vazquez

The Arab American Experience   233

17 Counseling Arab Americans   235
Morris L. Jackson and Sylvia Nassar-McMillan

The Multiracial Individual and Family Experience 249

18 Counseling Multiracial Individuals and Families 251
Kelley R. Kenney

The Gay/Lesbian/Transgendered Experience 267

19 Counseling Gay Men 269
A. Michael Hutchins

20 Counseling Lesbian Clients 291
Colleen R. Logan

21 Affirmative Counseling With Transgendered Persons 303
Jeffrey Mostade

The Experience of People With Disabilities 319

22 Counseling People With Disabilities: A Sociocultural Minority Group Perspective 321
William F. Hanjorgiris and John H. O'Neill

The Experience of Socioeconomic Disadvantage 343

23 The Culture of Socioeconomic Disadvantage: Practical Approaches to Counseling 345
Claire Bienvenu and Cara J. Ramsey

Part III ■ Professional Issues in Multicultural Counseling

24 Ethical Issues in Multicultural Counseling 357
Beth A. Durodoye

25 Research in Multicultural Counseling: Client Needs and Counselor Competencies 369
Gargi Roysircar

Index 389

Preface

Courtland C. Lee

Since its original publication in 1991 and subsequent second edition in 1997, *Multicultural Issues in Counseling: New Approaches to Diversity* has become an important book in the counseling profession. Both editions of the book have focused on culturally responsive counseling practice. They have provided professional counselors with strategies for culturally responsive intervention with many client groups. In addition, both books have been widely adopted as a textbook in counselor training programs.

Again, developments in the discipline of multicultural counseling have made it necessary to consider a new edition of this book. To stay relevant to counseling practice, it was decided that the time had again come to revisit the content of the book. In addition, three significant events have taken place since the second edition of this book was published. The first event is the start of the new millennium. For professional counselors, the new millennium encourages an examination of our philosophy and practice. It affords us the opportunity to reexamine and potentially redefine our commitment to the art of helping. The second event is the completion of the 2000 U.S. Census. The demographic data from the census suggest that the country has become increasingly diverse along a number of dimensions. This increased diversity underscores the need for counselors to become ever more culturally responsive. The third event involves the tragedies that occurred on September 11, 2001. A day that will live in infamy, it brought home at a number of levels the need to foster greater multicultural action and understanding. All of these events contributed to the decision to produce this third edition.

This edition represents a significant departure from its two predecessors. This book attempts to broaden the scope of multicultural counseling theory and practice. Specifically, this edition extends the concept of multiculturalism beyond the context of race/ethnicity into other important areas of cultural diversity. In addition to an examination of race/ethnicity, this edition also considers the important issues of sexual orientation, disability, and socioeconomic disadvantage.

Like its predecessors, the purpose of this book is to present culturally responsive intervention strategies for counselors and selected human development professionals working with, or preparing to work with, diverse client groups in a variety of settings. It provides practicing counselors and those preparing to enter the profession with direction for culturally responsive counseling with clients from a number of diverse backgrounds.

Focus of the Book

This book deals with multicultural counseling, defined as a relationship between a counselor and a client that takes both the personal *and* cultural experiences of each individual into consideration in the helping process. The focus of the book is on providing a broader perspective on diversity as a way to offer direction for multicultural counseling. The book is devoted to multicultural counseling practice with selected diverse client groups. The ideas presented have been developed out of both the professional and personal experiences of the chapter authors, who are scholars from the specific cultural group in question or have intimate knowledge of a particular group. Like the first two editions, although this book offers guidance for multicultural counseling practice, it is not intended to be a "cookbook" or a "how-to manual." It is designed to help counselors apply their awareness of and knowledge about cultural diversity to appropriate skills development with specific client groups.

Overview of Contents

This book is divided into three parts: Part I, Introduction; Part II, Direction for Culturally Responsive Counseling; and Part III, Professional Issues in Multicultural Counseling. The two chapters in the first part, Introduction, lay a conceptual foundation for the rest of the book. In chapter 1, "Multicultural Counseling: A New Paradigm for a New Century," Courtland C. Lee and Cara J. Ramsey offer a 21st-century paradigm for the discipline of multicultural counseling. They provide a broad perspective on diversity within this paradigm. They also consider the potential promise and possible pitfalls that are inherent in this important paradigm.

In chapter 2, "Entering the *Cross-Cultural Zone*: Meeting the Challenge of Culturally Responsive Counseling," Courtland C. Lee provides a conceptual framework for counseling across cultures and examines important issues that should be considered in addressing the challenges of culturally responsive counseling.

In the second part of the book, Direction for Culturally Responsive Counseling, approaches for counseling specific culturally diverse groups are presented. This section of the book is composed of 21 chapters, each offering ideas and concepts for culturally responsive counseling. These chapters include a review of the cultural dynamics of each group and their role in shaping mental health and the social challenges that often affect development. The authors introduce strategies for addressing these challenges. These counseling practices evolve from an understanding of and appreciation for the unique history and cultural experiences of each group. Significantly, the authors in this part of the book provide the reader with case studies that underscore their ideas on culturally responsive counseling.

The first section of Part II focuses on the Native American experience. In chapter 3, "When Eagle Speaks: Counseling Native Americans," Michael Tlanusta Garrett offers a comprehensive overview and understanding of this cultural group. He first discusses important terminology. Next, he provides a historical context for understanding the Native American experience. Garrett then explores Native American acculturation, traditional values, and worldview as well as spirituality, wellness, and healing practices. The chapter concludes with recommendations for counseling Native American clients.

The second section of Part II deals with the African American experience. In chapter 4, "A Cultural Framework for Counseling African Americans," C. Emmanuel Ahia provides a conceptual framework for counseling with African Americans. He examines a number of African assumptions and cultural traditions inherent in the philosophy known as *Afrocentrism*. Afrocentrism is considered by many scholars as the basis of an African

American worldview. Ahia discusses the relationship of Afrocentrism to the mental health of African Americans.

Donna Y. Ford and H. Richard Milner in chapter 5, "Counseling High-Achieving African Americans," focus attention on a segment of the African American population that has received little attention in the social science literature. They contend that high-achieving African Americans share problems associated with Blacks from all rungs of the socioeconomic ladder and all levels of achievement. However, the quality and quantity of the problems confronting these different groups of African Americans can be markedly different. Ford and Milner also address a dozen variables affecting the socioemotional and psychological well-being of high-achieving Blacks and offer recommendations for counseling with this group.

In chapter 6, "Counseling African American Women and Girls," Carla Adkison-Bradley and Jo-Ann Lipford Sanders provide directions for counselors on how to use culturally appropriate and meaningful interventions with African American women. The first part of the chapter focuses on the influences that affect the development and experiences of African American females. The second part of the chapter focuses on culturally responsive strategies for African American women and girls.

In a similar manner, Courtland C. Lee and Deryl F. Bailey explore the issues and challenges in counseling with African American male youth and men in chapter 7, "Counseling African American Male Youth and Men." Lee and Bailey offer historical and cultural perspectives on the psychosocial development of African American males and offer two case studies that provide strategies for counseling with this client group. The role of the Black church in promoting mental health is explored by Bernard L. Richardson and Lee N. June in chapter 8, "Developing Effective Partnerships in Order to Utilize and Maximize the Resources of the African American Church: Strategies and Tools for Counseling Professionals." They offer intervention strategies that use the resources of this important African American institution. In addition, they provide counselors with specific guidelines for working within a church context.

Part II continues with an exploration of the Asian American experience. In chapter 9, "Counseling Strategies for Chinese Americans," David Sue examines some important Chinese cultural values and their impact on Chinese Americans' development. He presents a case study that illustrates the importance of these values and their influence on the counseling process. An assertiveness group for Chinese Americans is also explored.

Satsuki Ina in chapter 10, "Counseling Japanese Americans: From Internment to Reparation," examines the internment experience of many Japanese Americans during World War II and the resulting psychological ramifications for both internees and members of their families. An intensive group counseling experience for former internees is presented that highlights the social, political, and cultural issues affecting the development of Japanese Americans.

In chapter 11, "Counseling Americans of Southeast Asian Descent: The Impact of the Refugee Experience," Rita Chi-Ying Chung and Fred Bemak examine the cultures of Southeast Asia and the refugee experience of many Americans from that part of the world. They discuss how the refugee experience presents mental health challenges to these people. Chung and Bemak present a comprehensive approach to counseling refugees called the Multilevel Model of psychotherapy. It takes into account the intricacy of the refugees' historical background, past and present stressors, the acculturation process, and the psychosocial ramifications of adapting to a new culture while providing a psychoeducational approach that includes cognitive, affective, and behavioral interventions.

The Korean American experience is examined in chapter 12, "Counseling Korean Americans." Catherine Y. Chang highlights the distinctiveness of Korean Americans. The immigration history, traditional values, acculturation, ethnic identity issues, and mental health issues of Korean Americans are explored in this chapter as well as counseling strategies for understanding and working with this client group.

The Latino American experience comprises the next section of Part II. Sandra I. Lopez-Baez in chapter 13, "Counseling Latinas: Culturally Responsive Interventions," examines important issues to consider when counseling women from this cultural group. Lopez-Baez discusses aspects of Latino culture that relate to the socialization of women. She then analyzes a series of case studies that highlight important counseling issues with Latinas.

In chapter 14, "Counseling Cuban Americans Using the Framework for Embracing Cultural Diversity," Silvia Echevarria-Doan and Martha Gonzalez Marquez expand on their work from the chapter on the framework for cultural awareness in the previous edition of this book. This framework is based on the belief that practitioners need to continually address their own individual issues toward diversity as part of their work with clients if they are to be culturally sensitive. The authors focus on counselors and their use of the framework through description, guidelines, and training/teaching exercises.

Madonna G. Constantine, Alberta M. Gloria, and Augustine Barón explore issues in counseling Mexican American college students in chapter 15, "Counseling Mexican American College Students." The authors explore cultural issues associated with counseling Mexican American college students. They briefly summarize conceptual frameworks that have been designed specifically for counseling Mexican American, Chicano, or Latino college students.

In chapter 16, "Puerto Ricans in the Counseling Process: The Dynamics of Ethnicity and Race in Social Context," Jesse M. Vazquez presents a historical and political overview of the Puerto Rican experience. He also discusses the impact of socioeconomic status on Puerto Ricans' development in the United States. Through a case study, he explores the challenges of racial/ethnic identity and the problems of racism that confront Puerto Ricans along with implications for counselors.

In chapter 17, "Counseling Arab Americans," Morris L. Jackson and Sylvia Nassar-McMillan examine this cultural group, which has not received a great deal of attention in the counseling literature. They examine the diversity of Arab Americans along with important dynamics of Arab culture. Jackson and Nassar-McMillan also consider barriers and possible intervention strategies when counseling Arab Americans. Through a case study, the authors offer specific intervention strategies that counselors can use to increase their effectiveness with Arab American clients.

Chapter 18, "Counseling Multiracial Individuals and Families," is new to this edition of the book. In this chapter, Kelley R. Kenney discusses the counseling issues and concerns of multiracial individuals and families. She first supplies some important definitions to characterize this growing population. Next, Kenney explores key issues and concerns confronting interracial couples and multiracial individuals, including children, adolescents, and adults. Through the use of case studies, she examines the unique issues of culturally responsive counseling with multiracial individuals and families.

The next three chapters are also part of a new addition to this book. They deal with the gay/lesbian/transgendered experience. In chapter 19, "Counseling Gay Men," A. Michael Hutchins explores issues associated with counseling gay men. He provides an overview of the dynamics of the cultural context of gay men. Then, through a series of case studies, Hutchins discusses key aspects of homosexual identity development. He focuses on the evolution of gay identity for men as well as the communities in which they live.

Colleen R. Logan in chapter 20, "Counseling Lesbian Clients," provides counselors with a better understanding of the many issues associated with counseling lesbian clients in an effective and affirming manner. Throughout the chapter are case studies of clinical work with lesbian clients derived from years of the author's experience. These case studies are designed to offer counselors greater insight into and appreciation of the experiences of lesbian individuals and their significant others.

In chapter 21, "Affirmative Counseling With Transgendered Persons," Jeffrey Mostade offers suggestions for affirmative counseling with this client group. He begins with a discussion of the history and content of sex, sexuality, and gender. This discussion is followed by an overview of the four groups of people on the transgendered spectrum. Mostade also discusses ethical issues and barriers to effective counseling with transgendered people.

Chapter 22, "Counseling People With Disabilities: A Sociocultural Minority Group Perspective," also represents a new part of the book. In this chapter, William F. Hanjorgiris and John H. O'Neill examine the issues associated with counseling people with disabilities. They compare and contrast the two predominant approaches to understanding disability— the social constructivist and the essentialist. However, in this chapter, the sociocultural aspects of the social constructivist approach to disability are emphasized.

Chapter 23 is also a new addition to this edition of this book. In this chapter, "The Culture of Socioeconomic Disadvantage: Practical Approaches to Counseling," Claire Bienvenu and Cara J. Ramsey explore the culture of socioeconomic disadvantage. After examining the important characteristics of the culture of poverty, they provide important directions for counseling across the socioeconomic divide. Two case studies illustrate important issues to consider when intervening as a counselor into the culture of poverty.

The third and final part of the book considers two important professional issues that need to be considered in a multicultural context: ethics and research. Beth A. Durodoye in chapter 24, "Ethical Issues in Multicultural Counseling," frames important ethical issues and concepts in a multicultural context and examines strategies relevant to ethical practice with culturally diverse client populations.

In chapter 25, "Research in Multicultural Counseling: Client Needs and Counselor Competencies," Gargi Roysircar concludes the book with a discussion of research concerning the impact of the counselor on the minority client in terms of the counselor's cultural and racial awareness, the counselor's application of cultural knowledge, the counselor's recognition of client–counselor racial dynamics, and the counselor's interface with minority client mistrust. Roysircar also addresses related research on multicultural counseling competencies and future directions.

Acknowledgments

Like its predecessors, this book owes its development to a number of people. As editor, I would like to use this space to acknowledge their contributions to the project. Again, I must start by thanking the contributors for the time and creative energy they put into preparing their chapters for this edition of the book. Their scholarly efforts are intensely admired and greatly appreciated.

A special note of appreciation goes to Carolyn Baker, ACA Director of Publications, for her support and incredible patience. Her quiet oversight and encouragement were most welcome. Carolyn's belief in this project helped to keep me motivated and focused through the challenging editorial process.

I am also deeply indebted to Kimberly Grillo and Cara Ramsey, who served as my editorial assistants in the development of this book. I am grateful to them for dealing effectively with all of the complex editing issues and "administrivia" associated with preparing the manuscript for this edition of the book.

Finally, I must acknowledge my wife, Vivian. Thank you for your love, support, and understanding. You said it could be done, and you were right!

About the Editor

Courtland C. Lee received his PhD in counseling from Michigan State University. He is professor and director of the Counselor Education Program at the University of Maryland, College Park. His areas of research specialization include multicultural counseling and men's issues in counseling. He has written, edited, or coedited four books on multicultural counseling. He has also written three books on counseling African American male youth. In addition, he has written numerous articles and book chapters on counseling across cultures. Dr. Lee is the former editor of the *Journal of Multicultural Counseling and Development* and serves on the advisory board of the *International Journal for the Advancement of Counselling.* Dr. Lee is a past president of the American Counseling Association and the Association for Multicultural Counseling and Development.

About the Contributors

Carla Adkison-Bradley is an associate professor and training director of the doctoral program in counselor education at Western Michigan University. She has served on the board of directors of the Council for Accreditation of Counseling and Related Educational Programs. Dr. Bradley has published numerous journal articles and book chapters that primarily focus on faculty development and doctoral preparation in counselor education. She is a Licensed Professional Clinical Counselor.

C. Emmanuel Ahia received his BA and MA from Wheaton College and his PhD from Southern Illinois University, Carbondale. He also received a JD from the University of Arkansas School of Law. He is associate professor of counseling and school psychology at Rider University Graduate School. He is a National Certified Counselor and is licensed to practice law in Pennsylvania. He has published in the areas of mental health law, family legal issues, conflict resolution, and sociopolitical aspects of multicultural identity development. He is a past president of the New Jersey Association for Multicultural Counseling and has served on the Pennsylvania Bar Association's committee on older persons' legal affairs.

Deryl F. Bailey is an assistant professor in the Department of Counseling and Human Development Services at the University of Georgia. Before earning his education specialist and doctorate degrees from the University of Virginia, he worked as a secondary school counselor. His areas of specialization include school counseling, group work, multicultural and diversity issues in schools, issues related to professional development for school counselors, adolescent African American male development, and the development and implementation of enrichment and empowerment initiatives for adolescents of color. He is the founder and director of the award winning initiative Empowered Youth Programs.

Augustine Barón received his PsyD in clinical psychology from the University of Illinois at Urbana–Champaign. He is on the psychology faculty of Walden University, a distance learning university based in Minneapolis. His areas of specialization include multicultural counseling, gay men's issues in counseling, clinical supervision, and psychotherapy outcome research. He has edited a book on Chicano psychology and has authored or coauthored a variety of journal articles and book chapters on multicultural counseling. Dr. Barón has served on the editorial boards of several journals, including the *Journal of Counseling & Development*. He is director of training emeritus of the Counseling and Mental Health Center at the University of Texas in Austin.

Fred Bemak is currently a professor and the program coordinator for the Counseling and Development Program in the Graduate School of Education at George Mason University.

He has done extensive work in the area of social justice and mental health, working in 30 countries and throughout the United States. He is a former Fulbright Scholar, a Kellogg International Fellow, and a recipient of the International Exchange of Experts and Research Fellowship through the World Rehabilitation Fund. At George Mason University, Dr. Bemak has facilitated the development of master's and doctoral training programs that emphasize multiculturalism, social justice, leadership, and advocacy, and has been working with these issues for over 30 years. He is a former director of an Upward Bound program, the Massachusetts Department of Mental Health Region I Adolescent Treatment Program, and a program funded by the National Institute of Mental Health that provided national consultation and training to community-based mental health programs. Dr. Bemak continues to provide consultation, training, and workshops for many community and school-based programs and has published numerous professional journal articles and book chapters, and four books that emphasize cross-cultural counseling, equity, and social justice.

Claire Bienvenu received her PhD in higher education administration with a concentration in college counseling from Louisiana State University. She is director of the University Success Program and an adjunct faculty member of the College of Education at the University of New Orleans. Her areas of specialization include retention of at-risk populations in higher education and college counseling. Dr. Bienvenu is a past president of the Louisiana Counseling Association.

Catherine Y. Chang is an assistant professor in the Department of Counseling and Psychological Services at Georgia State University. Previously, she was an assistant professor in the Counseling Program at Clemson University. She received her doctorate in counselor education from the University of North Carolina at Greensboro. Her areas of interest include multicultural counseling and supervision, Asian and Korean concerns, and multicultural issues in assessment.

Rita Chi-Ying Chung is an associate professor in the Counseling and Development Program, College of Education and Human Development, George Mason University. Her research focuses on social justice and multiculturalism through the psychosocial adjustment of refugees and immigrants, interethnic group relations and racial stereotypes, trafficking of Asian girls, coping strategies in dealing with racism and its impact on psychological well-being, cross-cultural and multicultural issues in mental health, and cross-cultural achievement motivation and aspirations. Dr. Chung has lived and worked in the Pacific Rim, Asia, and Latin America. She is currently coauthoring a book with Dr. Fred Bemak on social justice and multiculturalism.

Madonna G. Constantine is professor of psychology and education and chair of the Department of Counseling and Clinical Psychology at Teachers College, Columbia University. She received her PhD in counseling psychology from the University of Memphis. Dr. Constantine has numerous publications related to her research and professional interests. She currently serves as associate editor of *Cultural Diversity and Ethnic Minority Psychology* and the *Journal of Black Psychology*. Her research and professional interests include the mental health of persons of African descent; multicultural competence issues in counseling, training, and supervision; and career development of people of color and psychologists in training.

Beth A. Durodoye received her EdD in counselor education from the University of Virginia. She is an associate professor of counseling at the University of North Texas. Her specialty area is multicultural counseling. Dr. Durodoye's scholarly interests include cross-cultural advocacy, race and ethnic relations, and the mental health needs of persons of African descent. She is the author or coauthor of numerous publications, including a book, articles, and book chapters. She has also presented papers at local, state, regional, and national conferences.

Silvia Echevarria-Doan is an associate professor of marriage and family counseling at the University of Florida in Gainesville. Her scholarly work reflects her interest in strength-based family therapy and resilience, multicultural approaches in family therapy, qualitative research methodology, family therapy training, and family violence. She has presented internationally, nationally, and at state and local conferences on many of these topics and has received awards recognizing her research, teaching, and focus on cultural diversity issues as an educator.

Donna Y. Ford received her PhD in urban education from Cleveland State University. She is Betts Chair of Education and Human Development at Peabody College, Vanderbilt University. Dr. Ford's areas of research include gifted education, with a focus on identification and assessment; underrepresentation; underachievement; and multicultural curricula. She has written three books and several articles on gifted African American students. Dr. Ford consults on a national level with school districts and organizations in their efforts to become culturally competent and in their efforts to identify and serve more gifted students of color.

Michael Tlanusta Garrett, Eastern Band of Cherokee, is associate professor of counseling and chair of the Department of Educational Leadership and Counseling at Old Dominion University. He holds a PhD in counseling and counselor education and an MEd in counseling and development from the University of North Carolina at Greensboro and a BA in psychology from North Carolina State University. He is author and coauthor of more than 50 articles and chapters dealing with multiculturalism, group work, wellness and spirituality, school counseling, working with youth, and counseling Native Americans. Dr. Garrett also has authored the book *Walking on the Wind: Cherokee Teachings for Harmony and Balance* (1998) and coauthored the books *Medicine of the Cherokee: The Way of Right Relationship* (1996), *Cherokee Full Circle: A Practical Guide to Ceremonies and Traditions* (2002), and *Native American Faith in America* (2003).

Alberta M. Gloria received her doctorate in counseling psychology from Arizona State University and is a professor in the Department of Counseling Psychology and adjunct faculty with the Chicana/Latina Studies Program at the University of Wisconsin–Madison. Her primary research interests include psychosociocultural factors for Latina/Latino and other racial and ethnic students in higher education. Addressing issues of cultural congruity, educational and social coping supports, and academic well-being, her work has appeared in journals such as *Cultural Diversity and Ethnic Minority Psychology, Hispanic Journal of Behavioral Sciences*, and *Journal of College Student Development*. An active member of the American Psychological Association, she is currently chair of the Section on Ethnic and Racial Diversity for Division 17 (Society of Counseling Psychology) and member-at-large of Division 45 (Society for the Psychological Study of Ethnic Minority Issues). She was awarded the 2002 Emerging Professional Award from Division 45 for outstanding early career contributions in promoting ethnic minority issues in the field of psychology. More recently, Dr. Gloria received the 2003 Kenneth and Mamie Clark Award from the American Psychological Association of Graduate Students for her contributions to the professional development of ethnic minority graduate students.

William F. Hanjorgiris received his PhD in counseling psychology from Fordham University. He maintains a private psychotherapy practice in New York City and specializes in men's concerns. He is also the staff psychologist responsible for behavioral health at Rivington House–The Nicholas A. Rango Healthcare facility, the largest residential AIDS treatment facility in the United States. Dr. Hanjorgiris provided crisis intervention and support to recovery workers at ground zero shortly after 9/11 and is a member of the New York State Psychological Association Disaster Response Network. His research interests focus on men, stress, coping, disability, stigma, and identity development.

A. Michael Hutchins received his PhD in counseling from the University of Idaho. He is a licensed professional counselor in private practice in Tucson, Arizona, and is an adjunct faculty member in the Department of Education Psychology at the University of Arizona, Tucson. He specializes in working with men who have histories of sexual abuse and trauma and with the sexual identity developmental concerns of adolescent and adult males. He is a past president of the Association for Specialists in Group Work and of Counselors for Social Justice and is a past chair of the Association for Gay, Lesbian, and Bisexual Issues in Counseling. He currently serves on the editorial board of *The Journal of Gay, Lesbian, Bisexual, and Transgendered Issues in Counseling*. In addition, he is a member of the City of Tucson Gay, Lesbian, Bisexual, and Transgendered Issues Commission, where he chairs the Social Services Committee. He has written in the areas of multicultural group work, social justice/human rights, and sexual identity development.

Satsuki Ina received her PhD in counselor education from Oregon State University. She is professor emeritus at California State University, Sacramento. She is founder and director of the Family Study Center in Sacramento, a community-based counseling service and postgraduate clinical training program with an emphasis on multicultural counseling. In her private practice, she specializes in working with transracial adoption issues, cross-cultural marriages, diversity in the workplace, and ethnic identity and victimization from racism. She has produced and directed two documentary films about the World War II incarceration of Japanese Americans, *Children of the Camps* (2000) and *From a Silk Cocoon* (2005). She has developed viewers' guides and teachers' guides to accompany the documentaries.

Morris L. Jackson received his BS and MEd from the University of Hartford and his EdD from George Washington University. His contribution to the counseling profession has focused on multicultural and diversity counseling for the last 30 years. He studied the Arabic language and culture at the King Saud University in Riyadh, Saudi Arabia, and worked for several years as a full-time educational consultant to the Royal Embassy of Saudi Arabia Cultural Mission in Washington, DC. Currently, he is director of community relations and gift officer for American University in Washington, DC. He has been a board member for several nonprofit organizations and has served on the editorial board for the *Journal of Multicultural Counseling* and the *Journal of Psychology in Africa*. He is also adjunct professor of counseling at George Mason University in Fairfax, Virginia. Having traveled throughout Europe, Northern Africa, the Middle East, and the Caribbean, he has interest in cross-cultural counseling and training and has provided consultations to both the private and public sectors.

Lee N. June serves as assistant provost for academic student services and multicultural issues, vice president for student affairs and services, and professor of education at Michigan State University. He is editor or coeditor of four books: *The Black Family: Past, Present, and Future* (1991); *Men to Men* (1996); *Evangelism and Discipleship in African American Churches* (1999); and *Counseling in African American Communities* (2002). He earned a bachelor of science in biology from Tuskegee University, and a master of education in counseling and a master of arts and doctorate of philosophy in clinical psychology from the University of Illinois at Urbana–Champaign. He also did further studies at Haverford College in psychology and at Duke University's Divinity School. Some of his research and writing have been in the areas of effective psychological service delivery, psychology of the African American church, short-term counseling, and factors affecting the retention of undergraduate students.

Kelley R. Kenney received her EdD in counseling from George Washington University in Washington, DC. She is a professor in the graduate Department of Counseling and Human Services at Kutztown University in Kutztown, Pennsylvania, and serves as the program coordinator for the student affairs administration and student affairs college counseling program tracks. Dr. Kenney's areas of specialization are college students' development and multicultural counseling related to the multiracial population. Dr. Kenney has conducted workshops and written several articles and book chapters on counseling the multiracial population. She is also a coauthor of the book *Counseling Multiracial Families* and the counseling training videotape *Counseling the Multiracial Population: Couples, Individuals, and Families.* Dr. Kenney is a past chair of the North Atlantic Region of the American Counseling Association (ACA), is cochair of the Multiracial/Multiethnic Counseling Interest Network of ACA, and has been president of Pennsylvania's Counselor Educators and Supervisors Association.

Colleen R. Logan received her PhD in counselor education from the University of Virginia. She is an associate professor and program chair of the Counseling Psychology Program at Argosy University, Washington, DC. She currently serves on the American Counseling Association's Governing Council. She has presented both locally and nationally on myriad issues related to counseling gay, lesbian, bisexual, and transgendered clients. She has also authored or coauthored a number of articles and chapters as well as a book regarding how to work effectively with gay, lesbian, bisexual, and transgendered clients and their significant others.

Sandra I. Lopez-Baez received her PhD in counseling from Kent State University. She is an associate professor and coordinator of the Mental Health Counseling Track in the Counselor Education Program at the University of Virginia. Her research interests include multicultural counseling and diversity, counselors' sense of self across cultures, and the use of Gestalt therapy with Latinos. She has written a number of chapters, columns, and articles for counseling publications. She is a past president of Counselors for Social Justice, a division of the American Counseling Association, and has served on various committees of ACA.

Martha Gonzalez Marquez received her PhD in marriage and family therapy from Purdue University. She is a clinical member and approved supervisor for the American Association for Marriage and Family Therapy (AAMFT). She is also an active member of the American Family Therapy Academy. She currently pursues her qualitative research and clinical interests in cultural awareness and diversity as an associate and faculty member of the Gainesville Family Institute, a postgraduate institute accredited by the Commission on Accreditation of Marriage and Family Therapy Education of the AAMFT.

H. Richard Milner earned his PhD in curriculum studies from The Ohio State University. He is assistant professor of education in the Department of Teaching and Learning at Peabody College of Vanderbilt University. His areas of research include teachers' influences on students' opportunities to learn and academic achievement and persistence among African American students.

Jeffrey Mostade received his PhD in counseling and human services from Kent State University. He is in private practice as a trainer and geriatric care manager with Senex Eldercare, Counseling, and Training in Cleveland, Ohio. His areas of research specialization include diversity counseling, gay and lesbian aging, and the use of reflecting teams as a group modality. He has written two book chapters on diversity counseling and has also published peer-reviewed articles. Dr. Mostade presently serves on the Leadership Council of the Lesbian and Gay Aging Interests Network of the American Society on Aging. He also serves on the Advisory Council of the Department of Senior and Adult Services in Cuyahoga County, Ohio.

Sylvia Nassar-McMillan is an associate professor of counselor education at North Carolina State University. Her scholarship and service revolve around ethnic and gender diversity, specifically around issues of Arab American acculturation and ethnic identity development. She has been involved with the professionalization of counseling, both domestically and internationally, for over 15 years and currently serves on the board of directors of the National Board for Certified Counselors, the Advisory Committee of the Arab American Institute Census Information Center, and the Scientific Committee of the Arab American Community Center for Economic and Social Services. Both of her parents are foreign born, and her paternal heritage is Palestinian.

John H. O'Neill received a PhD in rehabilitation counselor education from Syracuse University and is a Nationally Certified Rehabilitation Counselor. Currently, he is professor and coordinator of counselor education at Hunter College, City University of New York. His research focuses on the community integration and employment of individuals with disabilities.

Cara J. Ramsey received her MEd in school counseling from the University of Maryland, College Park, concentrating on counseling in the urban school setting. She received her BA in psychology from Ohio University. She is currently a school counselor at Col. E. Brooke Lee Middle School in Silver Spring, Maryland.

Bernard L. Richardson received a BA in sociology from Howard University, an MA and PhD in counseling from Michigan State University, and a master of divinity from Yale University. He is currently the dean of the Andrew Rankin Memorial Chapel and associate professor of pastoral care and counseling in the School of Divinity at Howard University. He is coeditor of the first edition of *Multicultural Issues in Counseling: New Approaches to Diversity.* His research, teaching, and writing are in the area of pastoral care and counseling.

Gargi Roysircar is the founding director of the Multicultural Center for Research and Practice (www.multiculturalcenter.org) and professor of clinical psychology at Antioch New England Graduate School. She does research on the interface of acculturation and ethnic identity with the mental health of immigrants and ethnic minorities, worldview differences between and within cultural groups, multicultural competencies and training in professional psychology, and multicultural assessment and instrumentation. She has written numerous journal articles and book chapters on these topics. Her recent coedited books are *Multicultural Competencies: A Guidebook of Practices* (2003), *Multicultural Counseling Competencies 2003: Association for Multicultural Counseling and Development* (2003), and *Handbook for Social Justice in Counseling Psychology* (2005). She is a fellow of the American Psychological Association and a past president of the Association for Multicultural Counseling and Development. She is the editor of the *Journal of Multicultural Counseling and Development.*

Jo-Ann Lipford Sanders received her PhD in counseling from Kent State University. She is an associate professor and director of the Counseling Program at Heidelberg College in Tiffin, Ohio. Her areas of research specialization include multicultural counseling and African American girls'/women's issues in counseling. She has written and edited articles, book chapters, and a monograph on counseling with African Americans. She is a professional clinical counselor.

David Sue is a professor of psychology and an associate of the Center for Cross-Cultural Research at Western Washington University. He has served as the director of the psychology clinic and was the chairperson of the Mental Health Counseling Program for 12 years. He received his PhD in clinical psychology at Washington State University. His research interests revolve around process and outcome variables in cross-cultural counseling. He is the coauthor of *Counseling the Culturally Diverse, Understanding Abnormal Behavior,* and *Essentials of Abnormal Behavior* and is currently writing a text on counseling with his wife, Diane.

Jesse M. Vazquez received his PhD in counseling from New York University. He is professor of counselor education and currently chairperson of the Department of Educational and Community Programs at Queens College, City University of New York. He has served as coordinator of the Counselor Education Program and for more than 25 years was the director of the Puerto Rican Studies Program at Queens College. He has worked as a counselor and consultant in a variety of social service agencies and educational settings. He is past president of the National Association for Ethnic Studies and continues to serve on its board of directors. In addition, Dr. Vazquez was a founding board member of the Puerto Rican Studies Association. His articles, chapters, and monographs have focused on issues related to ethnic studies, multicultural education, and counseling across cultures.

Introduction

Multicultural Counseling: A New Paradigm for a New Century

1

Courtland C. Lee and Cara J. Ramsey

Counseling as a profession has always been influenced by the society in which it is practiced. To understand the nuances of counseling, it is necessary for one to appreciate the prevailing social context that influences its theory and practice. In the United States in the 21st century, counseling as a profession must be understood within the context of cultural diversity. This is because American society has experienced tremendous change over the past five decades. The social changes in the last half of the 20th century contributed to a wider recognition that the United States is truly a culturally pluralistic nation. An understanding of the dynamics of this cultural pluralism must underscore the theory and practice of counseling in the diverse realities of the 21st century.

To fully appreciate counseling and human development within the context of the cultural diversity of American society, one must understand that the notion of diversity is dramatically affected by changing demographics. For many years, cultural diversity was considered within the confines of racial or ethnic differences. However, in the demographic realities of the 21st century, diversity as a concept must be considered in a broader context. This broader diversity context should form the basis for effective multicultural counseling.

The purpose of this chapter and indeed this entire book is to provide this broader perspective on diversity as a way to offer direction for multicultural counseling. The chapter begins with an overview of the changing demographic realities that form the basis of cultural diversity in American society. Within the context of this overview, a definition for multicultural counseling is offered next. A new paradigm for considering the discipline of multicultural counseling along with its promise and pitfalls concludes the chapter.

Changing Demographics: The New Reality

Contemporary counseling theory and practice are greatly influenced by the new realities that have been promulgated by changing demographics. Although changes in the racial/ethnic makeup of the country are occurring, it is important to note that there are other demographic considerations to the new emerging level of diversity in the country. Data indicate that groups of people long marginalized or disenfranchised along other dimensions are making their voices heard or being recognized. These areas of diversity include sexual orientation, disability, and socioeconomic status.

Race and Ethnicity

Projections of the U.S. population into the 21st century indicate that by the year 2050, the non-Hispanic White population will decrease to 53% of the total population, while 25% of the population will be Hispanic; 15% Black; 1% American Indian, Eskimo, or Aleut; and 9% Asian or Pacific Islander (Day, 1996). Contributing factors to the shift in population distribution include higher birth rates of people of color, increased immigration from non-European parts of the world, and higher White mortality rates as more of this population enters old age (Day, 1996). Significantly, with the projected increase in the U.S. minority population, people of color are now the fastest growing portion of the labor force (U.S. Department of Labor, Bureau of Labor Statistics, 2004). Moreover, by 2020, most school-age children attending public schools will come from diverse cultural, ethnic, and/or racial backgrounds (National Center for Educational Statistics, 1997).

Sexual Orientation

It is difficult to determine the number of lesbian, gay, and transgender (LGT) youth in the United States, in part because LGT youth may fear the consequences of coming out or may not have self-identified their sexual orientations or gender identities yet. However, conservative estimates based on the U.S. high school population in 2002 suggest that there were approximately 689,000 students who may have identified themselves as homosexual or bisexual, have same-sex attractions, or have same-sex sexual experiences (Cianciotto & Cahill, 2003).

Although there are only conservative estimates regarding the number of LGT youth today, the 2000 U.S. Census collected data for same-sex unmarried partner households and has released information on gay and lesbian coupled households (Smith & Gates, 2001). However, these demographics may be a dramatic undercount of the actual lesbian and gay population. That being said, it is estimated that gays and lesbians comprise approximately 5% of the total U.S. population over age 18 (Smith & Gates, 2001). Moreover, substantially disproportionate increases in same-sex cohabiting unmarried partners were reported in the 2000 Census, with nearly all of the U.S. counties having self-reporting same-sex couples compared with slightly more than half of the counties in the 1990 Census (Bradford, Barrett, & Honnold, 2002). Thus, conservative estimates and limited information depict a growing LGT population that is still underrepresentative of the true LGT population in the United States.

Disability

Children and adults with disabilities make up a notable portion of the U.S. population. In fact, a 6-year study currently examining students with disabilities has found that students between the ages of 6 and 13 made up 11% of all children receiving special education services (National Dissemination Center for Children With Disabilities, 2003).

At the turn of the 21st century, it was reported that there were 53 million adults with disabilities in the United States in 1997. Out of this population, 33 million had a severe disability, and 10 million needed assistance with activities of daily living. These figures are consistent with the Survey of Income and Program Participation that estimated that 1 in 5 adults had some level of disability (U.S. Census Bureau, 2001).

Socioeconomic Disadvantage

Although the United States continues to be an affluent country, there are still large numbers of individuals who experience socioeconomic disadvantage. Census data indicate that 12.1% of the U.S. population were living below the official poverty thresholds in 2002 (Proctor & Dalaker, 2003). The number of people classified in "severe poverty" represented 40.7% of this population. In 1999, although the child poverty rate dropped to the lowest rate in 20 years, it was still significantly high with 1 in 6 children living in poverty (U.S. Census Bureau, 2001). The rates of socioeconomically disadvantaged people disaggregated by race in 2002 were 8% for non-Hispanic Whites, approximately 10% for Asians, approximately 24% for Blacks, and approximately 22% for Hispanics (Proctor & Dalaker, 2003). Other demographics included a rise in the number of families in poverty between 2001 and 2002, including married-couple families and female householder families. In fact, in 2002, half of all families in poverty were composed of a female householder and no husband present. Thus, the poverty experience varies on a number of dimensions, including age group, race/ethnicity, and family type (U.S. Census Bureau, 2001).

Multicultural Counseling Defined

The changing demographics of American society delineated in the previous section make it imperative that we consider a definition of multicultural counseling that is appropriate for the process of counseling across cultures. Broadly conceptualized, multicultural counseling considers the personality dynamics and cultural backgrounds of both counselor and client in creating a therapeutic environment in which these two individuals can purposefully interact. Multicultural counseling, therefore, takes into consideration the cultural background and individual experiences of diverse clients and how their psychosocial needs might be identified and met through counseling (Lee, 1997; Sue & Sue, 2002). Within this context, professional counselors must consider differences in areas such as language, social class, gender, sexual orientation, disability, and ethnicity between helper and client. These factors may be potential impediments to effective intervention, and counselors need to work to overcome the barriers that such variables might produce in the helping process.

Significantly, the concept of multicultural counseling has become the impetus for the development of a generic theory of multiculturalism that has become recognized as the fourth theoretical force in the profession (Pedersen, 1991). As such, multicultural theory joins the other three major traditions—psychodynamic theory, cognitive–behavioral theory, and existential–humanistic theory—as primary explanations of human development. Basic to the theory of multiculturalism is the notion that both client and counselor bring to the therapeutic dyad a variety of cultural variables related to things such as age, gender, sexual orientation, education, disability, religion, ethnic background, and socioeconomic status. In essence, cultural diversity is a characteristic of all counseling relationships; therefore, all counseling is multicultural in nature (Pedersen, 1991; Sue, Ivey, & Pedersen, 1996). A generic theory of multiculturalism provides a broad conceptual framework for counseling practice.

This evolution of multicultural counseling into a theoretical force with a broad framework for practice implies some important tenets for theory and practice. According to the definition discussed above, there are four basic tenets of multicultural counseling:

1. Culture refers to any group of people who identify or associate with one another on the basis of some common purpose, need, or similarity of background.

2. All counseling is cross-cultural in nature.
3. Multicultural counseling places an emphasis on human diversity in all of its many forms.
4. Culturally responsive counselors develop awareness, knowledge, and skills to intervene effectively into the lives of people from culturally diverse backgrounds.

Multicultural Counseling: A New Paradigm

The definition of multicultural counseling and its four basic tenets suggest a new paradigm. For most of the last four decades, multicultural counseling has been considered the discipline that focuses on the mental health and development of ethnic minority populations. Culturally responsive counselors were considered those who had developed the awareness, knowledge, and skills to work effectively with clients of color, in particular, African American, Hispanic American, Asian American, and Native American individuals.

The idea that counseling clients of color requires awareness, knowledge, and skills that differ from the traditions of the profession was formally developed in the 1960s and 1970s. Those decades, a period of social and political ferment in America, saw the rise of a generation of scholars of color who made major contributions to the profession. Many of these thinkers (Padilla, Ruiz, & Alvarez, 1975; Sue & Sue, 1977; Trimble, 1974; Vontress, 1969), ethnic minority counterparts to Carl Rogers, Albert Ellis, and Fritz Perls, stated that the cultures of people of color were qualitatively different from European-based White culture. Therefore, the validity of theories and techniques grounded in European and European American cultural traditions had to be questioned when applied to counseling interactions with people of color. These pioneering scholars established new theoretical and practical directions for multicultural counseling.

It is important that in the last two decades of the 20th century, other groups of people who had been marginalized, disenfranchised, or oppressed in different but similar ways to people of color became empowered and pressed for access to societal rights and privileges. Movements among women, gay/lesbian/bisexual/transgendered individuals, people with disabilities, and older individuals have underscored the importance of diversity and inclusiveness within American society.

It is not surprising that these movements have affected the theory and practice of counseling. New ideas about counseling individuals from these distinct groups have emerged in recent years (Barret & Logan, 2002; Hershenson, 1990; Kopala & Keitel, 2003; Myers & Schwiebert, 1996; Pope-Davis & Coleman, 2000). One theme that is evident in the literature on counseling with individuals from these groups is that therapeutic effectiveness must be considered within a context that encompasses the tenets of multicultural counseling.

Given this important theme, a new multicultural counseling paradigm has emerged. This paradigm is based on a consideration of diversity from a multifaceted perspective. No longer can multicultural counseling be focused exclusively on concepts of race and ethnicity; rather, it must take into consideration broader issues of diversity. In the new paradigm, multicultural counseling is expanded beyond notions of race and ethnicity to include other important aspects of cultural diversity, such as sexual orientation, disability, and socioeconomic disadvantage.

In this paradigm, culturally responsive counselors must have the awareness, knowledge, and skills to effectively address the many facets of cultural diversity that clients may present. Not only must culturally responsive counselors have competencies to deal with race and ethnicity, but they also must have the ability to address broader issues of cultural diversity.

The New Promise of the Multicultural Counseling Paradigm

The promise of the new paradigm of multicultural counseling can be considered in several significant ways. First, it is evident that traditional counseling theory has been enriched by the diverse notions of optimal mental health and normal development inherent in multicultural thought. The ideas on counseling theory and practice put forth by scholars from diverse cultural backgrounds that have emerged in the counseling literature, particularly in the past several decades, have generated an important new knowledge base. This base includes the fundamental concept that cultural differences are real and must be actively considered in counseling interventions. The awareness emerging from the multicultural paradigm has generated a realization that counseling as a profession must be inclusive of a variety of ways of thinking, feeling, and behaving as well as responsive to diverse worldviews (Barret & Logan; 2002; Hershenson, 1990; Kopala & Keitel, 2003; Myers & Schwiebert, 1996; Pope-Davis & Coleman, 2000).

A second example of the promise of the new paradigm is the fact that multicultural notions of counseling have fostered a new sense of social responsibility and activism within the profession. Working with culturally diverse clients, counselors have often been forced to consider the negative effects of phenomena such as racism, sexism, homophobia, ageism, and other forms of oppression on the development of culturally diverse client groups (Lee, 1998). This appreciation for the nature of oppression has led to an awareness that the etiology of problems often lies not in clients but rather in intolerant or restrictive environments. The only way that many client groups will be able to maximize abilities and interests is to eradicate these systemic impediments to their development (Lee, 1998).

Counselors who work with culturally diverse client groups, therefore, have been called on to become agents of systemic change by channeling energy and skill into helping clients from diverse backgrounds break down institutional and social barriers to optimal development. When necessary, mental health professionals must be willing to act on behalf of disenfranchised clients in an advocacy role, actively challenging long-standing traditions and preconceived notions that may stand in the way of optimal mental health and development. With the evolution of multicultural counseling, counselors are realizing, perhaps as never before, that if they are not a part of the solution, then they are a part of the problem (Lee, 1998).

Third, the promise of the multicultural counseling paradigm is evident in the emergence of the culturally competent counselor. Such an individual is one who has the awareness, knowledge, and skills to successfully intervene in the lives of clients from diverse backgrounds. A culturally competent counselor uses strategies and techniques that are consistent with the life experiences and cultural values of clients. To implement these strategies and techniques, such a professional must have awareness and knowledge related to issues of cultural diversity (Roysircar, Arredondo, Fuertes, Ponterotto, & Toporek, 2003).

A culturally responsive counseling professional is able to view each client as a unique individual while simultaneously taking into consideration his or her common experiences as a human being (i.e., the developmental challenges that face all people) as well as the specific experiences that come from his or her cultural background. In addition, a culturally responsive counseling professional must constantly be in touch with his or her own personal and cultural experiences as a unique human being who happens to be a professional counselor.

The growing demand for this type of helper has brought about a renaissance in the professional development of counselors. The need to be culturally responsive has put the responsibility on counselors to examine their own cultural heritage, values, and biases and how they might affect clients from diverse backgrounds. In addition, counselors have been required to gain knowledge about the history, experiences, and cultural values of diverse client groups. The acquisition of such cultural knowledge has been found to be important in developing empathy toward culturally diverse clients. It also forms the basis for using counseling skills that are consistent with clients' cultural backgrounds and individual experiences (Roysircar et al., 2003).

Potential Pitfalls of the Multicultural Counseling Paradigm

Although the multicultural counseling paradigm holds much promise within the profession, there are some potential pitfalls to its realization. First, in considering the concept of cultural diversity in counseling, there is the danger of assuming that all people from a specific cultural group are the same and that one methodological approach is universally applicable in any counseling intervention with them. Indeed, if one reviews much of the psychological or counseling literature related to multicultural issues, one might be left with the impression that there is an all-encompassing reality for any particular cultural group and that all people from that group act, feel, and think in a homogeneous fashion. Such an impression invariably leads to a monolithic perspective on the experiences of a specific group of people as well as stereotypical thinking, in which individuals are considered indistinguishable from one another in terms of attitudes, behaviors, and values. Counseling professionals with such a perspective run the risk of approaching clients not as distinctive human beings with individual experiences but rather merely as cultural stereotypes.

Second, in a similar vein, it has been implied that the focus on cultural dissimilarities in multicultural counseling theory and practice serves to accentuate human differences and has the potential for fostering renewed forms of intolerance (Patterson, 1996; Weinrach & Thomas, 2002). This is certainly a distinct possibility if counselors reduce cultural realities to a stereotypic level.

The third potential pitfall of the discipline has to do with perceived and actual counselor competence. As multicultural counseling continues to question the validity of traditional counseling practice with diverse groups of people, there is a danger that professional counselors will become self-conscious about their level of competence to work with diverse clients. A question often asked by counselors in a frustrated tone is "How can I really be effective with a client whose cultural background is different from mine?" Groping for an answer to this crucial question has the potential of driving many talented professionals away from cross-cultural counseling encounters.

Likewise, those professional counselors who are not aware of cultural dynamics and their impact on the psychosocial development of clients from diverse backgrounds may run the risk of engaging in unethical conduct in their interventions (Delgado-Romero, 2003; LaFromboise, Foster, & James, 1996; Ridley, Liddle, Hill, & Li, 2001). In recent years, major steps have been taken to ensure that ethical codes that guide counseling practice are responsive to diverse cultural realities (Delgado-Romero, 2003; Pack-Brown & Williams, 2003). Without a solid understanding of changes in ethical codes, ethical conduct could be a constant challenge and the fourth potential pitfall to avoid when counseling across cultures.

Fifth, it must be understood that when traditional counseling is considered in a multicultural context, it often becomes a sociopolitical process. Specifically, for many people from culturally diverse backgrounds, counseling has been perceived as a tool of oppression and social control (Sue & Sue, 2002). This perception is due, in large measure, to the fact that the only counseling many culturally diverse people have often received has been a forced, rather than a voluntary, experience with a culturally insensitive or unresponsive agent of some aspect of the broad social welfare system. Counseling in the perception of many people from diverse cultural backgrounds, therefore, becomes a process that agents of the dominant society use to forcibly control their lives and well-being.

The final pitfall of the multicultural counseling paradigm involves the challenge of moving beyond awareness and knowledge into actual practice. Although the renaissance in the professional development of counselors has advanced the notion of culturally responsive helpers, the concept of multicultural counseling "skills" is actually still rather tenuous. In many instances, pre- and in-service training experiences provide opportunities for counselors to develop a new level of awareness and an updated knowledge base to address the concerns of culturally diverse clients. However, such training tends to stop short of actual comprehensive skill acquisition. There is generally little exposure to counseling modalities that incorporate cultural dynamics or indigenous aspects of helping. A sentiment often expressed by counselors on the front lines of multicultural service delivery is the need for less theory and more practical direction for addressing client concerns in a culturally responsive manner.

It must be pointed out that there are no "cookbooks" or "how-to manuals" that can be realistically developed for working with culturally diverse clients. However, if multicultural counseling is to continue evolving as a discipline, then comprehensive approaches to service delivery must be developed, implemented, and evaluated. Personal awareness and cultural knowledge must be translated into culturally responsive practice.

Conclusion

American society in the 21st century is characterized by ever-increasing diversity and cultural pluralism. These phenomena have had a profound effect on the discipline known as multicultural counseling. No longer can multicultural counseling be considered exclusively within the confines of race and ethnicity; rather, a new paradigm that includes other important aspects of diversity, such as sexual orientation, disability, and socioeconomic disadvantage, must become the cornerstone of effective cross-cultural counseling practice. This new paradigm brings with it great promise as well as potential pitfalls. If counselors are to have an impact on the development of increasingly diverse client groups, then counseling practice must be grounded in responsiveness to cultural diversity. Developing such responsiveness should be an integral part of the personal growth process of all counselors. This process involves acquiring not only the awareness and knowledge but also the skills for effective multicultural intervention. This book attempts to capitalize on the promise of multicultural counseling by providing professional counselors with direction to enhance not only awareness and knowledge but also counseling skills.

References

Barret, B., & Logan, C. (2002). *Counseling gay men and lesbians: A practice primer.* Pacific Grove, CA: Brooks/Cole.

Bradford, J., Barrett, K., & Honnold, J. A. (2002). *The 2000 Census and same-sex households: A user's guide.* New York: National Gay and Lesbian Task Force Policy Institute, Survey and Evaluation Research Laboratory, and Fenway Institute. Retrieved June 10, 2004, from http://www.ngltf.org

Cianciotto, J., & Cahill, S. (2003). *Education policy: Issues affecting lesbian, gay, bisexual, and transgender youth.* New York: National Gay and Lesbian Task Force Policy Institute.

Day, J. C. (1996). *Population projections of the United States by age, sex, race, and Hispanic origin: 1995 to 2050* (Current Population Reports, P25-1130). Washington, DC: U.S. Government Printing Office.

Delgado-Romero, E. (2003). Ethics and multicultural competence. In D. B. Pope-Davis, H. L. K. Coleman, W. M. Liu, & R. L. Toporek (Eds.), *Handbook of multicultural competencies in counseling and psychology* (pp. 313–329). Thousand Oaks, CA: Sage.

Hershenson, D. B. (1990). A theoretical model for rehabilitation counseling. *Rehabilitation Counseling Bulletin, 33,* 268–278.

Kopala, M., & Keitel, M. (2003). *Handbook for counseling women.* Thousand Oaks, CA: Sage.

LaFromboise, T. D., Foster, S., & James, A. (1996). Ethics in multicultural counseling. In P. B. Pedersen, J. G. Draguns, W. J. Lonner, & J. E. Trimble (Eds.), *Counseling across cultures* (4th ed., pp. 47–72). Thousand Oaks, CA: Sage.

Lee, C. C. (1997). Cultural dynamics: Their importance in culturally responsive counseling. In C. C. Lee (Ed.), *Multicultural issues in counseling: New approaches to diversity* (2nd ed., pp. 15–30). Alexandria, VA: American Counseling Association.

Lee, C. C. (1998). Counselors as agents of social change. In C. C. Lee & G. R. Walz (Eds.), *Social action: A mandate for counselors* (pp. 3–14). Alexandria, VA: American Counseling Association and ERIC Counseling and Student Services Clearinghouse.

Myers, J. E., & Schwiebert, V. L. (1996). *Competencies for gerontological counseling.* Alexandria, VA: American Counseling Association.

National Center for Educational Statistics. (1997). *The social context of education.* Washington, DC: Author.

National Dissemination Center for Children With Disabilities. (2003). *Who are the children in special education?* Washington, DC: Author. Retrieved June 10, 2004, from http://www.nichcy.org/pubs/research/rb2.pdf

Pack-Brown, S. P., & Williams, C. B. (2003). *Ethics in a multicultural context.* Thousand Oaks, CA: Sage.

Padilla, A. M., Ruiz, R. A., & Alvarez, R. (1975). Community mental health services for the Spanish-speaking/surnamed population. *American Psychologist, 30,* 892–905.

Patterson, C. H. (1996). Multicultural counseling: From diversity to universality. *Journal of Counseling & Development, 74,* 227–231.

Pedersen, P. (1991). Multiculturalism as a generic approach to counseling. *Journal of Counseling & Development, 70,* 6–12.

Pope-Davis, D. B., & Coleman, H. L. K. (2000). *The intersection of race, class, and gender in multicultural counseling.* Thousand Oaks, CA: Sage.

Proctor, B. D., & Dalaker, J. (2003). *Poverty in the United States: 2002* (Current Population Reports, P60-222). Washington, DC: U.S. Government Printing Office.

Ridley, C. R., Liddle, M. C., Hill, C. L., & Li, L. C. (2001). Ethical decision making in multicultural counseling. In J. G. Ponterotto, J. M. Casas, L. A. Suzuki, & C. M. Alexander (Eds.), *Handbook of multicultural counseling* (2nd ed., pp. 165–188). Thousand Oaks, CA: Sage.

Roysircar, G., Arredondo, P., Fuertes, J. N., Ponterotto, J. G., & Toporek, R. L. (2003). *Multicultural counseling competencies 2003: Association for Multicultural Counseling and Development.* Alexandria, VA: Association for Multicultural Counseling and Development.

Smith, D. M., & Gates, G. J. (2001). *Gay and lesbian families in the United States: Same-sex unmarried partner households.* Washington, DC: Human Rights Campaign.

Sue, D. W., Ivey, A. E., & Pedersen, P. B. (1996). *A theory of multicultural counseling and therapy.* Pacific Grove, CA: Brooks/Cole.

Sue, D. W., & Sue, D. (1977). Barriers to effective cross-cultural counseling. *Journal of Counseling Psychology, 24,* 420–429.

Sue, D. W., & Sue, D. (2002). *Counseling the culturally diverse: Theory and practice* (4th ed.). Indianapolis, IN: Wiley.

Trimble, J. E. (1974, August). *The intrusion of Western psychological thought on Native American ethos.* Paper presented at the Second International Conference of the International Association for Cross-Cultural Psychology, Kingston, Ontario, Canada.

U.S. Census Bureau. (2001). *Population profile of the United States: 1999* (Current Population Reports, P23-205). Washington, DC: U.S. Government Printing Office.

U.S. Department of Labor, Bureau of Labor Statistics. (2004). *Working in the 21st century.* Retrieved June 10, 2004, from http://www.bls.gov/opub/working/home.htm

Vontress, C. E. (1969). Cultural barriers in the counseling relationship. *Personnel and Guidance Journal, 48,* 11–17.

Weinrach, S. G., & Thomas, K. R. (2002). A critical analysis of the multicultural counseling competencies: Implications for the practice of mental health counseling. *Journal of Mental Health Counseling, 24,* 20–35.

Entering the *Cross-Cultural Zone*: Meeting the Challenge of Culturally Responsive Counseling

Courtland C. Lee

Understanding the complex role of culture is a major challenge in counseling practice. Knowledge of cultural realities has become a professional imperative as counselors encounter increasingly diverse client groups. However, when culture is considered as a variable in the counseling process, it has the potential to become a source of conflict and misunderstanding. This may create barriers between helper and helpee who differ in terms of cultural background. The purpose of this chapter is twofold: first, to present a conceptual framework for counseling across cultures—the *cross-cultural zone*—and second, to examine some important issues that should be considered in addressing the challenges of culturally responsive counseling when entering this zone.

The Cross-Cultural Zone

It is obvious that entering a cross-cultural counseling relationship brings with it certain unique challenges and inherent opportunities. Facilitating such a relationship involves entering an important and potentially problematic area of helping. This helping space can be conceptualized as the *cross-cultural zone.* A counselor enters the cross-cultural zone whenever he or she significantly differs from a client in terms of cultural background. In much of the multicultural counseling literature, this helping space has been traditionally conceptualized as a White counselor engaging in a helping relationship with a client of color (Lee, 1997; McFadden, 1993). However, the cultural gaps that exist between counselor and client in the cross-cultural zone may also consist of distinct differences in aspects such as sexual orientation, disability status, religion, socioeconomic status, gender, or age.

It is important to point out that counseling in the cross-cultural zone can be a sociopolitical process related to a power differential between counselor and client (Cook, 1993; Lee, 1997; Lewis & Arnold, 1998; McWhirter, 1994; Sue & Sue, 2002). This is particularly true if, because of skin color, gender, sexual orientation, or disability status, a client occupies a subordinate cultural position in society. Such a position is usually characterized by forces of racism, sexism, homophobia, or ableism that negatively affect academic, career, or personal–social development. It is significant that in many instances, counseling practice has been perceived as a tool of power, oppression, or social control among many groups of people (Cook, 1993; Lee, 1997; Lewis & Arnold, 1998; McWhirter, 1994; Sue & Sue, 2002).

Counseling in the cross-cultural zone is often a forced, as opposed to a voluntary, experience, with a counselor perceived as a culturally insensitive or unresponsive agent of the broad and repressive social welfare system. Therefore, rather than being an empowering process, counseling can become disenfranchising, contributing to social marginalization for scores of client groups.

The dynamics of power, therefore, must be factored into the counseling equation in the cross-cultural zone (Cartenuto, 1992). This is particularly the case for those clients whose counseling issues relate to the stress of prejudice, discrimination, or socioeconomic disadvantage. In the cross-cultural zone, counselors must be aware of how power and cultural privilege play out within the helping process.

What is evident in the cross-cultural zone is that the cultural differences between counselor and client can be a significant impediment to the counseling process. Metaphorically, these counselor–client differences in the cross-cultural zone can hang between the counselor and the client like an impenetrable brick wall, impeding or negating counseling. This brick wall emphasizes the cultural distance between the counselor and the client. In many instances, the cultural differences in the cross-cultural zone are ignored, thereby widening the distance between helper and helpee.

Figure 2.1 presents another way to view the cross-cultural zone. Situated between the counselor and the client are significant differences in culture, which may take on the aura of a huge dead elephant if they are not addressed in a responsive manner.

The goal when entering the cross-cultural zone, therefore, is to scale the brick wall or remove the dead elephant and decrease the possible cultural distance that may exist between counselor and client. It is important that cultural differences are acknowledged and factored into the counseling relationship.

Best Practice in the Cross-Cultural Zone

If counselors are to be effective in the cross-cultural zone, then they must approach helping from a perspective that simultaneously acknowledges human similarity and celebrates

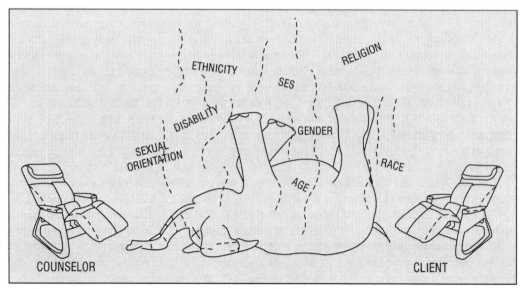

Figure 2.1
The Cross-Cultural Zone

human difference. They must adopt a philosophy that views each client as a unique individual while, at the same time, taking into consideration the client's common experiences as a human being (i.e., the universal developmental challenges that all people face regardless of cultural background) and the specific experiences that come from his or her cultural background. It is important that counselors consider each client within a cultural group context and a broader global human perspective (Lee, 2001).

Counselors who are responsive to clients from diverse cultural backgrounds have heightened awareness and an expanded knowledge base and use helping skills in a culturally responsive manner (Pope-Davis, Coleman, Liu, & Toporek, 2003; Roysircar, Arredondo, Fuertes, Ponterotto, & Toporek, 2003). This premise provides a framework for best practice in the cross-cultural zone.

Counselor Self-Awareness

The prerequisite for effective counseling in the cross-cultural zone is counselor self-awareness. It is important that counselors fully experience themselves as cultural beings. An individual who expects to work cross-culturally must first be anchored in his or her own cultural realities. This process should start with exploration of how one's own cultural background has influenced his or her psychosocial development. It is of critical importance that a person considers the role that cultural heritage and customs play in shaping his or her personality characteristics. It is also crucial that a person assess his or her own process of cultural identity development. An overview of this process is presented later in this chapter. The significant questions that one must ask in this regard are "How do I experience myself as a member of cultural group *X*?" "How do I experience other members of cultural group *X*?" and "How do I experience people of other cultural backgrounds?"

As part of this self-exploration process, it is also important that a counselor evaluate the influences that have shaped the development of his or her attitudes and beliefs about people from different cultural backgrounds. It is important to evaluate the explicit as well as the often subtle messages that one has received throughout his or her life about people who are culturally "different." A counselor must evaluate how his or her personal attitudes and beliefs about people from different cultural groups may facilitate or hamper counseling effectiveness.

Upon actually entering the cross-cultural zone and encountering a client from a different cultural context, a counselor must consider "What buttons does this client push in me as a result of the obvious cultural difference between us?" "What are some cultural blindspots I may have with respect to this client?" "As a result of my cultural realities, what strengths do I bring to this counseling relationship?" and "As a result of my cultural realities, what limitations do I bring to this counseling relationship?"

Culturally responsive counselors explore personal issues and questions, no matter how uncomfortable, in an attempt to discern how their own cultural heritage, values, and biases might affect the counseling process. Self-exploration leads to self-awareness, which is crucial in developing a set of personal attitudes and beliefs to guide culturally responsive counseling practice. Culturally responsive counselors are sensitive to cultural group differences because they are aware of their own identity as cultural beings.

Counselor Knowledge

It is imperative that counselors have a knowledge base from which to plan, implement, and evaluate their services in the cross-cultural zone. There are several basic aspects of a knowledge base for counseling intervention in the cross-cultural zone. First, counseling effectiveness in this zone must include knowledge of cultural identity development. Cultural identity refers to an individual's sense of belonging to a cultural group and the part of one's personality that is attributable to cultural group membership. Cultural identity may be considered as the inner vision that a person possesses of himself or herself as a member of a cultural group and as a unique human being. It forms the core of the beliefs, social forms, and personality dimensions that characterize distinct cultural realities and worldviews for an individual. Cultural identity development is a major determinant of a person's attitudes toward himself or herself, others of the same cultural group, others of a different cultural group, and members of a dominant cultural group (Sue, Ivey, & Pedersen, 1996).

The development of a cultural identity has been theorized within the context of several dimensions of culture. Given this, there are developmental models that explain various aspects of cultural identity, including racial/ethnic identity (Atkinson, Morten, & Sue, 1993; Cross, 1995; Helms, 1995), homosexual/gay/lesbian/bisexual identity (Cass, 1979; Coleman, 1982; Marszalek & Cashwell, 1999; McCarn & Fassinger, 1996; Troiden, 1988), feminist and womanist identity (Downing & Roush, 1985; Ossana, Helms, & Leonard, 1992), biracial identity (Kerwin & Ponterotto, 1995; Poston, 1990), and disability identity (Gill, 1997; Vash, 1981).

Cultural identity development occurs in a milieu characterized by complex social interaction among groups of people. Therefore, it is important to point out that most models of cultural identity development have been developed in a context in which one group of people has been in a position of social and cultural dominance while another group has been in a subordinate position. For example, Whites have traditionally enjoyed cultural privilege in their relationship with people of color (McIntosh, 1989). Likewise, heterosexuals have been in a dominant and privileged social position with respect to gays, lesbians, and bisexuals. The cultural privilege inherent in the dominant–subordinate relationship profoundly influences the attitudes of members of the dominant cultural group toward members of the subordinate group. Likewise, the perceptions of this cultural privilege held by people from subordinate groups profoundly influence attitudes they hold of themselves and members of the dominant group (Atkinson et al., 1993; Helms, 1995; Sue et al., 1996).

The various aspects of cultural identity have traditionally been conceptualized as developing through an evolutionary linear stage process (Atkinson et al., 1993; Cass, 1979; Cross, 1995; Downing & Roush, 1985; Poston, 1990) or, more recently, as a dynamic personality status process in which cultural information is simultaneously interpreted and internalized at a variety of levels (Helms, 1995). Though theorists have presented different speculations about the specifics, the stages or levels of cultural identity development appear to progress in the following manner (Sue et al., 1996):

- *Stage 1:* An individual experiences naïveté about his or her cultural realities and those of other people. He or she may have limited awareness of himself or herself as a cultural being.
- *Stage 2:* An individual encounters the reality of cultural issues, either his or hers or those of other cultural groups.
- *Stage 3:* An individual fully embraces his or cultural realities and attempts to relate to other groups of people as a cultural being.
- *Stage 4:* An individual reflects on the meaning of himself or herself as a cultural being.
- *Stage 5:* An individual internalizes his or her awareness of self as a cultural being.

The second basic aspect of knowledge for the cross-cultural zone is an understanding of how economic, social, and political systems operate with respect to their treatment of culturally diverse groups of people (Pope-Davis et al., 2003; Roysircar et al., 2003). Culturally responsive counselors should have an understanding of the historical impact of environmental forces such as racism, sexism, homophobia, classism, and ableism on the psychosocial development of people.

Third, counselors who enter the cross-cultural zone acquire working knowledge and information about specific groups of people. This should include general knowledge about the histories, experiences, customs, and values of culturally diverse groups. From such knowledge should come an understanding of specific cultural contexts and how they may influence personal and social development (Pope-Davis et al., 2003; Roysircar et al., 2003).

Counselor Skills

It is imperative that counselors enter the cross-cultural zone with a repertoire of responsive skills. They should be able to use counseling strategies and techniques that are consistent with the life experiences and cultural values of their clients.

Culturally responsive skills should be based on the following premises. First, cultural diversity is real and should not be ignored. Second, cultural differences are just that—differences. They are not necessarily deficiencies or pathological deviations. This suggests having the ability to meet clients where they are, despite obvious cultural gaps between helpers and helpees. Third, when counselors are working with clients from culturally diverse groups, it is important to avoid stereotypes and a monolithic perspective. It is crucial that counselors consider clients as individuals within a cultural group context.

In the cross-cultural zone, a number of theoretical approaches should be included in a counselor's repertoire. It is important that a counselor's style be eclectic enough that he or she can use a variety of helping approaches. These approaches should incorporate diverse worldviews and practices.

An important dimension to responsive practice in the cross-cultural zone is willingness on the part of a counselor to assume the role of systemic change agent or advocate. When working with culturally diverse clients, a counselor might need to consider the negative effects of phenomena such as racism, sexism, homophobia, ableism, classism, or other forms of cultural, economic, or social oppression on human development. The etiology of problems is often not in clients but rather in intolerant or restrictive environments. The only way in which clients will be able to solve problems or make decisions is to eradicate these systemic impediments. A culturally responsive counselor often must assume the role of systemic change agent and help clients to challenge such impediments (Lee, 1998).

The aspects of best practice in the cross-cultural zone not only are the basis of culturally responsive counseling but also can be considered as the foundation of quality counseling in general. As counselors strive to be aware of and responsive to the needs of culturally diverse client groups, they raise the standard of the profession for all.

Conclusion

An important question that must be considered with respect to culturally responsive counseling is "As a counselor, what feelings do you have, have you had, or do you contemplate having when entering the cross-cultural zone?" In most instances, the response to this question is the feelings of anxiety and fear. The cross-cultural zone can be a very challenging place for a counselor. He or she must understand the personal and cultural dynamics of his or her worldview while simultaneously attempting to comprehend those of his or her client. This process can be compounded when counselor and client differ significantly in terms of their cultural realities.

The next two sections of this book are intended to address the challenges of culturally responsive counseling. They expand on best practice in the cross-cultural zone presented in this chapter. The remainder of the book explores counseling concepts, issues, and practices to effectively meet the challenges and seize the opportunities of counseling in the cross-cultural zone.

References

Atkinson, D. R., Morten, G., & Sue, D. W. (1993). *Counseling American minorities: A cross-cultural perspective* (4th ed.). Madison, WI: Brown & Benchmark.

Cartenuto, A. (1992). *The difficult art: A critical discourse on psychotherapy.* Wilmette, IL: Chiron.

Cass, V. C. (1979). Homosexual identity formation: A theoretical model. *Journal of Homosexuality, 4,* 219–235.

Coleman, E. (1982). Developmental stages of the coming out process. *Journal of Homosexuality, 7,* 31–43.

Cook, E. P. (Ed.). (1993). *Women, relationships, and power: Implications for counseling.* Alexandria, VA: American Counseling Association.

Cross, W. E. (1995). The psychology of Nigrescence: Revising the Cross model. In J. G. Ponterotto, J. M. Casas, L. A. Suzuki, & C. M. Alexander (Eds.), *Handbook of multicultural counseling* (pp. 93–122). Thousand Oaks, CA: Sage.

Downing, N., & Roush, K. (1985). From passive acceptance to active commitment: A model of feminist identity development for women. *The Counseling Psychologist, 13,* 695–709.

Gill, C. J. (1997). Four types of integration in disability identity development. *Journal of Vocational Rehabilitation, 9,* 39–46.

Helms, J. E. (1995). An update of Helms's White and People of Color racial identity models. In J. G. Ponterotto, J. M. Casas, L. A. Suzuki, & C. M. Alexander (Eds.), *Handbook of multicultural counseling* (pp. 181–198). Thousand Oaks, CA: Sage.

Kerwin, C., & Ponterotto, J. (1995). Biracial identity development. In J. G. Ponterotto, J. M. Casas, L. A. Suzuki, & C. M. Alexander (Eds.), *Handbook of multicultural counseling.* (pp. 199–217). Thousand Oaks, CA: Sage.

Lee, C. C. (1997). Cultural dynamics: Their importance in culturally responsive counseling. In C. C. Lee (Ed.), *Multicultural issues in counseling: New approaches to diversity* (pp. 15–30). Alexandria, VA: American Counseling Association.

Lee, C. C. (1998). Counselors as agents of social change. In C. C. Lee & G. R. Walz (Eds.), *Social action: A mandate for counselors* (pp. 3–14). Alexandria, VA: American Counseling Association and ERIC Counseling and Student Services Clearinghouse.

Lee, C. C. (2001). Defining and responding to racial and ethnic diversity. In D. C. Locke, J. E. Myers, & E. L. Herr (Eds.), *The handbook of counseling* (pp. 581–588). Thousand Oaks, CA: Sage.

Lewis, J. A., & Arnold, M. S. (1998). From multiculturalism to social action. In C. C. Lee & G. R. Walz (Eds.), *Social action: A mandate for counselors* (pp. 51–65). Alexandria, VA: American Counseling Association and ERIC Counseling and Student Services Clearinghouse.

Marszalek, J. F., & Cashwell, C. S. (1999). The gay and lesbian affirmative development (GLAD) model: Facilitating positive gay identity development. *Adultspan Journal, 1,* 13–31.

McCarn, S. R., & Fassinger, R. E. (1996). Revisioning sexual minority identity formation: A new model of lesbian identity and its implications for counseling and research. *The Counseling Psychologist, 24,* 508–534.

McFadden, J. (Ed.). (1993). *Transcultural counseling: Bilateral and international perspectives.* Alexandria, VA: American Counseling Association.

McIntosh, P. (1989). White privilege: Unpacking the invisible knapsack. *Peace and Freedom, 2,* 10–12.

McWhirter, E. H. (1994). *Counseling for empowerment.* Alexandria, VA: American Counseling Association.

Ossana, S. M., Helms, J. E., & Leonard, M. M. (1992). Do "womanist" identity attitudes influence college women's self-esteem and perceptions of environmental bias? *Journal of Counseling & Development, 70,* 402–408.

Pope-Davis, D. B., Coleman, H. L. K., Liu, W. M., & Toporek, R. L. (2003). *Handbook of multicultural competencies in counseling and psychology.* Thousand Oaks, CA: Sage.

Poston, W. S. C. (1990). The biracial identity development model: A needed addition. *Journal of Counseling & Development, 69,* 152–155.

Roysircar, G., Arredondo, P., Fuertes, J. N., Ponterotto, J. G., & Toporek, R. L. (2003). *Multicultural counseling competencies 2003: Association for Multicultural Counseling and Development.* Alexandria, VA: Association for Multicultural Counseling and Development.

Sue, D. W., Ivey, A. E., & Pedersen, P. B. (1996). *A theory of multicultural counseling and therapy.* Pacific Grove, CA: Brooks/Cole.

Sue, D. W., & Sue, D. (2002). *Counseling the culturally diverse: Theory and practice* (4th ed.). Indianapolis, IN: Wiley.

Troiden, R. (1988). Homosexual identity development. *Journal of Adolescent Health Care, 9,* 105–113.

Vash, C. L. (1981). *Springer series on rehabilitation: Vol. 1. The psychology of disability.* New York: Springer.

Direction for Culturally Responsive Counseling

The Native American Experience

Contemporary Native Americans (a term that encompasses American Indians as well as Eskimos and Aleuts) are the descendants of the indigenous inhabitants of the North American continent. As a cultural group, they have a long and troubled history. The basis of their trouble has been their relationship with the U.S. government—a relationship often marked by conflict and oppression. There is a great deal of diversity among this cultural group, but culturally responsive counselors need to be aware of some common elements that contribute to Native Americans' mental health and psychosocial development. These elements include spirituality, a strong reverence for nature, and a deep respect for one's people.

When Eagle Speaks:
Counseling Native Americans

Michael Tlanusta Garrett

"Hoop Dancer"
*It's hard to enter
circling clockwise and counter
clockwise moving no
regard for time, metrics
irrelevant to this dance
where pain is the prime number
and soft stepping feet
praise water from the skies:*

*I have seen the face of triumph
the winding line stare down all moves
to desecration: guts not cut from arms,
fingers joined to minds,
together Sky and Water
one dancing one
circle of a thousand turning lines
beyond the march of gears—
out of time, out of
time, out
of time.*
            —Paula Gunn Allen (1991)

The poem by Paula Gunn Allen, Laguna Pueblo/Lakota, shows the movement, stamina, and skill of the hoop dancer, considered widely by many to be one of the most difficult and most revered of the Native dance styles on the powwow circuit. However, the poem also illustrates a number of concepts central to the experience of Native people in general, with an extraordinary emphasis on the harmony and balance required to survive and thrive. For Native people, the balance of multiple identities, pressures, and expectations can take on a new meaning as it relates to the metaphorical movements of the hoop dancer. To better understand the lives and worldviews of these people, it is important to hear their voices, their stories, and their experiences.

Native Americans consist of 2.5 million people with a population that is steadily growing. Although this number represents only 1.5% of the total population of the United States (U.S. Bureau of the Census, 2001), Native people have been described as representing "fifty percent of the diversity" in our country (Hodgkinson, 1990, p. 1). Across the United States, there are more than 557 federally recognized and several hundred state-recognized Native American nations (Russell, 1997). Given the wide-ranging diversity of this population consisting of 2.5 million people, it is important to understand that the term *Native American* encompasses the vastness and essence of tribal traditions represented by hundreds of Indian nations. Navajo, Catawba, Shoshone, Lumbee, Cheyenne, Cherokee, Apache, Lakota, Seminole, Comanche, Pequot, Cree, Tuscarora, Paiute, Creek, Pueblo, Shawnee, Hopi, Osage, Mohawk, Nez Perce, and Seneca are but a handful of the hundreds of Indian nations that exist across the United States.

Native Americans have been described as a group of persons facing enormous problems, including unemployment rates that are 3 to 11 times greater than that of the general population, a median income half that of the majority population, high school dropout rates exceeding 60% in many areas, arrest rates 3 times those for African Americans, and a rate of alcoholism double that of the general population (Heinrich, Corbine, & Thomas, 1990). Fetal alcohol syndrome rates for Native people are 33 times higher than those of non-Native people. One in six Native adolescents has attempted suicide, a rate 4 times that of all other groups. Alcohol mortality is 6 times the rate for all other ethnic groups. Tuberculosis is 7.4 times greater than for non-Indians. Diabetes is 6.8 times greater than for non-Indians (Russell, 1997).

Only 52% of Native youth finish high school, and only 4% graduate from college. Seventy-five percent of the Native workforce earns less than $7,000 per year. Forty-five percent of Native people live below the poverty level. As for living conditions, 46% have no electricity, 54% have no indoor plumbing, and 82% live without a telephone. Some of the possible challenges that Native people bring with them to the counseling process are evident (Russell, 1997).

Native Americans represent a wide-ranging diversity illustrated, for example, by approximately 252 different languages (Thomason, 1991). At the same time, a prevailing sense of "Indianness" based on common worldview and common history seems to bind Native Americans together as a people of many peoples (Herring, 1990; Thomason, 1991). Although acculturation plays a major factor in Native American worldview, there tends to be a high degree of psychological homogeneity, a certain degree of shared cultural standards and meanings, based on common core values that exist for traditional Native Americans across tribal groups (Choney, Berryhill-Paapke, & Robbins, 1995; DuBray, 1985; M. T. Garrett, 1999b; Heinrich et al., 1990; Oswalt, 1988; Peregoy, 1993; Sue & Sue, 1999).

Because approximately 50% of the Native American population resides in urban areas, the degree of traditionalism versus the degree of acculturation to mainstream American values and cultural standards for behavior is an important consideration in counseling Native people (J. T. Garrett & Garrett, 1994; Heinrich et al., 1990; Thomason, 1991). Native Americans come from different tribal groups with different customs, traditions, and beliefs; they live in a variety of settings, including rural, urban, and reservation (J. T. Garrett & Garrett, 1994). Both Cherokees and Navajos are Native Americans, but their regional cultures, climatic adaptations, and languages differ greatly (Garcia & Ahler, 1992). However, part of what they share in common is a strong sense of traditionalism based on basic cultural values and worldviews (Herring, 1990; Thomason, 1991).

To better understand how to provide Native clients with culturally responsive services in the counseling process, one must enter the world of a Native client. The purpose of this chapter is not to offer information dealing with many of the specific problems and issues that are of particular concern for this population, such as poverty and high unemployment, alcoholism and substance abuse, teenage pregnancy, suicide rates, delinquency, diabetes and other health concerns, or even whether casinos and the gaming industry have benefi-cial or destructive consequences for tribes. The purpose of this chapter is, instead, to offer a comprehensive overview and understanding of this population by discussing (a) termi-nology; (b) historical context; (c) acculturation; (d) traditional Native values and world-view; (e) spirituality, wellness, and healing practices; and (f) recommendations for counseling Native American clients.

Who Is Native American: "How Much Are You?"

The term *Native American* is often used to describe indigenous people of the Western hemi-sphere in an effort to provide recognition—viewed by many as long overdue—of the unique history and status of these people as the first inhabitants of the American continent. The U.S. Bureau of Indian Affairs (1988) has legally defined *Native American* as a person who is an enrolled or registered member of a tribe or whose blood quantum is one fourth or more ge-nealogically derived from Native American ancestry. The U.S. Bureau of the Census (2001), meanwhile, has relied on self-identification to determine who is a Native person. Oswalt (1988) pointed out, however, that

> if a person is considered an Indian by other individuals in the community, he or she is legally an Indian . . . [in other words], if an individual is on the roll of a federally recognized Indian group, then he or she is an Indian; the degree of Indian blood is of no real consequence, al-though usually he or she has at least some Indian blood. (p. 5)

Among some of the terms used historically or currently to refer to Native people are *American Indian, Alaskan Native, Native people, Indian, First American, Amerindian, Amerind, First Nations people, aboriginal people,* and *indigenous people.* The term *Native American* or *Native people* (and sometimes *Indian*) is used here to refer generally to those Native people indige-nous to the United States who self-identify as Native American and maintain cultural iden-tification as a Native person through membership in a Native American tribe recognized by the state or federal government or through other tribal affiliation and community recognition.

Surviving "History": Spirit Never Dies

Many authors have described the deliberate attempts throughout U.S. history by main-stream American institutions such as government agencies, schools, and churches to destroy the Native American institutions of family, clan, and tribal structure; religious belief systems and practices; customs; and traditional way of life (Deloria, 1988; Heinrich et al., 1990; Locust, 1988; Reyhner & Eder, 1992). Deloria (1988) commented, "When questioned by an anthropologist on what the Indians called America before the White man came, an Indian said simply, 'Ours' " (p. 166). Characterized by institutional racism and discrimination, U.S. dominant culture has a long history of opposition to Native cultures and of attempts to as-similate Native people (Deloria, 1988; Locust, 1988).

In the historical context of Native and White relations, as it became apparent that Native Americans had no interest in adopting White cultural standards and practices, Whites turned to the power of education to "civilize" Indian children early in life. Most treaty agreements included provisions for the education of Native American youth by establish-ing church-affiliated schools. Native American children were deliberately taken from their homes at a young age and forced to attend boarding schools as far away from home as possible. In the government-supported, church-run boarding schools, whose purpose was to assimilate Native Americans, the children were not allowed to speak their native language or practice their cultural traditions (which was often enforced through harsh physical punishment); they were required to speak only English, practice Christianity, and learn the tenets of White society (Hirschfelder & Kreipe de Montano, 1993). Moreover, these children, who had been removed from their homes typically around age 4 or 5 years, usually spent a minimum of 8 continuous years away from their families and communities (Deloria, 1988; Herring, 1989; Sue & Sue, 1999). Upon returning to their communities, many of these individuals discovered very quickly that they were not "White," yet they were not "Indian" either. What resulted was an intergenerational division that still remains today as a powerful influence on the cultural identity of many Native Americans, particularly the older generation.

The outlawing of Native religions in the late 1890s represented yet another dimension of the cultural onslaught. Once, having been asked why the Nez Perce had banned missionaries from their lands, Chief Joseph replied,

> They will teach us to quarrel about God, as Catholics and Protestants do. . . . We do not want to do that. We may quarrel with men sometimes about things on Earth, but we never quarrel about the Great Spirit. We do not want to learn that. (as quoted in Deloria, 1994, p. 194)

Missionaries divided up the Native population like slicing up a pie to determine which denominations would control which geographic regions. This governmental move, in conjunction with the churches, resulted, for the most part, in tribal religions being taken underground to avoid persecution. However, many Native Americans embraced Christianity, further disrupting the integrity of tribal traditions.

Yet another example of assimilation occurred in the early 1950s through a massive federal program designed to relocate reservation Indians to urban areas such as Chicago, Los Angeles, Denver, San Francisco, St. Louis, Cincinnati, Cleveland, and Dallas (Hirschfelder & Kreipe de Montano, 1993). After World War II, many Native Americans who had either served in the war or worked in factories returned home to reservations where times were hard and jobs were scarce. In what was officially called the Voluntary Relocation Program (later renamed the Employment Assistance Program), recruits were given a one-way bus ticket, temporary low-cost housing, and new clothing (Deloria, 1988). Given the competition for jobs and overt racism of the times, many Native Americans either were unable to obtain jobs or worked for very low wages. Although some prospered, many relocated Native Americans, separated from the support of extended family and tribal communities and cut off from ceremonial life, simply became yet another addition to the inner-city poor. Some Native Americans remained in urban centers (where there are still high concentrations of Native people today); yet others returned home once again to the reservations.

Needless to say, American policies of assimilation have had a pervasive impact on Native people and their way of life (Herring, 1990; Locust, 1988). It was not until 1924 that the U.S. citizenship of Native Americans, no longer a threat to national expansion, was recognized with the passage of the Citizenship Act (Deloria, 1988). In addition, Native Americans were not granted religious freedom until 1978 when the American Indian Religious Freedom Act was passed, overturning the Indian Religious Crimes Code, passed by Congress in 1889. This act guaranteed Native people the constitutional right to exercise their traditional religious practices for the first time in a century (Deloria, 1988; Loftin, 1989). On a more personal note, every time I pull out a $20 bill (which is not often), I am reminded of the betrayal of my tribe by the government back in 1838 when Andrew Jackson (depicted in all his glory on the $20 bill) signed off on an illegal act forcing the removal of over 16,000 Cherokees from parts of North Carolina, South Carolina, Tennessee, and Georgia to the Oklahoma territory (M. T. Garrett, 1998).

These are but a few examples of historical factors that have affected Native Americans psychologically, economically, and socially for generations. However, it is important not to lose sight of the most important considerations for counseling Native people on the basis of this information: trust versus mistrust. Oppression is and continues to be a very real part of the Native experience, something that Native clients bring to counseling, and must be dealt with either directly or indirectly. Counselors are trained professionals who encourage clients to tell their "story," make sense out of their story, and actively create their story through intentional living. In working with clients of color, it is important to understand the influence of oppression on that person's experience and to assess the extent to which the process of acculturation has affected or continues to affect the client's cultural identity (Lee, 2001; Robinson & Howard-Hamilton, 2000).

The cultural discontinuity experienced by Native Americans in response to federal policies may best be depicted through a brief narrative. In the quote that follows, a Navajo elder describes what her first experiences in school were like over 40 years ago, unable to speak any English and having never left the reservation before attending boarding school at the age of 7.

> It was the first time I've seen a brick building that was not a trading post. The ceilings were so high, and the rooms so big and empty. It was so cold. There was no warmth. Not as far as "brrr, I'm cold," but in a sense of emotional cold. Kind of an emptiness, when you're hanging onto your mom's skirt and trying hard not to cry. Then when you get up to your turn, she thumbprints the paper and she leaves and you watch her go out the big metal doors. The whole thing was cold. The doors were metal and they even had this big window with wires running through it. You watch your mama go down the sidewalk, actually it's the first time I seen a sidewalk, and you see her get into the truck and the truck starts moving and all the home smell goes with it. You see it all leaving.
>
> Then the woman takes you by the hand and takes you inside and the first thing they do is take down your bun. The first thing they do is cut off your hair, and you been told your whole life that you never cut your hair recklessly because that is your life. And that's the first thing them women does is cut off your hair. And you see that long, black hair drop, and it's like they take out your heart and they give you this cold thing that beats inside. And now you're gonna be just like them. You're gonna be cold. You're never gonna be happy or have that warm feeling and attitude towards life anymore. That's what it feels like, like taking your heart out and putting in a cold river pebble.
>
> When you go into the shower, you leave your squaw skirt and blouse right there at the shower door. When you come out, it's gone. You don't see it again. They cut your hair, now they take your squaw skirt. They take from the beginning. When you first walk in there, they take everything that you're about. They jerk it away from you. They don't ask how you feel about it. They never tell you anything. They never say what they're gonna do, why they're doing it. They barely speak to you. They take everything away from you. Then you think, mama must be whackers. She wants me to be like them? Every time you don't know what they're doing, they laugh at you. They yell at you. They jerk you around. It was never what I wanted to be. I never wanted to be like them. But my mom wanted me to be like them. As I got older, I found out that you don't have to be like them. You can have a nice world and have everything that mama wanted, but you don't have to be cold. (McLaughlin, 1994, pp. 47–48)

The institutional racism and trauma of cultural shock experienced by this Navajo woman over 40 years ago are still evident in her vivid description of the experience. Although the experiences of many Native Americans have changed as circumstances and policies have changed, historical factors and the process of acculturation remain a powerful influence on the lives of Native people as seen in varying forms across different generations (M. T. Garrett, 1996b; Herring, 1990; Little Soldier, 1985; Locust, 1988; Mitchum, 1989; Reyhner & Eder, 1992; Sue & Sue, 1999).

Acculturation: Circles With No Beginning and No End

Although many of the core traditional values permeate the lives of Native Americans across tribal groups (see Table 3.1), Native Americans are not a completely homogeneous group, differing greatly in their level of acceptance of and commitment to specific tribal values, beliefs, and practices through a variance of customs, language, and family structure (J. T. Garrett & Garrett, 1996). *Acculturation* has been described as

> the cultural change that occurs when two or more cultures are in persistent contact. In this process, change may occur in each of the cultures in varying degrees. . . . A particular kind of acculturation is assimilation, in which one culture changes significantly more than the other culture and, as a result, comes to resemble it. This process is often established deliberately through force to maintain control over conquered peoples, but it can occur voluntarily as well. (Garcia & Ahler, 1992, p. 24)

Thus, individuals differ in terms of their level of acculturation, geographic setting (urban, rural, or reservation), and socioeconomic status (J. T. Garrett & Garrett, 1994; Herring, 1996). The following levels of acculturation have been identified for Native Americans:

1. *Traditional*—May or may not speak English but generally speak and think in their native language; hold only traditional values and beliefs and practice only traditional tribal customs and methods of worship.
2. *Marginal*—May speak both the native language and English; may not, however, fully accept the cultural heritage and practices of their tribal group nor fully identify with mainstream cultural values and behaviors.
3. *Bicultural*—Generally accepted by dominant society and tribal society/nation; simultaneously able to know, accept, and practice both mainstream values/behaviors and the traditional values and beliefs of their cultural heritage.
4. *Assimilated*—Accepted by dominant society; embrace only mainstream cultural values, behaviors, and expectations.
5. *Pantraditional*—Assimilated Native Americans who have made a conscious choice to return to the "old ways." They are generally accepted by dominant society but seek to embrace previously lost traditional cultural values, beliefs, and practices of their tribal heritage. Therefore, they may speak both English and their native tribal language. (LaFromboise, Trimble, & Mohatt, 1990, p. 638)

These five levels represent a continuum along which any given Native American individual may fall (see Table 3.2). Regardless of blood quantum, the most popular and most deceiving means of determining a person's "Indianness," a person's degree of traditionalism, comes not only from his or her ethnic heritage but also from his or her life experiences and life choices (J. T. Garrett & Garrett, 1994). Is it okay for an Indian person to live and work in the city during the week and "go home" to the reservation or rural community during the weekend to be with family and friends? Is it okay for a person who was not raised in the traditional way to follow a life path that leads him or her back to the old ways? Is it okay

Table 3.1
Comparison of Cultural Values and Expectations

Traditional Native American	Contemporary Mainstream American
Harmony with nature	Power over nature
Cooperation	Competition
Group needs more important than individual needs	Personal goals considered important
Privacy and noninterference; try to control self, not others	Need to control and affect others
Self-discipline in both body and mind	Self-expression and self-disclosure
Participation after observation (only when certain of ability)	Trial-and-error learning; new skills practiced until they are mastered
Explanation according to nature	Scientific explanation for everything
Reliance on extended family	Reliance on experts
Emotional relationships valued	Concerned mostly with facts
Patience encouraged (allow others to go first)	Aggressive and competitive
Humility	Fame and recognition; winning
Win once; let others win also	Win first prize all of the time
Follow the old ways	Climb the ladder of success; importance of progress and change
Discipline distributed among many; no one person takes blame	Blame one person at cost to others
Physical punishment rare	Physical punishment accepted
Present-time focus	Future-time focus
Time is always with us	Clock watching
Present goals considered important; future accepted as it comes	Plan for future and how to get ahead
Encourage sharing freely and keeping only enough to satisfy present needs	Private property; encourage acquisition of material comfort and saving for the future
Speak softly, at a slower rate	Speak louder and faster
Avoid singling out the listener	Address listener directly (by name)
Interject less	Interrupt frequently
Use fewer "encouraging signs" (uh-huh, head nodding)	Use verbal encouragement
Delayed response to auditory messages	Use immediate response
Nonverbal communication	Verbal skills highly prized

Note. Compiled From Sanders, 1987.

for a person raised in the traditional way to forego the old ways in favor of a modern lifestyle? Is it okay for an Indian person to completely disregard the old ways and to be offended at the suggestion that he or she should know or practice this way of life purely because of his or her racial/ethnic heritage?

It is ironic that derogative terms such as *apple* or *uncle tomahawk* reflect a racial/cultural no-win situation that some Native Americans experience at being caught between two cultures in which they are "red" on the outside and "white" on the inside (LaFromboise, Coleman, & Gerton, 1993). This is what several authors have referred to as the "marginal" person. According to Little Soldier (1985), marginal Native Americans are the ones most likely to experience a variety of difficulties resulting from cultural conflict. "They may become trapped between their birthright and the dominant society, losing touch with the former but not feeling comfortable in the latter . . . [leading to] conflicts and resulting in serious identity crises" (Little Soldier, 1985, p. 187). These are the Native Americans who are most

Table 3.2
Levels of Acculturation Across Personality Domains

Domain	Level of Acculturation				
	1	2	3	4	5
Cognitive					
English	Some	Yes	Yes	Yes	Yes
Native language	Yes	Yes	Yes	No	Some
Understands mainstream customs	Yes	No	Some	Yes	Yes
Understands tribal customs	Some	Yes	Some	Yes	No
Behavioral					
Acts in tribally appropriate ways	Yes	No	Yes	No	Some
Acts in appropriate ways for mainstream	No	No	Yes	Yes	Some
Participates in tribal social activities	Some	Yes	No	Yes	No
Participates in mainstream social activities	Some	No	No	Yes	Yes
Affective/Spiritual					
Embraces traditional spirituality or Native American Church	Some	Yes	No	Some	No
Feels emotionally connected to the tribe	Yes	No	Yes	No	Yes
Social/Environmental					
Socializes with other Indian people	Yes	Yes	Some	Yes	No
Socializes with non-Indian people	No	Some	Yes	Yes	Yes
Chooses to live in Indian communities	Yes	Some	Some	No	Some
Chooses to live in non-Indian communities	Some	No	Some	Some	Yes

Note. For level of acculturation, 1 = *traditional,* 2 = *marginal,* 3 = *bicultural,* 4 = *assimilated,* and 5 = *pantraditional.* Table compiled From Choney, Berryhill-Paapke, & Robbins, 1995.

likely to experience a sense of being caught between two worlds (in a danger zone) as they struggle for identity and a sense of place (M. T. Garrett, 1995). By contrast, bicultural Native Americans are identified as having less personal, social, and academic difficulties because of their ability to effectively utilize a greater range in modes of social behavior and cultural communication that are appropriately used in a variety of contexts and situations (LaFromboise & Rowe, 1983; Little Soldier, 1985; see Figure 3.1).

Through *enculturation,* defined as "the process by which individuals learn their home culture" (Little Soldier, 1985, p. 185), many Native American children learn traditional values, beliefs, and modes of behavior and communication as a primary frame of reference. In the school environment and elsewhere, however, Native American students are often faced with pressure to compromise their basic cultural values and behaviors in order to successfully meet the expectations and standards of that context (Sanders, 1987). Hulburt, Kroeker, and Gade (1991) reported a higher incidence of feelings of rejection, depression, and anxiety reported by Native American students in comparison to other students. Around fifth and sixth grades, many Native American students begin to withdraw, becoming sullen, resistant, and indolent. The apparent decline of academic functioning and motivation in Native American students along with corresponding personal and social difficulties has been attributed, in part, to the difficulty that many Native American students have in reconciling existing cultural differences (Garcia & Ahler, 1992; M. T. Garrett, 1999a; Little Soldier, 1985; Sanders, 1987; Tierney, 1992). According to Sue and Sue (1999), the split between Native American traditions and mainstream expectations provides added stress to the already difficult challenge of identity formation. Consequently, cultural conflict has been hypothesized as a factor in the large percentage of Native American students who drop out of school (Colodarci, 1983; National Center for Education Statistics, 1991; Sanders, 1987).

MONOCULTURAL	*danger*	BICULTURAL	MONOCULTURAL
o----------------------------<--->-----------------------------------<--->---------------------------------o			
	zone		
TRADITIONAL		**ACCULTURATED**	**ASSIMILATED**
Identifies/enculturated with traditional Native American values, behaviors, and expectations.		Raised/enculturated with traditional Native American values/ worldview but has acquired the behaviors required for functioning in mainstream American culture.	Identifies/enculturated with mainstream American values, behaviors, and expectations.

Figure 3.1
The Acculturation Continuum

Note: Compiled From Little Soldier, 1985.

Cultural values and the influence of acculturation as a mediating factor in the process of identity development are of critical importance for Native Americans (Deyhle, 1992; Hornett, 1990; Sanders, 1987). According to LaFromboise et al. (1993), "it is possible for an individual to have a sense of belonging in two cultures without compromising his or her sense of cultural identity" (p. 399). Brendtro, Brokenleg, and Van Bockern (1990) have suggested that in order to establish a healthy cultural identity, Native Americans must find ways of satisfying the need for purpose through a sense of belonging, mastery, independence, and generosity. The institutional racism and the process of acculturation experienced by many Native Americans from early adolescence to early adulthood influence not only their definition of themselves as individuals but also their social, emotional, intellectual, and spiritual well-being (Cummins, 1992; Little Soldier, 1985; Mitchum, 1989; Tierney, 1992). This presents an additional challenge for Native Americans in achieving a meaningful sense of personal/cultural identity through *bicultural competence*, defined as the ability of an individual to effectively utilize "dual modes of social behavior that are appropriately employed in different situations" (LaFromboise & Rowe, 1983, p. 592). To be culturally competent, according to LaFromboise et al. (1993), an individual must

> (a) possess a strong personal identity, (b) have knowledge of and facility with the beliefs and values of the culture, (c) display sensitivity to the affective processes of the culture, (d) communicate clearly in the language of the given cultural group, (e) perform socially sanctioned behavior, (f) maintain active social relations within the cultural group, and (g) negotiate the institutional structures of that culture. (p. 396)

Thus, the biculturally competent individual possesses a high degree of resiliency through a strong sense of himself or herself in one or more cultural contexts. Understanding the experience of the biculturally competent individual becomes important in understanding what it means to cross cultural boundaries and how to best work with others who also must successfully cross these boundaries (M. T. Garrett, 1996b; Herring, 1995). In counseling, then, it becomes necessary to assess self-identity as indicated by that person's level of acceptance of and commitment to tribal culture in relation to mainstream American culture.

Native Traditions: Living the Ways

Several authors have described common core values that characterize Native "traditionalism" across tribal nations (Heinrich et al., 1990; Herring, 1990; Little Soldier, 1992; Peregoy, 1993; Thomason, 1991). Some of these Native traditional values (see Table 3.1) include the importance of community contribution, sharing, acceptance, cooperation, harmony and balance, noninterference, extended family, attention to nature, immediacy of time, awareness of the relationship, and a deep respect for elders (Dudley, 1992; Dufrene, 1990; J. T. Garrett & Garrett, 1994, 1996; M. T. Garrett, 1996a, 1998, 1999b; M. T. Garrett & Myers, 1996; Heinrich et al., 1990; Herring, 1990, 1999; Lake, 1991; Plank, 1994; Red Horse, 1997). All in all, these traditional values show the importance of honoring, through harmony and balance, what is believed to be a very sacred connection with the energy of life; this is the basis for traditional Native worldview and spirituality across tribal nations.

This section offers a general description of traditional values and worldview; however, it is important to remember that this is a general description (applying to one end of the acculturation spectrum) and may not apply universally across all Native nations with all Native people. Nonetheless, there does exist a common core of traditional values that can be identified for traditional Native people.

The Tribe/Nation

Traditional Native people experience a unique relationship between themselves and the tribe. In a very real sense, Native American individuals are extensions of their tribal nation—socially, emotionally, historically, and politically. For many Indian people, cultural identity is rooted in tribal membership, community, and heritage. Many Native nations are matriarchal/matrilineal or matriarchal/patrilineal, but there are those that follow patriarchal/patrilineal ways, too (or other variations of gender dominance and tracing of family heritage); this, in turn, affects not only communal and social structure and functioning but also family/clan structure and functioning. The extended family (at least three generations) and tribal group take precedence over all else. The tribe is an interdependent system of people who perceive themselves as parts of the greater whole rather than a whole consisting of individual parts. Likewise, traditional Native people judge themselves and their actions according to whether they are benefiting the tribal community and its continued harmonious functioning.

Among tribal members, there is always a strong sense of belonging based on social relationships and cultural values as well as a sacred sense of connection with one's ancestry and tribal history. These are all important determinants in the way a Native person sees himself or herself. In mainstream American society, worth and status are based on "what you do" or "what you have achieved." For Native Americans, "who you are is where you come from." Again, Native Americans essentially believe that "if you know my family, clan, or tribe, then you know me." As a result, traditional Native people who are asked to talk about themselves might be likely to describe some aspect of their family or tribal heritage.

Wisdom Keepers

Indian elders, the "Keepers of the Wisdom," are considered highly respected people because of the lifetime's worth of wisdom they have acquired through experience. Elders have always played an important part in the continuance of the tribal community by functioning in the role of parent, teacher, community leader, and spiritual guide (M. T. Garrett & Garrett, 1997). To refer to an elder as grandmother, grandfather, uncle, or aunt is to refer to a very special relationship that exists with that elder through deep respect and admiration. To use these terms and other more general terms such as *old woman* or *old man* is to greatly honor someone who has achieved the status of elder.

In the traditional way, elders direct young children's attention outward to the things with which they coexist (e.g., trees, plants, rocks, animals, elements, the land) and to the meaning of these things. They show the children the true relationship that exists with all things and the way in which to honor this relationship. In this way, children develop a heightened level of sensitivity for everything of which they are a part and which are a part of them, for the circular (cyclical) motion and flow of life energy, and for the customs and traditions of their people.

There is a very special kind of relationship based on mutual respect and caring between Indian elders and Indian children as one moves through the life circle from "being cared for" to "caring for," as Red Horse (1980) put it. With increase in age comes an increase in the sacred obligation to family, clan, and tribe. Native American elders pass down to the children the tradition that their life force carries the spirits of their ancestors. With such an emphasis on connectedness, children are held in great reverence, not only as ones who will carry on the wisdom and traditions but also as "little people" who are still very close to the spirit world and from whom there is much to learn. Brendtro et al. (1990) related the following story shared with them by Eddie Belleroe, a Cree elder from Alberta, Canada:

> In a conversation with his aging grandfather, a young Indian man asked, "Grandfather, what is the purpose of life?" After a long time in thought, the old man looked up and said, "Grandson, children are the purpose of life. We were once children and someone cared for us, and now it is our time to care." (p. 45)

The power of caring and relation is immeasurable in Native culture. Relationship focuses on a sense of connectedness, thankfulness, and the importance of giving back. Native elders are the keepers of the sacred ways, as protectors, mentors, teachers, and support givers, regardless of their social status.

As Native people move from being a child to being an elder in a traditional way, they learn to listen to the spirit of a person and to respect every individual for his or her intrinsic worth and being. As they begin "caring for," they are reminded of the spirit of playfulness, innocence, and curiosity through the realization that there is always something to learn and always something to appreciate. Indian elders direct young people's attention to the importance of certain values in a traditional way.

Humility

In the Native traditional way, we are important and unique as individuals, but we are also part of the greater circle of life. As we come to view ourselves in relation to the greater circle, we begin to view our actions or intentions in terms of how they affect the circle, whether it be the family, clan, tribe, community, or universe. One of the greatest challenges in life is to recognize our place in the universe and to honor this always.

Modesty and humility are essential to a harmonious way of life where the emphasis is placed on relation rather than domination. Individual praise should be welcomed if it has been earned, but this praise need not be used to bolster one in thinking or acting as though he or she is greater than any other living thing in the circle. Boasting of one's accomplishments and loud behavior that attracts attention to oneself are discouraged in the traditional way, where self-absorption and self-importance bring disharmony on oneself and one's family.

In the circle, the group must take precedence over the individual, and the wisdom of age takes precedence over youth, though it does not make anyone better or more worthy than anyone else. Many times, a traditional Native person may drop his or her head and eyes or at least be careful not to look into the eyes of another as a sign of respect for any elder or other honored person. No one is worthy of staring into the eyes of an elder or looking into the spirit of that honored person. This is also an act that signifies that a person does not view himself or herself as better than anyone else.

Generosity

Traditional Native views concerning property accentuate the underlying belief that whatever belongs to the individual also belongs to the group, and vice versa. It should come as no surprise to see Indian people sharing and/or giving their possessions away to others in certain circumstances. Generosity is considered a sign of wisdom and humility.

Traditional Native people are accustomed to cooperating and sharing. As a result, they participate well in group activities that emphasize cooperation and group harmony. Individual competition for the sake of beating others or showing others up is highly frowned upon in Native American culture. Many Indian people do very poorly in activities that emphasize competition among individuals. However, activities (especially sports) that emphasize intergroup competitions can be quite lively, to say the least, but all in good fun. The idea of seeking group harmony through cooperation and sharing takes precedence above all else.

Patience

Everything has its place. Very often, it is simply a matter of time before one recognizes where and how things fit together. In Native traditions, there is a sacred design to the world in which we live, to the process of life itself. And very often, it is not a matter of whether "things" fall into place but whether our capacity for awareness and understanding of "things" falls into place.

It is important to be able to learn through careful observation, listening, and patience, as well as through asking questions or thinking things through. Everything offers us a valuable lesson, from all of our surroundings to each of our experiences. It takes time and a special kind of willingness or openness to receive all of the lessons that are offered to us throughout life.

Time

Life offers us opportunities to think in terms of what is happening now and to be aware of what is taking place all around us by focusing on current thoughts, ideas, feelings, and experiences. Where you are *is* where you have come from and where you are going. We do not always have to live by the clock. Mother Earth has her own unique rhythms that signal the beginnings and endings of things. Again, one need only observe and listen quietly to know when it is time. So-called Indian time says that things begin when they are ready and things end when they are finished.

Being

Native tradition (the "Medicine Way") emphasizes a unique sense of "being" that allows one to live in accord with the natural flow of life energy. Being says "It's enough just to be; our purpose in life is to develop the inner self in relation to everything around us." Being receives much of its power from connectedness. Belonging and connectedness lie at the very heart of where we came from, who we are, and to whom we belong. True "being" requires that we know and experience our connections and that we honor our relations with all of our heart.

The Meaning of Family

It has been said by DuBray (1985), Rosebud Sioux, that "about the most unfavorable moral judgment an Indian can pass on another person is to say 'he acts as if he didn't have any relatives'" (p. 36). The concept of "relation" is a way of life for many Native American people, and it is very important for good reason. Everything is thought of in terms of relation of one kind or another. That is the natural order of things. Thus, it is believed that one cannot possibly know where one stands without knowing where he or she is in relation to everything else. Upon meeting for the first time, many Indian people will ask "Where do you come from? Who's your family? Who do you belong to? Who are your people?" This is because they want to know where they stand in relation to this new person and what commonality exists. In fact, this is a simple way of building bridges or recognizing bridges that already exist but are as yet unknown. It is also a way of honoring those bridges by appreciating them for what they are and by sharing.

In the traditional way, we are connected with all things, and we call on all of our relations for strength, for guidance, and for wisdom. We call on our relations for comfort and for sharing. There is harmony and balance in the energy of our connections. And it is believed that one of the most powerful sources of strength and wisdom comes from the family with whom we are truly connected. Of course, family may or may not consist of blood relatives. It is common practice in the Indian way, for instance, to "claim" another as a relative, thereby welcoming him or her as real family. From that point on, that person *is* a relative and that is that. After all, "family" is a matter of blood *and* of spirit.

In Native tradition, because the survival and well-being of the individual are synonymous with those of the community, family plays a prominent role in our lives, whether we realize it or not. Many Native people *are* their family in a real sense, because they identify themselves not by their own accomplishments but by the nature of their relations and the energy they draw from those connections. However, it is important to realize that what the mainstream defines as "family" takes on a much broader view in the traditional way. Family relationships include much more than the biological connections of the nuclear family. For example, as mentioned before, the claiming of nonblood relatives as family members is commonly practiced among Indian people who try to listen to the "spirit" of the relationship and honor it accordingly. Very often, we come into this world with many relatives not limited only to blood relation.

In the traditional way, the prevalence of cooperation and sharing in the spirit of community is essential for harmony and balance. It is not unusual for a Native child to be raised in several different households over time. This is generally not because no one cares enough to keep a child around very long, or because Native American people are lazy and irresponsible, but because it is considered both an obligation and a pleasure to share in raising and caring for the children in one's family. Grandparents, aunts, uncles, and other members of the community are all responsible for the raising of children, and they take this responsibility very seriously. After all, children are the fresh green leaves unfolding on the outermost branches of the tree, and they give the tree and its roots much strength and beauty.

The traditional view of family is universal in scope. "Family" extends well beyond one's immediate relatives to extended family relatives through second cousins, members of one's clan, members of the community or tribe, all other living creatures in this world, the natural environment, and the universe itself. The entire universe is thought of as "a family" with each and every one of its members having a useful and necessary place in the circle of life.

The animals are our four-legged brothers and sisters; the earth is mother; the sky, father; the moon, grandmother; and the sun, grandfather to all living creatures (gender references vary from tribe to tribe, but the essence of honoring intent remains consistent). All of these things are our relatives and should be treated with kindness and respect deserving of any family member. Traditionalists believe that the connection we all have with others (not just people) can be considered nothing short of sacred. "Relation" is something that extends beyond that of biological connection to one of a spiritual nature. For every connection that we have, we are part of it, and it is part of us. And there is energy there that we call "life." The traditional view of "family" symbolizes a unique approach to the entire process of living as we move through the circle of life.

Harmony Ethic

The Native cultural value of harmony in interpersonal relationships as well as in one's relationship with the environment speaks to the essence of Native tradition (Dudley, 1992; Dufrene & Coleman, 1992, 1994; M. T. Garrett, 1995, 1996a, 1996b; Good Tracks, 1973; Herring, 1992; Lake, 1991; Locust, 1988; Mitchum, 1989; Plank, 1994; Red Horse, 1980). This traditional value has been referred to as the *harmony ethic* (Neely, 1991). The harmony ethic (J. T. Garrett & Garrett, 1994, 1996; Neely, 1991) guides both the beliefs and the behaviors of Native people in the communal spirit of cooperation and contribution as a way of maintaining the natural harmony and balance that exist within oneself and with the world around oneself. The basic tenets of the harmony ethic are as follows:

1. *A nonaggressive and noncompetitive approach to life.* This is especially true if the goal of aggression or competition is individual success. If the goal of competition is to benefit the family, clan, tribe, or community, then competition is considered acceptable. Intertribal sports competitions, for example, can become quite aggressive in nature. Competition or aggression for personal gain, however, is frowned upon.
2. *The use of intermediaries, or a neutral third person, as a way of minimizing face-to-face hostility and disharmony in interpersonal relations.* This involves the conscious avoidance of interpersonal conflict in an attempt to maintain reciprocally harmonious relations with all of one's relations. This is a common strategy in the traditional way for resolution of conflict without upsetting the natural balance of things.
3. *Reciprocity and the practice of generosity.* This occurs even when people cannot afford to be generous. The acts of respectfully giving and of receiving are believed to be necessary to maintain the proper functioning of the community. Being able to share unselfishly frees the individual to learn important lessons that are offered in life.
4. *A belief in immanent justice.* This relieves people from feelings of needing to control others through direct interference. There is a natural order to things, and sometimes, there are situations or experiences that are out of our hands, so to speak. It is very important to be able to release rather than harm oneself or others with destructive emotions, thoughts, or actions. There is an old Indian saying that one should never speak ill against another for the wind will carry it to that person, and eventually, the ill will return on the wind, seven times stronger.

The harmony ethic is a system based on caring for fellow human beings through the expression of deep respect and kindness. It is a system based on harmonious survival among people in their social and environmental community. It also emphasizes the importance of choice. To the people of many Native nations, a person has just as much choice in creating harmony as he or she does in creating disharmony and social disruption.

Noninterference

From a traditional view, all things are alive and possess intrinsic worth. Native American spirituality focuses on the harmony and balance that come from our connection with all parts of the universe in which everything has the purpose and value exemplary of "personhood," including all plants (e.g., "tree people"), animals ("our four-legged brothers and sisters"), rocks and minerals ("rock people"), the land ("Mother Earth"), the winds ("the Four Powers"), "Father Sky," "Grandfather Sun," "Grandmother Moon," and the "Red Thunder Beings." As with humankind, all of these beings possess intrinsic worth and natural purpose in the greater scheme of things. Within this view lies the most powerful sense of belonging and connectedness as well as a deep respect for all of our relations. Spiritual "being" essentially requires only that we seek our place in the universe; everything else will follow in good time. Because everyone and everything were created with a specific purpose to fulfill, no one should have the power to interfere or to impose on others what the best path is to follow. This is the value of choice.

In the Medicine Way, the significance of relationship lies in a balance struck between an all-encompassing sense of belonging and connectedness with one's relations and the practice of noninterference. The highest form of respect for another person is respecting his or her natural right to be self-determining. This means not interfering with another person's ability to choose, even when it is to keep that person from doing something foolish or dangerous. Every experience holds a valuable lesson—even in death, there is valuable learning that the spirit carries forth. Noninterference means caring in a respectful way, and it is the way of "right relationship."

Interfering with the activity of others, by way of aggression, for example, cannot and should not be encouraged or tolerated. Not only is this disrespectful, but it violates the natural order of harmony and balance in which each being has to learn and experience life in his or her own way. Each person, each living being on Mother Earth, has his or her own Medicine that should not be disrupted or changed without that person choosing it. This is part of learning. What moves the circle is choice, and what keeps the circle are kindness and respect for the natural flow of life energy.

According to Good Tracks (1973), patience is the number one virtue governing Indian relationships. Respect often demands patience of us because things are rarely going to go the way that we expect them to. Yet, we have the tendency to want to change how things are rather than change what we expect. From a traditional way, "pain" is really nothing more than the difference between what is and what we want it to be. To be respectful of all things, we often must sacrifice expectation.

Sacred space is more than just physical space. It consists of all four directions, in the realm of mind, body, spirit, and natural environment. Just as we all have had the experience of someone bumping into us and not saying that he or she was sorry, we all have had the experience of someone telling us what to do, pressuring us, criticizing us, or manipulating us and not giving us the choice or the chance. All of these things take away choice, disrespect choice, and show little sign of regarding with interest, deference, and admiration. And we have done the same to others as well. No one likes to be controlled. People are not meant to be controlled. No one wants to feel as though his or her choice is being violated. It does not feel good. Such things as asking intrusive questions, interrupting, speaking for others, telling others what to do, arguing, blaming, using sarcasm, sulking, being condescending, nit-picking, or using threats (both spoken and unspoken) are all fairly common occurrences, and we wonder why we may not feel well so much of the time. It is because we are violating the natural laws of creation. It does not matter why we do it; what matters are the consequences of such actions that result in disharmony and discord.

Noninterference stresses the importance of always asking permission and not making unnecessary assumptions about others. It reminds us to always be thankful for what we have and not expect more than that but rather show respect for what we do have and for the greater circle of which we all are a part.

Above all, respect for others through patience, openness, and flexibility ultimately shows respect for oneself and one's community. It is not uncommon in the traditional way for the group to allow or accept a person's withdrawal without question or expectation. In addition, that person is to be welcomed back into the group without a required explanation for his or her absence. There is no need to interfere by asking what is wrong or offering solutions. Respect for another dictates that when a person is ready to share information, he or she will do so. Likewise, if a person is in need of assistance or advice, he or she will ask.

Patience is a virtue. Noninterference shows us that caring and respect are not one and the same but that both are required for harmonious relations. One of the highest forms of caring for another person comes through the expression of respect, that is, respecting a person's right and ability to choose for himself or herself and practicing the patience to allow him or her to do just that. Every person deserves the opportunity and respect to make his or her own choices. There are lessons to be learned through the making of choices and certain truths to be experienced through respect for the autonomy and presence of all living things. The following anecdote illustrates this:

> I think it is time you knew of Tagoona, the Inuit. Last year one of our white men said to him, "We are glad you have been ordained as the first priest of your people. Now you can help us with their problem." Tagoona asked, "What is a problem?" and the white man said, "Tagoona, if I held you by your heels from a third-story window, you would have a problem." Tagoona considered this long and carefully. Then he said, "I do not think so. If you saved me, all would be well. If you dropped me, nothing would matter. It is you who would have the problem." (Craven, 1973, p. 74)

The same philosophy applies, in a traditional way, to our relation with nature, in which permission must be asked before taking and thanks must be expressed by giving back in some way. This could be as simple as a small prayer giving thanks. It might mean sprinkling a little tobacco as an offering of gratitude for whatever has been received. Noninterference may take many different forms depending on the tribe and specific Native person, but the essence of respectful intent remains the same.

Spirituality and Wellness: Walking in Step

Different tribal languages have different words for or ways of referring to the idea of honoring one's sense of connection, but the meaning is similar across nations in referring to the belief that human beings exist on Mother Earth to be helpers and protectors of life. In Native communities, it is not uncommon, as an example, to hear people use the term *caretaker*. Therefore, from the perspective of a traditionalist, to see one's purpose as that of caretaker is to accept responsibility for the gift of life by taking good care of that gift and the surrounding beauty of the world in which we live.

More or less, the essence of Native American spirituality is about feeling. The feeling of connection is something that is available to all of us, though experienced in differing ways. It is important to note that the spiritual beliefs of Native Americans depend on a number of factors, including level of acculturation (traditional, marginal, bicultural, assimilated, pantraditional), geographic region, family structure, religious influences, and tribal-specific traditions (for further discussion of levels of acculturation, see J. T. Garrett & Garrett, 1994; M. T. Garrett & Pichette, 2000; LaFromboise et al., 1993). However, it is possible to generalize, to some extent, about a number of basic beliefs characterizing Native American traditionalism and spirituality across tribal nations. The following, adapted from Locust (1988, pp. 317–318), elaborates on a number of basic Native American spiritual and traditional beliefs:

- There is a single higher power known as Creator, Great Creator, Great Spirit, or Great One, among other names (this being is sometimes referred to in gender form but does not necessarily exist as one particular gender or another). There are also lesser beings known as spirit beings or spirit helpers.
- Plants and animals, like humans, are part of the spirit world. The spirit world exists side by side and intermingles with the physical world. Moreover, the spirit existed in the spirit world before it came into a physical body and will exist after the body dies.
- Human beings are made up of a spirit, mind, and body. The mind, body, and spirit are all interconnected; therefore, illness affects the mind and spirit as well as the body.
- Wellness is harmony in body, mind, and spirit; unwellness is disharmony in mind, body, and spirit.
- Natural unwellness is caused by the violation of a sacred social or natural law of Creation (e.g., participating in a sacred ceremony while under the influence of alcohol or drugs or having had sex within 4 days of the ceremony).
- Unnatural unwellness is caused by conjuring (witchcraft) from those with destructive intentions.
- Each of us is responsible for our own wellness by keeping ourselves attuned to self, relations, environment, and universe.

This list of beliefs in Native American spirituality crosses tribal boundaries but is by no means a comprehensive list. It does, however, provide a great deal of insight into some of the assumptions that may be held by a "traditional" Native client. To better understand more generally what it means to "walk in step" according to Native American spirituality, one can remember the following four Native principles as a general rule of thumb for living in harmony and balance:

1. Everything is alive.
2. Everything has purpose.
3. All things are connected.
4. Embrace the Medicine of every living being, and embrace your vision. (M. T. Garrett & Wilbur, 1999)

The Medicine of Healing

As counselors, we have the responsibility and privilege of being able to serve as facilitators and guides for our Native clients as they walk their own Medicine path, seeking their own vision. Archie Fire Lame Deer, Lakota Medicine Man, described the role of the caretaker through the following words:

> To be a Medicine person, you have to experience everything, live life to the fullest. If you don't experience the human side of everything, how can you help teach or heal? To be a good Medicine person, you've got to be humble. You've got to be lower than a worm and higher than an eagle. (as quoted in M. T. Garrett, 1998, p. 41)

Though it is not our job as counselors to be a Medicine person, it seems that we walk a parallel path as another form of helper.

The process of healing in the traditional way varies from tribe to tribe, but there are some general commonalities. First of all, someone seeking a Medicine person might never have any direct contact with that person but rather communicate through a mediator (maybe a relative or a mutually trusted person) who goes between helper and helpee; of course, this depends on the situation, on the specific Medicine person, and on the person being helped.

It is generally true that someone seeking a Medicine person will make an offering of some kind to the Medicine person as a sign of respect and good intent, and this offering is done without expectation of anything in return, although it is a request for help. The Medicine person might pray about the situation and make a decision about whether to help and, if so, how to help. Often, a form of ceremony will be implemented. The Medicine person might talk at length with the helpee or might not talk at all. A specific task might be given to the helpee for completion. Regardless, personal cleansing is usually a given. Again, all of this varies from tribe to tribe and from one Medicine person to another. However, two very important things that the Medicine person will often include as part of the healing process are (a) the support system for the person, such as family, friends, or other trusted persons, and (b) some type of ceremony or ritual (sometimes including a family or communal meal) that helps restore the person and his or her environment to harmony and balance. Finally, there is the philosophy with which the Medicine person approaches the entire process of healing, as best summarized by Godfrey Chips, Lakota Medicine Man: "I'm the spirit's janitor. All I do is wipe the windows a little bit so you can see out for yourself" (as quoted in M. T. Garrett, 1998, p. 145).

Given the cultural context of healing from a traditional Native perspective, it is important to consider how this fits with a contemporary mode of intervention. A major goal of counseling is to promote the wellness of the client by facilitating his or her optimum development through positive human change (M. T. Garrett, 1999a; Myers, 1991; Myers, Sweeney, & Witmer, 2001; Myers, Witmer, & Sweeney, 1995). Individual worldviews and cultural value orientations have been identified as critical variables that facilitate the therapeutic process. According to Ivey (1991), "by understanding the client's frame of reference, we can better plan interventions to facilitate change and life-span development within the appropriate cultural framework" (p. 8).

The primary goal of being able to informally assess and more fully understand Native clients' cultural identities as they understand them is to promote the wellness of Native clients. By developing better ways for helping Native Americans to deal with personal, social, and environmental difficulties resulting from cultural discontinuity and the process of acculturation, counselors can focus on wellness while also emphasizing culturally appropriate methods and communication style, depending on level of acculturation. This might be accomplished, for example, through counseling interventions designed to facilitate culturally appropriate identity development and (possibly) bicultural competence in Native Americans through techniques such as values clarification, self-awareness exercises, stress management, and communication skills enhancement. Understanding the client's cultural worldview as expressed through his or her voices, experiences, and stories is essential in understanding and utilizing culturally responsive counseling interventions and modes of communication to promote the wellness of the client.

Implications for Counseling

Identity

It is interesting to note the tendency of many Native Americans in the company of fellow in-group members to refer to each other as "Indian," whereas in the company of outsiders, they refer to themselves as "Native American" and expect non-Indians to do the same out of respect. Ironically, confusion regarding appropriate terminology, derogatory meanings associated with certain labels (e.g., "Indian") used by outsiders, and the tendency of mainstream culture to focus on blood quantum and physical characteristics as a sign of who is Indian underline the historical context and process of acculturation experienced by many

Native Americans. Rather, understanding the Native person is understanding the mental, physical, social, emotional, and spiritual experience of what it means to be "Indian" from that person's perspective.

As a counselor, Native or non-Native, respect for individual Native clients means finding out from which tribe that client comes, and possibly whether that person is directly affiliated with that tribe (federal, state, and/or community recognition). This can be approached out of interest or the need to better understand who that person is. However, it is not the job of a counselor to pass judgment on who is Indian and who is not. More specifically, a counselor should not ask a Native client how much Indian he or she is or relate personal stories of Indian heritage in the counselor's family as a way of connecting with that client. That is the quickest way to lose a Native person's receptivity and trust. If a client says he or she is Indian, then it must be assumed that he or she is and, more important, that that is an important part of the client's self-definition. It is another way of better understanding that client without having to get into the painful (and sometimes irrelevant) politics of categorization. It gives a counselor insight into that person's perception of his or her experience and place in the world.

History

The underlying issue in terms of counseling Native clients given the historical and political context is trust versus mistrust. The question to ask yourself as a counselor is "What can I do to create and maintain trust with a Native client?" By recognizing the need for further self-education about the history of specific tribes from which clients come, the counselor can better understand the context of trust versus mistrust that a particular Native client may bring to the counseling relationship. A natural next step to understanding a particular Native client is to better understand not only the historical context and meaning of the Native American experience but also the specific contemporary context from which that client comes as a function of his or her personal/cultural identity as a Native person.

Acculturation

The following Native American Acculturation Scale: Informal Assessment/Interview (M. T. Garrett & Pichette, 2000) is a set of statements or questions that provide areas for exploration and that can serve as an informal way of assessing level of acculturation in a Native client:

1. What is your tribal affiliation, if any?
2. Do you speak any other languages, and if so, which do you prefer?
3. Tell me how you see yourself in terms of your own identity.
4. How does/did your mother identify herself?
5. How does/did your father identify himself?
6. Tell me where you come from or where you grew up, and who were some of the important people to you there (e.g., friends, family, mentors).
7. Tell me where you live now and who are some of the important people to you there (or at this point in your life).
8. What kind of music, movies, foods, and so forth do you prefer?
9. Tell me where you see yourself in relation to your (tribal) culture and heritage.
10. What other things would you like for me to know about you as a person?

The Native American Acculturation Scale offers an operationalized means for counselors to informally assess a Native client's level of acculturation in order to better understand his or her worldview and cultural identity as a person of color (for quantitative assessment of acculturation, see M. T. Garrett & Pichette, 2000). Institutional racism, oppression, and the pressure to assimilate, very much a part of our country's history in dealings with minority groups, is a reality that continues to affect the lives of Native Americans through struggles to reconcile two very different cultures.

Counselors must avoid making assumptions about the cultural identity of Native American clients without gathering further information. By understanding a Native American client's cultural identity (traditional, bicultural, or assimilated), counselors are better prepared to work collaboratively with their client's needs, concerns, and goals through appropriate interventions that underscore the importance of that person's cultural identity, and that provide a way to recognize where that person is and where he or she wants to be (J. T. Garrett & Garrett, 1994). Therefore, counseling can be approached as a developmental process of helping Native American clients come to a better understanding of themselves, others, society, and life. Counselors who understand the acculturation continuum as a reflection of historical events/circumstances and life choices that shape the worldview of Native American clients will be able to see the clients as they see themselves—through their hopes, dreams, struggles, pain, strength, relations, history, and perceptions of what is real and meaningful in life.

Practitioners are encouraged to use the interview format to explore and identify a Native client's worldview. However, caution is necessary. Regardless of findings from formal or informal assessments of cultural identity, counselors should always maintain a flexible perspective that avoids stereotyping or inaccurate assumptions of meaning. Further, to better understand the essence of traditional Native culture, it is important to explore the meaning of the core values and beliefs that characterize what it means to be Native.

Native Values and Worldview

In contrast to many of the traditional Native values and beliefs discussed thus far, mainstream American values tend to emphasize self-promotion, saving for the future, domination of others, getting things done (doing), competition and aggression, individualism and the nuclear family, mastery over nature, a time orientation toward living for the future, a preference for scientific explanations of everything, clock watching, winning as much as possible, and reverence of youth (Charleston, 1994; DuBray, 1985; Garcia & Ahler, 1992; M. T. Garrett, 1995, 1999b; Little Soldier, 1992; Peregoy, 1993; Rotenberg & Cranwell, 1989; Sanders, 1987; Sue & Sue, 1999). Between the two very different value orientations of traditional Native Americans and mainstream Americans lies a whole continuum from the very traditional Native American raised on the reservation who speaks the Native language to the Native American raised in an urban setting who speaks only English, is completely assimilated with the mainstream American value system, and may feel little identification with a tribe (Herring, 1994; Thomason, 1991).

Acculturation and the effects of oppression have created changes for many Native people across the generations. For majority culture society, a person's worth is generally measured according to accomplishment and ambition. The so-called inactivity associated with old age has coincided with a general devaluing of elders in American society. Traditionally, it is the primary responsibility of the grandparents to raise the children and that of the parents to provide economic support. The Native American family is based on a multigenerational support system of interdependence that provides cultural continuity for all. Today, Indian children are influenced, among other things, by mainstream attitudes promoting the worthlessness of elders. The effects of mainstream views of elder people have, in many cases, split the Native American multigenerational support system by removing Indian elders from their roles as honored persons in the community. This is but one example of systemic indicators of value conflicts and cultural discontinuity.

For Native people, the potential for cultural conflicts due to differing values within the context of the larger society is evident. Assessment of level of acculturation, as discussed in the previous section, may offer valuable insight into a particular Native client's worldview, but further exploration of cultural conflicts may be a viable goal for counseling, if appropriate. Native clients can be encouraged to talk about the meaning of family, clan, or tribe to them as a way of exploring worldview, especially in light of intergenerational differences or the effects of oppression as contributing factors in issues being presented.

Spiritual Ways

Having a general understanding of Native American spirituality does not prepare one to participate in or conduct Native ceremonies as part of the counseling process (Matheson, 1996). That is the responsibility of those who are trained as Medicine persons (e.g., traditional spiritual healers, Medicine men or Medicine women, Indian doctors), individuals who can serve as important resources to counselors working with Native clients. However, having this understanding does prepare one to recognize culturally specific meanings and practices that may play a critical role not only in understanding the client's issues and appropriate ways of dealing with them but also in understanding the very world in which the client lives. Just because an Indian client is sitting in front of a counselor, the counselor cannot assume that the client is a traditionalist. Even if that person is traditional, the counselor must accurately understand what that means for that person. To be more specific, Native spirituality manifests in so many different forms, including traditional Native spiritual ways (specific to each Indian nation), Christian traditions, or the Native American Church, to name but a few.

When working with an Indian client, it is important for the counselor to get a sense of that person's level of acculturation by informally assessing (a) values (traditional, marginal, bicultural, assimilated, pantraditional), (b) geographic origin/residence (reservation, rural, urban), and (c) tribal affiliation (tribal structure, customs, beliefs; for further discussion of formal and informal assessment of Native American acculturation, see M. T. Garrett & Pichette, 2000). Both verbal and nonverbal cues will give counselors a good sense of a Native American client's level of acculturation (J. T. Garrett & Garrett, 1994). If questions remain, it is important to pose them in a respectful, unobtrusive way. Following are some examples of general leads intended to respectfully elicit important culturally relevant information:

- Where do you come from?
- Tell me about your family.
- What tribe/nation are you? Tell me a little bit about that.
- Tell me about you as a person, culturally and spiritually.
- Tell me how you identify yourself culturally.
- Tell me how your culture/spirituality plays into how you live your life.
- Tell me about your life as you see it, past, present, or future.

It is important not to assume that because a person looks Indian that he or she is traditional in his or her spiritual ways, or that because a person does not look Indian that he or she is not traditional. Moreover, with a client who seems to have more traditional values and beliefs, it may be particularly helpful to suggest that family or other significant persons (e.g., a Medicine man or Medicine woman) participate in the process to support the client as he or she moves through important personal transitions and any subsequent personal cleansing.

Communication

Once the counselor has some general information concerning the client's cultural background and spiritual ways, he or she has a better understanding of what may or may not be considered appropriate with and for the client. The following recommendations (M. T. Garrett, 1999b; M. T. Garrett & Pichette, 2000) are intended as culturally responsive ways for working with a traditional Native client.

1. *Greeting.* For traditional Native Americans, a gentle handshake is the proper way of greeting. Sometimes, t48here is no handshake at all, just a word of greeting or a non-verbal acknowledgment such as a head nod. To use a firm handshake, as is expected in mainstream American society as a sign of confidence and enthusiasm, is considered an insult in the traditional way because it is interpreted as an aggressive show of power. It may be important to follow, rather than lead, the client.

2. *Hospitality.* Given the traditional emphasis on generosity, kindness, and "gifting" as a way of honoring the relation, hospitality is an important part of Native American life. Therefore, it is helpful to be able to offer the Native client a beverage or snack as a sign of good relation. In the traditional way, to not offer hospitality to a visitor or guest is to bring shame on oneself and one's family.

3. *Silence.* In the traditional way, when two people meet, very little may be said between them during the initial moments of the encounter. Therefore, quiet time at the beginning of a session is an appropriate way of transitioning into the therapeutic process by giving both counselor and client a chance to orient themselves to the situation, get in touch with themselves, and experience the presence of the other person. This brief time (maybe a couple of minutes or so) can be nonverbal, noninteractive time that allows the client to be at ease. This is an important show of respect, understanding, and patience.

4. *Space.* Taking care to respect physical space is an extension of the importance in traditional Native culture that one need not always fill relational space with words. In Native tradition, both the physical form and the space between the physical are considered sacred. In counseling, it is important to respect the physical space of the client by not sitting too close and not sitting directly across from the client. Although the intention is to allow the counselor to focus in on the client and vice versa, this is a subtle invasion of space. A more comfortable arrangement, traditionally, is sitting together side by side in two different chairs at a slight angle. The burning of sage, cedar, or sweetgrass (a method of spatial cleansing for many tribal nations, commonly known as "smudging") should be done only at the request or with permission of the Native client.

5. *Eye Contact.* Native American clients with traditional values (and possibly those who are marginal or bicultural) may tend to avert their eyes as a sign of respect. To subtly match this level of eye contact is respectful and shows an understanding of the client's way of being. The eyes are considered to be the pathway to the spirit; therefore, to consistently look someone in the eye is to show a level of entitlement or aggressiveness. It is good to glance at someone every once in a while, but listening, in the traditional way, is something that happens with the ears and the heart.

6. *Intention.* One of the biggest issues with many Indian clients in the counseling relationship is trust. This should come as no surprise given the history of broken promises and exploitation survived by many tribal nations. Typically, an Indian client will "read" the counselor's nonverbal behaviors fairly quickly to determine whether the counselor is someone to be trusted or not. Therefore, counselors can focus on honor-

ing the mental space between counselor and client by seeking to offer respect and humility in the counseling process. Acceptance by the counselor means not trying to control or influence the client. This is considered "bad Medicine."

7. *Collaboration.* In counseling, more traditional clients may welcome (or even expect) the counselor to offer helpful suggestions or alternative ways of dealing with things. From a traditional perspective, respect for choice is utmost, but healing is a collaborative process. Therefore, the counselor should offer suggestions without offering directions. There is a difference between encouraging and pushing. And once again, with traditional Native American clients, actions will always speak louder than words. As a part of this, it is sometimes helpful to incorporate humor (appropriately) because this is an important part of Native culture and communication style, as well as a powerful tool for many Native Americans.

Counseling Recommendations

When working with Native people, counselors must make several important considerations based on historical context, level of acculturation, cultural values and worldview, spiritual tradition, and communication style. It is important for counselors to demonstrate sincere interest in and respect for clients. For non-Native counselors, having a general understanding of Native American worldview and spirituality does not prepare them to participate in or conduct Native ceremonies as part of the counseling process. That is the responsibility of those who are trained as Medicine people (e.g., traditional spiritual healers, Medicine men or Medicine women, Indian doctors), individuals who can serve as important resources to counselors working with Native clients. However, recognizing culturally specific meanings and practices may play a critical role in understanding not only the client's issues and appropriate ways of dealing with these but also the very world in which the client lives (M. T. Garrett & Wilbur, 1999). Just because an Indian client is sitting in front of a counselor, the counselor cannot assume that that person is traditional. Even if that person is traditional, the counselor must accurately understand what that means for that person.

As mentioned earlier, it is important to get a sense of the client's level of acculturation by informally assessing (a) values (traditional, marginal, bicultural, assimilated, pantraditional), (b) geographic origin/residence (reservation, rural, urban), and (c) tribal affiliation (tribal structure, customs, beliefs). Both verbal and nonverbal cues will give counselors a good sense of a Native American client's level of acculturation. If questions remain, it is important to pose them in a respectful, unobtrusive way, for example, "Tell me a little bit about where you come from," "Tell me about your family," or "Tell me which nation/tribe you are," and so on.

For the counselor, establishing trustworthiness with a Native client means being attentive, respectful, and culturally responsive to the client, giving appropriate structure and direction to the process while also being flexible enough to incorporate helpful resources or interventions (J. T. Garrett & Garrett, 1994). Showing respect could also mean being open to or suggesting the possibility of client consultation with a traditional healer. In fact, linking services could prove to be very effective if counselors encourage that such services be provided by traditional healers in conjunction with counseling or therapy. This would be a clear demonstration of respect for traditional ways while providing a more comprehensive service to Native clients in need. But this also means being familiar with and having good rapport with those resources in and around those communities.

Another method of demonstrating respect for the traditional way is to encourage extended family members to participate in the healing process (Attneave, 1985). Working in the presence of a group, giving people a choice about the best way to proceed with the process, and encouraging the participation of family members and friends are all natural components of the traditional healing way. Of course, this must and can be done while also respecting confidentiality of clients. The key is collaboration.

In addition to contemporary counseling interventions and treatment modalities, counselors can incorporate tribal-specific interventions as appropriate to meet the cultural/ spiritual needs of specific Native clients. As a major part of collaboration with Native clients in the counseling process, the following (M. T. Garrett & Carroll, 2000) are offered as practical recommendations.

Sociodemographics: Native clients can reconnect with a sense of purpose by finding ways to combat the high rates of unemployment, inadequate housing, low educational levels, poverty-level incomes, and isolated living conditions. Participation in community-wide volunteer programs to help those in need has proven to be a successful part of healing for many Indian people.

Physiology: Native people should be encouraged to get regular physical checkups and have blood tests done to monitor any difficulties regarding blood sugar or any other physiological difficulties.

Historical Context: A critical component of counseling could include a psychoeducational piece or dialogue designed to provide insight concerning many of the historical factors such as exploitation of Native people through discrimination, assimilation through boarding schools and relocation programs, and disruption of traditional cultural and familial patterns. This could provide important topics for discussion as well as help Native clients explore their own level of cultural identity development.

Acculturation/Identity: Native clients can be assisted with exploration of cultural identity issues by focusing on the cultural themes of belonging, mastery, independence, and generosity. Counselors can utilize the following general questions for each of the four respective areas: (a) Where do you belong? (b) What are you good at? What do you enjoy doing? (c) What are your sources of strength? What limits you? (d) What do you have to offer/ contribute?

Isolation/Social Connections: Participation in other social events such as family gatherings and powwows allows Native clients to experience social cohesion and social interaction in their communities. Moreover, some Native clients can benefit from a sense of reconnection with community and traditional roles. This could and has been accomplished through reviving tribal ceremonies and practices (e.g., talking circles, sweat lodges, powwows, peyote meetings), thus reestablishing a sense of belonging and communal meaningfulness for Native people and "returning to the old ways" or, at least, integrating many of these ways into modern-day life.

Generational Splits: Native clients of all ages can benefit from acting as or learning from elders serving as role models/teachers for young people. This, too, has become more commonly practiced by tribal nations across the country in therapeutic programs as well as in the schools.

Coping Mechanisms: Native clients can learn other methods of dealing with stress, boredom, powerlessness, and the sense of emptiness associated with acculturation and identity confusion. Consultation with or participation of a Medicine person (i.e., traditional Native healer) may prove very helpful.

Noninterference: The avoidance behavior of community members in maintaining the cultural value of not imposing one's will on another is something that can be addressed with the Native client as well as with community members to the extent that it may be destructive. Attneave's (1969, 1985) network therapy has been very effective with Indian clients as a way of working with an individual in a family and community context.

Other forms of intervention based on Native culturally responsive individual or group formats can be implemented as appropriate given the client's needs and openness to such interventions (see, e.g., Brendtro et al., 1990; Four Worlds Development Project, 1984; J. T. Garrett & Garrett, 1996; M. T. Garrett, 1998; M. T. Garrett, Brotherton, & Garrett, 2001; M. T. Garrett & Carroll, 2000; M. T. Garrett & Crutchfield, 1997; M. T. Garrett & Garrett, in press; M. T. Garrett & Osborne, 1995; Heinrich et al., 1990; Herring, 1999; Lake, 1991; Roberts-Wilbur, Wilbur, Garrett, & Yuhas, 2001; Thomason, 1991; Vick, Smith, & Iron Rope Herrera, 1998).

From a traditional Native American perspective, being well means "walking in step with the universe." This highlights the cultural importance of understanding, participating in, maintaining, and revering relationships and the art of relation. Counselors are trained as professionals to use this same "Medicine" for healing and for helping people learn from their experiences in order to make life choices. It is in everything in which power moves.

Conclusion: Circles Within Circles

As you hear the sound of the drum rumbling low to the sharp, impassioned cries of the singers, the vibration moves through you like a storm that rises in the distance, building slowly in the azure sky, then unloading in a rhythmic yet gentle pounding of the soil. Anyone, Native or non-Native, who has ever had the opportunity to experience the colors, movement, sounds, tastes, and smells of the powwow understands the feeling that passes through you. It is different for every person, but if you really experience the feeling, you know that it is connection. For some, it is a matter of seeing old friends or making new ones. For some, it is the image of the dancers moving in seemingly infinite poses of unity and airy smoothness to every flowing pound of the drum. For some, it is the laughter and exchange of words and gestures. For some, it is silent inner prayer giving thanks for another day of life. For some, it is the delicious taste of their second and third helpings of that piping-hot fry-bread. Whatever it is, in the end, it is coming together in one way or another and walking in step with the greater circle. And just when you think you have seen all there is to see, the hoop dancer quietly emerges from the crowd and enters the circle.

References

Allen, P. G. (1991). Hoop dancer. In A. R. Velie (Ed.), *American Indian literature: An anthology* (p. 235). Norman: University of Oklahoma Press.

Attneave, C. L. (1969). Therapy in tribal settings and urban network intervention. *Family Process, 8,* 192–210.

Attneave, C. L. (1985). Practical counseling with American Indian and Alaska Native clients. In P. Pedersen (Ed.), *Handbook of cross-cultural counseling and therapy* (pp. 135–140). Westport, CT: Greenwood.

Brendtro, L. K., Brokenleg, M., & Van Bockern, S. (1990). *Reclaiming youth at risk: Our hope for the future.* Bloomington, IN: National Education Service.

Charleston, G. M. (1994). Toward true Native education: A treaty of 1992 final report of the Indian Nations At Risk Task Force Draft 3. *Journal of American Indian Education, 33*(2), 1–56.

Choney, S. K., Berryhill-Paapke, E., & Robbins, R. R. (1995). The acculturation of American Indians: Developing frameworks for research and practice. In J. G. Ponterotto, J. M. Casas, L. A. Suzuki, & C. M. Alexander (Eds.), *Handbook of multicultural counseling* (pp. 73–92). Thousand Oaks, CA: Sage.

Colodarci, T. (1983). High school dropout among Native Americans. *Journal of American Indian Education, 23*(1), 15–22.

Craven, M. (1973). *I heard the owl call my name.* New York: Laurel.

Cummins, J. (1992). The empowerment of Indian students. In J. Reyhner (Ed.), *Teaching American Indian students* (pp. 3–12). Norman: University of Oklahoma Press.

Deloria, V., Jr. (1988). *Custer died for your sins: An Indian manifesto.* Norman: University of Oklahoma Press.

Deloria, V., Jr. (1994). *God is red.* Golden, CO: Fulcrum.

Deyhle, D. (1992). Constructing failure and maintaining cultural identity: Navajo and Ute school leavers. *Journal of American Indian Education, 31*(2), 24–47.

DuBray, W. H. (1985). American Indian values: Critical factor in casework. *Social Casework: The Journal of Contemporary Social Work, 66,* 30–37.

Dudley, J. Iron Eye. (1992). *Choteau Creek: A Sioux reminiscence.* Lincoln: University of Nebraska Press.

Dufrene, P. M. (1990). Exploring Native American symbolism. *Journal of Multicultural and Cross-Cultural Research in Art Education, 8,* 38–50.

Dufrene, P. M., & Coleman, V. D. (1992). Counseling Native Americans: Guidelines for group process. *Journal for Specialists in Group Work, 17,* 229–235.

Dufrene, P. M., & Coleman, V. D. (1994). Art and healing for Native American Indians. *Journal of Multicultural Counseling and Development, 22,* 145–152.

Four Worlds Development Project. (1984). *The sacred tree: Reflections on Native American spirituality.* Wilmot, WI: Lotus Light.

Garcia, R. L., & Ahler, J. G. (1992). Indian education: Assumptions, ideologies, strategies. In J. Reyhner (Ed.), *Teaching American Indian students* (pp. 13–32). Norman: University of Oklahoma Press.

Garrett, J. T., & Garrett, M. T. (1994). The path of good medicine: Understanding and counseling Native Americans. *Journal of Multicultural Counseling and Development, 22*(3), 134–144.

Garrett, J. T., & Garrett, M. T. (1996). *Medicine of the Cherokee: The way of right relationship.* Santa Fe, NM: Bear.

Garrett, M. T. (1995). Between two worlds: Cultural discontinuity in the dropout of Native American youth. *The School Counselor, 42,* 186–195.

Garrett, M. T. (1996a). Reflection by the riverside: The traditional education of Native American children. *Journal of Humanistic Education and Development, 35*(1), 12–28.

Garrett, M. T. (1996b). "Two people": An American Indian narrative of bicultural identity. *Journal of American Indian Education, 36,* 1–21.

Garrett, M. T. (1998). *Walking on the wind: Cherokee teachings for harmony and balance.* Santa Fe, NM: Bear.

Garrett, M. T. (1999a). Soaring on the wings of the eagle: Wellness of Native American high school students. *Professional School Counseling, 3,* 57–64.

Garrett, M. T. (1999b). Understanding the "medicine" of Native American traditional values: An integrative review. *Counseling and Values, 43,* 84–98.

Garrett, M. T., Brotherton, D., & Garrett, J. T. (2001). Inner circle/outer circle: Native American group technique. *Journal for Specialists in Group Work, 26,* 17–30.

Garrett, M. T., & Carroll, J. (2000). Mending the broken circle: Treatment and prevention of substance abuse among Native Americans. *Journal of Counseling & Development, 78,* 379–388.

Garrett, M. T., & Crutchfield, L. B. (1997). Moving full circle: A unity model of group work with children. *Journal for Specialists in Group Work, 22,* 175–188.

Garrett, M. T., & Garrett, J. T. (1997). Counseling Native American elders. *Directions in Rehabilitation Counseling: Therapeutic Strategies With the Older Adult, 3,* 3–18.

Garrett, M. T., & Garrett, J. T. (in press). Ayeli: Centering technique based on Cherokee spiritual traditions. *Counseling and Values.*

Garrett, M. T., & Myers, J. E. (1996). The rule of opposites: A paradigm for counseling Native Americans. *Journal of Multicultural Counseling and Development, 24,* 89–104.

Garrett, M. T., & Osborne, W. L. (1995). The Native American sweat lodge as metaphor for group work. *Journal for Specialists in Group Work, 20,* 33–39.

Garrett, M. T., & Pichette, E. F. (2000). Red as an apple: Native American acculturation and counseling with or without reservation. *Journal of Counseling & Development, 78,* 3–13.

Garrett, M. T., & Wilbur, M. P. (1999). Does the worm live in the ground? Reflections on Native American spirituality. *Journal of Multicultural Counseling and Development, 27,* 193–206.

Good Tracks, J. G. (1973). Native American noninterference. *Social Work, 17,* 30–34.

Heinrich, R. K., Corbine, J. L., & Thomas, K. R. (1990). Counseling Native Americans. *Journal of Counseling & Development, 69,* 128–133.

Herring, R. D. (1989). The American Native family: Dissolution by coercion. *Journal of Multicultural Counseling and Development, 17,* 4–13.

Herring, R. D. (1990). Understanding Native American values: Process and content concerns for counselors. *Counseling and Values, 34,* 134–137.

Herring, R. D. (1992). Seeking a new paradigm: Counseling Native Americans. *Journal of Multicultural Counseling and Development, 20,* 35–43.

Herring, R. D. (1994). The clown or contrary figure as a counseling intervention strategy with Native American Indian clients. *Journal of Multicultural Counseling and Development, 22,* 153–164.

Herring, R. D. (1995). Developing biracial ethnic identity: A review of the increasing dilemma. *Journal of Multicultural Counseling and Development, 23,* 29–38.

Herring, R. D. (1996). Synergetic counseling and Native American Indian students. *Journal of Counseling & Development, 74,* 542–547.

Herring, R. D. (1999). *Counseling with Native American Indians and Alaska Natives: Strategies for helping professionals.* Thousand Oaks, CA: Sage.

Hirschfelder, A., & Kreipe de Montano, M. (1993). *The Native American almanac: A portrait of Native America today.* New York: Macmillan.

Hodgkinson, H. L. (1990). *The demographics of American Indians: One percent of the people; 50% of the diversity.* Washington, DC: Institute for Educational Leadership.

Hornett, D. (1990). Elementary-age tasks, cultural identity, and the academic performance of young American Indian children. *Action in Teacher Education, 12,* 43–49.

Hulburt, G., Kroeker, R., & Gade, E. (1991). Study orientation, persistence, and retention of Native students: Implications for confluent education. *Journal of American Indian Education, 30*(3), 16–23.

Ivey, A. E. (1991). *Developmental strategies for helpers: Individual, family, and network interventions.* Pacific Grove, CA: Brooks/Cole.

LaFromboise, T. D., Coleman, H. L. K., & Gerton, J. (1993). Psychological impact of biculturalism: Evidence and theory. *Psychological Bulletin, 114,* 395–412.

LaFromboise, T. D., & Rowe, W. (1983). Skills training for bicultural competence: Rationale and application. *Journal of Counseling Psychology, 30,* 589–595.

LaFromboise, T. D., Trimble, J. E., & Mohatt, G. V. (1990). Counseling intervention and American Indian tradition: An integrative approach. *The Counseling Psychologist, 18,* 628–654.

Lake, M. G. (1991). *Native healer: Initiation into an ancient art.* Wheaton, IL: Quest.

Lee, C. C. (2001). Defining and responding to racial and ethnic diversity. In D. C. Locke, J. E. Myers, & E. L. Herr (Eds.), *The handbook of counseling* (pp. 581–588). Thousand Oaks, CA: Sage.

Little Soldier, L. (1985). To soar with the eagles: Enculturation and acculturation of Indian children. *Childhood Education, 61,* 185–191.

Little Soldier, L. (1992). Building optimum learning environments for Navajo students. *Childhood Education, 68,* 145–148.

Locust, C. (1988). Wounding the spirit: Discrimination and traditional American Indian belief systems. *Harvard Educational Review, 58,* 315–330.

Loftin, J. D. (1989). Anglo-American jurisprudence and the Native American tribal quest for religious freedom. *American Indian Culture and Research Journal, 13*(1), 1–52.

Matheson, L. (1996). Valuing spirituality among Native American populations. *Counseling and Values, 41,* 51–58.

McLaughlin, D. (1994). Critical literacy for Navajo and other American Indian learners. *Journal of American Indian Education, 33*(3), 47–59.

Mitchum, N. T. (1989). Increasing self-esteem in Native American children. *Elementary School Guidance and Counseling, 23,* 266–271.

Myers, J. E. (1991). Wellness as the paradigm for counseling and development: The possible future. *Counselor Education and Supervision, 62,* 3–10.

Myers, J. E., Sweeney, T. J., & Witmer, J. M. (2001). Optimization of behavior: Promotion of wellness. In D. C. Locke, J. E. Myers, & E. L. Herr (Eds.), *The handbook of counseling* (pp. 641–652). Thousand Oaks, CA: Sage.

Myers, J. E., Witmer, J. M., & Sweeney, T. J. (1995). *The WEL manual.* Greensboro, NC: Author.

National Center for Education Statistics. (1991). *Dropout rates in the United States: 1990.* Washington, DC: U.S. Department of Education, Office of Educational Research and Improvement.

Neely, S. (1991). *Snowbird Cherokees: People of persistence.* Athens: University of Georgia Press.

Oswalt, W. H. (1988). *This land was theirs: A study of North American Indians* (4th ed.). Mountain View, CA: Mayfield.

Peregoy, J. J. (1993). Transcultural counseling with American Indians and Alaska Natives: Contemporary issues for consideration. In J. McFadden (Ed.), *Transcultural counseling: Bilateral and international perspectives* (pp. 163–191). Alexandria, VA: American Counseling Association.

Plank, G. A. (1994). What silence means for educators of American Indian children. *Journal of American Indian Education, 34*(1), 3–19.

Red Horse, J. G. (1980). Indian elders: Unifiers of families. *Social Casework, 61,* 490–493.

Red Horse, J. G. (1997). Traditional American Indian family systems. *Families, Systems, and Health, 15,* 243–250.

Reyhner, J., & Eder, J. (1992). A history of Indian education. In J. Reyhner (Ed.), *Teaching American Indian students* (pp. 33–58). Norman: University of Oklahoma Press.

Roberts-Wilbur, J., Wilbur, M., Garrett, M. T., & Yuhas, M. (2001). Talking circles: Listen or your tongue will make you deaf. *Journal for Specialists in Group Work, 26,* 368–384.

Robinson, T. L., & Howard-Hamilton, M. F. (2000). *The convergence of race, ethnicity, and gender: Multiple identities in counseling.* Upper Saddle River, NJ: Merrill.

Rotenberg, K. J., & Cranwell, F. R. (1989). Self-concept in American Indian and White children. *Journal of Cross-Cultural Psychology, 20,* 39–53.

Russell, G. (1997). *American Indian facts of life: A profile of today's tribes and reservations.* Phoenix, AZ: Russell.

Sanders, D. (1987). Cultural conflicts: An important factor in the academic failures of American Indian students. *Journal of Multicultural Counseling and Development, 15,* 81–90.

Sue, D. W., & Sue, D. (1999). *Counseling the culturally different: Theory and practice* (3rd ed.). New York: Wiley.

Thomason, T. C. (1991). Counseling Native Americans: An introduction for non-Native American counselors. *Journal of Counseling & Development, 69,* 321–327.

Tierney, W. (1992). *Official encouragement, unofficial discouragement: Minorities in academe—The Native American experience.* Norwood, NJ: Ablex.

U.S. Bureau of the Census. (2001). *The American Indian and Alaska Native population: 2000.* Washington, DC: Author.

U.S. Bureau of Indian Affairs. (1988). *American Indians today.* Washington, DC: Author.

Vick, R. D., Sr., Smith, L. M., & Iron Rope Herrera, C. (1998). The healing circle: An alternative path to alcoholism recovery. *Counseling and Values, 42,* 132–141.

The African American Experience

Counseling interventions with African Americans should be predicated on an understanding of their culture and its crucial role in fostering development. An examination of this culture reveals that Americans of African descent have developed a worldview that is grounded in African-oriented philosophical assumptions.

Professional counselors need to find ways to incorporate African/African American cultural dimensions into the helping process. Likewise, within African American communities, institutions that provide a network of indigenous social support, such as the Black church, may need to be incorporated into the counseling process.

Within the social sciences literature, the African American experience has traditionally been viewed as a monolithic entity. It is important for counselors to remember that there are many aspects and facets to this cultural experience.

A Cultural Framework for
Counseling African Americans

C. Emmanuel Ahia

Counseling African Americans presents counselors with an opportunity to become more aware of the cultural issues that form a basic worldview for this client group. Although these issues affect each African American in a different way, they underlie African Americans' psychosocial development and are important in establishing a cultural context for counseling interactions. This chapter provides a cultural framework for counseling African American clients. It presents an overview of the concept of Afrocentricity and its relationship to African Americans' mental health.

Afrocentricity: A Theoretical Overview

Afrocentricity Defined

Any contemporary discussion of counseling African Americans must begin with an examination of Afrocentricity. Afrocentricity is an existential point of view that puts Africa at the center of one's cosmology (Asante, 1992). The central theme of Afrocentrism is the idea that people of African descent must acknowledge, understand, and love their "Africaness" in order to understand and effectively deal with the past, present, and future. Afrocentricity reframes many psychoeducational concepts, often considered deviant or pathological in a "Eurocentric" context, into positive developmental notions for people of African descent.

Afrocentric scholars are in general agreement that there exists a composite of African-oriented existential tendencies, philosophies, behaviors, ideas, and artifacts among people worldwide who trace their roots to Black Africa (Asante, 1991, 1992; Asante & Asante, 1993). The fact that these African universals are theorized to exist suggests that mental health and psychosocial development among people of African descent are related to the degree and nature of their awareness of and responsiveness to Afrocentricity (Akbar, 1979; Baldwin, 1981; Belgrave et al., 1994; Brookins, 1994; Nobles, 1986; Nobles & Goddard, 1992).

As a psychological resource, Afrocentricity represents what Jung (1958) referred to as the "collective unconscious" among African peoples. This collective unconscious is made up of African folklore, mythology, and historical, social, and political events.

Afrocentricity is evident in a number of African-oriented traditions and customs. These include such concepts as perception of reality, concept of time, spirituality, human relations, family membership, and holism. In traditional African societies, these concepts are significant representations of a collective African cultural ethos. The work of Mbiti (1970) on African religion and philosophical traditions offers, perhaps, the best explanation of these concepts.

Perception of Reality

The traditional African-oriented perception of reality can be described as field dependent or field sensitive. This pattern of conceptualizing and processing reality tends to take into consideration the interactions between and among objective and subjective realities as well as the consequences or implications of such interactions. Among the Ibos of eastern Nigeria, for example, a common way to test the manner in which a child perceives reality is with the "birds on a tree" quiz. The child is told that 100 birds are on a tree when a hunter shoots one of them. The child is then asked, "How many birds are left on the tree?" In Western thinking, the obvious answer would be 99. However, for an Ibo child, the correct answer is always zero, because the child is expected to factor in all other realities, not just the numerical. In this case, it is the greater reality of the birds' natural behavior to fly away if one of them is shot.

Concepts of Time

The African concept of time embodies a people-oriented or event-oriented utility. Time is fluid and gets its meaning and importance from the essence of people and events. Social events, as opposed to fixed calendars or mechanical devices, control responses to time.

Most traditional African cultures are concerned with two dimensions of time: the past and the present. The concept of the "future" was considered "no time." Individuals could reflect only on "what has been" and "what is." "What will be" was generally out of the realm of consideration.

Spirituality

In traditional African societies, religion/spirituality permeated human existence. An individual's entire life was a spiritual phenomenon. Spirituality was an integral part of a unity principle in which humans, animals, plants, and natural phenomena were interrelated in a natural order with God being the driving force.

A strong belief in a spirit world pervades traditional African worldviews. Spirits belong to the ontological realm of existence between human beings and God. Africans generally recognized two categories of spiritual beings: those who were created as spirits and those who were once human beings. Human fate is controlled by the spirit world.

Human Relations

The African-oriented view of human nature is characterized by cooperative interdependence and group centeredness in human relationships. Every human life is deemed to be existentially relevant to the functioning, well-being, and dynamics of a community.

Achieving adult status has considerable social implications because African societies are adult oriented, as opposed to youth oriented. Age and maturity affect leadership selection, social interaction, respect, responsibility, and cultural education. A younger person is expected to unconditionally respect older persons. Advanced age, in and of itself, is deemed respectable and honorable. Young people who show disrespect for their elders encounter different forms and degrees of social sanctions and isolation.

Family Membership

The traditional African family is extended in nature. For example, individuals with strong African identity tend to take obligatorily financial responsibility for even distant relatives.

Most African languages do not have words for cousin, nephew, second cousin, niece, uncle, aunt, and so forth. In many cases, these family relations are described simply as "brother" or "sister." This is done not merely for simplicity but reflects the true African-oriented family structure and close sense of family belongingness.

Holism

Traditional Africans generally make little distinction between body, mind, and spirit. Africans perceive a strong interconnectedness among the cognitive, affective, and behavioral realms of personality. The traditional African personality responds to external stimuli in a holistic fashion. In social gatherings, for example, Africans are more likely to participate rather than merely spectate. A traditional African is more likely than not to become cognitively, affectively, and behaviorally expressive in response to music or other affective stimuli.

It is important to note that given the vast cultural and ethnic group differences among African people, these concepts may be manifested in a variety of ways. There are significant geographic, language, religious, ethnic, and historical variations in the manifestation of these concepts throughout Black Africa.

Afrocentricity and the Mental Health of African Americans

African American scholars have concluded that there are aspects of the African American cultural experience that have evolved out of African realities that have a significant relationship with psychosocial development and mental health (Cross, 1974; Guthrie, 1980; Lee, 2004; Nobles, 1991; Pasteur & Toldson, 1982; White & Parham, 1990). These conclusions have led to the development of an Afrocentric conceptual framework for understanding African Americans' psychosocial development.

An examination of traditional African American culture, in which rudimentary Afrocentric ways of life have been preserved in relatively large measure, reveals that Americans of African descent have developed a worldview that is grounded in many of the African-oriented philosophical assumptions previously discussed. These assumptions constitute a cultural tradition that places a high premium on harmony among people and their internal and external environments, fosters self- and group development through behavioral expressiveness, and recognizes the need for holistic development (Nobles, 1991).

Nobles (1991) identified kinship or collective unity as an important foundation for African Americans' psychological and social development. In spite of all of the challenges to its integrity, for example, the family is the bedrock of African Americans' psychosocial well-being (Billingsley, 1992; Hill, 1972; McAdoo, 1988).

In addition to the family, the African American cultural experience offers other institutions that provide a network of psychosocial support. The Black church, for example, has been a historical bastion of group solidarity. It is an institution that has traditionally been devoted to nurturing both spirituality and Black consciousness.

Spirituality is a hallmark of African American life and culture and has been identified by Pasteur and Toldson (1982) as "Black Expressiveness." This phenomenon represents a healthy fusion of the cognitive, affective, and behavioral aspects of personality characteristic of Afrocentricity. This expressiveness is generally characterized by a high degree of affective energy exhibited in interpersonal interactions and behavior among African Americans.

Implications of Afrocentricity for Counseling With African Americans

A number of issues relative to Afrocentricity should be considered by counseling practitioners. African American scholars have suggested that the counseling profession seek new directions in its efforts to help African American clients empower themselves. These new directions should include modalities that incorporate Afrocentric elements to promote psychosocial development (Belgrave et al., 1994; Lee, 2003; Pasteur & Toldson, 1982).

Counselors, therefore, should consider the African American family and community as major therapeutic resources. Family intervention must provide for the inclusion of significant others and the inherent strength of kinship social support processes, where appropriate, as integral parts of counseling. In promoting African Americans' psychosocial development, counseling should be considered within the context of the family unit. Whenever possible, counseling services should be offered in a supportive family group format in which members can draw on each other's strengths for problem resolution or decision making.

In addition to the family, the African American community offers other institutions that provide a network of social support that can be incorporated into the counseling process. The Black church represents the oldest and perhaps most important of these indigenous community support systems. As appropriate and effective, counseling approaches should incorporate aspects of the multifaceted African American religious/spiritual experience.

Within the context of indigenous support systems available to African Americans for help with problem resolution or decision making, counselors should find ways to promote Black expressiveness. This holistic concept is often the key to optimal mental health. It should form the basis of many counseling modalities for African American clients.

Conclusion

Counseling with African Americans must be conducted with the knowledge that African American culture fosters attitudes, behaviors, and values that are psychologically healthy and that within this culture are the resources for addressing mental health challenges and problems. Counseling interventions, therefore, should be undertaken from an Afrocentric perspective that focuses on promoting optimal mental health and well-being. Counselors should strive to promote African Americans' development within an Afrocentric context of kinship, behavioral and emotional expressiveness, and holistic development.

There is an old saying, "You can take the Black man out of Africa, but you cannot take Africa out of the Black man." To varying degrees, African Americans possess attitudes, values, and behaviors that are characteristic of their African heritage. The essence of Afrocentricity suggests that this may provide an important key to culturally responsive counseling with African Americans.

References

Akbar, N. (1979). African roots of Black personality. In W. D. Smith, K. Burlew, M. Mosley, & W. Whitney (Eds.), *Reflections on Black psychology* (pp. 79–98). Washington, DC: University of America Press.

Asante, M. K. (1991). Multiculturalism: An exchange. *The American Scholar, 60,* 267–272.

Asante, M. K. (1992). *Afrocentricity.* Trenton, NJ: African World Press.

Asante, M. K., & Asante, K. W. (1993). *African culture: The rhythms of unity.* Trenton, NJ: African World Press.

Baldwin, J. A. (1981). Notes on an Africentric theory of Black personality testing. *Western Journal of Black Studies, 5,* 172–179.

Belgrave, F. Z., Cherry, V. R., Cunningham, D., Walwyn, S., Letlaka-Rennert, K., & Philips, F. (1994). The influence of Africentric values, self-esteem, and Black identity on drug attitudes among African American fifth graders. *Journal of Black Psychology, 20,* 143–156.

Billingsley, A. (1992). *Climbing Jacob's ladder: The enduring legacy of African American families.* New York: Simon & Schuster.

Brookins, C. C. (1994). The relationship between Afrocentric values and racial identity attitudes: Validation of the Belief Systems Analysis Scale on African American college students. *Journal of Black Psychology, 2,* 128–142.

Cross, A. (1974). The Black experience: Its importance in the treatment of Black clients. *Child Welfare, 52,* 158–166.

Guthrie, R. V. (1980). The psychology of Black Americans: A historical perspective. In R. L. Jones (Ed.), *Black psychology* (2nd ed., pp. 97–108). New York: Harper & Row.

Hill, R. (1972). *The strengths of Black families.* New York: Emerson-Hall.

Jung, C. (1958). *The archetypes and the collective unconscious.* In G. Adler, M. Fordham, & H. Reed (Eds.), *Collected works* (Vol. 9, Pt. 1; Bollingen Series XX, pp. 55–67). New York: Pantheon Books.

Lee, C. C. (2003). *Empowering young Black males III: A systematic modular training program for Black male children and adolescents.* Alexandria, VA: American Counseling Association and CAPS Press.

Lee, C. C. (2004). Counseling African Americans. In R. L. Jones (Ed.), *Black psychology* (4th ed., pp. 631–650). Hampton, VA: Cobb & Henry.

Mbiti, J. S. (1970). *African religions and philosophy.* Garden City, NY: Doubleday.

McAdoo, H. P. (Ed.). (1988). *Black families.* Newbury Park, CA: Sage.

Nobles, W. W. (1986). *African psychology: Toward its reclamation, reascension, and revitalization.* Oakland, CA: Black Family Institute.

Nobles, W. W. (1991). African philosophy: Foundations of Black psychology. In R. L. Jones (Ed.), *Black psychology* (3rd ed., pp. 47–63). Berkeley, CA: Cobb & Henry.

Nobles, W. W., & Goddard, L. L. (1992). *An African-centered model of prevention for African-American youth at high risk* (DHHS Publication No. ADM 92-1925:87-92). Washington, DC: U.S. Government Printing Office.

Pasteur, A. B., & Toldson, I. L. (1982). *Roots of soul: The psychology of Black expressiveness.* Garden City, NY: Anchor Press/Doubleday.

White, J. L., & Parham, T. A. (1990). *The psychology of Blacks: An African American perspective.* Englewood Cliffs, NJ: Prentice Hall.

Counseling High-Achieving African Americans

Donna Y. Ford and H. Richard Milner

National reports highlight a crippling loss of faith and hope among African Americans, most often those in poverty. Excessive poverty, unemployment, underemployment, and poor school achievement have become a reality for far too many people of color. However, much of what we know or presume to know about African Americans is based on poorly achieving and low socioeconomic status (SES) groups. That is, seldom are high-achieving or middle-class African Americans the focus of research and practice. Subsequently, counselors and other helping professionals are left with impressionistic data and speculations on the perceptions, values, experiences, and struggles of an important segment of the Black population. This heavy focus on poor-achieving minorities, lower SES minorities, and the minuscule research on successful Blacks raises serious questions about the generalizability of the findings and conclusions. It paints a deficit-oriented picture of African Americans (Ford & Grantham, 2003; Ford & Harmon, 2001; Milner, 2003) and paints a profile of homogeneity that ignores the unique issues facing African Americans of different SES and achievement levels.

In this chapter, we contend that high-achieving African Americans share problems associated with Blacks from all rungs of the socioeconomic ladder and all levels of achievement. However, the quality and quantity, or nature and extent, of the problems confronting these different groups of African Americans can be markedly different. There is a need to fill the void in our awareness and understanding of the various factors that contribute to socioemotional and psychological concerns among high-achieving Black children and adults. An underlying premise of this chapter is that high achievement status does not inoculate African Americans from the harsh realities of race in American society. This chapter also addresses variables affecting the socioemotional and psychological well-being of high-achieving Blacks in particular and makes some recommendations for improving the mental health of successful Black children and adults.

High Achievement: An Elusive Concept

The concept of achievement itself is elusive and becomes even more difficult to define when we speak of "high" or "low" achievement. Some individuals, families, and cultures define achievement in academic terms. High academic achievement is viewed as a function of school performance, reified in the form of grades or grade point average. Those in school settings, for example, are considered high achievers if they have As or Bs. A high academic achiever, thus, is someone who is above average in school performance. Many of these students are identified as gifted and talented.

Others define achievement outside of academic settings. Thus, performance and rank on one's job constitute achievement. Those holding the higher ranked positions (e.g., manager, administrator) are often viewed as successful (e.g., attending college) or high achievers.

The term *achievement* is also relative. It is often said that an individual is doing well, "given his ability" or "given her circumstances." Thus, what is deemed high achieving or successful for one individual may not be considered so for another. As Sternberg (1985), Gardner (1983), and others have stated about the terms *intelligent* or *gifted*, they are social constructs, and what is valued as gifted or intelligent in one culture may not be valued as gifted or intelligent in another.

The term *achievement* is also relative in a different way, based on perception. For instance, a student earning primarily Cs in school might be considered a high achiever by his or her classmates because most students in that particular school are receiving Ds and failing grades. Finally, students and adults can have different perceptions of students' achievement level or status. For example, a student may think that he or she is doing well in school because he or she has not failed any courses or has a certain grade point average, but teachers and/or parents may disagree. A common statement is "But he (or she) can do better."

In this chapter, we focus on at least two groups of high-achieving African Americans— those in school settings and in employment settings. We define high-achieving students in school settings as those (a) whose grade point average is above average (e.g., 3.0 or higher on a 4.0 scale), (b) whose achievement test scores are at or above the 80th percentile, or (c) who are involved in leadership and service roles (e.g., head of a student organization or committee). Relative to adults, we define vocational achievement as (a) having a position that is commensurate with one's education or (b) in the process of achieving or having achieved one's career goals. As the examples in the previous paragraph illustrate, these criteria are themselves subjective and arbitrary, but they are the consensus of the authors and are used to place the forthcoming issues into context.

Social Factors Affecting the Mental Health of High-Achieving African Americans

It is often assumed that success is associated with mental—emotional and psychological— well-being. After all, if one's grades and finances are in order, one should be "happy" and somewhat free of mental health problems. This Western or European perspective of success and achievement—success defined in terms of grades and income—may not bode well for people of color, in particular African Americans. Essentially, this chapter contends that high achievement status can take its toll on the mental well-being of some African American children and adults, that with success comes a new or unique set of mental health issues.

Our collective experiences suggest that the following issues can pose mental health issues for high-achieving African American children and adults.

Limited Access and Glass Ceilings

As adults, Blacks seldom reach their full potential, due in large part to limited access and glass ceilings. Despite having high grades, educational credentials, and high incomes, many high-achieving Blacks find that certain doors are still closed to them. Despite laws against housing and employment discrimination, for example, many homeowners and businesses still find ways to prevent integration. An African American physician seeking residence in a racially segregated community may find that "the house has just been purchased," or a Black professor may find that "the apartment was rented yesterday" or "is no longer available." In educational settings, discrimination takes on a different form. For example, Black students have less access to academically rigorous programs, such as gifted education, advanced placement, and honors courses. Yet, they are severely overrepresented in special education classes, low-ability groups, and vocational tracks (Ford, 1996a, 1999; Gutman & McLoyd, 2000).

According to Cose (1993), although the number of African Americans earning high incomes has risen in the last decade, only a handful have climbed near the top of the corporate structure. Compared with their White counterparts, African Americans are less likely to be promoted, to be the chief executive officer or administrator, or to receive salaries commensurate with training and experience. Thus, they are underemployed and underpaid. This harsh reality regarding the consequences of social injustices is illustrated in depth by MacLeod (1995) in *Ain't No Makin' It*. MacLeod chronicled the experiences of four groups of students as they moved into adulthood: high-achieving Blacks, high-achieving Whites, low-achieving Blacks, and low-achieving Whites. As adults, the former high-achieving Black students—those who epitomized the ideal of the American dream and the Protestant work ethic—fared no better than the former low-achieving White students.

Such glass ceilings in schools and workplaces limit the potential of Black children and adults, as well as contribute to anger, frustration, resentment, boredom, and apathy. These glass ceilings limit access and reinforce the reality that even high-achieving Blacks are victims of the great social injustice of differential reward.

Double Standards

High-achieving or successful Blacks may complain of having to expend more time and energy to arrive at the same position as their White counterparts or working "twice as hard to get half as far." One academically successful Black male reported, "If you want to be successful, you have to work twice as hard as White people" (Ford, 1995). These double standards relative to energy expenditure place additional pressures on Blacks, resulting in burnout, apathy, and hopelessness. Black students, for example, may refuse to exert the effort necessary to be placed into academically advanced courses because they see their chances for placement or admission as being too small; they see the price for admission as too high. This perception is apparent in the following comment: "Why should I try to get good grades and do well on the achievement tests? They [administrators and teachers] don't put Black kids in gifted programs, no matter how well we do." Thus, the student's cost–benefit analysis suggests that the costs—the price one pays to succeed in school—outweigh the benefits.

Exclusion and Isolation

Blacks who have moved up the socioeconomic ladder often find it lonely at the top. Many African Americans discover that the racial demons that have plagued them all their lives do not recognize business hours (Cose, 1993, p. 55). Thus, even if Blacks succeed in cracking or jarring closed doors, they risk rejection and isolation from their White counterparts. For example, Black students in predominantly White schools may have great difficulty finding a close friend, finding company for lunch, getting a date, or getting an invitation to social events, and they may feel uneasy at such events if invited. These feelings of alienation may leave African American students with the perception that they have little option but to avoid classes and social events where they are the only person of color or one of few. For example, if honors courses, debate teams, school organizations, and so forth are predominantly White, Black students are less likely to seek admission. These decisions have unfortunate long-term implications by limiting the future potential of Black students.

Powerlessness

High-achieving Blacks may find that success is more evident in their title than actual power. A Black vice president of a company, or a school administrator, may find himself or herself relegated to tasks pertaining to minorities only, thereby having restricted or focused authority. Some African Americans may find that their supervisors are reluctant to release control, and as a result, the breadth of their responsibilities is reduced. Others find that they were never intended to have real decision-making authority but were hired or promoted to serve as "window dressing." Further, high-achieving Blacks may find that the political pressures are so great that they retard the development of equitable and credible initiatives; subsequently, they find themselves perpetuating the status quo. The result of such limitations associated with this facade of power is apathy, discouragement, frustration, and anger.

Voicelessness and Invisibility

When African Americans are few in numbers, they have a limited voice. Although they may express concerns related to injustices on the job or in school, their concerns may be ignored or given lowered priority. In other instances, the limited presence of African Americans renders them invisible and easy to ignore. Voicelessness and invisibility can lead not only to frustration, anger, and resentment toward the person(s) rendering them but also to a sense of hopelessness and powerlessness.

Token Status

Too often, Black students and adults are not considered successful. Consequently, when they do succeed, they may be perceived as a "credit" to their race, as "truly exceptional" persons (see Corwin, 2001; Suskind, 1998). As the only or one of few Blacks in a particular setting, Black students and adults are often expected to be the expert on all issues related to Blacks and other minorities. This expectation of having to "know it all" places a heavy burden on the shoulders of African Americans and increases their level of stress or overload. There may also be discomfort when Blacks realize that they actually know little about their racial and cultural heritage. Students may comment, "Every time we talk about Blacks in school, which is rare, I am expected to know everything. This is the only time my classmates and teachers try to learn something from me. I don't have all of the answers. Who could?"

Similarly, Black professors at institutions of higher education may be expected to teach multicultural classes, even if this is not their area of expertise (or interest); they are also expected to mentor all or most minority students, and they are asked to serve on numerous committees, which gives the committees an image of diversity. These multiple roles and expectations contribute to frustration, burnout, and overload among high-achieving Blacks.

Second Guessing

An additional stress for high-achieving African Americans is the constant scrutiny to which they are subjected, including constant questioning of competence, questioning about motives underlying decisions, and minimization of the quality of their work and efforts. Questions of competence come in many guises—full-scale attacks or subtle comments. For example, White administrators or teachers may express surprise when a Black employee or student does well but are not surprised when he or she fails or are less surprised when a White employee or student does well. Second guessing, whether direct or indirect, blatant or subtle, serves to build a superior–inferior hierarchy, with Blacks at the bottom. It also communicates the underlying message that the individual has "overachieved," perhaps due to luck or good fortune. Anger, resentment, and frustration are only a few possible responses that African Americans may have to these painful tactics.

Pigeonholing

Blacks may be pigeonholed into certain positions. For example, they may be hired as vice presidents, but the position is in minority affairs, a Black community, or a poverty-stricken area. These positions have a narrow focus, have limited power, and are accompanied by issues that are complex and difficult to resolve. Similarly, when identified as gifted, Black students are often identified as gifted in creativity, leadership, or visual and performing arts rather than as intellectually and academically gifted (Ford, 1995, 1996b). The implicit message is that Blacks can sing and dance, for example, but do not need or cannot succeed in academically rigorous coursework. Not surprisingly, students become bored in school when they are underchallenged and become angry and resentful at the messages that undermine their competence and smack of their being intellectually inferior (see Ford & Grantham, 2003; Ford & Harmon, 2001).

Guilty by Association

Black students and adults may be stereotyped by White Americans when they are seen as members of a group rather than as individuals. Hence, the stereotypes and fears associated with Blacks in general are attributed to high-achieving Blacks. Black males often complain of being stopped by police officers or followed in stores without cause. In essence, high-achieving African Americans are presumed to be guilty because they are Black. As in the previous examples, anger, frustration, confusion, and apathy can result.

Steele (1997, 1999) studied the concept of "stereotype threat" among African American students. His work reveals that the performance of Black students can suffer on standardized intelligence tests when these students believe that the test result will reflect negatively on their racial group. Specifically, when told that the test measures how smart Blacks are, Black students perform poorly or refuse to take the test.

Taking Their Toll: The Impact of Social Sources of Stress on African Americans

The issues just described represent social or external sources of stress that place a socioemotional and psychological price on success for Black children and adults. The price that some Blacks pay for success is described in this section.

Identity Conflicts

Race and racial identity affect one's socioemotional and psychological health in significant ways. The issue of race may be more salient for Blacks than for other groups. For instance, White Americans are much less likely to experience the chronic stress and problems associated with race because the color of their skin is not viewed with a deficit orientation (Ford & Grantham, 2003; Ford & Harmon, 2001) and, thus, is not a barrier to academic and social success.

Racism, prejudice, and discrimination can negatively affect the extent to which Blacks identify with their racial background and heritage and can affect their racial identity. In his revised model of racial identity, entitled the psychology of Nigrescence, Cross (1995; see also Cross & Vandiver, 2001) described more completely how African Americans progress and regress in the process of becoming Afrocentric. According to the model, Blacks in Stage 1 (preencounter) hold one of at least three attitudes toward race: (a) low-salience attitudes, (b) social stigma attitudes, or (c) anti-Black attitudes. Those holding a low-salience attitude do not deny being physically Black, but they consider their Blackness as having an insignificant role in their daily lives, their well-being, or how they define themselves. Cross contended that these individuals are unlikely to give much thought to race issues and appear unaware of such problems. Overall, they view themselves as "human beings who just happen to be Black" (Cross, 1995, p. 98). However, African Americans who hold social stigma attitudes not only have low-salience attitudes but also see their racial orientation as something to be ashamed of. By default, race is attributed some significance, but not in the positive sense. Anti-Black attitudes constitute the third and most extreme type of preencounter individual. Such persons see their racial status as negative. They loathe other Blacks, feel alienated from other Blacks, and do not perceive the Black community as a potential resource or support base.

All three preencounter types favor European cultural perspectives, such as beauty, art, communication modes, and academic preferences. Cross (1995; see also Cross & Vandiver, 2001) contended that preencounter attitudes transcend social class boundaries, with low-salience, social stigma, and anti-Black attitudes being expressed at all economic levels.

Next (encounter), the individual experiences an "identity metamorphosis" (Cross, 1995, p. 104) in which a major event or series of events induce cognitive dissonance. These events, either positive or negative, tear away at the person's preencounter attitudes and push him or her toward increased awareness of his or her status as a racial being. The encounter, therefore, results in great emotionality, guilt, anger, and anxiety for having previously minimized or denied the significance of race. Racism, prejudice, discrimination, and issues discussed in the previous sections—pigeonholing, glass ceiling, and so forth—are encounters that many high-achieving Blacks face. Without effective coping mechanisms and a support base, Blacks become increasingly frustrated, resentful, and angry.

Stage 2 (immersion–emersion) represents what Cross (1995) referred to as the "vortex of psychological Nigrescence" (p. 106). African Americans in this stage begin to rid themselves of their raceless identities and begin constructing their new frame of reference. Yet, this stage is also characterized by anxiety, primarily about becoming the "right kind of Black person" (Cross, 1995, p. 106). Equally problematic, all that is White is perceived as evil, oppressive, and inhuman, whereas all that is Black is proclaimed superior.

In the immersion phase, African Americans immerse themselves in the world of Blackness or anti-Whiteness. For example, they attend political or cultural meetings that focus on Black issues, along with issues of justice and equity. Cross (1995) described this stage as being energized by rage, guilt, and a developing sense of pride. The individual accepts himself or herself as a racial being. Common themes are selflessness, dedication, and commitment to Blacks. They may experience creative, inspirational bursts of energy that communicate the richness of their racial heritage. Taken to the extreme, African Americans in the immersion stage have difficulty controlling the impulse to confront White authority figures, even on a life-or-death basis. That is, the threat of death is not feared. There is also an anti-White orientation in which White is viewed as evil and distrustful and Blacks have little appreciation or respect for White Americans.

In the emersion phase, there is a marked decline in the racist and emotional attitudes. This leveling off occurs when African Americans encounter a role model or mentor, for instance, who displays a more sophisticated and calmer persona. Through role models and mentors, Blacks learn to substitute romantic and romanticized notions of Blackness with a deeper and more serious understanding of Blackness.

The third stage (internalization) is marked by the integration of a new identity, an identity that is more authentic and naturalistic. This identity includes high salience to Blackness, which can take on several manifestations, including biculturalism. An internalized identity serves several functions: (a) It defends and protects the person from psychological problems associated with living in a society in which race matters; (b) it provides a sense of belonging and social affiliation; and (c) it provides a basis for interacting and communicating with people, cultures, and situations beyond the world of Blackness (Cross, 1995; Cross & Vandiver, 2001).

The final stage (internalization) is action oriented. Here, African Americans devote much time and energy, perhaps a lifetime, to finding ways to translate their personal sense of Blackness into a plan of action, a commitment to Black affairs and improving the circumstances of African Americans. The three types of identities are nationalist, biculturalist, and multiculturalist.

Although a stage model, Cross and Vandiver (2001) acknowledged that individuals can regress or get stuck at one stage. Whether a person regresses, becomes stuck, or progresses through the stages of racial identity depends, in large part, on the individual's personality, support base, resources, and his or her experiences. For example, Black children and adults in predominantly White settings may experience more negative encounters based on race than those in predominantly Black settings. They may also experience such encounters at an earlier age than Blacks in predominantly Black settings.

Allegiance Issues

Allegiance issues and peer pressures often have a negative influence on Blacks. High-achieving Blacks may experience conflict relative to supporting the beliefs, values, and norms of the dominant culture as opposed to their parent culture. Consequently, they show ambivalence about their abilities and consider them as envied by others—yet personally undesirable. W. E. B. DuBois (1965) described this phenomenon when he wrote about two warring souls fighting with each other to be accepted in White America. Leanita McClain, the first Black female elected to the board of directors of the *Chicago Tribune*, was subsequently perceived by many as acting White. She described the dilemma of bicultural stress most poignantly in her newspaper column entitled "The Middle Class Black's Burden":

> I run a gauntlet between two worlds, and I am cursed and blessed by both. I travel, observe and take part in both; I can also be used by both. I am a rope in a tug of war. If I am a token in my downtown office, so am I at my cousin's tea. I assuage white guilt. . . . I have a foot in each world, but I cannot fool myself about either. . . . Whites won't believe that I remain culturally different; blacks won't believe that I remain culturally the same. (McClain, 1986, p. 14)

McClain (1983) described this identity issue as hellish confusion whereby successful Blacks feel guilty and stressful about their success. Success sometimes leads African Americans to ask themselves, as did McClain, "I have made it, but where?" (see Campbell, 1984, p. 74). McClain eventually committed suicide. This frustration, confusion, and anger were more recently discussed in *The Rage of a Privileged Class* (Cose, 1993). With success comes a unique set of issues for Blacks.

Not surprisingly, therefore, many educators and counselors have noted a significant change in the aspirations of Blacks toward academic achievement and social mobility. Specifically, whereas previous generations had defined success for one Black person as success for all Blacks, more recently Blacks are less apt to view the achievements of individual Blacks as progress for all Blacks. The "all for one and one for all" collective sense of success has all but disappeared for some Blacks to be replaced by the perception that successful Blacks have "sold out" and are "acting White" when they achieve (Corwin, 2001; Fordham, 1988; Suskind, 1998).

Smith (1989) argued that race serves to create a common referent of peoplehood such that individuals tend to define themselves in terms of membership in a particular group. Thus, this collective identity represents the sense of belonging that is psychologically important for people of color. To reinforce the belief that they are still legitimate or authentic members of the Black community, Blacks may sabotage any chance they have of succeeding outside of it. With this antiachievement ethic, Blacks may underachieve, drop out, refuse to participate in gifted programs, refuse to accept certain positions, and otherwise fail to reach their academic potential in school and life (Corwin, 2001; Ford, 1996b; Fordham, 1988; Suskind, 1998).

In short, detachment from one's race, whether perceived or real, threatens the survival of the Black community and its culture, and it creates suspicion among Blacks about member loyalty. Hence, the Black community may reject successful Blacks not because they have achieved but because they appear removed and detached from their indigenous community. The Black community may reject Blacks who identify with the dominant culture, desire to join it, and accept its behaviors as paradigms worth copying. Which culture, then, should African Americans emulate when trying to fulfill their potential? Which belief and value system should they incorporate?

Survival Guilt

The notion of survival guilt can shed light on the many socioemotional and psychological factors affecting the motivation and achievement of African Americans who may feel guilt, anxiety, depression, and ambivalence over having "survived" when others who seem to be equally, if not more, rewarded did not. Survival conflict is a negative reaction to surpassing the accomplishments of family and/or peers. These feelings become debilitating if not recognized, resulting in a devaluation of one's sense of self, one's accomplishments, and one's ambitions. As with fear of success, individuals suffering from survival conflict fear or anticipate negative consequences from competitive striving.

African Americans who succumb to negative feelings associated with success do so to help maintain loyalty and a sense of belonging to their family and peers. They seek social and cultural continuity. Piorkowski (1983) noted that as individuals move from a lower social class standing to a higher one, they often experience "social class change anxiety." These successful persons find themselves in a quandary because as achievement increases, so too does guilt. To escape survival conflict, Blacks may resort to self-sabotage, procrastination, dropping out, or other behaviors that thwart success. High-achieving Blacks may also overcompensate to allay their feelings. For instance, they may overextend themselves to prove to other Blacks, particularly less successful Blacks (and themselves), that they have not forgotten who they are or where they came from. In an effort to assuage the guilt, many go home for visits with gifts, money, and so forth. Coner-Edwards and Edwards (1988) reported that middle-class Blacks may save most of their earnings or dress less well than they can afford out of fear of appearing hedonistic or overindulgent. Others become absorbed in their work and refrain from involvement in social activities. In essence, they must resolve their guilt at the risk of losing ties or feeling rejected by their community, or they may never be able to enjoy their attainment.

Achievement Ideology

The American dream has been defined in both the popular press and scholarly work in terms of the life chances associated with the middle class—a home, a car or two, a good neighborhood, a college education, the ability to purchase adequate health care, and so forth. However, Blacks have historically been blocked from the realization of the American dream in these areas. Even when middle-class status was achieved, African Americans found that money still could not buy them a meal at certain restaurants, a home in certain neighborhoods, or a job in certain businesses or professions. Similarly, middle-class Black families could not educate their children at the school of their choice. Although laws have wiped away, at least on paper, the aforementioned inequities, middle-class Blacks may still find certain doors closed and locked. Thus, having achieved the American dream relative to the key characteristics just listed, it would be unrealistic to assume that high-achieving Blacks have truly "arrived." As illustrated above, counselors must examine whether Blacks have invested realistically in the notion of the achievement ideology. To what extent are high-achieving Blacks failing to achieve balanced lives because they work all the time? Are they riddled with guilt when they take time off or attempt to enjoy work and leisure? How secure do they feel about their grades and academic accomplishments, SES, and other indices of success?

Within-Group Competition

The previous sections have centered primarily on conflicts between Blacks and Whites, leaving the misperception that conflict is only between groups. Another unfortunate consequence of Black achievement is within-group conflict, as depicted by jealousy, envy, and competition. As mentioned earlier, Blacks who are successful in school and/or at work may be accused of acting White. Research on high-achieving Black students, conducted by Fordham (1988), has revealed that many face negative peer pressures; they are discouraged from achieving by their Black classmates. Similarly, Ford (1995) noted that a disproportionate percentage of high-achieving Black students (compared with low achievers) were teased and/or accused of acting White by Black classmates. Similar pressures can occur on one's job, particularly when resources and opportunities for Blacks to achieve are scarce. Black coworkers may resort to sabotaging each other (e.g., withholding important information, providing misinformation, attempting to outperform others through dishonesty, unjustly criticizing each other's work, withholding compliments).

The aforementioned problems represent attacks on the sense of identity of successful Black children and adults. The factors that determine how an individual will respond are varied and complex. However, some general guidelines can be used as a basis for developing coping strategies among high-achieving Blacks.

Potential Barriers to Counseling African Americans

In general, Blacks and other racially and culturally diverse groups underutilize counseling services. In their study of the reasons why minority students do not seek counseling, Atkinson, Jennings, and Liongson (1990) found the counselor's race to be significantly related to seeking counseling. Specifically, findings indicated that the availability of culturally similar or culturally sensitive counselors is an important determinant of counseling service utilization for those minority students most closely identified with their ethnic culture (Atkinson et al., 1990, p. 348). The issue of race may be particularly important for Black children and adults in the immersion–emersion stage of identity development, as described by Cross (1995).

A similar explanation for underutilization is that Black students may not believe that White counselors have the cultural skills and competencies necessary to meet the needs of those who are racially and culturally diverse. They anticipate negative or inappropriate counseling experiences.

Meager attention has been given to understanding how an individual's racial identity affects his or her mental health. And as just indicated, it also affects individuals' willingness to seek counseling. This consideration of racial identity is essential because attitudes that both denigrate an individual as a successful Black person and promote wishes to be White may be psychologically maladaptive and non-self-actualizing.

Because of the myriad problems associated with racial identity development, it must be considered as a potential issue in the counseling process. Parham (1989) cogently delineated issues that counselors might need to address when working with Black children and adults: (a) self-differentiation versus preoccupation with assimilation, in which the individual strives to become comfortable with the recognition that he or she is a worthwhile human being, irrespective of valuation and validation from Whites, and (b) ego transcendence versus self-absorption, whereby successful African Americans strive to become secure enough with themselves to develop personal ego strength.

Black children and adults must achieve congruence between their real self and their ideal/perceived self to become fully functioning individuals who have well-integrated identities. A positive racial identity may result when counselors provide the support necessary to free successful Blacks from the racial stereotypes others impose on them. Therefore, counselors are urged to work with Black students and adults on problems associated with academic achievement and upward mobility because achieving success in society is difficult for African Americans.

Defense mechanisms, those techniques used to protect oneself from pain or discomfort, can be destructive to the helping process. As Yalom (1985) stated, individuals with neurotic defenses are frozen in a closed position; they are not open for learning, and they are generally searching for safety rather than growth. Through defense mechanisms, one can withdraw from, distort, or attack problems. These defenses include denial of having a problem or projecting one's problems onto others. These issues result in a general inability of African American clients to grow and to overcome the issues for which they have sought counseling.

Denial is the conscious screening out of unpleasant information that might threaten one's sense of self and peoplehood. When thoughts or feelings are unacceptable, one tries to disown and/or deny them (Perls, 1976). African Americans who rationalize and deny reality may be unable to progress toward healthier stages of socioemotional and psychological development. Dudley (1988) noted that Blacks may spend an inordinate amount of time and energy maintaining the belief that racial factors have little to do with their current status. (Such individuals may be in the preencounter stage of racial identity.) This belief may be maintained by a narcissistic psychological defense consisting of denial of the devalued status assigned to the Black individual and a more grandiose view of the self. Such a defense enables Blacks to view themselves as special, as a special subgroup of Blacks, or as beyond racial categorization. However, by denying external barriers to achievement, African Americans may come to internalize them, or to believe that the attacks are justified or based on substance. Consequently, they may be falsely led to believe that their capabilities and competencies are seriously limited. If attacks are persistent, Black children and adults may have lowered self-perceptions and become devastated. In essence, because of the myriad defense mechanisms that can interfere with counseling, a major task of the counselor will be to help preencounter, encounter, and immersion–emersion African Americans to explore their defense mechanisms.

In the next section, we present a case study of an African American adolescent from a middle-class family who has "learned" to underachieve because it is uncomfortable being a high-achieving Black student. The case illustrates many of the issues explored in this chapter.

Case Study

Joseph, a 14-year-old Black male, currently attends high school in a middle-class community. Joseph's parents (a professor and an accountant) brought him to counseling because of depression and bouts of anger. During counseling, Joseph often reflects on his school experiences. Joseph attended a predominantly Black public elementary school. He has happy, positive memories about these school years and often boasts about his school achievement. His mother indicated that Joseph was identified as gifted and placed in the district's gifted education program in the second grade. He had also received numerous awards and other recognition for his academic achievement.

The family moved to a predominantly White suburb when Joseph was in middle school. Shortly thereafter, his parents began to notice a significant decline in Joseph's interest in school and academic performance. Joseph, for example, no longer made the honor roll, nor was he interested in doing so. His teachers, all of whom were White females, expressed concern that Joseph was a behavioral problem: He often disrupted class, was off task, seldom completed assignments, talked out of turn, and thrived on his status as the class clown. Joseph presented a different picture; he described his teachers as mean, unfair, and boring. He reported that many of the teachers ridiculed and embarrassed him. He complained that teachers were insensitive and often seemed to enjoy demeaning Blacks. Joseph also recalled being teased by both Black and White students, many of whom could not understand why Joseph spoke "proper English." Joseph was teased most often when he visited friends in his former neighborhood.

By the end of the first grading period, one teacher requested that Joseph be referred for child services for special education evaluation. Joseph's parents were shocked—how could their son be identified as gifted in one school and referred to special education in another? They refused to have Joseph evaluated. They held numerous meetings with administrators and teachers regarding why Joseph was not placed in the gifted program, as he had been identified earlier. Unable to resolve this issue and their differences with several teachers, Joseph's parents transferred him to another school, which was also predominantly White and middle class. The problems were similar in this school. Teachers complained that Joseph talked too much and asked too many questions, particularly about minority groups and issues of justice. For example, Joseph questioned teachers when they stated that Christopher Columbus discovered America; he questioned their constant focus on slavery and their inattention to the contribution of Blacks to American history. Joseph also expressed frustration and anger at being what he called a "token" at certain times during the school year. For instance, he recalled having to be the "expert" on all issues related to African Americans. One student asked Joseph to explain why "so many Blacks commit crimes." Another student wanted to know why "Black people are so good at sports." Others asked how his parents could "afford a nice house and to live in their neighborhood." Joseph also described his experience when trying out for both tennis and basketball. When he failed to make the basketball team but made the tennis team, Joseph was teased unmercifully.

Much of what Joseph discussed in counseling had not been shared with his parents. For the most part, they thought that Joseph was adjusting well to school, although his grades were not at the level they expected. They were also unaware that Joseph attempted to buy friendships and peer acceptance. During one counseling session, Joseph described how he stole money from his parents so that he would "always have it to show the White students." He stated, "I did not want them to think that I was just another poor Black kid." When this did not work and the teasing, isolation, and rejection continued, Joseph became more frustrated and angry. When his parents brought Joseph to counseling, he had been suspended for fighting.

What are Joseph's major concerns? What needs is he trying to meet? What factors have contributed to his difficulties? How could they have been prevented? How can a counselor help Joseph to deal effectively with his concerns? To what extent will peers, teachers, and family members be involved in the counseling process?

Counseling Interventions for High-Achieving African Americans

Counseling Black children and adults requires gathering information from a variety of sources (students, parents, teachers, and several objective measurements) to better understand how successful Blacks feel about themselves, including their social relationships, satisfaction with life, and future. An important question to explore is how racial identity development can be enhanced or facilitated. According to Erikson (1968), the process of racial identity development is a major developmental task that occurs during the fifth stage of psychosocial development. His stages of psychosocial development are mediated by successful resolution of conflicts in earlier stages of psychosocial development. Accordingly, if Blacks do not progress successfully through Stages 1 to 4, healthy racial identity is jeopardized. As indicated so often, threats to the mental health of Blacks include conflicts with members of one's racial group over issues of commitment to one's indigenous culture, that is, fear of being perceived as acting White or rejecting the Black culture in any way.

Banks's (1979) five-stage framework for understanding ethnic identity development can help ensure effective counseling for successful Blacks. Counselors must help successful Blacks reach higher stages of racial identity. At such stages, Blacks can function well within several racial and cultural settings and appreciate the differences among these cultures as well. For Black adults and children to reach this level of functioning, however, counselors must attend to the affective and cultural dimensions of being not only Black but also successful.

Accordingly, counselors must teach Blacks how to cope effectively with feeling isolated from White Americans or rejected by other African Americans. Exploring feelings of isolation may be especially important during the preencounter, encounter, and immersion–emersion stages of racial identity development. Just as important, counselors are advised to speak openly with Blacks about racial issues. For example, Kochman (1981) stated that Blacks often prefer to speak openly about issues of racism and discrimination rather than ignore or avoid such discussions. Thus, counselors who are culturally sensitive work earnestly to develop open and trusting relationships with their Black clients.

Injustices associated with race are a reality in America. As Cose (1993) noted, "For most Blacks in America, regardless of status, political persuasion, or accomplishments, the moment never arrives when race can be treated as a total irrelevancy. Instead, too often it is the only relevant factor defining our existence" (p. 28). Because racially motivated attacks strike at the core of the Black person's identity, a strong emotional response is normal. To survive, Blacks must expect such feelings, recognize that they are normal, learn not to be frightened by them, and learn how to use emotions to their own best interests. Given the intensity of the racial attacks on Blacks, it is especially important that African Americans learn how to manage their emotional responses to racism. A supportive system that provides an avenue for expressing feelings and exploring alternatives for managing these feelings is invaluable.

As described below, a trusting counseling relationship, role models and mentors, family counseling, group counseling, and multicultural counseling are potentially hopeful intervention strategies.

A Trusting Relationship

The emphasis placed on the counseling relationship versus the techniques as the major counseling strategy is an important issue when counseling Black children and adults. Again, it cannot be emphasized enough that the quality of the counseling relationship is measured, at least in part, by the degree of empathy, unconditional positive regard, congruence, and active listening on the part of counselors. These strategies enhance the relationship and encourage greater disclosure on the part of Black children and adults.

Counseling must include intervention techniques designed for specific cultural groups. Counselors must avoid being culturally encapsulated, disregarding cultural differences in favor of applying blindly the same techniques to all clients and across all situations. Essentially, when working with successful Blacks, counselors must attend to universal needs common among all populations while also attending to cultural needs. The counseling relationship requires that counselors emphasize similarities among diverse groups or individuals and the universality of the human experience. Perhaps most important, the counseling relationship is enhanced when counselors respect and appreciate not only individual differences but also between-group and within-group differences.

Role Models and Mentors

Mentoring can facilitate the intellectual or vocational development of persons identified as protégés (Grantham, 2004). Whatever form it takes, mentoring provides emotional support, enhances self-esteem, corrects dysfunctional attitudes and behaviors, and teaches values and ethics (Pasch, Krokow, Johnson, Slocum, & Stapleton, 1990). Counselors must take an active role in facilitating the mentor relationships for African Americans, particularly children. Without role models, Black children may have a lower probability of being positive about success and achievement. Thus, mentors and role models serve as important and powerful resources in the prevention of academic, psychological, and socioemotional problems.

Group Counseling

Group counseling can be especially effective with Black children and adults because of their cultural orientation to communal work. Group counseling encourages Black children and adults to view themselves as a central part of the larger social community. Sharing, cooperation, and reciprocity are essential elements of social interaction among Blacks (Harrison, Wilson, Pine, Chan, & Buriel, 1990; Shade, Kelly, & Oberg, 1997). Group counseling might also enhance the self-esteem and racial identity of Black children and adults, letting them know that others share their concerns. When African Americans have the opportunity to speak with others who share their concerns, they may become more comfortable with being "different." From group counseling experiences, African Americans may increase their sense of hope and optimism, decrease their feelings of alienation, develop more effective coping techniques, and acquire more effective socialization skills.

Family Counseling

The family, as a primary socialization agent, has an integral part in child development, including racial identity (Ford, 2004). Counselors must consider carefully the family's stage of racial identity development. Specifically, families in the encounter stage of identity development may be too preoccupied with self-discovery to benefit fully from counseling with White counselors. Depending on the extent of preoccupation, Exum (1983) recommended referring such families to multicultural counselors. Exum also cautioned that families in the immersion stage are the most difficult to work with because of their strong anti-White feelings. Such families may reject counseling or insist on working only with a Black counselor.

Equally important, fearing that schools will emphasize competitiveness and individualism, which are antithetical to values espoused in the Black culture, some parents resist placing their children in predominantly White schools (Ford, 2004). Counselors (and, of course, teachers) must help African American parents to believe that high-level academic courses and programs (e.g., gifted education, honors) should not be perceived as prerogatives of White students. Increasing the participation of Black students in these programs requires the support and participation of parents and significant others in the students' lives. Other strategies include conducting parent workshops and seminars as well as providing resource materials on issues related to being both Black and successful (Ford, 1996b, 2004). Interventions must educate Black parents about the psychological and socioemotional needs of their children and any sacrifices successful Black children may have to make.

Black families, particularly extended families, also play an important role in promoting the socioemotional health of their members. Their involvement in counseling, therefore, may be highly facilitative. Family members can increase the sense of cohesion, connectedness, and understanding that may be necessary for some successful Blacks to appreciate their achievements. Key issues worth exploring in family counseling are (a) family achievement orientations; (b) support networks within the home and community; (c) educational involvement; (d) self-differentiation (individual versus group identity and achievement); and (e) maintaining cultural values and heritage as well as ties to the larger, less economically advantaged Black community.

Summary and Conclusion

Although racial discrimination and economic stratification continue to be major sources of stress for many people of color, some nonetheless have been able to acquire the requisites for upward mobility. Successful Blacks have been able to emerge through the narrow window of opportunity that exposes them to the "good life." Yet, class analysis is a neglected approach to understanding the Black experience in America. Few scholarly works have stimulated any real discussion of the Black experience in terms of differential achievement status. High-achieving African Americans are victims of both racial injustice and social injustice. They represent a group who approached the door of equal opportunity and opened it by the handle of equal opportunity. As described in this chapter, there is both promise and peril among successful Blacks, many of whom find that high achievement does not mitigate racial injustices.

There is much diversity among African Americans relative to income, education, occupation, lifestyle, values, and family background. Thus, Blacks represent a unique mixture of racial, historical, and cultural heritages. More often than not, however, high-achieving Blacks are omitted from discussions of "Blacks," "the Black community," and "inner-city Blacks," despite the reality that successful Blacks exist among all three (Pinderhughes, 1988, p. v).

It is naive to assume that Blacks who are achieving have "arrived" in America, that this group is free from discrimination faced by other Blacks. Long-standing oppression and deprivation continue to affect the psychology and achievements of many Blacks, including those who achieve in school and at work. The results of social injustices can be deeply embedded and outside of one's awareness. Yet, negative self-perceptions, serious role conflicts, bicultural stress, and self-defeating behaviors are realities in the lives of high-achieving

Black children and adults. Nonetheless, as described in this chapter, counselors are an integral part of the helping equation. Counselors have both the presence and the power to help successful Black children and adults to lead rewarding lives.

References

Atkinson, D. R., Jennings, R. G., & Liongson, L. (1990). Minority students' reasons for not seeking counseling and suggestions for improving services. *Journal of College Student Development, 31,* 342–350.

Banks, J. A. (1979). *Teaching strategies for ethnic studies* (2nd ed.). Boston: Allyn & Bacon.

Campbell, B. M. (1984, December). To be Black, gifted, and alone. *Savvy,* 67–74.

Coner-Edwards, A. F., & Edwards, J. (1988). The Black middle class: Definitions and demographics. In A. F. Coner-Edwards & J. Spurlock (Eds.), *Black families in crisis: The middle class* (pp. 1–9). New York: Brunner/Mazel.

Corwin, M. (2001). *And still we rise: The trials and triumphs of 12 gifted inner-city high school students.* New York: HarperPerennial.

Cose, E. (1993). *The rage of a privileged class.* New York: HarperCollins.

Cross, W. E., Jr. (1995). The psychology of Nigrescence: Revising the Cross model. In J. G. Ponterotto, J. M. Casas, L. A. Suzuki, & C. M. Alexander (Eds.), *Handbook of multicultural counseling* (pp. 93–122). Thousand Oaks, CA: Sage.

Cross, W. E., Jr., & Vandiver, B. J. (2001). Nigrescence theory and measurement: Introducing the Cross Racial Identity Scale (CRIS). In J. G. Ponterotto, J. M. Casas, L. A. Suzuki, & C. M. Alexander (Eds.), *Handbook of multicultural counseling* (2nd ed., pp. 371–393). Thousand Oaks, CA: Sage.

DuBois, W. E. B. (1965). The souls of Black folk. In A. Mandelbaum (ed.), *Three Negro classics* (pp. 209–389). New York: Avon Books.

Dudley, R. G., Jr. (1988). Blacks in policy-making positions. In A. F. Coner-Edwards & J. Spurlock (Eds.), *Black families in crisis: The middle class* (pp. 15–27). New York: Brunner/Mazel.

Erikson, E. H. (1968). *Identity: Youth and crisis.* New York: Norton.

Exum, H. A. (1983). Key issues in family counseling with gifted and talented Black students. *Roeper Review, 5*(3), 28–31.

Ford, D. Y. (1995). *Correlates of underachievement among gifted and nongifted Black students.* Storrs: University of Connecticut, National Research Center on the Gifted and Talented.

Ford, D. Y. (1996a). Desegregating gifted education: A need unmet. *Journal of Negro Education, 64*(1), 52–62.

Ford, D. Y. (1996b). *Reversing underachievement among gifted Black students: Promising practices and programs.* New York: Teachers College Press.

Ford, D. Y. (1999). The recruitment and retention of Black students in gifted programs. In S. Cline & K. T. Hegeman (Eds.), *Gifted education in the 21st century: Issues and concerns* (pp. 135–152). New York: Winslow Press.

Ford, D. Y. (2004). A challenge for culturally diverse families of gifted children: Forced choices between affiliation or achievement. *Gifted Child Today, 27*(3), 26–29.

Ford, D. Y., & Grantham, T. C. (2003). Providing access for gifted culturally diverse students: From deficit thinking to dynamic thinking. *Theory Into Practice, 42*(3), 217–225.

Ford, D. Y., & Harmon, D. (2001). Equity and excellence: Providing access to gifted education for culturally diverse students. *Journal of Secondary Gifted Education, 12*(3), 141–147.

Fordham, S. (1988). Racelessness as a factor in Black students' school success: Pragmatic strategy or Pyrrhic victory? *Harvard Educational Review, 58*(1), 54–84.

Gardner, H. (1983). *Frames of mind: The theory of multiple intelligences.* New York: Basic Books.

Grantham, T. C. (2004). Multicultural mentoring to increase Black male representation in gifted programs. *Roeper Review, 48*(3), 232–248.

Gutman, L. M., & McLoyd, V. C. (2000). Parents' management of their children's education within the home, at school, and in the community: An examination of African American families living in poverty. *The Urban Review, 32*(1), 1–24.

Harrison, A. O., Wilson, M. N., Pine, C. J., Chan, S. Q., & Buriel, R. (1990). Family ecologies of ethnic minority children. *Child Development, 61,* 347–362.

Kochman, T. (1981). *Black and White styles in conflict.* Chicago: University of Chicago Press.

MacLeod, J. (1995). *Ain't no makin' it: Aspirations and attainment in a low-income neighborhood.* Boulder, CO: Westview Press.

McClain, L. (1983, July 24). How Chicago taught me to hate Whites. *The Washington Post,* pp. C1, C4.

McClain, L. (1986). *A foot in each world.* Evanston, IL: Northwestern University Press.

Milner, H. R. (2003). Teacher reflection and race in cultural contexts: History, meaning, and methods in teaching. *Theory Into Practice, 42*(3), 173–180.

Parham, T. A. (1989). Cycles of psychological Nigrescence. *The Counseling Psychologist, 17,* 187–226.

Pasch, M., Krokow, M. C., Johnson, C., Slocum, H., & Stapleton, E. M. (1990). The disappearing minority educator—no illusion. A practical solution. *Urban Education, 25*(1), 207–218.

Perls, F. (1976). *Gestalt therapy verbatim.* New York: Vintage Books.

Pinderhughes, C. A. (1988). Foreword. In A. F. Coner-Edwards & J. Spurlock (Eds.), *Black families in crisis: The middle class* (pp. iii–v). New York: Brunner/Mazel.

Piorkowski, G. K. (1983). Survivor guilt in the university setting. *The Personnel and Guidance Journal, 61,* 620–622.

Shade, B. J., Kelly, C., & Oberg, M. (1997). *Creating culturally responsive classrooms.* Washington, DC: American Psychological Association.

Smith, E. M. J. (1989). Black racial identity development. *The Counseling Psychologist, 17,* 277–288.

Steele, C. M. (1997). A threat in the air: How stereotypes shape the intellectual identities and performance of women and African Americans. *American Psychologist, 52,* 613–629.

Steele, C. M. (1999, August). Thin ice: "Stereotype threat" and Black college students. *The Atlantic Monthly, 284*(2), 50–54.

Sternberg, R. J. (1985). *Beyond IQ: A triarchic theory of human intelligence.* Cambridge, England: Cambridge University Press.

Suskind, R. (1998). *A hope in the unseen: An American odyssey from the inner city to the Ivy League.* New York: Broadway.

Yalom, I. D. (1985). *The theory and practice of group psychotherapy* (3rd ed.). New York: Basic Books.

Counseling African American Women and Girls

Carla Adkison-Bradley and Jo-Ann Lipford Sanders

At the beginning of the 21st century, the voice of the African American female client has remained relatively obscure. Although the counseling literature has seen a proliferation of writings and research on multicultural counseling, little discussion or information is available on the strengths and developmental aspects that affect African American women and girls. A perusal of recent counseling literature identified few articles and books on effective therapeutic interventions with this particular population.

Several African American women scholars (Greene, 1994; Jackson & Greene, 2000; Sanchez-Hucles, 1997) have attributed the absence of the African American female perspective in the psychological literature to her dual identity as a member of a racially oppressed group and as a woman. More specifically, the counseling profession has historically ignored or minimized the significance of race in the therapeutic process. Although other cultural identities such as ethnicity, gender, sexual orientation, spirituality, and class have been recognized and incorporated into discussions of client diversity, the saliency of race in general, and racism in particular, continues to be a point of contention within the counseling profession. Moreover, counseling scholars who have attempted to address "the woman question" have had a similar myopic approach, with the assumption that gender is the primary locus of oppression for all women, leaving the viewpoints of African American women out of the discourse (Jackson & Greene, 2000). As a result, professional counselors have been left to draw their own conclusions about the identities and experiences of African American women, which have often led to negative and stereotypical images derived from print and television media.

To work effectively and competently with African American women, counselors need to have a more accurate and informed understanding of the developmental aspects, strengths, and challenges of African American women and girls. This chapter provides directions for counselors on how to utilize culturally appropriate and meaningful interventions with African American women. The first half of this chapter focuses on the cultural and environmental influences that affect the development and experiences of African American females. With knowledge of these critical issues, counselors are in a better position to establish rapport, obtain accurate information, and formulate meaningful intervention strategies. The second half of this chapter focuses on culturally responsive strategies. Case studies are presented to illustrate applications of these strategies.

Environmental and Cultural Influences

A discussion of the environmental and cultural experiences that affect the development of the African American woman is complex because society has defined her in constraining and degrading ways. A recent review of the literature revealed several interesting points. Many of the empirical studies have focused on African American females from a "problem-centered" perspective (i.e., teenage mothers, poor women, or substance users) often in comparison with their White American counterparts. Furthermore, scholars have paid scant attention to the multifaceted dimensions of African American women's historical experiences beyond their enslavement and participation in the women's movement.

A residual of slavery that continues to be a cultural constraint for African American women is the paradigm of a "strong Black woman." African American women have been depicted as aggressive, self-sacrificing, and caretakers of their families and others. These characteristics are often descriptive of the "mammy" stereotype. The role of mammy is rooted in the history of slavery when an actual mammy was the primary caretaker of the master's household (Mitchell & Herring, 1998). She was often stout, dark-skinned, and obsequiously devoted to the master and his family.

Several writers have acknowledged that contemporary society continues to expect "mammy" behavior from African American women whether or not they fit the physical description (Giddings, 1984; Greene, 1994; Jackson & Greene, 2000). Mitchell and Herring (1998) cited a poignant example of an African American woman whose coworkers expected this type of stereotypical behavior and were disappointed when she did not comply.

> I received a less-than-positive review from my supervisor, which I didn't understand. I knew I had done my job well. When I went in to question the review, my supervisor, a White woman, told me that several of my coworkers complained that I was intimidating and hard to get along with. I knew what she meant—I didn't make them feel good, I didn't make them laugh, put them at ease, socialize with them at lunch. I was there to do a job, but I was being rated on how comfortable I made Whites I worked with feel. (Mitchell & Herring, 1998, p. 55)

The above illustration demonstrates one of the subtle realities of workforce racism and sexism that African American women face as they attempt to gain acceptance and respect from their colleagues. It also signifies the penalty of being censored and often ostracized when African American women do not acquiesce to the unwritten rule of serving and nurturing coworkers.

Similarly, when African American women are not being judged by their behavior, they are being evaluated by their level of facial and physical attractiveness. Perhaps the most jutting theme in the literature on women of color is that African American women must often negotiate an environment that lauds European American standards of beauty and behavior that ultimately could diminish their feelings of worth. It has been generally recognized that Western societies' paradigm of feminine beauty excluded females of African ancestry (Giddings, 1984; Lipford Sanders, 1996; Neal & Wilson, 1989). Western culture's paradigm of facial beauty, inclusive of White skin color, straight hair, light eyes, and angular features, refers back to the "Cult of True Womanhood." During the early 1800s, femininity was defined by the cult's central tenets of purity, homemaking, submissiveness, and piety. Failure to measure up to any of these tenets, which most African American women could not do, made a woman immoral and "a different kind of humanity" (Giddings, 1984). Thus, being womanly and feminine in American culture was, and still is, defined by being a White American woman. When compared with White American standards of beauty/femininity, traditional African features—kinky hair texture; darker skin, eye, and hair colors; and broad or thick facial features—are deemed unattractive and inferior by mainstream culture (Jackson & Greene, 2000).

Transmission of Cultural Values

The research on women often underscores gender as the key to obtaining information about and understanding development for women. Some researchers have further suggested that ethnicity be included in this understanding (Hanson & Johnson, 2000). These perspectives seem to propose that gender and ethnicity are separate and distinct issues necessary to understand development for women. However, from conception to birth and throughout life, both gender and ethnicity are equally important to the development of Black women and therefore to Black girls.

Although traditional researchers have theorized gender development as a singular dimension independent of context, current researchers have suggested that gender development for African American women and other women of color is best understood through a multidimensional focus. This multidimensional focus may be noted in the transmission of cultural values.

Examining the effects of race and gender on identity development of African American women should begin with an understanding of their socialization. A focus on the socialization of Black girls offers insights into developmental concerns of adult women. Researchers have included them as a small part of global women's issues but seldom acknowledge their contextually unique experiences. What typically occurs is that aberrant behaviors attributed to the label of "at risk" are presented without a consideration of mediating circumstances.

Socialization is the process of social conditioning through which children learn the established language, customs, laws, expectations, cultural ideologies, and symbols of a given society. Racial socialization should be understood as the process by which Black children learn how language, customs, laws, cultural ideologies, and the like affect their experience as a Black person within a given society. Even in the racial socialization literature, there are many messages for Black boys, mostly dealing with safety issues, but few published studies about socialization messages for Black girls, who must also navigate through muddy waters of racism, sexism, and classism. Racial socialization is most effective when included in a proactive discourse. Another aspect of the racial socialization process involves the demystification and demythologization of cultural ideology about Black females in general. There are many issues in relation to the *quadripartite discrimination* associated with gender, race, age, and class seen in some African American girls:

- As females in a patriarchal society, they may struggle to understand such issues as a predefined paradigm of beauty, the historical divisiveness of colorism, the relevance of a personal style (i.e., talk, walk, and attitude) unique to Black women, the importance of defining and understanding power, and friendship difficulty with other Black girls.
- As students labeled "at risk," they could feel a need to overcompensate toward a mythical stereotypical attitude about low academic expectations of Black children. They may mediate academic concerns and personal expectations by stating "THEY don't want us here anyway" or "Whatever, I'll never see these people again" or "I could do better if I really wanted to, but school is boring" and "Black kids get treated differently... anyway." They could manifest behaviors associated with powerlessness and hopelessness relative to their ability to become scholars. Some of their acting out behaviors that have been labeled as "aggressive," "defiant," and "unmotivated" have often been explained by this population as "they only see us when we act out, otherwise we are invisible," and "even if we get together and laugh, we are told to be quiet because we are disruptive. How can a person be disrupting when we were only talking? Our teacher said that we are too loud and just trying to get attention ... and she don't know what she talkin' bout."

- As adolescents in an adult world, they may manifest cautiousness and lack of trust of most adults. Some may state, "I don't trust anybody, and certainly not most adults . . . except my mother."
- As Blacks in a race-conscious society, they may express a great deal of ambivalence and anger that racism and discrimination ever occurred. Some African American girls may state that "race didn't matter," and others may feel that they are perceived differently than their White counterparts because they are Black.

African American girls are bombarded early with negative messages about their worth, intelligence, and beauty. These negative messages can adversely affect the development of self-concept and self-esteem. Many researchers have suggested that one way to combat the negative societal messages is to strengthen the racial self. Researchers have shown that there is a positive relationship between a strong Afrocentric understanding and self-concept in African American children (Neal-Barnett & Smith, 1996).

Strengths and Effective Coping Methods

It is not enough to know only about the injustices and exploitations that African American females have endured. Counselors need to also recognize the strengths and resilient nature of this particular population. hooks (1993) averred that not all African American women are debilitated by society's daily assaults on their beauty and dignity. She asserted that some have managed to heal these painful wounds by creating healthy representations of their own world. Magazines published by African Americans, such as *Essence, Body and Soul, Ebony,* and *Black Enterprise,* have had a long history of attending to the "Black woman question." These periodicals are replete with stories about African American women overcoming environmental challenges. They also provide culturally relevant information about career advancement, health, and strategies to counteract negative societal forces.

Spirituality also plays a central role in fortifying African American women. Moreover, both religion and spirituality are cornerstones of African American culture. Religion, in particular, provides an avenue for African American women to transcend issues of racism, sexism, and other concerns with prayer, fellowship, and mediation with others in their congregation (McRae, Thompson, & Cooper, 1999). Further, studies on the psychology of religion have consistently found that African American women attend church more frequently and participate in more church-related activities than any other racial group (Chatters, Levin, & Taylor, 1992; Mattis, 2000). These findings were consistent for African American girls and adolescents as well. Eugene (1995) acknowledged that church activities provide a mechanism "for African American women to perform, function, feel, and express themselves without the invidious distinctions which White judgments bring to bear" (p. 69). In many predominantly African American churches, this sense of free expression and rejuvenation occurs in evening prayer meetings. Often in this setting, African American women convey their problems or concerns and ask for prayers by the membership to alleviate their suffering. They also ask for assistance in bearing their burdens in the same manner (Eugene, 1995). Several researchers have affirmed that prayer is an important coping strategy for African American females (e.g., Paragament et al., 1990).

Culturally Responsive Counseling Strategies

This chapter advances the basic tenets of multicultural counseling in that counselors should have or receive training in working with clients from diverse populations. The Association for Multicultural Counseling and Development (Arredondo et al., 1996) recommended that counselors have specific knowledge about their own racial and cultural backgrounds and how their personal backgrounds affect their definition and biases of normality/abnormality and the process of counseling. It is also equally important that counselors explore their own attitudes, behaviors, and beliefs about African American females and be willing to do some personal work to become comfortable in working with this client population. Perhaps the most salient theme evident from this body of work is that counselor educators, students, and practitioners may have limited exposure to the strengths, coping methods, and environmental challenges often encountered by African American women and girls. Therefore, additional training is recommended so that counselors can increase their capacity to care, listen, respect, mutually engage, and validate African American female clients. Turner (1997) suggested that acquiring a deeper understanding of African American womanhood and her experiences will help counselors to have a more collaborative and proactive stance with African American female clients. She suggested that counselors explore the following six areas as they relate to the client's identified presenting problem:

1. How she feels about and experiences her race and ethnicity, along with her perception about how others experience her;
2. Her strength and coping mechanisms in negotiating race and gender;
3. Those parts of herself and her experience which cause her pain, hurt, and frustration internally and externally;
4. Those parts of herself that are responding resourcefully to forces both within and beyond her control;
5. The interactive parts of herself, family, work, and social environment, which work beneficially for her in fostering healthy growth and change, as well as those that interfere with this healthy process;
6. An examination of the extent to which she has acquired internalized and externalized meaningful connections and bicultural support systems. These systems include significant others, groups, organizations, and religious affiliations. (Turner, 1997, p. 81)

Illustrations of Culturally Responsive Counseling

The following case examples illustrate culturally relevant counseling strategies for African American women and girls. These examples are composites and experiences drawn from our own clinical and supervisory experiences.

Group Approach: A Sister-Friend Intervention

Group counseling and support groups have long been regarded as a treatment of choice for African American females. The main reason for utilizing a group approach with African American women is to assist group members with giving voice to joy and pain. According to hooks (1993), "we [African American women] do not heal in isolation. Healing is by integration. . . . it is participatory" (p. 15). Empowering consequences of group validation of career, racial, and cultural experiences include not only letting go of internalized negative stereotypes but also internalizing more affirming messages about oneself and others (Vasquez & Han, 1995).

Group counseling for African American women was first introduced to the counseling profession by Jordan (1991). She developed a proactive group counseling experience entitled "Sister Friends." The purpose of the group was to assist African American women "to move toward fulfilling their fullest potential in a challenging, but supportive, atmosphere" (Jordan, 1991, p. 55). The following case example demonstrates how counselors can utilize the "sister friend" counseling concept in an individual counseling relationship.

Allison

Allison is a 43-year-old woman referred to the counseling agency by her two girlfriends, who were concerned about Allison's emotional state after the recent breakup with her fiancé. One of her girlfriends initially called the agency, and then Allison called to set up her intake appointment. Both of her girlfriends came with Allison to the appointment and remained in the waiting room while Allison spoke with the counselor.

Over the last 2 weeks, Allison has been tearful and upset about the ending of her engagement with Anthony. The wedding would have been next month. She had called in sick to work a couple of days, but when she was at work she was able to function well. When she was not at work, however, she spent most of her time talking with her parents and seeking advice from her girlfriends and a female assistant pastor at her church.

Allison has a promising career as a medical records manager at a large hospital. She always performed well on her job evaluations, and the hospital administration considers her to be "nice, easy to get along with, and a team player." She is the only girl of three siblings. She has two older brothers who have been married for 20 years, and her parents had just celebrated their 50th wedding anniversary.

Anthony, her ex fiancé, is a successful electrician and has recently taken over his family's 60-year-old construction company, which was the first African-American-owned business in the city. She and Anthony had dated for 6 years, and her parents and relatives consider him to be a "member of the family." About 1 month prior to their breakup, Anthony told Allison that "he needed space." Although she had sensed that their relationship might be in jeopardy, she proceeded with the wedding plans, hoping that he was just having "prewedding jitters."

Since the breakup, Allison has been feeling embarrassed and angry. This would have been her first marriage. She felt that she let her parents down as well as members of her church who had assisted her with the wedding plans. Allison shared with the intake counselor, "I don't understand why I'm not married. I have always considered myself to be attractive and smart. I don't have many vices, and I'm dedicated to my church and community."

Discussion

Third-party or family interventions are often used as a last resort when a client is in denial. The most common use is with the substance abuse client. Family and friends are asked to assemble to tell the client how destructive his or her behavior is. Clients are often taken by surprise. The focus of the intervention is on how the client's destructive behavior affects him or her and other family members.

When designing a sister-friend intervention, none of the above premises are true. Whereas families are usually the primary participants in third-party interventions, sister-friend interventions more often include female familial others. The client is fully aware of notification. The focus of this intervention tends to be the impact of the client's behavior on herself.

Sisterhood is a prevailing ethos within Black culture. The special closeness of Black women has been intergenerationally transmitted from its cultural roots in African society to its earliest experiences with bondswomen. Although it has often been understood as a survival mechanism, sisterhood bonds also offer a way for Black women to obtain daily nurturance, provide the support of individuals whose experiences are similar, and serve as a social network. Although the term *sister-friend* has been used loosely, it implies the attainment of emotional intimacy among women.

Several factors determined if and when a sister-friend intervention would be appropriate for Allison. First, Allison had women emotionally attached enough to independently seek help for her (i.e., they made the initial inquiry). Second, Allison accepted their concern as an acknowledgment of their right to be concerned (i.e., she made and kept the appointment). Third, they had a shared history and a long-standing relationship (i.e., this was noticed and confirmed as her friends brought her to therapy and her continual references to them). Fourth, she had a counselor who was perceptive enough to notice the significance of these social supports in Allison's life.

Upon agreement with Allison, a sister-friend intervention session was scheduled. The counselor contacted all participants to meet in her office. Confidentiality was discussed, and Allison was encouraged to divulge as much information about her concerns as she felt comfortable. Invited members also presented their perspectives of the situation, highlighted Allison's strengths, and noted her irrational thinking.

In a sister-friend intervention, the counselor plays a dual role. She serves as a facilitator mediating truth-telling while also offering a supportive and safe climate. The latter is made easy because there is established emotional intimacy. The most important role of the counselor is to serve as a perceptive listener categorizing information in theoretical contexts. Sister-friend interventions tend to be very dynamic with individuals quickly moving to the source of the problem. The conversations tend to be blunt. As the only stranger in the session, the counselor must be cautioned not to rescue the client but to listen and take mental notes of her reactions. The following serves as an example of the dialogue within the group:

"Allison, he just isn't right. You are unwilling to hear anything negative about him, and that is just silly. You wanted to believe everything was okay, but there were a million signs that he is just a dog! I realize that this is hard to hear, but you must come to understand it was about him not wanting you and not about you not being okay." As Allison began to cry, several women joined her. The dialogue continued, "And this whole thing about you serving the church faithfully and feeling sorry for yourself is just a way to say you are mad at God. It ain't about God; it's about your refusal to listen. You are really mad at yourself because you think there is something wrong with you."

The counselor listened and sparingly facilitated movement. What the counselor noticed were themes of denial, damaged self-perception, challenged belief in positive reciprocity, a belief that the breakup was Allison's sole problem, an inability to consider negative thoughts about her ex fiancé, and possible effects of internalized oppression for the "American dream marriage." After all members and Allison had shared, the counselor summarized the session. She spent a few minutes applauding the strength and power of their love for one another.

The counselor used the themes from the intervention as building blocks for continued therapy with Allison. She noted, "I was able to learn more about my client in this one night than I could have in several sessions." Specifically, one aspect of Allison's problem that became clearer from the intervention surrounded cultural and gender expectations about marriage. The counselor noticed an element of sexism, namely, "I am not okay without marriage and children; my family, church, and community expect it," and was able to assist Allison in reframing this view that the only place she could find true happiness was within the institution of marriage.

Psychoeducational and Life Preparation Group for Adolescent African American Girls

The following 10-week group was developed for Black adolescent females on the basis of the Afrofemcentric (African-female-centered) perspective that embraces the significance of socializing African American females to redefine themselves as well as an Afro-cognitive orientation that teaches them to change their thinking about themselves and Black people. To answer the questions about who they are, what they think, and how to effectively work with them, counselors need to know how race, class, spirituality, and gender intersect throughout African American female development. Its primary goal is to provide a format for understanding the principle of self-empowerment. Empowerment here is understood as learning the ways that power can be useful in mediating the adolescent task between one's evolving self and a societally defined self.

The group was held for 10 weeks during a school term. They met during alternating mornings and afternoons so as not to miss much class. The group's curriculum was designed to address the theme "Girls and Their Pearls":

Peace Within
Excellence
Achievement (intellectualism)
Respect for Self and Others
Love for Self and Others
Spirituality as place of Centeredness

Each participant was given a notebook with the following affirmation included:

> I was a girl.
> I am now a young woman.
> I am kind and honest.
> Within me, I have the ability to change the world.
> I am in control of myself.
> I am responsible for myself.
> Many others support me.
> I will be proud to spell my name . . . W.O.M.A.N. I will be proud to spell my name . . . W.O.M.A.N.

Each session opened with the playing of "You Can Count On Me" by Whitney Houston and Ce Ce Winans (BabyFace, 1995). The girls then recited the mantra. Although there are many activities that can be offered using African values and principles, several activities from Sessions 1–10 are detailed below.

Session 1: "When I Look in the Mirror"

Goals: Begin rapport building. Increase participants' self-awareness, self-reflection, and self-disclosure.

All rules and procedures for effective group processes were initiated. Participants were given 5- × 7-inch index cards to indicate their academic schedules. A mirror was passed around, and each girl described who she saw in the mirror. The process of journaling was discussed.

- *Journal Assignment:* They were given a poem by an African American writer and asked to list three things that they saw when looking into a mirror.

Session 2: "My Voice Has the Power to Hurt and Heal"

Goal: Examine the voices of African American women through music, poetry, and literature.

Participants were introduced to varying ways in which Black females have expressed themselves through the written word. A female African American poet was the guest speaker and read some of her poetry. Additionally, the participants read and discussed the poetry of other Black female poets such as Sonia Sanchez and Nikki Giovanni. The use of bibliotherapy is very successful with Black girls. Other activities:

- Discussed power of journaling and its power of perceived reality, that is, people tend to believe that which is written down.
- Introduced the power of silence in role plays. Silence was very difficult because the participants stated, "If you don't talk, then people think you're scared, and you can't be scared."
- Developed group definition of self-esteem.
- Discussed writing as preparation for successful academic year.
- Introduced *Phenomenal Woman Series.* This is a series in which each girl has to bring a picture and biography of a Black woman whose life she perceives as being phenomenal. She is then responsible for presenting this woman to the entire group, and the facilitators make a copy for each participant's journal. Examples used throughout the group included Black women in the fields of education, television, music, and politics, as well as grandmothers and writers.
- Began academic check in which girls with academic problems are identified so as to partner participants with an academic mentor.
- Took pictures of each participant and placed them in the journals.
- Discussed last week's journal article.
- *Journal Assignment:* Write a short poem about one's voice.

Session 3: "Where I'm Coming From—Herstory"

Goals: Increase participants' knowledge and understanding of the history and accomplishments of their ancestors. Increase awareness of the significant events of diverse women in the formation of the United States.

Activities:
- Discussed addressing ways to effectively conduct an oral interview with an elder in the community.
- Discussed terms like *ethnicity, culture, gender, discrimination, power,* and *voice.*
- Discussed history of Black people naming themselves.
- Discussed ways to do computer searches for historical contributions of Black people. A good reference workbook is entitled *Herstory: Black Female Rites of Passage* by M. C. Lewis (1988).
- *Homework Assignment:* To interview an elder from the community and write a short narrative.
- *Journal Assignment:* Participants were given journal sheets with caricatures of Black women with varying facial expressions. Participants were asked to write a few words depicting what they imagined the person was trying to say.

Session 4: "Where Am I Going—NIA (Purpose)"

Goals: Expand vocational and educational choices. Help identify personal strengths to facilitate successful goal completion. Stress the importance of academic excellence as empowerment.

Activities:
- A career counselor was the guest speaker and discussed possible career choices. She also discussed the history of work relating to African American women. Participants then role-played several scenes in which they practiced telephone etiquette, a job

interview and college interview, effectual speech techniques, and how to address authority figures.
- *Journal Assignment:* "What is my favorite thing about school?"

Session 5: "She-Roses"

Goal: Increase participants' awareness of women and men who overcame obstacles to become great contributors to society. Establish a broad range of role models.

Activities:
- Discussed tolerance and respect of different ideas and perspectives.
- Discussed importance of friendship, namely, how to be a friend and how to make a friend.
- Discussed assertive and aggressive behaviors.
  During this session, several African American women attended and engaged in a discussion called "granny talk." Grannies are not necessarily grandmothers or identified using this label. They are women who have been "seasoned" by life experiences and whose mission is to help adolescent African American girls become quality African American women. These adult African American women have returned to the principles and experiences taught by history and refuse to allow the historical denigration of African American women to prevail. They spoke to the girls of hope and wisdom, but more important, they listened to the girls' stories.
- *Journal Assignment:* Free thoughts expressing their feelings about the group, about whatever learning has occurred, and something specific they have learned about themselves that is reflected from a historical Black "She-Rose."
- *Homework Assignment:* Participants were asked to bring something from their room that best described how they were feeling since beginning the group (nothing alive!).

Session 6: "Caring for Myself"

Goals: Promote awareness and knowledge of personal appearance. Expand participants' understanding of a healthy lifestyle. Offer insights regarding "first impressions being lasting impressions."

Activities:
- Viewed the film *400 Years Without a Comb* (Morrow, 1973), which discusses the care of Black women's hair since African enslavement. Each participant was given a sheet of questions to listen for in the film. The majority of the girls had no knowledge about the difficulties of their foremothers.
- Discussed body image and facial beauty. The participants wrote a television show honoring Black women. They were encouraged to notice areas within society that incorrectly defined them and to redefine the Black women they wanted to be. Issues of colorism and the worth of a person assigned to women who possess skin tones, hair textures, and facial features that are lighter hued and angular are still affecting Black girls in the 21st century.
- *Journal Assignment*: Free choice.

Session 7: "Laying in the Bed I Make"

Goals: Introduce and practice coping strategies useful in stressful situations. Help participants evaluate possible choices in uncomfortable dilemmas. Teach impulse control techniques relating to interpersonal relations (family, teachers, school, and peers).

- Role played various conflict mediation situations. During this session a great deal of time was spent discussing perceptions of femininity. Discussions centered on what the participants labeled as "unfairness" if they "acted like Black girls." This depiction was detailed as laughing loud, talking loud, and wearing large hoop earrings.

Session 8: "My Community—My House"

Goal: Identify personal and family strengths. Increase understanding of the importance of one's community and the varying ways this is defined for African Americans.

- A guest speaker discussed the seven principles of the Nguzo Saba. The Nguzo Saba are principles associated with the celebration of Kwanzaa, which means "first fruits of the harvest." Kwanzaa, created by M. Ron Karenga in 1966, offers an opportunity for Black people to reaffirm their commitment to themselves, their families, and their communities and to remember their ancestors. The seven principles are Umoja (unity), Kujichagulia (self-determination), Ujima (collective work and responsibility), Ujamaa (cooperative economics), Nia (purpose), Kuumba (creativity), and Imani (faith). A nice workbook for this activity is entitled *Afrocentric: Self Inventory and Discovery Workbook* by Useni Perkins (1989).
- *Journal Assignment:* Free choice.

Section 9: "Great Power Within M.E." (M.E. = Mental Energy)

Goal: Empowerment through knowledge, and knowledge through legacy building.

- The participants discussed the phrase "going mental" and what knowledge was able to do for their foremothers—Sojourner Truth, Mary McCloud Bethune, and others who understood that just because someone says something negative about you does not mean that you must accept it. Within some areas of the Black community, this is called "prophesyin." The importance of defining oneself was discussed at great length.
- This was one of the most difficult sessions because these young ladies had been defined as "at risk," and many of them articulated what this meant. For example, "They said this is a group for bad girls and dumb girls, but I ain't dumb." The girls made a video in which the cofacilitators asked them to voice their concerns and frustrations about being labeled "at risk." They were also asked to share how their life experiences were similar to those of their foremothers and other significant Black women in their lives. This experience was very cathartic for these girls. As they watched themselves in the video, group participants felt validated and encouraged as they reflected on their shared legacy with significant and courageous African American women.

Session 10: Closing Festival

Goal: Termination

- Took group pictures for journal.
- Completed evaluations that allowed self-expression of learning of self.

Conclusion

It is important that counselors view the information presented in this chapter regarding African American women and girls as a "cultural lens" that should be adjusted with each client (Boyd-Franklin & Garcia-Preto, 1994). Among African American women and girls, there is great diversity based on class, religion, skin color, and age. These cultural factors can add an additional layer of complexity to the counseling process. Therefore, it is imperative that the African American female perspective become a central focus in the supervision and education of counselors.

References

Arredondo, P., Topororek, R., Brown, S., Jones, J., Locke, D., Sanchez, J., & Stadler, H. (1996). *Operationalization of the multicultural counseling competencies*. Alexandria, VA: Association for Multicultural Counseling and Development.

BabyFace. (1995). Count on me [Recorded by W. Houston & C. C. Winans]. On *Waiting to exhale* [CD]. New York: Sony/Epic.

Boyd-Franklin, N., & Garcia-Preto, N. (1994). Family therapy: The cases of African American and Hispanic women. In L. Comas-Diaz & B. Greene (Eds.), *Women of color: Integrating ethnic and gender identities in psychotherapy* (pp. 239–264). New York: Guilford Press.

Chatters, L., Levin, J., & Taylor, R. J. (1992). Antecedents and dimensions of religious involvement among older Black adults. *Journal of Gerontology, 47,* 269–278.

Eugene, T. M. (1995). There is a balm in Gilead: Black women and the Black church as agents of a therapeutic community. *Women and Therapy, 16,* 55–71.

Giddings, P. (1984). *When and where I enter: The impact of Black women on race and sex in America.* New York: Morrow.

Greene, B. (1994). Diversity and difference: Race and feminist psychotherapy. In M. P. Mirkin (Ed.), *Women in context: Toward a feminist reconstruction of psychotherapy* (pp. 333–351). New York: Guilford Press.

Hanson, S. L., & Johnson, E. P. (2000). African American girls inclined to science early. *Journal of Minorities in Science and Engineering, 6,* 4–8.

hooks, B. (1993). *Sisters of the yam: Black women and self-recovery.* Boston: South End Press.

Jackson, L. C., & Greene, B. (2000). *Psychotherapy with African Americans: Innovations in psychodynamic perspectives and practice.* New York: Guilford Press.

Jordan, J. M. (1991). Counseling African American women: Sister friends. In C. C. Lee & B. L. Richardson (Eds.), *Multicultural issues in counseling: New approaches to diversity* (pp. 51–63). Alexandria, VA: American Counseling Association.

Lewis, M. C. (1988). *Herstory: Black female rites of passage.* Chicago: African American Images.

Lipford Sanders, J. (1996). My face holds the history of my people and the feelings in my heart: The perceptions of adolescent African American females toward perceived facial attractiveness and racial socialization messages. *Dissertation Abstracts International, 57*(12), 7760. (UMI No. 9716998)

Mattis, J. S. (2000). African American women's definitions of spirituality and religiosity. *Journal of Black Psychology, 26,* 101–122.

McRae, M. B., Thompson, D. A., & Cooper, S. (1999). Black churches as therapeutic groups. *Journal of Multicultural Counseling and Development, 27,* 207–220.

Mitchell, A., & Herring, K. (1998). *What the blues is all about: Black women overcoming stress and depression.* New York: Berkley.

Morrow, W. L. (1973). *400 years without a comb.* New York: Milady.

Neal, A., & Wilson, M. (1989). The role of skin color and features in the Black community: Implications for Black women and therapy. *Clinical Psychology Review, 9,* 323–333.

Neal-Barnett, A. M., & Smith, J. M., Sr. (1996). African American children and behavior therapy: Considering the Afrocentric approach. *Cognitive and Behavioral Practice, 3,* 351–369.

Paragament, K., Ensing, D., Falgout, K., Olsen, H., Reilly, B., Van Haitsma, K., & Warren, R. (1990). God help me: Religious coping efforts as predictors of the outcomes of significant negative life events. *American Journal of Community Psychology, 18,* 693–824.

Perkins, U. E. (1989). *Afrocentric: Self-inventory and discovery workbook. For African-American youth.* Chicago: Third World Press.

Sanchez-Hucles, J. V. (1997). Jeopardy not bonus status for African American women in the workforce: Why does the myth of advantage persist? *American Journal of Community Psychology, 25,* 565–580.

Turner, C. W. (1997). Clinical applications of the Stone Center theoretical approach to minority women. In J. Jordan (Ed.), *Women's growth in diversity: More writings from the Stone Center* (pp. 74–90). New York: Guilford Press.

Vasquez, M. J., & Han, A. (1995). Group interventions and treatment with ethnic minorities. In J. F. Aponte, R. Y. Rivers, & J. Wohl (Eds.), *Psychological interventions and cultural diversity* (pp. 109–127). Needham, MA: Allyn & Bacon.

Appendix

Additional Resources

African American Women

Boyd, J. A. (1995). *Girl to girlfriend: Everyday wisdom and affirmations from the sister circle.* New York: Dutton.

Danquah, M. N. (1998). *Willow weep for me: A Black woman's journey through depression.* New York: Norton.

Feagin, J. R., & Sikes, M. P. (1994). *Living with racism: The Black middle-class experiences.* Boston: Beacon Press.

Vanzant, I. (1993). *Acts of faith: Daily meditations for people of color.* New York: Simon & Schuster.

African American Girls

Flake, S. G. (1999). *The skin I'm in.* New York: Hyperion Books.

Rand, D., Foster, S., & Parker, T. (1998). *Black books galore: Guide to great African American books for children.* New York: Wiley.

Rand, D., & Parker, T. (2000). *Guide to great African American books about girls.* New York: Wiley.

Tarply, N. (1997). *I love my hair.* New York: Little, Brown.

Tarply, N. (1999). *Girl in the mirror: Three generations of Black women in motion.* New York: Beacon Press.

Tatum, B. (1997). *Why are all the Black kids sitting together in the cafeteria? And other conversations about race.* New York: Basic Books.

Counseling African American Male Youth and Men

Courtland C. Lee and Deryl F. Bailey

Amerian men find themselves constantly evaluating their role and meaning in life and society. They are besieged from all sides with messages about and images of what it means, or should mean, to be a man. Feminists, for example, have called on men to use their masculine privilege and power to change the larger community for the good of all (Pleck, 1981; Stoltenberg, 2000). Mythopoetic writers have advocated that men get in touch with and celebrate primal, mythic, or poetic images of manhood (Barton, 2000; Bly, 1990; Keen, 1991; R. L. Moore & Gillette, 1990). Religious groups, such as "Promise Keepers," offer men a chance to recommit themselves not only to religion but also to their families (McManus, 2003). Madison Avenue exhorts men to "just do it." The often conflicting nature of these images and messages has left many men confused about the nature of manhood and the essence of masculinity.

For African American men, the thrust of these images and messages concerning manhood is often blunted by compelling data that suggest that, as a group, they are in a state of psychosocial crisis. Evidence from both popular and social science literature indicates that African American males constitute a population at risk (Allen-Meares & Burman, 1995; Blake & Darling, 1994; Boyd & Allen, 1996; Conner, 1995; Johnson & Watson, 1990; King, 1993; Majors & Bilson, 1992; McCall, 1994; Randolph, 1990; Salholz, 1990; Shakur, 1994; Weathers, 1993; White & Cones, 1999; Wright, 1992).

Besides facing struggles with social and economic problems common to many men, African American men as a group experience a higher rate of homicide (Walker, Spohn, & Delone, 1996), imprisonment (Mauer, 1994; U.S. Department of Justice, 1995), unemployment, and racism ("Most Black Men Profiled," 2001) than any other group.

Central to the challenges confronting African American males are significantly low levels of educational attainment. Data on the educational attainment of African American male youth (Garibaldi, 1992; National Urban League, 2000; Porter, 1998; Roach, 2001; Slaughter-Defoe & Richards, 1995; Watson, 1999) present a profile of widespread failure. What is evident from this profile is that African American males tend to experience massive alienation from the educational process in America's schools. There is a serious stifling of achievement, aspiration, and pride on the part of many African American male youth in school systems throughout the country.

It is apparent that African American males face major psychosocial hurdles. Although many achieve significant economic, educational, and social success, it is also evident that across the life span African American men often face a series of significant challenges to such success. These challenges can take a heavy toll, often manifesting themselves in significant levels of stress and depression (Evans & Evans, 1995; Gary & Berry, 1985).

This chapter offers direction for counseling with African American male youth and men. Although many of Bradley and Lipford Sanders's ideas and concepts presented in chapter 6 for counseling with African American women and girls have applicability here, the unique historical and social challenges that confront African American males make this chapter necessary. After an overview of historical and cultural perspectives, crucial issues and strategies for counseling African American male youth and men are presented.

Historical and Cultural Perspectives on Counseling African American Males

Responsive counseling with African American males, at any age, must be predicated on an understanding of the historical and cultural context that shapes the psychosocial development of this client group. Professional counselors must possess not only solid intervention skills but also knowledge of the historical forces that have affected African American males' development. Likewise, they must appreciate the dynamics of African American culture and their influence on optimal mental health.

Historically, unlike his White male counterpart, achieving masculine privilege in the United States has not been a birthright for the African American male (Lee, 1990). Social and economic forces throughout American history have combined to keep African American males from assuming traditional masculine roles (Staples, 1978; Wilkinson & Taylor, 1977). This process has been an integral part of the dynamics of oppression and racism that have pervaded the Black experience in America (Grier & Cobbs, 1968). Beginning with the slavery experience, the African American male has been an object of fear (Hilliard, 1985; Staples, 1978). He and his implied physical prowess and leadership ability have been perceived as a significant threat to the social order and economic power structure. During the era of slavery and the decades that have succeeded it, the American power structure has initiated various social and economic actions that have resulted in the subordination of the African American male and the virtual elimination of his masculine advantage in the larger society (Staples, 1978). The racism inherent in such actions has operated to impede the sex role socialization of African American males and has kept them, in many instances, from realizing even the most basic aspects of masculine privilege and power, namely, life-sustaining employment and the ability to support a family (Staples, 1978).

The historical persistence of barriers to manhood has significantly affected the psychosocial development of African American males (Crawley & Freeman, 1993). The general inability to fulfill masculine roles has made rage, frustration, powerlessness, and hopelessness pervasive themes in the developmental dynamics of African American males. These themes are often evident in antisocial and self-destructive behavior patterns (Williams, 1998). In a society where a man's worth (and ultimately his manhood) has seemingly been judged by his ability to accumulate a degree of wealth and power, the African American male's general inability to obtain little of either has had serious consequences for his psychosocial development.

Although scores of African American men have developed the survival strategies, coping mechanisms, and forms of resistance to successfully overcome societal barriers, it must be understood that systemic forces have historically been stacked against their psychosocial development. For this reason, counseling with African American male youth and men must be based on an understanding of the historical context in which their psychosocial development occurs. It is important to appreciate that such development is complex and challenging in a society that has historically placed the African American male at social and economic risk.

Although American society has characteristically stifled the expression of African American manhood, the cultural context of the Black experience has served to nurture the socialization and psychosocial development of male youth and men. African American scholars have concluded that the African American cultural experience has a positive relationship with optimal mental health and psychosocial development for men and male youth (Akbar, 1991; Crawley & Freeman, 1993; Lee, 1996; Majors & Bilson, 1992).

A synthesis of the ideas of these scholars suggests that African American males' development and socialization are enhanced in a cultural environment characterized by rudimentary African- and African-American-oriented philosophical assumptions. These assumptions constitute a cultural tradition among African Americans that has placed a high premium on dynamics such as kinship, cooperation, mutual respect, commitment, and spirituality.

Collectively, these dynamics have contributed to the development of positive attitudes, values, and behaviors among African Americans, often despite the social pressure of racism and oppression in the larger American society. Significantly, these dynamics have been the foundation of optimal African American male socialization. From an early age, African American males are generally socialized into these cultural traditions in the home and larger African American community (Barnes, 1991; Crawley & Freeman, 1993; Lee, 1996; Majors & Bilson, 1992). These traditions form the meaning of psychosocial development and help African American males interpret the larger American social milieu. They are the basis of optimal mental health for African American males. Counseling intervention with African American males, therefore, should be predicated on an appreciation of their cultural context and its crucial role in promoting psychosocial development.

Within the context of these historical and cultural perspectives, the next section of the chapter presents issues and concepts to consider in counseling with African American male youth. Issues and guidelines for counseling practice with African American men then follow.

Counseling African American Male Youth

Issues to Consider in Counseling With African American Male Youth

The psychosocial development of African American male youth needs to be interpreted within the context of psychosocial issues that may impede development of this client group. Counselors who work with African American male youth need to understand and be sensitive to these crucial psychosocial issues, which include negative environmental stressors, additional developmental tasks, and a lack of positive role models. The effects of these impediments to psychosocial development in childhood and adolescence can often be seen in negative and self-destructive attitudes, behaviors, and values among African American males. Results include educational underachievement, unemployment, delinquency, substance abuse, homicide, and incarceration in disproportionate numbers (Hawkins, 1999; Leonard, Lee, & Kiselica, 1999). Working with an awareness of these issues will allow counselors to develop effective intervention strategies that promote education and social empowerment for African American male youth.

Negative Environmental Stressors

African American male youth may be extremely vulnerable to social forces and negative societal expectations. Society has far too often indoctrinated African American male youth with the belief that their future is limited to athletics, entertainment, prison, or the morgue (Cordes, 1985; Gibbs, 1988). The expectations of poor academic performance, drug use, violence, teenage fatherhood, and disrespect for authority in many instances become self-fulfilling prophecies for young African American males. What is not often considered, however, is that these represent secondary responses to negative environmental stressors for many African American male youth. These environmental stressors include cultural insensitivity and a generally oppressive system that fears the empowerment of African American male youth (Patton, 1995).

According to Patton (1995), the responses of African American male youth to these stressors have been identified as dysfunctional cultural adaptations and can include fathering a child out of wedlock, disrespecting women, and adopting a macho image. Such behavioral responses represent functional and immediate reactions to systemic insensitivity toward African American males. In their attempt to attain manhood, young African American males often use these adaptations without understanding why or realizing their possible self-destructive nature.

When working with African American male youth, counselors need to be aware of the context in which such behaviors occur. Counselors must understand the nature of these reactions and adaptations and their direct relationship to the socioeconomic status, social injustices, and educational constraints that often confront young African American males. An awareness of the relationship among environmental stressors (social, economical, political, and educational limitations), the challenges generated by these stressors, and the resulting secondary adaptations will assist counselors in helping many African American male youth address the issues confronting them. Thus, although counselors may not be able to alleviate the environmental stress caused by cultural insensitivity and an oppressive system, they can effectively help African American male youth attain workable solutions to their often self-destructive secondary adaptations.

Two realities must occur for the implementation of workable solutions via the counselor. First of all, the counselor should not pretend that racism does not occur or should just be ignored. Affirmation of their reality is an important step in establishing a working relationship between adults and adolescents; for African American male youth, that reality is the strain and pressure of dealing with racism on a daily basis. They need to be able to talk and express their emotions, fears, and doubts as well as their dreams, hopes, and aspirations (Boyd-Franklin & Franklin, 2000; Leonard et al., 1999). Second, counselors must become advocates for this population. Whether in the schools or the community, the counselor needs to help educate adults working with this population about the danger of low expectations and the easy acceptance of stereotypes; instead, they need to learn how to become encouragers and find ways to challenge this population in a positive way. Advocates find ways to open doors to opportunity for adolescent African American males rather than allowing them to close (Bailey, Getch, & Chen-Hayes, 2003).

Additional Developmental Tasks

Theorists and researchers have suggested that major aspects of human development unfold in a series of life stages and are influenced by both heredity and environment (Erikson, 1950; Havighurst, 1972; Kohlberg, 1966; Piaget, 1970). As individuals progress through the life stages, they must master a series of developmental tasks. Mastery of tasks at one stage of life influences success with those in succeeding stages. Conversely, failure to master developmental tasks at one stage can negatively influence success in later stages.

For young African American males, successfully completing these early developmental stages and tasks has often been problematic because of a complex set of historical and social factors. These tasks are often negatively affected by the convergence of environmental forces (Lee, 1996; Madhubuti, 1990; Majors & Bilson, 1992), including extreme environmental stress in the home, community, or school during the crucial early years of life (Boyd-Franklin & Franklin, 2000). Successful completion of developmental tasks can, for example, be hampered by school experiences distinguished by ineffective teaching strategies as well as predetermined negative views on African American male youth and their learning potential on the part of educators (Boyd-Franklin & Franklin, 2000; Irvine, 1990; Lee, 1996). Thus, instead of developing the sense of industry that comes with mastering fundamental skills in reading, writing, and computing during the all-important elementary school years, many young African American male students experience a sense of frustration with the teaching–learning process, which lays the groundwork for future academic and social failure.

The historical and social factors, which serve as environmental stressors for African Americans, present yet another problem for adolescent African American males. These factors interact in such a way that African American adolescent males are forced to deal with additional developmental tasks in their psychosocial development. These tasks are most directly affected by race, ethnicity, and culture (Crawley & Freeman, 1993; Griffin, 2000). The adolescent African American male peer culture demands more large group conformity than other ethnic same-sex groups, thus endangering the development of independent decision making (Harris, 1995). As discussed earlier, environmental stressors can result in self-destructive behaviors for this population and negative peer pressure that can be extremely damaging. Too often adolescent African American males are described as having untapped academic and social potential—untapped because it is easier to conform to group behavior than to strike out on their own. Another developmental task negatively stressed for this group includes career selection, an important prerequisite for healthy identity formation. Career selection stems from a student's academic strengths, and low expectations from teachers and counselors for this population place barriers rather than providing opportunities for positive development (Boyd-Franklin & Franklin, 2000; Harris, 1995; Irvine, 1990). With respect to identity formation, adolescent African American males must try to construct a healthy identity in spite of conflicting messages concerning race from the dominant society.

Because African American male youth are often prevented from mastering both the crucial universal and race-specific developmental tasks in childhood and adolescence, this lack of mastery negatively influences their academic, career, and social success in the later stages of life (Lee, 1994, 1996). It is not unusual, therefore, for African American males to reach adolescence with a basic mistrust of their environment, doubts about their abilities, and confusion about their place in the social structure. This makes developing an identity during the crucial boyhood-to-manhood transition of the adolescent years extremely problematic.

Lack of Role Models

The social reality that many African American male youth may have to engage in the process of identity formation with minimal or no positive adult male role modeling compounds the issues. Significantly, identity formation during adolescence is a process in which youth develop aspects of their personal and social identities by selecting and identifying with various role models. Given the historical, social, and economic limitations placed on Black manhood in America, the range of adult African American male role models available to adolescent males may often be severely restricted. The developmental passage to adulthood can thus become a confusing experience for many African American male youth because the evolution of gender-appropriate roles and behaviors for African American men has often been stifled by historical and social powerlessness.

A Framework for Counseling With African American Male Youth

The psychosocial challenges that confront African American male youth suggest a pressing need for programmed intervention on the part of professional counselors. Such initiatives must focus on helping these youth develop the attitudes, behaviors, and values necessary to function at optimal levels.

Counseling may need to be provided through culture-specific empowerment experiences. These experiences should develop the attitudes and skills necessary for academic achievement, foster positive and responsible behavior, provide opportunities to analyze the image of African American men, critically expose participants to African American male role models, and develop a sense of cultural and historical pride in the accomplishments of African American men.

Lee (1996) offered five guidelines that provide the framework for culture-specific counseling with African American male youth in educational or community mental health settings:

1. *Be developmental in nature.* Far too often the only counseling that young African American males receive comes after they have committed an offense against the social order. The goal of such an intervention is generally not development but rather punishment. Counseling should focus on helping African American male youth to meet challenges that often lead to problems in school and beyond in a proactive manner.
2. *Be comprehensive.* When working with adolescent African American males, counselors should utilize counseling strategies that are comprehensive in nature. All areas of the young men's lives (school, family, community, religious/spiritual, work, etc.) should be taken under consideration.
3. *Provide for competent adult African American male resources as appropriate.* Only African American men can teach African American male youth how to be African American men. By virtue of attaining adult status as African Americans and males, they alone have the gender and cultural perspective to accurately address the developmental challenges facing African American male youth. Although African American women and individuals of both sexes from other ethnic backgrounds can play a significant role in helping to empower young African American males, it is only an adult African American man who can model the attitudes and behaviors of successful African American manhood. As necessary, therefore, efforts should be made to actively recruit, train, and support competent African American men to serve as facilitators or consultants in counseling interventions.
4. *Incorporate the strengths of Black families.* Counseling initiatives for African American male youth must be based on an appreciation of the historical strength of the African American family. Such an appreciation is critical because much of the social science literature presents the generally pathological view of African American family life rather than the long-standing alternative view that disputes pathological notions of Black family life. This alternative view reveals a legacy of continuity, hard work, kinship, love, pride, respect, and stability in the evolution of African American families—despite the history of discrimination, racism, oppression, and poverty that has characterized much of the African American experience. In the face of extreme environmental hardship, scores of African American families have found the inner resources to cope effectively, promote the positive development of children, and prevail ultimately across generations. Promoting family involvement in counseling with African American male youth, therefore, should be approached with the understanding that this institution is a strong and viable force for enhancing psychosocial development.

5. *Incorporate African/African American culture.* Counselors should find ways to incorporate African and African American cultural dimensions into interventions for male youth. Culture-specific approaches to counseling transform basic aspects of African American life, generally ignored or perceived as negative in a traditional psychoeducational framework, into positive developmental experiences. For example, African and African American art forms (e.g., music, poetry, and graphic expression) and culture-specific curriculum materials can be incorporated into counseling.

In addition to using these five guidelines, counselors could develop and implement intervention programs that incorporate these same principles to work with groups of adolescent African American males. Following is a description of such a program that has been successful in working with this population.

Project: Gentlemen on the Move

The mission of Project: Gentlemen on the Move (GOTM) is to develop and nurture academic and social excellence in adolescent African American males. This particular model is both developmental and comprehensive in its approach. Developmentally, this model identifies where members are academically and socially and compares this information to where they should be (based on age and academic ability level) and then assists them in developing the necessary skills to reach their full potential. This is referred to as the "transformation." The transformation is defined as a positive change or modification in the social and academic performance of adolescent African American males; therefore, the transformation is unique to each student. For some, these transformations begin to manifest shortly after joining the group, and for others, they emerge in stages over varying periods of time. Second, GOTM is comprehensive in that it takes a holistic approach to the empowerment and transformation of adolescent African American males by addressing multiple aspects of their lives. The program intentionally and directly deals with issues that members are confronted with on a daily basis (e.g., how to appropriately respond to prejudice/racism in school and the community, how to combat peer pressure). GOTM members participate in community service projects as a way to develop leadership skills and unity among its members while providing a service to members of their communities and establishing a sense of ownership and responsibility for the well-being of the community at large. GOTM also provides avenues (e.g., dances, community service projects, and forums) for its members to interact with other groups of students who are normally outside of their circle of friends. The intent is to remove the social barriers that exist between them and their peers from different cultures. GOTM also enlists the support and assistance of the families via a parent support group, Parents of Gentlemen on the Move (PGOTM). Parent participation in PGOTM is mandatory. Parents meet monthly to discuss school and community issues that affect their sons' lives. Through PGOTM, parents receive information critical to their sons' school experience, support from other parents and program staff, and information regarding activities of GOTM.

Critical Components

The program consists of four components: (a) attention to process, (b) focus on identified areas of content, (c) support through individual and group counseling, and (d) specifically designed activities to achieve the goals of the program. Although each component serves an important role, it is the intermingling of these four components that creates a system in which the effectiveness of one component is important to the effectiveness of the next and is critical to the overall success of the program.

The *process component* includes elements such as recruitment and referral, selection, invitation, and monitoring. The *content component* involves skill development and the integration of new information pertinent to academic and social growth.

Academic topics include a study of African, African American, and family histories; health-related issues; and tips on enhancing academic excellence. Topics promoting social development include the improvement of self-efficacy, personal and business etiquette training, the importance of giving back to the community, and appreciation and acceptance of individual differences. This last element of the social topics focuses on respect for self, elders, women, and culturally different individuals. Opportunities to be exposed to traditional African American culture as well as interactions with individuals from other cultures are considered crucial. Both the academic and social topics are covered during miniworkshops held weekly and are referred to as Saturday Institutes. The third component is the *support component*. Within this component, group members are involved in individual and group counseling sessions. These sessions enable group members to establish short-term and long-term academic and social goals. Other areas of support include structured study sessions held during the first 2 hours of the Saturday Institutes and intense exam preparation, known as exam lock-ins. The exam lock-ins are held the weekend prior to the end-of-semester exams, and participation is mandatory. Members who earn an overall exam average of 93 or above earn the privilege to have their membership elevated from GOTM members to GOTM scholars for the upcoming semester. Also apart of the support component is the Give Me a Reason: An Academic Incentive Program. This program provides a variety of rewards for academic progress and excellence, such as money, T-shirts, travel, dining, and tickets for sporting and cultural events, to name a few.

The final component is the *activity component*, which includes educational field studies, college visitations, special event opportunities, and community service projects. Past community service projects have included community-wide Easter egg hunts for youngsters in grades K–5, an annual 5-k road race called Project: Gentlemen on the Move Race Against Drugs, and a 1-day basketball clinic for elementary and middle school students. The first three activities (field trips, college visitations, and special event opportunities) help to broaden members' worldviews. The remaining activities provide avenues for developing leadership skills and a positive work ethic while fulfilling an identified need within the community. During the summer, group members are invited to participate in the Project: Gentlemen on the Move Summer Academy; this 1-week academy focuses on leadership development and self-improvement for group members.

When adolescents are provided adequate direction, support, and opportunities, they are better able to overcome many of the academic and social challenges that oftentimes hinder their development. This is especially true for African American adolescent males (Bailey, 2001). Over the past 15 years, GTOM has been well received by schools and communities. Although many participants continue to view their academic and social challenges as barriers, others have been able to accept the challenges for what they are, devise a plan of action, and move forward. Counselors who choose to use such programs must be prepared to invest much time and energy if the program is to meet the needs of its members.

Counseling African American Men

Issues to Consider in Counseling With African American Men

Although much has been written about counseling men in recent years, very little of this literature has focused on specific issues of counseling with African American men. The literature suggests that although there are issues common to counseling all men (Moore & Leafgren, 1990; Scher, Stevens, Good, & Eichenfield, 1987), the unique psychological and social pressures on African American men make mental health intervention with this client group particularly challenging (Baker, 1999; Franklin, 1999; Lee, 1999; White & Cones, 1999). In order to provide a framework for counseling African American men, a number of important issues need to be considered. These include racism, problems of aggression and control, cultural alienation, self-esteem, dependency, and help-seeking attitudes and behaviors.

Racism

When discussing important issues in counseling with African American men, it should be stressed that, as a client group, they differ significantly in terms of their socioeconomic status, educational attainment, lifestyles, and value orientations. However, all African American men share the common reality of racism (Lee, 1999). Although reactions to this oppressive dynamic may differ, its persistence significantly affects the quality of life for African American men and should be considered as a significant factor in both problem etiology and counseling intervention (Lee, 1999).

The stresses of daily life are compounded for African American men by both overt and covert racism. As mentioned previously, racism operates, in many instances, to limit African American men from a full measure of life-sustaining employment and the ability to support a family. In addition, racism has spawned a number of negative stereotypes about African American manhood (Majors & Bilson, 1992).

The historical persistence of racism has significantly affected the mental health of adult African American males. The general inability to totally fulfill masculine roles has made anger, frustration, diminished self-esteem, and depression pervasive mental health issues for African American men (Lee, 1999).

Significantly, African American men have developed a number of ways of coping with and adapting to the dynamics of racism and its inherent challenges, many of which may manifest themselves as presenting issues in counseling. Several of these are discussed below.

Problems of Aggression and Control

The problems that African American men experience with aggression and control often present themselves in one of three ways. First, African American men may exhibit too much control over their anger, frustration, or other strong emotions, resulting in repression or suppression of such affect. Second, they may exhibit too little control over such emotions. In this case, they often demonstrate limited or immature coping skills. Third, African American men may engage in inappropriate channeling processes in which they direct strong emotions inward. Such channeling processes can often lead to stress-related illness such as hypertension or maladaptive behaviors including substance abuse.

Cultural Alienation/Disconnection

Often perceiving themselves to be marginalized or powerless in American society, many African American men cope with their anger, frustration, or sense of hopelessness by disconnecting from meaningful personal relationships or roles valued by society. Such disconnection often leads to cultural alienation. With a limited sense of interconnectedness and a perceived sense of rejection by many sectors of society, the attitudes, behaviors, and values of many African American men often reflect significant disengagement from the world of work, family, and community. This cultural alienation often leads to an identity built on an "outlaw" or "outsider" image among many African American men.

Self-Esteem Issues

The general inability to totally fulfill masculine roles often contributes to diminished self-esteem among many African American men. An internalized negative self-image generally results when African American men perceive that they are socially or economically handicapped by negative stereotypes or exclusion from a full measure of employment opportunities. Such perceptions may lead to concerted and often misdirected efforts to assert manhood and attain a sense of self-esteem. In many instances, such efforts result in maladaptive or antisocial behaviors.

Dependency Issues

The dimensions of coping and adaptation among African American men can often be related to issues of dependency. African American men often relieve environmental or interpersonal stress by developing unhealthy or unproductive dependencies. For example, the release of anger, frustration, or other negative affect may be associated with a dependency on drugs or alcohol. Similarly, the release of such affect may be linked to dependency on a process. This might be seen among men whose problem solving or coping behavior consists of a relatively constant process of maladaptive or violent behavior.

Help-Seeking Attitudes and Behaviors

In considering these issues, it is important to examine the help-seeking attitudes and behaviors among African American men. Consistent with the literature on counseling men in general, African American men, as a rule, do not seek counseling. In many cases, African American men consider the need to seek traditional counseling as an admission of weakness or as being perceived as "unmanly." Although this is a phenomenon that can be observed among men from a number of racial or ethnic groups, it takes on a different dimension for African American men. For many of them, doing anything that seems unmanly can threaten a masculine self-concept already diminished by society's views and stereotypes of African American manhood. As a rule, therefore, African American men are generally socialized to not open up to strangers.

African American men often find "counseling," however, within community kinship networks (Taylor & Chatters, 1989). For example, many men will seek out family members or close and trusted friends for help with problem resolution or decision making. They may also seek the guidance of a minister or other religious leader associated with the Black church. In addition, African American men have traditionally found "counseling" services in community centers of male social activity, such as barbershops, taverns, or fraternal/social organizations. These are places where men engage in informal conversation and significant male bonding. Such centers allow men to informally, and often indirectly, discuss personal issues with trusted confidants in a nonthreatening atmosphere.

In many instances, African American men are referred for counseling by some societal agent, be it judge, social worker, or probation officer, after they have committed some offense against the social order. Counseling, therefore, becomes a forced-choice process, and the implicit goal is rehabilitation or punishment. It is not unusual, therefore, to find many African American men approaching the counseling process with apathy, suspicion, or hostility. The resistant attitude about counseling may be a defense mechanism among many African American males (Majors & Nikelly, 1983; Vontress, 1995). African American men generally view counseling as an activity that is conducted by agents of a system that has rendered them virtually powerless. The counseling process, therefore, may come to be perceived as another infringement on African American manhood (Lee, 1999).

A Framework for Counseling With African American Men

Although the issues discussed above may present barriers to effective counseling with African American men, they also provide the basis of a framework for effective intervention with this client group. A number of key factors comprise this framework:

- *Developing Rapport.* Given the possible degree of alienation or distrust of the counseling process, it is important to find ways to make an initial personal connection with African American male clients. Counselors may need to adopt an interpersonal orientation when counseling with African American men. Such an orientation places the primary focuses on the verbal and nonverbal interpersonal interactions between counselor and client as opposed to counseling goals or tasks (Gibbs, 1980).
- *Pacing the Engagement of the Actual Counseling Process.* It is important to pace the counseling relationship and be mindful of engaging in therapeutic work too rapidly with many African American men. The process is often more effective when it evolves naturally from a personal relationship, based on openness and trust, that emerges between the counselor and the client.
- *Counselor Self-Disclosure.* It is important that a counselor be prepared to self-disclose, often at a deep and personal level, to an African American male client. A counselor's willingness to forthrightly answer direct, and often intimate, questions about his or her life increases credibility and promotes rapport with many African American men in counseling. A counselor should self-disclose, however, only to the level of his or her comfort about revealing personal information to a client.
- *Introspection Process.* Given cultural alienation or disconnection among many African American men, a counselor may need to foster a climate that encourages client introspection. The veneer of aloofness, strength, and control characteristic of alienation among African American men may preclude the sharing of intimate feelings that is generally a major aspect of the counseling process. Counselor credibility and openness can promote a climate that facilitates an introspection process with many African American male clients.
- *Spirituality.* Counseling with African American men can often be enhanced if a counselor can engage clients in an exploration of how they approach living and dying (i.e., spirituality). Helping clients to explore their sense of spirituality or personal meaning in life can provide a focus for processing issues of alienation, anger, or frustration. Such an existential/philosophical exploration can be facilitated only if rapport and trust have been established.
- *Racism–Sensitive Counseling.* Counseling with African American men must be predicated on sensitivity to the dynamic of racism. Although there is a great deal of variation in the effects of racism on the psychosocial development of African American men, its influence on the quality of their lives cannot be overstated. A culturally responsive counselor, therefore, should factor this variable into problem etiology and resolution, as appropriate. It is important to avoid discounting clients' perceptions of how this dynamic affects their lives.
- *Psychoeducational Counseling.* Counseling should be viewed as an educative process for many African American men. The primary focus of the process may need to be developing new skills or behaviors to deal more effectively with social and economic challenges.

Crucial Stages in a Counseling Process With African American Males

The counseling framework can be seen in the following crucial stages of a counseling process with African American men. The stages are similar in their structure and content to a framework advanced by Gibbs (1980) for conceptualizing the initial response of African American consultees to the use of mental health consultation. Gibbs suggested the importance of considering an interpersonal orientation in mental health interventions with African Americans. This clinical orientation focuses on process rather than content in interpersonal interactions. Adopting such an orientation requires interpersonal competence, which is the ability to evoke positive attitudes and to obtain favorable responses to one's actions. Culturally responsive counseling with African American men, therefore, is predicated on promoting an interpersonal orientation. The following five stages imply interpersonal competence on the part of a counselor.

Stage 1: Initial Contact/Appraisal Stage

Upon entering counseling, many African American men will be aloof, reserved, passive—aggressive, or openly hostile. Conversely, they may be superficially pleasant and appear to acquiesce to the counselor's wishes. Underlying such behavior may be a lack of trust in or hostility toward the counselor and the therapeutic process. At this stage, therefore, personal authenticity on the part of the counselor is critical. It is critically important that an African American male client see the counselor from the outset as genuine or "being for real."

Stage 2: Investigative Stage

Equalitarian processing characterizes this stage. In specific terms, this may consist of attempts on the part of an African American male client to minimize any social, economic, professional, or educational distinctions he perceives between himself and the counselor. A client may seek to relate to the counselor on a level that minimizes degrees, licenses, and other forms of professional identification. An African American male client may "check out" the counselor by investigating possible areas of personal commonality that exist between them. It is important, therefore, that a counselor become comfortable with stepping outside of his or her professional role to interact with an African American male client at such a level of personal commonality.

Stage 3: Involvement Stage

It is at this stage that an African American male client often decides whether he can identify with the counselor as a person. This decision is generally predicated on open and honest self-disclosure on the part of the counselor. At this stage of the counseling process, a client will often engage in an identification process that is characterized by asking the counselor personal questions. The degree to which a counselor is able to get personal and engage in self-disclosure with an African American male client can often promote a sense of trust and facilitate movement into a working counseling relationship.

Stage 4: Commitment Stage

At this stage, an African American male client generally makes a decision about whether he can trust and work with a counselor. This decision is usually based on his evaluation of the counselor as an open and honest individual whom he can relate to on a personal level.

Stage 5: Engagement Stage

At this stage, the client makes a decision that the counselor is "for real" and can be trusted. This is the working stage in which the counselor and the client engage in the process of counseling.

The following case study highlights some of the possible issues and challenges associated with counseling African American men:

> Curtis is a 57-year-old African American male. He is currently a midlevel manager with a major electronics firm. He is married with three children. His wife is a middle school teacher in an urban public school system. Curtis and his family live in a middle-class suburb of a major city. His oldest child is a student at a prestigious university, and his other two children attend secondary school.
>
> Curtis grew up in a working-class neighborhood in a large city. His father worked two manual labor jobs to support Curtis and his mother, younger brother, and sister. Today, Curtis's sister is a nurse who is married and lives with her family in a distant city. His brother became involved in drugs during adolescence and is now serving time in a nearby prison for manslaughter.
>
> When he graduated from high school, Curtis enlisted in the Marine Corps and served a tour of duty in Vietnam, where he was wounded and received the Purple Heart. Upon his discharge from the Marines, Curtis got married and started his family. He also enrolled in college part-time. After 6 years of working full-time in a factory and attending college part-time, Curtis received a BS degree in electrical engineering. He was then hired as a management trainee by the electronics firm. He was the only African American hired as a management trainee.
>
> Recently, Curtis's performance at work has been slipping. He appears at work looking tired and, according to his boss, often seems detached from his coworkers. Suspecting problems at home, Curtis's boss suggests that he talk with the firm's employee assistance counselor.
>
> Curtis is extremely reluctant to talk with the counselor. He initially attends the counseling sessions because he feels that he has been ordered to do so. Curtis gradually reveals to the counselor, however, that he has recently been under a great deal of stress. His father passed away several years ago, and now he finds that he must take care of his mother, who is beginning to have health problems. This, in addition to paying college tuition for his oldest child and addressing the needs of his two younger children, has begun to strain his relationship with his family. Curtis says he and his wife are constantly arguing over finances and other family matters. He also never seems to have time for his children and seems to be constantly yelling at them.
>
> However, he is most upset because he has watched younger White males with less experience than he advance beyond him in the management of the firm. In many instances, Curtis was responsible for the initial training of these men. When he has discussed his progress in the company with his supervisor, he has been told that these younger employees attended better training programs and that their knowledge of the electronics field is more current. This, despite the fact that his performance evaluations have always been outstanding. He claims he has watched White men in the company form networking groups that have generally excluded him. He knows that the key to advancement in the firm lies in being a part of one of these groups. Curtis reluctantly confides to the counselor that he has begun drinking to deal with his stress, fears, anger, and frustration.

Case Interpretation

Curtis is an African American man dealing with a significant amount of stress in his life. His anger, frustration, fears, and perceptions of racism have actually moved him beyond stress to a state of distress. Ironically, he did what the "system" expects and sought the so-called American dream. He got an education, honorably served his country in a time of crisis, found gainful employment, worked hard, raised a family, and joined the ranks of the middle class. His achievements refute many of the statistics and stereotypes associated with Black men in contemporary American society.

Despite his accomplishments, however, Curtis perceives that he has not been able to fully participate in or cash in on the American dream. Although his financial and family challenges are characteristic of many middle-class American men, the dynamics associated with his ethnicity play a major role in Curtis's perceptions. Despite his qualifications and job performance, he has been unable to feel fully integrated into his work setting. More important, he has not been afforded the opportunity to advance in a manner commensurate with his job performance.

Curtis considers his failure to move up the corporate ladder a reflection of how he, as an African American, is viewed and treated in the workplace. It is obvious that he has reached the infamous "glass ceiling," which confronts many ethnic minorities and women in the workplace. It is a barrier that is characterized by racial or gender insensitivity and exclusion in the workplace. This unseen but pervasive barrier generally stifles both talent and career goals. It can also have a damaging effect on many aspects of an individual's life. For African Americans, this barrier to career advancement has fostered significant amounts of anger among members of the middle class (Cose, 1993; Thomas, 1993). This is certainly the case with Curtis.

Significantly, Curtis's anger, frustration, and the associated stress have begun to affect the quality of his home and family life. His perceived inability to fulfill his multiple masculine roles of provider and head of his family has severely affected his well-being.

Presenting Issues

As is often the case with African American men in counseling, the major presenting issue in Curtis's case is anger. He is angry at a system that has thwarted his ability to reach his full potential. Curtis appears to have channeled this anger and the other strong emotions associated with it inward, which has no doubt precipitated his drinking. As his level of stress rises, he attempts to cope by disconnecting from his environment, both at home and in the workplace.

It is obvious that being constantly passed over for career advancement has severely affected Curtis's self-esteem. As family pressures increase, his ability to fulfill increasing responsibilities as a provider is in direct proportion to his inability to advance professionally. Curtis's career stagnation is particularly hard on him because, in his perception, the only thing blocking his advancement is the color of his skin.

Counseling Intervention

Initial Contact

At the outset, it was important to gain Curtis's trust and allay his fears about talking about personal issues to a stranger. The counselor wanted Curtis to see him as a person first and as a mental health professional second. The counselor adopted an interpersonal approach that was focused more on the relationship between the two of them than any specific counseling goals. The counselor engaged Curtis in conversation about a variety of nonthreatening issues (e.g., sports, events in the community, the firm's ranking in the electronics field).

Appraisal

As Curtis and the counselor continued to talk over the first few sessions, it was obvious that they had much in common. The counselor was forthcoming with information about his own family origins, educational background, and military experience. It turned out that Curtis and the counselor shared similar political views, religious views, and opinions about the local sports teams. Several times Curtis asked direct questions about the counselor's home and family life. The counselor, while not altogether comfortable in revealing such information, was generally open and honest with Curtis. Although Curtis had not yet revealed anything of any substance related to his anger and frustrations, he and the counselor established a solid personal relationship. This was evidenced by the fact that Curtis began to refer to the counselor as "my man."

Curtis and the counselor shared much in common. If this had not been the case, however, it would have been important for the counselor to be open with Curtis in a personal way. Finding ways to equalize the status between Curtis and the counselor would have been an important aspect in establishing a counseling relationship.

Involvement

Curtis began to reveal his anger at the firm's promotion policies. As he spoke, his anger became increasingly evident. It was important at this point for the counselor to let Curtis tell his story and vent his anger. As his story unfolded, Curtis periodically turned to the counselor and asked, "You understand what I'm saying?" or "You see where I'm coming from?" This was Curtis's way of checking to see if the counselor was really hearing what was being said. It was important for the counselor to answer these questions in a forthright and often personal way. In other words, Curtis needed to hear from the counselor, "Hey man, I've been there."

Commitment

After several sessions, it was obvious to Curtis that the counselor was someone he could definitely talk to and possibly work with. Curtis proclaimed that the counselor was "alright!" With this stamp of approval, Curtis proclaimed that he was ready to work with the counselor on finding concrete solutions to the challenges facing him. In Curtis's words, it was "time to take care of some business."

Engagement

At this point, because of the personal nature of the professional relationship that had been established between himself and Curtis, the counselor encouraged Curtis to explore meaning in his life. He asked Curtis to consider how he saw himself as a human being, a man, and an African American. He asked what meaning being an African American man had for him. The counselor encouraged Curtis to consider what gave his life meaning as an African American man. Curtis talked about the importance of family, God, and work to his life. Curtis claimed that all of these things were important to him because things were so bad for Black men in general.

As the meaning and purpose of his life became more focused for Curtis, the counselor helped him to see the interrelatedness of his challenges: He now bears the financial responsibility for not only his children but also his ailing mother. Career advancement would no doubt make this responsibility easier to bear. However, the glass ceiling appears to be preventing him from moving up the corporate ladder to greater economic reward. All of this contributes to his sense of anger and frustration, which affects his relationships both at home and at work. It also has him questioning his worth as a man. At this point, Curtis was ready to engage in a plan of action.

His first step was to admit that he was drinking too much and that this excessive behavior would not effectively relieve his stress. The counselor helped him to engage in a concrete problem-solving process. The primary goal was to find ways to more effectively channel his strong emotions. Curtis and the counselor explored a variety of options.

Curtis decided that one way to deal with the drinking and to relieve stress was to get some exercise. He had played some basketball in high school and had put a net in his driveway for his children's recreation many years ago. In the past, he had enjoyed "shooting hoops with his kids." The counselor suggested that he might find time to shoot baskets again with his two younger children. This not only would provide him with exercise but also would help him to reconnect with his children.

Although his wife and children went to church on a regular basis, Curtis did not. He and the counselor also discussed the possibility that spiritual direction within the African American religious tradition might be important in dealing with his challenges. The counselor strongly supported Curtis's decision to attend church again with his family on a regular basis. The counselor and Curtis considered ways that this could become important family time. Part of family time would include talking about and planning for family challenges with his wife.

A particularly difficult family issue and one that, heretofore, had not been discussed was Curtis's relationship with his incarcerated brother. Curtis visited his brother several times a year but had minimal contact with him. When talking about his brother, Curtis got extremely emotional. He experiences tremendous guilt with respect to his brother. He discussed his regret at not having spent more time with his brother when they were younger. Curtis feels that if he had spent more time as a role model or mentor for his brother, perhaps he would not have gotten into trouble.

He made a commitment that part of his family time would entail visiting his brother on a regular basis. Curtis would use his visits with his brother as a time to reestablish his relationship with him and possibly help him plan for his life after incarceration.

With respect to his work situation, Curtis discussed with the counselor the possibility of confronting his supervisor about his perceptions concerning racism in the firm's promotion practices. Curtis rehearsed with the counselor what he might say to the supervisor about his concerns. His goal was to be able to state his perceptions about the promotion practices in a calm and logical but forceful manner.

The counselor at this point also decided to engage in some advocacy efforts on Curtis's behalf. He helped Curtis network with several local civil rights associations that could serve as a resource in his efforts to affect the firm's promotion policies. He promised to help Curtis locate and work with a lawyer in preparing a discrimination suit against the firm if that became necessary. The counselor also coordinated some training sessions on diversity issues in the workplace for the firm's management team.

Follow-Up

As a result of his efforts and the threat of external legal and political action, Curtis was eventually promoted to an upper-level management position. His family-focused efforts also improved the quality of his home life. He had found important new ways to channel his anger. His drinking behavior moderated significantly. After terminating the formal relationship with the counselor, Curtis periodically dropped by the counselor's office whenever he was feeling stressed out and needed to talk.

Reviewing this case, a culturally responsive counselor needs to address the challenges associated with issues such as those which confronted Curtis with intervention at the interpersonal and systemic levels. The first level of intervention involves the direct service to the client. There is much that a culturally responsive counselor can do to help empower a client such as Curtis to effectively challenge his stress, fears, anger, and frustrations. Such service delivery must be predicated, however, on an understanding and appreciation of the culture-specific issues that may hinder or facilitate responsive counseling with African American men.

In addition to direct client intervention with a client such as Curtis, a culturally responsive counselor may need to intervene into the work setting to effect institutional change. In this case, the counselor readily assumed the role of advocate for Curtis. As an advocate, the counselor intervened within the firm on behalf of Curtis, and indirectly for other minority employees, in a way that was designed to eradicate both overt and covert racism.

Conclusion

Within the panorama of the changing face of manhood in America, the realities of African American males often stand out in a striking and troublesome manner. The future status of African American males depends, in some measure, on the ability of counselors to help empower this client group for maximum psychoeducational achievement and meaningful, productive lives. This will require not only an understanding of the social and cultural context that frames African American males' realities but also a willingness to expand the boundaries of counseling practice.

References

Akbar, N. (1991). *Visions for Black men.* Nashville, TN: Winston-Derek.

Allen-Meares, P., & Burman, S. (1995). The endangerment of African American men: An appeal for social work action. *Social Work, 40,* 268–274.

Bailey, D. F. (2001). Empowering and transforming African American adolescent males: A personal reflection. *Georgia School Counselors Association Journal, 10,* 42–47.

Bailey, D. F., Getch, Y., & Chen-Hayes, S. (2003). School counselors as social advocates. In B. Erford (Ed.), *Transforming the school counseling profession* (pp. 411–434). Upper Saddle River, NJ: Merrill/Prentice Hall.

Baker, F. M. (1999). Psychiatric treatment of older African American males. In L. E. Davis (Ed.), *Working with African American males: A guide to practice* (pp. 29–38). Thousand Oaks, CA: Sage.

Barnes, E. J. (1991). The Black community as a source of positive self-concept for Black children: A theoretical perspective. In R. L. Jones (Ed.), *Black psychology* (3rd ed., pp. 667–692). Berkeley, CA: Cobb & Henry.

Barton, E. R. (Ed.). (2000). *Mythopoetic perspectives of men's healing work: An anthology for therapists and others.* Westport, CT: Bergin & Garvey.

Blake, W. M., & Darling, C. A. (1994). The dilemmas of the African American male. *Journal of Black Studies, 24,* 402–415.

Bly, R. (1990). *Iron John: A book about men.* Reading, MA: Addison-Wesley.

Boyd, H., & Allen, R. (Eds.). (1996). *Brotherman: The odyssey of Black men in America—An anthology.* New York: One World.

Boyd-Franklin, N., & Franklin, A. J. (2000). *Boys into men.* New York: Penguin Putnam.

Conner, M. J. (1995). *What is cool: Understanding Black manhood in America.* New York: Crown.

Cordes, C. (1985, January). At risk in America: Black males face high odds in a hostile society. *APA Monitor,* pp. 9, 10, 11, 27.

Cose, E. (1993). *The rage of a privileged class: Why are middle-class Blacks angry? Why should America care?* New York: HarperCollins.

Crawley, B., & Freeman, E. M. (1993). Themes in the life views of older and younger African American males. *Journal of African American Male Studies, 1,* 15–29.

Erikson, E. (1950). *Childhood and society.* New York: Norton.

Evans, R. C., & Evans, H. L. (1995). Coping: Stressors and depression among middle-class African American men. *Journal of African American Men, 1,* 29–40.

Franklin, A. J. (1999). Therapeutic support groups for African American men. In L. E. Davis (Ed.), *Working with African American males: A guide to practice* (pp. 5–14). Thousand Oaks, CA: Sage.

Garibaldi, A. M. (1992). Educating and motivating African American males to succeed. *Journal of Negro Education, 61,* 4–11.

Gary, L. E., & Berry, G. L. (1985). Depressive symptomatology among Black men. *Journal of Multicultural Counseling and Development, 13,* 121–129.

Gibbs, J. T. (1980). The interpersonal orientation in mental health consultation: Toward a model of ethnic variations in consultation. *Journal of Community Psychology, 8,* 195–207.

Gibbs, J. T. (Ed.). (1988). *Young, Black, and male in America: An endangered species.* New York: Auburn House.

Grier, W. H., & Cobbs, P. M. (1968). *Black rage.* New York: Basic Books.

Griffin, S. T. (2000). *Successful African American men—From childhood to adulthood.* New York: Kluwer Academic/Plenum.

Harris, S. M. (1995). Psychosocial development and Black male masculinity: Implications for counseling economically disadvantaged African American male adolescents. *Journal of Counseling & Development, 73,* 279–287.

Havighurst, R. J. (1972). *Developmental tasks and education* (3rd ed.). New York: McKay.

Hawkins, J. A. (1999). An absence of a talented tenth. In V. C. Polite & J. E. Davis (Eds.), *African American males in schools and society* (pp. 108–124). New York: Teachers College Press.

Hilliard, A. G. (1985). A framework for focused counseling on the African American man. *Journal of Non-White Concerns in Personnel and Guidance, 13,* 72–78.

Irvine, J. J. (1990). *Black students and school failure.* New York: Praeger.

Johnson, J. M., & Watson, B. C. (Eds.). (1990). *Stony the road they trod: The African American male.* Washington, DC: National Urban League.

Jones, K. M. (1986). Black male in jeopardy. *Crisis, 93,* 16–21, 44–45.

Keen, S. (1991). *A fire in the belly: On being a man.* New York: Bantam Books.

King, A. E. O. (1993). African American males in prison: Are they doing the time or is the time doing them? *Journal of Sociology and Social Welfare, 20,* 9–27.

Kohlberg, L. (1966). Moral education in the schools: A developmental view. *School Review, 74,* 1–30.

Lee, C. C. (1990). Black male development: Counseling the "native son." In D. Moore & F. Leafgren (Eds.), *Problem-solving strategies and interventions for men in conflict* (pp. 125–137). Alexandria, VA: American Counseling Association.

Lee, C. C. (1994). Adolescent development. In R. Mincy (Ed.), *Nurturing young Black males: Challenges to agencies, programs, and social policy* (pp. 33–44). Washington, DC: Urban Institute Press.

Lee, C. C. (1996). *Saving the native son: Empowerment strategies for young Black males.* Greensboro, NC: ERIC Counseling and Student Services Clearinghouse.

Lee, C. C. (1999). Counseling African American men. In L. E. Davis (Ed.), *Working with African American males: A guide to practice* (pp. 39–53). Thousand Oaks, CA: Sage.

Leonard, S., Lee, C. C., & Kiselica, M. S. (1999). Counseling African American male youth. In A. M. Horne & M. S. Kiselica (Eds.), *Handbook of counseling boys and adolescent males* (pp. 75–86). Thousand Oaks, CA: Sage.

Madhubuti, H. (1990). *Black men: Obsolete, single, dangerous? African American families in transition: Essays in discovery, solution, and hope.* Chicago: Third World Press.

Majors, R., & Bilson, J. M. (1992). *Cool pose: The dilemmas of Black manhood in America.* New York: Lexington Books.

Majors, R., & Nikelly, A. (1983). Serving the Black minority: A new direction for psychotherapy. *Journal of Non-White Concerns in Personnel and Guidance, 11,* 142–151.

Mauer, M. (1994). *Americans behind bars: The international use of incarceration, 1992–1993.* Washington, DC: Sentencing Project.

McCall, N. (1994). *Makes me wanna holler: A young Black man in America.* New York: Random House.

McManus, E. R. (2003). *Uprising: A revolution of the soul.* Nashville, TN: Nelson Books.

Moore, D., & Leafgren, F. (Eds.). (1990). *Problem-solving strategies and interventions for men in conflict.* Alexandria, VA: American Counseling Association.

Moore, R. L., & Gillette, D. (1990). *King, warrior, magician, lover: Rediscovering the archetypes of the mature masculine.* San Francisco: Harper.

Most Black men profiled by police, poll says. (2001, June 21). *The Washington Post,* pp. 1, 35.

National Urban League. (2000). *The state of Black America 2000: Blacks in the new millennium.* New York: Author.

Patton, J. M. (1995). The education of African American males: Frameworks for developing authenticity. *Journal of African American Men, 1,* 5–27.

Piaget, J. (1970). *Science of education and the psychology of the child.* New York: Onion Press.

Pleck, J. H. (1981). *The myth of masculinity.* Cambridge, MA: MIT Press.

Porter, M. (1998). *Kill them before they grow: Misdiagnosis of African American boys in American classrooms.* Chicago: African American Images.

Randolph, L. (1990, August). What can we do about the most explosive problem in Black America—the widening gap between women who are making it and men who aren't. *Ebony,* p. 52.

Roach, R. (2001, May). Where are the Black men on campus? *Black Issues in Higher Education, 18,* 18–20.

Salholz, E. (1990, December). Short lives, bloody deaths: Black murder rates soar. *Newsweek,* p. 116.

Scher, M., Stevens, M., Good, G., & Eichenfield, G. A. (1987). *Handbook of counseling and psychotherapy with men.* Newbury Park, CA: Sage.

Shakur, S. (1994). *Monster: The autobiography of an L.A. gang member.* New York: Penguin.

Slaughter-Defoe, D., & Richards, H. (1995). Literacy for empowerment: The case of Black males. In V. L. Godsen & D. A. Wagner (Eds.), *Literacy among African American youth: Issues in learning, teaching, and schooling* (pp. 125–147). Cresskill, NJ: Hampton.

Staples, R. (1978). Masculinity and race: The dual dilemma of Black men. *Journal of Social Issues, 34,* 169–183.

Stoltenberg, J. (2000). *Refusing to be a man: Essays on sex and justice.* New York: Routledge.

Taylor, R. J., & Chatters, L. M. (1989). Family, friend, and church support networks of Black Americans. In R. L. Jones (Ed.), Black adult development and aging (pp. 37–59). Berkeley, CA: Cobb & Henry.

Thomas, C. (1993). *Black and blue: Profiles of Blacks in IBM.* Atlanta, GA: Aaron Press.

U.S. Department of Justice. (1995). *Prisoners in 1994.* Washington, DC: U.S. Government Printing Office.

Vontress, C. E. (1995). The breakdown of authority: Implications for counseling young African American males. In J. G. Ponterotto, J. M. Casas, L. A. Suzuki, & C. M. Alexander (Eds.), *Handbook of multicultural counseling* (pp. 457–472). Thousand Oaks, CA: Sage.

Walker, S., Spohn, C., & Delone, M. (1996). *The color of justice: Race, ethnicity, and crime in America.* Belmont, CA: Wadsworth.

Watson, B. (1999). African American higher education: Differences between men and women. *Just the Facts, 1,* 19–22.

Weathers, D. (1993, December). Stop the guns. *Essence,* pp. 70–71, 132–137.

White, J. L., & Cones, J. H. (1999). *Black man emerging: Facing the past and seizing a future in America.* Freeman.

Wilkinson, D. Y., & Taylor, R. L. (1977). *The Black male in America: Perspectives on his status in contemporary society*. Chicago: Nelson-Hall.

Williams, O. J. (1998). Healing and confronting the African American man who batters. In R. Carrillo & J. Tello (Eds.), *Family violence and men of color: Healing the wounded male spirit* (pp. 67–83). New York: Springer.

Wright, W. (1992). The endangered Black male child. *Educational Leadership, 49,* 14–16.

Developing Effective Partnerships in Order to Utilize and Maximize the Resources of the African American Church: Strategies and Tools for Counseling Professionals

Bernard L. Richardson and Lee N. June

Professional counselors who are effective in the broader African American community are those who have discovered and are proficient in using nontraditional methods of service delivery (June, 1986, 1988; Lee, 1990). June (1986), for example, suggested an aggressive outreach strategy that utilizes indigenous helping resources. Therefore, effective counseling practice with African Americans incorporates those institutions, organizations, and strategies that are consistent with their cultural and life experiences.

The African American church is an indigenous institution that counseling professionals can partner with, interact with, and turn to in providing counseling services to African Americans (Boyd-Franklin, 2003; June, 1986; B. L. Richardson, 1989). In this chapter, the term *African American church* is used in a generic sense to describe the traditions of those religious institutions in African American communities represented by a variety of Christian denominations. Lincoln and Mamiya (1990), for example, stated that "any black Christian person is included in the 'black church' if he or she is a member of a black congregation" (p. 1). According to them, 80% of all Black Christians are in the seven independent, historic, and totally Black-controlled denominations, which were founded after the Free African Society of 1787, whereas another 6% are in smaller communions. These seven denominations constitute the following:

1. African Methodist Episcopal,
2. African Methodist Episcopal Zion,
3. Christian Methodist Episcopal,
4. National Baptist Convention, U.S.A., Incorporated,
5. National Baptist Convention of America, Unincorporated,
6. Progressive National Baptist Convention, and
7. Church of God in Christ.

Smith (1982) described the African American church as having been born in bondage: "It was, from its inception, a servant church embedded and engaged in the anguish and freedom of an oppressed people" (p. 15). Slavery and then segregation denied African Americans access to the full rights and privileges accorded other Americans. The church was the only institution that African Americans had to meet their emotional, spiritual, and material needs. DuBois (1899), in his classic work *The Philadelphia Negro*, described how the church met the needs of Blacks in the latter part of the 19th century.

Today, as we experience the early part of the 21st century, the church remains at the center of community life, attending to the social, spiritual, and psychological needs of scores of African Americans. No other institution has claimed the loyalty and attention of African Americans as has the church.

Boyd-Franklin (2003) described the church as "multifunctional community institutions" serving the needs of a disenfranchised population. The significance of the church among African Americans has important implications and potentials for providing mental health services. Many associate traditional counseling settings with institutional or individual racism. Settings perceived as oppressive or racist might promote a defensive posture among many African Americans, which may hinder therapeutic progress (Katz, 1985; Sue, McKinney, Allen, & Hall, 1974). The African American church, however, as an indigenous institution offers a familiar and supportive environment for counseling. In this environment, individuals may confront in an open and honest way a full array of issues that affect their lives.

In what is still the most recent exhaustive study of the African American church, Lincoln and Mamiya (1990) estimated the Black church membership at 23.7 million. They further stated that on the basis of various indices of church membership, approximately 78% of the African American population claimed church membership and had attended at least once in the last 6 months. They also noted that Blacks tended to have higher rates of church attendance than White Protestants (44% vs. 40%, respectively). If one assumes that these figures continue to hold, then on the basis of the March 2002 census (U.S. Census Bureau, 2003), which listed a Black population of 36,023,000, the Black church membership is now at least 28,097,940. Taylor, Thornton, and Chatters (1987) reported that 82.1% of African Americans believed that the church has helped the conditions of Blacks in America, 4.9% indicated that it has hurt, and 12.1% indicated that it has made no difference. Malone (1994) estimated the annual income of the Black church to be $1.7 billion.

These indicators clearly suggest the important influence of the church on the lives of scores of African Americans. Therefore, the purpose of this chapter is to discuss the importance of African American churches in the context of (a) indicating how counseling professionals can interact successfully with this important institution and (b) suggesting tools and strategies necessary to forge this relationship such that clients can be better served.

African American Religion and Spirituality: Their Role in Mental Health

God and religious institutions are prominent in the lives of the majority of Americans. Gallup and Jones (2000) reported from a survey that 96% of Americans believe in God or a universal spirit (83% of whom consider themselves to be a part of the Christian religious tradition), whereas Gallup and Lindsay (1999) put the figure at 95% and further stated that over the past 50 years the figure has never dropped below 90%. Although we do not have the specific figures for African Americans (but Gallup and Jones, 2000, placed the figures at virtually 100%), on the basis of other indicators, the figures are undoubtedly higher than for the population at large. Although the percentage of Americans overall who believe in God is high, Bergin (1980) indicated that only 50% of psychologists do.

There are many reasons why the African American church is and should be considered as a vehicle for providing mental health services. One important reason is related to the historical and contemporary role of religion and spirituality in the lives of African Americans (Frazier, 1963; Lincoln & Mamiya, 1990; Mbiti, 1990; Woodson, 1921). Boyd-Franklin (2003) noted, "Some of the most important historical and psychological experiences of African Americans and their families are strongly rooted in religious and spiritual backgrounds and experiences" (p. 143).

The church is, therefore, the key symbol and the vehicle of expression of religion and spirituality for many African Americans. Ironically, it is this spiritual and religious orientation that may be at the root of why the African American church has not been utilized by many counseling professionals, who may have a conscious or unconscious desire to stay clear of religious or spiritual issues and symbols in the treatment process. This, however, is changing, as Cook and Wiley (2000) have noted. Nevertheless, too many counselors still are not trained to deal with such issues and thus often ignore religion and spirituality as therapeutic concerns even when initiated by clients. This failure to consider the issues of religion and spirituality in counseling, especially when they play such an important role in the lives of many African Americans, undoubtedly results in less than successful outcomes.

Therefore, counseling professionals who work with African Americans must be sensitive to the role that religion and spirituality play in many of their clients' lives. This does not mean that a counselor must be formally trained in theology to work with those African Americans for whom religion and spirituality are important. To be sensitive within this context means a willingness to explore with clients the role that these issues play in their lives as well as to demonstrate a respect for and some level of understanding of the worldview that emanates from the religious belief. Some specific recommendations for increased effectiveness are discussed in the latter part of this chapter.

Knox (1985) documented, in her work with African American alcoholics and their families, that spiritual beliefs have become a part of the survival system of African Americans. She argued that these "coping methods" should be explored just as any other psychosocial area in the assessment process. Accordingly, Lovinger's (1984) insight about the role of religion in the lives of clients is especially relevant for working with African Americans. He noted that

> a patient's religious belief and experiences contain important meanings about past experiences and can characterize the quality of a patient's relationship with others. When these issues emerge in therapy, they can aid therapy if approached with interest and respect. None of this requires any change in the therapist's own attitudes toward religion, other than relinquishing (if held) that religion is silly or meaningless. No phenomena can be usefully approached this way. (Lovinger, 1984, pp. xi–xii)

The proclivity toward religion and spirituality does not mean that African Americans are not amenable to psychological interpretations and insights. Often observed in counseling African Americans in both pastoral and secular situations is that many interpret the events of their lives theologically as well as psychologically. For example, the following was related to the senior author of this chapter at the close of an initial session in a pastoral context by an African American client who was himself a mental health worker:

> This session made me realize that I am now ready to deal with some of the issues that I have been resisting for some time. I wish the process didn't have to be so painful. I guess it is true that it sometimes hurts to grow. I wonder what God is trying to teach me by this trial?

Accordingly, we agree with Smith (1982) that many African Americans seek out certain counselors because of their religious and pastoral identification.

It must be acknowledged that the reluctance of many counseling professionals to engage in any dialogue concerning religious or spiritual beliefs is most likely due to a fear that they cannot or could not integrate the information into their own understanding of human behavior rather than to any disregard for the clients' belief. However, such a fear on the part of the counselor can lead to unsuccessful therapeutic outcomes in counseling situations in which a client's religious belief is counterproductive to positive mental health. Counseling professionals should consider enlisting the aid of the church and clergy in working through this type of impasse. Particularly when a mental health professional feels that a client's belief is counterproductive to positive mental health, he or she should consult with a clergyperson. The counseling professional should not assume that the client's belief is supported by the client's pastor or church. After consulting with the client's pastor, the counselor might recommend that the client receive instruction from the church about particular beliefs. A counselor should be as comfortable consulting a member of the clergy about a client's religious belief and its possible effect on the helping process as consulting a physician about a physical condition that might affect medical treatment. This kind of collaborative relationship will enhance the quality of care that counseling professionals provide.

The Role of African American Clergy

At the center of the church is the African American clergy, who have traditionally been recognized as major leaders in their respective communities (Hamilton, 1972; Woodson, 1921). In attending to spiritual needs, they have had and still have a significant influence on mental health intervention. Often the pastoral counseling activity has represented the only resource available to address emotional and psychological crises (Washington, 1964). An important aspect of the clergyperson's role that has important implications for mental health practitioners is that of pastoral initiative. Historically, clergy are expected to go where the people are and intervene when necessary on their own initiative and without specific invitation (Switzer, 1986). Further, with their freedom of entry to homes, clergy are able to discover problems in their early stages (Switzer, 1986).

Another important aspect of the counseling that clergy perform is that they usually have prior relationships with those who seek them out for counseling. Therefore, clergy often may have an understanding of the family dynamics and living conditions of their parishioners. The unique role of African American clergy also affords them the opportunity to provide counseling that is proactive and preventive. Through activities such as educational programs, sermons, and interaction in organizations and business meetings, the clergy, unlike other professionals, have an ongoing opportunity to educate people about potentially harmful situations in the community and potentially harmful individual behaviors. In discussing the role of clergy in crisis intervention, Switzer (1986) suggested that the clergyperson is unique in that no other professional has the kind of "platform or organizational context" in which to engage in sound education for mental health and problem solving. With the support of pastors and church leaders, the resources of the church can be available to counseling professionals. Thus, counseling professionals have tremendous opportunities to be an instrumental part of the proactive and preventive aspect of the African American church. For example, workshops on such topics as addiction, parenting, male–female relationships, education, racism, sexism, and HIV/AIDS are greatly needed. With the assistance and the cooperation of the pastor, counseling professionals can provide preventive education and counseling services to these communities.

The Need for Partnership With Clergy

The clergy's role is unique, and the mental health professional may not be able to duplicate their strategies and techniques. However, mental health practitioners in partnership with clergy can use the unique resources of the African American church to offer more comprehensive, aggressive, and indigenous outreach programs in African American communities. Nowhere is this more evident than in the area of referral. The counseling professional who has developed a working relationship with an African American pastor has access to a referral system that can enhance the relationship between counselor and client. A person is more likely to participate in counseling and feel more comfortable with a counselor who has the respect and trust of his or her pastor and church community.

Considering the importance of counseling services, it is a cause for concern that the majority of these services aimed at African American communities historically have not had working relationships with churches and clergy. Boyd-Franklin (2003), drawing from her work with African American families, noted with amazement that mental health practitioners routinely contact clinics, hospitals, or counselors who have previously worked with clients, but not pastors. She further noted that when a family counselor recognizes the significance of religious values for a client and is aware of the resources of the African American church, four types of intervention are possible: (a) involving a clergyperson as a consultant, a cocounselor, or an integral part of the treatment process; (b) mobilizing the resources of the Black church network to help a family in crisis; (c) utilizing or deploying church networks as support for a family during times of illness, death, or loss; and (d) helping isolated African American families cut off from their original networks to create new ones.

That members of the African American clergy were not supportive of mental health professionals, was a popular notion that existed as the reason for the absence of working relationships between African American clergy and mental health professionals. It was believed that African American clergy were threatened and feared the loss of parishioners who might seek only psychological solutions to their problems. Although this may have been true, research evidence has now suggested, however, that African American clergy hold favorable attitudes toward mental health professionals (B. L. Richardson, 1989). An important implication of this research is that the possibility exists for African American clergy and mental health professionals to work together in partnership to foster the social, spiritual, and psychological well-being of people in African American communities.

Intervention Strategies Using the Resources of the African American Church

The African American church provides counselors with a setting that can facilitate various intervention strategies. Two modes of intervention can be used in counseling African Americans: intervention that focuses on the church as a support system and intervention that addresses systemic problems that affect African Americans (Gunnings, 1976). These intervention strategies, which can utilize and maximize the many resources within the African American church, are discussed in this section.

Intervention That Focuses on the Church as a Support System

True religion has an element of increasing self-esteem. Increasing self-esteem is critically important when it has been negatively affected by the forces of racism and oppression, which is often the case with African Americans. Historically, the African American church has been a primary source for the development of African Americans' self-esteem; as such, it is in a powerful position to bolster the self-esteem of its members. The African American church provides avenues of self-expression and efficacy via church titles and responsibilities and via its theology or conception of God. Individuals who find their level of self-efficacy diminished by limited opportunities and who have jobs that do little to enhance self-esteem gain a strong sense of self-respect and community recognition as a result of positions they hold in African American churches.

The communal aspect of working within the church serves to strengthen individual and group identity. The heritage of African Americans lends credence to this cultural phenomenon. In his research on West African civilization, Mbiti (1990) maintained that group membership is the preeminent source of identification in the development of a sense of self for Africans. Nobles (1980) stressed the importance of the African philosophical notion of kinship or collective unity as an important foundation for African American mental health intervention. Within this context, counselors must see and use the African American church as a support system for individuals facing various life challenges. For example, the church could be an important helping resource for individuals recently released from prison or for others needing assistance in adjusting to community life.

The African American church has always emphasized the need for strong families and, as part of its religious tradition, provides teachings and programs that support family life. The African American church, therefore, can also be utilized as a support system in the treatment of African American families. Boyd-Franklin (2003) argued that it is important for counselors to understand the concept of the church family as it relates to African Americans. She noted that for many African Americans the church functions as an extended family and for single mothers as a surrogate family. She also noted that the African American church provides role models for young people and serves a social function by providing families the opportunity to mingle. It is significant to note that many African American parents who live in predominantly White neighborhoods and whose children attend predominantly White schools seek out African American churches not only for spiritual edification but also for the positive African American identity that the churches instill in children.

Counselors can utilize these unique resources in working with African American families. Boyd-Franklin (2003) suggested that counselors should identify the church as a social support resource for isolated families who have a religious orientation. She noted that some African American families entering community mental health centers are "very socially isolated and emotionally cut off from their extended families" (p. 143) and that assisting isolated African American families in identifying and locating a new church network could be a significant intervention. Boyd-Franklin rightly cautioned that this intervention is not for everyone and stated, "It should be made only if it appears syntonic with the family's belief systems and earlier experiences" (p. 143).

Even though the church can be a potent and supportive resource, mental health professionals have traditionally considered it to be an institution that is uncompromising and holds a narrow perspective on morals and values. Those who hold this view often fail to recognize that in certain cases the identification with the church can appropriately reinforce an individual's moral and ethical belief system. As an example, clergy, working in concert with counseling professionals, can offer alternatives and support to people contemplating and/or engaging in self-destructive and community-disruptive economic enterprises such as the illegal drug trade. Such alternatives and support might include church-sponsored community forums that offer testimonials by former addicts and drug dealers who can point out the short- and long-term negative effects of selling drugs.

Intervention That Addresses Systemic Problems Affecting African Americans

The African American church has historically played a key role in fostering social change at the community and societal levels (Smith, 1982). The civil rights movement of the 1960s and the leadership of Dr. Martin Luther King, Jr., attest to the role of the African American church and clergy in social change. Thus, the counselor who works within the context of the African American church can educate clients about how systemic problems affect their lives and can also be part of the process that seeks to change these conditions. Counselors working in African American communities should seek to empower their clients to challenge and confront racist and oppressive structures and policies that unjustly govern their lives. Counselors should also be willing to be advocates on behalf of clients. The church is a vehicle that counselors can use to help them become effective advocates and to assist them in empowering clients. For example, counselors can identify clients who have been victimized by unfair hiring practices, discrimination in housing, inadequate educational facilities, or inadequate health care. They can then refer these clients to pastors and church leaders who can in turn help them organize and collectively confront oppressive systems and practices by using the church as a base of operations. The use of the church, the support of pastors, and the identification with other victims of systemic injustice can give clients a sense of control over their lives.

Guidelines for Working Within a Church Context

Although the proposal that counseling professionals should enlist the resources of the African American church in providing mental health services to African American communities has been made (June, 1986; B. L. Richardson, 1989), this is still a relatively new concept for most counseling professionals, and some direction is needed in establishing working relationships with African American churches. The guidelines that follow are based on our own experience and represent suggestions for facilitating the development of such relationships and enhancing counselor effectiveness.

1. Earn Acceptance

Some well-meaning counseling professionals come into the church believing that they will be immediately accepted because of their education or their professional accomplishments. However, they soon find that it takes more than credentials to be accepted as helping professionals within the African American church. To earn acceptance, counseling professionals must be perceived as being sincere and trustworthy, as not flaunting professional status, and as having a genuine interest in the betterment of African Americans. Hunt (1988) rightly stated that "it is not what you know but who you are and how you use the information about a person's cultural characteristics that eventually allows the client to trust" (p. 116). With other conditions being right, when these attributes are perceived, the word quickly spreads among church members that the counselor is a professional who is "down to earth and easy to talk to"—a description that is a sign of acceptance within the African American church community.

2. Explore Personal Beliefs

If counselors are to be sensitive to the role of spirituality and religion in the lives of clients, they must examine their own beliefs. Counselors should determine what aspects of their personal religious beliefs (or nonbeliefs) could interfere with being competent in working with certain problems. This is especially important in handling such delicate issues as abortion and homosexuality. More personal beliefs, such as those concerning spiritual gifts such as healing, also require counselors to possess a certain spiritual affinity with the concept in order to be effective. Counselors should not attempt to undertake this process alone but should explore their attitudes toward religion and spirituality with a clergyperson or religious professional. When the counselor's attitude is negative or when there is a core value conflict, referring the client to another counselor is appropriate.

3. Develop a Relationship With Pastors

As noted earlier, in the African American church tradition there is a great deal of respect for the office and authority of the pastor. Therefore, regardless of how skillful the counselor is, all efforts to use the African American church as a therapeutic ally will fail unless positive relationships are developed with pastors. An excellent way to meet and establish contact with pastors is through ministerial alliances or pastors' conferences. Most communities have such alliances or conferences at which clergy meet regularly to discuss clerical and community concerns, and these alliances and conferences can provide counseling professionals with an opportunity to meet African American clergy from various denominations. Rather than merely articulating their skills and concerns, however, counseling professionals should use the alliances and conferences as an opportunity to demonstrate them concretely. Presenting a workshop on a relevant problem confronting African Americans, such as the problems facing youth, could be an excellent way to demonstrate expertise while delivering a needed service.

4. Establish and Maintain a Relationship With Local Churches

After developing a relationship with the pastor of a local church, the next step is to be introduced to a local congregation. Again, the workshop format is a dramatic and efficient way to present counseling skills to the African American church community. Workshops on topics such as addiction, parenting, peer pressure, male–female relationships, racism, and prejudice are usually well received in church settings. If the workshop is successful, individual counseling referrals usually follow. Speaking to the issue of referrals from clergy and church congregations, Cook and Wiley (2000) stated the following:

> Workshops, retreats, educational programs around issues such as bereavement, forgiveness, depression, and other life issues can be of value in promoting referrals for treatment. Annual depression and anxiety screening days are services that, when offered in the church, appear less threatening. (p. 382)

It is also possible for mental health professionals, in collaboration with the host church, to establish a counseling center on site. Such a model has been outlined by Solomon (1990).

Over the last decade, churches (particularly larger ones—megachurches) have increasingly begun to develop their own counseling centers and have regular counseling hours. These centers tend to focus on pastoral and Biblical counseling techniques. The number of such centers has increased as the concept of megachurches has evolved and as faith-based initiatives have spread. The counselor who is familiar with this field can also participate in this setting. This is particularly true for the counselor who is a Christian.

Additionally, if one is a Christian and a member of a local church, membership will allow one to routinely exercise his or her talents and skills in that congregation in a variety of areas including counseling.

5. Become Acquainted With the Religious Tradition of the Local Church or Denomination

The religious traditions of the African American church are represented by various denominations. As noted earlier, these include African Methodist Episcopal Zion, African Methodist Episcopal, Baptist of various sorts, Congregational, Church of God in Christ, Church of God, Seventh Day Adventist, Apostolic, Lutheran, Episcopal, and Roman Catholic. In addition, an increasing number of African Americans follow Islam. Counseling professionals need to have some knowledge of these denominations and religions because of possible therapeutic and/or customary issues that may affect a client's ability to function. Counseling professionals can become familiar with the religious beliefs and practices of various Christian denominations by requesting denominational handbooks from pastors and by taking survey courses on American religion and Black theology. An excellent source for background information on the African American church is *The Black Church in the African American Experience* (Lincoln & Mamiya, 1990). Information on Islam can be obtained by contacting the leader of a Muslim congregation or by taking a course on world religions.

In becoming familiar with the various traditions, counselors should pay close attention to local church and denominational laws, as well as attitudes toward the role of women in the church and society; attitudes toward divorce and remarriage; prohibitions against drugs and alcohol; and teachings on abortion, homosexuality, healing, and health practices. These issues may become therapeutic issues or the focus of counseling.

6. Become Acquainted With the Field of Biblical Counseling

Over the last few decades, increasing attention has been given to developing theories and techniques of Christian and Biblical counseling. In Black church settings, Biblical and Christian counseling must be distinguished from spiritual and religious counseling. Although Biblical and Christian counseling is a form of religious or spiritual counseling, it is more narrowly defined as a form of counseling that views the Bible as the word of God and whose principles and techniques are based on and consistent with its views. Spiritual and religious counseling, in contrast, refers to a broader type of counseling that acknowledges and respects God or the Divine in any religious or spiritual tradition and whose principles and techniques are based on this respect and acknowledgment.

Many churches and pastors have been trained in principles of Biblical counseling, and an increasing number of Black parishioners are seeking such counseling. Several Black churches have set up their own counseling centers and have regular counseling hours. Thus, mental health professionals need to become acquainted with this field, its literature, and these types of counseling resources.

Representative materials that give good general overviews of the field of Christian and Biblical counseling include *The Psychology of Counseling* (Narramore, 1960), *Christian Counseling: A Comprehensive Guide* (Collins, 1988), *Effective Biblical Counseling* (Crabb, 1977), *Basic Principles of Biblical Counseling* (Crabb, 1975), *Competent to Counsel* (Adams, 1970), *The Christian Counselor's Manual* (Adams, 1973), and *The Integration of Psychology and Theology* (J. D. Carter & Narramore, 1979).

Writings that are more African American oriented in the field of Biblical and Christian counseling include *Biblical Counseling With African Americans* (Walker, 1992) and *Counseling in African American Communities* (June, Black, & Richardson, 2002). Others are by Edward Wimberly, one of the more prolific writers on pastoral counseling, and his book *Pastoral Care in the Black Church* (1979) and particularly his chapter "Pastoral Counseling and the Black Perspective" (1989) are must readings. The chapter entitled "Psychotherapy With Members of African American Churches and Spiritual Traditions" by Cook and Wiley (2000) in the *Handbook of Psychotherapy and Religious Diversity* is also highly recommended.

Additional materials that can give mental health professionals a perspective on how counseling, mental health, and other pertinent issues are perceived and conceptualized within the Black church include *The Black Family: Past, Present, and Future* (June, 1991); *How to Equip the African American Family* (Abatso & Abatso, 1991); *Reclaiming the Urban Family* (W. Richardson, 1995); *From Holy Power to Holy Profits* (Malone, 1994); *Men to Men* (June & Parker, 1996); *Women to Women* (N. Carter & Parker, 1996); *Adam! Where Are You?* (Kunjufu,

1994), and, as already mentioned, *The Black Church in the African American Experience* (Lincoln & Mamiya, 1990).

In addition to the materials just listed, the National Biblical Counseling Association, organized in 1999, annually holds a national conference on Biblical counseling that brings together a variety of African American professionals in the counseling, health, and religious fields who operate within African American churches and are sensitive to the need for sound psychological counseling and counseling interventions that are consistent with the Biblical tradition. Anyone interested in this association and its resources may contact Christian Research and Development, 27 West Township Line Road, Suite 2, Upper Darby, Pennsylvania 19082; phone: 610-449-8112 or 1-800-551-1CRD; Web site: www. crdonline.org.

Over the last decade, the psychology and counseling professions have also become more accepting of the need for psychologists and counselors to become more conversant with religious issues that clients might present. Richards and Bergin (2000) observed that "the alienation that has existed between the mental health professions and religion for most of the 20th century is ending" (p. 3). Their observation is based on the fact that the American Psychological Association has done publications on this topic, recent books on the topic by "mainstream" publishers have appeared, and the latest revisions of the ethical codes of the American Psychological Association and the American Counseling Association have recognized that religion is also a type of diversity that mental health professionals are obligated to respect.

Counselors who wish to gain an understanding of the literature related to the broader field of religious and spiritual counseling are encouraged to read *Religion and the Clinical Practice of Psychology* (Shafranske, 1996), *A Spiritual Strategy for Counseling and Psychotherapy* (Richards & Bergin, 1997), *Integrating Spirituality Into Treatment: Resources for Practitioners* (Miller, 1999), and *Handbook of Psychotherapy and Religious Diversity* (Richards & Bergin, 2000).

7. Develop and Nurture a Collaborative Research Program

Counselors who have shown a genuine interest in the Black church and have developed effective relationships could further aid both the mental health field and the congregation by developing a collaborative research agenda. According to Cook (1993),

> collaborative research efforts between mental health counseling researchers and African American churches can advance the knowledge of mental health resources within the church, and can assist churches in using their resources in productive ways that will benefit the surrounding communities. (p. 320)

The areas that Cook (1993) suggested as ripe for research are individual interventions, individual counseling practices, collaboration with African American clergy, group interventions, and outreach interventions. Her article also discussed the issues surrounding access to African American churches, such as gaining entry, negotiating collaborative relationships, and selecting appropriate methodologies.

Conclusion

The emergence of counseling professionals who recognize cultural diversity has initiated a search for new skills, innovative strategies, and appropriate techniques for delivering mental health services to African American communities. The African American church, with its rich history, continuing significance, and great influence in African American communities, can be a valuable resource, an avenue of service delivery and cooperative research. Those counseling professionals who wish to work with and assist the full range of African American clients will be wise to seek out and work in partnership with the African American church.

The strategies put forth in this chapter necessitate that counselors serve as advocates of social change, as consultants, as mediators, as research collaborators, and as continual learners. Counselors are also encouraged to develop alliances and partnerships with African American religious professionals and to become familiar with their literature and counseling techniques. Further, counselors need to become more aware of personal biases, fears, and skill deficits that could prevent them from embracing indigenous resources such as the African American church. Counselors who are willing to meet these challenges will build a foundation that could ultimately lead to the discovery of new strategies and techniques for mental health practices in African American communities.

References

Abatso, G., & Abatso, Y. (1991). *How to equip the African American family.* Chicago: Urban Ministries.

Adams, J. (1970). *Competent to counsel.* Grand Rapids, MI: Baker.

Adams, J. (1973). *The Christian counselor's manual.* Grand Rapids, MI: Zondervan.

Bergin, A. (1980). Psychotherapy and religious values. *Journal of Consulting and Clinical Psychology, 481,* 95–105.

Boyd-Franklin, N. (2003). *Black families in therapy* (2nd ed.). New York: Guilford Press.

Carter, J. D., & Narramore, B. (1979). *The integration of psychology and theology.* Grand Rapids, MI: Zondervan.

Carter, N., & Parker, M. (Eds.). (1996). *Women to women.* Grand Rapids, MI: Zondervan.

Collins, G. R. (1988). *Christian counseling: A comprehensive guide* (Rev. ed.). Dallas, TX: Word.

Cook, D. A. (1993). Research in African American churches: A mental health counseling imperative. *Journal of Mental Health Counseling, 15,* 320–333.

Cook, D. A., & Wiley, C. Y. (2000). Psychotherapy with members of African American churches and spiritual traditions. In P. S. Richards & A. E. Bergin (Eds.), *Handbook of psychotherapy and religious diversity* (pp. 369–396). Washington, DC: American Psychological Association.

Crabb, L. J. (1975). *Basic principles of biblical counseling.* Grand Rapids, MI: Zondervan.

Crabb, L. J. (1977). *Effective Biblical counseling.* Grand Rapids, MI: Zondervan.

DuBois, W. E. B. (1899). *The Philadelphia Negro: A social study.* Philadelphia: University of Pennsylvania Press.

Frazier, E. F. (1963). *The Negro church in America.* New York: Schocken Books.

Gallup, G., Jr., & Jones, T. (2000). *The next American spirituality: Finding God in the 21st century.* Colorado Springs, CO: Victor.

Gallup, G., Jr., & Lindsay, D. M. (1999). *Surveying the religious landscape: Trends in U.S. beliefs.* Harrisburg, PA: Morehouse.

Gunnings, T. S. (1976). *A systemic approach to counseling.* East Lansing: Michigan State University.

Hamilton, C. V. (1972). *The Black preacher in America.* New York: Morrow.

Hunt, P. (1988). Black clients: Implications for supervision of trainees. *Psycho-Counseling, 24,* 114–119.

June, L. N. (1986). Enhancing the delivery of mental health and counseling services to Black males: Critical agency and provider responsibilities. *Journal of Multicultural Counseling and Development, 14,* 39–45.

June, L. N. (1988, November). *Psychotherapy (mental health counseling) and the Black church.* Paper presented at the International Congress on Christian Counseling, Atlanta, GA.

June, L. N. (Ed.). (1991). *The Black family: Past, present, and future.* Grand Rapids, MI: Zondervan.

June, L. N., Black, S., & Richardson, W. (Eds.). (2002). *Counseling in African American communities.* Grand Rapids, MI: Zondervan.

June, L. N., & Parker, M. (Eds.). (1996). *Men to men.* Grand Rapids, MI: Zondervan.

Katz, J. H. (1985). The sociopolitical nature of counseling. *The Counseling Psychologist, 13,* 615–624.

Knox, D. H. (1985). Spirituality: A tool in the assessment and treatment of Black alcoholics and their families. *Alcoholism Treatment Quarterly, 2,* 31–44.

Kunjufu, J. (1994). *Adam! Where are you?* Chicago: African American Images.

Lee, C. C. (1990). Black male development: Counseling the "native son." In D. Moore & F. Leafgren (Eds.), *Problem solving strategies and interventions for men in conflict* (pp. 125–137). Alexandria, VA: American Association for Counseling and Development.

Lincoln, C. E., & Mamiya, L. H. (1990). *The Black church in the African American experience.* Durham, NC: Duke University Press.

Lovinger, R. J. (1984). *Working with religious issues in therapy.* New York: Aronson.

Malone, W., Jr. (1994). *From holy power to holy profits.* Chicago: African American Images.

Mbiti, J. S. (1990). *African religions and philosophies* (2nd ed.). Portsmouth, NH: Heinemann.

Miller, W. R. (Ed.). (1999). *Integrating spirituality into treatment: Resources for practitioners.* Washington, DC: American Psychological Association.

Narramore, C. M. (1960). *The psychology of counseling.* Grand Rapids, MI: Zondervan.

Nobles, W. (1980). African philosophy: Foundations for Black psychology. In R. L. Jones (Ed.), *Black psychology* (pp. 23–36). New York: Harper & Row.

Richards, P. S., & Bergin, A. E. (1997). *A spiritual strategy for counseling and psychotherapy.* Washington, DC: American Psychological Association.

Richards, P. S., & Bergin, A. E. (Eds.). (2000). *Handbook of psychotherapy and religious diversity.* Washington, DC: American Psychological Association.

Richardson, B. L. (1989). Attitudes of Black clergy toward mental health professionals: Implications for pastoral care. *Journal of Pastoral Care, 43,* 33–39.

Richardson, W. (1995). *Reclaiming the urban family.* Grand Rapids, MI: Zondervan.

Shafranske, E. P. (Ed). (1996). *Religion and the clinical practice of psychology.* Washington, DC: American Psychological Association.

Smith, A. (1982). *The relational self.* Nashville, TN: Abingdon Press.

Solomon, B. B. (1990). Counseling Black families at inner-city church sites. In H. Cheatham & J. B. Stewart (Eds.), *Black families: Interdisciplinary perspectives* (pp. 353–372). New Brunswick, NJ: Transaction.

Sue, S., McKinney, H., Allen, D., & Hall, J. (1974). Delivery of community mental health services to Black and White clients. *Journal of Consulting and Clinical Psychology, 42,* 594–601.

Switzer, D. K. (1986). *The minister as crisis counselor.* Nashville, TN: Abingdon Press.

Taylor, R. L., Thornton, M. C., & Chatters, L. M. (1987). Black Americans' perception of the sociohistorical role of the church. *Journal of Black Studies, 18,* 123–138.

U.S. Census Bureau. (2003). *The Black population in the United States. Current population survey, March 2002.* Washington, DC: Racial Statistics Branch, Population Division. Retrieved March 29, 2005, from http://www.census.gov/population/www/socdemo/race/black.html

Walker, C. (1992). *Biblical counseling with African Americans.* Grand Rapids, MI: Zondervan.

Washington, J. R. (1964). *Black religion: The Negro and Christianity in the United States.* Boston: Beacon Press.

Wimberly, E. P. (1979). *Pastoral care in the Black church.* Nashville, TN: Abingdon Press.

Wimberly, E. P. (1989). Pastoral counseling and the Black perspective. In G. S. Wilmore (Ed.), *African American religious studies* (pp. 420–428). Durham, NC: Duke University Press.

Woodson, C. G. (1921). *The history of the Negro church.* Washington, DC: Associated.

The Asian American Experience

Americans of Asian descent trace their cultural origins to countries such as Cambodia, China, Japan, Korea, and Vietnam. Each Asian American ethnic group has its own unique cultural history and traditions. However, some dynamics are rooted in centuries-old Asian religious traditions and play a major role in shaping the cultural values of Asian Americans, regardless of ethnic background. These dynamics must be appreciated if culturally responsive counseling is to occur with Asian American clients and include factors such as moderation in behavior, self-discipline, patience, and humility. Many of these behaviors and values are dictated by family relationships that emphasize honor and respect for elders.

Chapter

Counseling Strategies for Chinese Americans

David Sue

Of the 10,242,998 Asian or Pacific Island Americans living in the United States, the largest subgroup is Chinese Americans, who number 2,432,585 (U.S. Department of Commerce, 2001). Because of the relaxation of immigration quotas, the majority of individuals in this group are either foreign born or recent immigrants. The continuing influx of immigrants demonstrates the importance of gaining knowledge of Chinese culture. The Chinese in America are a heterogeneous group with differences in political, linguistic, economic, and geographical backgrounds. Although most are from mainland China, Hong Kong, or Taiwan, many refugees and immigrants from southeast Asia are also of Chinese origin. Chinese Americans vary in terms of acculturation levels, ethnic identity, educational levels, and socioeconomic status. Despite these differences, this chapter focuses on the experiences and traditions that they share.

There is a pervasive view that Chinese Americans are a highly successful group with few problems (Yin, 2000). This is reflected in articles such as "To America With Skills" (1985) and "Asian Americans: Are They Making The Grade?" (1984). It is true that Chinese Americans are well represented in higher education at the undergraduate and graduate school levels. However, included in these data are graduate students from Asian countries who stay in the United States for advanced degrees (Wang, 1993). Although many Chinese Americans are well educated, others have very low educational levels. A close examination of the statistics reveals a bimodal distribution: one group is highly successful and acculturated, and the other is poor, living in poverty, and traditional in orientation (Kitano & Daniels, 1988; D. W. Sue & Sue, 1999). Compared with White Americans, nearly 4 times as many Chinese Americans have less than 4 years of schooling (Nishi, 1982). English proficiency continues to be a problem. The majority of Asian American students have a bilingual background. The inability to communicate well in English contributes to low self-esteem and self-consciousness (Kiang & Lee, 1993). Even among college-educated Chinese Americans, academic success has not led to commensurate rewards. Salaries are less than would be predicted according to educational levels, and Chinese Americans are underrepresented in managerial and supervisory positions (Ong & Hee, 1993; S. Sue & Okazaki, 1990).

Chinese Americans continue to face issues of discrimination and prejudice in U.S. society. Although some are fourth- or fifth-generation Americans, most are still identified as "foreign" and regarded with suspicion. In a representative sample of 1,216 adults surveyed involving attitudes toward Chinese Americans, several disturbing findings were reported (Committee of 100, 2001). Nearly one third of the respondents thought that Chinese Americans would be more loyal to China than to the United States, and nearly half believed that Chinese Americans would pass secret information to China. This survey was done before the crash of the U.S. spy plane in China.

Chinese American Cultural Values and Their Impact

Values have a tremendous impact in terms of how we view the world, what we consider to be right, the standards we uphold, and the way we assess and evaluate situations. Many Asian American adolescents continue to hold traditional cultural values of deference and respect for their parents (Ying, Coombs, & Lee, 1999). However, it must be remembered that these values are influenced by acculturation. Leong and Tata (1990) found that highly acculturated Chinese American children were more likely to value self-actualization than were those with low acculturation. In addition to the stressors faced by adolescents, Asian American youngsters must also learn to deal with multicultural issues at school and with their family and peers. Many feel pressures for commitment from their own ethnic group as well as from majority group members (Chiu & Ring, 1998).

Some values and traditions seem to change at different rates. Chen and Yang (1986) found that with acculturation, Chinese American adolescents' attitudes toward dating and sex became more similar to those of White adolescents but that the Confucian values of loyalty, conformity, and respect for elders remained. The continuing arrival of Chinese from Asian countries to the United states ensures the survival of traditional cultural values. In this section, I present some traditional Chinese values, contrast them with Western values, and discuss the implications of these differences for individual counseling. In later sections I describe family therapy based on Chinese values and provide a format for an assertiveness training program for Chinese Americans.

Filial Piety

Filial piety is a very strong value in Chinese American families. As one daughter responded,

> I must find a way to repay my parents for all they have sacrificed for me. I remind myself as often as they remind me that if it weren't for them, I would be that dirty Chinese girl working in the rice paddy. (Ying et al., 1999, p. 356)

Filial piety refers to the obligations, respect, and duty that a person has to his or her parents. Parents are to be obeyed and held in high esteem. Allegiance to them is primary and is expected from male offspring even after they have married and begun a family of their own (Blair & Qian, 1998). Many Chinese tales for children reflect the theme of filial piety. One such story tells of a destitute couple whose husband's parents were living with them. Because there was not enough food for his parents, children, and wife, the couple decided to bury their youngest child. While digging the grave, they discovered gold (Tseng & Hsu, 1972). The willingness to sacrifice their child for the parents resulted in a reward.

In Western culture, although parents are also honored, the emphasis on the nuclear family and independence reduces the importance of the family of origin. In fact, obligation to children is often stressed. It is their feelings and desires that are paramount. As Hsu (1953) observed more than 50 years ago, "the most important thing to Americans is what parents should do for their children: to Chinese, what children should do for their parents" (p. 75).

Proper parenting is thought to inculcate filial piety in the children. Chinese mothers are rated higher on parental control and are significantly more directive in dealing with their children than are Caucasian American mothers. This reflects the "parents are always right" notion of Confucian philosophy (Jose, Huntsinger, Huntsinger, & Fong-Ruey, 2000; Lin & Fu, 1990). The emphasis on politeness and control may be the reason why Chinese American males and females were less likely to receive a conduct disorder diagnosis than were other subgroups of Asian American adolescents receiving therapy in the mental health system (Kim & Chun, 1993). In Chinese families, the parents often choose their children's careers. For example, Taiwanese college students, as opposed to White American college students, were more likely to report being influenced by their parents for a particular field of study. In contrast, White college students indicated being influenced in career choice by peers and friends (Kuo & Spees, 1983). Obeying parents is emphasized in Chinese American families as an indication of filial piety, leaving little room for self-determination.

Such situations may lead to conflict, especially among Chinese Americans who have become more acculturated and exposed to the notion of personal choice. In working with individuals who experience conflict between filial piety and individual goals, the counselor could help the clients identify the reasons for their stress. Chinese clients often will not know the source of their conflict other than it involves their parents. Being able to understand that this conflict is connected with differences in cultural expectations may lead the way to resolution. Exposure to Western values of self-determination and independence often produces conflicts in family relationships.

Stress on Family Bonds and Unity

Among Chinese Americans, child-rearing practices are focused on emphasizing the importance of family ties and obligations, not on helping individuals separate and become independent. Individual growth is not the accepted norm (Blair & Qian, 1998). Praise is given for actions that are seen as benefiting the family, and guilt-inducing techniques are used to maintain discipline. Children are expected to retain emotional ties with the mother and a respectful attitude toward the father, even when they become adults. An individual who agonizes over career choices because of concern over upsetting parental wishes might be seen as being overly dependent according to the Western perspective. Expecting and assisting the Chinese client to become more independent without considering the cultural implications, however, may lead to even greater conflict.

Roles and Status

Communication patterns among Chinese Americans are based on cultural tradition and flow down from those of higher status. Men and elders are accorded greater importance than women or younger individuals. In a family, the father makes the major decisions with little input from others (D. W. Sue & Sue, 1999). A well-functioning family is one that adheres to prescribed communication rules. Negotiations and democratic discussions to arrive at decisions, which are typical of White families, may be foreign to many Chinese American families (Saner-Yiu & Saner-Yiu, 1985; Soo-Hoo, 1999). Indeed, such discussions may be seen as challenges to the authority figure, the father. Because the mother is responsible for socializing the children, it is a reflection of poor parenting if the children become rebellious or overly acculturated. She has to mediate between the dictates of her husband and the complaints of her children. If the mother has done her job well, the children will be respectful and provide for her in old age. The greatest responsibility is placed on the eldest son. He is expected to help raise his younger siblings and to be a role model for them. He inherits the family leadership upon the death of the father and is expected to provide financial and emotional support for his mother. Daughters are expected to help in the household. Fewer demands are placed on them because they become members of the husband's family when they marry.

These role prescriptions make it necessary to alter traditional forms of therapy. For example, family counseling might seem to be an ideal modality for Chinese families. However, family therapy is also based on the Western perspective of what constitutes a well-functioning family. For example, Bowen (1978) believed that dysfunctional families are the result of fused identities and overemotional dependence. In this approach, family members are assisted to develop greater interdependence and differentiation. This approach would conflict with the Chinese American practice of maintaining interdependent family ties. Other possible problems with some forms of family therapy could be the emphasis on freely expressing emotions to one another; egalitarian role relationships; confrontational methods; role-playing; and little focus on environmental issues affecting the family, such as economics, prejudice, and acculturation conflicts (D. Sue, 1994). Without modification, family therapy could threaten the traditional roles and values of the Chinese culture.

Does this mean that family counseling should not be used in working with Chinese American families? With modification that includes an assessment of cultural values, acculturation conflicts, and the possible impact of racism, family therapy can be useful. Ho (1987) made the following suggestions when dealing with a Chinese American family in a counseling situation: Promote differences in roles by first addressing the father and the mother. Reframe or relabel statements that family members make. If a child becomes angry, restate the issue in terms of parental expectations. Do not encourage the child to communicate strong negative feelings to the parents. Promote filial piety also by gently reminding parents of the necessity of being positive role models for their children. Focus on the use of positive and respectful feelings between family members.

Somatization Versus Psychologization

In general, Chinese Americans combine reports of emotional distress with physical symptoms. Discomfort and disturbance are expressed in terms of somatic complaints, such as headaches. Because of this, biological explanations as well as physical treatments for psychological problems are acceptable to many Chinese clients (Kung, 2001). In fact, they are more likely to have a somatopsychological perspective. Physical illnesses are believed to cause psychological problems. For example, having a headache may result in feelings of depression. White Americans, in contrast, have a psychosomatic perspective. Physical symptoms and illnesses are often thought to be the result of psychological states.

In working with Chinese Americans, it would be a mistake to discount physical complaints. They are real problems. Both physical and psychological concerns have to be dealt with. One approach might be to inquire about the physical symptom and discuss its impact on individual or family functioning. Physical or medical treatments can be used with suggestions for improvement in other aspects of the client's life. The effectiveness of the intervention is based on the alleviation of both physical and psychological symptoms. The focus on biological causes alleviates the guilt of the individual or family members for having the illness.

Control Over Strong Emotions

In traditional Chinese culture, emotional expression was restrained to prevent challenges to tradition and order. This is not to say that Chinese Americans do not show a variety of emotional reactions. Just like other human beings, they can be angry, sad, happy, jealous, confident, or anxious. However, these displays do not typically occur outside of the family. Feelings are not openly expressed except in the case of young children. Parents rarely show signs of physical affection, such as holding hands or saying "I love you" (Shon & Ja, 1982). Instead, love is acknowledged through behaviors that benefit the family and its members. Children are rarely praised directly for their contribution. Parents indirectly express pride by telling friends or other siblings about the achievements or work of a particular offspring.

White Americans believe that the expression of feelings is healthy and leads to better adjustment. In counseling, the Western focus on expressing emotions may present difficulties for the Chinese American client, especially when negative emotions are aired. The Chinese American client may lack the experience to identify, acknowledge, or communicate emotional states. Forcing Chinese clients to express emotions directly will meet with resistance and will be counterproductive. Instead, the emphasis should be on the indirect expression of positive and respectful feelings. Because love, respect, and affection are shown through behaviors, one approach might be to make the following statement, "We do different things to show that we care for our family; I would like to learn from you the ways you have of caring for your family" (Ho, 1987). Such an approach focuses on behavior, is respectful, and is indirect.

Family Therapy Based on Chinese Values

Soo-Hoo (1999) discussed the use of brief strategic family therapy that incorporates a cultural frame of reference and includes many elements from Chinese cultural values that were presented earlier.

The case involved a 26-year-old Chinese American man who requested counseling for himself and his 63-year-old father. His mother had died 3 years ago, and his father responded by losing interest in life and becoming depressed. Because of his father's emotional difficulties, the son had moved back home to provide caretaking duties. His attempts to provide for his father were often met with angry outbursts and lecturing. The two of them had initially sought counseling from a White therapist who had conceptualized the problem in the following manner: The father needed to grieve and emotionally express his feelings over the loss of his wife, and in trying to deal with this situation, the father and the son had become overinvolved or overly dependent on one another and needed to individuate. This conceptualization may or may not have been accurate. However, it did not fit the cultural frame of reference of the clients, and they terminated therapy and sought counseling from a Chinese counselor who analyzed and approached the problem from a cultural perspective.

Cultural Frame of Reference

From the father's perspective, the family is very important in Chinese culture and became even more so with the death of his wife. Because parents, especially the mother, are supposed to instruct their children on ways to achieve success in life, the burden was now completely on the father. With the loss of his wife, he urgently felt the need to prepare his son from lessons learned in life and the hardships that needed to be overcome. His attempt to educate his son was in the form of lecturing and nagging. In trying to fulfill his parental role, he was actually driving his son away, which made him feel even more depressed. The son believed he was meeting his obligation of filial piety by coming back to care for his father. He was confused and angry that instead of receiving appreciation, he became the object of criticism. He resented his father's controlling nature.

Cultural Family Intervention

Instead of having each member talk about his issues or encouraging communication with one another, which is inconsistent with Chinese cultural patterns, Soo-Hoo (1999) initially

131

offered his observations to the father and the son. He acknowledged the father by describing the difficulties of raising a family in this society and praised his strength in persevering. He pointed out that the family was very important and that the father genuinely cared for his son and wanted the best for him. The father agreed with this interpretation and expressed gratitude for being understood. The son was also validated by reference to his display of filial piety by being caring and dutiful to his father. The lack of appreciation for his effort was also noted. In this way, the counselor was able to express the concerns of each in a manner that did not engender confrontation.

Reframing

Instead of viewing the problem as an interpersonal issue, emphasis was thus placed on the forces that were pulling the family apart. Both the father and the son had roles to play in saving the family. The two were then seen separately with the father coming in first. In support of the Chinese view of parenting, the counselor indicated that the father's role was to teach his son lessons in life. The father said that his son would not listen. The counselor asked if the father would like to try a new strategy. He eagerly accepted. The son was next seen separately, and aspects of filial piety were emphasized. The counselor acknowledged that the son was very caring but asked him to try something new that would be difficult for him. He explained that the father needed to feel respected and useful and asked if the son would he be willing to try to make a further sacrifice. The son agreed. Both the father and the son were brought in to discuss a new solution that involved homework assignments. The father would have a fixed time period each day to share the hardships that he had experienced in life with his son. He was to do this calmly and share not only his failures but also his successes in life. Lecturing and advice giving were to be discontinued, and he was to teach by example. The son's role was to listen to the father and respond by saying in a sincere manner, "Dad, I understand." Two weeks after the homework assignment, the two indicated that the relationship had improved greatly.

This cultural approach to family therapy involved several components. First, the problem was interpreted within a cultural context. Second, the problem was reframed from one involving interpersonal conflicts to forces pulling the family apart. Third, the solution involved culturally sanctioned roles and behaviors. The father was to be a teacher and lead by example. The son was to demonstrate filial piety. Deep emotional exploration of interpersonal conflicts was avoided. The behavioral homework solutions were culturally based. Although not all Chinese American families will do well with this culturally based intervention (some are acculturated and amenable to Western approaches), problems can be avoided before intervening by assessing the family's cultural frame of reference.

Academic and Career Orientation

In most Chinese families, there is great stress on academic achievement (Eaton & Dembo, 1997). This emphasis may exist even if the parents received few years of formal education. It is not individual achievement that is desired, however. The work is for the enhancement of the family. The emphasis on academics is reflected in the statistic that Chinese Americans complete a college education at nearly double that of the average in the United States (Population Reference Bureau, 1998). Paradoxically, the academic success of Chinese Americans has led to the revision of standards by certain institutions of higher education to reduce the number of admissions to Asian Americans (Wang, 1993).

Achievement comes at a price, however. Chinese American students show a high level of fear of academic failure (Eaton & Dembo, 1997). S. Sue and Zane (1985) reported that foreign-born Chinese American university students achieved higher grade point averages but accomplished this by taking reduced course loads, studying more hours per week, and limiting their career choices. Partly because of this, the students reported greater anxiety, loneliness, and feelings of isolation as compared with other college students.

The amount of parental pressure for their children to succeed academically can be great. Anything less than an A may be considered inferior and an indication that the student no longer cares for the family. There is also pressure to choose a career that the parents approve of. Chinese American students continue to go predominantly into the scientific fields and not into the social sciences. Counselors must be careful to expose Chinese Americans to a wide range of career options.

To aid readers in understanding the importance of Chinese American cultural values and their influence in the counseling process, the following case study is presented.

The Case of John C.

John C. is a 23-year-old student majoring in electrical engineering. He is the oldest of five children and sought counseling because of headaches, indigestion, and insomnia. A visit to the student health service resulted in a referral to the counseling center. Although John was an outstanding student in terms of grades, he seemed unhappy and isolated at the campus.

During the initial interview, John seemed depressed and anxious. He was difficult to counsel because he responded to inquiries with short but polite statements and seldom volunteered information about himself. He avoided any statements that involved feelings and presented his problem as a strictly educational one. Although he never directly expressed it, John seemed to doubt the value of counseling and needed much reassurance and feedback about his performance in the interview.

After several sessions, the counselor was able to discern one of John's major concerns. John did not like engineering and felt pressure by his parents to go into this field. Because the health center had found no physical reasons for John's somatic complaints, the counselor suspected that the complaints were psychophysiological in nature. The counselor felt that John was unable to take responsibility for any of his actions, was excessively dependent on his parents, and was afraid to express the anger he felt toward them.

Using the Gestalt "empty chair technique," the counselor had John pretend that his parents were seated opposite him. The counselor had John express his true feelings toward them. Although ventilating true feelings was initially very difficult, John was able to eventually do so under constant encouragement by the counselor. Unfortunately, the following sessions with John proved nonproductive in that he seemed more withdrawn and guilt-ridden than ever.

Cultural Analysis

In analyzing this case, a culturally aware counselor might entertain the following thoughts and hypotheses about John and the counseling process. Restraint of strong feelings, the stigma of personal problems, and cultural conflicts with his family may be the basis for the headaches, insomnia, and indigestion reported by John. It might be wise to address the physical symptoms first and design treatment strategies for them before proceeding to the inter- and intrapersonal conflicts.

Western culture values taking responsibility for one's life (individual responsibility and decisions). Chinese culture values a family decision. The family is harmonious, and one is part of the family, not separate from it. To infer that John is avoiding responsibility and is excessively dependent on his parents is a serious distortion of cultural values. From this case, one can see how Chinese American values such as filial piety, definition of family roles and status, somatization, control of feelings, and pressures to excel may strongly influence the counseling process.

The techniques that the counselor used may be culturally inappropriate. "Expressing your feelings to parents" in the empty chair technique may ask the client to violate a basic cultural value of "honor thy parents." John's withdrawal and apparent depression may have been the result of guilt he experienced after the therapeutic intervention. Indirect and subtle strategies might have been more effective with this client.

Culturally Based Strategies

Use of culturally consistent strategies could include the following: First, the somatic complaints should be taken as authentic and means of treating them discussed. Events associated with the onset of headaches or stomach problems can be identified. Actions and treatments that have been useful in the past in reducing the physical problems could be determined with John's help.

Second, John might be asked to consider the possibility that the problem may involve cultural or acculturation conflicts that he and his parents were facing. The counselor would discuss what they and he would define as being successful and also explore possible difficulties in being the oldest son in the family.

Third, cognitive and problem-solving approaches could be developed and utilized. John's counselor valued openness and the elaboration of personal feelings. This is a Western value perhaps not shared by the client. Even acculturated Asian American students seem to prefer counseling roles that involve consultation or the facilitation of indigenous support systems (Atkinson, Kim, & Caldwell, 1998). John could be asked whether he knew of friends or family that were going through similar types of issues and the types of solutions they came up with. Different strategies could be evaluated and their possible impact on both John and his family considered. The parents may be highly traditionally oriented in terms of their definitions of filial piety and expectations for the oldest male child. John could be asked about the best way of approaching his parents regarding their expectations. The mother often plays the role of intermediary between the children and parents. He might first approach his mother and explain that he understands and respects his parents but ask if they would still be proud of him if he succeeded in an area outside of engineering. He might present his interest in a different field and ask about their thoughts on it. This culturally based conceptualization and counseling approach would be more consonant with the Chinese value system.

Personality Tests and Assertiveness

On paper-and-pencil tests, Chinese Americans score high on deference, self-restraint, abasement, external locus of control, and need for structure. They also show a lower tolerance for ambiguity, lower dominance, and lower aggression (Abbott, 1976; Fenz & Arkoff, 1962; D. W. Sue & Kirk, 1972). Chinese American boys are more cooperative and have a more external locus of control than do White children (Cook & Chi, 1984). These characteristics seem to make sense in terms of the cultural values and traditions presented. Chinese children and adolescents also report greater fear of criticism and failure than do comparison groups (Dong, Yang, & Ollendick, 1994). Some groups of Chinese Americans describe themselves as quiet and nonassertive. They report being uncomfortable in situations in which an evaluative component is present (D. Sue, Ino, & Sue, 1983; D. Sue, Sue, & Ino, 1990). It is interesting that during a presentation that I gave on research on Asian Americans, the Chinese American students attending voiced many questions and were quite responsive. However, when asked if they participated in classroom discussions at the university, few indicated that they did. Most saw the value of assertiveness training.

Caution must be used in interpreting the findings of personality assessment. There is a lack of data to determine the reliability and validity of the measures for Chinese Americans or other Asian American groups (Okazaki & Sue, 2000). Personality characteristics can also be interpreted from a cultural perspective. For example, deference and self-restraint may represent Chinese values of modesty and politeness rather than negative attributes. Some "personality" characteristics may also be a result of racism. Asian Americans often feel stereotyped by White society and develop negative feelings about themselves when compared with White students (Yeh & Huang, 1996).

Assertiveness Training for Chinese Americans

Because Chinese American men and women often feel uncomfortable in social situations and believe that they lack assertiveness, many have voiced an interest in assertiveness training. Guidelines for group assertiveness training are as follows:

1. *Pregroup screening.* A short 15-minute individual meeting with prospective group members is conducted. During this time, the procedures and approaches used in the group are explained. Client expectations and the assessment of the appropriateness of assertiveness training group work for the individuals are determined at this time. Some group leaders believe that having homogeneous members (same sex, same generational status, etc.) is important in the smooth operation of the groups. This has not been found to be necessary, although individuals who actively reject their own cultural identity may be screened out.
2. *First group meeting.* Information about the purpose of the group, the materials that will be covered, and the techniques that will be used is presented. The importance of confidentiality is discussed and stressed. Personal introductions begin with the group leader, who serves as a model. To reduce anxiety, the counselor might then designate the order for the rest of the group for the introductions.
3. *Culture and racism.* During subsequent sessions, the origin of nonassertiveness of Chinese Americans is discussed. Child-rearing patterns and family experiences are shared. For example, the use of shame and guilt in families is discussed. They discuss why this value and other values were important in their development. It is pointed out that in Chinese culture, nonassertiveness has often been viewed positively. Being quiet and respectful indicates filial piety. Feelings of being a "person of color" in America and its possible impact on assertion are discussed, along with stereotypes and prejudice. Active participation is encouraged by directing specific questions to individuals. The idea of assertiveness is brought up and defined, and its advantages and disadvantages are discussed with respect to both traditional Chinese and Western values. In general, members of these groups have agreed that assertiveness is useful in American society.
4. *Situational assertiveness.* Situational assertiveness is discussed next. It is pointed out that an individual may be assertive in some situations but not in others. Experiences in which assertive behaviors have been exhibited, such as with friends or siblings, are shared. It is pointed out that individuals can decide to be assertive with professors, classmates, and employers but remain deferential to parents and relatives if they so desire.
5. *Group members are asked to write down on paper some situations in which they have difficulty being assertive.* Suggestions can be gained from the assertion questionnaire completed earlier. Cultural contexts are considered. If more assertion is desired with parents, the members brainstorm to come up with suggestions that are respectful and

culturally appropriate. Distinctions among nonassertiveness, aggression, and assertiveness are made. Demonstrations of these behaviors are provided for different situations. Feelings and thoughts are elicited after each performance. The group leader first models each procedure and then structures an easy situation for each participant.

6. *From his or her list, each group member chooses a simple assertive response to practice outside of the group setting.* The situation is first practiced in the group. Cognitions and affect about the situation are discussed. Possible consequences, both positive and negative, are acknowledged. Cognitive approaches that reframe or focus on task performance and realistic appraisal are used. Use of the minimal effective response to achieve the desired goal is practiced, and alternative responses are also discussed. The members are asked to try out their assertive responses outside of the group. The easiest tasks are assigned first. The members are to note their feelings and thoughts during the assertion.

7. *Group meetings involve discussion of homework assignments and cognitive coping strategies used.* Members share what has worked for them. More complex assignments are given, and progress is assessed.

8. *Final group sessions involve a summary by group members in terms of understanding the factors associated with nonassertiveness, their evaluation of their own progress, and suggestions for improvement in the program.*

With some modifications, the basic format of the group training can be used to discuss issues such as filial piety, conflicts over acculturation, sex-role conflicts and expectations, and career options.

Conclusion

Chinese Americans represent a growing and heterogeneous population. It is currently the largest Asian group in the United States of which the majority are foreign born. Consequently, counselors and other mental health professionals need to become aware of the possible impact of cultural values on the process of counseling. Specifically, counselors have to become aware of their own worldview and assumptions about what constitutes successful counseling when working with Chinese American clients. Issues such as independence, the necessity of eliciting emotional reactions, and equality of relationships must be seen from a cultural perspective. Group experiences can be highly effective with Chinese Americans, especially when cultural influences on behavior are discussed.

References

Abbott, K. A. (1976). Culture change and the persistence of the Chinese personality. In G. DeVos (Ed.), *Response to change: Society, culture, and personality* (pp. 87–119). New York: Van Nostrand.

Asian Americans: Are they making the grade? (1984, April 2). *U.S. News and World Report,* pp. 41–47.

Atkinson, D. R., Kim, B. S. K., & Caldwell, R. (1998). Ratings of helper roles by multicultural psychologists and Asian American students: Initial support for the three-dimensional model of multicultural counseling. *Journal of Counseling Psychology, 45,* 414–423.

Blair, S. L., & Qian, Z. (1998). Family and Asian students' educational performance. *Journal of Family Issues, 19,* 355–374.

Bowen, M. (1978). *Family therapy in clinical practice.* New York: Aronson.

Chen, C., & Yang, D. (1986). The self-image of Chinese American adolescents. *Pacific/Asian American Mental Health Research Center Review, 3/4,* 27–29.

Chiu, Y.-W., & Ring, J. M. (1998). Chinese and Vietnamese immigrant adolescents under pressure: Identifying stressors and interventions. *Professional Psychology: Research and Practice, 29,* 444–449.

Committee of 100. (2001). *American attitudes toward Chinese Americans and Asian Americans.* New York: Author.

Cook, H., & Chi, C. (1984). Cooperative behavior and locus of control among American and Chinese American boys. *Journal of Psychology, 118,* 169–177.

Dong, Q., Yang, B., & Ollendick, T. H. (1994). Fears in Chinese children and adolescents and their relations to anxiety and depression. *Journal of Child Psychology and Psychiatry, 35,* 351–363.

Eaton, M. J., & Dembo, M. H. (1997). Differences in the motivational beliefs of Asian American and non-Asian students. *Journal of Educational Psychology, 89,* 433–440.

Fenz, W. D., & Arkoff, A. (1962). Comparative need patterns of five ancestry groups in Hawaii. *Journal of Social Psychology, 58,* 67–89.

Ho, M. K. (1987). *Family therapy with minorities.* Newbury Park, CA: Sage.

Hsu, F. L. K. (1953). *Americans and Chinese: Two ways of life.* New York: Abelard-Schuman.

Jose, P. E., Huntsinger, C. S., Huntsinger, P. R., & Fong-Ruey, L. (2000). Parental values and practices relevant to young children's social development in Taiwan and the United States. *Journal of Cross-Cultural Psychology, 31,* 677–702.

Kiang, P. N., & Lee, V. W. (1993). Exclusion or contribution? In P. P. Ong (Ed.), *The state of Asian Pacific America* (pp. 25–48). Los Angeles: LEAP Asian Pacific American Public Policy Institute and UCLA Asian American Studies Center.

Kim, L. S., & Chun, C.-A. (1993). Ethnic differences in psychiatric diagnosis among Asian American adolescents. *Journal of Nervous and Mental Disease, 181,* 612–617.

Kitano, H. H. L., & Daniels, R. (1988). *Asian Americans: Emerging minorities.* Englewood Cliffs, NJ: Prentice Hall.

Kung, W. W. (2001). Consideration of cultural factors in working with Chinese families with a mentally ill patient. *Families in Society, 82,* 97–107.

Kuo, S. Y., & Spees, E. R. (1983). Chinese American student lifestyles: A comparative study. *Journal of College Student Personnel, 42,* 407–413.

Leong, F. T. L., & Tata, S. P. (1990). Sex and acculturation differences in occupational values among Chinese American children. *Journal of Counseling Psychology, 37,* 208–212.

Lin, C.-Y. C., & Fu, V. R. (1990). A comparison of child-rearing practices among Chinese, immigrant Chinese, and Caucasian American parents. *Child Development, 61,* 429–433.

Nishi, S. M. (1982). The educational disadvantage of Asian and Pacific Americans. *Pacific/Asian American Mental Health Research Center Review, 1,* 4–6.

Okazaki, S., & Sue, S. (2000). Implications of test revisions for assessment with Asian Americans. *Psychological Assessment, 12,* 272–280.

Ong, P., & Hee, S. J. (1993). The growth of the Asian Pacific population: Twenty million in 2020. In P. P. Ong (Ed.), *The state of Asian Pacific America* (pp. 11–24). Los Angeles: LEAP Asian Pacific American Public Policy Institute and UCLA Asian American Studies Center.

Population Reference Bureau. (1998). *Population bulletin.* Washington, DC: U.S. Government Printing Office.

Saner-Yiu, L., & Saner-Yiu, R. (1985). Value dimensions in American counseling: A Taiwanese-American dimension. *International Journal for the Advancement of Counselling, 8,* 137–146.

Shon, S. P., & Ja, D. Y. (1982). Asian families. In M. McGoldrick, J. K. Pearce, & J. Giordano (Eds.), *Ethnicity and family therapy* (pp. 208–228). New York: Guilford Press.

Soo-Hoo, T. (1999). Brief strategic family therapy with Chinese Americans. *American Journal of Family Therapy, 27,* 163–179.

Sue, D. (1994). Incorporating cultural diversity in family therapy. *The Family Psychologist, 10,* 19–21.

Sue, D., Ino, S., & Sue, D. M. (1983). Nonassertiveness of Asian Americans: An inaccurate assumption? *Journal of Counseling Psychology, 30,* 581–588.

Sue, D., Sue, D. M., & Ino, S. (1990). Assertiveness and social anxiety in Chinese-American women. *Journal of Psychology, 124,* 155–164.

Sue, D. W., & Kirk, B. A. (1972). Psychological characteristics of Chinese-American college students. *Journal of Counseling Psychology, 6,* 471–478.

Sue, D. W., & Sue, D. (1999). *Counseling the culturally different: Theory and practice* (3rd ed.). New York: Wiley.

Sue, S., & Okazaki, S. (1990). Asian-American educational achievements: A phenomenon in search of an explanation. *American Psychologist, 45,* 913–920.

Sue, S., & Zane, N. W. S. (1985). Academic achievement and socioemotional adjustment among Chinese university students. *Journal of Counseling Psychology, 32,* 913–920.

To America with skills. (1985, July 8). *Time,* pp. 42–44.

Tseng, W. l., & Hsu, J. (1972). The Chinese attitude toward parental authority as expressed in Chinese children's stories. *Archives of General Psychology, 26,* 28–34.

U.S. Department of Commerce. (2001). *Profiles of general demographic characteristics 2000.* Washington, DC: U.S. Government Printing Office.

Wang, L. L.-C. (1993). Trends in admissions for Asian Americans in colleges and universities. In P. P. Ong (Ed.), *The state of Asian Pacific America* (pp. 49–60). Los Angeles: LEAP Asian Pacific American Public Policy Institutes and UCLA Asian American Studies Center.

Yeh, C. J., & Huang, K. (1996). The collectivistic nature of ethnic identity development among Asian-American college students. *Adolescence, 31,* 645–661.

Yin, X.-H. (2000, May 7). Asian Americans: The two sides of America's "model minority." *The Los Angeles Times,* p. M1.

Ying, Y.-W., Coombs, M., & Lee, P. A. (1999). Family intergenerational relationship of Asian American adolescents. *Cultural Diversity and Ethnic Minority Psychology, 5,* 350–363.

Chapter

Counseling Japanese Americans:
From Internment to Reparation

10

Satsuki Ina

A fter the Japanese attack on Pearl Harbor on December 7, 1941, President Franklin D. Roosevelt issued Executive Order 9066, which enabled the military, in absence of martial law, to circumvent the constitutional safeguards of American citizens of Japanese descent. The order authorized the mass evacuation of 110,000 Japanese Americans residing on the West Coast, who were interned from 1 to 5 years without due process of law. Although implemented as a "military necessity," it has been documented that "the grave injustices were perpetrated in spite of the fact that our government had in its possession proof that not one Japanese American, citizen or not, had engaged in espionage, not one had committed any act of sabotage" (Weglyn, 1976, p. 29). It has also been documented that in this bleak period in American history, the decision to create concentration camps, bounded by barbed wire and guard towers, was, in fact, a result of hysteria, racism, and economic exploitation (Weglyn, 1976).

Almost 50 years later, through the indefatigable efforts of leaders and advocates of the Japanese American community, the Civil Liberties Act of 1988 was passed. Popularly known as the Japanese American Redress Bill, this bill mandated Congress to pay each victim of the internment $20,000 in reparation for a most grievous error perpetrated on Americans of Japanese descent.

The following story was written by a 45-year-old Japanese American woman who participated in an intensive group therapy session that focused on the internment experience during World War II:

> Once upon a time there was a little soldier girl who grew up surrounded by barbed wire. She was scared, and so were her mommy and daddy and brother. But they all marched together and pretended to be unafraid. The father wrote poems about guard towers and guns while the brother played with his toy truck made with broken checkers for wheels. Then one day, the little soldier girl's daddy was taken away and no one could pretend to be unafraid anymore. No one knew where her daddy was. And when she grew up she kept searching for her daddy. She often recognized him because he always went away when she needed him. And she still today sleeps in her soldier clothes, trying to be unafraid.

This story captures the quiet trauma of this woman's internment camp experience and the impact of this event on her later development. Like the other participants, this woman presented the classic image of the successful Japanese American. She was highly educated with a successful career and all of the outward appearances of the so-called model minority. And yet, like the others as well, she suffered from the invisible consequences of low-grade depression and psychosomatic illness. Lack of spontaneity, low risk taking, workaholism, and difficulty in interpersonal relationships were issues with which all participants in the group were able to identify.

The psychological consequences of having been born a political prisoner in her own country was something this woman was reluctant, and yet compelled, to explore within the safety of a supportive group of men and women who had also been *Children of the Camps*. This term, coined by the author, is used to identify individuals who either were born or spent some portion of their formative years in the U.S. internment camps during World War II. This intensive therapy process is presented in detail as a means of highlighting the social, political, and cultural issues that affect the psychological development of the Japanese American client.

Traditional Japanese Values and Norms

To acquire an in-depth understanding of the matrix of traditional Japanese values and norms that influence the Japanese American personality and family structure, the reader is referred to the Appendix at the end of this chapter. However, a brief sketch of significant cultural variables may help to clarify the process and content issues in counseling Japanese Americans. Keeping in mind variations due to social class, geographical origin, and generation in the United States, some common themes can be identified in terms of cultural values and norms.

Much of traditional Japanese culture can be traced to the philosophical precepts of life that were dictated by Confucianism and Buddhism. Within this system of thought, the individual is superseded by the family, specific hierarchical roles are established for all family members, and rules of behavior and conduct are formalized; an individual's adherence to this code of conduct is a reflection not only on the immediate family but also on the extended kinship network.

Regarding the nuclear family, Shon and Ja (as cited in McGoldrick, Pearce, & Giordano, 1982) described the father as the leader and decision maker. His authority is unquestioned. The welfare of the family rests squarely on the father's shoulders. He enforces family rules and is the primary disciplinarian. The successes or failures of the family and its individual members are viewed essentially as the father's responsibility. The traditional role of the mother is that of the nurturant caretaker of both her husband and her children. The mother is clearly the emotionally devoted, nurturant parental figure. The strongest emotional attachments, therefore, tend to be with the mother.

Highly developed feelings of obligation govern many of the interpersonal relationships of Japanese Americans. Shame and loss of face are frequently used to reinforce adherence to prescribed sets of obligations. The interdependent quality of relationships suggests that harmony in these relationships is best achieved through proper conduct and attitudes. The often unspoken obligatory reciprocity within relationships is a serious consideration in the life of a Japanese American. Respect and obedience to parents and others in authority positions reflect the indebtedness of the individual and serve to express affection and gratitude.

In a social structure in which interdependence is so highly valued, the fear of losing face can be a powerful motivating force for conforming. The withdrawal of the family's, community's, or society's confidence and support, and the exposure of one's wrong actions for all to see, is a profound shaming experience to be avoided at all costs.

Harmonious interpersonal relationships are maintained by avoiding direct confrontation. Therefore, much of the communication style of the Japanese American is indirect and is characterized by talking around the point. Problem solving occurs within the prescribed family structure. There is a strong dictum that problems be kept within the family and solved there. The ability to endure hardships and to demonstrate unflagging loyalty and sacrifice for the good of the whole is often called on for resolution of problems.

The Acculturation Variable

Empathic understanding of a client's experience is based on the principles of similarity and identification. Therefore, it is essential that counselors avoid projecting their unconscious stereotypes onto the culturally different client. This benevolent blindness can lead the counselor to discount or deny differences in values, behavior, family structure, and communication style that can serve as rich resources for change and growth. To minimize the dangers of assumed similarities or differences, a careful evaluation of the extent to which the client has adopted American mainstream values, attitudes, and behaviors must be made.

Japanese Americans typically identify themselves in terms of numbers of generations since immigrating to the United States. Issei, the first generation, are currently in their 80s and older. They are the immigrant group that arrived in the United States during the late 1800s. Targeted by the Oriental Exclusion Act of 1924, Issei were prohibited from gaining citizenship or owning land (Kitagawa, 1967). Today they are the elders in the community and the least likely cohort group to utilize Western mental health services. Because of the language barrier and traditional Japanese values of shame associated with having emotional problems, Issei are more likely to cope with personal problems by relying on their religious beliefs and drawing on the cultural coping mechanisms of stoicism, privacy, fatalism, and family support (Maykovich, 1972). Issei interned in the camps during the war typically did not talk about the shame and humiliation that they experienced, nor of the guilt they felt about their children who had to be imprisoned because of their parents' nationality (Kiefer, 1974). Traditional loyalty, propriety, and fear of retribution were also likely factors that inhibited complaining or being openly critical of the government (Kitagawa, 1967). A study by Hallenberg (1988) of the Japanese American elders who had experienced internment indicated that 55% of the subjects interviewed hardly ever talked about the internment even 15 years later and that 42% rarely talked about it more than 40 years later.

Nisei, the second generation, currently range in age from 60 to 80 years. They are the American-born children of the Issei. Educated in American schools, this cohort group tends to reflect a more bicultural approach to life. Some are bilingual, but because of the internment experience, most felt the social and familial pressure to acculturate and adopt American ways that would ensure success and acceptance in the larger community. The questioned loyalty and assimilability of Japanese Americans raised by the wartime hysteria intensified the urgency to become "good Americans." Consequently, this generation of Japanese Americans, encouraged by their immigrant parents, were deeply committed to educational and professional achievement as the mechanism for being accepted by the dominant culture. Thus, I feel that the unconscious influence of Japanese culture on the Nisei personality is more prominent than may be outwardly acknowledged.

In the group process, Nisei and Sansei (third-generation) participants were asked to rate themselves on a scale of *very Japanese* to *very American*. Nisei tended to rate themselves in the *very American* range along with their Sansei counterparts. Although Nisei participants were older than the Sansei, and therefore during their early years were raised in a closed Japanese cultural system within the camps, they tended to deny the impact of this early Japanese socialization on their self-perception. However, in the discussion that followed regarding traditional Japanese values and coping styles, Nisei participants often expressed surprise at how Japanese they really were.

Sansei, the third generation, are now approximately 40 to 60 years old. They may have been born in the camps or are likely to have experienced the reentry process after the internment as young children. This generation is, almost without exception, English speaking only. Though more fully acculturated, the intense striving to be "good Americans" has been perpetuated in Sansei. Although national loyalty was no longer an issue, Sansei in the group reflected the divided loyalty between familial expectations and personal desires.

Several Sansei participants in the group talked about their dissatisfaction with their jobs. In the discussion, it became clear that for some, their original career choice was fostered more by parental definitions of success and the more accessible or socially appropriate career paths for Asian Americans rather than by personal preference. When asked to describe any persistent problems in his life, a 45-year-old dentist reported, "I have difficulty handling paper work, official forms, book-keeping, business information, and documents. I am easily distracted from priority work. I procrastinate. I am tentative and unclear as to my life's primary work." Although initially he was unable to label his feelings and understand the roots for his chronic state of depression, with the support of the group, he was eventually able to recognize the depth of his feelings of obligation to his parents as well as his guilt for resenting his role as the dutiful son. Angry feelings surfaced as he described the faceless oppression that plays a part in his psychic dilemma.

This Sansei client was surprised to discover the extent to which he adheres to the values of filial respect and avoidance of losing face. His experience as a child internee, the possible internalized anxiety that his parents felt during the trauma of internment, and the subsequent discrimination and displacement led him to choose an acceptable career that would ensure his security and status in society. "It's hard work being Japanese, and it's damn painful to be a minority."

It is therefore important that the counselor be sensitive to the conscious and unconscious cultural identification processes operating in the Japanese American client. It is incumbent on the counselor to have a working knowledge of traditional Japanese values and norms and to use this cultural information as the background from which the client emerges as a unique individual. McGoldrick et al. (1982) suggested that cultural information is best used as a filter to determine the extent to which cultural factors contribute to the presenting problem and as a resource in choosing clinical interventions.

The counselor's ability to appreciate the impact of social, cultural, and familial processes can help the client understand the source of his or her pain as well as enable the client to make more conscious choices about staying within or stepping outside of cultural and societal boundaries. A culturally responsive counselor will thoroughly explore the possible social and psychological consequences of the client's choices.

Although generational identification of the Issei, Nisei, and Sansei can provide the counselor with a general sense of their degree of acculturation, other acculturation indicators can be helpful. Rural Japanese American communities tend to be more traditional in contrast to urban communities, which have been disturbed by urban renewal efforts. Affiliation with specific ethnic, social, civic, and religious organizations can also be a helpful indicator. Peer group affiliation in schools and dating preferences also help to determine the degree of acculturation. It is important to keep in mind, however, that the influences of culture and racial discrimination are often more unconscious than conscious, and the counselor will do well to explore these issues jointly with the client. Assessing the degree of acculturation will enable the counselor to clarify the presenting problem and to select appropriate culture-specific interventions.

The Presenting Problem

Human problems are at once unique and universal. What brings the client into therapy, however, is the inappropriate or ineffective ways in which he or she is coping with the problem. For ethnic minority clients, it is essential that these coping styles be understood in terms of both their cultural and defensive overlay. Grier and Cobbs (1968), in their classic text *Black Rage*, described the concept of the "paranorm," which can be applied to all minority group members who have been victims of racial bigotry and oppression. As a psychological defense against the dehumanizing effects of racism, minority subgroups develop a norm of appropriate paranoia against which they check their perceptions of safety and trust.

It is impossible to ferret out how much of the client's coping style is cultural, defensive, or uniquely individual. Two types of errors in understanding the presenting problems, however, could bring the therapeutic process to a standstill. The first error is to assume that cultural or defensive factors are insignificant in influencing the client's coping style, and the second error is to assume that the client's coping style can be explained completely by cultural or defensive factors, without consideration for individual uniqueness. Thus, the workaholism that some group participants describe will be only superficially understood if the clients' historical experience of being viewed as unassimilable as a race was not explored. Japanese Americans who experienced the confinement possess a group consciousness that should not be minimized. Fear of failure for this group is understandably high. The counselor's task is to facilitate the client's awareness of this socially imposed defense mechanism to enable him or her to see the problem in the contextual as well as the uniquely personal framework.

To further illustrate this point, the participant whose story introduced this chapter spoke of her difficulty in finding lasting relationships with men. She typically picked men who tended to be emotionally unavailable to her. As an adult, she consciously understood that her father was taken away suddenly in the middle of the night and incarcerated in a separate prison. In the course of the group process, however, she realized that as a child she experienced her father's disappearance as abandonment and felt overwhelmed by the anguish and fear of her mother, who was left to care for two small children alone behind barbed wires.

This early childhood trauma was then exacerbated not by a dysfunctional family's no-talk rule but by cultural mandates that discouraged discussion about what was internalized as a shameful experience. The precarious balance of maintaining dignity in the face of the loss of their personal freedom was a challenge to the Japanese American internees. As a coping style influenced by Japanese culture and reinforced by the larger society's amnesia about the camps, silence was used in an effort to heal the injury. The consequences of both the cultural and defensive coping mechanism are depicted in Hallenberg's (1988) study, which found a significant relationship between not talking about the internment and chronic depression. The group helped the woman challenge her mistaken belief that somehow she was unlovable and that was why her father left her. She was also able to recognize how the silence into which she withdrew mirrored the silence of her parents, the community, and the government regarding her internment experience.

The counselor's ability to attend to the personal, cultural, and defensive variables that influence the client's coping style enables the counselor to understand the backdrop for the presenting problem.

Intervention Strategies

In working with Japanese American clients, the entire range of clinical interventions may be considered for treatment. However, the counselor who has assessed the degree of acculturation, cultural constraints and prescriptions, and defense mechanisms against racism is better able to make a sensitive choice of intervention. To minimize resistance in a cross-cultural therapeutic relationship, it is recommended that the interventions selected serve to challenge, not conflict with or negate, existing coping mechanisms. Consequently, the counselor must be willing to adapt interventions to the client's need. This requires the counselor to have a wide repertoire of clinical interventions from which to choose.

To better understand the psychological effects of the internment experience on Japanese Americans, a clinical analogy may be appropriate. Like the incest victim in a dysfunctional family, American citizens of Japanese descent were singled out, and their fundamental rights to due process were violated by the very arm of the government designated to protect those rights. The social amnesia and denial subsequent to the internment further traumatized the victims and led to internalized shame and repressed anger. Not unlike the child victim who manages to cope by developing psychic barriers against vulnerability (Courtois, 1988), Japanese Americans as a group committed themselves to being good citizens and made every effort to be accepted by the larger society. After years of suppressing and denying the anger because of the dependency on the perpetrator, clients in this classic "incest bind" can experience symptomatic behaviors.

What follows is the examination of a group experience for Japanese Americans who experienced internment. Important stages of the group experiences as well as critical issues are explored.

Creating a Safe Environment

As the group experience began, the facilitator acknowledged and opened for discussion the cultural prohibitions against disclosing family problems and the open expression of feelings. The reluctance to reopen the painful experience of the internment required an extensive trust-building process. Participants were encouraged to be aware of their physical and emotional boundaries, and the facilitator modeled, with respect, each person's right to say "no." This was particularly crucial for people whose rights had been so blatantly violated. Participants were told that any level of self-disclosure was acceptable, and every member agreed to honor confidentiality for the material presented by the group.

Telling Your Story

Not unlike the incestuous family's "secret," the unacknowledged crime against the Japanese Americans was rationalized with euphemisms such as "wartime hysteria," "protective custody," and "national security." Consequently, many of the victims themselves, culturally primed to respect authority and shamed by the experience, kept the story of their internment to themselves. Rather than complaining and revolting, they practiced silent endurance. Until recently, very little about the camp experience was acknowledged in the classroom, the media, or government policy. For the participants, then, telling their story, talking about what they experienced and how they coped, was the beginning of the healing process. To have others in the group mirror back empathic acceptance, without judgment, served as an invaluable intervention in empowering the victim.

Prior to the session, each person was asked to talk to at least one other family member about his or her intention to participate in this group. This served not only to prepare the participants emotionally but to begin effecting a challenge to the previous no-talk rule to which the family may have adhered.

Often, implicit in the minority experience is the absence of acknowledgment and validation by the majority power structure. Just as in the family, when this validation is not provided, self-doubt prevails. Thus, the facilitator's role was to model and support, emphatically and affirmatively, the acknowledgment of each participant's story. Participants were asked to bring photographs of themselves, share stories that were told about them, and describe what happened to their family. The participants expressed shame in terms of loss of face. Therefore, assisting the participants to look into the faces reflecting back acceptance and understanding served as a powerful shame reduction intervention. This section of the workshop was given no time limit. It was completed only after each person felt that he or she had finished.

Identifying Developmental Needs

Participants were encouraged to identify their developmental tasks and needs at the time of the internment and to consider how those tasks and needs were affected by the internment. Many participants were able to understand for the first time what it must have been like for their parents to have children behind barbed wire fences. One of the significant issues that surfaced was the disorganization of family roles and rules with the imposition of the military superstructure on the family. Just the very physical structure of the barracks and mess hall affected family privacy, communication, and control. In addition, participants described the pervasive fear and anxiety that gripped their parents as they attempted to raise a family in a prison compound surrounded by tanks and armed guards standing on watchtowers.

Using the Adlerian early childhood recollections process (Dinkmeyer, Pew, & Dinkmeyer, 1979), participants reexperienced that period of their development and identified what it was that they needed from their parents at the time. The group was then asked to respond to each individual's needs with verbal affirmations as the participant returned to the early experience but this time with an empowered parental source. Cultural injunctions against violating filial piety carry a heavy burden of guilt. Therefore, during the debriefing, the facilitator actively reframed blaming of parents for their child's unmet needs as limitations compounded by external forces.

One woman described the images that came up for her as she regressed to her early infancy. She was born in the camps. She recalled that as she looked up from her straw mat "crib" she saw her parents' faces. Rather than being joyful at her birth, she realized that what she saw were faces that were fearful and anxious. She wept as she recognized that her arrival was not a welcome blessing. She realized that her need for security was only tenuously provided because her parents were likely to have been ambivalent about having an offspring when their own security was in question. With the help of the group, she further realized that the egocentric "child" decided that somehow she was the source of her parents' fear and anxiety.

Themes that emerged from these early recollections and consequent decisions included issues of trust, abandonment, powerlessness, fear of risk, pessimism, and self-discounting. Participants were able to relate these issues to current persistent problems in their work and love relationships.

Expressing the Unexpressed

Having identified the source of the hurt that had been so long buffered by culturally and socially induced guilt and shame, the participants were encouraged to express the emotions that had been suppressed so long. Anger directed at parents could be identified; anger directed at an amorphous government that had violated their right to freedom, however, was difficult to identify and justify. It was expressed as anger without a target, as a diffuse, unlabeled rage.

Because of cultural prescriptions of emotional constraint, anger release techniques were presented in progressive steps of intensity from passive to more active forms of release. Participants were invited to participate at a level that was just over their comfort zone and no more. The first step was to discuss the effects of suppressed emotions on the body and the relationship of this suppression to somatic illnesses and depression. People were then encouraged to relate their experiences to these concepts. The next step was to listen to music written and performed by Japanese Americans that expressed the trauma and humiliation of the internment experience. This process enabled participants to hear the feelings of others poignantly and emotionally expressed. For many, this released tears and feelings of affirmation.

Each step progressively intensified the release of feelings. To reduce anxiety about the public display of emotions, people were paired for each exercise, and partners were instructed to affirm and nonverbally support the other person's feelings. Most preferred to pair up and go to separate rooms to have some privacy. Participants were then encouraged to move their bodies by using Bioenergetic (Lowen, 1975) movements and to vocalize their feelings.

Debriefing was extensive, and inhibitions were discussed and acknowledged. The facilitator explained that reluctance or refusal to participate was honored as a choice and was not a sign of emotional inadequacy. Participants were assured that no judgment or clinical assessment would be assigned as a result of their choices. For all victims, choice without judgment is crucial to the healing process.

Grieving the Losses

As anger gave way to sadness, participants identified their grief over their losses. One man said, "When my parents lost their freedom, I guess I lost some of my childhood." Participants recalled discussion about material losses but rarely about emotional losses. Children grew up or were born into a family environment where parents had lost the dignity of self-determination. Though most of the internees faced the situation with courage, the experience took away 2, 3, or sometimes 4 years from the lives of innocent people. Participants were encouraged to identify ways to continue to heal the wounds of the inner child. Personal work, family work, and even political work were discussed.

Personal work was the need to acknowledge the losses that the child had experienced and to work to fulfill unmet needs. One man said, "I really need to let the child in me play joyfully and without guilt." Another woman said, "I'd like to let the fearful child in me have new experiences."

Family work included discussion of the detrimental effects of the no-talk rule and how beginning to talk to parents and learning about their experiences could help participants integrate these feelings and experiences into their personal history. Discovering how parents had coped, how the internment had affected their relationships, and their feelings about their children were all issues that remained cloaked in silence for members of the group.

At the political level, of course, the monetary reparation of $20,000 and a presidential apology to all of the surviving internees was discussed. Many participants felt that the reparation represented a symbol of the long-awaited acknowledgment of the crime against the Japanese Americans. The guilt and loss of face shrouded in government silence could now be lifted and guilt assigned to the appropriate perpetrator. Foremost, acknowledgment and a formal apology would facilitate the healing of an insidious wound.

Termination

The group grew very close. A simulated family had been created in which the pain could be identified, shared, and validated. The grief work could be completed, and the participants could move forward in their development. For most, the group experience was just the beginning of a therapeutic journey. One participant closed the final session with, "Now, maybe I can really do something with my freedom!"

Nuts and Bolts

In attempting to replicate this group experience, it is highly recommended that at least one of the facilitators be a member of the Japanese American community because of the highly sensitive nature of the issues involved and the cultural constraints against involving outsiders. A facilitator who has also been an internee can facilitate some of the more difficult processes through self-disclosure and role modeling. Ideally, a male and female cotherapy team would be helpful. Because fewer men than women are likely to participate, the presence of a male role model can serve to validate the different gender perspectives. A small group size of five or six can serve to minimize the public quality of the group and also allow each member as much time as needed to tell his or her story and express deeply buried emotions that are likely to surface. A tight, safe context is essential for trauma victims; therefore, a weekend intensive with a 1-month and 6-month follow-up was adopted to prevent time disruption and screen out possible dropouts.

Because it is not generally acknowledged by the Japanese community or the community at large that people suffer today from the consequences of the internment, this group experience is not likely to be one that a participant would want to publicize. Therefore, participation is more likely to be enhanced by working within the community through notifying key people such as clergypersons, education and medical personnel, and social service providers who can, by word of mouth, inform people about such a group experience.

As with other groups, it is essential that the group leader conduct an individual intake to assess the psychological well-being of potential participants. Due to the social, cultural, and political influences that have caused much of the emotions around the internment experience to be suppressed, it is important that individual members possess the necessary ego strength to process intense emotions and that they have a relatively supportive environment to which they will return. Because an essential feature of the healing process is the ability to bond and experience acceptance, individuals with personality disorders that could interfere with this process are referred for individual therapy to deal with internment issues.

Conclusion

Because the evacuation of the Japanese Americans in 1942 occurred on the West Coast of the United States and Canada (Daniels, 1971; Weglyn, 1976), not every Japanese American client will have the direct experience of the internment as did those participating in the group discussed in this chapter. This description of the group experience, however, can help counselors to understand the acculturation process, cultural constraints and resources, and defensive strategies for coping with racism and discrimination when working with Japanese American clients. Additionally, the group process presented in this chapter can serve to demonstrate methods for modifying traditional interventions to make them culturally appropriate for the Japanese American client.

Implications of the internment experience on subsequent generations of Japanese Americans need to be addressed. Possible clinical issues to be considered include the intergenerational effects of cultural coping mechanisms with respect to the trauma of internment.

References

Courtois, C. A. (1988). *Healing the incest wound: Adult survivors in therapy.* New York: Norton.
Daniels, R. (1971). *Concentration camps USA: Japanese Americans and World War II.* New York: Holt, Rinehart & Winston.

Dinkmeyer, D. C., Pew, W. L., & Dinkmeyer, D. C. (1979) *Adlerian counseling and psychotherapy*. Monterey, CA: Brooks/Cole.

Grier, W. H., & Cobbs, P. M. (1968). *Black rage*. New York: Basic Books.

Hallenberg, K. (1988). *Internment experience of the Japanese American elderly and their emotional development*. Unpublished master's thesis.

Kiefer, C. W. (1974). *Changing cultures, changing lives*. San Francisco: Jossey-Bass.

Kitagawa, D. (1967). *Issei and Nisei: The internment years*. New York: Seabury Press.

Lowen, A. (1975). *Bioenergetics*. New York: Penguin Books.

Maykovich, M. (1972). *Japanese American identity dilemma*. Tokyo: Waseda University Press.

McGoldrick, M., Pearce, J. K., & Giordano, J. (1982). *Ethnicity and family therapy*. New York: Guilford Press.

Weglyn, M. (1976). *Years of infamy: The untold story of America's concentration camps*. New York: Morrow Press.

Appendix

Additional Resources

Armor, J., & Wright, P. (1989). *Manzanar*. New York: Vintage Books.

Broom, L., & Reimer, R. (1949). *Removal and return: The socioeconomical effects of the war on the Japanese Americans*. Berkeley: University of California Press.

Chuman, F. F. (1976). *The bamboo people: The law and Japanese Americans*. Chicago: Japanese American Citizens League.

Collins, D. (1985). *Native American aliens: Disloyalty and the renunciation of citizenship by Japanese Americans during World War II*. Westport, CT: Greenwood Press.

Commission on Wartime Relocation and Internment of Civilians. (1997). *Personal justice denied: Report of the Commission on Wartime Relocation and Internment of Civilians*. Seattle: University of Washington Press.

Daniels, R. (1993). *Prisoners without trial: Japanese Americans in World War II*. New York: Hill & Wang.

DeVos, G. A. (1955). A qualitative Rorschach assessment of maladjustment and rigidity in acculturating Japanese Americans. *Genetic Psychology Monograph, 52*, p. 51.

Doi, T. (1973). *The anatomy of dependence*. Tokyo: Kodansha International.

Exec. Order No. 9066, 7 Fed. Reg. 1407 (1942). As of March 31, 1942, Pub. L. No. 503, 18 U.S.C. § 47(a) (1942).

Grier, W. H., & Cobbs, P. M. (1968). *Black rage*. New York: Basic Books.

Guterson, D. (1995). *Snow falling on cedars*. New York: Vintage Books.

Harth, E. (Ed.). (2001). *Last witnesses: Reflections on the wartime internment of Japanese Americans*. New York: St. Martin's Press.

Hosokawa, B. (1969). *Nisei: The quiet Americans*. New York: Morrow.

Ichioka, N. (Ed.). (1989). *Views from within: The Japanese American Evacuation and Resettlement Study*. Los Angeles: University of California Asian American Studies Center.

Inada, L. (Ed.). (2000). *Only what we could carry: The Japanese American internment experience*. Berkeley, CA: Heyday Books.

Ishigo, E. (1972). *Lone heart mountain*. Los Angeles: Anderson, Ritchie, & Simon.

Kashima, T. (1980). Japanese American internees' return, 1945 to 1955: Readjustment and social amnesia. *Phylon (The Atlanta University), 41*(2), 107–115.

Kashima, T. (2003). *Judgment without trial: Japanese American imprisonment during World War II*. Seattle: University of Washington Press.

Kikumura, A. (1981). *Through harsh winters: The life of a Japanese immigrant woman.* Novato, CA: Chandler & Sharp.

Kitano, H. (1969). *Japanese Americans: The evolution of a subculture.* Englewood Cliffs, NJ: Prentice Hall.

Kogawa, J. (1983). *Obasan.* Harmondsworth, England: Penguin Books.

Marsella, A., Friedman, M., Gerrity, E., & Scurfield, R. (1996). *Ethnocultural aspects of post-traumatic stress disorder: Issues, research, and clinical applications.* Washington, DC: American Psychological Association.

Nagata, D., & Takeshita, Y. (1998). Coping with resilience across generations: Japanese Americans and the World War II internment. *Psychoanalytic Review, 85,* 557–613.

Nishi, S. M., Bannai, L., & Tomihiro, C. (1983). Bibliography on redress: Wartime relocation and internment of Japanese Americans. *P/AAMHRC Research Review, 2*(1), 6–8.

Ogawa, D. M. (1971). *From Japs to Japanese: The evolution of Japanese American stereotypes.* Berkeley, CA: McCutchan Press.

Okihiro, G. (1996). *Whispered silences: Japanese Americans and World War II.* Seattle: University of Washington Press.

Okubo, M. (1946). *Citizen 13660.* New York: Columbia University Press.

Sone, M. (1953). *Nisei daughter.* Seattle: University of Washington Press.

Sue, S., & Morishima, J. K. (1982). *The mental health of Asian Americans.* San Francisco: Jossey-Bass.

Sue, S., & Wagner, N. N. (1973). *Asian-American psychological perspective.* Palo Alto, CA: Science and Behavior Books.

Takaki, R. (1989). *Strangers from a different shore.* Boston: Little, Brown.

Thomas, D. S., & Nishimoto, R. S. (1946). *The spoilage.* Berkeley: University of California Press.

Tsukamoto, M., & Pinkerton, E. (1987). *We the people.* Elk Grove, CA: Laguna.

Wake, M. N. (1983). Acculturation and clinical issues affecting the mental health of Japanese Americans. *P/AAMHRC Research Review, 2*(4), 5–7.

Wilson, R. A., & Hosokawa, B. (1980). *East to America: A history of the Japanese in the United States.* New York: Morrow Press.

Yamamoto, J., Machizawa, S., & Steinberg, A. (1986). The Japanese American relocation center experience. *P/AAMHRC Research Review, 5*(3/4), 17–20.

Counseling Americans of Southeast Asian Descent: The Impact of the Refugee Experience

11

Rita Chi-Ying Chung and Fred Bemak

Since 1975, more than 1.5 million Southeast Asians have fled from their homes and sought refuge in the United States. The mass exodus of Southeast Asian refugees was prompted by political turmoil and genocide, causing them to become one of the fastest growing ethnic groups in the United States. This population consists of five main Southeast Asian groups: Vietnamese, Cambodians, Laotians, Hmong, and Chinese-Vietnamese. They have settled in every state in the United States but are especially concentrated in California, Texas, and Washington, DC.

To fully understand the refugee situation, it is important to distinguish between refugee and immigrant status. Murphy (1977) differentiated between "forced versus free" or involuntary versus voluntary migration. According to this definition, refugees are forced to leave their country of origin and are displaced from their countries by events outside of their control, such as war or genocide, because it is dangerous to remain in their home countries and impossible to continue their customary way of life. The refugee population is therefore distinguished from other migrants such as immigrants or sojourners because of their involuntary and sudden departure (Bemak & Chung, 2000). Similar to the general population of refugees, the Southeast Asian refugees have been ill prepared for the sudden departure from their familiar world and faced uncertainty, confusion, high risk for personal safety, and complete disruption of their normal lives. Such chaos often caused the loss of personal identity accompanied by the loss of reference groups such as family, community, culture, and country (Bemak & Chung, 2000).

Southeast Asian refugees primarily entered the United States in two main waves, with each wave having different demographic characteristics and experiences before and after migration. The first wave of Southeast Asian refugees left Vietnam prior to the fall of Saigon in 1975 and entered the United States directly or from refugee camps. During the fall of Saigon, because of their close association with the United States and/or South Vietnamese forces, these refugees were assisted by the American government and hastily evacuated by helicopters or sealifts. This first wave was mainly Vietnamese and tended to be relatively well educated and able to speak some English (Chung & Okazaki, 1991).

The second main wave of Southeast Asian refugees entered the United States between 1978 and 1980 and consisted of Vietnamese, Laotians, Hmong, and Cambodians. The second wave of refugees escaped from their homes by sea or made hazardous journeys through the jungle. Those from Vietnam left in small, overcrowded, and unseaworthy boats. The "boat people" frequently encountered brutal attacks by sea pirates, and many were subjected to severe violence or were raped or killed (Chung & Okazaki, 1991). The Cambodians, Hmong, and Laotians escaped by land through the jungle, crossing minefields and avoiding ambushes by military soldiers. They encountered tropical diseases, death, hunger, starvation, and exhaustion. Further compounding the trauma, the escape from countries of origin for many of those in the second wave did not result in an immediate resettlement to a host country. Instead, they were forced to wait in overcrowded and unsanitary refugee camps in nearby countries such as Thailand, the Philippines, or Hong Kong for months or even years before they were permanently resettled in the United States or other resettlement countries. In contrast to the first wave, the second wave of refugees generally tended to be less educated with no prior English language skills. Furthermore, many, especially those from the rural areas, had little or no exposure to Western culture prior to arriving in resettlement countries (Chung & Okazaki, 1991).

The first wave of Southeast Asian refugees tended to adjust more successfully than the second wave because of the premigration differences. Because the first wave managed to escape Vietnam before the fall of Saigon, they were exposed to less premigration trauma, and they were better educated and possessed more wealth and resources (S. Nguyen, 1982). As the political repression intensified in Cambodia, Vietnam, and Laos after 1975, many in the second wave experienced human atrocities and genocide and were victims of incarceration, torture, brutal beatings and violence, sexual abuse, rape, and starvation. Many also witnessed killings and torture or were forced to commit human atrocities themselves (Mollica, Wyshak, & Lavelle, 1987). These atrocities not only were confined to countries of origin but also occurred during their escape and in the refugee camps (Mollica & Jalbert, 1989).

This chapter first discusses the psychosocial adjustment and adaptation of Southeast Asian refugees, followed by a discussion on the types of distress predictors and the level of psychological distress encountered by this group. Cultural belief systems and their barriers to mental health services and use of traditional healing methods are also presented. Finally, the chapter discusses counseling issues and presents the Multilevel Model (MLM) approach to psychotherapy with refugees, using a case study to illustrate application of the model.

Psychosocial Adjustment and Adaptation

Two major factors are associated with Southeast Asian refugees' psychosocial adjustment and adaptation in the United States. One factor is the degree of premigration trauma experienced in home countries during the war, the escape process, and life in the refugee camps. Mollica, Lavelle, and Khoun (1985) classified the different types of premigration trauma for refugees into four general categories: deprivation (e.g., food and shelter), physical injury and torture, incarceration and reeducation camps, and witnessing and experiencing killing and torture. The second factor is the level of difficulties in adjusting to the resettlement country that is often culturally significantly different from their home country (e.g., Bemak, 1989; Chung & Bemak, 2002b; Chung & Kagawa-Singer, 1993; K. M. Lin, Masuda, & Tazuma, 1982; K. M. Lin, Tazuma, & Masuda, 1979; Nicholson, 1997; Westermeyer, 1986).

The emotional survival mechanism used by the Southeast Asian refugees to cope with traumatic experiences of torture, rape, and other human atrocities prior to migration was to act "dumb" (Mollica & Jalbert, 1989). To survive, individuals acted as if they were deaf, dumb, foolish, confused, or stupid. They had also learned to obediently comply with orders without question or complaint because they knew that appearing smart would result in torture or execution. The fear of being killed or tortured has remained for many refugees, causing them to continue acting dumb or being afraid to speak up or show their true feelings in the resettlement country (Mollica & Jalbert, 1989). Such behavior among the refugees, which originally served as survival skills, may appear to be aversive, antisocial, or even pathological when viewed within the culture of the host country (Stein, 1986). Furthermore, it has been found that Vietnamese Amerasians (children with American fathers and Vietnamese mothers) experience the psychological recoil effect to cope with traumatic experiences (Bemak & Chung, 1998). This phenomenon suggests that for this group to survive in physically and psychologically dangerous environments, strong defenses are developed, causing emotional numbness to the painful environment. It is only when they are in the resettlement country and feel safe that the psychological effects of trauma are displayed, making it critical for psychotherapists to be aware of this phenomenon (Bemak & Chung, 1998).

Resettlement in a foreign country poses additional challenges for Southeast Asian refugees. Premigration trauma may be exacerbated by hardships experienced after resettlement. For example, Vietnamese Amerasian refugees frequently experienced racism in Vietnam. Their hopes that such discrimination would end once in the United States were often shattered as they found themselves facing prejudice and racism in the United States (Bemak & Chung, 1998). Some Amerasian youths have responded aggressively and sometimes violently, resulting in legal problems. Tayabas and Pok (1983) found that problems with adjustment were more accentuated during the initial 1- to 2-year resettlement period during which refugees commonly focused on meeting their basic needs of housing and employment.

During resettlement, refugees may become motivated to recover what has been lost as they attempt to rebuild their lives. However, they may also encounter a loss of control over decision making with regard to basic life issues such as the geographical location of where they will live in the resettlement country, job opportunities, and social networks. These difficulties may hinder their enthusiasm to acculturate and create emotional and psychological problems as they confront the loss of their culture and identity. Tasks such as catching a bus, handling money, or going shopping, which were routine tasks in their home countries, may become major ordeals in the process of acculturation (Chung & Okazaki, 1991).

Acculturative Stress

Southeast Asian refugees also undergo acculturative stress during resettlement. Acculturative stress is a combination of ameliorating effects of environmental, familial, demographic, and other factors (Miranda & Matheny, 2000) and refers to a unique type of distress that involves adjusting to a foreign culture and possibly changing one's identity, values, behaviors, cognitions, attitudes, and affect (Berry, 1990; Berry & Annis, 1974; Liebkind, 1996; Miranda & Matheny, 2000). For refugees, acculturative stress is influenced by multiple factors, as stated above, as well as premigration experiences, the social and political context of the resettlement society, and postmigration acculturation experiences (Liebkind, 1996).

Bemak (1989) described a three-phase developmental model of acculturation associated with successful adjustment and adaptation to the host country. In the first phase, the refugee attempts to use skills to master the new environment and establish security and psychological safety. The second phase follows after the successful completion of the first phase and is the integration of former skills that were developed in the home country with the newly acquired skills learned in the host country. The third phase is achieved when the refugee develops a growing sense of the future. It is only after the mastery of culture, language, and a sense of psychological safety that the refugee begins to plan for future attainable goals and implement strategies to achieve those goals.

Survivor's Guilt

It is common for refugees to experience survivor's guilt after resettlement (Brown, 1982; K. M. Lin, Inui, Kleinman, & Womack, 1982; Tobin & Friedman, 1983). They are haunted by the guilt of successfully escaping from their home country while leaving family, relatives, and friends behind in a politically volatile and potentially dangerous situation (Bemak & Chung, 2000; Chung, 2000). Many refugees have little or no information regarding those they left behind. The lack of knowledge about their safety and well-being adds to refugees' already existing guilt, resulting in some refugees experiencing nostalgia, depression, anxiety, and frustration that interferes with successful adjustment (Bemak & Chung 2000). For example, in one study 22% of Cambodian women reported the loss of their spouse; therefore, many of them made the decision to leave Cambodia (Chung, 2000). The findings showed that those who made the decision to leave Cambodia were more likely to experience psychological distress. This may relate to feelings of guilt about subjecting their families in the United States to financial hardship, especially for those who are fully dependent on welfare; concerns about family and friends left behind; and survivor's guilt, which intensifies as the refugees become more successful in the resettlement country (Chung & Bemak, 1995).

Employment and English Language Proficiency

To rebuild one's life in a foreign country is a difficult task. A high percentage of Southeast Asian refugees remain dependent on welfare even after being in the United States for a long period of time, largely due to unemployment (Chung & Bemak, 1995). Acquiring a job poses particular difficulties for refugees because educational training and skills obtained in their home country are most often not transferable to resettlement countries. This may cause a dramatic change in socioeconomic status, causing some refugees to take jobs for which they are overqualified. Chung and Bemak (1995) indicated that there was a tendency for refugee men to remain unemployed and welfare dependent while waiting for a suitable position that matched their skills because taking any employment could result in downward mobility and loss of status. Although refugees make remarkable progress in their adjustment, K. M. Lin et al. (1979) and K. M. Lin, Masuda, and Tazuma (1982) found only a small percentage regained their former socioeconomic status.

Furthermore, English language skills play an important part in refugees' adjustment and are a key factor to gainful employment. However, for those who are illiterate in their own language, learning English proves to be a challenge. Chung and Kagawa-Singer (1993) found that attendance in English as a Second Language (ESL) classes was significantly associated with distress in this population. It has been suggested that emotional and mental fatigue as well as memory and concentration difficulties due to premigration trauma may also inhibit learning performance in ESL classes (Mollica & Jalbert, 1989).

Changing Family Dynamics

Resettlement for Southeast Asian refugees also creates changes in the family structure. Because of high rates of unemployment and underemployment among Southeast Asian men, it is often necessary for women to work in order to provide adequate financial family support. Whereas refugee men may experience a downward turn in their socioeconomic status, women may experience upward mobility in their socioeconomic status (Chung, Bemak, & Kagawa-Singer, 1998). Working outside of the home and community and being exposed to American culture, refugee women may begin to question their traditional cultural gender roles and seek more independence. Such shifts in roles and attitudes frequently cause marital conflicts.

Similar to immigrants, refugee children and adolescents tend to acculturate faster than their parents, which also contributes to changing roles and shifting family dynamics. Attending school and having exposure to nonrefugee children through ESL or other classes, children are apt to learn the English language and the American customs faster than their parents. This often results in a shift in family dynamics, with the children assuming the role of a language and cultural translator for their parents. When this happens, children frequently witness a transformation of their parents from previously competent, autonomous caretakers to depressed, overwhelmed, and dependent individuals. Confidence in their parents as caregivers and providers is inevitably undermined, and the traditional family structure may change dramatically as a result. Furthermore, some children may experience feeling ashamed of their parents in the resettlement country because their parents lack English language skills, dress "funny," and behave according to non-Western manners and customs. There may also be embarrassment to publicly speak in their mother tongue with parents or family members because peers in the resettlement country may laugh at them.

Child-Rearing Practices

Another area of possible change within families is child-rearing practices. Usual disciplinary measures, such as corporal punishment, that were used before migration may be prohibited by resettlement country laws. This issue presents a serious dilemma for Southeast Asian refugee parents, who may already feel diminished in their status as parents and constricted in raising their children in ways that have been culturally acceptable for generations. Intergenerational conflict between parents and children may also occur regarding issues such as dating, marriage, curfew, and/or parental supervision. Many refugee children face the difficult position of bridging two worlds—acculturating and adopting the customs and behaviors similar to their resettlement country peer group while maintaining the role as a child in a traditional family. In attempts to curtail their children from adopting patterns of behavior and values that are incongruent with traditional values and beliefs, some refugee parents try to maintain a strict traditional upbringing. Despite this, many parents experience the loss of traditional authority and control as their children become more outspoken and challenge their authority and the "old culture."

School

Paralleling the home experience are the difficulties faced in schools by many refugee children and adolescents. They may experience racial prejudice and tension manifested in fighting or in being punched, mimicked, harassed, or robbed by non-Asian students (Huang, 1989; Schaprio, 1987). The norms regulating classroom and school behavior are usually different than those in their home countries. Although the acquisition of a new language is one of the most important factors in acculturation, according to Bemak and Chung (2003), it is highly complicated and symbolic of other facets of adjustment. For example, a school counselor may insist that Vietnamese students are not allowed to speak Vietnamese during group activities. This rejection of their native language sends a negative message about the students' culture and may have multiple adverse effects on Vietnamese students' psychosocial adjustment, racial identity, and academic performance.

Furthermore, children wishing to participate in extracurricular activities may have difficulties with parents who cannot understand these "foreign activities" that do not emphasize studying. Many Southeast Asian refugee parents see educational success as a tool for upward mobility and do not understand the relevance of extracurricular activities. These issues, combined with the desire to belong and adjust, may generate both internalized and externalized tensions and conflicts for refugee children and adolescents.

Psychological Distress

Due to the extent of and exposure to trauma prior to migration, it is not surprising to find that premigration trauma is a major predictor of psychological problems (Bemak & Greenberg, 1994; Chung & Bemak, 2002b; Chung & Kagawa-Singer, 1993; Hinton, Tiet, Tran, & Chesney, 1997; Mollica et al., 1998; Nicholson, 1997). The major psychological problems exhibited by Southeast Asian refugees as an outcome of premigration trauma are post-traumatic stress disorder (PTSD), depression, somatization, and suicide (e.g., Carlson & Rosser-Hogan, 1994; Cheung, 1982; Chung & Kagawa-Singer, 1995; Fawzi et al., 1997; Nicholson, 1997). Studies have found that there may be a delay in the onset of PTSD until years after the initial trauma (Sack, Him, & Dickason, 1999) and that premigration trauma tends to wane with time as other postmigration variables, such as employment and housing, assume more importance (Hinton et al., 1997; Rumbaut, 1989). Nevertheless, it has been clearly established that premigration trauma has a long-standing negative impact on mental health after resettlement (e.g., Chung & Kagawa-Singer, 1993; Hauff & Vaglum, 1995; Hinton et al., 1997). Given the multiple forms of stress that include key concerns such as war trauma and resettlement, it is essential for counselors to sort out these various forms of trauma and stress in a sequential and developmental order (Sack, 1998).

Studies have found intergroup differences among Southeast Asian populations with respect to psychological distress. Cambodians have been found to experience more psychological distress compared with other groups (e.g., Chung & Bemak, 2002b; Chung & Kagawa-Singer, 1993; Mollica et al., 1987), which has been attributed to the Cambodian refugees' experience of the genocide orchestrated by the Pol Pot regime. Vietnamese and Chinese-Vietnamese have been found to be the least distressed compared with other groups, which Chung and Kagawa-Singer (1993) found was associated with higher levels of education, better English language skills, the fact that some had managed to arrive with financial assets, and access into the already established Chinatown communities in the United States. Furthermore, Beiser (1988) suggested that the relative size of ethnic communities may be responsible for ethnic differences in the rate of depression among this population. A larger ethnic community may provide more social support, thus buffering stress and reducing depression.

At-Risk Groups

Specific subgroups within the Southeast Asian refugee population have been identified as at risk for developing serious mental health problems. For example, older refugees may be at risk for psychological problems. This may be due to older refugees encountering more difficulties in adjustment, such as downward social mobility, conflicts with children, changing family dynamics, more difficulty in learning English, and difficulty finding work (Bemak & Chung, 2000; Buchwald, Manson, Ginges, Keane, & Kinzie, 1993; Chung & Kagawa-Singer, 1993). Refugees who are less proficient in English are also at higher risk for depression because of the linkage of poor English proficiency and employment status (Chung & Kagawa-Singer, 1993; Hinton et al., 1997).

Gender differences in psychological distress have also been found for Southeast Asian refugees, with women reporting a significantly higher level of psychological distress than their male counterparts. In 1980, the United Nations High Commissioner for Refugees designated refugee women as a high-risk group for developing serious psychological problems due to their premigration war experiences of rape, sexual abuse, and violence (Refugee Women in Development, 1990). In addition, in the resettlement country, refugee women not only have to cope with their premigration traumas but also encounter significant challenges in postmigration adjustment (Chung, 2000).

Although refugee women in general are at risk, within the Southeast Asian refugee population, Cambodian women specifically have been found to be at greater risk for developing serious mental health problems due to their experiences during the Pol Pot Khmer Rouge government (Chung, 2000; Mollica, et al., 1985). It has been found that Cambodian refugee women reported nearly 9 times more trauma than other Southeast Asian refugee groups (Mollica, Lavelle, & Khoun, 1985). For example, in one study 95% of the Cambodian women reported that they had been sexually abused or raped (Mollica, 1986). In a community sample of 300 Cambodian refugee women, 22% reported death of a spouse, and 53% reported loss or death of other family members (Chung, 2000). Three specific subgroups of Cambodian refugee women have been identified as high risk: (a) those who have been raped or sexually abused, (b) those who are widowed, and (c) those who have lost their children (Caspi, Poole, Mollica, & Frankel, 1998). In response to the severity of the premigration traumatic experiences, some older Cambodian women have displayed nonorganic or psychosomatic blindness (Van Boemel & Rozee, 1992). The degree of this disorder is significantly related to the number of years the women were interned in the camps and the degree and level of traumatic events they witnessed. Gender differences were also found in the predictors of psychological distress between and within Southeast Asian refugee groups (Chung & Bemak, 2002b; Chung et al., 1998). To be effective, it is critical that counselors examine in depth the differences between refugee women and men with regard to the type of distress predictors and the level and degree of psychological distress.

Children and adolescents have also been identified as a group at risk. Premigration trauma is a precursor to high school dropout rates and low grade point averages (Ima & Rumbaut, 1989). Parental stress and depression have a negative impact on children's psychosocial adjustment and academic achievement (Chung & Bemak, 2000; Rumbaut, 1989). Dealing with racial prejudice at school and other stressors such as learning English can affect successful adjustment (Schaprio, 1987). In addition, differences have been found between the first and second waves of refugees, with children from the second wave reporting more difficulties in adjustment (Chung & Bemak, 2000), demonstrating that it is important to examine inter- and intragroup differences. Vietnamese Amerasians and unaccompanied minors are specifically at risk given their unique circumstances (Bemak & Chung, 1998, 1999).

Cultural Belief Systems

Studies have found that Southeast Asian refugees report high frequencies of somatic symptoms with no apparent organic pathology, including headaches, weakness, dizziness, abdominal pain, and fatigue (Caspi et al., 1998; Chung & Kagawa-Singer, 1995; E. H. Lin, Carter, & Kleinman, 1985). Similar to clients from non-Western backgrounds, Southeast Asian refugees exhibit distress through bodily complaints (Farooq, Gahir, Okeyere, Sheikh, & Oyebode, 1993; Kleinman & Kleinman, 1985; Ohaeri & Odejide, 1994; Roberts, 1994). It has been suggested that Southeast Asian refugees express depression and other psychological problems in a manner that is consistent with their cultural belief systems (e.g., Chung & Kagawa-Singer, 1995; K. M. Lin et al., 1979). These studies have indicated that Southeast Asian refugees, like other Asian populations, tend to express psychological distress as neurasthenia, which is comprised predominantly of somatic symptoms (e.g., headaches, weakness, pressure on the chest or head) but with depression, anxiety, and psychosocial dysfunction. Mental illness is highly stigmatized in most Asian cultures; therefore, the expression of neurasthenic symptoms may be a culturally sanctioned method of expressing psychological distress (Cheung, 1982; Chung & Kagawa-Singer, 1995; Kleinman, 1982). However, it is important to acknowledge that although many Southeast Asian refugees exhibit distress through somatic channels, they are also capable of discussing their problems in psychological terms (Cheung, 1982; Kinzie et al., 1982; Mollica et al., 1987).

Southeast Asian refugees' conceptualization of mental health differs from the Western framework, which in turn influences their help-seeking behavior and therefore treatment expectations. How can a Western counselor be effective with this population if there is disparity regarding the conceptualization of mental illness between therapist and client? It is critical for the counselor to be aware of and understand the client's conceptualization of problems within the context of the client's culture and to use culturally sensitive therapeutic interventions and skills (Bemak & Chung, 2000; Kagawa-Singer & Chung, 1994; Kleinman, Eisenberg, & Good, 1978; Kleinman & Good, 1985; Pedersen, 2000). Furthermore, the counselor must acknowledge the fact that many Southeast Asian refugees are unfamiliar with Western mental health concepts because few had ever been exposed to mental health treatment in their home countries (Chung & Kagawa-Singer, 1995; Chung & Lin, 1994; K. M. Lin & Masuda, 1983). There were no psychiatrists in Laos; South Vietnam had only a handful of psychiatrists in 1975; and it is doubtful that there were mental health professionals in Cambodia. Consequently, when Southeast Asian refugees seek help from Western counselors, they expect a medical approach and quick symptom relief. Given their view of mental illness as akin to physical disorders, they often request injections or medication (Chung & Okazaki, 1991).

Even so, many Southeast Asian refugees reject Western practices and prefer traditional healing practices that involve belief in possession, soul loss, and witchcraft (Chung & Lin, 1994). Rituals for exorcism, performed by shamans and Taoist priests in Vietnam (Hickey, 1964) and by Buddhist monks in Laos and Cambodia (Westermeyer, 1973), consist of calling back the soul of individuals believed to be suffering from soul loss and asking local guardian gods for protection. Fortune-telling with cards and coins, the Chinese horoscope, and physiognomy (palm reading and reading of facial features) are also popular methods of treatment.

A major influence on the Southeast Asian belief system is Chinese medical practices. Vietnamese, Cambodians, and Hmong regularly use Chinese folk remedies including herbal concoctions and poultices; forms of acupuncture; acupressure and massage; and the dermabrasive practices of cupping, pinching, rubbing, and burning (D. L. Nguyen, Nguyen, & Nguyen, 1987). Because mental illness is seen as a disturbance of the internal vital energy, acupuncture is often used as a remedy for depression and psychosis.

Although religious beliefs differ among Southeast Asian refugee groups, health and mental health practices are influenced by religious and medical practices. For example, Vietnamese religious beliefs consist of a combination of Buddhism, Taoism, and Confucianism. The Vietnamese values share commonalities with Chinese cultural concepts such as filial piety, ancestor worship, interpersonal relationships based on hierarchical roles and reciprocal obligations, high regard for education, a strong family orientation, and loss of face. Thervada Buddhism, in which the attainment of spiritual enlightenment is valued over the achievement of material success, plays a central role in every aspect of a Cambodian's life. Laotians strongly believe in animism (belief in the supernatural, gods, demons, and evil spirits) as an essential part of everyday life. Illnesses are commonly treated by the shaman through practices such as "string tying," in which a cord is tied around the wrist to enable a person to communicate with the spirit of deceased ancestors or to prevent the loss of a sick person's soul. The string may be perceived as a symbol of a patient's spiritual wholeness and his or her social and familial support system (Muecke, 1983).

Furthermore, culture influences the expression of grief and bereavement. Under the Pol Pot regime, Cambodians were forbidden to perform traditional mourning rituals that are fundamental to the Buddhist belief (Ross, 1990). Any open display of grief was a sufficient pretext for death threats and even murder (Vickery, 1984). Given the death and loss experienced by this population, it is critical that counselors take into account cultural styles of grief and bereavement as well as allow refugee clients to display a cultural manifestation of bereavement.

Barriers to Mainstream Mental Health Services and Use of Traditional Methods

Many studies have identified the serious need for mental health services among the Southeast Asian refugee population (e.g., Gong-Guy, 1987; Kinzie & Manson, 1983; Mollica, Wyshak, Coelho, & Lavelle, 1985). Although there is a great need for mental health services, only a small percentage of this group have utilized mainstream mental health services or even those services targeting Asian clients (S. Sue, Fujino, Hu, Takeuchi, & Zane, 1991). The main reason for the low utilization of mainstream mental health services is that these services are not culturally responsive (Kagawa-Singer & Chung, 1994; S. Sue et al., 1991). When refugees enter mainstream mental health services, the environment is unfamiliar to them. There might be not only a language barrier between the client and the counselor but also cultural differences in both verbal (e.g., tone and volume of speaking) and nonverbal (e.g., eye contact and personal space) behaviors. For example, if the counselor should happen to have his or her soles of the feet facing the Southeast Asian refugee client or pat the head of a child, it would be considered to be extremely offensive. The counselor may not be aware of the effect of this nonverbal behavior. Poor accessibility may also be a hindrance to the utilization of mainstream mental health services (K. M. Lin, Inui, et al., 1982). Clinics and private offices are often located in places that cannot easily be reached, and using public transportation to get to these places may be a difficult task for Southeast Asian refugees, especially those individuals with poor English skills. Simple tasks such as working out a bus timetable, a bus route, or the payment may be highly stressful. Furthermore, many refugees may be unaware of the types and availability of mental health services (Van Deusen, 1982).

When considering or providing mainstream mental health services for Southeast Asian refugees, the cultural frame of reference must be kept in mind. Southeast Asian refugees' help-seeking behavior is influenced by culturally based attitudes (Van Deusen, 1982; Vignes & Hall, 1979). For example, traditional beliefs, superstitions, and belief in the supernatural are common barriers to mainstream mental health care (Tung, 1983). This population often relies on indigenous healers and folk medicine (Egawa & Tashima, 1982; Muecke, 1983; Yeatman & Dang, 1980). Many Southeast Asian refugees reject Western practices and prefer traditional healing (Hickey, 1964; Westermeyer, 1973).

Chung and Lin (1994) found that many Southeast Asian refugees reported concurrent utilization of both traditional and Western mainstream health care methods. This population of refugees in Chung and Lin's study reported a preference for traditional methods of healing, and their utilization of mainstream services in the United States was a reflection of the unavailability of traditional methods. Such behavior suggests a critical need for health and mental health services for this population. Hence, it is important for counselors to be aware, acknowledge, and accept that Southeast Asian refugee clients may concurrently utilize both Western and traditional healing methods.

Counseling Southeast Asian Refugees

In view of the cultural beliefs and preference for traditional health care methods, it is crucial that counselors work cooperatively with bilingual/bicultural mental health professionals, community leaders, elders, and traditional healers (e.g., spiritual leaders, monks, priests, herbalists, and shamans). Bilingual/bicultural mental health professionals not only are interpreters or translators but also serve as specialized mental health professionals who are familiar with both Western models of mental health and the unique medical and psychological worldview of Southeast Asian cultures. Bilingual/bicultural mental health professionals play an important role because they not only bridge the language gap and interpret subtle cultural messages between clients and therapists but also help to establish a culturally sensitive treatment environment.

Because language differences pose a major barrier to help seeking for Southeast Asian refugees, the use of trained translators and interpreters is essential in areas where bilingual/bicultural mental health professionals are not available. Training of translators and interpreters is imperative to facilitate effective interventions and to minimize inaccuracies in communications. For example, an untrained Southeast Asian translator may be too embarrassed to tell the Western-trained counselor that certain questions may be culturally offensive to the Southeast Asian client. Sometimes inadequately trained translators may answer for the refugee client, interpreting what they believe to be the "right" answer or a respectful response. Problems can also arise because of confidentiality, poor paraphrasing of questions, or inadequate translation of problems and psychological terms into the client's language.

Even with accurate translations, misdiagnoses may occur because of cultural misunderstandings. In one instance, a Southeast Asian man was committed to a psychiatric institution and was heavily medicated because his sponsor reported that he kept referring to seeing dead relatives and speaking with them. What the sponsor failed to realize was that referring to the dead is a common and accepted behavior among people from Southeast Asian cultures (Chung & Okazaki, 1991).

Many of the principles for counseling Asian Americans also apply to Southeast Asian refugees. To be effective, counselors need to maintain both ascribed and achieved credibility with their clients in order to continue with the counseling process and avoid premature termination (S. Sue & Zane, 1987). Ascribed credibility is determined by the counselor's status (e.g., age, education, or gender), whereas achieved credibility, or gaining the trust and confidence of the client, is determined by the counselor's competency in the therapy sessions. Therefore, if the counselor initially has a low ascribed credibility, he or she can acquire credibility by being culturally aware and sensitive. To achieve trust and credibility, counselors need to be aware of the Southeast Asian refugee client's premigration history, postmigration adjustment issues, cultural belief systems pertaining to health and mental health, and the potential concurrent use of traditional and Western methods of health care.

Refugee clients are frequently preoccupied, especially in early sessions, with resolving problems associated with basic needs and services rather than working on more serious mental health concerns. This may result in refugee clients requesting help for social services, such as assistance with housing, employment, welfare, and so on. Responding to these requests rather than discounting them as inappropriate in the process of counseling will develop trust and credibility. It is important for counselors to be aware that the client's need to address these problems may be associated with personal despair and fear concerning basic needs, which may overshadow other therapeutic issues. Because these social problems about daily living are often presented to counselors rather than to other social service providers, there is a need for a linkage between existing resettlement programs, social and human service providers, and the mental health and counseling services. It is important that counselors understand the refugee client's unfamiliarity with the Western psychotherapeutic method of talk therapy and the low ascribed credibility of talk therapy. Subsequently, one way of beginning counseling sessions with refugee clients is to discuss everyday survival issues, such as asking clients about their employment situation, housing, and income. These discussions over critical life issues are natural ways to lead into the pressing psychological problems that are often associated with premigration trauma and postmigration adjustment issues. The general aims of a counselor working with Southeast Asian clients should be the following: (a) to alleviate hopelessness, (b) to instill in clients faith in themselves and hope for the future, (c) to identify existing coping strategies, (d) to explore new alternative coping strategies, and (e) to help clients attain a sense of mastery and confidence over their lives.

The Multilevel Model (MLM) of Psychotherapy: An Approach to Counseling With Refugees

To effectively provide counseling for Southeast Asian refugees, counselors must be culturally sensitive and understand the individuals' and families' cultural worldview, premigration history and experience, and the extent of identification with their culture of origin. This requires not only the knowledge of Western counseling and counseling techniques but also the ability to incorporate such theories into a multicultural counseling framework. Therefore, as a critical first step in achieving cultural responsiveness, it is essential that counselors acquire multicultural skills and competencies (D. W. Sue et al., 1998). This also includes the counselors' ability to display cultural empathy (Chung & Bemak, 2002a). To be effective with refugees, it is also crucial to understand the factors associated with severe trauma and to take a multidisciplinary approach that incorporates constructs in psychology, counseling, anthropology, psychiatry, public health, social work, and sociology.

To address the complexity of these diverse bases of knowledge and skills, Bemak and Chung (Bemak, Chung, & Pedersen, 2003) have designed a comprehensive approach to counseling refugees called the Multilevel Model. The MLM takes into account the intricacy of the refugees' historical and sociopolitical background, past and present stressors, the acculturation process, and the psychosocial ramifications of adapting to a new culture while providing a psychoeducational approach that includes cognitive, affective, and behavioral interventions. Cultural foundations and their relation to community and social processes are critical in this model. The MLM includes the following four levels: Level I—Mental Health Education; Level II—Individual, Group, and/or Family Psychotherapy; Level III—Cultural Empowerment; and Level IV—Indigenous Healing. The four levels are interrelated, and there is no fixed sequence for their implementation so that they may be used simultaneously or independently. Although each level can be viewed independently, working with a client on all levels is essential to attain the desired goals of counseling. The treatment planning emphasizing or using any one level or combination of levels must be based on the assessment of the counselor. It is important to note that the use of this model does not require additional funding or resources, but rather it is anticipated that the counselor assumes a different and more diverse role as a helper.

In Level I (Mental Health Education), there is a focus on the counselor educating clients about mainstream mental health services. Many refugees are not familiar with the types of services available or with the process of mental health treatment; thus, the counselor must educate the client about issues such as the norms of behavior in the physical environment of a mental health clinic, the purpose of the intake assessment, the roles and expectations for the client and the counselor, the role of the interpreter, the types and use of intervention, the appointment system, and so on. Such information helps the Southeast Asian refugee client understand the nature of a therapeutic relationship and formulate expectations for counseling.

Level II (Individual, Group, and/or Family Psychotherapy) builds on the traditional Western techniques of counseling. The counselor must make an assessment about the individual's needs and then determine which type of counseling (i.e., individual, group, or family) would be most suitable for the particular client. Although traditional Western techniques are foreign to Southeast Asian refugee clients, it has been suggested that these traditional methods of individual and family therapy are effective with Asian clients (Zane & Sue, 1991). In particular, some specific techniques have been identified to be effective in working with this population. For example, the counselor may take a more directive and active role during counseling sessions with Southeast Asian refugees (Kinzie, 1985). Cognitive–behavioral interventions have also been recognized as being helpful with Southeast Asian refugees (Bemak & Greenberg, 1994; Egli, Shiota, Ben-Porath, & Butcher, 1991). De Silva (1985) and Mikulas (1981) suggested that this approach may be effective with refugees because of its comparability with Buddhist beliefs. Beiser (1987) maintained that cognitive–behavioral interventions are helpful to this population because the techniques assist them to reorient to the present rather than to maintain a painful preoccupation with past memories or to worry about an uncertain future.

Other techniques that can be incorporated into MLM Level II are storytelling and projective drawing. Pynoos and Eth (1984) described how these techniques can assist children who have experienced trauma to regain control over their response to the traumatic event. Bemak and Timm (1994) demonstrated the efficacy of using dream work in the therapeutic process with refugees. Other techniques that may be used in individual counseling include gestalt, relaxation, role-playing, and psychodrama.

Although group therapy has not been used extensively as a therapeutic intervention with Southeast Asian refugees, a few studies have pointed toward its effectiveness with this population. Friedman and Jaranson (1994) indicated that highly traumatized refugees have found solace in group therapy. Kinzie et al. (1988) instituted a 1-year therapy group for Southeast Asian refugees that incorporated discussions about somatic symptoms, cultural conflicts, and loss, with the group structure allowing flexibility with therapy session times and duration. The group approach may naturally lend itself to include psychoeducational information sessions (MLM Level I), traditional group counseling (MLM Level II), and cultural empowerment group meetings (MLM Level III).

Southeast Asian refugees are from collectivistic cultures that emphasize interdependence, a focus on family and group rather than on oneself, and obligation and responsibility to the family and group (Morris & Silove, 1992; Rechtman, 1997). Hence, group and family counseling may be more culturally appropriate than individual counseling because family is central to the Southeast Asian culture. It is important to note that given the emphasis on extended rather than nuclear family, family therapy for this population may include the extended family members. Mental health professionals have stated the importance of family therapy with refugees, explaining that the roots, experiences, and subsequent family system problems with acculturation make family counseling an ideal intervention strategy (Bemak, 1989; Lee, 1989). Counselors who use family therapy must have a clear understanding and knowledge about the cultural background and traditional relationships in the family.

Level III (Cultural Empowerment) provides another important dimension in the healing of the refugee client. Cultural empowerment consists of assisting the Southeast Asian refugee client in gaining a better sense of environmental mastery. Frequently, the counselor is unfamiliar with a multicultural framework and may focus exclusively on mental health concerns while neglecting basic issues of adaptation in daily life. Many counselors find themselves faced with refugee clients who are initially more interested in working on survival issues, such as housing and employment. The refugees may be more interested in trying to understand and make sense of their new environment rather than in discussing psychosocial adjustment and interpersonal issues. As mentioned earlier, it is important to address these issues as fundamental concerns before other psychological problems can be explored. Cultural empowerment directly addresses these adjustment issues. Counselors must therefore be sensitive to the difficulties inherent in adjusting to a new culture and provide case management through assistance and guidance that will lead to a sense of empowerment for the refugee clients. In MLM Level III—Cultural Empowerment, the counselor is not expected to be a case manager for the client but rather assume the role of a "cultural guide," providing the client with relevant information about how the American social service system works and answering questions about the host culture. In addition, by serving as a cultural broker, the counselor may educate the refugee client about the legal system governing certain practices and information that may be neglected by social agencies. For example, school teachers and police have often mistaken coin rubbing, an Asian traditional medical treatment method that leaves bruises on the skin, for child abuse (D. L. Nguyen et al., 1987).

In fostering cultural empowerment, the counselor may also become an advocate to ensure that clients' rights and entitlements are not violated. For example, if Southeast Asian clients share with the counselor their experiences of racism in the United States, the counselor may inform the clients about legal and personal methods of dealing with this situation. Furthermore, the counselor may also assume the role of a change agent and facilitate the education of Southeast Asian refugee communities as well as the wider society regarding racism and discrimination toward this group. Another example is assisting refugees who feel exploited by employers, especially if their qualifications and training were not recognized in the resettlement country, or who are underemployed or given jobs that require training that they already had without adequate pay. Compounding the situation is the report by Southeast Asian refugees that their fellow workers discriminate against them because they have a reputation of working hard and long hours, behaviors that may be resented and envied by others (Pernice & Brook, 1996). Therefore, assisting Southeast Asian clients in accessing community resources and opportunities, and helping them to develop cultural and self-empowerment leading toward successful adjustment, are important expansions in the role of the counselor.

In Level IV (Indigenous Healing), the counselor integrates Western and traditional healing methodologies. The World Health Organization (1992) described how an integration of indigenous healing with Western traditional healing practices resulted in more effective outcomes. Such integration may be best accomplished in cooperation with indigenous healers who are known to refugee community members. As indicated previously, Chung and Lin (1994) found that there was a preference among Southeast Asian refugees to utilize traditional methods of healing rather than Western counseling and that a large percentage of this population concurrently used both traditional and Western methods. Counselors working with this population not only must acknowledge that their clients may prefer traditional practices or want to combine traditional and Western methods but also must be willing to integrate the refugee clients' healing methods with the Western treatment techniques. To this end, counselors will benefit from approaching healers or community elders to work cooperatively and in conjunction with them in the treatment (Chan, 1987; Hiegel, 1994). This may require counselors to identify traditional healers within the Southeast Asian community, form therapeutic alliances, and work in partnership to provide an integration of conventional Eastern counseling interventions and traditional healing. This requires the counselor to be flexible, open, and culturally sensitive (Bemak et al., 2003). It should be noted that not all traditional healers are legitimate, so it is important to use community members to assist in identifying legitimate healers.

Case Study

The case study of Mrs. N is provided to assist readers in understanding the complex issues that Southeast Asian refugee clients present in counseling.

Mrs. N is a 52-year-old Cambodian woman who came to the United States in 1984. Her husband had worked as an engineer in Cambodia and, because he was educated, was placed in a detention facility during the Pol Pot regime. Acquaintances told Mrs. N that her husband was subjected to forced labor in the camp, without adequate food, clothing, or water. She also learned that he was routinely tortured and once after trying to escape was brutally beaten and burned. Mrs. N learned that her husband had died in the camps and often found herself wondering about how he had died, imagining many awful possibilities.

When she learned that her husband had died, Mrs. N, her daughter (at the time 10 years old), and her sister fled through the jungles of Cambodia to Thailand. Because of dangerous and terrible travel conditions, it was a very difficult journey. They narrowly escaped death by hiding from soldiers three times and were hungry, tired, and ill for much of their journey through the jungle. Mrs. N's sister was shot and killed when they were only 5 miles from Thailand. At the time of the shooting, Mrs. N grabbed her daughter and ran deep into the woods, hiding there for 2 days before attempting again to cross the river into Thailand. Once safely across, they were escorted to a refugee camp and hoped to gain entry into the United States. The living conditions in the camp were poor, and Mrs. N and her daughter shared a tent with two other families. After a year and a half of waiting, a church in Springfield, Massachusetts, became her sponsor, and Mrs. N and her daughter relocated to the United States.

It has been more than 20 years since Mrs. N and her daughter moved to the United States. Her daughter, now in her late 30s, appears to be well adjusted and has a number of Cambodian and American friends. However, Mrs. N continues to have many problems. She still has frequent nightmares about the war atrocities she witnessed and the deaths of her husband and her sister. Mrs. N is generally quiet about her nightmares and does not talk about them much with others. Apart from attending special ceremonies and occasional parties, she remains quietly by herself or with two other widowed Cambodian women her own age. Having taken many ESL courses, Mrs. N's English skills have improved, and she holds a job as a baker in a local food store. She often feels sad and has frequent thoughts of ending her life. She explains that the only reason for staying alive is her daughter. Mrs. N came to the clinic on the recommendation of an El Salvadorian coworker who was familiar with mental health treatment.

The intervention model used for the case of Mrs. N is the MLM of psychotherapy for refugees. The levels of the model are explained below.

Level I—Mental Health Education

Although Mrs. N came to the clinic through a referral of a friend, the counselor (Dr. A) wanted to assess her understanding and expectations about counseling. Dr. A quickly determined that the friend who had referred Mrs. N had provided a good overview about the counseling process. One area that needed clarification was Dr. A's role as a counselor. Mrs. N had assumed that Dr. A would be directive in telling her what to do to feel better. Dr. A carefully explained how she would assist Mrs. N to gain better self-understanding and feel better and how their work together might help Mrs. N.

Level II—Individual, Group, and/or Family Psychotherapy

In the assessment of Mrs. N, it was clear to Dr. A that she was experiencing PTSD. Dr. A decided that initially Mrs. N would benefit from individual short-term therapy to address her PTSD symptomatology and depression. As Dr. A heard Mrs. N describing her loneliness and lack of companionship, she thought about the Cambodian culture and Mrs. N's background. Exploring with Mrs. N about her days in Cambodia, she learned that Mrs. N had many friends and an active social life in Cambodia. Mrs. N commented, "I really enjoyed that time at home. There was always someone to talk with then." On the basis of an understanding that the Cambodian culture emphasizes family and community, combined with the fact that Mrs. N was lonely, Dr. A recommended that after short-term individual counseling Mrs. N continue with group counseling to deal with unresolved issues related to leaving her home country, adapting to a new culture, and losing her husband and sister.

Dr. A was conducting an open membership group in the clinic for refugee women who had lost family members and felt that the format, shared experiences with peers and interpersonal communication, would be beneficial for Mrs. N. The group therapy sessions consisted of bereavement and grief counseling sessions and explorations to identify, acknowledge, and cope with loss and bereavement. The structure of the group also allowed for an examination of associated issues so that in later sessions Mrs. N could explore her forced migration from Cambodia and problems in adapting to a new culture.

Level III—Cultural Empowerment

In the later group sessions, there would be an incorporation of Level III, Cultural Empowerment, focusing on psychoeducational training to enhance acculturation skills. Difficulties in adjusting to a foreign culture; strategies for adaptation; cognitive, emotional, and behavioral responses to cultural and identity loss; and other available resources were all presented and discussed during this time. Furthermore, Dr. A had established a relationship with one of the Cambodian community leaders who worked in a resettlement agency to periodically meet and discuss the general themes emerging in the group (maintaining confidentiality) related to cultural realities for Cambodian single women.

Level IV—Indigenous Healing

Dr. A believed that it was important to learn about the Cambodian culture because she had been identified by the Cambodian community as a professional with cultural sensitivity and an openness to perspectives about traditional healing methods that are important to the Cambodian community. Although Dr. A was not a Buddhist and did not understand many of the religious practices, she understood from her previous clients and contact with the community leader that there were important practices in the Buddhist religion that were closely aligned with the healing process. Despite her Western training as a counselor, she was open to incorporating traditional healing as a curative element to help her Southeast Asian clients. Thus, Dr. A acknowledged that if Mrs. N believed in traditional practices (Level IV—Indigenous Healing), they could readily be introduced and incorporated at any time during the individual or group therapy. In fact, the Cambodian community leader had told her that there were special ceremonies done by Buddhist monks that brought peace for the deceased. In the counseling sessions, Dr. A explored Mrs. N's belief in this practice and whether she was interested in participating in the ceremony with a Buddhist monk. Mrs. N responded, "I am afraid to finally 'let go,' but I think it would be best for everyone if I did." The support and integration of cultural healing practices in conjunction with Western counseling practices were instrumental in providing culturally sensitive treatment for Mrs. N.

Conclusion

The case of Mrs. N can be viewed as a typical situation for many Southeast Asian refugees. The implementation of the MLM provides an important framework from which to work with the Southeast Asian refugees. The model does not require the counselor to work sequentially on each level and does not necessitate additional resources or funding. To have a more in-depth understanding of the MLM regarding such issues as the concurrent usage of multiple levels of the MLM; incorporation of bilingual/bicultural mental health workers in the psychotherapeutic process; gaining cross-cultural understanding and awareness; skill development in cross-cultural work; selection of individual, group, and/or family therapy as a method of treatment; and so on, refer to the book by Bemak et al. (2003) entitled *Counseling Refugees: A Psychosocial Approach to Innovative Multicultural Interventions*. More important, the utilization of the MLM is an expansion of the counselor's role to incorporate culturally sensitive intervention strategies specific for the Southeast Asian refugee.

References

Beiser, M. (1987). Changing time perspective and mental health among Southeast Asian refugees. *Culture, Medicine, and Psychiatry, 8,* 22–27.

Beiser, M. (1988). Influences of time, ethnicity, and attachment on depression in Southeast Asian refugees. *American Journal of Psychiatry, 145,* 46–51.

Bemak, F. (1989). Cross-cultural family therapy with Southeast Asian refugees. *Journal of Strategic and Systemic Therapies, 8,* 22–27.

Bemak, F., & Chung, R. C.-Y. (1998). Vietnamese Amerasians: Predictors of distress and self-destructive behavior. *Journal of Counseling & Development, 76,* 452–458.

Bemak, F., & Chung, R. C.-Y. (1999). Vietnamese Amerasians: The relationship between biological father, psychological distress, and self-destructive behavior. *Journal of Community Psychology, 27,* 443–456.

Bemak, F., & Chung, R. C.-Y. (2000). Psychological interventions with immigrants and refugees. In J. F. Aponte & J. Wohl (Eds.), *Psychological interventions and cultural diversity* (pp. 200–213). Needham Heights, MA: Allyn & Bacon.

Bemak, F., & Chung, R. C.-Y. (2003). Multicultural counseling with immigrant students in schools. In P. B. Pedersen & J. C. Carey (Eds.), *Multicultural counseling in schools: A practical handbook* (pp. 84–101). Boston: Allyn & Bacon.

Bemak, F., Chung, R. C.-Y., & Pedersen, P. (2003). *Counseling refugees: A psychosocial approach to innovative multicultural interventions*. Westport, CT: Greenwood Press.

Bemak, F., & Greenberg, B. (1994). Southeast Asian refugee adolescents: Implications for counseling. *Journal of Multicultural Counseling and Development, 22,* 115–124.

Bemak, F., & Timm, J. (1994). Case study of an adolescent Cambodian refugee: A clinical, developmental, and cultural perspective. *International Journal of the Advancement of Counseling, 17,* 47–58.

Berry, J. W. (1990). Psychology of acculturation. In R. W. Brislin (Ed.), *Applied cross-cultural psychology* (pp. 232–253). Newbury Park, CA: Sage.

Berry, J. W., & Annis, R. C. (1974). Acculturative stress: The role of ecology, culture, and differentiation. *Journal of Cross-Cultural Psychology, 5,* 382–406.

Brown, G. (1982). Issues in the resettlement of Indochinese refugees. *Social Casework, 63,* 155–159.

Buchwald, D., Manson, S. M., Ginges, N. G., Keane, E. M., & Kinzie, D. (1993). Prevalence of depressive symptoms among established Vietnamese refugees in the United States. *Journal of General Internal Medicine, 8,* 76–81.

Carlson, E. B., & Rosser-Hogan, R. (1994). Cross-cultural response to trauma: A study of traumatic experiences and posttraumatic symptoms in Cambodian refugees. *Journal of Traumatic Stress, 7*(1), 43–58.

Caspi, Y., Poole, C., Mollica, R. F., & Frankel, M. (1998). Relationship of child loss to psychiatric and functional impairment in resettled Cambodian refugees. *Journal of Nervous and Mental Disease, 186,* 484–491.

Chan, F. (1987, April). *Survivors of the killing fields.* Paper presented at the Western Psychological Association Convention, Long Beach, CA.

Cheung, F. H. (1982). Psychological symptoms among Chinese in urban Hong Kong. *Social Science and Medicine, 16,* 1339–1344.

Chung, R. C.-Y. (2000). Psychosocial adjustment of Cambodian refugee women: Implications for mental health counseling. *Journal of Mental Health Counseling, 23,* 115–126.

Chung, R. C.-Y., & Bemak, F. (1995). The effects of welfare status on psychological distress among Southeast Asian refugees. *Journal of Nervous and Mental Disease, 184,* 346–353.

Chung, R. C.-Y., & Bemak, F. (2000). Vietnamese refugees' levels of distress, social support, and acculturation: Implications for mental health counseling. *Journal of Mental Health Counseling, 22,* 150–161.

Chung, R. C.-Y., & Bemak, F. (2002a). The relationship between culture and empathy. *Journal of Counseling & Development, 80,* 154–159.

Chung, R. C.-Y., & Bemak, F. (2002b). Revisiting the California Southeast Asian mental health needs assessment data: An examination of refugee ethnic and gender differences. *Journal of Counseling & Development, 80,* 111–119.

Chung, R. C.-Y., Bemak, F., & Kagawa-Singer, M. (1998). Gender differences in psychological distress among Southeast Asian refugees. *Journal of Nervous and Mental Disease, 186,* 112–119.

Chung, R. C.-Y., & Kagawa-Singer, M. (1993). Predictors of psychological distress among Southeast Asian refugees. *Social Science and Medicine, 36,* 631–639.

Chung, R. C.-Y., & Kagawa-Singer, M. (1995). Interpretation of symptom presentation and distress: A Southeast Asian refugee example. *Journal of Nervous and Mental Disease, 183,* 639–648.

Chung, R. C.-Y., & Lin, K. M. (1994). Help-seeking behavior among Southeast Asian refugees. *Journal of Community Psychology, 22,* 109–120.

Chung, R. C.-Y., & Okazaki, S. (1991). Counseling Americans of Southeast Asian descent: The impact of the refugee experience. In C. C. Lee & B. L. Richardson (Eds.), *Multicultural issues in counseling: New approaches to diversity* (pp. 107–126). Alexandria, VA: American Association for Counseling and Development.

De Silva, P. (1985). Buddhism and modern behavioral strategies for the control of unwanted intrusive cognitions. *The Psychological Record, 35,* 437–443.

Egawa, J. E., & Tashima, N. (1982). *Indigenous healers in Southeast Asian refugee communities.* San Francisco: Pacific Asian Mental Health Research Project.

Egli, A., Shiota, N., Ben-Porath, Y., & Butcher, J. (1991). Psychological interventions. In J. Westermeyer, C. Williams, & A. Nguyen (Eds.), *Mental health services for refugees* (pp. 157–188). Washington, DC: U.S. Government Printing Office.

Farooq, S., Gahir, M. S., Okeyere, E., Sheikh, A. J., & Oyebode, F. (1993). Somatization: A transcultural study. *Journal of Psychosomatic Research, 39,* 883–888.

Fawzi, M. C. S., Pham, T., Lin, L., Nguyen, T. V., Ngo, D., Murphy, E., & Mollica, R. F. (1997). The validity of posttraumatic stress disorder among Vietnamese refugees. *International Society for Traumatic Stress Studies, 10*(1), 101–108.

Friedman, M., & Jaranson, J. (1994). The applicability of the posttraumatic stress disorder concepts to refugees. In A. J. Marsella, T. Bornemann, S. Ekblad, & J. Orley (Eds.), *Amidst peril and pain: The mental health and well-being of the world's refugees* (pp. 207–288). Washington, DC: American Psychological Association.

Gong-Guy, E. (1987). *The California Southeast Asian mental health needs assessment.* Oakland, CA: Asian Community Mental Health Services.

Hauff, E., & Vaglum, P. (1995). Organized violence and the stress of exile. *British Journal of Psychiatry, 166,* 360–367.

Hickey, G. G. (1964). *Village in Vietnam.* New Haven, CT: Yale University Press.

Hiegel, J. P. (1994). Use of indigenous concepts and healers in the care of refugees: Some experiences from the Thai border camps. In A. J. Marsella, T. Bornemann, S. Ekblad, & J. Orley (Eds.), *Amidst peril and pain: The mental health and well-being of the world's refugees* (pp. 293–310). Washington, DC: American Psychological Association.

Hinton, W. L., Tiet, Q., Tran, C. G., & Chesney, M. (1997). Predictors of depression among refugees from Vietnam: A longitudinal study of new arrivals. *Journal of Nervous and Mental Disease, 185,* 39–45.

Huang, L. N. (1989). Southeast Asian refugee children and adolescents. In J. T. Gibbs & L. N. Huang (Eds.), *Children of color: Psychological interventions with minority children* (pp. 264–304). San Francisco: Jossey-Bass.

Ima, K., & Rumbaut, R. (1989). Southeast Asian refugees in American schools: A comparison of fluent-English-proficient students. *Topics in Language Disorders, 9*(3), 54–75.

Kagawa-Singer, M., & Chung, R. C.-Y. (1994). A paradigm for culturally based care in ethnic minority populations. *Journal of Community Psychology, 22,* 192–208.

Kinzie, J. D. (1985). Overview of clinical issues in the treatment of Southeast Asian refugees. In T. C. Owan (Ed.), *Southeast Asian mental health: Treatment, prevention, services, training, and research* (pp. 113–135). Washington, DC: National Institute of Mental Health.

Kinzie, J. D., Leung, P., Bui, A., Ben, R., Keopraseuth, K. O., Riley, C., et al. (1988). Group therapy with Southeast Asian refugees. *Community Mental Health Journal, 23*(2), 157–166.

Kinzie, J. D., & Manson, S. (1983). Five years' experience with Indochinese refugee psychiatric patients. *Journal of Operational Psychiatry, 14*(3), 105–111.

Kinzie, J. D., Manson, S., Do, V., Nguyen, T., Anh, B., & Pho, T. (1982). Development and validation of a Vietnamese language depression rating scale. *American Journal of Psychiatry, 139,* 1276–1281.

Kleinman, A. (1982). Neurasthenia and depression: A study of somatization and culture in China. *Culture, Medicine, and Psychiatry, 6,* 117–190.

Kleinman, A., Eisenberg, L., & Good, B. (1978). Culture, illness, and care. *Annals of Internal Medicine, 88,* 251–258.

Kleinman, A., & Good, B. (Eds.). (1985). *Culture and depression: Studies in the anthropology and cross-cultural psychiatry of affect and disorder.* Berkeley: University of California Press.

Kleinman, A., & Kleinman, J. (1985). Somatization: The interconnections in Chinese society among culture, depressive experiences, and the meaning of pain. In A. Kleinman & B. Good (Eds.), *Culture and depression: Studies in the anthropology and cross-cultural psychiatry of affect and disorder* (pp. 149–160). Berkeley: University of California Press.

Lee, E. (1989). Assessment and treatment of Chinese American immigrant families. *Journal of Psychotherapy, 6*(102), 99–122.

Liebkind, K. (1996). Acculturation and stress: Vietnamese refugees in Finland. *Journal of Cross-Cultural Psychology, 27,* 161–180.

Lin, E. H., Carter, W. B., & Kleinman, A. M. (1985). An exploration of somatization among Asian refugees and immigrants in primary care. *American Journal of Public Health, 75,* 1080–1084.

Lin, K. M., Inui, T. S., Kleinman, A. M., & Womack, W. (1982). Sociocultural determinants of the help-seeking behavior of patients with mental illness. *Journal of Nervous and Mental Disease, 170,* 78–85.

Lin, K. M., & Masuda, M. (1983). Impact of the refugee experience: Mental health issues of the Southeast Asians. In *Bridging cultures: Southeast Asian refugees in America* (pp. 32–52). Los Angeles: Special Services for Groups, Asian American Community Mental Health Training Center.

Lin, K. M., Masuda, M., & Tazuma, L. (1982). Adaptational problems of Vietnamese refugees: Part III. Case studies in clinic and field: Adaptive and maladaptive. *Psychiatric Journal of the University of Ottawa, 7*(3), 173–183.

Lin, K. M., Tazuma, L., & Masuda, M. (1979). Adaptation problems of Vietnamese refugees: II. Life changes and perception of life events. *Archives of General Psychiatry, 37*, 447–450.

Mikulas, W. (1981). Buddhism and behavior modification. *The Psychological Record, 31*, 331–342.

Miranda, A. O., & Matheny, K. B. (2000). Sociopsychological predictors of acculturative stress among Latino adults. *Journal of Mental Health Counseling, 22*, 306–317.

Mollica, R. F. (1986, August). *Cambodian refugee women at risk*. Paper presented at the annual convention of the American Psychological Association, Washington, DC.

Mollica, R. F., & Jalbert, R. R. (1989). *Community of confinement: The mental health crisis on Site Two: Displaced persons' camps on the Thai-Kampuchean border*. Boston: Committee on World Federation for Mental Health.

Mollica, R. F., Lavelle, J., & Khoun, F. (1985, May). *Khmer widows at highest risk*. Paper presented at the Cambodian Mental Health Conference, New York.

Mollica, R. F., McInnes, K., Pham, T., Fawzi, M. C. S., Murphy, E., & Lin, L. (1998). The dose—effect relationships between torture and psychiatric symptoms in Vietnamese ex-political detainees and a comparison group. *Journal of Nervous and Mental Disease, 186*, 543–553.

Mollica, R. F., Wyshak, G., Coelho, R., & Lavelle, J. (1985). *The Southeast Asian psychiatry patient: A treatment outcome study*. Boston: Indochinese Psychiatric Clinic.

Mollica, R. F., Wyshak, G., & Lavelle, J. (1987). The psychosocial impact of war trauma and torture on Southeast Asian refugees. *American Journal of Psychiatry, 144*, 1567–1572.

Morris, P., & Silove, D. (1992). Cultural influences in psychotherapy with refugee survivors of torture and trauma. *Hospital and Community Psychiatry, 43*, 820–824.

Muecke, M. A. (1983). Caring for Southeast Asian refugees in the U.S.A. *American Journal of Public Health, 73*, 431–438.

Murphy, H. B. (1977). Migration, culture, and mental health. *Psychological Medicine, 7*, 677–681.

Nguyen, D. L., Nguyen, P. H., & Nguyen, L. H. (1987). *Coin treatment in Vietnamese families: Traditional medical practice vs. child abuse*. Unpublished manuscript.

Nguyen, S. (1982). Psychiatric and psychosomatic problems among Southeast Asian refugees. *Psychiatric Journal of the University of Ottawa, 7*(3), 163–172.

Nicholson, B. F. (1997). The influence of premigration and postmigration stressors on mental health: A study of Southeast Asian refugees. *Social Work Research, 21*, 19–31.

Ohaeri, J. U., & Odejide, O. A. (1994). Somatization symptoms among patients using primary health care facilities in a rural community in Nigeria. *American Journal of Psychiatry, 151*, 728–731.

Pedersen, P. (2000). *A handbook for developing multicultural awareness*. Alexandria, VA: American Association for Counseling and Development.

Pernice, R., & Brook, J. (1996). Refugees' and immigrants' mental health: Association of demographic and postimmigration factors. *Journal of Social Psychology, 136*, 511–519.

Pynoos, R., & Eth, S. (1984). Children traumatized by witnessing acts of personal violence: Homicide, rape, or suicide behavior. In S. Eth & R. Pynoos (Eds.), *Posttraumatic stress disorder in children* (pp. 17–44). Washington, DC: American Psychiatric Press.

Rechtman, R. (1997). Transcultural psychotherapy with Cambodian refugees in Paris. *Transcultural Psychiatry, 34*, 359–375.

Refugee Women in Development. (1990). *What is refugee?* (Available from www.refwid.org)

Roberts, S. M. (1994). Somatization in primary care: The common presentation of psychosocial problems through physical complaints. *Nurse Practitioner, 19*(47), 50–56.

Ross, R. R. (Ed.). (1990). *Cambodia: A country study*. Washington, DC: Federal Research Division, Library of Congress.

Rumbaut, R. G. (1989). Portraits, patterns, and predictors of the refugee adaptation process: A comparative study of Southeast Asian refugees. In D. W. Haines (Ed.), *Refugees and immigrants: Cambodians, Laotians, and Vietnamese in America* (pp. 138–190). Totwa, NJ: Rowman & Littlefield.

Sack, W. H. (1998). Multiple form of stress in refugee and immigrant children. *Child and Adolescent Psychiatric Clinics of North America, 7,* 153–167.

Sack, W. H., Him, C., & Dickason, P. (1999). Twelve-year follow-up study of youths who suffered massive war trauma as children. *Journal of the American Academy of Child and Adolescent Psychiatry, 38,* 1173–1179.

Schaprio, A. (1987). Adjustment and identity formation of Lao refugee adolescents. *Smith College Studies in Social Work, 58*(3), 157–181.

Stein, B. N. (1986). The experience of being a refugee: Insights from the research literature. In C. L. Williams & J. Westermeyer (Eds.), *Refugee mental health in resettlement countries* (pp. 5–23). Washington, DC: Hemisphere.

Sue, D. W., Carter, R. T., Casas, J. M., Fouad, N. A., Ivey, A. E., Jensen, M., et al. (1998). *Multicultural counseling competencies: Individual and organizational development.* Thousand Oaks, CA: Sage.

Sue, S., Fujino, D., Hu, L., Takeuchi, D., & Zane, N. (1991). Community mental health services for ethnic minority groups: A test of cultural responsive hypothesis. *Journal of Consulting and Clinical Psychology, 59,* 533–540.

Sue, S., & Zane, N. (1987). The role of culture and cultural techniques in psychotherapy: A critique and reformulation. *American Psychologist, 42,* 37–45.

Tayabas, T., & Pok, T. (1983). The arrival of the Southeast Asian refugees in America: An overview. In *Bridging cultures: Southeast Asian refugees in America* (pp. 3–14). Los Angeles: Special Services for Groups, Asian American Community Mental Health Training Center.

Tobin, J. J., & Friedman, J. (1983). Spirits, shamans, and nightmare death: Survivor stress in a Hmong refugee. *Journal of Orthopsychiatry, 53,* 439–448.

Tung, T. M. (1983). Psychiatric care for Southeast Asians: How different is different? In T. C. Owan (Ed.), *Southeast Asian mental health: Treatment, prevention, services, training, and research* (pp. 5–40). Washington, DC: National Institute of Mental Health.

Van Boemel, G., & Rozee, P. D. (1992). Treatment for psychosomatic blindness among Cambodian refugee women. In E. Cole, O. M. Espin, & E. D. Rothblum (Eds.), *Refugee women and their mental health: Shattered societies, shattered lives* (pp. 239–266). New York: Haworth.

Van Deusen, J. (1982). Part 3. Health/mental health studies of Indochinese refugees: A critical overview. *Medical Anthropology, 6,* 213–252.

Vickery, M. (1984). *Cambodia 1975–85.* Boston: South End Press.

Vignes, A. J., & Hall, R. G. W. (1979). Adjustment of a group of Vietnamese people to the United States. *American Journal of Psychiatry, 136*(4A), 442–444.

Westermeyer, J. (1973). Lao Buddhism, mental health, and contemporary implications. *Journal of Religion and Health, 12,* 181–187.

Westermeyer, J. (1986). Migration and psychopathology. In C. L. Williams & J. Westermeyer (Eds.), *Refugee mental health in resettlement countries* (pp. 39–59). Washington, DC: Hemisphere.

World Health Organization. (1992). *Refugee mental health: Draft manual for field testing.* Geneva, Switzerland: Author.

Yeatman, G. W., & Dang, V. V. (1980). Cao Gio (coin rubbing): Vietnamese attitudes towards health care. *Journal of the American Medical Association, 247,* 1303–1308.

Zane, N., & Sue, S. (1991). Culturally responsive mental health services for Asian Americans: Treatment and training issues. In H. Myers, P. Wohlford, P. Guzman, & R. Echemendia (Eds.), *Ethnic minority perspectives on clinical training and services in psychology* (pp. 47–58). Washington, DC: American Psychological Association.

Counseling Korean Americans

Catherine Y. Chang

Korean Americans are a subpopulation of the Asian group, which has become the fastest growing ethnic minority group in the United States (Hamilton, 1996, Leong, Wagner, & Kim, 1995; Sandhu, 1997). Population trends suggest that within the Asian population, Korean Americans are one of the most rapidly increasing immigrant groups, representing 11% of the total Asian population (U.S. Census Bureau, 2000).

To understand Korean Americans as a distinct subgroup of Asian Americans, it is important to understand the commonalities shared by the Asian American population as a whole while studying the distinctiveness of Korean Americans. The purpose of this chapter is to highlight the distinctiveness of the Korean American population, keeping in mind the commonalities shared by the Asian American population as a whole. Immigration history, traditional Korean values, acculturation and ethnic identity issues, and mental health issues of Korean Americans are discussed as well as counseling strategies for understanding and working with Korean American clients.

Immigration History

Since the passing of the Immigration and Naturalization Law of 1965, the rate of immigration by Koreans has increased dramatically. In 1980, there were approximately 350,000 Korean Americans living in the United States; by 1990, that number had more than doubled to 800,000 (U.S. Department of Commerce, 1995); and by the 2000 census, there were 1,076,872 Korean Americans (U.S. Census Bureau, 2000). Other estimates suggest that the Korean American population is over 2 million (Van der Woude, 1998). Having immigrated since 1965, the majority of Korean Americans are foreign born (U.S. Department of Commerce, 1993) and have a shorter immigration history compared with Japanese and Chinese Americans (Chen, Edwards, Young, & Greenberger, 2001). Thus, research on Koreans in the Untied States is still in the exploratory stage, and most of the empirical research has been accomplished since 1976 (Hurh & Kim, 1990a).

Koreans immigrated to improve the quality of life for themselves as well as their family members; therefore, they tend to immigrate to this country as family units rather than as individuals (Hurh & Kim, 1990b; Min, 1984). Also, the current immigration policy emphasizes family reunification, and with the growing number of Korean Americans presently in the United States, there will be more individuals in Korea eligible to apply for entry under the family reunification category (Ishii-Kuntz, 1997).

Traditional Korean Values

Korean tradition is based predominantly on Confucian ideology, which has been most influential in shaping the behavior pattern and structure of the family and community (Chang & Myers, 1997; I. H. Park & Cho, 1995). The family is seen as the central pillar of Confucianism, and thus, family cohesion and continuity serve as the foundation for sustaining the human community and the state (I. H. Park & Cho, 1995).

Also according to Confucian ideology, the parental role is authoritarian in nature. The paternal and maternal roles are complementary rather than symmetrical, with the father's task guided by its emphasis on guidance, instruction, discipline, and financial support and the mother's role serving as emotional monitor, nurturer, and healer within the family (Rohner & Pettengill, 1985; Song, 1999). Fathers express their devotion to the children through strictness and mothers through indulgence. Parents are to dispense wisdom, responsibility, and benevolence to their children, and children are expected to obey, be loyal, and respect their parents (Hyun, 2001).

Filial piety, "to respect one's parents and to care for one's parents" (Sung, 1995, p. 240), regulates the intergenerational relationship between parents and children throughout the life cycle (K. C. Kim, Kim, & Hurh, 1991). Filial obligation dictates that children will provide for the parents physically, financially, and sociopsychologically as well as honor and respect them by consulting parents concerning family and personal matters (K. C. Kim et al., 1991; Youn & Song, 1991). Filial piety ensures harmony and order in the family and thus society (Hyun, 2001) by reducing intergenerational conflicts (Kauh, 1997). Despite changes in family structure and exposure to American cultural values, Korean Americans tend to maintain their filial obligation. Ishii-Kuntz (1997) reported that Korean American adults are more likely to provide various types of support, including financial and emotional, compared with their Chinese and Japanese counterparts.

Closely connected to filial piety is the importance of family and group orientation, or the idea of collectivism, because it is in the family context that filial piety is practiced. The family and society are viewed as more important than the individual; the family's and society's needs take precedence over individual needs (Ho, 1990). It is more important to fulfill one's expected roles both within the family and in society even at the cost of individuality (Hyun, 2001). Koreans are taught to respect their traditions and to adhere to standards of proper behavior without emphasizing a private self that is separate from the social context. The importance of group behavior can be found in the Korean word for conformity, which means maturity and inner strength (H. Kim & Markus, 1999). From an early age, Korean children are taught that all members of the family are responsible for the protection and welfare of the family and that the family is primary (Y. R. Lee & Sung, 1998; Sung, 1995).

Related to this family and group orientation are the concepts of shame and guilt. In the Korean tradition, the concept of "loss of face" implies that the entire family loses respect and community status when an individual is shamed. This places an inordinate burden on the individual to maintain harmony and order and to minimize any conflicts and problems that may bring shame and guilt to the family (Thomas, 2000). By placing such value on harmonious relations, Korean culture reflects a restrained rather than an expressive orientation. Any form of communication, expression, and behavior that undermines harmony in relationships is viewed as undesirable; therefore, confrontational, directive, or harsh behavior is avoided (J. C. Lee & Cynn, 1991).

This tendency to avoid confrontation and situations that may bring shame onto someone else places a great deal of importance on silence and high context communication. For Koreans, silence is seen as a way to promote harmony and politeness. Spoken words are often viewed suspiciously and disregarded. According to Confucianism, true communication is believed to occur from feelings and not from talking (Franks, 2000). Koreans value high context communication in which meanings are derived indirectly from the context of the communication, contrary to the United States, which values low context communication with its emphasis on clarity and explicitness of messages. This tentative style of communication emphasizes indirect, evasive messages (Yook & Albert, 1998).

Like many Asian American cultures, academic achievement and education are highly valued in the Korean American culture (Asakawa & Csikszentmihalyi, 2000; Y. E. Choi, Bempechat, & Ginsburg, 1994). In fact, Korean American parents identified educational opportunities for their children as one of the most common reasons for immigrating to the United States (Yagi & Oh, 1995). Related to this importance of education, Asian American parents expect their children to continue their education beyond college and are more likely to decide whether their children should go to college as well as discuss ACT/SAT preparation with their children compared with Caucasian American parents (Asakawa & Csikszentmihalyi, 2000). Education for Koreans is seen as one of the main channels to higher social position, and academic achievement is synonymous with prestige for the family (E. Y. Kim, 1993; S. E. Smith, 1996). The importance of education and effort is further displayed by Korean parents in that they regulate their children's time by supervising work habits, limiting free-time activities, providing the necessary resources for educational activities, and not assigning chores in an effort to leave more time for academic endeavors (Y. E. Choi et al., 1994).

Acculturation and Ethnic Identity

Acculturation and ethnic identity development, two core processes shared by all ethnic minorities, were identified by Leong (1986) as focal points for understanding Asian Americans. Acculturation involves adapting to and adopting a new culture. This process can create demands on immigrants that may conflict with their native cultural system, therefore leading to cultural conflicts. These cultural conflicts generated by the acculturation process can lead to mental health problems (Atkinson & Gim, 1989; Berry, 1997; Huang, 1994; Suinn, Khoo, & Ahuna, 1995; Ying, 1995). The process of acculturation changes over time and across generations, and it is influenced by gender, age, and length of stay in the host culture (Nah, 1993; J. Y. Shin, Berkson, & Crittenden, 2000; Wong-Rieger & Quintana, 1987).

Studies support that acculturation plays an important role in promoting understanding of ethnic minority individuals and, therefore, is an important factor to consider in counseling. The effectiveness of counseling can be influenced by the client's degree of acculturation into the dominant society (Sodowsky, Lai, & Plake, 1991). Acculturation also has been associated with patterns of conflicts, attitudes toward counselors, willingness to seek counseling services, perceived counselor credibility, client behaviors, mental health status, and well-being (Atkinson & Gim, 1989; Chang, 1998; Suinn et al., 1995).

In addition to the acculturation process, Korean Americans must go through the process of ethnic identity development. Ethnic identity refers to "a subjective sense of social boundary or self-definition" (Meleis, Lipson, & Paul, 1992, p. 99). It involves coming to terms with one's ethnic membership group as a salient reference group (E. J. Smith, 1991). One's ethnic identity develops through the experiences of ethnic group membership and integration of the group's specific values and traditions into the self. Many ethnic minorities struggle to understand their ethnic identity. Of importance to counselors, ethnic identity has been found to influence quality of life and as such acts as a mediator of mental health (S. Kim & Rew, 1994). The process of ethnic identity development interacts with contextual factors including society, family, peers, and school/work environments (Kvernmo & Heyerdahl, 1996).

Related to ethnic identity is ethnic attachment. Korean Americans maintain a high level of ethnic attachment. Many speak the Korean language, eat mainly Korean food, subscribe to Korean newspapers, maintain Korean friendships, and practice Korean customs most of the time (Hong & Min, 1999; Hurh & Kim, 1984; Min, 1991). Regardless of length of residence in the United States and level of acculturation, Hurh and Kim (1984) found that Korean immigrants maintained a high level of ethnic attachment as measured by subscribing to Korean newspapers, associating with other Koreans, and also attending a Korean church. The Koreans in this study indicated a strong sense of family priority, ethnic pride, and a preference for teaching the Korean language to their children as well as participating in Korean associations. Similarly, Hong and Min (1999) reported that second-generation Korean American adolescents tended to retain the Korean language, friendships, and ethnic identity. K. C. Kim, Hurh, and Kim (1993) also found that regardless of age or length of residence in the United States, Koreans retained a strong social and cultural ethnic attachment, including a commitment to filial piety. Kitano (1997) reported that Korean Americans had the lowest rate of outmarriages compared with other Asian American cultures. Chen et al. (2001) reported that Korean Americans were least positive about relationships with non-Asians. In addition, Hyun (2001) reported that there was no significant difference in traditional value endorsement of Korean immigrants in the United States compared with Koreans living in Korea, thus demonstrating Korean immigrants' strong connection to their ethnic values.

The Korean church serves both as a place to worship and as the social, cultural, and educational center for most Koreans. In fact, Ng (1995) estimated that 70% to 80% of Korean immigrants attend church regularly and that there is one Korean church for every 400 Koreans in the United States. The Korean church provides a reception center for new immigrants, a place of fellowship, a place where Korean customs and traditions are practiced, and a place where children are taught traditional Korean values, such as filial piety (Min, 1991; H. S. Park, Murgatroyd, Raynock, & Spillett, 1998). Thus, the Korean church assists in maintaining a high level of Korean ethnicity for many Koreans. The Korean church also serves as a buffer for depression; Koreans with a higher intrinsic religious orientation had lower depressive symptoms (H. S. Park et al., 1998).

Mental Health Issues

All immigrant minority groups are at risk for certain mental health issues. In this section, issues specific to Korean Americans are addressed with respect to stressors related to the immigration process, downward occupation mobility, interfamilial conflicts, and being a member of the "model minority."

Studies have shown that immigrants are likely to experience stresses due to minority status, prejudice and discrimination, changes in employment, communication problems, identity confusion, and differences in customs (Nah, 1993; J. Y. Shin et al., 2000; K. R. Shin, 1994). Because of the recency of immigration, many Korean Americans are especially at risk for suffering from mental health problems. Stress related to the immigration process seems to contribute significantly to family violence, alcoholism, juvenile delinquency, alienation of elders, marital and intergenerational conflicts, and mental health disorders in Korean Americans (Koh & Upshaw, 1987; Kuo, 1984).

Kuo (1984) found that Korean Americans exhibited more depressive symptoms than did Chinese, Japanese, or Filipino Americans. Lin et al. (1992) also reported elevated depression scores in Korean immigrants. K. R. Shin (1994) found that Korean American women were considerably more depressed than the average adult American, and the respondents, on average, reported moderate levels of acculturative stress. Korean American college students scored significantly lonelier than their American counterparts (Simmons, Klopf, & Park, 1991), thus putting them at risk for depression. Crittenden, Fugita, Bae, Lamug, and Lin (1992) reported that Korean college students had higher self-reported frequencies of depressive symptoms and higher rates of alcohol abuse and suicide than American students.

Many middle-class families in Korea fall to working-class status after immigrating to the United States, thus increasing the stress due to downward occupational mobility and the stresses associated with unfulfilled expectations and aspirations (Rohner, Hahn, & Koehn, 1992). Korean immigrants arrive in the United States dreaming of a better life for themselves and their children. However, many soon discover that because of language barriers and lack of acceptance of professional degrees earned at Korean universities, they cannot maintain their professional status. Therefore, they are forced to settle for manual-labor jobs in the United States. To increase their standard of living, many Korean fathers acquire second full-time jobs, and many Korean mothers seek work outside the home for the first time (Rohner et al., 1992). This downward occupational mobility may lead to loss of face, feelings of personal failure, loss of a sense of personal control and personal efficacy, impairments in self-esteem and self-adequacy, and possibly other mental health disturbances (Newman, 1988; Rohner et al., 1992).

An additional stressor for the newly immigrated Korean family involves the increase in parent–child conflicts that may result from differences in acculturation between parents and children. While parents are busy adjusting to their new life, they may have less time to spend with their children, and the children are preoccupied with adjusting to school and language acquisition (Nah, 1993). Korean children tend to adopt American values of autonomy and freedom more quickly than their traditional parents, who continue to follow Korean traditional parenting, which emphasizes authority and strict control over the children (Shrake, 1999). This can lead to cultural conflicts between the parents and the children.

Because of children's exposure to school and greater learning facility, Korean children tend to acquire the English language more quickly than their parents, leading to communication barriers between the parents and the children (J. C. Lee & Cynn, 1991), which can negatively affect the development of a functional family. Family cohesion is further threatened by parents' expectation that their children succeed academically. Korean children may feel guilt, shame, and worthlessness if they cannot meet their parents' academic expectations (Hong, 1996), which can become a major psychological burden resulting in mental health problems, social delinquency, and strained parent–child relationships (S. E. Smith, 1996).

In addition to conflicts in the parent–child relationship, Korean Americans may also experience marital discord as Korean men and women acculturate at different rates. Because of occupational downward mobility, many Korean women are forced to work outside the home for the first time. Often the women find employment more quickly than the men because they are less concerned about status and are therefore less selective. This creates a double burden for the Korean wife as she continues to perform her household tasks mandated by traditional gender-role ideology and begins to work outside the home (Hurh & Kim, 1990b). Korean men engrained with the male-dominated culture influenced by Confucian teaching may feel threatened and become more defensive and resistant to change and adaptation (Nah, 1993). Hyun (2001) found that Korean women endorsed traditional values to a lesser degree than did Korean men. These individual differences in rate of adaptation seem to complicate interpersonal relationships between men and women and between other family members.

The myth of the "model minority" may be limited to particular areas such as school and work and does not appear to extend to social relationships. Academic success does not necessarily translate to effective functioning in life (Ying et al., 2001). Chen et al. (2001) reported that European American attitudes toward Asian Americans, and more specifically Korean Americans as a subpopulation, were less positive than attitudes toward Mexican Americans and African Americans. This is consistent with Liu, Campbell, and Condie's (1995) study that showed that Latino Americans and African Americans also rated Asian Americans low in their dating preferences. Additionally, the myth of the model minority may engender a sense of pride in some Koreans, but this image may increase levels of stress and anxiety as Korean Americans attempt to live up to this stereotype.

Downward occupational mobility, language difficulties, and family stresses experienced by Korean Americans place their mental health at significant risk. Despite this risk, they are less likely to utilize social and mental health resources than the general public (K. H. Choi & Wynne, 2000). The result is emotional stress and strain without mental health intervention, which can lead to a lower quality of life and a decreased ability to adjust to stresses that occur in their lives (Chang & Myers, 1997).

Barriers to Mental Health Service

Like many Asian Americans, Korean Americans are reluctant to approach government agencies because of language and cultural barriers, whereas others are unaware of community resources (Thomas, 2000). Western-style psychotherapy with its emphasis on emotional and verbal expression may be contrary to Korean cultural values of emotional restraint and internalization of individual problems. Individuals may be reluctant to discuss their personal problems outside of the family because their behavior is a direct reflection on the entire family. By publicly admitting and discussing personal problems, the individual is bringing shame to the family name. Korean Americans who seek counseling are violating traditional cultural values by discussing the personal feelings and issues that they have been taught to repress and control (S. E. Smith, 1996).

Because of the perception that mental illness is stigmatizing and brings shame onto the family, many Korean Americans believe that mental health can and should be obtained by exercising will power and avoiding bad thoughts (Atkinson & Gim, 1989). Instead, they present somatic complaints when they need to express emotional distress or social problems. This has become so common that the somatic complaint has been named *hwa-byung*. The symptoms of *hwa-byung* include constricted or oppressed sensations in the chest, palpitations, heat sensation, flushing, headache, epigastric mass, dysphoria, anxiety, irritability, and difficulty in concentration (Lin et al., 1992). *Hwa-byung* provides a socially accepted way for Korean Americans to discuss their depressive reactions by classifying them within somatic afflictions.

Like other Asian groups, Koreans are more.likely to seek help from their family and friends, religious leaders, and church groups before seeking the help of mental health professionals (Ishii-Kuntz, 1997; Yeh & Wang, 2000). Yeh and Wang (2000) found that Koreans were significantly more likely to talk with religious leaders or engage in religious activities in coping with problems compared with other Asian groups. Consequently, when Korean Americans seek help from mental health professionals, they tend to be more psychologically disturbed than European Americans who seek help (Sue & Sue, 1977).

The myth of the model minority (i.e., hard-working, well-educated, self-contained, and self-supporting community) may divert needed resources from Korean Americans toward communities perceived to be more in need (Harris-Hastick, 1996). Mental health agencies may not be providing the needed services to Korean Americans because they perceive the Korean community to be self-sufficient.

There are many other factors that contribute to biased perceptions of Korean American clients and the lack of services provided. These factors include Korean Americans' view of mental health, their help-seeking behavior, language difficulties, the personal and cultural background of the counselor, and inadequacies in counselor training programs (Leong, 1986).

Counseling Strategies

Many Korean Americans may be unfamiliar with the concepts of Western "talk therapy" and medical approaches; therefore, mental health professionals must utilize treatment strategies that are culturally appropriate. Traditional insight-oriented therapy may be contrary to Korean values, which emphasize harmonious relationships, interdependence, self-control, emotional restraint, and result-oriented solutions (Song, 1999).

In considering counseling strategies, it is important to remember that Korean Americans may exhibit help-seeking behaviors that are different from those of White Americans. Korean Americans are more likely to solve problems on their own or rely on family members or friends (J. Y. Shin et al., 2000). They also are more likely to express psychological distress in the form of somatic illness. Korean Americans typically seek professional help as a last resort (Song, 1999).

It is also important to consider previous research on Asian American attitudes and participation in help-seeking behaviors. Studies have shown that Asian American college students are more willing to participate in academic or vocational counseling than in traditional counseling (Atkinson, Lowe, & Matthews, 1995; Gim, Atkinson, & Whiteley, 1990; S. E. Smith, 1996). Problems reflecting interpersonal or intrapersonal concerns are underendorsed by Asian Americans (Tracey, Leong, & Glidden, 1986), and Asian American women are more willing to endorse counseling-related problems than are Asian American men (Gim et al., 1990). Additionally, Korean American students reported less comfort with classroom guidance than did Caucasian students (S. E. Smith, 1996). In terms of coping strategies, Korean Americans were more likely to cope with problems by engaging in religious activities than were their other Asian American counterparts (Yeh & Wang, 2000).

In applying the research to working with Korean Americans, researchers have proposed many practical suggestions for culturally appropriate counseling. Because of Korean Americans' strong emphasis on family and reliance on family to resolve problems, counselors working to help solve problems within the family may be more effective than directly focusing on psychological and relationship problems (J. Y. Shin et al., 2000). In working within the family, it is important for the counselor to define and to respect the family members' roles, remembering the importance of hierarchical role structure. The counselor will want to work within the existing hierarchy of the family rather than changing the system. The counselor may want to consider addressing and deferring to the father as a sign of respect. If the father is not present in the counseling session, the counselor may want to encourage the mother to consult with her husband before making any counseling commitments (J. C. Lee & Cynn, 1991). To respect the family hierarchical structure, the counselor may want to consider interviewing the parents first, allowing them to discuss adult issues and express their emotions freely without loosing parental control. Interviewing the children separately from their parents will also allow the children to discuss issues they may not feel comfortable discussing in front of their parents (Song, 1999).

The Korean church plays an integral role in the lives of many Koreans. Although mental health professionals may be reluctant to discuss the role of religion and church with their clients in general, counselors may want to consider discussing religion and church with their Korean American clients (H. S. Park et al., 1998). Because Korean Americans may seek advice from their church leaders prior to seeking counseling, the mental health professional may want to consider consulting with church leaders and/or inviting them to participate in the counseling process.

For many Korean Americans, seeking counseling can be seen as bringing shame to the family. To decrease this shame, the counselor can normalize the issue for the family by explaining that their issue is a normal part of adjusting to immigration and dealing with the acculturation process (J. C. Lee & Cynn, 1991). Also, counselors may want to appropriately integrate positive reframing and compliments in the counseling process; these methods avoid shaming the clients while preserving their dignity and proper roles in the family (Song, 1999). Because Korean Americans tend to associate counseling with their children's education and are more willing to seek counseling for educational matters, it may be advantageous to initiate counseling with the focus on the children's educational planning and slowly move the family to consider additional issues (J. Y. Shin et al., 2000).

Because Korean Americans value authority and hierarchy, this may be utilized in treatment and education. Korean American clients may believe the counselor is in a higher position because of his or her professional status and professional knowledge. Counselors can use this hierarchical structure to join with the client (Song, 1999). Consistent with the hierarchical structure, Korean American clients may prefer a structured counseling situation with a directive, paternalistic, and authoritarian approach. An autocratic rather than a democratic counselor will be viewed as more credible and helpful with these clients.

Counselors also need to be aware of possible differences in communication styles. Koreans tend to value emotional restraint and silence. Counselors from a European American background may value more direct language and expression while devaluing silence. For these counselors, silence may symbolize that the person is being ignored, a sign of anger, or a sign of discomfort (Franks, 2000). Silence may not carry the same connotation for many Korean Americans. In addition to silence, self-disclosure may also become a communication obstacle. Korean Americans may avoid discussing their inner feelings, especially negative feelings. Instead, the Korean American client may discuss events or factual information or analyze problems related to other people or to people in general, thus avoiding the focus on himself or herself. By self-disclosing, the Korean client has violated the private self as well as betrayed the family, which can lead to an increase in guilt feelings. Counselors need to be mindful of Koreans' use of silence and reluctance to self-disclose in the counseling process (Yu, 1999). Also, respect for authority figures may lead Korean American clients to nod in agreement even when they do not understand or agree with what is being said (Chang & Myers, 1997).

In setting treatment goals with Koreans, it is important to be aware that traditionally Koreans are family oriented and that they value harmony, emotional restraint, and hierarchical role structure; thus, establishing individual-oriented goals will be difficult for Koreans. Korean American families are more likely to respond to treatment goals that are family oriented with a focus on the children (Song, 1999). Additionally, many Asian Americans expect a quick diagnosis and some form of treatment benefit in the early stages of counseling (Huang, 1994). Thus, focusing on symptom relief in the early stages may be helpful.

Before progressing too quickly with the Korean American client, it is important for the counselor to conduct a thorough assessment of the client, which includes not only a standard assessment but also cultural information. This will provide the counselor with valuable information, which will influence the counselor's choice of treatment. Congress's (1994) culturagram provides a useful structure for collecting cultural information and for assessing ethnic identity and acculturation. The culturagram divides cultural information into the following categories: (a) length of time in the community; (b) spoken language, native language, and English or bilingual ability; (c) contact with cultural institutions; (d) health beliefs; (e) holidays and special events; (f) educational and work values; (g) family patterns of support; (h) crisis events and stressors; and (i) education and career selection. These factors can provide the counselor with insight regarding the acculturation level and ethnic identity of the Korean American client. Although acculturation level and ethnic identity are important, counselors need to be aware that cultural issues are not always relevant or the primary issues with all Korean American clients. Counselors need to learn to differentiate between acculturation as an issue for intervention and as the basis for planning successful interventions (Chang & Myers, 1997).

Case Study

The following case study illustrates the importance of traditional Korean values and the influence of acculturation and ethnic identity development.

Sun-Hy Kim (Sunny) is a 19-year-old second-semester freshman attending an elite university. She immigrated to the United States with her parents and two younger brothers when she was 10 years old. Throughout high school, Sunny struggled with her studies, but with long hours of studying and extra tutoring, she managed to receive good grades and did well on the SAT. While in college she has experienced a world of independence. She no longer has to report to anyone about her whereabouts, she is able to go out on a school night, and she is able to socialize with people of both sexes and different ethnic backgrounds.

Sunny's parents sent her to college with the explicit direction that she was to study hard, receive good grades, and go to medical school. Sunny has discovered that she does not enjoy her science classes and does not want to become a medical doctor. She is not sure what she wants to study, but she knows that it is not medicine. She also has discovered that she enjoys having a social life, even if it means sacrificing her studies. Sunny has been convincing her parents that she is a serious student by having her roommates lie to them about her being in the library or the lab when she is out.

Sunny has been trying to fool her parents by being the obedient daughter while she is at home. She brings home many of her science books and spends hours in her bedroom telling her parents that she is studying. She hid her grades from her parents but knows that they will be very disappointed in her because she is the first person in her family to attend college. Her parents are very proud of her and tell everyone that she is an excellent student who is going to be a doctor.

While at school, Sunny feels angry and frustrated with her parents. While at home, she feels guilty and ashamed. Why can't her parents be like her roommates' parents and just let her study what she wants to and not put so much pressure on her to do well? Sunny also has been receiving pressure from her first Caucasian boyfriend, who doesn't understand why their relationship has to be a secret. Sunny is confused because she feels like she is two different people. At home, she is the obedient daughter; at school, she is the fun-loving coed.

Sunny entered the university health center complaining of headaches and stomach pains. After several visits to the health center with no success, the doctor referred her to the university counseling center. Sunny went only after receiving pressure from her boyfriend and roommates.

In conceptualizing this case, the counselor may want to consider the following questions: (a) How will you assess Sunny from a multicultural perspective? (b) What roles do acculturation and ethnic identity play in this case? (c) What major issues do you identify? (d) To what extent would you involve the family in the counseling process?

This is a typical case of a Korean American adolescent's struggle between her Korean culture and her American culture. It will be important for the counselor working with Sunny to conduct a thorough assessment that will provide information regarding her acculturation level and ethnic identity. Congress's (1994) culturagram may be a useful assessment tool. On the basis of the assessment, the counselor will want to work toward culturally responsive intervention techniques that not only recognize and respect her Korean heritage but also recognize that these values may be in conflict with her adopted American values. There are several issues present is this case, including Sunny's cultural conflicts, conflicts with parents' expectations, struggles with her school work, pressure from her boyfriend, and her somatic complaints. It will be up to the counselor to prioritize these concerns while remembering that Sunny, like many Asians, expects immediate relief. Because Sunny is away at school, family counseling may not be a consideration, but it will be important for the counselor to remember that regardless of whether the family is physically present during the counseling session, they have a great influence on Sunny's life.

Conclusion

Korean Americans are a subgroup of Asian Americans, and as such, they share many similarities to this group. However, Korean Americans also have distinct characteristics that need to be considered. Traditional Korean values include filial piety, family and group orientation, restrained communication styles, and academic achievement. Because of the recency of immigration and language difficulties, many Korean Americans are at risk for mental illness, including depression and interpersonal conflicts. This chapter has tried to address the mental health issues related to Korean Americans and has suggested some intervention strategies.

References

Asakawa, K., & Csikszentmihalyi, M. (2000). Feelings of connectedness and internalization of values in Asian American adolescents. *Journal of Youth and Adolescence, 29,* 121–145.

Atkinson, D. R., & Gim, R. H. (1989). Asian-American cultural identity and attitudes toward mental health services. *Journal of Counseling Psychology, 36,* 209–212.

Atkinson, D., Lowe, S., & Matthews, J. (1995). Asian-American acculturation, gender, and willingness to seek counseling. *Journal of Multicultural Counseling and Development, 23,* 130–138.

Berry, J. W. (1997). Immigration, acculturation, and adaptation. *Applied Psychology: An International Review, 46,* 5–34.

Chang, C. Y. (1998). *The role of distinctiveness in acculturation, ethnic identity, and wellness in Korean American adolescents and young adults.* Unpublished doctoral dissertation, University of North Carolina at Greensboro.

Chang, C. Y., & Myers, J. E. (1997). Understanding and counseling Korean Americans: Implications for training. *Counselor Education and Supervision, 37,* 35–49.

Chen, C., Edwards, K., Young, B., & Greenberger, E. (2001). Close relationships between Asian American and European American college students. *Journal of Social Psychology, 141,* 85–100.

Choi, K. H., & Wynne, M. E. (2000). Providing services to Asian Americans with developmental disabilities and their families: Mainstream service providers' perspective. *Community Mental Health Journal, 36,* 589–595.

Choi, Y. E., Bempechat, J., & Ginsburg, H. P. (1994). Educational socialization in Korean American children: A longitudinal study. *Journal of Applied Developmental Psychology, 15,* 313–318.

Congress, E. P. (1994). The use of culturagrams to assess and empower culturally diverse families. *Families in Society, 75,* 531–540.

Crittenden, K., Fugita, S., Bae, H., Lamug, C., & Lin, C. (1992). A cross-cultural study of self-report depressive symptoms among college students. *Journal of Cross-Cultural Psychology, 23,* 163–178.

Franks, P. H. (2000, March). *Silence/listening and intercultural differences.* Paper presented at the annual meeting of the International Listening Association, Virginia Beach, VA.

Gim, R., Atkinson, D., & Whiteley, S. (1990). Asian-American acculturation, severity of concerns, and willingness to see a counselor. *Journal of Counseling Psychology, 37,* 281–285.

Hamilton, B. (1996). Ethnicity and the family life cycle: The Chinese American family. *Family Therapy, 23,* 199–212.

Harris-Hastick, E. F. (1996). Voices of Korean American women. *Community Review, 14,* 34–44.

Ho, C. K. (1990). An analysis of domestic violence in Asian Americans. *Women and Therapy, 9,* 129–150.

Hong, J. J. (1996). *The Korean American family: Assimilation and its toll on the first and second generation relationship.* Brookville, NY: Long Island University. (ERIC Document Reproduction Service No. ED401348)

Hong, J., & Min, P. G. (1999). Ethnic attachment among second generation Korean adolescents. *Amerasia Journal, 25,* 165–178.

Huang, L. N. (1994). An integrative approach to clinical assessment and intervention with Asian American adolescents. *Journal of Clinical Child Psychology, 23,* 21–31.

Hurh, W. M., & Kim, K. C. (1984). Adhesive sociocultural adaptation of Korean immigrants in the U.S.: An alternative strategy of minority adaptation. *International Migration Review, 18,* 188–215.

Hurh, W. M., & Kim, K. C. (1990a). Adaptation stages and mental health of Korean male immigrants in the United States. *International Migration Review, 24,* 456–479.

Hurh, W. M., & Kim, K. C. (1990b). Correlates of Korean immigrants' mental health. *Journal of Nervous and Mental Disease, 178,* 703–711.

Hyun, K. J. (2001). Sociocultural change and traditional values: Confucian values among Koreans and Korean Americans. *International Journal of Intercultural Relations, 25,* 203–229.

Ishii-Kuntz, M. (1997). Intergenerational relationships among Chinese, Japanese, and Korean Americans. *Family Relations, 46,* 23–32.

Kauh, T. O. (1997). Intergenerational relations: Older Korean Americans' experiences. *Journal of Cross-Cultural Gerontology, 12,* 245–271.

Kim, E. Y. (1993). Career choice among second-generation Korean Americans: Reflections of a cultural model of success. *Anthropology and Education Quarterly, 24,* 224–248.

Kim, H., & Markus, H. R. (1999). Deviance or uniqueness, harmony or conformity? A cultural analysis. *Journal of Personality and Social Psychology, 77,* 785–800.

Kim, K. C., Hurh, W. M., & Kim, S. (1993). Generation differences in Korean immigrants' life conditions in the United States. *Sociological Perspectives, 36,* 257–270.

Kim, K. C., Kim, S., & Hurh, W. M. (1991). Filial piety and intergenerational relationship in Korean immigrant families. *International Journal of Aging and Human Development, 33,* 233–245.

Kim, S., & Rew, L. (1994). Ethnic identity, role integration, quality of life, and depression in Korean American women. *Archives of Psychiatric Nursing, 8,* 348–356.

Kitano, H. H. L. (1997). *Race relations* (5th ed.). Upper Saddle River, NJ: Prentice Hall.

Koh, S. D., & Upshaw, H. (1987). An experimental inquiry into depressive affect in Asian Americans. In *The Pacific/Asian American Mental Health Research Center report* (pp. 1–9). Chicago: Pacific/Asian American Mental Health Research Center.

Kuo, W. H. (1984). Prevalence of depression among Asian Americans. *Journal of Nervous and Mental Disease, 172,* 449–457.

Kvernmo, S., & Heyerdahl, S. (1996). Ethnic identity in aboriginal Sami adolescents: The impact of the family and the ethnic community context. *Journal of Adolescence, 19,* 453–463.

Lee, J. C., & Cynn, V. E. H. (1991). Issues in counseling 1.5 generation Korean Americans. In C. C. Lee & B. L. Richardson (Eds.), *Multicultural issues in counseling: New approaches to diversity* (pp. 127–140). Alexandria, VA: American Association for Counseling and Development.

Lee, Y. R., & Sung, K. T. (1998). Cultural influences on caregiving burden: Cases of Koreans and Americans. *International Journal of Aging and Human Development, 46,* 125–141.

Leong, F. T. L. (1986). Counseling and psychotherapy with Asian Americans: Review of the literature. *Journal of Counseling Psychology, 33,* 196–206.

Leong, F. T. L., Wagner, N. S., & Kim, H. H. (1995). Group counseling expectations among Asian American students: The role of culture-specific factors. *Journal of Counseling Psychology, 42,* 217–222.

Lin, K. M., Lau, J. K. C., Yamamoto, J., Zheng, Y. P., Kim, H. S., Cho, K. H., & Nakasaki, G. (1992). *Hwa-byung*: A community study of Korean Americans. *Journal of Nervous and Mental Disease, 180,* 386–391.

Liu, J. H., Campbell, S. M., & Condie, H. (1995). Ethnocentrism in dating preferences for an American sample: The ingroup bias in social context. *European Journal of Social Psychology, 25,* 95–115.

Meleis, A. I., Lipson, J. G., & Paul, S. M. (1992). Ethnicity and health among five Middle Eastern immigrant groups. *Nursing Research, 41,* 98–103.

Min, P. G. (1984). An exploratory study of kin ties among Korean immigrant families in Atlanta. *Journal of Comparative Family Studies, 15,* 59–75.

Min, P. G. (1991). Cultural and economic boundaries of Korean ethnicity: A comparative analysis. *Ethnic and Racial Studies, 14,* 225–241.

Nah, K. H. (1993). Perceived problems and service delivery for Korean immigrants. *Social Work, 38,* 289–296.

Newman, K. S. (1988). *Falling from grace: The experience of downward mobility in the American middle class.* New York: Free Press.

Ng, F. (Ed.). (1995). *The Asian American encyclopedia* (Vol. 3). New York: Marshall Cavendish.

Park, H. S., Murgatroyd, W., Raynock, D. C., & Spillett, M. A. (1998). Relationship between intrinsic–extrinsic religious orientation and depressive symptoms in Korean Americans. *Counseling Psychology Quarterly, 11,* 315–324.

Park, I. H., & Cho, L. J. (1995). Confucianism and the Korean family. *Journal of Comparative Family Studies, 26,* 117–134.

Rohner, R. P., Hahn, B. C., & Koehn, U. (1992). Occupational mobility, length of residence, and perceived maternal warmth among Korean immigrant families. *Journal of Cross-Cultural Psychology, 23,* 366–376.

Rohner, R. P., & Pettengill, S. M. (1985). Perceived parental acceptance–rejection and parental control among Korean adolescents. *Child Development, 56,* 524–528.

Sandhu, D. S. (1997). Psychocultural profiles of Asian and Pacific Islander Americans: Implications for counseling and psychotherapy. *Journal of Multicultural Counseling and Development, 25,* 7–22.

Shin, J. Y., Berkson, G., & Crittenden, K. (2000). Informal and professional support for solving psychological problems among Korean-speaking immigrants. *Journal of Multicultural Counseling and Development, 28,* 144–159.

Shin, K. R. (1994). Psychosocial predictors of depressive symptoms in Korean American women in New York City. *Women and Health, 21,* 73–82.

Shrake, E. K. (1999, April). *The effects of parenting styles on adolescent problems: A case study of Korean Americans.* Paper presented at the annual meeting of the American Educational Research Association, Montreal, Quebec, Canada.

Simmons, C. M., Klopf, D. W., & Park, M. S. (1991). Loneliness among Korean and American university students. *Psychological Reports, 68,* 754.

Smith, E. J. (1991). Ethnic identity development: Toward the development of a theory within the context of majority/minority status. *Journal of Counseling & Development, 70,* 181–188.

Smith, S. E. (1996). Willingness of Korean American elementary school children to participate with counselors in a developmental guidance program. *Early Child Development and Care, 125,* 85–94.

Sodowsky, G. R., Lai, E. W. M., & Plake, B. S. (1991). Moderating effects of sociocultural variables on acculturation attitudes of Hispanics and Asian Americans. *Journal of Counseling & Development, 70,* 194–204.

Song, S. J. (1999). Using solution-focused therapy with Korean families. In K. S. Ng (Ed.), *Counseling Asian families from a systems perspective* (pp. 127–141). Alexandria, VA: American Counseling Association.

Sue, D. W., & Sue, D. (1977). Barriers to effective cross-cultural counseling. *Journal of Counseling Psychology, 24,* 420–429.

Suinn, R. M., Khoo, G., & Ahuna, C. (1995). The Suinn–Lew Asian Self-Identity Acculturation Scale: Cross-cultural information. *Journal of Multicultural Counseling and Development, 23,* 139–148.

Sung, K. (1995). Measures and dimensions of filial piety in Korea. *The Gerontologist, 35,* 240–247.

Thomas, E. K. (2000). Domestic violence in the African American and Asian American communities: A comparative analysis of two racial/ethnic minority cultures and implications for mental health service provision for women of color. *Psychology: A Journal of Human Behavior, 37,* 32–43.

Tracey, T. J., Leong, F. T., & Glidden, C. (1986). Help seeking and problem perception among Asian Americans. *Journal of Counseling Psychology, 33,* 331–336.

U.S. Census Bureau. (2000). *Profiles of general demographic characteristics: 2000.* Retrieved June 22, 2004, from http://www.census.gov/prod/cen2000/dp1/2k00.pdf

U.S. Department of Commerce. (1993). *We the Americans: Asians.* Washington, DC: U.S. Government Printing Office.

U.S. Department of Commerce. (1995). *Statistical abstract of the United States.* Washington, DC: U.S. Government Printing Office.

Van der Woude, M. (1998, January/February). Korean students in the United States. *ESL Magazine,* 28–29.

Wong-Rieger, D., & Quintana, D. (1987). Comparative acculturation of Southeast Asian and Hispanic immigrants and sojourners. *Journal of Cross-Cultural Psychology, 18,* 345–362.

Yagi, D. T., & Oh, M. Y. (1995). Counseling Asian American students. In C. C. Lee (Ed.), *Counseling for diversity: A guide for school counselors and related professionals* (pp. 61–83). Boston: Allyn & Bacon.

Yeh, C., & Wang, Y. W. (2000). Asian American coping attitudes, sources, and practices: Implications for indigenous counseling strategies. *Journal of College Student Development, 41,* 94–103.

Ying, Y. W. (1995). Cultural orientation and psychological well-being in Chinese Americans. *American Journal of Community Psychology, 23,* 893–911.

Ying, Y. W., Lee, P. A., Tsai, J. L., Hung, Y., Lin, M., & Wan, C. T. (2001). Asian American college students as model minorities: An examination of their overall competence. *Cultural Diversity and Ethnic Minority Psychology, 7,* 59–74.

Yook, E. L., & Albert, R. D. (1998). Perceptions of the appropriateness of negotiation in educational settings: A cross-cultural comparison among Koreans and Americans. *Communication Education, 47,* 18–29.

Youn, G., & Song, D. (1991). Aging Koreans' perceived conflicts in relationships with their offspring as a function of age, gender, cohabitation status, and marital status. *Journal of Social Psychology, 132,* 299–305.

Yu, M. M. (1999). Multimodal assessment of Asian families. In K. S. Ng (Ed.), *Counseling Asian families from a systems perspective* (pp. 15–26). Alexandria, VA: American Counseling Association.

Appendix

Additional Resources

Hurh, W. M. (1998). *The Korean Americans.* Westport, CT: Greenwood Press.

Institute for Korean-American Culture
    www.ikac.org
Korean Cultural Service
    www.koreanculture.org
Korean Heritage Library
    www.usc.edu/isd/locations/ssh/korean/
Korean International Service
    www.korea.net
National Korean American Service and Education Consortium
    www.nakasec.org

The Latino American Experience

Latino *is a sociological/political term that identifies a culture shared by several ethnic groups in the United States, including Mexicans, Puerto Ricans, and Cubans as well as other ethnic groups with origins in Central and South America. Latino culture developed as a result of the fusion of Spanish culture (brought to the Americas by missionaries and soldiers) with native indigenous cultures and African (the result of the slave trade) cultures in Mexico, South America, and the Caribbean Basin. Commonality among Latino American ethnic groups is found in the use of the Spanish language, the influence of Roman Catholic traditions, and strong kinship bonds between family members and friends. However, there is a wide variety within each Latino American group based on variables such as degree of acculturation, socioeconomic status, language preference, and generation in the United States.*

Counseling Latinas: Culturally Responsive Interventions

Sandra I. Lopez-Baez

Bienvenidos, amigos y amigas! Because of the rapid growth of the Latino population in the United States and the increased demand for mental health services from this group, there is a need for counselors to understand Latinos and their culture. This chapter offers a brief synthesis of the interrelatedness of Latino values and mental health function within a cultural context. The three cases that are presented illustrate the complex interface between ethnicity, culture, and mental health as addressed by the *Diagnostic and Statistical Manual of Mental Disorders* (*DSM–IV–TR;* American Psychiatric Association, 2000). In the *DSM–IV–TR,* an outline for cultural formulation is presented. This outline helps counselors understand the individual's cultural and social influence group and the cultural context relevant to clinical care. The outline consists of five categories:

1. *Cultural identity* of the individual,
2. *Cultural explanations* of the individual's illness,
3. *Cultural factors* related to psychosocial environment and level of functioning,
4. *Cultural elements of the relationship* between the individual and the clinician, and
5. Overall *cultural assessment* for diagnosis and care. (American Psychiatric Association, 2000, pp. 879–880)

The items in this outline provide counselors with information related to individuals' environmental and social supports directly affecting their daily functioning. Vontress, Johnson, and Epp (1999) presented an analogy of cultural groups serving a similar purpose to humans as their prenatal attachment to the mother's womb, nourishing and sustaining the fetus. Upon birth, an individual's cultural group shapes and molds the individual to adjust to a referent social order. Vontress et al. (1999) stated, "It is visible and invisible, conscious and unconscious, cognitive and affective. It provides rules, mores, or psychological principles that people live by" (p. 14). Therefore, it is imperative that counselors incorporate a way of understanding their own as well as the client's cultural context in assessment, diagnosis, and treatment considerations.

Case 1

Idalia is a 30-year-old, Catholic, Peruvian woman married for 10 years to Osvaldo. They have four children: 9-year-old twins, Carlos and Marife; 8-year-old Jaime; and 6-year-old Pedro. Idalia has been growing more anxious every day. Anxiety has interfered with her sleep and daily functions; she complains of "nervios." She and Osvaldo are arguing more frequently because Idalia wants to work full-time now that all of the children are in school until 3:00 p.m. She had a part-time job at the children's school as a teacher aide, and the principal has made her an offer, a full-time position, come fall. However, Osvaldo wants her to stay at home like his mother did. He claims there is enough for her to do at the house. Her dilemma stems from trying to be a good mother and wife, plus attempting to work outside of the home to secure a college fund for the children. "Whom should I let down?" she asks her counselor.

Case 2

Carmen is 24 years old, Catholic, Puerto Rican (native islander), and single. She is a graduate student in accounting at a state university. Her faculty adviser and mentor, Dr. White, has also been supportive and encouraging as she pursues her studies. Her family is proud of her accomplishments. They are a tight-knit group and have sacrificed much to help her complete her education. Carmen's boyfriend, Ismael, has been with her since high school. He joined the Navy after high school graduation and served 6 years. Their relationship continued while he was serving in the military. He wrote frequently, and they saw each other while he was on shore leave. Upon discharge, Ismael came back as a certified welder and was employed by a contractor who mentored and showed him the details of the business. Ismael is planning to start his own company with the savings he has accrued over the years. He has asked Carmen to marry him; the problem is that he and Carmen have grown apart as she furthered her schooling. Ismael is happy to marry her and have her stay at home as a homemaker, taking care of him and the children. Carmen and her family expect her to be a professional woman with managerial responsibilities, following a "career path." Dr. White has recommended her to several Fortune 500 companies that are willing to hire her as a comptroller as soon as she graduates. This entails a lot of travel and business meetings as well as earning a six-figure salary. Ismael is very uncomfortable with all of this. He has told her how "out of place" he feels with her colleagues and acquaintances. They both realize there is a "chasm" growing between them, but they do not know what to do. If they marry and she does what Ismael wants, she lets her family and Dr. White down. "Ismael is a good man, just very traditional. My family likes him but disagrees with his views." She states that the combined pressure of the situation and school demands are affecting her appetite and eating habits. She has lost over 30 pounds in 6 weeks, feels cold all of the time, and has trouble concentrating. "How do I choose?" she asks her counselor.

Case 3

Consuelo is 55 years old, a mother of three children, and a grandmother with two grandchildren. She is a widow who married at age 18 in Mexico. Her husband was killed when Consuelo was 30 years old, and she was left to raise the children on her own. Both her and her husband's family helped as much as they could, but it was hard to make ends meet. Consuelo migrated to New Jersey to live with a relative and work as a seamstress. Her success was such that she set up her own store and made enough money to put all three of her children through college and professional school. One is a physician; one is an architect; and her youngest is a nurse. She is very involved with her church, community, and grandchildren, whom she sees frequently. Her concern stems from her two grandchildren, a boy and a girl born to her oldest son. Her oldest son married a divorced American woman who had no children from her prior marriage. Consuelo disapproves of divorce because she is Catholic. Furthermore, the children are being raised "with no religion" and "no respect for their elders." They do not speak Spanish or like "traditional" Mexican foods or music. Consuelo feels like a failure. "Where did I go wrong? Is this someone's envidia toward me?" she asks her counselor.

In reading these cases, one questions whether it matters what culture or ethnic background these women come from. It seems that the problems presented by these women share a universal theme concerning women of all cultures. In truth, many human problems are universal in nature. However, ethnicity and culture have a direct impact on the manner in which symptoms are manifested by individuals and addressed by clinicians.

Latino is a pan-ethnic label applied to a heterogeneous group of people (Romero, 2000). Governmental institutions and media also use the term *Hispanic* in lieu of *Latino* to refer to this growing population of individuals who were born in or trace their ancestral background to one of the Spanish-speaking Latin American countries, the Caribbean, or Spain (Marin & Marin, 1991). Individuals within this population use their country of origin (e.g., Mexico, Chile, Puerto Rico) as a self-identifier, rather than the label *Hispanic*. Because the term *Hispanic* is used interchangeably with *Latino*, for purposes of this chapter, the term *Latino/Latina* is used as the descriptor for this population that shares a Latino/Hispanic origin.

The U.S. Census Bureau has reported an increasing demographic growth trend in the Latino population since 1999. In the year 2000, the U.S. Census (Guzman, 2000) reported the Latino population as increasing to 35.5 million or 12.5% of the total U.S. population (not including the 3.8 million Latinos in the Commonwealth of Puerto Rico). The Latino population in the United States has been increasing since 1990 by 2% to 4% each year. This rate of growth is expected to continue throughout the year 2050, so that by the year 2050 Latinos will outnumber all other U.S. minorities and represent between 18% and 25% of the U.S. population. This growth trend is highly significant because it will affect communities, services, and systems both public and private. Counselors must develop an understanding of the cultural framework from which to reach this population.

Latinas and Their Cultural Values

Latinas are a diverse group within the U.S. population. They represent 1 out of every 14 women in the United States. Latinas share a core of common cultural values as well as differences in degrees of monolingualism to bilingualism, traditionalism to assimilation in their cultural characteristics, and ethnic identity and degree of acculturation. They are active participants in a growing female workforce (Amaro & Russo, 1987; Arredondo, 1991).

Counselors who understand values embraced by Latino culture can adjust their interventions to meet this population's needs. Many authors (Arredondo, 1991; Canino, 1982; Marin & Marin, 1991; Paniagua, 1998; Vasquez, 1994) have discussed *familismo* as a salient culture-specific value among Latinos. Familismo is described as a strong identification with and attachment to both nuclear and extended family members. This is accompanied by strong feelings of loyalty, reciprocity, and solidarity among members of the family. Three value orientations accompany familismo: a perceived obligation to provide material and emotional support to the members of the extended family, the reliance on relatives for help and support, and the perception of relatives as behavioral and attitudinal referents.

Familismo includes the extended family composed of blood relatives and those considered kin, who may not be blood relatives but are in close relationship and actively involved with the family. This family orientation is frequently misunderstood by counselors unfamiliar with familismo. If construed as a clinically significant entity, it is most often interpreted as dependence, immaturity, enmeshment, and inability to take initiative. The counselor may perceive the client as uncooperative and even paranoid if the client is unwilling to discuss family issues on the first visit. Familismo emphasizes interdependence over independence, whereas independence is valued as a sign of adjustment in American culture.

Paniagua (1998) defined *respeto* as valuing and acknowledging hierarchies that define an individual's "proper" place in society by age, gender, race, and class. For Latinas, respeto dictates that behavior toward older individuals or toward men should be characterized by a respectful, subordinate attitude. Direct assertive behavior or a confrontational manner aimed at an authority figure such as an older man or a parental figure is not culturally supported.

Simpatia is another Latino characteristic described by Paniagua (1998) as the need for behaviors that promote smooth and pleasant social relationships that move individuals to show conformity and empathy toward others. There is a tendency to avoid interpersonal conflict and emphasize positive behaviors by being agreeable. Simpatia may interfere with decision-making ability through unassertiveness and indirect client expressions. This may be perceived as a Latina's inability or resistance to be forceful and direct.

Another characteristic discussed by various authors (Marin & Marin, 1991; Paniagua, 1998; Vasquez-Nutall, Romero-Garcia, & DeLeon, 1987) is *fatalismo*, or the belief in fate. Fatalismo is the conviction that life's events are inevitable and attributed to God's will. Individuals feel at the mercy of natural and supernatural forces that they cannot control and must resign themselves to their fate. This implies vulnerability and lack of control in the presence of adverse events. Conversely, it can be a potentially adaptive response to uncontrollable life situations, making the person resilient.

Other characteristics have converse counterparts in U.S. cultural values. Paniagua (1998), Marin and Marin (1991), and Triandis (1989) described *colectivismo* or *alocentrismo* as a value central to Latino culture. This value emphasizes interdependence, field sensitivity, conformity, mutual empathy, willingness to sacrifice for the welfare of others, and trust in members of their group. It represents a tendency for the individual to place the collective's needs over his or her own, focusing on the needs, objectives, and points of view of the reference group. Latinos prefer nurturing, loving, intimate, and respectful relationships rather than confrontational, superordinated ones. Group orientation, rather than individual objectives, tends to be the norm for this group. This contrasts with the *individualismo* valued by U.S. culture. Individualismo focuses on competition that leads to success. When colectivismo is devalued and individualismo is preferred, collectivistic behavior may be misconstrued as maladaptive. Problems with setting boundaries, inability to be assertive, exhibiting resistance to therapeutic change, passivity, or a passive–aggressive stance are behavioral outcomes of colectivismo that are frequently misconstrued by counselors as significant symptoms in need of clinical interventions.

Personalismo can be contrasted to *formalismo*, preferred in many settings within U.S. culture. *Personalismo* (Paniagua, 1998) is an orientation toward people characterized by warmth, sharing personal information, and preference for physical closeness to others. There is a preference for contacts that are personal over impersonal or institutional ones. High importance is given to the qualities of positive interpersonal and social skills as well as trust. *Formalismo* stresses proper formal relationships that focus on consideration and respect, showing compliance with those in power, and observing personal respect to allow individuals to feel that their personal power is being acknowledged.

Marianismo is a label for the expectation that women should be yielding, obedient, dependent, timid, sentimental, gentle, and sexually pure until marriage. Latinas are expected to model themselves after the Virgin Mary (virtuous) so as to be spiritually superior to men and capable of enduring a lot of suffering produced by men. Taking care of the husband and children, and placing their needs above their own, is a trademark of marianismo expected of Latinas.

Clinical Considerations

Latinas tend to present their problems in a culturally prescribed fashion. Their symptoms or problems are not readily apparent to non-Latino counselors unless they are familiar with the culture. In following the outline for cultural context specified by the *DSM–IV–TR*, it is important to understand how to elicit cultural information. Castillo (1997) equated this process to conducting "clinical ethnography" in that each item of the outline probes further into the individual's cultural framework or worldview.

In exploring the *cultural identity* of a Latina, the counselor must address issues related to her ethnic or cultural reference group. The counselor needs to consider questions such as the following: How involved is she with her culture of origin and with the host (American) culture? How fluent is she in her native language and in English? Which language does she prefer? Consider that each culture has typical forms of mental illness with idiosyncratic manifestations. An example that may consternate counselors is the different manifestations of marianismo. The Latina may appear to passively accept oppression and mistreatment yet relate how depressed she feels about it. Cultural schemas vary, and expression of illness has varying degrees of acceptance by the group. Counselors must attempt to familiarize themselves with these cultural manifestations to better understand a Latina's cultural identity and her understanding of it.

Cultural explanations of the individual's illness/problems require the counselor to understand how the client expresses symptoms or distress. In addition, the meaning and perceived severity of symptoms in relation to cultural reference group norms must also be understood. The counselor may ask the client what she thinks is the nature of the problem in an attempt to understand the client's experience. Fatalismo dictates that the client's fate is preordained; thus, it may be the will of God in action and must not be challenged. Counselors may interpret this as resistance or passivity when what is needed is a reframe of the problem and possible alternatives to solving it. It is important to explore how the Latina's reference group has historically described the problem or concern and what actions her culture endorses to address such concerns. Is there social support within the client's community for individuals who are experiencing these concerns or problems? These questions should be explored in the counseling sessions to better understand the client's cultural realm.

Cultural factors related to the psychosocial environment address culturally relevant or culture-based sources of social or environmental stress and their impact on the client's social supports. Castillo (1997) contended that these factors also affect level of functioning, level of impairment, recovery process, and relapse. Additional considerations include the role of religion, relatives, and kinship networks in providing emotional and informational support. Counselors working with Latinas need to assess the client's degree of involvement with extended family as a response to familismo needs. Another important consideration is a Latina's colectivismo outlook, in which the reference group becomes a powerful influence in her life.

In the *client/counselor relationship*, differences in culture and social status between client and counselor are important considerations. These influence the diagnosis and prescribed treatment of the presenting symptoms or problem. The counselor's demeanor is crucial in the establishment of rapport. Personalismo dictates a degree of warmth and caring different from a detached professional stance. Offering the proper respeto by addressing the person by title rather than by first name is important. Keep in mind that simpatia dictates a non-confrontational approach by the client and the counselor. Castillo (1997) defined *diagnostic ethnocentrism* as the use of a counselor's own cultural schemas in diagnosing a client's symptoms. Such schemas bias the counselor's understanding of the client's behavior, method of relating, and reaction to rapport. Language can become a serious barrier when the client has limited use of English in narrating her problem and the counselor assumes a different meaning than the one intended by the client. An illustration is the Latina who, in trying to relate her anxiety about a stressful day, used the phrase "dropped acid" (referring to the acid in her stomach). The counselor referred her for drug screening. The client's verbal ability to communicate symptoms must be understood to avoid such mistakes.

In the overall *cultural assessment*, the counselor has explored the seven cultural values of familismo, respeto, simpatia, fatalismo, colectivismo, personalismo, and marianismo, leading to a culture-based assessment summary. This can become the foundation for a culture-based treatment plan. Counselors working with Latinas need to be thorough in their cultural assessment and include cultural patterns, their effect on treatment decisions, and recommendations for care. Vasquez (1994) suggested that counselors working with Latinas must address the foundation for the development of their mental health problems. She discussed lack of confidence due to gender role attributions, tendency to blame self (or one's lack of ability) for failures, and the inability to take credit for success (related to collectivism) as the underlying base for most problems that Latinas experience. Latino values encompass many positive aspects. However, when the context in which these values are embraced changes, the same values become an obstacle to adaptation and a source of stress that create difficulties in coping.

Review of the Three Cases

The case of Idalia presents a Latina facing the common anxiety of a modern-day two-working-parents household. Compounding this is the cultural tenet that married Latinas are responsible for domestic work, their children, and their husband. This is further compounded by the marianismo expectation to yield to her husband's wishes and endure suffering.

Cultural values need not interfere with Idalia's adaptation to American culture. She and Osvaldo will be straddling two cultures and raising children who will hopefully be competent bicultural individuals. Idalia's dilemma can be addressed by helping her understand how resilient she is and how helpful her financial contribution will be to the family and the children's education. This reinforces her need to be a good mother and wife as well as caring for herself within the context of the family. It is important to empower Idalia by recognizing cultural role expectations as mother and wife as well as working with her to create a bridge between her culture of origin and American culture. Her connection to Latinas, the church, and the community can become powerful allies to support and sustain her. This can become a suitable substitute for an extended network of kin who lend support to her nuclear family, an alternative to their natural environment.

The case of Carmen is colored by gender role expectations from Latino culture that clash with her new American environment. Her "self-construal" (Garcia-Prieto, 1998), or deeper cultural structure, affects her cognitions, emotions, motivations, and behaviors. Her family's support for her studies and career path nurtured her success. Her adviser has been encouraging and well meaning but fails to understand her hesitation regarding such good job offers. Dr. White's expectations are that she "make up her own mind" while failing to realize that colectivismo has been ingrained in Carmen as a cultural value and that empathy and respect to authority are operating at an unconscious level. Her need for personalismo and simpatia dictate compliance with those in power and create serious problems for her. Her weight loss may be indicative of an eating disorder of clinical significance. A thorough evaluation is necessary to recommend a course of treatment. The need to educate Carmen regarding decision making, the process of acculturation, and its stressful effects is evident. In addition, the need for same-culture peer support and validation of her dilemma are significant parts that must be considered in formulating a treatment plan. Helping her sort out self-expectations as well as what others expect of her is important. Carmen needs to work on strategies to cope with stress and a way to balance the different areas of her life to include her culture, family, professional business culture (a clash with personalismo), and American culture.

The case of Consuelo presents a first-generation immigrant who has retained her traditional cultural values and identifies with such cultural schemas, including her sense of extended family and kin. Her children represent second-generation individuals who, though born in Mexico, grew up in the United States and participated in the educational system that immersed them in American culture. Thus, their level of acculturation and understanding of both cultures give them the flexibility to comfortably operate in both cultures. Consuelo's grandchildren were born and raised in the United States and have had little exposure to Mexican culture, so their cultural schema is different from Consuelo's. This reality is hard for Consuelo to understand and accept.

Consuelo's need for respeto from her grandchildren is not met. Her expectation of their behavior toward her as an elder parental figure is also not met. Furthermore, her equating this to the children being disrespectful or *mal educado* (ill educated in Latino customs) leads her to believe that in some way this is her fault or failure. Somehow she failed to convey to her children the notions and values related to child rearing espoused by Latino culture. She considers this as her fate or punishment for her failure, as fatalismo dictates. The grandchildren's lack of religion is of great concern because religion is tied to culture for Latinos. The observance of certain holidays and participation in church-related activities become support systems that reinforce cultural values.

As the family networks deteriorate, her sense of familismo is affected because the support of the extended family is missing. If this is not replaced, stress and illness may result. The counselor must explore Consuelo's involvement with church and community as systems of support and as kinship groups that help validate her feelings. Garcia-Prieto (1998) addressed the issue of "role strain" that is affecting Consuelo. This is the psychological and accompanying psychosomatic symptoms indicative of role and culture conflict. The results of this conflict are stress, identity crises (What is the role of a grandmother?), feelings of isolation (Am I the only one with these expectations?), alienation (I do not understand my children or grandchildren; I don't feel as close to them as I should), and depression. Consuelo's Latina notion that a mother "lives for her children and grandchildren" is at the root of her distress. Exploring alternatives as to how she can share the love of her culture with her grandchildren is important. She may want to reconnect with her extended family in Mexico because members of this group may offer opportunities to foster her sense of cultural self.

Vasquez (1994) recommended the following when counseling Latinas: (a) helping them learn how to use energy for not feeling badly about themselves; (b) teaching them coping skills, how to manage both hurt and anger, conflict management skills, and decision-making skills; (c) facilitating their talking openly about discrimination; and (d) teaching them strategies such as positive self-talk, how to seek support, and behavioral rehearsal.

Empowerment through validation is a key issue in counseling the Latina population. Addressing their concerns and symptoms within their cultural framework through the counseling process is vital to optimize the level of functioning of Latinas in the American culture. A respectful demeanor for the individual and her cultural background are important for counselors to observe when working with Latinas.

Conclusion

A counselor's understanding and exploration of the client's cultural values have two outcomes: They will provide a culturally based assessment, and they allow the individuals to retain their Latino identity with adaptive variations to the demands of U.S. culture. The attempt to treat a culturally adaptive behavior for the client's culture of origin results in failure through misdiagnosis and ill-suited treatment plans. Although it is true that U.S. cultural norms differ from those of Latino culture, they are not necessarily incompatible. Many Latinos seeking help need to find balance to cope with the process of acculturation. This becomes a challenge for counselors to address and consider in the assessment, diagnosis, and treatment of this population.

References

Amaro, H., & Russo, N. F. (1987). Hispanic women and mental health: An overview of contemporary issues in research and practice. *Psychology of Women Quarterly, 11,* 393–407.

American Psychiatric Association. (2000). *Diagnostic and statistical manual of mental disorders* (4th ed., text rev.). Washington, DC: Author.

Arredondo, P. (1991). Counseling Latinas. In C. C. Lee & B. L. Richardson (Eds.), *Multicultural issues in counseling: New approaches to diversity* (pp. 143–156). Alexandria, VA: American Counseling Association.

Canino, G. (1982). The Hispanic woman: Sociocultural influences on diagnoses and treatment. In R. Becerra, M. Karno, & J. Escobar (Eds.), *Mental health and Hispanic Americans* (pp. 117–138). New York: Grune & Stratton.

Castillo, R. J. (1997). *Culture and mental illness: A client-centered approach.* Pacific Grove, CA: Brooks/Cole.

Garcia-Prieto, N. (1998). Latinas in the United States: Bridging two worlds. In M. McGoldrick (Ed.), *Re-visioning family therapy: Race, culture, and gender in clinical practices* (pp. 330–346). New York: Guilford Press.

Guzman, B. (2000). *The Hispanic population census 2000 brief.* Washington, DC: U.S. Census Bureau.

Marin, G., & Marin, B. V. (1991). *Research with Hispanic populations.* Newbury Park, CA: Sage.

Paniagua, F. A. (1998). *Assessing and treating culturally diverse clients: A practical guide* (2nd ed.). Thousand Oaks, CA: Sage.

Romero, A. J. (2000). Assessing and treating Latinos: Overview of research. In I. Cuellar & F. A. Paniagua (Eds.), *Handbook of multicultural mental health* (pp. 209–223). San Diego, CA: Academic Press.

Triandis, H. C. (1989). The self and social behavior in differing cultural contexts. *Psychological Review, 96,* 506–520.

Vasquez, M. J. (1994). Latinas. In L. Comas-Diaz & B. Greene (Eds.), *Women of color: Integrating ethnic and gender identities in psychotherapy* (pp. 114–138). New York: Guilford Press.

Vasquez-Nutall, E., Romero-Garcia, I., & DeLeon, B. (1987). Sex roles and perceptions of femininity and masculinity of Hispanic women: A review of the literature. *Psychology of Women Quarterly, 11,* 409–425.

Vontress, C. E., Johnson, J. A., & Epp, L. R. (1999). *Cross-cultural counseling: A casebook.* Alexandria, VA: American Counseling Association.

Counseling Cuban Americans Using the Framework for Embracing Cultural Diversity

Silvia Echevarria-Doan and Martha Gonzalez Marquez

Latinos now constitute about 12.5% (nearly 35 million) of the total U.S. population and 36% of the total ethnic minority population (U.S. Census Bureau, 2001); Cubans make up 5% of the entire Latino population (Garcia & Marotta, 1997). By 2025, it is expected that Latinos will constitute about 18% of the population (U.S. Census Bureau, 2001), a 20% growth rate compared with 10% between 1980 and 1990 (Schick & Schick, 1991, as cited in Garcia & Marotta, 1997). By the year 2050, some projections of Latinos/Hispanics in the United States are as high as 133 million, or 25% of the total population (U.S. Census Bureau, 1998, as cited in Bean, Perry, & Bedell, 2001). Immigration accounts for the majority of these projected increases in the Hispanic/Latino population, with almost one third of all immigrants coming from Latin America (Garcia & Marotta, 1997). Migration patterns of Cubans into the United States have not changed much since they were described in the previous edition of this book. The only new development since then is a "lottery system" allowing a very limited number of Cubans to migrate to the United States. This is associated with the lifting of some restrictions related to U.S. travel to and from Cuba during the Clinton presidency. The increase in sanctioned travel essentially opened doors and channels of communication in ways that lifted decades of limited (or no) contact between families (with the exception of the short-lived open dialogue and travel to Cuba in 1979, which led to the Mariel Boatlift in 1980).

On the basis of these projections, there is a strong likelihood that counselors will face the possibility of working with Hispanic/Latino families. Clearly, the importance of preparing counselors to be culturally responsive is quite evident given these changing demographics. The purpose of this chapter is to expand on Martha Gonzalez Marquez's Framework for Embracing Cultural Diversity, which was introduced in our previous chapter in the second edition of this book, as the Framework for Cultural Awareness. This is done by focusing primarily on the framework's emphasis on awareness of self as part of culturally responsive practice. As we stated in our previous chapter, "the Framework for Cultural

Awareness (Marquez, 1992) is based upon the belief that practitioners need to continually address their own individual issues toward diversity as part of their work with clients if they are to be culturally sensitive" (Rafuls & Marquez, 1997, p. 270). We hope to do this by focusing on therapists and their use of this framework. The Framework for Cultural Awareness (Marquez, 1992; Rafuls & Marquez, 1997) has been developed further since the last edition of this book. Therefore, the focus of this chapter is to highlight these developments and discuss how therapists can be trained in the use of this framework through description, guidelines, and training/teaching exercises.

Culturally Competent Practice With Hispanic Families: Recent Developments

In a highly influential challenge to the field of counseling advocating for culturally responsive practice, Sue, Arredondo, and McDavis (1992) conceptualized that multicultural competence is demonstrated in three distinct ways. These ways included therapists' awareness of their own culture, their knowledge about the client's worldview/experiences in the United States, and their behaviors in terms of using culturally appropriate interventions and strategies. In a recent review of family therapy with Hispanic families, Bean et al. (2001) noted that the most common measure of therapist knowledge was associated with the therapist's behaviors in terms of strategies and interventions.

Bean et al. (2001) discussed culturally appropriate practice with Hispanic families by generating several guidelines based on a content analysis of professional literature on family therapy with Hispanics. They discussed what counselors should be prepared to do rather than defining what they must do with every Hispanic family. The guidelines included using family therapy as the preferred treatment modality, acting as an advocate for the family, assessing immigration experiences, assessing acculturation, showing respect for the father, interviewing family subsystems separately, not forcing changes, providing concrete suggestions, and warmly engaging the family. The majority of the empirical studies in their analysis utilized Mexican American and Cuban American samples, mostly of lower- or working-class backgrounds often addressing externalized problems such as substance abuse or delinquency.

There are several notable practice models with Hispanic/Latino families that have been developed in the last few years. These include Falicov's (1998) Multicultural Ecosystem Comparative Approach (MECA) and Szapocznik et al.'s (1997) Brief Strategic Family Therapy Model and Szapocznik and William's (2000) Structural Ecosystemic Theory. The latter two were developed specifically with Cuban American families in South Florida). Of these models, the MECA model deliberately addresses the importance of making the therapist aware of how therapist–client cultures influence each other through a process called "cultural mapping." By making distinctions between the therapist's map and the family's map of unique cultural experience (i.e., based on specific dimensions of culture), therapists and clients are able to connect along dimensions of similarity and provoke interest and curiosity along dimensions of difference. For example, in some cases, a therapist and a client family may share similar levels of education and social class but have different ethnic and religious backgrounds. In other cases, they may share similar developmental niches (as parents of adolescents) or may share different forms of similar experiences like relocation, marginalization, or prejudice. Falicov (1998) explained, "[An] ability to compare cultural maps relies on an attitude of close attention, curiosity, empathic understanding, and sociological imagination in the therapist" (p. 19).

By combining an emphasis on the therapist's own cultural experience like the MECA model and offering practical guidelines as Bean et al. (2001) did to prepare culturally responsive therapists, we delineate guidelines to develop a therapist's own self-awareness of culture, the cornerstone of the Framework for Embracing Cultural Diversity. This framework is not exclusively designed for therapy with Hispanic/Latino families. Yet, it has been used in teaching and supervising therapists who work with Cuban American families.

A Framework for Embracing Cultural Diversity: New Developments

This framework provides a method of teaching counselors how to be more culturally aware of, sensitive to, and accepting toward their clients. Counselors ideally begin the process long before seeing clients and continue the process throughout their development. This framework embraces the idea that awareness is a lifelong endeavor that is dynamic and multidimensional. The Framework for Embracing Cultural Diversity is based on four tenets that are described in this section and illustrated through experiential exercises outlined in the next section. The assumptions underlying this framework are as follows:

1. It is believed that families and their situations are systemic and contextual in nature. That is, families bring with them a number of interconnected variables that occur within different dimensions of lived experience. All of these variables affect their presenting problem. From an individual perspective, clients experience internally and biologically influenced processes with which they may struggle that also affect the family just as the family influences their individual internal processes. Individuals are also affected by their interpersonal relationships with others in their lives.
2. Neglecting to incorporate contextual variables in a working hypothesis in therapy can be disrespectful and potentially dangerous. Focusing primarily on the problem or a solution could devalue the life experiences in a family by assuming that all families with a particular presenting problem are the same. It might also covertly convey that all families should assimilate to the host culture and adopt its values. Assimilation could be interpreted as the norm rather than being a choice.
3. The counselor's culture becomes part of the family's system as they are affected by the counselor and the counselor is affected by the family. Thus, the counselor's own life experiences have an impact on the assumptions that underlie the questions asked by the counselor, the direction of therapy, and the change process (Karrer, 1989). Because of this assumption, the framework focuses heavily on the self of the therapist and ways in which the therapist can increase and embrace cultural awareness for himself or herself and, as a result, for clients.
4. All cultural experiences should be validated within the context of uniqueness and strengths. As McGoldrick (1982) asserted, "There is a common tendency for human beings to fear, and therefore reject, that which they can't understand" (p. 4). Clinically, this leads to labeling that which is different as wrong or bad; thus, families from different cultural backgrounds could easily be pathologized. Resource-oriented research (Echevarria-Doan, 2001; Rafuls, 1994) has found that resource-oriented language and resource-based interviewing had a positive influence on how families perceived themselves and how therapists viewed their ability to change. Thus, an overarching theme of strength and resource orientation is included in this framework.

Tenet 1: Consider a Larger Multidimensional Definition of Culture

So often the term *culture* is narrowly defined to include only race or ethnicity. What we have discovered through such fields as anthropology, archeology, and methods of ethnography is that an individual's culture is much broader and can include multiple variables.

Combining this concept of the individual's culture with that of the family and the meaning of culture makes for a wonderfully complex therapist–client experience. Below is a partial list of factors that should be considered when developing an idea of the family's cultural identity:

- Shared historical contexts
- Political status
- Immigration for purposes of political asylum
- Immigration for purposes of saving family and self
- Leaving behind valued elements
- Similar dialects/languages
- Similar attire
- Interpersonal space
- Beliefs about gender and power
- Shared values regarding marginalization and oppression
- Shared experiences: disasters/climate
- Social class
- Appearance: skin color/shades, eye shape/color, height
- Similar habits
- Similar lifestyles
- Levels and value of education
- Religious practices
- Spiritual orientation.

The multidimensional nature of culture is evident with the various combinations of these factors that can be influencing individuals at different life stages and at different times. For instance, the factors that are most influential for adolescents may be related to appearance and issues of fitting in with their peer culture rather than being concerned about sociopolitical issues. Conversely, adults in that same family may be more aware of social class and issues of marginalization, unlike those of the younger members in the family, because of differences in their developmental stage and their levels of acculturation to the mainstream culture. For the entire family then, all of these issues, whether similar or different, are a part of the family's cultural context.

Tenet 2: Interact With Others and Examine Similarities and Differences

Immersion into the life of others who are culturally different is an optimal method for learning about life experiences. Attempting to embrace emotionally what others have experienced will assist in sensitizing to and appreciating their perspective. This is not a passive but an active concept. Therapists do not have to wait for the culturally different client for this to take place. Opportunities abound to learn about other cultures: art festivals, museums, concerts, books, movies, neighbors, community centers, organizations, historical readings, and so forth. Counselors can make a concentrated effort to increase their own repertoire of friends and acquaintances to include those from different cultures. In addition, they can make deliberate attempts to dialogue about meaningful cultural issues and examine differences and similarities. This can help to reduce fears of the unfamiliar, help to learn to talk comfortably about cultural issues, and help to dispel stereotypes that may have developed. A probable side effect could be the discomfort that results from an awareness of the often painful struggles that others have experienced because of their differences and also a discomfort at one's own realizations of flawed biases and assumptions. Often counselors must dwell in discomfort and examine its nature in order to move forward, a thread that is present in all aspects of this framework.

Tenet 3: Accept and Celebrate a Personal Journey Toward Self-Awareness

In conjunction with embracing the cultural differences in others, counselors must examine their own cultural identity both past and present. They can begin by considering the factors addressed in Tenet 1 from their own life experience perspective. Interviewing family members from different generations can illuminate intergenerational customs and beliefs that may still be present in one's life.

Furthermore, counselors should examine their own biases and assumptions regarding different cultural factors such as race, gender, ethnicity, and family constellation. For example, many counselors do not readily admit that they are biased in thinking that two-parent families are healthier than one-parent families; however, this kind of bias can guide their thinking in counseling practice. Likewise, one's assumptions regarding certain cultural factors can also affect counseling. Many assume that all Hispanic parents are conservative, old-fashioned, and generally strict. This can be in part accurate; however, this can also serve to narrow one's vision as a counselor. Identifying and addressing these biases and assumptions is a necessary step toward cultural self-awareness. A further examination into the roots of these biases and assumptions can help counselors deconstruct their own experiences and develop a fuller understanding of them.

Finally, counselors can request critical feedback from others regarding their perceptions of our own biases and assumptions. The purpose is to genuinely learn about oneself through the lenses of those close colleagues. For this exercise to be meaningful, it will require a true level of honesty and disclosure and of acceptance on one's part. Openness on the part of a counselor will be essential. Once again, discomfort could arise; however, the benefits will far outweigh the risks.

Tenet 4: Examine Individual Personal Experiences With Differences

This tenet is overarching, tying together the previous three tenets in a manner that is recursive in nature. While considering a larger multidimensional definition of culture, interacting with others and examining similarities and differences, and accepting and embracing a personal journey toward self-awareness, counselors need to examine how they are influenced by their own individual personal experiences with differences. What personal experiences do we have where we felt prejudice from someone? On what grounds were we marginalized? Religion, appearance, language? How did we feel? How has that experience influenced our lives today? How has that experience influenced how we feel toward that group or individual who made us feel marginalized? The answers to these questions can broaden a counselor's vision of culture and can help him or her realize the roots of personal biases and assumptions. Counselors can learn about the lens through which they see others as well as themselves. It is vital that counselors accept their own place along the journey toward cultural identity formation.

Consider also the effects on counseling if one learns about cultural differences solely through his or her own personal experiences. For many, these experiences are broad and can indeed contribute to the understanding and progress of therapy. However, for others, relying on their own life experiences may be too narrow a base from which to draw. One may still be healing from the wounds left by past experiences with prejudice, discrimination, marginalization, or oppression and be unaware of their residual presence in one's thinking. One may very well unintentionally project his or her sentiments onto those whom one works with in counseling. Learning from our own painful experiences can serve to assist others in our work if we are careful to differentiate our experience from that of our clients.

Use of Framework for Embracing Cultural Diversity With Students and Supervisees

In most cases, we recommend that classroom or supervisory experiences utilizing the Framework for Embracing Cultural Diversity first provide participants with an overview of the tenets that have been explained. Normally, a discussion of this material should follow in order to open up dialogue regarding thoughts, ideas, and reactions to these tenets. Acquisition of knowledge and skill in working with diverse groups is encouraged through active participation in exercises that facilitate "doing and being" ourselves with others who may be different. It is often helpful to divide groups into pairs or small groups for many of the discussions and practice activities that we are recommending (see Project 1).

For instance, to accomplish the stated tasks under Tenet 1 (considering a larger multidimensional definition of culture) and Tenet 2 (interacting with others while examining similarities and differences), students can take part in paired interview projects. Generally, it is best to pair individuals of different ethnicities, races, and/or cultures. Students are then asked to interview each other using questions that correspond to different dimensions of culture (listed under Project 1). Usually this will take an entire class period (of 2 to 3 hours) with time allotted for interviewing and processing responses. In case of extreme class homogeneity, this can also be assigned as an interview project outside of class wherein students can deliberately select culturally diverse respondents who are not classmates.

Project 1

Interview your assigned classmate (preferably from a culture different than your own). Have him or her respond to as many of the questions that you would like to ask from each of the dimensions of culture listed below. Take some time to converse about these in terms of contrast (i.e., similarities and differences) between you and your respondent.

History

What are your family's origins?
What political/historical/environmental events have affected you and your family?
How does your family respond to being unique historically and now?
How has your family changed throughout the generations? How has it stayed the same?

Relational Issues

How do family members communicate?
What are the rules of respect?
What did you learn about intimate relationships?
How were you expected to treat your siblings?
What are your parents' views about parenting?
What did you learn from your parents about parenting?
What will you pass on to future generations of your family?
What did you learn about sexual orientation?
What did you learn from your other interpersonal relationships that you did not learn at
    home concerning the above issues?

Gender Issues

What are the messages about gender differences that you received?
What messages about gender roles were you comfortable with and uncomfortable with?
How did gender affect power in your family?

Appearances

What languages are spoken in your family across generations? Did that ever change?
How does your family dress? Does that differ during special events?
How is your family's appearance unique? Does this differ between individual members?

Rituals

How do you celebrate special events?
What are some traditions that your family holds?
What kinds of foods do you eat?

Spirituality

What are your family's views about religion?
How is your life affected by religion?
In what ways did your family demonstrate their spirituality?
How was your family treated when demonstrating their spiritual beliefs?

Education/Work

How does your family view education?
How does your family view holding a job?
What did you learn from your educational experiences that you did not learn at home concerning the above issues?

Economics

How does your family's socioeconomic status affect them?
What were some of the rules surrounding allowances/asking for money?
How did your family respond to those from a different social class?
In what manner were issues related to finances discussed in your family?

External Influences

What does your family think about what is on television/radio?
What kind of discussions did your family have about the media?
What kind of political discussions did your family engage in?

Self-Guided Activities

Tenet 3 addresses acceptance and celebration of our personal journey toward self-awareness. This includes examining our own cultural identity along with our biases and assumptions regarding different cultural factors such as race, gender, ethnicity, and family constellation. To deconstruct some of these biases and assumptions, we must become aware of our own origin. Below are several self-guided activities that can facilitate some of these experiences.

Activity 1

1. Immerse yourself into the world of media (television, radio, music, magazines, newspapers, billboards, etc.). Consider such cultural issues as family makeup, gender roles, religion, socioeconomic status, education, ethnicity, and sexual orientation.
2. Think about the cultural messages the media sends (whether intentionally or unintentionally) concerning families, men, women, relationships, and therapy.
3. How do these messages fit within your own cultural framework, and how don't they fit?
4. Interview someone from a different culture than your own about the same media messages. How do these messages fit or not fit within that person's culture?

Activity 2

Locate and read a book written about a culture or cultural experience different than your own. This book can be fiction, nonfiction, poetry, or something else. The purpose is for you to immerse yourself in another culture and experience it as much as possible. Possibilities include books relating to the Holocaust, migration, slavery, sociopolitical changes (communism, feminism, etc.), oppression, and individual or group experiences. Consider the following:

1. Your reactions to the book
2. How this book has affected you
3. How your assumptions/biases about the culture were challenged or altered
4. How your clinical work might be affected by this experience.

Activity 3

Locate articles concerning any type of cultural issue. The articles can be theoretical or research based. However, each article must be from a field other than your own. Consider the following:

1. What made you choose this article?
2. How does the information in this article differ from the information on cultural issues commonly found in the literature in your field?
3. How is the information presented in this article similar to the information commonly found in the literature in your field?
4. On the basis of this article, how can the different fields inform each other about this particular cultural issue?
5. What did you find most interesting about this article?
6. How will this article affect your clinical work?

In-Class Exercises

Tenet 4 within the Framework for Embracing Cultural Diversity involves examining individual personal experiences with differences. Some of the ways to assist students and supervisees in this process include exercises that have them personalize emotions associated with diversity.

Exercise 1

Have students/supervisees isolate themselves in the room. Students are to visualize the scenarios you will be describing. They are to especially note their emotional responses to the scenarios. The purpose of this exercise is for the students to personalize the emotions associated with difference, oppression, and prejudice, thus assisting them to become more sensitive to others.

1. Picture a time when someone made you feel different because of your appearance. How did you feel?
2. Picture a time when your views about abortion were strongly challenged. How did you feel?
3. Picture a time when someone spoke disparagingly about your faith/religion. How did you feel?
4. Picture a time when you were made to feel financially limited or incapable. How did you feel?
5. Picture a time when someone ridiculed a friend or family member. How did you feel?

6. Picture a time when a foreign language was spoken in front of you. Then picture those same people laughing. How did you feel?
7. Picture a time when someone laughed at a belief you had. How did you feel?
8. Picture a time when someone minimized a crisis you experienced. How did you feel?
9. Picture a time when you were challenged about your choice of careers or schooling. How did you feel?
10. Picture a time when someone ridiculed a project you cared a great deal about. How did you feel?
11. Picture a time when you felt misunderstood and the other person was not willing to try to understand. How did you feel?

A Personal Journey

The Framework for Embracing Cultural Diversity underscores how important it is for therapists to examine their own cultural identity (both past and present) while also embracing cultural differences in others. We believe this is often less difficult for individuals who have had to stand outside of the mainstream culture themselves. This is true for both of us as we constantly navigate through our own personal journeys of cultural identity and cultural awareness. We have chosen to illustrate how this remains a continual process by sharing part of Silvia Echevarria-Doan's personal journey of cultural identity as a Cuban American woman after she visited her homeland for the first time since immigrating to the United States.

As a first-generation Cuban immigrant, the first author feels that she has led a bicultural existence for most of her life. This bicultural existence has required her to deal with a constant interplay of being Cuban and/or American depending on the context in which she exists. It is what Shorris (1992) referred to in his book *Latinos: A Biography of the People* as the "in-between," when one is not totally Cuban and not totally American. Identifying with either one or both has a great deal to do with whom one interacts with, where the interaction takes place, and the language used throughout the interaction, among other variables. It is a constant foreground/background experience. Therefore, awareness of others in comparative ways comes easily, as does cultural awareness of self. However, this is not to say that this should free us from the work involved in becoming culturally responsive therapists.

As part of her own cultural journey, one of the first author's dreams was to return to her homeland of Cuba with her parents. This dream became a reality in May 2000 when she was joined by her parents (and husband) on their first visit back to Cuba since they immigrated to the United States in 1962. This was an emotionally intense and draining experience, which will remain carved in her memory forever. As a cultural lesson in time, going back to one's original homeland has different meanings to each of those who return. For the author, it was a chance to make connections with her past and the origin of her cultural identity (i.e., the Cuban in her) in ways that were not possible in the United States. Of greater importance was the opportunity to experience this with her parents as they also came to terms with their past, especially as it related to their decision to immigrate. It was a sense of relief (and perhaps even forgiveness of self) for them to know and feel that they had done the right thing despite the impact that immigration continues to have on their family today. She is thankful to be a part of her parents' affirmation that their decision to leave was not in vain despite the pain and separation from family members and familiar surroundings, many of which were hardly recognizable after all of these years, thus the bittersweet emotional memories associated with this trip.

The most meaningful aspect of this personal journey was being reminded of the courage that it takes to make the decision to leave one's homeland forever (without truly knowing what lies ahead). It is absolutely necessary to keep this in mind when working with Cuban American immigrant families because so much is revealed and resolved when they have the opportunity to explore this decision in depth as part of their past, present, and future. Both Falicov (1998) and Bean et al. (2001) addressed this issue in their models of practice and guidelines. Falicov promoted what she called a "migration narrative." The construction of this narrative helps the therapist address

> questions about premigration and the entry experience, provides a tool to explore the motivations behind the move and sense of responsibility of the people who initiated the process, [and informs us of] their choice points, the ordeals suffered to get here, the attachments to those family members who stayed and those who already left, and the reception by those already here. (Falicov, 1998, p. 47)

Ignoring the importance of this intervention with Cuban American clients proves to be a great disservice to the clients as well as a sorely missed opportunity for any therapist or counselor.

Conclusion

This chapter has expanded on the development of the Framework for Embracing Cultural Diversity (created by the second author) by introducing in detail each of its tenets and basic assumptions. On the basis of recommendations to move beyond cultural awareness and knowledge into actual skill acquisition, we have demonstrated how this framework can be taught and utilized in class or supervision by presenting specific experiential activities. We also chose to focus on the framework's emphasis on awareness of self as part of culturally responsive practice. In particular, the first author's own personal journey of cultural identity as it pertains to culturally responsive practice with Cuban American families was highlighted. The significance of migration history as it pertains to one's decision to leave one's homeland was emphasized in this personal journey. Although the Framework for Embracing Cultural Diversity has been used to address culturally responsive therapy with Cuban American families, it is applicable to a variety of clients and cultures because of its broadened view of culture.

References

Bean, R. A., Perry, B. J., & Bedell, T. M. (2001). Developing culturally competent marriage and family therapists: Guidelines for working with Hispanic families. *Journal of Marital and Family Therapy, 27,* 43–54.

Echevarria-Doan, S. (2001). Resource-based reflective consultation: Accessing client resources through interviews and dialogue. *Journal of Marital and Family Therapy, 27,* 201–212.

Falicov, C. J. (1998). *Latino families in therapy: A guide to multicultural practice.* New York: Guilford Press.

Garcia, J. G., & Marotta, S. (1997). Characteristics of the Latino population. In J. G. Garcia & M. C. Zea (Eds.), *Psychological interventions and research with Latino populations* (pp. 1–14). Boston: Allyn & Bacon.

Karrer, B. M. (1989). The sound of two hands clapping: Cultural interactions of the minority family and the therapist. In G. W. Saba, B. M. Karrer, & K. V. Hardy (Eds.), *Minorities and family therapy* (pp. 209–237). New York: Haworth Press.

Marquez, M. G. (1992). *Cultural awareness in the field of marriage and family therapy: A qualitative analysis of multiple perspectives.* Unpublished doctoral dissertation, Purdue University, West Lafayette, IN.

McGoldrick, M. (1982). Ethnicity and family therapy: An overview. In M. McGoldrick, J. K. Pearce, & J. Giordano (Eds.), *Ethnicity and family therapy* (pp. 3–30). New York: Guilford Press.

Rafuls, S. E. (1994). *Qualitative resource-based consultation: Resource-generative inquiry and reflective dialogue with four Latin American families and their therapists.* Unpublished doctoral dissertation, Purdue University, West Lafayette, IN.

Rafuls, S. E., & Marquez, M. G. (1997). La Familia Fernandez: Directions for counseling Cuban Americans. In C. C. Lee (Ed.), *Multicultural issues in counseling: New approaches to diversity* (2nd ed., pp. 269–294). Alexandria, VA: American Counseling Association.

Shorris, E. (1992). *Latinos: A biography of the people.* New York: Norton.

Sue, D. W., Arredondo, P., & McDavis, R. J. (1992). Multicultural counseling competencies and standards: A call to the profession. *Journal of Counseling & Development, 70,* 477–486.

Szapocznik, J., Kurtines, W., Santisteban, D. A., Pantin, H., Scopetta, M., Mancilla, Y., et al. (1997). The evolution of structural ecosystemic theory for working with Latino families. In J. G. Garcia & M. C. Zea (Eds.), *Psychological interventions and research with Latino populations* (pp. 166–190). Boston: Allyn & Bacon.

Szapocznik, J., & Williams, R. A. (2000). Brief strategic family therapy: Twenty-five years of interplay among theory, research, and practice in adolescent problem behaviors and drug abuse. *Clinical Child and Family Psychology Review, 3,* 117–134.

U.S. Census Bureau. (2001, March). *The Hispanic population in the United States* (Current Population Reports, P20-535). Washington, DC: U.S. Government Printing Office.

Counseling Mexican American College Students

Madonna G. Constantine, Alberta M. Gloria, and Augustine Barón

A recent U.S. Census report indicates that nearly 22 million Mexican Americans reside in the United States (U.S. Bureau of the Census, 2000). Over the course of a decade, the overall Latino population has grown from 22.4 million in 1990 to 35.3 million in 2000. This increase (57.9%) is more than 4 times the increase for the total U.S. population (Guzmán, 2001). Further, U.S. Census projections estimate that in less than 50 years, almost 1 in 4 persons will be Latino, with Latinos constituting 63 million persons by 2030 and 88 million persons by 2050 (U.S. Bureau of the Census, 2000).

Although Latinos are the fastest growing and youngest racial and ethnic group in the United States, they are not proportionally represented in the larger educational system (U.S. Department of Education, National Center for Education Statistics [NCES], 2000a). For example, Latino children constitute a substantial portion of elementary and secondary school children (U.S. Department of Education, NCES, 2000b). However, college entry numbers are dissimilar (U.S. Department of Education, NCES, 1998, 2000a). More specifically, Latino students comprised 9% of all undergraduate students in the United States, although they earned only 5.3% of all bachelor's degrees in 1997 (Wilds, 2000). Throughout their educational experiences, many Latino students encounter educational tracking, lower educational expectations from teachers, schools with fewer resources, and teachers who have not been trained to incorporate a diversity of cultural values into the classroom curriculum (Gay, 2001).

By subpopulations, Mexican Americans comprise the largest segment of Latinos (i.e., 64%), have the lowest median age, and are the most uneducated (U.S. Bureau of the Census, 2000). For example, individuals of Mexican descent are least likely to have a high school education relative to other Latino subgroups (Therrien & Ramirez, 2000). The college completion rates are also similar, with only 5% of Mexican Americans having completed college. Overall, Latinos tend to enroll part-time and, as a result, are more likely to take more than 6 years to earn a bachelor's degree (U.S. Department of Education, NCES, 1996). Despite the lower college completion rates and extended time frame for college completion, Latinos have equal or higher educational aspirations than do other college students (Quintana, Vogel, & Ybarra, 1991). Thus, there are various circumstances that may contribute to the discrepancy between Mexican Americans' educational aspirations and their educational attainment.

Taking into account the particular educational patterns of Latinos, unique cultural considerations may need to be weighed when counseling Mexican American college students. Thus, this chapter explores vital cultural issues associated with counseling Mexican American college students and briefly summarizes conceptual frameworks that have been designed specifically for counseling Mexican American, Chicano, or Latino college students. In extending context-based and culturally integrative counseling, the differential helping roles that culturally competent college counselors can assume in working with Mexican American students are discussed and illustrated with the use of case vignettes.

Salient Cultural Considerations in Counseling Mexican American College Students

Despite the inclusion of different cultures and ways of knowing, the culture of academia continues to be based on White, middle-class, male values (e.g., competition, individualism, and separatism; Feagin, Vera, & Imani, 1996; Gloria & Pope-Davis, 1997). Hence, for Mexican American students who attend predominantly White colleges and universities, it is possible that they may experience incongruence between their own personal values and the values of their environments (Constantine, Robinson, Wilton, & Caldwell, 2002), particularly among less acculturated individuals. Cultural congruity is described as the fit between students' personal values and the values of the environment in which they operate (Gloria & Robinson Kurpius, 1996). Prior investigations have revealed that noncognitive factors, such as the environment or social support systems, may affect how Mexican American students experience college (Constantine et al., 2002). For example, Gloria and Robinson Kurpius (1996) found that greater cultural congruity was a significant predictor of Mexican American college students' decision to remain in college. Prolonged exposure to culturally incongruent circumstances may result in undue distress for students, which may in turn propel them to seek counseling services. When Mexican American students seek such services, there are various psychological, social, cultural, and environmental issues that should be considered by counselors who work with these clients (Gloria & Rodriguez, 2000).

Prior to discussing counseling service considerations for Mexican American college students, it is important to note that assumptions of uniformity about Latinos held by some individuals may create misconceptions about the changing educational demography and particular needs of college students of Mexican descent (Echeverry, 1997; Reyes & Valencia, 1993). Specifically, a "typical Latino" or "typical Mexican American" does not exist. Beliefs in this vein create the detrimental belief of essentialism (Martinez, 1998) within different Mexican-descended communities. Essentialism is the notion that there are certain aspects or minimal requirements (e.g., culture, language, and behaviors) for individuals to adhere to in order to be "real" Latinos or Mexican Americans. Nonetheless, some of the key elements that need to be considered in counseling Mexican American college students include acculturation and generational status, ethnic identity, language, gender roles, familial roles, socioeconomic status, sexual orientation, and spirituality and religion.

Acculturation and Generational Status

Many Mexican American college students experience acculturation stress or conflict depending on their length of residence in the United States (e.g., generational status), the strength of their cultural values, and the values of the college environment (Barón & Constantine, 1997; Gloria & Rodriguez, 2000; Wilton & Constantine, 2003). Acculturation has been defined as a bidirectional interactive process between an individual and the host culture (Berry, 1993; Casas & Vasquez, 1996). In particular, acculturation occurs when an individual's attitudes, values, beliefs, customs, and behaviors may become more like those of the host culture as a result of continued exposure. In turn, the host culture may also adopt certain elements associated with an individual's cultural group. Mexican American individuals who are first-generation college students often experience greater difficulties in adjusting to college, as compared with their second- and third-generation counterparts, because of their lack of familiarity with the norms, values, and expectations associated with various college environments.

Levels of acculturation among Mexican American college students may differ greatly, but Latino students who are raised in highly acculturated families and environments may begin to question their cultural orientation as they encounter other Latinos in the college environment who hold different values and attitudes (Gloria & Rodriguez, 2000). Some Mexican American college students may experience both direct and indirect pressure to acculturate to White American culture, and such pressures may result in feelings of isolation from aspects of Mexican American culture (Cervantes, 1988). Hence, many Mexican American students adopt bicultural ways of functioning within academic environments to avoid feeling isolated or alienated from their culture of origin and the academic culture (Constantine et al., 2002).

Ethnic Identity

Ethnic identity refers to one's understanding of one's own ethnic group and of oneself as a member of that group (Bernal, Knight, Ocampo, Garza, & Cota, 1993). Although acculturation and ethnic identity are interrelated and have been used interchangeably (Phinney, 1990), they are distinct constructs (Arbona, Flores, & Novy, 1995). Most models conceptualize ethnic identity development in stages, phases, or statuses that may be experienced by people of color as they actively negotiate cultural issues. This development involves movement from harboring negative attitudes and stereotypes about one's own ethnic or racial group to a position wherein one has internalized healthier self-esteem and cultural pride and greater appreciation of cultural differences that exist among all individuals.

The choice of one's self-referent may be linked to one's ethnic identity. For example, the terms *Chicano* and *Chicana* have sociopolitical connotations of political consciousness, in contrast to the broader self-referent of *Mexican American*. Throughout this chapter, however, the use of the term *Mexican American* denotes individuals who are of Mexican descent who are currently residing in the United States. For a current explanation of the different self-referents for all Latinos, the reader is referred to Comas-Díaz's (2001) recent taxonomy of reference terms.

Language

Fluency in the English language is a dimension that cannot be overlooked by counselors when considering interactions with and approaches to working with Mexican American college students. Although not all Mexican-descended individuals are fluent in Spanish, the impact of language issues on the educational process has received considerable attention. For example, approximately 75% of all Latinos between the ages of 16 and 24 years reported speaking Spanish at home (Frase, 1992). Having an adequate working knowledge of English and maintaining one's native language have also been identified as crucial to future workforce placement (Macias, 1993) and to Mexican American students feeling culturally connected with others. It has long been debated as to whether decreased English language fluency has a negative influence on academic achievement, but a more recent study found that language use did not influence stress or academic achievement among Mexican American university students (Garcia-Vasquez, Vasquez, & Huang, 1998).

It is critical for counselors to determine the language that Mexican American college students feel most comfortable speaking. The manner in which this determination is made, however, requires more than a simple question (e.g., "Do you feel more comfortable speaking in English or Spanish?"). Although Mexican American students may be able to function in their daily lives (e.g., speak and interact with faculty and other students in English), the discussion of private and potentially painful issues may be best described, processed, and expressed in their first language (Koss-Chioino & Vargas, 1999). It is also important to note that few counselors are bilingual (Patterson, 1996), much less able to conduct psychological assessments and therapy in Spanish.

Gender Roles

Mexican American culture often emphasizes the elevated status of males and the subsequent double standards that tend to negatively affect women (Constantine & Barón, 1997). An example of this socialization is the value of *machismo*, which has come to mean hypermasculinity or male chauvinism. Originally, the word held positive connotations in Mexican culture, but it has lost its positive references when translated (Barón, 1991; Barón & Constantine, 1997) and has been subsequently pathologized. For example, machismo could represent Latinos who are family protectors and supporters and who hold benign and flexible attitudes in providing structure to family relationships or those who rigidly adhere to gender roles through extreme authoritarianism, domination of women, hypersexuality, or consumption of alcohol (Gloria, Ruiz, & Castillo, 2004).

For Latino women, the interconnected concepts of *marianismo* and *hembrismo* are commonly espoused and create "cultural paradoxes" in that these women are expected to be "morally and spiritually superior to men, while [at the same time being] expected to accept male authority" (Boyd-Franklin & Garcia-Preto, 1994, p. 253). Specifically, marianismo is the value that women endure suffering and emulate La Virgen (the Virgin Mary; Mirandé, 1985; Rivers, 1995), creating a standard against which women are judged (Dernersesian, 1993). Hembrismo connotes "femaleness," as Latino women are expected to competently fulfill multiple roles both in and out of the home (Comas-Díaz, 1989).

Several scholars (e.g., Gloria, 1999; Haro, Rodriguez, & Gonzales, 1994; Vasquez, 1982) have identified social and cultural pressures and barriers to completion of higher education among Mexican American females. For example, although more Mexican American females than males enroll in colleges and universities, their male counterparts tend to persist to graduation at a higher rate. Despite changes in gender and culturally ascribed roles for males and females of Mexican descent, gender-role influences continue to affect academic persistence and graduation rates. Labeling or assuming behaviors as *machista* or *marianista* without understanding the origin or cultural context of the behavior will limit counselors' therapeutic impact (Gloria et al., 2004). As a result, assessment of adherence to traditional gender roles is an important aspect when working with Mexican American college students (Constantine & Barón, 1997).

Family and Familial Roles

Social support has been defined as the helpfulness of social relationships, human attachments, and the supportive resources that are exchanged among members of a social system (Gottlieb, 1981). In facing the difficulties of academic life, Mexican American college students may often look to family and school personnel for social support (Constantine et al., 2002; Gloria & Rodriguez, 2000). Traditionally, many may adhere to the value of *familismo*, a strong sense of family centrality and importance (Gloria & Rodriguez, 2000) and a value that is often closely linked to and supported by gender roles. Familismo may be manifested by providing resources and emotional support to other family members, primarily relying on family for support, expressing attitudes and behaviors held by the family, and placing one's need after those of the family's (Knight, Bernal, Garza, & Cota, 1993).

The social and cultural pressure to create and maintain a family can create stress for many Mexican American college women, as motherhood is often viewed as the pinnacle of womanhood by many Latino communities (Trujillo, 1997). Consequently, Latino families often exert overt and covert pressures on female college students to return and attend to daily family activities and special events (Gloria & Rodriguez, 2000; Vasquez, 1982). Although this "tug" is also present for Mexican American males, culturally ascribed gender roles for women create additional pressures and guilt for leaving behind or moving beyond their families (Arredondo, 1991). Thus, it is important that counselors and their clients clarify and understand gender-role values and work to incorporate these values into treatment plans rather than simply pathologizing such perspectives.

Mobilizing social support networks may help many Mexican American students to function more effectively within academic systems (Constantine, Wilton, & Caldwell, 2003; Gloria & Rodriguez, 2000). In particular, social support from family and school personnel (e.g., faculty mentors) has been found to be predictive of Latino students' academic persistence in higher education (Alva, 1991; Gloria & Robinson Kurpius, 1996; Lango, 1995). Determining whether Mexican American students have someone who is academically successful to whom they can look or emulate to some degree is imperative (Gloria & Rodriguez, 2000), because Latino students who perceive themselves to be mentored are more likely to academically succeed than those who do not hold such perceptions (Aguirre & Martinez, 1993; Gándara, 1995).

Finances and Socioeconomic Status

The practical aspect of financing higher education is a central issue for many Mexican American college students. It is estimated that almost half of incoming Latino first-year students come from families with incomes of less than $20,000, and almost half of these students receive financial aid. Similarly, 40% of students receive some form of federal aid, and 15% receive institution-specific aid (O'Brien, 1993). These statistics are of notable importance because less than one quarter of Latinos earn $35,000 or more, as compared with almost one half of non-Latino Whites who are employed full-time. Similarly, individuals of Mexican descent reported the lowest percentage of persons earning $35,000 or more (20.6%) as compared with other Latino subpopulations (Therrien & Ramirez, 2000).

Despite their financial need, Latino students often borrow less money than other racial or ethnic groups to pay for their education. Although money can be borrowed to finance school, federal and institutional financial support generally does not consider the economic needs of these students' families (Gloria & Castellanos, 2003). Many Mexican American students often delay or discontinue their educational pursuits to help their families meet financial obligations (Pappas & Guajardo, 1997; Quintana et al., 1991). Not wanting to accumulate debt, many Mexican American college students hold full-time positions to help pay for school and help financially support their families. In a study of Latino college students, Haro et al. (1994) reported that 80% of these students held jobs, with 75% working off-campus. Further, many of these students were living at or below poverty level and were dependent on their families for financial support. Hence, assessing Mexican American students' financial obligations, work schedules, and stress related to finances may be helpful in creating a treatment plan that is feasible and relevant to the educational experiences of students. Further, providing after-hours counseling sessions may be necessary to meet the school and work schedules of some Mexican American college students.

Sexual Orientation

Although the gay, lesbian, and bisexual (GLB) literature often does not attend to racial and ethnic differences among Mexican-descended individuals, many GLB Mexican American college students find themselves as "minorities among minorities." Morales (1990, 1992) indicated that racial and ethnic minorities within GLB communities frequently struggle with racial and ethnic prejudice and discrimination. Specifically, Mexican American GLB college students are often shunned by the larger U.S. society and by the Latino community both within and outside of the university setting (Morales, 1992). For example, Mexican American lesbians face the status of a quadruple minority (Yep, 1995)—a member of a racial/ethnic minority group, a woman, an individual who often is socioeconomically disadvantaged, and a sexual minority. Furthermore, Mexican-descended lesbians often are perceived as a threat to the established social male hierarchy commonly espoused within many Latino and Mexican American communities (Trujillo, 1997).

If Mexican-descended individuals are to openly declare their sexual orientation, then the issue of sexuality must be a topic of discussion, which is a difficult effort because sexual silence is often supported by Latino culture (Marín & Gómez, 1997). Regardless of familial emphasis, Latino families generally do not discuss matters of sex and sexuality with their Latino youth (Centers for Disease Control, 1991). Contributing to a lack of information about sex, traditional Latino beliefs assume that "good women" do not know about sex or sexual matters (Marín & Gómez, 1997). When appropriate, counselors need to assess internalized messages and assumptions regarding sexual comfort and practices of Mexican American college students to aid them in making healthy and safe decisions about sexual behaviors. Such decisions are particularly relevant given the increased level of sexual activity among Latino adolescents over the past 30 years (Newcomer & Baldwin, 1992) and the increased number of AIDS-related deaths among Latinos (Marín & Gómez, 1997).

Spirituality and Religion

As commonly overlooked factors, spirituality and religion play major roles in the lives of many Mexican American individuals. Not typified by any one religious or spiritual tradition, Mexican Americans are most predominantly Catholic (Falicov, 1998), but Mexican Americans are also represented in Judaic, Baptist, Evangelical, Lutheran, Mormon, and Pentecostal communities (Zea, Mason, & Murguía, 2000). Similarly, the traditional spiritual beliefs (ethnomedical healing systems) of *curanderismo, espiritismo,* and *santería* are espoused by many U.S. Latinos (Koss-Chioino, 1995). The mind, body, and spirit are viewed as compartmentalized entities in some mental health settings, and this perspective may leave many Mexican-descended individuals feeling that a part of their overall worldview is missing if only the mind is the focus of counseling (Constantine, Myers, Kindaichi, & Moore, 2004; Lopez-Baez, 1997). As a result, the locus of etiology of students' concerns may need to be addressed as many Latinos often believe that emotional or personal concerns are caused by spiritual weakness, bad luck, supernatural events, or God's will (Echeverry, 1997).

Although the dimensions of belief and faith are being more readily integrated into the field of counseling (Richards & Bergin, 2000; Richards & Smith, 2004), these dimensions have long represented important aspects of many Mexican Americans' lives. Counselors who are open to integrating spiritual and religious issues into the counseling process may find some Mexican American college students to be more responsive to treatment approaches or interventions. This is particularly relevant as Latino youth are more likely than their White counterparts to turn to religion as a means of coping (Copeland & Hess, 1995). Counselors who are willing to integrate such issues, however, need to establish strong rapport and engender *confianza* (trust and confidence) because religion and spirituality are considered to be deeply personal issues and are often outside the purview of public discussion or dialogue (Gloria et al., 2004).

Counseling Frameworks for Addressing the Psychological Issues of Mexican American College Students

There is extensive conceptual and empirical literature regarding the educational aspects and academic experiences of Mexican American college students. Although the literature pertaining to Mexican American or Chicano/Chicana college students, in particular, is readily available (e.g., Arellano & Padilla, 1996; Gloria, 1997; Solberg & Villareal, 1997), integrating the literature into counseling frameworks for this population is comparatively sparse. The theoretically based counseling frameworks that address the experiences of Mexican American college students (i.e., Ruiz & Casas, 1976; Barón, 1991; Barón & Constantine, 1997; Gloria, 1999; Gloria & Rodriguez, 2000) are briefly reviewed.

Ruiz and Casas (1976)

The earliest counseling framework identified for Chicano students was introduced by Ruiz and Casas (1976). This model proposed four counselor characteristics: bilingualism, biculturality, image, and outreach. The authors asserted that counselors working with Chicano students must have command of both English and Spanish as well as familiarity and comfort with Chicano and Anglo cultures. According to Ruiz and Casas, the concept of "image" referred to counselors needing to be aware of how they were perceived by the clients, ideally as change agents who are responsive to sociocultural aspects of Chicanos. Similarly, counselors must provide outreach, making deliberate efforts to get to know Chicano college students. Behavioral in nature, Ruiz and Casas recommended that counselors (a) actively direct their clients toward resolution, (b) deal only with a limited number of issues, (c) rank clients' concerns relative to the associated stress, and (d) contract with clients for specific therapeutic objectives. Although this model advocated for counselors to teach Chicano students how to resist and eliminate prejudicial practices and encouraged counselors to take a community psychology approach, the underlying motives of students' presenting issues were not addressed. Also, the model was designed, delivered, and intended for Chicanos. Although a culturally specific counseling model is important, the likelihood of available Latino or Mexican American counselors for all students who desire a same-race or same-ethnic counselor is low.

Barón (1991)

Fifteen years later, Barón (1991) presented a broader and psychologically inclusive framework for counseling Chicano college students. This approach stressed the importance of addressing key cultural concepts of acculturation, ethnic identity development, and machismo. In particular, Barón emphasized the interrelatedness of the proposed key concepts for male Chicanos. From this framework, Barón also outlined the structure for a process-oriented group intervention for Hispanic male college students. This group addressed the dynamics of Chicano identity formation and served as a venue to gain intellectual and emotional insights, thereby emphasizing educational persistence and success. Although Barón's model focused on relevant concepts (i.e., acculturation, ethnic identity, and machismo), it did not address the broader aspects of traditionality and gender roles for Chicano males and females. Similarly, environmental or campus-related contexts were not specifically or directly included within the counseling framework, despite the integration of educational persistence issues and sociocultural aspects of counseling Chicanos.

Barón and Constantine (1997) and Constantine and Barón (1997)

The basis of the next two frameworks was taken from Barón's (1991) previous model. More recently, Barón and Constantine (1997) and Constantine and Barón (1997) presented an integrated framework of counseling for Latino students. The models assessed via a standard clinical interview core psychosocial and cultural constructs. These constructs included ethnic identity development, level of acculturation, and gender-role socialization. In particular, the construct of machismo was addressed relative to male–female differences and sexual orientation. Central to the model was the assessment of the psychosocial and cultural constructs across cognitive, affective, and behavioral domains. The authors also described interactive culture strain as the emotional distress or conflict that is experienced when individuals attempt to integrate various developmental challenges related to acculturation, ethnic identity development, and gender-role socialization. The strain is a result of the existence of differences in the levels of awareness and progression across all of the dimensions of the three psychosocial/cultural constructs. For many Mexican American college students, "psychic energy" (Anzaldúa, 1990) is needed to deal with the strain of defining and understanding their ethnic identity, managing their acculturation stress, and negotiating the university culture and environment (Gloria & Robinson Kurpius, 1996). Although, Barón and Constantine's approach addressed important psychosocial and cultural factors, it did not integrate environmental and sociocontextual influences of the academic environment.

Gloria (1999)

In creating a psychoeducational support group for Chicana college students, Gloria (1999) integrated Yalom's (1995) therapeutic factors, Chicano/Chicana cultural values, and academic persistence issues of Chicanas in higher education. The cultural values of *familismo, personalismo, respeto, simpatía, dignidad,* and *confianza* were noted to be central to group dynamics. Recommendations proposed for group facilitators were to (a) actively participate in Chicano/Chicana communities, thereby establishing trust and credibility; (b) build cohesion and establish alliances among group members to validate educational and emotional experiences; (c) increase feelings of academic and cultural efficacy to develop skills and strategies for balancing home and school demands; (d) promote group members' awareness and understanding of value systems regarding traditionality and acculturation; (e) develop group members' interpersonal skills and strategies for dealing with campus racism and discrimination; (f) help group members create a "university family"; and (g) validate Chicana students' educational experiences, thereby decreasing feelings of campus alienation and isolation. Although Gloria incorporated psychological, social, cultural, and environmental aspects into the group framework, her framework did not focus on process-oriented aspects of counseling, as the group was theme based and educational in nature. Further, the mode of delivery was intended for gender- and ethnic-specific groups.

Gloria and Rodriguez (2000)

More recently, Gloria and Rodriguez (2000) delineated a psychosociocultural approach for university counseling center staff who provide counseling services to Latino university students. Their approach emphasized the dynamic and interdependent relationships of psychological concerns, social support systems, cultural factors, and university environmental contexts—a psychosociocultural approach. Gloria and Rodriguez asserted that addressing the dynamic and interdependent relationships of these constructs is necessary in providing more comprehensive and context-specific counseling. In creating a structure for university counseling center service providers, the authors designed a set of minimal competencies for each dimension. Although Gloria and Rodriguez's framework addressed the differential roles of counselors, it did not fully integrate the multiplicity of roles and functions that counseling center staff could perform on Mexican American students' behalf.

Possible Roles of Counselors Working With Mexican American College Students

The frameworks described in the preceding section create bases from which counseling center practitioners may counsel many Mexican American students. Nonetheless, there continues to be a need for a more comprehensive framework that discusses how counselors can adopt culturally relevant roles in addressing psychological issues, social support systems, cultural values, and environmental context issues in this population. Hence, in this section, we discuss the application of Atkinson, Thompson, and Grant's (1993) three-dimensional model of counseling racial and ethnic minority individuals to Mexican American college students who seek counseling services and their counselors.

Atkinson et al. (1993) presented a three-dimensional model for counselors working with racially and ethnically diverse clients, and this model can be easily applied to Mexican American college students who present for counseling center services. Within the model, three factors should be considered when selecting the roles and strategies necessary to work with Mexican American college students: (a) the locus of the problem's etiology, (b) the client's level of acculturation, and (c) the goals of helping. Atkinson et al. proposed eight potential roles that counselors can fulfill within the therapeutic relationship. These roles include adviser, advocate, facilitator of indigenous support systems, facilitator of indigenous healing systems, consultant, change agent, counselor, and psychotherapist. It is important that the specific role or roles assumed by counselors at any given time depend on the specific combination of the three aforementioned issues for Mexican American students.

Within the *adviser* role, for example, counselors educate clients about forms of discrimination and oppression that they might face as members of a particular racial or ethnic group. An adviser role may be assumed with particularly low-acculturated clients who may be experiencing psychological distress because of racism or prejudice in their lives. An example of this counselor role is illustrated in working with Angela, a second-generation Mexican American college freshman. Despite having lived all of her life in the United States, she was low in acculturation, having grown up in the barrio and spending most of her time within her large extended family and close-knit Mexican community. Within her community, Angela was virtually isolated from mainstream culture until she left home to attend a large 4-year, predominantly White public university.

In this first time away from home, Angela experienced difficulty adjusting to college life and had trouble making friends. Despite believing that she was very introverted, Angela had made several attempts to get to know her roommate better. Angela's roommate, Kristen, a White American woman, did not speak to Angela, displayed a Confederate flag in their room, and consistently made racist comments to her friends about Blacks, Asians, Native Americans, and Jews. Angela noted that although Kristen did not say anything discriminatory about Latinos in front of her, she was reasonably sure that Kristen discussed her in a negative fashion with her friends when she was not around. Angela was unaware of what the Confederate flag symbol means, but she believed that it likely represented something unfavorable to certain racial or ethnic groups. In this instance, Angela's counselor could intercede as an adviser to explain the meanings of the Confederate flag and answer questions that Angela may have about some of Kristen's potential ideological beliefs about cultural differences. The counselor may also help Angela to identify other social support systems that she could access in order to feel more connected to her college peers, especially individuals who value and appreciate cultural diversity. The advising role assumed by

Angela's counselor may also help alleviate some of her adjustment difficulties of being away from home for the first time and dealing with a stressful living situation.

Next, the role of *advocate* can be assumed when working with Mexican American college students. This role may involve counselors literally speaking for their clients when low English-speaking ability or low acculturation may make it difficult for the clients to be understood by others (Atkinson et al., 1993). An example is the case of José and his counselor, who had been addressing his difficulties in adjusting to college life. José was born in Mexico and attended high school there. More recently, a pressing concern for José was being abruptly cut from the university soccer team because of his current language skills. Despite being a first-string player and tremendously enjoying soccer, José was stunned that he was dismissed from the team because he could not communicate well in English to his teammates and coach. Because of his adherence to certain cultural values (e.g., collectivism and deference to authority) and his English language proficiency, José may feel reluctant to approach his coach to inquire about his being cut from the team. In this situation, his counselor could assume an advocacy role, with José's written consent, that may involve speaking directly with the coach to ask about José's dismissal from the team and identifying ways to help José gain entry back onto the team. Similarly, José's counselor could serve as an advocate in helping José to file a grievance against his coach, if appropriate. Hence, in an advocate role, counselors work as a liaison between their clients and the sources of their specific problems.

According to Atkinson et al. (1993), counselors can also serve as *facilitators* of indigenous support systems. That is, counselors can identify available cultural resources and support networks primary to Mexican American students. An example of this facilitative role is reflected in the case of Mario, a third-generation self-identified Chicano. Since starting college and leaving his parents, siblings, and girlfriend, Mario has felt lonely and depressed. Because this is his first year of school, Mario does not want to worry his family about his concerns, and simultaneously, he feels uncomfortable telling his concerns to "total strangers." Although he has made a few college acquaintances, Mario is not willing to seek counseling because he is not "crazy" like others who receive services at the campus counseling center. When attending a mandatory outreach program on dating and relationships in his residence hall, Mario met and informally spoke to the presenter, a mental health counselor from the university counseling center. Curious as to whether he might get other ideas about meeting people, Mario visited the counselor for one session to identify ways that he could gain more social support. Realizing that Mario was reluctant to share his personal issues within a formal mental health relationship, Mario's counselor assessed with whom Mario might feel most comfortable talking about his concerns, rather than addressing the issues of depression and loneliness in a formal counseling context. During the conversation, Mario's counselor was able to ascertain that he received a great deal of support from his girlfriend Elsa and his older brother Francisco, or "Cisco." Also, Mario revealed that he and Cisco participated in campaigns for education and strikes for local migrant farmworker rights. Along with his parents, Mario and Cisco also attended mass every Sunday and then gathered with extended family for dinner.

From this information, Mario and his counselor brainstormed various indigenous support systems that could be mobilized. First, through the use of technology, Mario would coordinate with Elsa and Cisco to have daily e-mail conversations and schedule with his parents to have consistent bimonthly phone conversations. Next, the counselor arranged to introduce Mario to the student coleaders of the Movimiento Estudiantil Chicanos de Atzlán. These student leaders were active in campus politics and provided Saturday tutoring services for Latino elementary and secondary school children who did not know English. Further, a small group of the mechistas (i.e., students belonging to the Movimiento Estudiantil Chicanos de Atzlán) gathered on Sunday afternoons to attend the local Spanish mass and make dinner afterward. Although Mario and his counselor indirectly addressed his issues, the counselor intervened in a culturally relevant and useful manner in reconnecting Mario to university-based indigenous support systems.

Further, Mario's counselor also served as a facilitator of indigenous healing systems (Atkinson et al., 1993). Specifically, counselors may participate in traditional religious practices or ethnomedical healings (Koss-Chioino, 1995) that clients believe may be helpful to them, or counselors may refer clients to these systems if they are unable to assist clients more directly. In the assessment of Mario's family activities, the counselor recognized the importance of Mario's religious and spiritual beliefs. In addition to attending mass with other mechistas, Mario was given contact information for a Catholic priest (i.e., to receive pastoral counseling) because he reported feeling comfortable confiding to his community priest on past occasions at home.

The fifth role that counselors can assume is that of *consultant*. This role is often used with more highly acculturated individuals who may seek counseling to aid them in preventing or mitigating externally caused problems stemming from discrimination (Atkinson et al., 1993). Mili, a junior and third-generation Mexican American college student, has experienced difficulties in her work-study job and is in need of a consultant. For the past three semesters as a work-study student, she has been filing paperwork for a college department and has become disinterested with the tedious work. Traditionally, work-study students in this department perform filing work for one semester, after which they get promoted to less tedious jobs such as answering phones, greeting visitors, and taking copying and word-processing requests from faculty. Because Mili has a thick accent, her male supervisor believes she would have difficulties communicating with others. Subsequently she has been passed over twice for a promotion. Serving as a consultant, Mili's counselor can help her to devise ways of addressing this issue with her supervisor and identify any recourse she might have in being passed over for promotion. As a last option, the counselor could also help Mili to identify other work-study positions in which she might find more fulfillment.

The counselor working with Mili could also assume the role of *change agent*. In this role, counselors attempt to change social environments that may lead to discrimination (Atkinson et al., 1993). For example, Mili's counselor could volunteer his or her services to department chairpersons to provide "cultural sensitivity" or "culture in the workplace" seminars. As a change agent, Mili's counselor could also participate in activities (e.g., training seminars, local and national conferences) that involve publicly speaking to others about discrimination and cross-cultural issues faced by Mexican American college students.

Along with the roles described above, Atkinson et al. (1993) included the traditional *counselor* role. In this role, counselors seek to prevent problems. This role is mainly used for more acculturated clients like Mili who might feel comfortable talking about personal issues. This role can also be performed with Mexican American students of differing levels of acculturation if counselors are knowledgeable and integrative of cultural values and nuances for students (Constantine & Barón, 1997; Gloria & Rodriguez, 2000). In the counselor role, the therapist could help Mili to explore her feelings of frustration and anger associated with being passed over for promotion. In particular, the therapist could address the messages that Mili has internalized about her personal and academic skills and abilities as a result of her supervisor making assumptions about her accent. Further, Mili's counselor could address adjustment difficulties and developmental issues that she may encounter as a Mexican American female on a college campus.

The final role of *psychotherapist* is somewhat different from that of the counselor role. The psychotherapist role is typically applicable to highly acculturated clients who want relief from an existing problem caused by an internal etiology (Atkinson et al., 1993). This type of role may be difficult to establish with some Mexican American college students because certain problems or issues faced by this population may be the direct result of external factors such as discrimination or oppression. If counselors assume this role, they must be cautious not to overattribute clients' problems to internal or intrapsychic causes. For example, in Angela's case (the first vignette presented), the counselor would be inappropriate in solely attributing Angela's difficulties with her roommate to her need for acceptance. Instead, an effective and culturally competent counselor would be mindful that others' prejudices or negative attributions may be contributing to Angela's difficulties in her current situation. It is important to note, however, that psychotherapy could also be conducted that addresses externally focused concerns.

Conclusion

Although the experiences of Mexican American college students on U.S. campuses are varied and diverse, counselors may better attend to the psychological needs of this population by being cognizant of important culturally based issues in the context of providing mental health treatment. Moreover, college counselors' flexibility in adopting various helper roles when working with this population may be vital to their delivery of effective and multiculturally competent counseling services (Constantine et al., 2003). In fulfilling these multifaceted roles, counselors must examine their biases or hesitancies with regard to performing some of the roles. For example, counselors must contend with their potential biases against indigenous healing methods and alternative counseling services, interventions that some counselors may have been socialized against within their clinical training programs (Constantine et al., 2004; Gloria et al., 2004). Similarly, counseling center counselors need to contend with the organizational culture of their settings that either support or hinder the effectiveness of their services to Mexican American college students (Constantine et al., 2002). Understanding how various service delivery modalities and interventions may positively affect the experiences of Mexican American college students seems crucial to these counseling centers' ability to provide holistic and culturally relevant services to this population.

References

Aguirre, A., Jr., & Martinez, R. O. (1993). *Chicanos in higher education: Issues and dilemmas for the 21st century* (ASHE-ERIC Higher Education Rep. No. 3). Washington, DC: George Washington University, School of Education and Human Development.

Alva, S. A. (1991). Academic invulnerability among Mexican American students: The importance of protective resources and appraisals. *Hispanic Journal of Behavioral Sciences, 13,* 18–34.

Anzaldúa, G. (1990). La conciencia de la mestiza: Towards a new consciousness. In G. Anzaldúa (Ed.), *Making face, making soul/haciendo caras: Creative and critical perspectives by feminists of color* (pp. 377–389). San Francisco: Aunt Lute.

Arbona, C., Flores, C. L., & Novy, D. M. (1995). Cultural awareness and ethnic loyalty: Dimensions of cultural variability among Mexican American college students. *Journal of Counseling & Development, 73,* 610–614.

Arellano, A. R., & Padilla, A. M. (1996). Academic invulnerability among a select group of Latino university students. *Hispanic Journal of Behavioral Sciences, 18,* 485–507.

Arredondo, P. (1991). Counseling Latinas. In C. C. Lee & B. L. Richardson (Eds.), *Multicultural issues in counseling: New approaches to diversity* (pp. 143–156). Alexandria, VA: American Association for Counseling and Development.

Atkinson, D. R., Thompson, C. E., & Grant, S. K. (1993). A three-dimensional model for counseling racial/ethnic minorities. *The Counseling Psychologist, 21,* 257–277.

Barón, A., Jr. (1991). Counseling Chicano college students. In C. C. Lee & B. L. Richardson (Eds.), *Multicultural issues in counseling: New approaches to diversity* (pp. 171–184). Alexandria, VA: American Association for Counseling and Development.

Barón, A., & Constantine, M. G. (1997). A conceptual framework for conducting psychotherapy with Mexican American college students. In J. G. García & M. C. Zea (Eds.), *Psychological interventions and research with Latino populations* (pp. 108–124). New York: Allyn & Bacon.

Bernal, M. E., Knight, G. P., Ocampo, K. A., Garza, C.A., & Cota, M. K. (1993). Development of Mexican American identity. In M. A. Bernal & G. P. Knight (Eds.), *Ethnic identity: Formation and transmission among Hispanics and other minorities* (pp. 31–46). Albany: State University of New York Press.

Berry, J. W. (1993). Ethnic identity in plural societies. In M. E. Bernal & G. P. Knight (Eds.), *Acculturation: Theory, model, and some new findings* (pp. 9–25). Boulder, CO: Westview.

Boyd-Franklin, N., & Garcia-Preto, N. (1994). Family therapy: The cases of African American and Hispanic women. In L. Comas-Díaz & B. Greene (Eds.), *Women of color: Integrating ethnic and gender identities in psychotherapy* (pp. 239–264). New York: Guilford Press.

Casas, J. M., & Vasquez, M. J. (1996). Counseling the Hispanic. In P. B. Pedersen, J. G. Draguns, W. J. Lonner, & J. E. Trimble (Eds.), *Counseling across cultures* (4th ed., pp. 146–176). Thousand Oaks, CA: Sage.

Centers for Disease Control. (1991). Characteristics of parents who discuss AIDS with their children—United States, 1989. *Morbidity and Mortality Weekly Report, 40,* 789–791.

Cervantes, O. F. (1988). The realities that Latinos, Chicanos, and other ethnic minority students encounter in graduate school. *Journal of La Raza Studies, 2,* 34–41.

Comas-Díaz, L. (1989). Culturally relevant issues and treatment implications for Hispanics. In D. R. Koslow & E. Salett (Eds.), *Crossing cultures in mental health* (pp. 31–48). Washington, DC: Society for International Education Training and Research.

Comas-Díaz, L. (2001). Hispanics, Latinos, or Americanos: The evolution of identity. *Cultural Diversity and Ethnic Minority Psychology, 7,* 115–120.

Constantine, M. G., & Barón, A. (1997). Assessing and counseling Chicano(a) college students: A conceptual and practical framework. In C. Lee (Ed.), *Multicultural issues in counseling: New approaches to diversity* (2nd ed., pp. 295–314). Alexandria, VA: American Counseling Association.

Constantine, M. G., Myers, L. J., Kindaichi, M., & Moore, J. L. (2004). Exploring indigenous mental health practices: The roles of healers and helpers in promoting well-being in people of color. *Counseling and Values, 48,* 110–125.

Constantine, M. G., Robinson, J. S., Wilton, L., & Caldwell, L. D. (2002). Collective self-esteem and perceived social support as predictors of cultural congruity among Black and Latino college students. *Journal of College Student Development, 43,* 307–316.

Constantine, M. G., Wilton, L., & Caldwell, L. D. (2003). The role of social support in moderating the relationship between psychological distress and willingness to seek psychological help among Black and Latino college students. *Journal of College Counseling, 6,* 155–165.

Copeland, E. P., & Hess, R. S. (1995). Differences in young adolescents' coping strategies based on gender and ethnicity. *Journal of Early Adolescence, 15,* 203–219.

Dernersesian, A. C. (1993). And, yes . . . the earth did part: On the splitting of Chicana/o subjectivity. In A. de la Torre & B. M. Pesquera (Eds.), *Building with our hands: New directions in Chicana studies* (pp. 34–56). Los Angeles: University of California Press.

Echeverry, J. J. (1997). Treatment barriers: Accessing and accepting professional help. In J. G. García & M. C. Zea (Eds.), *Psychological intervention and research with Latino populations* (pp. 94–107). Boston: Allyn & Bacon.

Falicov, C. J. (1998). *Latino families in therapy: A guide to multicultural practice.* New York: Guilford Press.

Feagin, J. R., Vera, H., & Imani, N. (1996). *The agony of education: Black students at White colleges and universities.* New York: Routledge.

Frase, M. (1992). *Are Hispanic dropout rates a result of recent immigration?* Washington, DC: U.S. Department of Education, National Center for Education Statistics.

Gándara, P. (1995). *Over the ivy walls: The educational mobility of low income Chicanos.* Albany: State University of New York Press.

Garcia-Vasquez, E., Vasquez, L. A., & Huang, C. Y. (1998). Psychological factors and language: Impact on Mexican American students. *College Student Journal, 32,* 6–18.

Gay, G. (2001). Educational equality for students of color. In J. A. Banks & C. A. McGee Banks (Eds.), *Multicultural education: Issues and perspectives* (4th ed., pp. 197–224). New York: Wiley.

Gloria, A. M. (1997). Chicana academic persistence: Creating a university-based community. *Education and Urban Society, 30,* 107–121.

Gloria, A. M. (1999). Apoyando estudiantes Chicanas: Therapeutic factors in Chicana college student support groups. *Journal for Specialists in Group Work, 24,* 246–259.

Gloria, A. M., & Castellanos, J. (2003). Latino/a and African American students at predominantly White institutions: A psychosociocultural perspective of educational interactions and academic persistence. In J. Castellanos & L. Jones (Eds.), *The majority in the minority: Retaining Latina/o faculty, administrators, and students* (pp. 71–92). Sterling, VA: Stylus.

Gloria, A. M., & Pope-Davis, D. B. (1997). Cultural ambience: The importance of a culturally aware learning environment in the training and education of counselors. In D. B. Pope-Davis & H. L. K. Coleman (Eds.), *Multicultural counseling competencies: Assessment, education and training, and supervision* (pp. 242–259). Thousand Oaks, CA: Sage.

Gloria, A. M., & Robinson Kurpius, S. E. (1996). The validation of the Cultural Congruity Scale and the University Environment Scale with Chicano/a students. *Hispanic Journal of Behavioral Science, 18,* 533–549.

Gloria, A. M., & Rodriguez, E. R. (2000). Counseling Latino university students: Psychosociocultural issues for consideration. *Journal of Counseling & Development, 78,* 145–154.

Gloria, A. M., Ruiz, E. L., & Castillo, E. M. (2004). Counseling Latinos and Latinas: A psychosociocultural approach. In P. S. Richards & T. Smith (Eds.), *Practicing multiculturalism: Internalizing and affirming diversity in counseling and psychology* (pp. 167–184). Boston: Allyn & Bacon.

Gottlieb, B. H. (1981). *Social networks and social support.* Beverly Hills, CA: Sage.

Guzmán, B. (2001). *The Hispanic population* (Current Population Reports, C2KBR/01-3). Washington, DC: U.S. Census Bureau.

Haro, R. P., Rodriguez, G., Jr., & Gonzales, J. L., Jr. (1994). *Latino persistence in higher education: A 1994 survey of University of California and California State University Chicano/Latino students.* (ERIC Document Reproduction Service No. ED380023)

Knight, G. P., Bernal, M. E., Garza, C. A., & Cota, M. K. (1993). A social cognitive model of the development of ethnic identity and ethnically based behaviors. In M. E. Bernal & G. P. Knight (Eds.), *Ethnic identity: Formation and transmission among Hispanics and other minorities* (pp. 214–234). Albany: State University of New York Press.

Koss-Chioino, J. D. (1995). Traditional and fork approaches among ethnic minorities. In J. F. Aponte, R. Y. Rivers, & J. Wohl (Eds.), *Psychological interventions and cultural diversity* (pp. 145–163). Boston: Allyn & Bacon.

Koss-Chioino, J. D., & Vargas, L. A. (1999). *Working with Latino youth.* San Francisco: Jossey-Bass.

Lango, D. R. (1995). Mexican American female enrollment in graduate programs: A study of the characteristics that may predict success. *Hispanic Journal of Behavioral Sciences, 17,* 33–48.

Lopez-Baez, S. I. (1997). Counseling interventions with Latinas. In C. C. Lee & B. L. Richardson (Eds.), *Multicultural issues in counseling: New approaches to diversity* (pp. 257–267). Alexandria, VA: American Association for Counseling and Development.

Macias, R. F. (1993). Language and ethnic classification of language minorities: Chicano and Latino students in the 1990s. *Hispanic Journal of Behavioral Sciences, 15,* 230–257.

Marín, B. V., & Gómez, C. A. (1997). Latino culture and sex: Implications for HIV prevention. In J. G. García & M. C. Zea (Eds.), *Psychological intervention and research with Latino populations* (pp. 73–93). Boston: Allyn & Bacon.

Martinez, E. (1998). *De colores means all of us: Latina views for a multi colored century.* Cambridge, MA: South End Press.

Mirandé, A. (1985). *The Chicano experience: An alternative perspective.* Notre Dame, IN: University of Notre Dame Press.

Morales, E. S. (1990). HIV infection and Hispanic gay and bisexual men. *Hispanic Journal of Behavioral Sciences, 12,* 212–222.

Morales, E. (1992). Latino gays and Latina lesbians. In S. Dworkin & F. Gutiérrez (Eds.), *Counseling gay men and lesbians: Journey to the end of the rainbow* (pp. 125–139). Alexandria, VA: American Association for Counseling and Development.

Newcomer, S., & Baldwin, W. (1992). Demographics of adolescent sexual behavior, contraception, pregnancy, and STDs. *Journal of School Health, 62,* 265–270.

O'Brien, E. M. (1993). Latinos in higher education. *Research Briefs, 4,* 1–13. (ERIC Document Reproduction Service No. ED383790)

Pappas, G., & Guajardo, M. (1997). Ethnic diversity as a measurement of quality in higher education. *Latinos in Colorado: A Profile of Culture, Changes, and Challenges, 5,* 19–22.

Patterson, C. H. (1996). Multicultural counseling: From diversity to universality. *Journal of Counseling & Development, 74,* 227–231.

Phinney, J. S. (1990). Ethnic identity in adolescents and adults: Review of research. *Psychological Bulletin, 108,* 499–514.

Quintana, S. M., Vogel, M. C., & Ybarra, V. C. (1991). Meta-analysis of Latino students' adjustment in higher education. *Hispanic Journal of Behavioral Sciences, 13,* 155–169.

Reyes, P., & Valencia, R. R. (1993). Educational policy and the growing Latino student population: Problems and prospects. *Hispanic Journal of Behavioral Sciences, 15,* 258–283.

Richards, P. S., & Bergin, A. E. (Eds.). (2000). *Handbook of psychotherapy and religious diversity.* Washington, DC: American Psychological Association.

Richards, P. S., & Smith, T. (Eds.). (2004). *Practicing multiculturalism: Internalizing and affirming diversity in counseling and psychology.* Boston: Allyn & Bacon.

Rivers, R. Y. (1995). Clinical issues and intervention with ethnic minority women. In J. F. Aponte, R. Y. Rivers, & J. Wohl (Eds.), *Psychological interventions and cultural diversity* (pp. 181–198). Boston: Allyn & Bacon.

Ruiz, R. A., & Casas, J. M. (1976). Culturally relevant and behavioristic counseling for Chicano college students. In P. B. Pedersen, J. G. Draguns, W. J. Lonner, & J. E. Trimble (Eds.), *Counseling across cultures* (pp. 181–202). Honolulu: University of Hawaii Press.

Solberg, V. S., & Villareal, P. (1997). Examination of self-efficacy, social support, and stress as predictors of psychological and physical distress among Hispanic college students. *Hispanic Journal of Behavioral Sciences, 19,* 182–201.

Therrien, M., & Ramirez, R. R. (2000). *The Hispanic population in the United States: March 2000* (Current Population Reports, P20-535). Washington, DC: U.S. Census Bureau.

Trujillo, C. M. (1997). Sexual identity and the discontents of difference. In B. Greene (Ed.), *Ethnic and cultural diversity among lesbians and gay men* (pp. 266–278). Thousand Oaks, CA: Sage.

U.S. Bureau of the Census. (2000). *The Hispanic population in the United States*. Washington, DC: U.S. Department of Commerce.

U.S. Department of Education, National Center for Education Statistics. (1996). *The condition of education* (NCES Rep. No. 1996-304). Washington, DC: U.S. Government Printing Office.

U.S. Department of Education, National Center for Education Statistics. (1998). *Racial and ethnic differences in participation in higher education* (NCES Rep. No. 1998-012). Washington, DC: U.S. Government Printing Office.

U.S. Department of Education, National Center for Education Statistics. (2000a). *Digest of education statistics 1999* (NCES Rep. No. 2000-031). Washington, DC: U.S. Government Printing Office.

U.S. Department of Education, National Center for Education Statistics. (2000b). *Racial and ethnic distribution of elementary and secondary students* (NCES Rep. No. 2000-005). Washington, DC: U.S. Government Printing Office.

Vasquez, M. J. T. (1982). Confronting barriers to the participation of Mexican American women in higher education. *Hispanic Journal of Behavioral Sciences, 4*, 147–165.

Wilds, D. J. (2000). *Minorities in higher education 1999–2000: Seventeenth annual status report*. Washington, DC: American Council on Education.

Wilton, L., & Constantine, M. G. (2003). Length of time, cultural adjustment difficulties, and psychological distress in Asian and Latin American international college students. *Journal of College Counseling, 6*, 177–186.

Yalom, I. D. (1995). *The theory and practice of group psychotherapy* (4th ed.). New York: Basic Books.

Yep, G. A. (1995). Communicating the HIV/AIDS risk to Hispanic populations. In A. M. Padilla (Ed.), *Hispanic psychology: Critical issues in theory and research* (pp. 196–212). Thousand Oaks, CA: Sage.

Zea, M. C., Mason, M. A., & Murguía, A. (2000). Psychotherapy with members of Latino/Latina religions and spiritual traditions. In P. S. Richards & A. E. Bergin (Eds.), *Handbook of psychotherapy and religious diversity* (pp. 397–419). Washington, DC: American Psychological Association.

Puerto Ricans in the Counseling Process: The Dynamics of Ethnicity and Race in Social Context

Jesse M. Vazquez

Although Puerto Rico has been a territory of the United States since 1898, many Americans still do not know, for example, where the island is geographically located, that all Puerto Ricans have been American citizens since 1917, that they are a racially heterogeneous population, that Puerto Rican monetary currency is the currency of the United States, and so on. The degree of cultural illiteracy that exists among many non-Puerto-Rican Americans about Puerto Rico and Puerto Ricans is astounding. Unfortunately, the lay public knows far more about the negative Puerto Rican stereotypes than it does about matters cultural, political, historical, and psychological.

Puerto Ricans now constitute the second largest (Chicanos are the largest) ethnically distinct Latino group in the continental United States. Over 3.4 million Puerto Ricans live in the United States, and about 3.8 million still reside in Puerto Rico (U.S. Bureau of the Census, 2001a, p. 4). Although emigration from Puerto Rico to New York had been occurring since the early 1900s (and well before that under Spanish rule), the early and middle 1950s marked the most dramatic high point of the Puerto Rican migration to the United States. During that high watermark of migration, approximately 80% of the migrants settled in New York City (Fitzpatrick, 1987). Since that time, for well over 40 years, Puerto Ricans have continued to migrate not only to New York but also to other major urban centers in the northeastern and midwestern parts of the United States. Boston, Chicago, Newark, Philadelphia, Trenton, and other urban centers across the country have become home to large concentrations of Puerto Rican settlements. New York City, however, continues to be home to the greatest number of Puerto Ricans in the continental United States, including Hawaii and Alaska. A significant colony of Puerto Ricans had taken root in Hawaii beginning in about 1902 when Puerto Rican workers were sent to the Hawaiian Islands to cut sugar cane and pick pineapples (Centro de Estudios Puertorriquenos, 1977; Silva & Souza, 1982).

According to recent estimates, 36.6% of all Hispanics in New York are Puerto Rican, and Latinos make up approximately 15.1% of that state's population (U.S. Bureau of the Census, 2001a, p. 7). Latinos in New York City constitute 27% of the total population, and Puerto Ricans continue to constitute the largest segment of all Latino subgroups, followed by Dominicans (Logan, Stowell, Stults, & Oakley, 2001, Table 1).

For a large segment of the Puerto Rican population, however, the pattern of migration is circular (between the United States and Puerto Rico), a phenomenon that sustains cultural, linguistic, and family connections and loyalties. According to Bonilla (1989), the circular migration—the dynamics and causes of which he placed into the larger framework of an advanced international capitalism—is also creating a startling similarity in worldviews and problems shared between those who reside on the island and those who, for a time, find themselves in the United States. This phenomenon is greatly facilitated by Puerto Ricans' U.S. citizenship, ease of travel, and the island's political and economic connection with the United States as well as the place that Puerto Rico occupies in the larger network of the global economy.

The first-person chronicles of the earlier migrants, the work of novelists, and the studies of historians, sociologists, anthropologists, and community activists reflect the toughness of spirit, the resistance to oppression, and the complexity of those Puerto Ricans who served as the pioneers and who formed the first barrios in New York City for those who followed in other cities throughout the United States (see Colon, 1982; Fitzpatrick, 1987; Haslip-Viera & Baver, 1996; Iglesias, 1977/1984; Mohr, 1985; Morales, 1986; E. Padilla, 1958; F. Padilla, 1987; Pantoja, 1989; Rivera, 1982, 1987; Rodriguez, 1989; Sanchez-Korrol, 1994; Torres & Velazquez, 1998).

There is a history of struggle among Puerto Ricans, both on the island and in the United States. It is a struggle against the abuses and oppression of a classic form of colonialism and imperialism under the Spanish and neocolonialism under U.S. rule since 1898. It is also a struggle to maintain a unique cultural heritage and identity amidst profound technological and environmental change and the overwhelming external and internal pressures to adopt and adapt to things North American.

For the Puerto Ricans in the United States, it is also a struggle to survive economically, culturally, linguistically, and psychologically. Tensions around ethnic/cultural and racial identity abound and play a central role in the process of acculturation as well as in the resistance to assimilating forces. Counselors who work with Puerto Rican clients must begin to appreciate the complexity and legacy of this social and historical reality. Unquestionably, the impact of these historical events has played a critical role in shaping the collective social, economic, and psychological worldviews of Puerto Ricans who continue to live in the United States as well as those who make their homes on the island. And then there are those whose circular pattern of migration has permitted them to live in both worlds in what is now seen as common in the transnational movements of millions of immigrants around the globe.

Socioeconomics: Implications for Counselors

Since the 1990 Census, it seems that between 1997 and 1998 a small percentage (2%) of Puerto Ricans and other Hispanics climbed out of poverty, but "there was no change statistically in the number of Hispanic families who were poor" (U.S. Bureau of the Census, 1999, p. 2). A significant portion of the Puerto Rican population in the United States continues to live at or below the poverty line. Incredibly, 30.9% of Puerto Rican families found themselves below the poverty level in the 1990s (U.S. Bureau of the Census, 1990).

Another statistical reality that continues to have significant implications for counselors in schools and social service agencies is that 37% of families in the Puerto Rican community are headed by females with no male spouse present (U.S. Bureau of the Census, 2000, Table 3.2). If one also considers that Puerto Ricans and other Hispanics—28% compared with 5% of the non-Hispanic White population—have less than a ninth-grade level of education, one can begin to see the emergence of a profile for a population at risk (U.S. Bureau of the

Census, 2000, Table 5.2). Of those 28%, many are school dropouts, are underemployed, and have school-age children.

Rodriguez (1989) suggested that this kind of statistical profile, however, does not necessarily portend the breakdown of the Puerto Rican family, as so many interpreters of these data might have one believe. It is critical that counselors who work within the Puerto Rican community suspend their own beliefs about what they consider a "typical" family as well as explore the sources of strengths that keep families together. However, as Rodriguez (1989) noted, it is not the increased number of female-headed households that is the issue but the persistent poverty—a distinction worth noting.

These issues represent aspects of the socioeconomic challenges that have a direct impact on the lives of Puerto Ricans and their children and, in one form or another, become the concerns of the counselor, even though they may seem far removed from the area of cultural beliefs, attitudes, and values of the Puerto Rican migrant. The challenges, by and large, are direct results of (a) the social and economic structure that exists in the United States; (b) the history of political, economic, and military control exercised over the people and resources of the island since the United States invaded and annexed Puerto Rico; and (c) the problems that spring from the fact that the "Puerto Ricans are both the only colonial group to arrive en masse, and the first racially heterogeneous group to migrate to the U.S. on a large scale" (Rodriguez, 1989, p. xiv). All of these conditions make for an environment guaranteed to create stress for the migrant who finds his or her way to an American metropolis. Counselors should be able to incorporate these kinds of observations into their work and to set them into a broader societal context.

Racial/Ethnic Identity: Implications for Counselors

In one of the earliest community studies of Puerto Rican adaptation to life in an urban American setting, E. Padilla (1958) focused on the issue of racial and ethnic identity of Puerto Ricans in the United States. She noted, "Both in Puerto Rico and in the United States social race is an important aspect of social life, but *race* is looked at, defined, and appraised in different ways in the two countries" (p. 69). This seemingly straightforward, yet complex, observation has been repeated many times in the literature since then and has been linked to psychological stress in response to the chronic and persistent racism and cultural dissonance that Puerto Ricans experience in the United States (Betances, 1971, 1972, 1973; De La Cancela, 1988; De La Cancela & Zavala-Martinez, 1983; Fitzpatrick, 1987; Longres, 1974; Martinez, 1986; Rodriguez, 1980, 1989; Zavala-Martinez, 1988, 1994a, 1994b).

If an individual is perceived to be phenotypically non-White in the United States, or if he or she is believed to be a member of an ethnic group (in this case Puerto Rican) that has been socially designated as non-White, then all members of that group are considered socially non-White regardless of within-group variability in phenotypes. Herein lies the psychological and social dilemma for many Puerto Ricans.

Puerto Ricans first identify culturally as Puerto Ricans but also proceed to make racial distinctions among a variety of physical traits, such as skin color, hair texture (the notion of "good" hair or "bad" hair), thickness of lips, and nose configuration. Different combinations of these traits place the individual—phenotypically, that is—into one of several racially rooted categories, which, as indicated, are based on more than skin color: *blanco* (phenotypically White with a variety of so-called Caucasian features), *trigueno* (brunette type, wheat color), *indio* (dark skin, straight black hair), *morenos* (dark skin with a variety of Negroid or Caucasian features), and *negro* (equivalent to dark-skinned Black people in the United States; Rodriguez, 1989).

When forced to identify within the framework of the prevailing racial–social structure of the United States, many Puerto Ricans, particularly during the earliest stages of their migration, face stress and confusion while trying to fit into the Black–White dichotomy offered by the American racial and social framework. If an individual's primary anchor of identity is cultural, and he or she is forced to identify as either White or Black, then that person is essentially being deprived of a personal sense of identity (Rodriguez, 1989). This is especially confounding in families and in a population in which racial phenotypes are quite varied. If I identify as Black, or am identified as White in a family that contains significant racial variation, what does that do to my sense of connection and identification as a member of that family? How do I feel about my lighter or darker brother or sister who may have benefited or not from these kinds of perceptual racial distinctions? Further, what is the emotional price paid when the experience is one that Rodriguez (1989) called "perceptual dissonance"? In such a case, the individual sees himself or herself in one way, and others see the individual quite differently. The experience, "particularly as it pertains to race, is clearly an unsettling process" (Rodriguez, 1989, p. 76).

This is particularly interesting in light of recent census data that show that a significant number—about 42%—of Puerto Ricans and other Latinos, when asked to racially identify themselves, opted for the "some other race" category, whereas only 0.2% of the non-Hispanic or Latino group checked this option (U.S. Bureau of the Census, 2001b, p. 10). In point of fact, 97% of the 15.4 million respondents who reported "some other race" alone were Latinos. This clearly reflects a different view of racial identification.

On an island where well into the latter part of the 19th century the merchants and landowners were primarily from Spain and other Western European countries, the "matter of color was also a matter of class" (Martinez, 1986, p. 39). According to Martinez, if "a non-White or racially mixed individual should rise in class status, then that person was accorded the deference of that class and the color disappeared" (p. 39). That is, racial identity, although not addressed directly, assumed less importance as measured against the individual's achievements as a university professor, accomplished musician, lawyer, engineer, or successful public servant.

The most recent census figures from the island of Puerto Rico yielded a very interesting statistical racial profile for those on the island. It seems that 80.5% identified as racially White, whereas only 8% identified as being Black or African American (Puerto Rican Legal Defense and Education Fund [PRLDEF], Institute for Puerto Rican Policy, 2001). This same report suggested that the most controversial aspect of the 2000 Census for the 3.8 million island Puerto Ricans was "the use of the Hispanic identifier and race questions, which had not been used in a census on the Island since 1950 "(PRLDEF, Institute for Puerto Rican Policy, 2001, p. 1). Only 7.3% selected the "some other race" option, whereas 4.2% indicated a multiracial identity. These results, according to this same report, are "harder to interpret" (PRLDEF, Institute for Puerto Rican Policy, 2001, p. 1). Conventional wisdom would have expected higher rates in the Black or African American category as well as in the multiracial category. Further analysis awaits.

Today, after nearly 100 years of an American presence on the island and more than 50 years since the beginning of the huge migrations to the U.S. mainland, the matter of racial identity and confusion persists in expressions of how Puerto Ricans see themselves and how they are racially perceived and designated by non-Puerto Ricans. For those who are involved in counseling Puerto Ricans, the issue of racial identity will be a repeated theme in the counseling process, sometimes central and at other times peripheral.

Conflicts or uncertainty regarding racial and ethnic intermarriage, incidents of racism and racial injustice, questions pertaining to racial/ethnic identity, and other related issues will continue to be raised in the counseling process as long as race and ethnicity continue to play a central role in the American social and political structure.

The Case Study of Nydia

The case study presented here illustrates the challenge in the counseling process of working with a client who specifically raises questions related to racial and ethnic identity.

Nydia is a 30-year-old Puerto Rican woman, born in Puerto Rico, who at the age of 2 migrated with her family to the United States. Nydia sought counseling shortly after her non-Latino fiancé made his first visit to meet her family. She came to me for counseling because she had heard that I was Puerto Rican and she believed that I would be able to help her sort out the tension and fears that she was experiencing after her fiancé's visit.

Although her fiancé knew that Puerto Ricans were racially heterogeneous, he had no idea that this broad range of variability of racial phenotypes could also be seen within one nuclear family. He quickly identified some of the darker complected members in Nydia's family as Black and was quite taken aback by this observation. Until that moment, he had assumed (based on his American perception and conceptualizations of race and racial categories) that because Nydia was phenotypically White that all of her siblings were also White. He asked her what she was: Was she Black, or was she White? As far as Nydia was concerned, she had always simply seen herself as a Puerto Rican who happened to be phenotypically White with some darker and some lighter complected siblings and cousins. However, his subsequent persistent probing about Nydia's racial identity and pressing inquiries about her family's racial origins were sufficient to create a panic in her. Was he really telling her that this might be sufficient reason to call off their engagement? Nydia was concerned about her fiancé's preoccupation with her racial identity; and she was also uncertain about her own racial/ethnic identity at this point. Although she never denied her identity as a Puerto Rican woman, she had never really come to terms with the complexity of her own racial identity.

After conducting a routine history, my approach was to encourage Nydia to examine her ethnic identity as a Puerto Rican woman in the United States. What did it mean to her to have grown up as a Puerto Rican in New York? What was it like for her? A detailed open exploration of the client's ethnic self or ethnic psychohistory will reveal a complex web of emotional experiences that ultimately allow the client an opportunity to examine more openly an aspect of the self that has heretofore remained vague, hidden, and undefined. This dynamic is quite common in American society. Although the American mythology espouses a so-called melting-pot ideology, the real message we receive is that we must hide (or make little mention of) who we are ethnically. Americans are asked to deny racial or cultural contradictions, especially when they are apparent or experienced as painful. Those who are unable to grasp the reality of racial and ethnic identity in American society have a tendency to create a kind of new personal mythology about who they are ethnically and racially.

As a society, Americans rarely challenge their ethnic perceptions of self and others and the societal myths that belie the trail of tears that is a central part of America's racial and ethnic history. How many times have we heard the expression "when I look at you I don't see color, I see a person." Many manage to construct personal notions about who they are ethnically and what other people think they are. Those who are members of the dominant society, particularly those who are considered White in this society, seem to have a greater tendency to accept an acculturated behavior pattern consistent with the core American society. However, people of color, and Puerto Ricans regardless of phenotype are placed in this social category, may be much more easily able to get in touch with this illusive ethnic self.

Nydia was no exception. She began to look carefully at her family's migration history, the existence of racism in American society, the covert and not so covert meanings about race and racial characteristics she was exposed to in her own family, and how a multiplicity of social and economic realities had shaped a good deal of her life and her family's life. What was the larger social context of her life that contributed to where her family lived, what kinds of schools existed in the community, and what kinds of jobs were her family members forced to take to earn a living and to survive in a large urban metropolis? And how was all of this connected to her interior psychological life and development?

Her need to drop out of school and her subsequent efforts to begin college again in her late 20s were events that she reexamined from a variety of perspectives. She reevaluated her own personal success in a blue-collar career in light of the choices she had made as well as in light of the limited and imposed choices available to her family and to thousands of other Puerto Ricans who had come to the United States in search of a better life. Looking at specific critical incidents in her life through the lens of her ethnic self gradually allowed Nydia to begin to come to terms with who she is ethnically and racially. Eventually, Nydia was able to effectively formulate some questions of her own, which sought to clarify her fiancé's own racial belief system and some of his current preoccupations with race and racial identity. She considered what the implications might be for their continued relationship.

A useful approach in cases in which ethnic or racial identity plays a role in shaping affect and cognition is to first explore the structural and functional aspects of race and ethnicity in American society, and the impact of these on the development of the individual, and then attempt to connect these sociological and anthropological domains with the feelings, experiences, and meanings of these events in the life of the client.

These kinds of explorations place the client's issues in a broader social and cultural context. How has the client historically experienced these events? What is the meaning of these events in the client's life? A blend of cognitive, phenomenological, existential, and didactic (sociological, anthropological, and historical discourse) strategies allows the counselor and the client to draw links that may exist between the many layers of experiences and external events that contribute to this kind of inner conflict.

The structural aspects of racial and ethnic identity issues need to be understood as part of the matrix of emotional and behavioral responses of the client to his or her world. The linkage between these domains is critical for movement in either the counseling process or the educational process. For school counselors, a psychoeducational approach, particularly in groups, will allow students the opportunity to begin to understand how their social selves are intricately entwined with their psychological selves.

There is no diagnosis, in the classical sense, because there is no identifiable disorder or disease process going on. However, there can be anger, distress, confusion, and sometimes self-doubt that grow out of the client's perception of self (ethnically and racially) and others' perceptions of the client.

The often heard comment "that's funny, you don't *look* Puerto Rican" tells worlds about the perception of the speaker. If the Puerto Rican accepts the phrase, then perhaps it can be assumed that there is confusion about the self in relation to others.

Martinez (1986) saw this racial identity confusion as a phenomenon that will continue to exist as long as Puerto Ricans "avoid or deny their reality in American society" (p. 45). Rodriguez (1989), however, considered that the very ambiguity of racial and cultural identity can be viewed as a potential source of strength and as a healthy sign of adaptation that perhaps will pose a direct "challenge to the U.S. bifurcation of race" (p. 77). She found that many Puerto Ricans have been able to move back and forth among the White, Black, and Hispanic worlds. This movement, she suggested, "may be rooted in the ability to see oneself in a variety of ways" (p. 77). A new generation of Puerto Ricans may be emerging as truly tricultural and perhaps bilingual or even trilingual. Is it a denial of a racial reality, or is it a forging of a new identity? Within the context of a rapidly changing racial and cultural America, this idea may begin to gain more meaning as racial–ethnic demographic balances shift in the 21st century. As noted earlier, this should be viewed in light of the 42% of Latino respondents who, when asked to identify racially, selected "some other race." Rodriguez (2000) reported that this figure was at 40% in a 1993 update from the 1990 Census. For many, this Latino response is a confounding phenomenon. And as Rodriguez (2000) pointed out, "For Latinos, responses to race are seldom as simple and straightforward as they tend to be for most non-Hispanic whites" (p. 11).

Do these figures represent racial denial or confusion, or is it perhaps the first step toward the formation of new identities and a breakdown of the old Black–White paradigm in America's racial construct?

Conclusion

Nydia's case raises a number of important psychoculturally rooted issues that are frequently encountered when counselors are working with Puerto Rican clients. To serve the Puerto Rican client more effectively, the counselor must attend to a wide range of issues, including not only racial identity but also the importance of the continuity of language, implications of class, changing family patterns, the salience of gender, and a societal and economic structure that has shaped the migration and the current and future life chances of Puerto Ricans in the United States and in Puerto Rico. And understanding the dynamics of acculturation and assimilation is naturally a central focus of concern. How rapidly or how slowly do Puerto Ricans assimilate into the American mainstream? What is the role of race, language, and culture in this process? In effect, the counselor must be fully prepared to explore issues that go well beyond the purview of the traditional counseling domain and to use techniques and strategies that may challenge the current order of things.

Because of the central role of culture in the field of multicultural counseling, we should remain constantly vigilant and question the emerging literature that attempts to broaden our understanding of other groups but that may also inadvertently reify cultural patterns or traits that may be situational and in the process of social change. The cultural inventory approach, so common in much of the current counseling literature, enumerates traits or characteristics such as eye contact, kinetics, gender roles, and family patterns of Puerto Ricans and other ethnic groups in American society. But it is an approach that can hinder our attempts to help and, in the final analysis, may reify and make static that which is by experience a most dynamic process.

Understanding cultural patterns in a vacuum, without engaging in a more complex dialectical assessment of the client's world at the present moment and historically, inevitably leads to the most superficial cultural pronouncements of a people. Without an appreciation of the dynamic nature of the "ethnic matrix" (Vazquez, 1975, 1977, 1986), the counseling process stagnates in a collection of cultural minutia.

Despite the strides that have been made in the last 20 years, we continue to read research literature that misinterprets cultural minutia and presents these as fixed, unchanging phenomena. For example, some authors continue to distort the concepts of *machismo* and *marianismo* by presenting misleading and flattened descriptions of a complex set of behaviors that are shaped by a multiplicity of forces. Others propose that "passivity and docility" of Puerto Ricans and other Latinos are still a part of the "character" study of a people, and still others are preoccupied with trying to establish a pan-Hispanic or pan-Latino psychological profile that defies the complex history of migration and immigration from the Caribbean and South and Central America. But Latinos in the United States are a complex people racially, culturally, politically, and historically, and efforts to homogenize the Latino in psychological terms is misleading. They do not fit easily into the old prevailing Euroethnic models of ethnicity, nor, as we are learning, do they easily fit into the traditional racial constructs of American society. Efforts to do so in a pseudoscientific way may contribute to the oversimplification of the psychocultural experience and the current choices that many Puerto Ricans and other Latinos are making. The rush to establish neat phases or stages in psychocultural or ethnic identity development can perhaps do more harm than good. As suggested, it may be far more effective to contextualize the issues at hand and to look at a broad range of factors contributing to and interacting with the individual's behavior and worldview and the process of continuing cultural and societal change.

Cultural observations, such as group identity, differing attitudes toward family, attitudes toward outsiders, and ideas of male and female roles—if erroneously reported in the literature—could have an adverse effect on the perceptions, strategies, and actions of counselors. This can be problematic, especially if these kinds of "cultural data" at one time or another are merged into the counseling process. Cultural data should never be seen as immutable. There is little argument with the idea that cultural specifics are valuable adjuncts in the counseling process, but how the cross-cultural practitioner validates, evaluates, and judiciously incorporates these observations into his or her intervention strategies warrants careful consideration.

Bock (1988), in his work in psychological anthropology, provocatively titled his prelude and postlude chapters with the following propositions: "All anthropology is psychological," and "All psychology is cultural." These seemingly paradoxical assertions are clearly intended to provoke consideration of the cultural roots of psychological thinking and practice and, at the same time, the psychological dimensions of all anthropological and social observations and conceptualizations and their sources.

This chapter on counseling Puerto Ricans should be seen simply as a guide to an approach, an effort to see the cultural in the psychology of the individual and the psychological in the culture. It is not a "cookbook" formula. It is suggestive of the complexities of the human experience and a snapshot of a people who continue to struggle in a rapidly changing world where transnational and transcultural phenomena are beginning to challenge the old static notions of culture and race.

Counselors can anticipate working with Puerto Rican clients who may express a wide range of degrees of acculturation as well as with those who have a clear sense of who they are ethnically and racially. Many may adapt to the mainland's cultural mode simply as an accommodation for the sake of survival, whereas others may reassert their identity in forms that may be outmoded and perhaps dysfunctional in a postindustrial world. Still others will fashion new ways of assuring their future while reaffirming and recapturing that which is valuable and enduring in their community of memory.

References

Betances, S. (1971). Puerto Rican youth: Race and the search for self. *The Rican, 1*(1), 4–13.

Betances, S. (1972). The prejudice of having no prejudice in Puerto Rico. Part I. *The Rican, 2*(1), 41–54.

Betances, S. (1973). The prejudice of having no prejudice in Puerto Rico. Part II. *The Rican, 3*(3), 22–37.

Bock, P. K. (1988). *Rethinking psychological anthropology: Continuity and change in the study of human action.* New York: Freeman.

Bonilla, F. (1989). La circulacion migratoria en la decada actual [Circular migration in the current decade]. *Boletin Del Centro De Estudios Puertorriquenos, 2*(6), 55–59.

Centro de Estudios Puertorriquenos. (1977). *Documents of the Puerto Rican migration: Hawaii, Cuba, Santo Domingo, and Ecuador.* New York: Research Foundation of the City University of New York.

Colon, J. (1982). *A Puerto Rican in New York and other sketches.* New York: International Universities Press.

De La Cancela, V. (1988). Labor pains: Puerto Rican males in transition. *Centro Boletin, 2,* 41–55.

De La Cancela, V., & Zavala-Martinez, I. (1983). An analysis of culturalism in Latino mental health: Folk medicine as a case in point. *Hispanic Journal of Behavioral Sciences, 5,* 251–274.

Fitzpatrick, J. P. (1987). *Puerto Ricans: The meaning of migration to the mainland* (2nd ed.). Englewood Cliffs, NJ: Prentice Hall.

Haslip-Viera, G., & Baver, S. L. (1996). *Latinos in New York: Communities in transition.* Notre Dame, IN: University of Notre Dame Press.

Iglesias, C. A. (1984). *Memoirs of Bernardo Vega: A contribution to the history of the Puerto Rican community in New York* (Juan Flores, Trans.). New York: Monthly Review Press. (Original work published 1977)

Logan, J., Stowell, J., Stults, B., & Oakley, D. (2001). *Immigrant enclaves in the American metropolis, 1990–2000.* Retrieved August 5, 2001, from University of Albany, Lewis Mumford Center for Comparative Urban and Regional Research Web site: http://www.albany.edu/mumford/census

Longres, J. F. (1974, February). Racism and its effects on Puerto Rican continentals. *Social Casework,* pp. 67–99.

Martinez, R. (1986). Puerto Ricans: White or non-White? *Explorations in Ethnic Studies: The Journal of the National Association for Ethnic Studies, 9*(2), 37–48.

Mohr, N. (1985). *Rituals of survival: A woman's portfolio.* Houston, TX: Artes.

Morales, J. (1986). *Puerto Rican poverty and migration: We just had to try elsewhere.* New York: Praeger.

Padilla, E. (1958). *Up from Puerto Rico.* New York: Columbia University Press.

Padilla, F. (1987). *Puerto Rican Chicago.* Notre Dame, IN: University of Notre Dame Press.

Pantoja, A. (1989). Puerto Ricans in New York: A historical and community development perspective. *Boletin Del Centro De Estudios Puertorriquenos, 2*(5), 20–31.

Puerto Rican Legal Defense and Education Fund, Institute for Puerto Rican Policy. (2001, May). *Puerto Rico: 2000 population and racial breakdown* (IPR Datanote on the Puerto Rican Community). New York: Puerto Rican Legal Defense Fund.

Rivera, E. (1982). *Family installments: Memories of growing up Hispanic.* New York: Morrow.

Rivera, E. (1987). The Puerto Rican colony of Lorain, Ohio. *Boletin Del Centro De Estudios Puertorriquenos, 2*(1), 11–23.

Rodriguez, C. E. (1980). Puerto Ricans: Between Black and White. In C. Rodriguez, V. Sanchez-Karol, & O. Alers (Eds.), *The Puerto Rican struggle: Essays on survival in the U.S.* (pp. 20–30). New York: Puerto Rican Migration Research Consortium.

Rodriguez, C. E. (1989). *Puerto Ricans born in the U.S.A.* Boston: Unwin Hyman.

Rodriguez, C. E. (2000). *Changing race: Latinos, the Census, and the history of ethnicity in the United States.* New York: New York University Press.

Sanchez-Korrol, V. E. (1994). *From colonia to community: The history of Puerto Ricans in New York City, 1917–1948.* Berkeley: University of California Press.

Silva, M. N., & Souza, B. C. (1982). The Puerto Ricans in Hawaii: On becoming Hawaii's people. *The Puerto Rican Journal, 1*(1), 29–39.

Torres, A., & Velazquez, J. E. (1998). *The Puerto Rican movement: Voices from the diaspora.* Philadelphia: Temple University Press.

U.S. Bureau of the Census. (1990). *The Hispanic population in the United States: March 1989* (Current Population Reports, Series P-20, No. 444). Washington, DC: U.S. Government Printing Office.

U.S. Bureau of the Census. (1999, September). *Household income at record high: Poverty declines in 1998, Census Bureau reports.* Washington, DC: U.S. Department of Commerce.

U.S. Bureau of the Census. (2000, November). *Family households by type and Hispanic origin group: 1999* (Current Population Survey, March 1999, PGP-2 and PPL-124: Table 3.2, Created June 23, 2000, and Revised November 2, 2000). Washington, DC: U.S. Department of Commerce. Retrieved August 4, 2001, from www.census.gov/population/socdemo/Hispanic/CPS99/99GIFshow/TSLD012/htm

U.S. Bureau of the Census. (2001a, May). *The Hispanic population: Census 2000 in brief.* Washington, DC: U.S. Department of Commerce. Retrieved August 5, 2001, from www.census.gov/population/www/cen2000/brief.html

U.S. Bureau of the Census. (2001b, March). *Overview of race and Hispanic origin: Census 2000 brief.* Washington, DC: U.S. Department of Commerce. Retrieved August 4, 2001, from www.census.gov/population/www/cen2000/brief.html

Vazquez, J. M. (1975). *Expressed ethnic orientation and its relationship to the quality of student–counselor rapport as reported by Puerto Rican college students.* Unpublished doctoral dissertation, New York University.

Vazquez, J. M. (1977). Accounting for ethnicity in the counseling relationship: A study of Puerto Rican college students. *Ethnic Groups, 1,* 297–318.

Vazquez, J. M. (1986). The ethnic matrix: Implications for human service practitioners. *Explorations in Ethnic Studies: The Journal of the National Association for Ethnic Studies, 9,* 1–18.

Zavala-Martinez, I. (1988). *En la lucha:* The economic and socioemotional struggles of Puerto Rican women. In L. Fulani (Ed.), *The psychopathology of everyday racism and sexism* (pp. 3–24). New York: Harrington Park Press.

Zavala-Martinez, I. (1994a). *Entremundos:* The psychological dialectics of Puerto Rican migration and its implications for health. In C. Lamberty & C. Garcia Coll (Eds.), *Puerto Rican women and children: Issues in health, growth, and development* (pp. 29–37). New York: Plenum Press.

Zavala-Martinez, I. (1994b). *Quien soy?* Who am I? Identity issues for Puerto Rican adolescents. In E. P. Salett & D. R. Koslow (Eds.), *Race, ethnicity, and self-identity in multicultural perspective* (pp. 89–116). Washington, DC: National Multicultural Institute.

Appendix

Community Agencies, Research Institutes, and Other Organizations

Aspira of New York, Inc., 332 East 149th Street, Bronx, NY 10451, (212) 292-2690

Center for Latino, Latin American, and Caribbean Studies (CELAC), Social Science 250, University at Albany, State University of New York, Albany, NY 12222

Center for Puerto Rican Studies (Centro de Estudios Puertorriquenos), Hunter College of the City University of New York, 695 Park Avenue, New York, NY 10021

Council of Puerto Rican and Latino Studies of the City University of New York, c/o Dr. Gabriel Haslip-Viera, City College of New York, Department of Sociology, Convent Avenue, New York, NY 10031

Hispanic Research Center, Fordham University, Bronx, NY 10458

Institute for the Puerto Rican/Hispanic Elderly, 105 East 22nd Street, New York, NY 10010

Institute for Puerto Rican Policy, 99 Hudson Street, 14th Floor, New York, NY 10013-2815, (212) 739-7516, e-mail: ipr@iprnet.org

National Congress for Puerto Rican Rights, 160 West Lippincott, Philadelphia, PA 19133.

Puerto Rican Family Institute, 116 West 14th Street, New York, NY 10011

The Arab American Experience

Dynamic international political and social events make it mandatory that Americans gain a greater understanding of the centuries-old cultural traditions of the Arab world. Within the context of rapidly changing events taking place in that part of the world, Americans of Arab descent and their cultural traditions are gaining greater recognition in the United States. It is therefore incumbent on professionals from every sector of American society to become more knowledgeable about important aspects of Arab and Arab American culture. As part of this, professional counselors must develop an understanding of the cultural dynamics associated with Arab Americans' mental health and psychosocial development.

Arab Americans trace their cultural origins to the Middle East and northern Africa. They are a heterogeneous cultural group differing in ethnic background and religious affiliation. The most significant dynamics of Arab American culture that need to be considered in counseling are religion and family unity. The traditions of both Christianity and Islam influence basic attitudes, values, and behavior of Americans of Arab descent. Family unity is also a highly valued cultural dynamic among Arab Americans.

Counseling Arab Americans

Morris L. Jackson and Sylvia Nassar-McMillan

As a cultural group, Americans of Arab ancestry have received scant attention in the counseling literature. Professional counselors have had little access to information that addresses the important cultural and developmental issues of this group. Significantly, the U.S. Bureau of the Census in 1990 granted Arab Americans the option to write *other* as their cultural designation on census forms. This event truly signaled the recognition of Arab Americans as a distinct cultural group in American society. History has recorded that the first Arabic-speaking people came to American shores between 146 and 480 B.C. and were believed to be Phoenicians, people of the country known today as Lebanon (Boland, 1961). John Zogby, author of *Arab America Today: A Demographic Profile of Arab Americans* (1990), estimated the number of Arab Americans to be in excess of 3 million (J. Zogby, personal communication, 1996). Arab Americans reside in cities throughout the United States. Metropolitan areas that represent significant Arab American population centers include Detroit, Michigan; Allentown, Pennsylvania; Birmingham, Alabama; Boston, Massachusetts; Houston, Texas; Jacksonville, Florida; New York, New York; Portland, Oregon; San Francisco, California; Utica, New York; and Worchester, Massachusetts (Zogby, 1984). Detroit has the largest population of Arabs outside of the Middle East (ACCESS, 1998).

Like other ethnic minority groups in American society, Arab Americans face daily challenges to their overall development and well-being. These challenges take the form of discrimination, stereotyping, and general negative reactions to them as an ethnic group. One such challenge can be linked to an individual's or family's reason for immigration. The voluntary or involuntary nature of migration can affect psychological as well as economic adjustment (Takeda, 2000). Anti-Arab prejudice, in particular, may be due to strained U.S.–Middle East relations. During the course of their development, Arab Americans encounter a crisis of cultural identity common to many minority groups in the United States, which is sometimes mediated by the circumstances of their individual or family migration issues.

This chapter first examines the diversity of Arab Americans. Second, it explores important dynamics of Arab culture such as religion and family and considers racial–religious–ethnic identification issues. The chapter next discusses the counselor's challenge in providing mental health services to Arab Americans, including barriers to successful counseling and possible intervention strategies and techniques, and then presents a case study that contains excerpts from counseling sessions to demonstrate this challenge.

Diversity of Arab Americans

Although Americans of Arab ancestry are generally perceived to be a homogeneous group, it is important to recognize that they originally came from approximately 20 different countries in the Middle East and northern Africa. They form a heterogeneous group whose members differ in terms of race, religion, and political ideology. Writers and researchers who have traced the history and explored the diversity of Arab Americans in the United States include Hooglund (1987), McCarus (1994), Naff (1994), Orfalea (1988), and Pulcini (1993).

The arrival of people of Arab ancestry in America occurred during three distinct time periods (Orfalea, 1988). The first of these was from 1878 to 1925. Census data indicated that in 1910 there were approximately 100,000 Arab Americans in the United States. Most Arabs who arrived during this period came from Greater Syria, the territory that today includes Iraq, Israel and the Occupied Territories (formerly known as Palestine), Jordan, Lebanon, and Syria. These first Arab immigrants were Christians. They were laborers, factory workers, and peddlers who lived primarily in urban areas. The majority were poor and uneducated and sought refuge and contentment in building close-knit communities.

The second major period of Arab immigration to the United States was shortly after World War II. The people in this group differed sharply from the earlier immigrants in that they were primarily Muslim and better educated. According to Orfalea (1988), this was the beginning of the brain drain from Egypt and other North African countries, Jordan, Iraq, and Syria. This period also was marked by the surge in Palestinian refugees and exiles who felt that they were without a country. Other countries represented in this wave, but with smaller numbers of immigrants, were Lebanon and Yemen. This second wave of immigrants often found themselves alienated from their Arab peers and American counterparts because of their Muslim religion and its accompanying culture.

The third period of Arab immigration has been since 1966. This influx of people, approximately 150,000 individuals, is primarily the result of an easing of immigration regulations. This third group shares much in common with members of the second immigrant group. They are mostly Muslim, with the largest ethnic group being Palestinian, and primarily professionals or technical workers.

In the last decade of the 20th century, there was a dramatic influx of refugee immigrants from Iraq. Some have estimated that number at 25,000 (Karmo, 2001). Mental health professionals working with this new group of Arab American clients report that their needs, both economic and psychological, are great (Karmo, 2001; Kira, 2001a).

Essential to obtaining a comprehensive understanding of and perspective on this cultural group is appreciating that Arab Americans migrated to the United States from a variety of countries in the Middle East. The first Arab American immigrants arrived in the United States over a century ago, and today they represent a diverse cultural group with a growing impact in this country. Particular attention should be paid to the recent increase in immigration from Iraq because of the extensive needs presented by this group.

Arab American Culture

Any discipline that seeks to understand the dynamics of Arab American development must take into account the experiences that shape that development. Counseling strategies and techniques for Americans of Arab ancestry, therefore, must be predicated on an understanding of Arabic cultural dynamics and their important role in fostering attitudes, behaviors, and values. In a counseling context, the most significant aspects of Arab American culture that must be considered are religion and family.

Religion

Religion is a major vehicle by which Arab culture is transferred. Most Arab Americans are either Christians or Muslims. Those who follow Christianity have found it somewhat easier to assimilate into the American cultural mainstream than have their Muslim counterparts.

An appreciation of Islam is key to understanding Arab and Arab American culture. For one fifth of the world's population, Islam is both a religion and a complete way of life. About 18% of those who follow Islam live in the Arab world. The very name of the religion—Islam—means both submission and peace, for it is in submitting to Allah's (God's) will that human beings gain peace in their lives in this world and in the hereafter.

Islam reveres not only Abraham, who is father of the Arabs as well as of the Jews, but also Moses and Jesus. Muhammad, the prophet and messenger of God, was the last of this long line of prophets. Importantly, there is a Judeo–Christian–Islamic tradition, for Islam shares with the other Abrahamic religions their sacred history, the basic ethical teachings contained in the Ten Commandments, and above all, belief in one God.

For Muslims, or followers of Islam, the Quran (Koran; 1983) is the actual word of God. Under the direction of Muhammad, the verses and chapters of the Quran were organized in the order used today. There is only one text of the Quran accepted by all schools of Islamic thought, and there are no other versions.

The Quran is the central sacred reality of Islam. As the direct word of God, the Quran is considered the primary guide for Muslim life. It is the source of all Islamic doctrines and ethics. Both the intellectual aspects of Islam and Islamic law are based on the Quran. The Quran emphasizes the significance of knowledge and encourages Muslims to learn and acquire knowledge of God's laws as well as of the world of nature. It places the gaining of knowledge as the highest religious activity.

Basic to an appreciation of the religion is understanding the Articles of Faith and the Pillars of Islam. The fundamental Articles of Faith are to have faith in God, His angels, His books, His messengers, and the Day of Judgment and God's determination of human destiny.

The five Pillars of Islam are affirmation of the faith (*shahadah*), five daily prayers (*salat*), fasting (*sawm*) from dawn to sunset during the month of Ramadan, making the pilgrimage (*hajj*) to the Holy Kaaba in Mecca at least once in a lifetime, and paying a tax (*zakat*) on one's capital, used for the needs of the community. Ethics lie at the heart of Islamic teachings, and all people are expected to act ethically toward one another at all times.

Islam possesses a religious law that governs the lives of Muslims and that they consider to be the embodiment of the will of God. This law, although rooted in the sources of Islamic revelation, is a living law that addresses the needs of Islamic society.

Islamic laws are basically preventative. The faith of the Muslim causes him or her to have respect for the rights of others, and Islamic law is such that it prevents most transgressions.

Nydell (1987) outlined some basic Islamic values and religious attitudes commonly found among Arabic-speaking peoples:

1. A person's dignity, honor, and reputation are of paramount importance.
2. Loyalty to one's family takes precedence over personal needs.
3. It is important to behave at all times in a manner that reflects well on others.
4. Everyone believes in one God and acknowledges His power.

5. Humans cannot control all events; some things depend on God.
6. Piety is one of the most admirable characteristics in a person.

Perhaps because approximately 80% of the Arab world practices Islam (Loza, 2001), many Islamic and Arabic traditions are overlapping. Christian Arabs often uphold similar values to those described. The strength of these values cannot be understated, and some have attributed satisfaction with life in the United States to religion among Arab individuals (e.g., Faragallah, Schumm, & Webb, 1997).

Family

The family is the foundation of Islamic society. The peace and security offered by a stable family are greatly valued and considered essential for spiritual growth. The Arab American family has evolved over time. During the early years of Arab immigration to the United States, many Arab families were not greatly affected by Western values. Newly arrived families cultivated and reinforced values derived from their Arabic tradition and heritage. However, as assimilation and acculturation began to occur, many Arab American families were faced with a choice. On the one hand, there was a strong desire to maintain traditional Arabic family values. On the other hand, there was an awareness of the need to adopt the values of American culture.

Most Arab Americans belong to an extended family system in which members experience loyalty, security, emotional support, and financial assistance (Nydell, 1987). Unfortunately, for some recent immigrants, particularly refugees, the family system has been uprooted, causing much stress and vulnerability. In general, though, immediate family members and extended relatives share a closeness that is evident in a high degree of family unity. For example, despite differences they may have with each other, family members will collude with and support one another against an outsider whom they perceive as interfering with family unity. A traditional Arabic expression illustrates this family unity: "It is me and my brother against my cousin, but it is me and my cousin against the outsider." Another term, *Asabiyah,* while also having a political meaning, commonly refers to an allegiance toward group aims and functions (Sayed, Collins, & Takahashi, 1998). In many Arab American families, men generally are viewed as the head of the household. Older men in the extended family demand the most respect. Grown sons are responsible for their parents and, in the absence of their father, are responsible for their unmarried sisters. This is not to suggest that Arab American women do not play a significant role in family dynamics. Although women may typically adopt a submissive role in public, in the privacy of their homes they may exert a considerable amount of influence, even to the extent of adamantly disagreeing with their husbands on important family matters. In the case of refugees, the family structure has been derailed, and women by default may become the head of the household (Nassar-McMillan & Hakim-Larson, 2003).

Children are raised in a manner that ensures that they will respect their parents. In Arabic culture, good children show respect for their parents as well as for all adults, particularly older adults. Recently, however, many Arab American children have been rejecting their cultural traditions. Parents now have to spend more time and effort to exert control and instill traditional discipline in their children. Peer pressure in schools, for example, has begun to compete with parental influence.

Racial–Religious–Ethnic Identification Issues

In the United States, skin color is a primary means of social identification and distinction. Americans of Arab ancestry, however, may trace their origins to countries that do not make skin color distinctions among people. The following classifications, based on racial, religious, and ethnic factors, may be appropriate for identifying Arab Americans: White Christian, White Muslim, Black Christian, and Black Muslim. The four groups are examined here to assist professional counselors in understanding the influence of race and religion in Arab American culture.

White Christian Arab Americans arrived in this country from Egypt, Iraq, Jordan, Lebanon, Palestine (currently recognized as Israel and the Occupied Territories), and Syria. Members of this racial–religious–ethnic group, despite cultural differences, have found it easier to assimilate into American society. This is primarily due to their racial and religious similarities with the majority American cultural group.

White Muslim Arab Americans in the U.S. population have come from all of the Arabic-speaking countries except Eritrea, Ethiopia, Somalia, and Sudan. This group has been subjected to various forms of discrimination and prejudice, primarily because their religious traditions differ significantly from those commonly found in the United States.

Black Christian Arab Americans are a relatively small group of people that may grow in the future. They are from Egypt and parts of northern Africa. Their experience in the United States parallels that of African Americans, who are often confronted with discrimination and prejudice because of the color of their skin.

Black Muslim Arab Americans may be divided into two groups. One group includes individuals whose mother tongue is Arabic or who were born in an Arab country. The second group is composed of African Americans who were originally Christians but who have adopted the Muslim faith. American society, however, often does not distinguish between these two groups. Black Muslim Arab Americans have two disadvantages in American society: They are both Black and Muslim. This generally means that this group has been the least accepted of the four groups.

If counseling is to be effective with a client of Arab ancestry, it may be necessary to first identify the client's racial–religious–ethnic background. In so doing, a counselor may discover how a client's attitude, values, and behaviors have been shaped by the experience associated with a particular identification.

Other factors to consider in understanding individual or family identification are level of acculturation, previous and current social class (Karmo, 2001), urban versus rural background, and the extent to which country of origin was influenced by Western values (Nassar-McMillan & Hakim-Larson, 2003). These issues of cultural identification interplay not only with how these individuals are perceived by other Americans but also with possible intergroup and intragroup prejudices and hostilities within Arab American communities themselves (Nassar-McMillan & Hakim-Larson, 2003).

Arab Americans' Mental Health: The Counselor's Challenge

In American culture, seeking the services of a professional counselor for assistance with problem resolution or decision making is a common practice for many groups. However, this is generally not the case with Arab Americans. The first line of psychological defense for Arab Americans is a conference or consultation with a family member about a problem. A man provides guidance for another man, whereas a woman is counseled by another woman. Cross-sex counseling is uncommon. Young men seek guidance from older men, and young women are advised by older women. When the nature of a problem is too sensitive to discuss with an immediate family member, a person looks to a more distant relative. If a family member is unavailable, then an Arab American might talk with a trusted friend.

General mistrust of outsiders is not uncommon among Arab Americans (Nassar-McMillan & Hakim-Larson, 2003). The concept of counseling is foreign to many clients of

Middle Eastern descent. Their mental health issues have historically been addressed by physicians, priests and imams, and magicians (Loza, 2001) as well as fortune-tellers and Koranic healers (Al-Krenawi & Graham, 2000). A professional counselor is considered a stranger who is outside of the Arab American support system. If none of the previously mentioned counseling sources are available, as a last resort, the Arab American may decide to seek the services of a professional counselor.

Barriers to Successful Counseling With Arab Americans

Racial and ethnic barriers that have been discussed as problematic in the cross-cultural counseling relationship with culturally different clients seem to be applicable to Arab American clients. Of particular significance is how culture, religion, language, and rapport affect the counseling relationship. As just noted, Arab Americans do not, as a rule, disclose personal and family matters to strangers. Arabic-speaking people feel more comfortable discussing academic and vocational matters. Some Arab American clients may be reluctant to engage in self-disclosure or experience considerable frustration during the counseling process because of their inability to fully express themselves in English. They may feel verbally handicapped when they are unable to communicate to the counselor exactly what they feel about problems.

Communication styles that may be characteristic of Arabic culture and that are likely to affect relationship development issues in counseling are the verbal assertiveness and gestures used by Arabs (Via, Callahan, Barry, Jackson, & Gerber, 1997). These behaviors may cause an American counselor to feel intimidated or even offended by the Arab American client. Culture-based communication styles and coping strategies can lead to overdiagnoses of a multitude of psychological conditions (Kamoo, Hakim-Larson, Nassar-McMillan, & Porcerelli, 2001). Arab American clients who present themselves as dependent, indecisive, or nonverbal emotionally may be labeled as "resistant" (Karmo, 2001).

Clients of Arab American backgrounds operate on a survival versus insight basis (Karmo, 2001; Sayed et al., 1998). This belief, rooted in the Islamic concept of predetermination, or fate, can make primary prevention and education efforts particularly challenging.

Issues specific to the new refugee population pose unique challenges for the counselor. Economic adaptation is particularly important to the successful acculturation of these individuals (Kamoo et al., 2001; Takeda, 2000). For example, a former physician compelled to take a position as a filling station attendant merely to support his family will undoubtedly suffer from depression as well as other self-esteem issues. In terms of psychological adaptation, alarming numbers of this group suffer from posttraumatic stress disorder (Jamil et al., 2002; Kira, 2001b), which mediates any other issues they may have. Although substance abuse is a serious issue for this group, pathological gambling has become an epidemic. Other issues are domestic violence (Abou El-Azayem, 2001) and generally impaired value processing systems, leading to paradoxical morality (Kira, 1999).

The traditional counseling process is an activity foreign to Arabic culture and, therefore, may be strange to many Arab Americans. Counselors interested in assisting their clients to self-disclose need to determine the degree of acculturation and assimilation of their clients. Failure to make this determination could cause culture-specific barriers, such as language and religion, to be erected between counselors and clients.

The most significant impediment to a possible counseling relationship with Americans of Arab ancestry is the hostility that has been fostered in American society through a continuous barrage of negative publicity about and stereotyping of Arabs (Matawi, 1996). This negative stereotyping has been perpetrated in the form of jokes, television programming, cartoons, comic strips, and movies (Stockton, 1994). Counselors need to be sensitive to the negative feelings, often undisplayed, of Arab American clients as a result of this hostility.

Intervention Techniques and Strategies

Professional counselors working with Arab Americans must consider new ways to maximize their chances of therapeutic success with this population. In the counseling literature, rapport has been discussed as a significant factor in the establishment of a positive therapeutic counselor–client relationship. The building of rapport is generally focused on during initial counselor–client interactions. Successful counseling with Arab Americans relies on the relationship between counselor and client, rather than interpretation or exploration of client issues (Al-Abdul-Jabbar & Al-Issa, 2000). Sensitive counselors committed to bridging cultural differences with Americans of Arab ancestry should consider the following suggestions to facilitate the development of rapport in the helping relationship:

1. Counselors should develop knowledge and understanding of the religion and culture of Arab Americans. This is important so that intelligent differentiations can be made between Christian and Muslim Arab Americans. Counselors should read books and articles and attempt to converse informally with Arab Americans to increase their understanding of Arabic religious and cultural differences. In general, Arab Americans are pleased and excited over opportunities to share information about their culture and religion.
2. Counselors should begin and end the counseling session with a ritual. It has been suggested that such a ritual could be as simple as standing and initiating a handshake (Karmo, 2001; Nobles & Sciarra, 2000).
3. Counselors should become attuned to common proverbs used by Arab American clients (Abou El-Azayem, 2001). Familiarity with a few Arabic expressions may be more beneficial to the counselor's effectiveness than any technique he or she may use.
4. Counselors should be mindful that Arabic-speaking people, as a rule, are not accustomed to, or comfortable with, expressing feelings about personal matters outside the context of the family. Such disclosures may be regarded as inappropriate assertiveness (Al-Abdul-Jabbar & Al-Issa, 2000). Counselors need to be respectful of this perspective. Communication styles among individuals of Middle Eastern descent may differ from the Western norm, and this behavior should be interpreted in its cultural context (Faragallah et al., 1997).
5. Because of the role of fate in the teachings of Islam, Arab Americans are survival oriented versus insight oriented. Therapies focused on insight tend to be ineffective and counterproductive with this population and can be highly anxiety provoking because of the conflicts between individual and collective focuses (Al-Abdul-Jabbar & Al-Issa, 2000). Multimodal, or eclectic, approaches may be most effective in counseling Arab Americans. Recommended are family or system approaches (Nobles & Sciarra, 2000), cognitive/behavioral approaches (Karmo, 2001), and problem solving that focuses on daily functioning (Al-Abdul-Jabbar & Al-Issa, 2000).
6. Counselors should establish relationships with Arab American clients prior to actually starting the counseling process. Establishing such a relationship is called *prerapport*. The significant point is for counselors to converse and interact with clients from the Arab American population in settings outside the traditional counseling office. Consequently, when an Arab American client comes to begin counseling, the amount of time spent on building rapport and trust may be significantly reduced. Therapeutic considerations regarding this rapport include the following:

a. Discussing confidentiality with the client is essential.
b. Because a definitive end to counseling is very likely to seem abrupt, given the extended boundaries of the therapeutic relationship, offering follow-up sessions to check in with clients is suggested.
c. Early in the establishment of a counseling relationship, professional counselors should determine the level of family involvement needed.
d. In the case of refugees, it is critical to assess for posttraumatic stress disorders so as to discern the possible interaction of its effects with any other diagnosis, and to provide treatment accordingly.

Beyond rapport building, there are some other strategies that counselors should consider in their work with Arab Americans. The importance of religion and the family system to Arab Americans cannot be overstated. Counselors familiar with aspects of the Christian and Muslim religions will be welcomed by Arab American clients to initiate a discussion about religion. The Quran indicates that the closer one is to Allah, the easier it is to cope with psychic problems. All counselors need to be aware that Muslim Arab Americans view the Quran together with the sunna, which is the body of Islamic custom and practice based on the words and deeds of the Prophet Muhammad, as providing them with a way of life. These two documents regulate and govern the lives and emotions of Muslim Arab Americans.

One method of intervention that the counselor may use to introduce religion into the therapeutic process is to explain to the client in the first session that part of the technique used includes a holistic approach to the resolution of the client's concerns. This approach focuses not only on the mind and body but also on the spirit. This may provide the counselor with an opportunity to identify the religion of the client and its significance in the client's life.

Another method for maximizing success with Arab American clients is to involve family members in counseling sessions. It is recommended that counselors first meet with the client. The head of the family should be contacted next to discuss the nature of the client's concerns and to share possible solutions. Next, the counselor should meet with family members and the client to jointly discuss the problem.

A final suggestion for successful counseling with this population is to learn six basic Arabic expressions that will enhance their counselor rapport. These are "Assalamu Alakum" ("Peace be unto you"), "Mahaba" ("Hello"), "Kafe Hallick" ("How are you?"), "In Sha Allah" ("If God is willing"), "Ma Sha Allah" ("This is what God wished"), and "Mas Alama" ("Goodbye").

The following are examples of how these expressions can be used in the counseling setting. The expression "Assalamu Alakum" is a formal greeting. The response is "Wa Lakum Salam," which means "And peace be unto you." This verbal exchange may be followed by a more informal statement such as "Mahaba," which prompts the response "Kafe Hallick." These three expressions may be used in the beginning of the counseling session. Another significant expression is "In Sha Allah." For example, it should be used in the following way. Should an Arab American client request that a counselor solve his or her problem, the counselor would preface a response with the preceding Arabic expression and then provide a normal counselor response. An example is as follows:

> *Client:* It was suggested that I come to see you today because you are an excellent counselor. I was told that you could solve my problem.
> *Counselor:* In Sha Allah, I will do my best to help you with your problem.

It is common practice for counselors to offer their clients reassuring and reinforcing statements to help them achieve a better state of well-being. For example, the Arabic expression "Ma Sha Allah" has particular relevance for counselors assisting Arab American clients in changing unproductive behavior. One way counselors may help clients is to give positive statements followed by the Arabic expression, or the Arabic expression may precede the counselor response. The examples below illustrate this point:

Counselor: You seem to be feeling much better today than you did during the last session, Ma Sha Allah.
Counselor: Ma Sha Allah, I am pleased to hear that your studies are going well.

The use of a few key Arabic expressions in counseling sessions, when appropriate, may have more meaning than the same idea expressed in English because it conveys the counselor's attempt to understand and respect Arab culture.

The Case Study of Hala

The case study presented here illustrates intervention strategies and techniques that are helpful with Arab American clients.

Hala is a 28-year-old Arab American female. She entered into counseling because it was becoming increasingly difficult for her to cope with stress and anxiety in her life. She indicated that this was caused by her parents' rejection of her choice of a marriage partner. Hala's primary complaint was her inability to get over her parents' disapproval of her plans to marry an Arab man who is of the Christian faith. Hala was raised in and continues to follow Islam. Despite the fact that she saw this young man only once a year because he lived and worked in Syria, Hala stated that she loved him dearly and wanted to marry him.

Hala was born in Syria and is currently a permanent resident in the United States and plans to become a naturalized citizen. Her father was born in Syria and her mother in Lebanon. They immigrated to the United States for professional opportunities. She has two older brothers.

Hala's primary language choice is Arabic. This is especially true at social and community Arab American activities. In the school environment, Hala is comfortable speaking English. She is bilingual but has greater fluency in Arabic. She studied English for 4 years in Syria during high school. Upon arriving in the United States approximately 10 years ago, Hala attended English language classes. Her family members converse in Arabic with each other at home and in other situations.

Islam has played a significant role in guiding Hala's life. Her family travels often to Syria to maintain a strong linkage to extended family members. Visiting grandparents and cousins was one of the ways in which Hala's parents were able to reinforce traditional Arabic values and beliefs in her. It is clear that Hala's parents wanted to ensure that she grew and developed with the guiding principles of Islam.

Hala has earned an associate degree at a community college. Currently at the university, she is an excellent college student and has a 3.5 grade point average. She plans to complete a bachelor of science degree in business administration. Hala then plans to attend law school. She did not have many friends while at the community college. She indicated that her relationships were restricted to having an occasional cup of tea or coffee with a classmate. Hala is currently employed full-time at an international organization. She has always worked since arriving in the United States.

Hala's parents were educated in Lebanon, Syria, and England. Her father earned a master's degree in England, and her mother received a bachelor's degree in Lebanon. Her father is employed full-time at a local university, and her mother currently does not work outside of the home. Her two brothers live in another city.

Hala has had several counseling sessions. Although some progress has been made in reducing the amount of anxiety and stress she is experiencing, Hala still harbors unresolved anxiety related to not finding a marriage partner pleasing to her parents. An excerpt from one of the counseling sessions with her male counselor follows:

Counselor: Good afternoon, Hala. How are you doing today?

Hala: All right, I could be better.

Counselor: What would make it better for you?

Hala: I tried to talk with my parents the other day about my situation. No matter how I expressed myself, they still did not seem to understand the problem I am having.

Counselor: By situation, are you referring to your desire to marry Abdulla?

Hala: Yes.

Counselor: It is important to you that your parents really understand that you love Abdulla and do not care that he is a Christian.

Hala: My parents know his parents, and we all are from the same town. I just don't get it. They know he is from a nice family. Abdulla is a medical doctor. I could have a good life with him.

Counselor: Despite the fact your parents have had a social relationship with his family, they still will not give their approval for you to marry Abdulla. And because you do not have their approval, you are not happy.

Hala: Well not exactly. Basically, I am a happy person. But since he will not be in my life, I have begun to spend more time alone. There is no one else that I can foresee having a relationship with who will meet my parents' qualifications.

Counselor: What do you do with yourself when you are alone?

Hala: I work every day and spend my evenings reading books.

Counselor: What else do you do with your time?

Hala: I am taking two courses at the university. Sometimes I get together with some of my girlfriends, but this does not happen often. My mother and I go to the movies. She is like my best friend. I think she is supportive of me marrying Abdulla. However, it is difficult for the both of us to convince my father.

Counselor: What I now understand is that your mother is supportive and empathetic to your situation even to the point of letting your father know how important Abdulla is to you.

Hala: You are right. I have had many conversations with my mother. She knew from the beginning that I wanted to marry Abdulla. I have always confided in her. She knows just about all of my secrets.

Counselor: Your mother has always been there for you when you needed her.

Hala: That is correct. I have even discussed with her in some detail the problem that my father has with Abdulla.

Counselor: What is the problem your father has with Abdulla that has led him to disapprove of your marrying him?

Hala: He stated that Abdulla has different values and beliefs. And since I was raised a Muslim, there is likely to be cultural conflict in the marriage. My father said that marriage is difficult by itself. And to add cultural differences would probably lead to divorce. You know my father has a point. But I believe that love can overcome all obstacles, even cultural differences.

Counselor: You place a greater emphasis on love and your father on values and beliefs. Was there anything else your father shared with you regarding his disapproval?

Hala: Yes. My father was quite direct in his objection. He asked me, "If I approved of your marrying Abdulla and children are born, will they be raised Christian or Muslim?" He was quite adamant in saying that his grandchildren will be Muslim not Christian.

Counselor: It is now quite clear to me what your problem is and why your father objects so strongly. You are so deeply in love with Abdulla that beliefs and values and difference in religion are not significant obstacles. On the other hand, your father is so deeply rooted in the Islamic tradition and raised you in the Islamic faith, and the fear that his grandchildren would not be raised Muslim is more than he can bear.

Hala: I think you are right. But what can I do so that he might change his mind?

Counselor: The reality of your situation may be that he may never change his mind. Hala, I want you to know that I am 100% supportive of helping you make the decision that you think is best for you.

Hala: I could just run away and marry Abdulla. However, if I was to do that my father may never talk to me again. I think my mother would always be there if I needed her. Another option I have is to continue trying to convince my father that this marriage would work and that I would do my best to influence Abdulla to be supportive of raising any children as Muslim. The other option I have is to do nothing and hope that time is a healer and my father changes his mind.

Counselor: You have mentioned several different options. Could you share with me the option that you are likely to choose?

Hala: Of course there are advantages and disadvantages to each of the options I mentioned. My heart tells me I should marry Abdulla. If I follow my heart, I take the risk of hurting my father so much he may not speak to me again. Also, if I do not marry Abdulla, I may never be able to find another potential marriage partner whom I feel comfortable with.

Counselor: What are your thoughts on the other options?

Hala: Try as I may, it would probably be almost impossible to get my father to change his mind. After all, he lives and breathes the Arabic traditions. So I do not think this is a viable option. I was being optimistic in stating that maybe time will have a favorable impact on him.

Counselor: Hala, you have just discussed in a general way the different options that you might have and some of the consequences. Are you ready to make a decision?

Hala: No. I was hoping that you would tell me what to do. That's why I entered into counseling. I thought for sure you would direct me in the right direction.

Counselor: Hala, the issue of marriage is a long-time commitment and is one of the most significant decisions that we have to make in life. I cannot tell you what to do. I am keenly aware that you are torn between selecting a marriage partner, and being joyous about that, and being sad about the fact that marriage could isolate you from your father. In addition, I understand that right now you are unhappy being single and approaching 30 years of age. I do not think you should feel compelled to make a decision right now. Maybe you can think about what we have discussed today and let me know at our next counseling session what you have decided.

Hala: That's not a bad idea because I am not ready to make a decision at this moment. I think I want to discuss some of the things we talked about today with my mother and understand what her thoughts might be on my situation.

This counseling session illustrates the challenge of an Arab American Muslim woman in cultural conflict with her parents because of her desire to marry a Christian Arab. The conflict arises because of different cultural values that may impact not only the marriage but any progeny from the union. The client is torn between her love of her parents, and wanting to respect the traditional Arab values she was taught, and her love for a marriage partner. It is obvious that the client has been affected by her father's disapproval of the marriage partner. The client is faced with the existential challenge of making a decision in the counseling session that could adversely affect her relationship with her parents. The counselor should make it clear to her that she bears the responsibility for any decision she makes and the action she takes on that decision.

Conclusion

In the emerging era of cultural diversity in American society, Arab Americans are stepping forward to proclaim their cultural heritage and traditions. These Americans of Arab ancestry are a flourishing cultural group whose diversity cannot be denied. They are representative of Arabic-speaking people from throughout the Middle East and northern Africa. Like other immigrant groups before them, Arab Americans are becoming acculturated, in varying degrees, to American lifestyles. In this process, they experience problems related to their cultural identity. Arab Americans face the challenge of blending two unique and different worldviews into one homogeneous culture.

Counselors are urged to obtain a comprehensive understanding of the religion and family systems of Arab Americans because they are a significant aspect of Arab American culture and are vital to Arab Americans' psychological well-being. Counselors concerned with bridging cultural barriers may need to rethink their techniques and strategies in order to effectively work with this population. Counselors can play a critical role in ensuring that Arab Americans are not an invisible cultural group.

References

Abou El-Azayem, A. (2001, May). *Programs for prevention of domestic violence in Arab cultures.* Paper presented at the 2nd Biennial National Conference on Arab American Health Issues, Dearborn, MI.

ACCESS. (1998). *The Arab Community Center for Economic and Social Services: Program guide.* Detroit, MI: Author.

Al-Abdul-Jabbar, J., & Al-Issa, I. (2000). Psychotherapy in Islamic society. In I. Al-Issa (Ed.), *Al-Junun: Mental illness in the Islamic world* (pp. 277–293). Madison, CT: International Universities Press.

Al-Krenawi, A., & Graham, J. R. (2000). Culturally sensitive social work practice with Arab clients in mental health settings. *Health and Social Work, 25,* 9–22.

Boland, C. M. (1961). *They all discovered America.* New York: Doubleday.

Faragallah, M. H., Schumm, H. R., & Webb, F. J. (1997). Acculturation of Arab American immigrants: An exploratory study. *Journal of Comparative Family Studies, 28,* 182–203.

Hooglund, E. J. (1987). *Crossing the waters.* Washington, DC: Smithsonian Institution Press.

Jamil, H., Hakim-Larson, J., Farrag, M., Kafaji, T., Duqum, I., & Jamil, L. H. (2002). A retrospective study of Arab American mental health clients: Trauma and the Iraqi refugees. *American Journal of Orthopsychiatry, 72,* 355–361.

Kamoo, R., Hakim-Larson, J., Nassar-McMillan, S. C., & Porcerelli, J. (2001, May). *An integrative approach to acculturation and mental health in immigrants of Arab and Chaldean descent.* Paper presented at the 2nd Biennial National Conference on Arab American Health Issues, Dearborn, MI.

Karmo, T. (2001, May). *Mental health management in Arab Chaldean Americans.* Paper presented at the 2nd Biennial National Conference on Arab American Health Issues, Dearborn, MI.

Kira, I. A. (1999, July). *Value processing and mental health.* Paper presented at the 6th European Congress of Psychology, Rome, Italy.

Kira, I. A. (2001a, May). *A departmental experience in the Arab American community in Michigan with emphasis on experience with Arab American children.* Paper presented at the 2nd Biennial National Conference on Arab American Health Issues, Dearborn, MI.

Kira, I. A. (2001b). A taxonomy of trauma and trauma assessment. *Traumatology: An International E-Journal, 2,* 1–14. Retrieved from http://www.fsu.edu/_trauma

Loza, N. (2001, May). *Insanity on the Nile: The history of psychiatry in Pharaonic Egypt.* Paper presented at the 2nd Biennial National Conference on Arab American Health Issues, Dearborn, MI.

Matawi, A. H. (1996). *Proxemics among male and female Saudi Arabian undergraduate students in Saudi Arabia and the United States.* Unpublished doctoral dissertation, Howard University, Washington, DC.

McCarus, E. (Ed.). (1994). *The development of Arab American identity.* Ann Arbor: University of Michigan Press.

Naff, A. (1994). The early Arab immigrant experience. In E. McCarus (Ed.), *The development of Arab American identity* (pp. 23–35). Ann Arbor: University of Michigan Press.

Nassar-McMillan, S. C., & Hakim-Larson, J. (2003). Counseling considerations among Arab Americans. *Journal of Counseling & Development, 81,* 150–159.

Nobles, A. Y., & Sciarra, D. T. (2000). Cultural determinants in the treatment of Arab Americans: A primer for mainstream therapists. *American Journal of Orthopsychiatry, 70,* 182–191.

Nydell, M. (1987). *Understanding Arabs: A guide for Westerners.* Yarmouth, ME: Intercultural Press.

Orfalea, G. (1988). *Before the flames: A quest for the history of Arab Americans.* Austin: University of Texas Press.

Pulcini, T. (1993). Trends in research on Arab Americans. *Journal of American Ethnic History, 12,* 27–60.

Quran [Koran]. A. Yusef, Trans. (1983). *Holy Koran* (Text, translation, and commentary). Beltsville, MD: Amana.

Sayed, M. A., Collins, D. T., &Takahashi, T. (1998). West meets East: Cross-cultural issues in inpatient treatment. *Bulletin of the Menninger Clinic, 62,* 439–454.

Stockton, R. (1994). Ethnic archetypes and the Arab image. In E. McCarus (Ed.), *The development of Arab American identity* (pp. 119–153). Ann Arbor: University of Michigan Press.

Takeda, J. (2000). Psychological and economic adaptation of Iraqi male refugees: Implications for social work practice. *Journal of Social Work Practice, 26,* 1–21.

Via, T., Callahan, S., Barry, K., Jackson, C., & Gerber, D. E. (1997). Middle East meets Midwest: The new health care challenge. *Journal of Multicultural Nursing and Health, 3,* 35–39.

Zogby, J. (Ed.). (1984). *Taking root: Bearing fruit—The Arab American experience.* Washington, DC: American-Arab Anti-Discrimination Committee.

Zogby, J. (1990). *Arab America today: A demographic profile of Arab Americans.* Washington, DC: Arab American Institute.

The Multiracial Individual and Family Experience

Multiracial individuals and families are gaining more prominence in U.S. society. Significantly, the 2000 U.S. Census marked the first time that people in the United States could describe themselves by selecting more than one racial category. Multiracial individuals are defined as persons whose biological parents are of two different racial backgrounds and whose lineage encompasses two or more distinctly different racial backgrounds. Because U.S. society has traditionally operated out of a monoracial model of race relations and racial identity development that does not allow for variations in physical appearance, multiracial individuals and interracial couples have historically evoked considerable controversy and scrutiny. Navigating and integrating multiple heritages in a monoracial society is often an ongoing challenge faced by multiracial individuals well into adulthood.

Counseling Multiracial Individuals and Families

Kelley R. Kenney

This chapter examines the counseling issues and concerns of multiracial individuals and families. In exploring this population, it is important to first identify and define who is included.

Definitions

Multiracial individuals are defined as persons whose biological parents are of two or more different racial backgrounds and whose lineage encompasses two or more distinctly different racial backgrounds (Funderburg, 1994; Gibbs, 1989; Root, 1992).

Interracial couples are described as couples, married or not, in which each partner is of a different racial background (Root, 1992; Spickard, 1989).

Multiracial families are composed of interracial couples and their multiracial offspring; single parents with biological offspring who are multiracial and single parents who have gone through a surrogate pregnancy process or artificial insemination process that results in the birth of a multiracial child; and families in which a cross-racial or transracial adoption has occurred, including gay and lesbian couples or single individuals who have adopted transracially or have gone through a surrogate pregnancy process or artificial insemination process that results in the birth of a multiracial child (Kenney, 2000).

Cross-racial or *transracial adoptions* are adoptions in which children are placed with families of another race (Stolley, 1993).

Multiracial individuals and families are a dramatically increasing segment of the U.S. population. The 2000 Census marked the first time that people in the United States could describe themselves by selecting more than one racial category (Root & Kelley, 2003). Census 2000 data reveal that 2.4% of the country's 281.4 million individuals described themselves as multiracial. Of these, 93% reported being of two racial backgrounds, whereas 7% reported being of three or more racial backgrounds. With the continuing increase in the rates of interracial marriages in the United States, the numbers of individuals claiming more than one racial heritage are expected to soar.

Families that have become multiracial through cross-racial and transracial adoption are also on the increase. Included in this group are children who are citizens of foreign countries and are adopted into U.S. families. Stolley (1993) indicated that 1 million children in the United States live with adoptive parents, of which 8% are children who were transracially adopted.

Issues and Concerns of Interracial Couples

Multiracial individuals and interracial couples have historically evoked considerable controversy and scrutiny. Although interracial unions between Blacks and Whites are far outnumbered by other interracial partnerships, particularly between Asians and Whites, Black–White relationships have borne the brunt of much of the controversy and ridicule (Okun, 1996). The historical context of this ridicule in the United States is based on a set of assumptions and societal myths regarding the superiority of Whites, which suggested that racial mixing was dangerous and resulted in mongrelization (Davis, 1991). These myths further suggested that individuals who engaged in interracial relationships had ulterior motives for doing so (Wardle, 1992). These motives included quests for the exotic, sexual curiosity and promiscuity, economic and social status or achievement, domination, potential citizenship, rebellion against society or family, or racial self-hatred (Root, 1992; Spickard, 1989). Other myths have implied that persons of color are more willing to accept children of interracial unions than are Whites (Wardle, 1992) and that the difficulties faced by interracial individuals and families are based on race (Root, 2001; Wehrly, 1996). Despite the increase in this population, U.S. society continues to have difficulty moving beyond these myths and stereotypes, hence the continued prevalence of prejudicial attitudes, acts of violence, discrimination, and rejection of interracial couples and multiracial individuals (Root, 1994; Solsberry, 1994).

Many interracial couples, particularly Black–White couples and their children, have had to deal with lack of acceptance, resulting in isolation and alienation from family, friends, and neighbors. Frankenberg (1995) indicated that unions between Black males and White females have often met with intense hostility. However, according to Solsberry (1994), the level of difficulty experienced by an interracial couple may vary on the basis of their socioeconomic status, educational background, and the community in which they reside.

The racial stratification of U.S. society, whereby races are viewed as inherently separate, has always made interactions among and between races a challenge. Societal concerns regarding interracial unions are representative of many unresolved issues about race (Root, 2001; Spickard, 1992). Interracial couples of all racial compositions have faced overt and covert challenges that seem to be directly related to the maintenance of racial and ethnic categorizations and identifications, sociopolitical hierarchies, and cultural values and mores (Azoulay, 1997; Comas-Diaz, 1996; Eschbach, 1995; Oriti, Bibb, & Mahboubi, 1996; C. W. Stephan & Stephan, 1989; W. G. Stephan & Stephan, 1991). These concerns, although prevalent in relationships between Whites and Blacks, may be even more prevalent in intermarriages involving Arabs, Asians, Latinos, and Native Americans.

Intermarriage is often viewed as an indicator of the assimilation process. The degree to which individuals of a particular group are likely to intermarry may be based on issues concerning level of assimilation and acculturation (Kitano, Fujino, & Sato, 1998; Saenz, Hwang, Aguirre, & Anderson, 1995). Lee (1996) indicated that although some interracial families involving Asians seem to be able to integrate multiple cultures with a high level of success, others have experienced conflicts related to differences in values, religious beliefs, communication styles, child-rearing practices, and in-law influences. This often seems to be related to issues of acculturation and assimilation. For immigrant and first-generation Asians, Latinos, and Arabs married to European Americans, concerns regarding communication styles, language, gender roles, parenting styles, customs, and food may be indicative of profound differences in cultural values and worldviews (Wehrly, Kenney, & Kenney, 1999). These cultural issues may become more cumbersome when both intermarried partners are persons of color (Blau, 1998).

Issues and Concerns of Multiracial Individuals

U.S. society operates out of a monoracial model of race relations and racial identity development that does not allow for variations in physical appearance (Root, 1997a, 1997b). Multiracial individuals, particularly those whose appearance makes it difficult for mainstream society to project onto them an identity from one of the sociopolitically defined single-race groups, challenge conventional racial ideology. An additional burden for multiracial individuals involves curtailing the ongoing challenge of responding to questions regarding who or what they are (Houston, 1997; Ramirez, 1996; Wijeyesinghe, 2001; Williams, 1996). Many multiracial individuals have reported that questions and concerns about their physical appearance and racial identity have been issues that they as well as their parents have needed to address even before birth (Wehrly et al., 1999). Hence, for many multiracial individuals, concerns and questions regarding identity are lifelong issues (Bradshaw, 1992; Williams, 1996).

Navigating and integrating multiple heritages in a monoracial society is often an ongoing challenge faced by multiracial individuals well into adulthood (Nishimura, 1998; Root, 1998). The issues and challenges faced by multiracial individuals as well as how they negotiate and deal with these concerns varies depending on their age and developmental stage in life. Thus, it is important to examine and discuss persons of multiple heritages from a developmental perspective.

Multiracial Children

Multiracial children experience a variety of stressors that are different from those of their parents. Many of these stressors are related to issues of racial identity and to the establishment of a sense of belonging among their peers and the greater society (Funderburg, 1994; Root, 1996; Rosenblatt, Karis, & Powell, 1995). According to McFadden (2001), it is important for interracial partners to recognize in the early stages of their relationship that children from their marriage not only are racially mixed but also have to adjust to being identified as "others." A family environment that fosters communication and provides love and security is key to wholesome development and to the emergence of ego strength and resilience in multiracial individuals (Nash, 1997; Root, 1996; Rosenblatt et al., 1995).

The issues and concerns of multiracial children may differ on the basis of age and developmental stage. Children begin to explore who they are during early childhood. In an attempt to understand their identity and how they fit into the family and other social environments, young children spend a lot of time and energy comparing themselves with others. They may even ask questions about their looks and those of others, specifically their parents, as a way of exploring their identity (Wardle, 1999). Confronted with frequent questions such as "What are you?" or "Are you Black, or are you White?" and quizzical and scrutinizing stares, multiracial children experience their uniqueness and discover at a young age that they do not fit traditional patterns of racial identification (Root, 1990, Wehrly, 1996; Wijeyesinghe, 2001). The development of a positive racial identity and ethnic identity is the most salient issue faced by multiracial children. Hence, according to Wardle (1999), an open, honest, and supportive environment is essential for helping multiracial children to explore their identity.

The complexities of navigating between their multiple heritages and those of their family and social environment can be confusing for young children. Those who are challenged to identify more with one aspect of their racial heritage than another experience an even greater level of confusion and dissonance. To endure these challenges and develop a healthy and positive self-concept, multiracial children must have the benefits of a secure and predictable family environment (Okun, 1996). In addition, Wardle (1999) pointed out the necessity of giving multiracial children exposure to supportive and positive influences in all aspects of their environments. This includes professionals involved in the child's care even before birth. Professionals do not function in a vacuum and may make race-based assumptions, thus treating the child and his or her family as a stereotype. Beginning at birth, it is important to expose the multiracial child to persons, books, dolls, pictures, and so forth, that are reflective of all races and cultures. During childhood, it is important to establish a solid foundation on which to build a strong self-concept in preparation for the more difficult challenges faced in adolescence.

Multiracial Adolescents

Establishing and maintaining social acceptance is one of the major tasks of adolescence. This normal aspect of the developmental process may be complicated by issues of racial identity (Okun, 1996). Multiracial adolescents experience this period of their development with varying degrees of anxiety and vulnerability; this is particularly true as involvement with their peer group, dating, and other social interactions become important (Okun, 1996; Root, 1994; Wardle, 1999). Multiracial adolescents often find themselves redefining and renegotiating their once stable relationships as a result of experiencing societal racism through stereotypical and prejudicial comments and actions directed toward their mixed ancestry (Wehrly, 1996). This is often the first time that multiracial individuals experience the barriers associated with being people of color (Root, 1990).

Another major challenge that may be experienced by multiracial adolescents is pressure to choose a racial identity or racial reference group (Gibbs & Hines, 1992; Pinderhughes, 1995). Desires to be accepted by peers, desires to conform to social expectations, or loyalties felt toward one parent over the other are often at the root of this pressure (Steel, 1995; Wehrly, 1996). The decision to choose or identify with one aspect of one's heritage over others can result in feelings of disloyalty and guilt. The racial dissonance often experienced by multiracial adolescents who are challenged in this way can be quite painful (Okun, 1996).

Many of the developmental issues and concerns that affect multiracial adolescents are similar to those experienced by all adolescents. Multiracial children who enter adolescence having a strong sense of themselves and their multiracial heritage as well as an ability to respond firmly and assertively to questions, remarks, and pressures have a greater chance of successfully meeting the challenges of adolescence (Wardle, 1999). Here again, the support provided within the individual's environment is critical.

Multiracial Adults

The issues that may be faced by multiracial adults are most often related to lack of resolution of concerns and questions regarding their mixed racial identity and heritage (Wehrly, 1996). Difficulties surviving earlier experiences of rejection or isolation and feelings of inferiority, as well as guilt related to embarrassments about parts (or all) of one's racial heritage, may be manifested in feelings of confusion or insecurity that may be experienced throughout the multiracial individual's lifetime (Okun, 1996; Wehrly, 1996; Wehrly et al., 1999).

The challenge of integrating dual or multiple heritages with other areas of their lives is ongoing for multiracial individuals (Root, 1998). The problem of institutionalized racism continues to permeate societal forces; hence, some multiracial adults continue to have their racial identities assigned or experience pressure to self-identify in a particular way. This is often based on their physical appearance (Root, 1997b). According to Root (1990), multiracial men in particular often have a difficult time overcoming social obstacles and constraints. Multiracial women, in contrast, are seen as less threatening and may therefore experience less overt obstacles to their success.

Root (1994) discussed six themes around which issues and challenges often arise for multiracial individuals: "(1) uniqueness, (2) acceptance and belonging, (3) physical appearance, (4) sexuality, (5) self-esteem, and (6) identity" (p. 462). Although these themes are not mutually exclusive, any one of them may be operating or related to concerns that a multiracial individual may be experiencing at any developmental stage.

1. *Uniqueness.* According to Root (1994), this theme interfaces with all of the other themes. Multiracial individuals often experience themselves as "different" from others because they are often treated as special or unique simply because of their multiple heritages. This may lead to behaviors or interactions that may be misinterpreted or misunderstood.
2. *Acceptance and belonging.* Multiracial individuals often feel that they must straddle both or all sides of the racial line. As a result, constant efforts are made to find a place where they can feel and experience a sense of connection or fit.
3. *Physical appearance.* According to Hall (1997), persons of mixed-race heritage often have physical features that are distinctly different than those of single-race heritage. Because of societal pressures, women tend to define themselves and their value on the basis of physical appearance; hence, for multiracial women, appearance seems to be of particular significance. Questions or judgments made about multiracial individuals' racial identity are typically based on perceptions of their physical appearance (Root, 1994).
4. *Sexuality.* Multiracial women continue to experience difficulties in relationships related to stereotypical myths about the exotic multiracial female that permeate societal views.
5. *Self-esteem.* Self-esteem interfaces with and is affected by the experiences of the multiracial individual with regard to the other five themes. Positive environmental support is essential for the development of a positive self-concept.
6. *Identity.* One's sense of identity can be equated with feelings of connectedness and belonging. Multiracial individuals who have had positive exposure and support for their exploration of their multiple heritages are more fluid in the affirmation and expression of their identity (Okun, 1996; Wehrly et al., 1999).

Counseling Interracial Couples: Case Study of Carlos and Sheila

The case study of Carlos and Sheila is a depiction of a married interracial couple dealing with acculturation and assimilation issues.

Carlos, a 33-year-old Latino of Mexican background, and Sheila, a 31-year-old of English heritage, have been married for 9 months. The couple has come to counseling to discuss how to deal with conflicts that have recently surfaced in their relationship. The two had met at a singles group offered by their parish church and had dated for about 3 years before getting married.

Carlos was born in a small town outside of Mexico City. His family came to the United States when Carlos was 4 years old. Carlos recalls that his mother worked outside of the home on a limited basis because she had to care for four children and a household. She worked as a seamstress and could, therefore, do much of her work at home. Carlos's father believed that the home and children were the woman's responsibility and that the man was the head of the household and the chief breadwinner. He was a skilled and licensed electrician in Mexico and upon arriving in the United States found employment with a contracting firm.

Carlos and his brother, Antonio, were the only children in the family to attend college. His two sisters were only allowed to attend cosmetology school. After completion of college, Carlos pursued a career as a teacher and coach and was very successful. Sheila and her two sisters had been encouraged by their parents to go to college. Sheila's mother worked as a registered nurse, and her father was a chemical engineer. Sheila had studied accounting as an undergraduate and pursued a master's degree in accounting. She entered a career as an investments accountant for a high-powered accounting firm.

Carlos and Sheila never talked much before they were married about the number of children they wanted to have or about each other's career or family roles. Shortly after the couple was married, Carlos began to talk about starting a family and spoke of dreams of having at least four children, as his parents had. Sheila was very excited and enthusiastic about her work and the social opportunities it provided her. The couple's conflicts and constant arguments began when Sheila shared at dinner one evening that she had accepted an account that in the future would require travel and long hours at the office. Sheila had difficulty understanding why Carlos was not happy about this new opportunity that she had been given, particularly because it was possible that he could accompany her on business trips that occurred at times when he was not teaching.

The above case example raises issues and questions regarding the backgrounds, cultural identities, and worldviews of both partners and how couples navigate around concerns in these areas. The counselor working with Carlos and Sheila needs to be aware of and sensitive to the cultural backgrounds of both partners as well as have an understanding for how counseling is viewed in a cultural context. Whereas the White spouse may view counseling as a natural solution to working out problems or difficulties, the non-White spouse may not, due to cultural beliefs regarding how one deals with personal and family issues (Okun, 1996). Hence, if Carlos and Sheila remain in counseling, this needs to be assessed and discussed upfront.

Another variable that needs to be addressed at the outset of counseling with this couple is the racial and cultural background of the counselor as well as his or her gender. Myths and stereotypes continue to cloud societal views of individuals who enter into interracial relationships and marriages. Counselors have an obligation to examine their own views and the manner in which these views affect their perceptions of clients, their clients' concerns, and the work they do with them (Solsberry, 1994). Similarly, it is important to consider the extent to which clients perceive the racial/cultural background of the counselor as a deterrent to the counselor's ability to understand their issues and concerns (Okun, 1996). Moreover, when counselors are working with partners whose country of origin is not the United States, they must examine their views regarding acculturation and assimilation. Awareness of the potential to impose American values on others through counseling is key. Hence, the counselor must openly dialogue with clients and assist them in developing goals that are conducive to the clients' values and needs (Okun, 1996).

Partners who are able to comprehend each other's worldview are often able to function more collaboratively and come up with mutually agreed-on solutions and decisions (Okun, 1996). According to Ibrahim and Schroeder (1990), partners benefit from assistance with clarifying and understanding each other's worldview and cultural background. This provides each with useful information for becoming aware of the values that each brings to the relationship and how these values affect views and interactions. Hence, to assist Carlos and Sheila in diffusing the conflict in their relationship, it is important that the counselor help them to examine the cultural context within which each of them was raised and has continued to operate. It is also important to educate each of them about the other's cultural values and mores. In working with Carlos and Sheila, cultural values related to work, family, child-rearing, and gender-role expectations and responsibilities require specific attention. Once their differing values have been delineated and understood, both partners can be assisted in dealing with disappointments they may experience related to unmet expectations. According to Okun (1996), helping couples to positively reframe their conflicts as being indicative of cultural differences, rather than being indicative of one being "right" and the other "wrong," enables couples to see their conflicts as differences with equal value. Thus, they are able to establish a climate in the relationship that is conducive to negotiation. Having greater awareness of and respect for their differences and similarities, couples are able to move beyond their conflicts and develop empathy and tolerance necessary for working more collaboratively on lifestyle choices and decisions (Okun, 1996).

It is important to address the fact that there has been an increase in the number of gay and lesbian interracial couples. According to Wehrly et al. (1999), the complexities of society's stigmatized perceptions of gays, lesbians, and people of color often result in a level of stress in these interracial relationships that is greater than the level of stress experienced by heterosexual interracial couples. Therefore, to be effective in helping these couples deal with the complexities of their relationships, counselors must not only assess their own attitudes and views about persons who engage in interracial relationships but also assess their attitudes and views about gay and lesbian relationships.

Counseling Multiracial Children

Counselors working with multiracial children must be sensitive to the possibility that the problems that may be presented by the children may be unrelated to their multiracial status (Wardle, 1999; Wijeyesinghe, 2001). According to Okun (1996), in assessing the problems or concerns of multiracial children, it is important to determine whether their problems or concerns are related to the children's developmental age or stage; child-rearing practices of the parents, the parents' relationship, or other familial issues; or racial/ethnic issues and concerns. The age, level of understanding, and cognitive abilities of the children are also important to consider because these influence the children's perceptions and experiences of the problem (Okun, 1996; Wehrly, 1996).

Children need to feel heard and validated; hence, the most important skill to utilize in working with multiracial children is that of supportive and culturally sensitive listening (Wehrly et al., 1999). This is particularly necessary for the development of trust and a positive relationship with the child, especially if the issues and concerns being presented are racially or ethnically oriented (Wehrly, 1996).

The establishment of a foundation for a positive self-concept is crucial to multiracial children's development. Counselors must assist children in identifying and acknowledging their strengths and abilities, in developing effective coping skills for dealing with conflict, and in developing and pursuing their own unique interests (Okun, 1996). According to Herring (1992), in helping children develop positive views of their racial and ethnic heritage, it is important to encourage and assist them in learning about all aspects of their heritage. This may be particularly important in cases in which conflict exists between parents, a parent is absent, and/or a parent's extended family is not available or involved. Working with both the child and significant adults in the child's life may also be crucial in this instance (Wehrly et al., 1999).

In the counseling process, the involvement of siblings and parents or significant adults in the child's life can be useful for understanding the interactions and dynamics of the family. Counselors may also intervene and work with teachers, specifically if it seems that a lack of understanding or sensitivity to issues related to the child's multiracial status is involved (Wehrly et al., 1999). Other effective treatment strategies include bibliotherapy, role-playing, journaling, creative writing, and various art mediums (Wehrly, 1996).

Counseling Multiracial Adolescents

Adolescents of mixed-race heritage may have the additional dilemma of dealing with stresses related to their multiple heritages; therefore, it is important that the counselor distinguish between typical developmental concerns of adolescence and concerns that may be related to the adolescents' mixed heritage (Gibbs & Moskowitz-Sweet, 1991). Gibbs (1989) suggested that the counselor's work with multiracial adolescents involves an assessment of potential conflicts in five major psychosocial areas: multiracial identity, social marginality, sexuality and choice of partners, separation from parents, and educational and career goals. This assessment should be conducted in the context of the adolescents' views and perceptions of their multiracial heritage. The perceptions and views of family members, including extended family members, toward family members' multiracial status should also be assessed. In addition, the availability of support resources and networks in the school and community should be examined (Gibbs & Moskowitz-Sweet, 1991). The support of individual, family, and other social support networks should be established from the start of the counseling process (Pinderhughes, 1995).

As with multiracial children, treatment and intervention with multiracial adolescents requires a solid working alliance built on trust and cultural sensitivity. According to Gibbs and Moskowitz-Sweet (1991), intervention must also be considerate of the adolescents' ego strength and should focus on the development of skills related to problem solving, clarification of values, decision making, and goal setting. Of salient importance is the counselor's ability to validate multiracial adolescents' feelings about their mixed-race status, assist them with understanding the relationship between problematic behavior and challenges they may be experiencing regarding their mixed-race heritage, and assist them in exploring all aspects of their heritage in order to develop a positive self-image (Pinderhughes, 1995).

Intervention strategies that are useful for assisting multiracial adolescents with exploring their racial identity and developing a positive self-concept include focused discussions, bibliotherapy, and homework assignments (Pinderhughes, 1995). Other useful strategies include role-playing, journaling, storytelling, and behavioral goal setting. Counselors working in school settings can also utilize peer counseling and peer support groups (Gibbs & Moskowitz-Sweet, 1991).

Counseling Multiracial Adults: Case Study of Cindy Malloy

The case study of Cindy Malloy is a depiction of a multiracial young adult attempting to come to terms with and understand her multiracial heritage.

> Cindy is a 23-year-old journalist of Japanese and Irish American ancestry. She has recently come in for counseling in hopes of learning how to cope with anxiety, which she has been experiencing since shortly after plans were made for her to go to Japan to work and meet her Japanese family members for the first time.
>
> Cindy's mother was raised in Kyoto, Japan, and was one of six children. Cindy's mother was young when her parents died, leaving her and her siblings to be raised by an aunt and an uncle who had no children. Cindy's father is an Irish American who was studying Japanese and martial arts in Japan about a decade after World War II. Cindy's parents met and secretly dated; 6 months later, they fled to Tokyo and were married, despite threats from Cindy's mother's family to disown her.
>
> A couple of years after they were married, Cindy's parents moved from Japan to Mr. Malloy's hometown of Wilton, Connecticut. Despite the estranged relationship that Cindy's parents had with other members of her mother's family, Cindy's mother and father managed

to maintain ongoing contact with Mrs. Malloy's two older sisters. Mrs. Malloy attempted to give Cindy and her older brother and sister a sense of connection to their Japanese family by sharing pictures that arrived of their aunts and their families. Cindy recalls occasions when packages would arrive for them from their aunts as well. The environment in which the Malloy children grew up was as prototypically American. Despite this, Mr. and Mrs. Malloy attempted to give their children a sense of their Japanese culture and roots, including the language. Cindy and her siblings enjoyed eating Mrs. Malloy's Japanese cooking and hearing their parents' stories of Japan; however, Cindy recalled that she and her siblings thwarted their parents' attempts to teach them the Japanese language and customs.

Mrs. Malloy eventually resumed contact with all of her siblings. This was followed by a trip home to Japan, which Mrs. Malloy made with Cindy's older sister shortly after she finished college. This trip served as an opportunity for Cindy's mother to reconcile with her family. Upon returning home, Mrs. Malloy and Cindy's sister shared stories of their experience. Hearing her sister tell stories about her Japanese aunts, uncles, and cousins as well as stories about the places she had visited made Cindy long for an opportunity to meet and see the people and places she had only heard about.

Cindy majored in journalism during college. A year before graduation, she learned from a Japanese exchange student about opportunities available for English-language journalists in Japan. Excited about the prospects that this would present, Cindy began investigating the idea of going to Japan to work. After graduation from college, she was fortunate to get a journalism position, working full-time for the newspaper where she had done her internship. This allowed her to gain additional experience and to save money for the trip that she was hoping she could make to Japan. With the help of cousins in Japan and a Japanese placement service referred by the career services officer at her alma mater, Cindy continued to explore possibilities for employment in Japan and eventually landed a position.

As time grew closer to her trip, Cindy began to worry about how she would be perceived and accepted by her family in Japan. More so than her siblings, Cindy has spent the majority of her life dodging curious questions and queries about her background. Although she has always had a circle of friends, Cindy has always felt that she has had to make an extra effort in order to be accepted. At times, she has wondered whether she is really accepted anywhere.

Multiracial individuals seldom use counseling to deal with overt issues related to their mixed heritage; however, it is important that counseling professionals be aware of the potential influence that being of mixed-race heritage may have on one's life (Root, 1994). The six aforementioned themes posited by Root (1994) provide an essential framework for counselors to assess and conceptualize the issues and concerns presented by multiracial individuals. In working with Cindy, these themes are important to consider because of their possible relevance to her interpersonal style, her perceptions of her environment, and her symptoms of anxiety. Consideration should also be given to the possible relevance of these themes in Cindy's life on the basis of the geographical area in which she grew up; the level of contact she has had with other multiracial individuals; and the degree to which her family provided her support, preparation, and validation for a multiracial existence (Root, 1992). Exploration of the underlying issues related to the themes will be helpful in reducing Cindy's anxiety and will be useful for the development of problem-solving strategies for helping her prepare positively for the journey that she is about to take (Root, 1994).

Root's (1998) ecological identity model is also useful in exploring the issues and concerns underlying Cindy's anxiety. Although this model may be applicable for other multiracial individuals, it was developed specifically from Root's work with multiracial Asian Americans. Root (1998) outlined numerous factors that influence the identity of multiracial Asians, including the historical conditions in the country of origin at the time of the Asian ancestor's immigration to the United States, the historical conditions of the United States at the time of the Asian immigrant's arrival in the United States, and the historical conditions in the United States since the time of the Asian immigrant's arrival. Other factors that can affect the multiracial Asian individual's identity are generation in the United States, age, physical appearance, gender, gender and ethnicity of each of the individual's parents, acceptance or rejection of the individual by paternal and maternal family members, and whether the individual had or has reclaimed an Asian name.

Utilizing the ecological identity model, the counselor could explore factors influencing Cindy's identity development. This process will be helpful in determining the potential impact that Cindy's identity development has had on her current difficulties. This process involves the counselor exploring the three major categories of the model, which are what Root (1998) referred to as inherited influences, traits, and social interaction with community. Factors in the model that fall under inherited influences include the following: languages in the home, parent's identity, nativity, extended family, names, values, sexual orientation, and phenotype. Factors included under traits include temperament, social skills, talents, and coping skills. Factors under social interaction with community consist of home, school/work, community, friends, and outside the community. It is also important to explore the regional history of race relations, which is seen as influencing the three major categories discussed above. An individual's racial or ethnic identity is determined by the interaction of all of these factors. Gender is a significant influence in that it surrounds all of the factors in the model.

Logan, Freeman, and McRoy's (1987) ecological approach may also be beneficial in working with multiracial clients like Cindy. This approach has three components—the genogram, ecomap, and cultural continuum—that can be utilized to assist multiracial individuals in exploring what it means to be multiracial (Logan et al., 1987). The genogram is useful in helping the client examine the potential impact of family relationships and dynamics, roles, and significant life events. The genogram can also be used to examine the racial and ethnic backgrounds of family members, the attitudes of immediate and extended family toward the multiracial individual, and the level of functioning of family relationships. The relationships that the multiracial individual and his or her family have had with social networks, including community, neighborhood, schools, and other community institutions, may also be explored. Specifics pertaining to the individual and his or her family's overall development and lifestyle may also be examined (Logan et al., 1987).

The ecomap uses connecting lines and symbols similar to those used in the genogram to illustrate relationships. The multiracial individual's family is shown in a large circle, with smaller circles drawn around it that signify connections with other family and social support networks. Connecting lines are used to show the individual's and family's relationships to other family and social support. The ecomap allows the counselor to explore with the client his or her own and the family's relationship with external networks. The information that can be gleaned regarding the positive or negative experiences that the client and his or her family has had with these networks can provide useful data about where and to whom the individual can go for empowerment and support. It can also provide information regarding the potential need for reevaluating or reframing relationships (Logan et al., 1987).

The cultural continuum consists of four cultural response categories, including denial of cultural or racial significance, assimilation with the dominant culture or race, assimilation with the minority culture or race, and multiracial identification. There are advantages and disadvantages associated with each response category. Utilizing these response categories, the counselor can help clients explore how they have responded to circumstances in their lives in which they have felt challenged about their mixed-race heritage while also examining the pitfalls and outcomes of earlier and more recent choices and decisions made related to aspects of their heritage (Logan et al., 1987).

Counseling Multiracial Individuals and Their Families

Counseling intervention with multiracial families varies depending on the issues and concerns of the family members (Wehrly et al., 1999; Wijeyesinghe, 2001). It is important to note that although the issues presented by multiracial families may at times differ from those presented by monoracial families, the fact that a multiracial family is coming for counseling is not indicative of pathology or dysfunction. Rather, multiracial families may often deal with issues concerning their multiple heritages, experience bouts of racism, and be challenged about their racial loyalties (Okun, 1996).

Counselors must examine their own views of interracial couples and their offspring. If the therapeutic environment is perceived to be unaccepting or biased, the family is not likely to continue the counseling process (Okun, 1996; Wehrly et al., 1999). In addition, the strategies utilized by the counselor must take into consideration the multiple racial and cultural backgrounds that may be present in the session and the multiple worldviews and perspectives that may be operating (Wehrly, 1996).

Multiracial families often present with child-related issues and concerns. In these instances, assessment should include examination of whether the concerns are related to developmental factors, inadequate parenting, marital or relationship conflicts in the environment, academic difficulties, or racial/ethnic-related challenges (Okun, 1996). The therapeutic strategies of structural family therapy, experiential family systems therapy, and extended family systems therapy are useful with multiracial families (Wehrly, 1996). Ibrahim (1998) advocated for the use of general systems theory in counseling multiracial families and suggested that the pragmatic and psychoeducational approach of primary intervention may be valuable in that it is proactive and prevention oriented and focuses on empowerment. Primary intervention should involve the home, the schools, and the community and entails educating parents, teachers, school personnel, community agencies, recreation groups, sports groups officials, and others who may be knowledgeable about the issues and challenges faced by youngsters and family members of multiracial families (Ibrahim, 1998).

Gibbs and Moskowitz-Sweet (1991) discussed the benefits of complete family involvement in activities that provide a sense of family pride and enhance children's self-esteem. Suggestions are made for family participation in ethnic and cultural activities as well as multiracial and multicultural social activities. Recommendations are also made for family involvement in religiously oriented activities that provide a spiritual component to cultural enhancement and politically oriented activities that emphasize the need for improvement of the social climate for multiracial families.

Kenney (2000) suggested that as advocates for multiracial families, counselors need to be familiar with resources available to provide support and affirmation for multiracial individuals and families. These resources include support groups and organizations (more than 30 across the country) and Internet Web sites. Many of these have been organized and facilitated by interracial couples, multiracial individuals, and multiracial families (Root & Kelley, 2003).

Issues of Transracial Adoption

Transracial adoptions both domestic and out-of-country have for decades met with extreme controversy. Domestic adoptions have typically involved White parents adopting Black, Latino, or Native American children. Prior to 1994, when Congress approved the Multiethnic Placement Act, which prevented child welfare agencies from discriminating against prospective parents on the basis of race, color, or national origin, restrictions existed that curtailed placements of Black and mixed-race Black children with White families (Okun, 1996).

In the early 1970s, the National Association of Black Social Workers (NABSW) passed a resolution against transracial adoptions involving Black and mixed-race Black children. The opposition of the NABSW toward these adoptions was largely related to concerns about the racial identity of these children and a fear that these adoptions would lead to cultural genocide (McRoy & Hall, 1996). Similar concerns regarding the adoption of Native American children resulted in the 1978 Indian Child Welfare Act that forbade the transracial adoption of Native American children (McRoy & Hall, 1996). Despite the 1994 Multiethnic Placement Act and the continued prevalence of transracial adoptions, there is still opposition, particularly from groups with political agendas and from factions of the Black community (Wardle, 1999).

Out-of-country adoptees have mostly come from parts of Central and South America, Asia, and Eastern Europe (Wehrly et al., 1999). The controversy surrounding these adoptions is mainly related to the dramatic cultural differences that often exist between the child's country of origin and the United States. Concerns have also been raised about the cultural exploitation seen as being prevalent in the adoptions of children from underdeveloped countries in need of political and economic reforms (Okun, 1996).

According to Okun (1996), a major issue for domestic transracial adoptees is the development of a positive racial identity and the ability to handle the challenges of racism. For intercountry transracial adoptees, the issues are most often related to the loss of cultural heritage and identity. The most salient issue confronted by both domestic and out-of-country transracial adoptive children and families is cross-racial and cross-cultural adjustment (Wehrly, 1996). The age of the child at the time of the adoption may also present some concerns, particularly with regard to the changes and adjustments that must be made by the child and his or her new family. How these changes and adjustments are attended to will determine the success of the placement (Miranda, 2003; Wardle, 1999).

According to Crumbley (1999), there are a number of issues that should be addressed when the suitability of prospective adoptive parents is being considered. Similar to other multiracial families, transracial adoptive families often encounter challenges about the racial and cultural makeup of their families. Hence, transracial adoptive parents must examine their motivation to adopt, the racial diversity of the community in which they live, the level of acceptance of family and friends, their knowledge of the child's cultural heritage and ancestry, their commitment to exposing the child to his or her racial and cultural roots, and their commitment to helping the child develop a positive sense of racial and cultural identity. The feelings and reactions that the biological children in the family have regarding the transracial adoption are also important to consider.

The feelings, comfort level, and welfare of the transracial adoptive child must come first. Therefore, parents must be able to prepare the child to face racism and discrimination and teach the child how to respond. To do this effectively, parents must acknowledge that racism exists and not make excuses for prejudice and discrimination, and they must have a sense of their own values and attitudes (Crumbley, 1999; Miranda, 2003). They must also provide their adoptive child with exposure to aspects of his or her racial and cultural heritage in a consistent, positive, and meaningful way in order to help the child develop a positive identity and strong sense of racial and cultural pride (Miranda, 2003; Wardle, 1999).

Counseling a Transracial Adoptee and Family: Case Study of Carl Hagerman

The following case study is an example of the potential issues faced by transracial adoptive families.

Carl, an 8-year-old African American child, was adopted as an infant by an affluent young White couple who are both physicians. Carl and his parents live in a predominately White suburb of a small city in the midwestern region of the United States. Carl's parents are bringing him for counseling because they have begun to notice that he is becoming isolated and withdrawn and does not want to go to school. Mornings at the Hagerman house have become challenging for all of them.

The school that Carl attends is predominately White with the exception of only a few other African American and Asian American students. Carl is in the third grade and is now the only student of color in his class. An Asian American student who had been in his class previously, and with whom Carl got along, is no longer there because his family has moved. All of the teachers, administration, and support personnel at Carl's school are White and have had little preparation for how to work with diverse students and their families.

Although it has been no secret to Carl that he is adopted, the Hagerman's have made an effort not to call attention to Carl's racial background. The Hagerman's extended family have all been very positive and supportive of the adoption of Carl. However, Mrs. Hagerman's sister who lives in the southwest and is a social worker expressed concern about the Hagerman's adopting an African American child and suggested the potential need for additional support, just as the adoption caseworker had recommended. Mrs. Hagerman's retort was that love and a financially secure environment were sufficient. The Hagerman's have not sought out support options or resources available to cross-racial adoptive families.

During his first session with the counselor, Carl discloses that he is unhappy at school and afraid of the children. Further probing reveals that some of the boys in his class and their older siblings have been calling him names and saying that "brown people are disgraceful and disgusting." Carl further revealed that he became fearful of going to school because a few of the older boys had made threats to hurt him. On one occasion, while in the lavatory, one of Carl's male classmates had tripped him. Carl indicates having shared this incident with his teacher, who did nothing to intervene.

Counselors working with transracial adoptive individuals and their families must determine how or whether the concerns being presented are influenced by the adoption and racial issues. Again, it is important that the counselor not make assumptions that the concerns are related to these factors (Okun, 1996). In working with Carl and his adoptive parents, the counselor must assess the manner in which the issue of Carl's adoption and his obvious racial difference has been addressed. The counselor must also assess the views that the extended family have about the adoption and determine the relationship that exists with the extended family as well as the level of support provided by the extended family. In addition, the counselor should explore the extent to which Carl's adoptive parents are aware of and have made use of support resources available to transracial adoptive families (Miranda, 2003; Okun, 1996).

In this case example, Carl informed the counselor that his unhappiness at school was a result of teasing and harassment that he was receiving because of his racial background. In trying not to call attention to Carl's racial background, his adoptive parents have not talked with Carl about prejudice and discrimination and how others may respond to the fact that he is Black. Thus, Carl was not prepared to deal with the onslaught of racial negativity that he experienced at school. Although the Hagerman's have a close relationship with and support from extended family, the fact that they have not sought assistance from support resources available to transracial adoptive families may be problematic.

In continuing to work with Carl and his parents, the counselor must assist the Hagerman's in becoming aware of the implications of their lack of attention to addressing Carl's racial background. The counselor must also emphasize the availability of resources for assisting transracial adoptive families in providing the level of support necessary not only for the success of the placement but also for the positive growth and development of their adoptive child (Miranda, 2003; Wardle, 1999). The counselor can serve as an advocate to the family by identifying and assisting the Hagerman's in getting connected to appropriate support resources geared toward helping transracial adoptive families.

According to Okun (1996), the specific strategies utilized in working with children in transracial adoptive families depend on the ages or developmental stages of the children. In working with transracial adoptive families with young children like the Hagerman's, play therapy, art therapy, and other expressive therapies may be useful. In addition, bibliotherapy is recommended for the entire family. When working with older transracial adoptees, counselors must be sensitive to special concerns that the children may have related to adjusting to the new environment and all that it encompasses. Some transracial adoptees experience conflicted and ambivalent feelings regarding their identities as they get older. They and their families need support, reassurance, and validation as they deal with these complexities (Okun, 1996). The therapeutic environment must be sensitive and conducive to allowing family members to freely express their feelings and concerns (Wehrly et al., 1999).

Gay and lesbian individuals and couples have been increasingly involved in transracial adoptions. These transracial adoptive families encounter the same issues faced in other transracial adoptive families; therefore, the same recommendations given for counseling with other transracial adoptive families should be followed. It should be noted, however, that these families may face additional challenges related to societal homophobia. Counselors working with these families may need to assess their own attitudes related to gay and lesbian relationships and transracial adoption by gay and lesbian individuals and couples (Wehrly et al., 1999).

Conclusion

With the continued increase in the numbers of interracial couples, multiracial individuals, multiracial families, and families that have become multiracial through transracial adoption comes the increasing need for counseling professionals to have an awareness of the unique issues, concerns, and strengths of this burgeoning population. In gaining greater awareness about this group and the history of oppression experienced by its members, counselors are challenged to examine their roles not only as counselors but also as advisers, advocates, consultants, and social change agents. As Oriti et al. (1996) suggested, the therapeutic strategy or approach utilized may not be as salient an issue in working with multiracial families as the extent to which the services provided are sensitive to and accepting of the diverse heritages, orientations, and worldviews of this population.

References

Azoulay, K. G. (1997). *Black, Jewish, and interracial: It's not the color of your skin, but the race of your kin and other myths of identity*. Durham, NC: Duke University Press.

Blau, M. (1998, December/January). Multiracial families. *Child, 12*(10), 96, 98, 103.

Bradshaw, C. K. (1992). Beauty and the beast: On racial ambiguity. In M. P. P. Root (Ed.), *Racially mixed people in America* (pp. 77–99). Newbury Park, CA: Sage.

Comas-Diaz, L. (1996). LatiNegra: Mental health issues of African Latinas. In M. P. P. Root (Ed.), *The multiracial experience: Racial borders as the new frontier* (pp. 167–190). Newbury Park, CA: Sage.

Crumbley, J. (1999). *Transracial adoption and foster care*. Washington, DC: CWLA Press.

Davis, P. J. (1991). *Who is Black? One nation's definition*. University Park: Pennsylvania State University Press.

Eschbach, K. (1995). The enduring and vanishing American Indian: American Indian population growth and intermarriage in 1990. *Ethnic and Racial Studies, 18*(1), 89–108.

Frankenberg, R. (1995). *White women, race matters: The social construction of Whiteness*. Minneapolis: University of Minnesota Press.

Funderburg, L. (1994). *Black, White, other: Biracial American talk about race and ethnicity.* New York: Morrow.

Gibbs, J. T. (1989). Biracial adolescents. In J. T. Gibbs, L. N. Huang, & Associates (Eds.), *Children of color: Psychological interventions with minority youth* (pp. 322–350). San Francisco: Jossey-Bass.

Gibbs, J. T., & Hines, A. M. (1992). Negotiating ethnic identity: Issues for Black–White biracial adolescents. In M. P. P. Root (Ed.), *Racially mixed people in America* (pp. 223–238). Newbury Park, CA: Sage.

Gibbs, J. T., & Moskowitz-Sweet, G. (1991). Clinical and cultural issues in the treatment of biracial and bicultural adolescents. *Families in Society: The Journal of Contemporary Human Services, 72,* 579–591.

Hall, C. C. I. (1997). Best of both worlds: Body image and satisfaction of a sample of Black-Japanese biracial individuals. *Amerasia Journal, 23*(1), 87–97.

Herring, R. D. (1992). Biracial children: An increasing concern for elementary and middle school counselors. *Elementary School Guidance and Counseling, 27,* 123–130.

Houston, H. R. (1997). "Between two cultures": A testimony. *Amerasia Journal, 23*(1), 149–154.

Ibrahim, F. A. (1998, March). *Counseling multiracial adolescents.* Paper presented at the annual conference of the American Counseling Association, Indianapolis, IN.

Ibrahim, F. A., & Schroeder, D. G. (1990). Cross-cultural couples counseling: A developmental, psychoeducational intervention. *Journal of Comparative Family Studies, 21,* 193–205.

Kenney, K. (2000). Multiracial families. In J. Lewis & L. Bradley (Eds.), *Advocacy in counseling: Counselors, clients, community* (pp. 55–70). Greensboro, NC: ERIC/CASS.

Kitano, H. H. L., Fujino, D. C., & Sato, J. T. (1998). Interracial marriages: Where are the Asian Americans and where are they going? In L. C. Lee & N. W. Zane (Eds.), *Handbook of Asian American psychology* (pp. 233–260). Thousand Oaks, CA: Sage.

Lee, E. (1996). Asian American families: An overview. In M. McGoldrick, J. K. Pearce, & J. Giordano (Eds.), *Ethnicity and family therapy* (2nd ed., pp. 227–248). New York: Guilford Press.

Logan, S. L., Freeman, E. M., & McRoy, R. G. (1987). Racial identity problems of biracial clients: Implications for social work practice. *Journal of Intergroup Relations, 15,* 11–24.

McFadden, J. (2001). Intercultural marriage and family: Beyond the racial divide. *The Family Journal: Counseling and Therapy for Couples and Families, 11*(1), 39–42.

McRoy, R. G., & Hall, C. C. I. (1996). Transracial adoptions—In whose best interest? In M. P. P. Root (Ed.), *The multiracial experience: Racial borders as the new frontier* (pp. 63–78). Newbury Park, CA: Sage.

Miranda, G. E. (2003). Domestic transracial and multiraciality. In M. P. P. Root & M. Kelley (Eds.), *Multiracial child resource book: Living complex identities.* Seattle, WA: MAVIN Foundation.

Nash, R. D. (1997). *Coping with interracial dating.* New York: Rosen.

Nishimura, N. J. (1998). Assessing the issues of multiracial students on college campuses. *Journal of College Counseling, 1*(1), 45–53.

Okun, B. F. (1996). *Understanding diverse families: What practitioners need to know.* New York: Guilford Press.

Oriti, B., Bibb, A., & Mahboubi, J. (1996). Family-centered practice with racially/ethnically mixed families. *Families in Society: The Journal of Contemporary Human Services, 76,* 573–582.

Pinderhughes, E. (1995). Biracial identity—Asset or handicap? In H. W. Harris, H. C. Blue, & E. E. H. Griffith (Eds.), *Racial and ethnic identity: Psychological development and creative expression* (pp. 73–93). New York: Routledge.

Ramirez, D. A. (1996). Multiracial identity in a color-conscious world. In M. P. P. Root (Ed.), *The multiracial experience: Racial borders as the new frontier* (pp. 49–62). Newbury Park, CA: Sage.

Root, M. P. P. (1990). Resolving "other" status: Identity development of biracial individuals. In L. S. Brown & M. P. P. Root (Eds.), *Diversity and complexity in feminist therapy* (pp. 185–205). New York: Haworth Press.

Root, M. P. P. (Ed.). (1992). *Racially mixed people in America*. Newbury Park, CA: Sage.

Root, M. P. P. (1994). Mixed-race women. In L. Comas-Diaz & B. Greene (Eds.), *Women of color: Integrating ethnic and gender identities in psychotherapy* (pp. 455–478). New York: Guilford Press.

Root, M. P. P. (Ed.). (1996). *The multiracial experience: Racial borders as the new frontier*. Thousand Oaks, CA: Sage.

Root, M. P. P. (1997a). Contemporary mixed-heritage Filipino Americans: Fighting colonized identities. In M. P. P. Root (Ed.), *Filipino Americans: Transformation and identity* (pp. 80–94). Thousand Oaks, CA: Sage.

Root, M. P. P. (1997b). Multiracial Asians: Models of ethnic identity. *Amerasia Journal, 23*(1), 29–41.

Root, M. P. P. (1998). Multiracial Americans: Changing the face of Asian America. In L. C. Lee & N. W. Zane (Eds.), *Handbook of Asian American psychology* (pp. 261–287). Thousand Oaks, CA: Sage.

Root, M. P. P. (2001). *Love's revolution: Interracial marriage*. Philadelphia, PA: Temple University Press.

Root, M. P. P., & Kelley, M. (2003). *Multiracial child resource book: Living complex identities*. Seattle, WA: MAVIN Foundation.

Rosenblatt, P. C., Karis, T. A., & Powell, R. D. (1995). *Multiracial couples: Black and White voices*. Newbury Park, CA: Sage.

Saenz, R., Hwang, S. S., Aguirre, B. E., & Anderson, R. N. (1995). Persistence and change in Asian identity among children of intermarried couples. *Sociological Perspectives, 38*, 175–194.

Solsberry, P. W. (1994). Interracial couples in the United States of America: Implications for mental health counseling. *Journal of Mental Health Counseling, 4*, 304–307.

Spickard, P. R. (1989). *Mixed blood: Intermarriage and ethnic identity in 20th-century America*. Madison: University of Wisconsin Press.

Spickard, P. R. (1992). The illogic of American racial categories. In M. P. P. Root (Ed.), *Racially mixed people in America* (pp. 12–23). Newbury Park, CA: Sage.

Steel, M. (1995). New colors: Mixed-race families still find a mixed reception. *Teaching Tolerance, 4*(1), 44–46, 48–49.

Stephan, C. W., & Stephan, W. G. (1989). After intermarriage: Ethnic identity among mixed heritage Japanese Americans and Hispanics. *Journal of Marriage and the Family, 51*, 507–519.

Stephan, W. G., & Stephan, C. W. (1991). Intermarriage: Effects of personality, adjustment, and intergroup relations in two samples of students. *Journal of Marriage and the Family, 53*, 241–250.

Stolley, K. S. (1993). Statistics on adoption in the United States. *The Future of Children: Adoption, 3*(1), 26–42.

Wardle, F. (1992). Supporting biracial children in the school setting. *Education and Treatment of Children, 15*, 163–172.

Wardle, F. (1999). *Tomorrow's children*. Denver, CO: Center for the Study of Biracial Children.

Wehrly, B. (1996). *Counseling interracial individuals and families*. Alexandria, VA: American Counseling Association.

Wehrly, B., Kenney, K. R., & Kenney, M. E. (1999). *Counseling multiracial families*. Thousand Oaks, CA: Sage.

Wijeyesinghe, C. L. (2001). Racial identity in multiracial people: An alternative paradigm. In C. L. Wijeyesinghe & B. W. Jackson, III (Eds.), *New perspectives on racial identity development: A theoretical and practical anthology* (pp. 129–152). New York: New York University Press.

Williams, M. G. (1996). Race as process: Reassessing the "What are you?" encounters of biracial individuals. In M. P. P. Root (Ed.), *The multiracial experience: Racial borders as the new frontier* (pp. 191–210). Newbury Park, CA: Sage.

The Gay/Lesbian/Transgendered Experience

Issues associated with sexual orientation have gained greater prominence in U.S. culture in recent years. Gay, lesbian, and transgendered individuals face a multitude of challenges as well as increasing rights and opportunities as they explore and proclaim their sexual orientation. For many individuals who identify as homosexual or who are exploring their sexual identity, coming to live in harmony with themselves can mean experiencing dissonance in the community at large.

Counseling Gay Men

A. Michael Hutchins

To understand a man's attraction to another man is to understand a unique way of being in the world. As a counselor, one hopes to invite clients to fully explore themselves and to be one with themselves and the world around them—to live in harmony and to creatively transcend dissonance. For many clients who identify as homosexual, or who are exploring their sexual identity, coming to live in harmony with themselves can mean experiencing dissonance in the community at large. As such, counselors may need to assist clients in developing the skills necessary to make choices that may create internal harmony while helping them develop the strength to face adverse conditions in the world at large. Additionally, it may mean counselors must take steps to advocate for and create greater understanding and inclusion in the community at large.

Counselors can better understand the dissonance experienced by men coming to an understanding of their sexual orientation if this search for clarity about sexuality is framed as a developmental process. There are several models for understanding sexual identity development (Cass, 1979; Coleman, 1982; Troiden, 1979, 1989). All of these models have stages of awareness, dissonance, acceptance, and synthesis. In understanding a man's sexual orientation, Appleby (2001) recommended understanding the levels of development on five interconnected levels: (a) historical, (b) environmental–structural, (c) cultural, (d) family, and (e) individual. He suggested that it is the counselor's task "to assist . . . in the process of developing a positive self and group identity, to manage the information around the stigmatized identity, and to advocate for more nurturing (nondiscriminatory) environments" (Appleby, 2001, p. 8). In this chapter, identity development is considered primarily from Cass's (1979) model integrating Appleby's (2001) recommendations.

While exploring the sexual identity of individual men, counselors must be aware of the environmental and cultural dynamics of the community in which that identity development is occurring. Some cultures and communities are supportive of healthy development of alternative lifestyles. However, other communities may be less tolerant of diverse worldviews. This may create dissonance for a man developing a sexual identity. In looking at individual development, a potential developmental process in communities is reflected upon.

In exploring personal identity development, it is important to acknowledge the communities in which the developing man lives. Each individual grows to maturity living in a community. Often, the standards and norms one holds for oneself are different from those of the community in which one lives. As individual men come to a greater understanding and acceptance of their sexual orientation, they may experience less and less harmony with the community at large. In such cases, counselors may need to become involved in community education and advocacy. In other cases, the community norms may be more accepting and celebratory of an individual's sexual orientation—perhaps even more so than he is. In such cases, counselors may need to assist the client in becoming aware of the resources in the community in which he lives and in working with the community as advocates to become more inclusive for men in all stages of sexual identity exploration. Where one sees the dissonance in individuals and in communities, one sees the results of a society that is reflecting a history of homophobia and heterosexism. It is incumbent on counselors to be aware of such dynamics and to work to create a more inclusive environment. When working with men who are members of communities that have already been marginalized, the task of addressing multiple arenas of discrimination becomes even more challenging.

Dynamics of the Cultural Context of Gay Men

Diversity

Historically, much of the understanding of male sexuality development has come from attempts to understand the development of middle-class, English-speaking, Caucasian men (Tobias, 1998). For many men who do not fit into that group, additional developmental issues can be most significant. In this chapter, issues of diversity within the gay male community and in the community at large are addressed. A comprehensive exploration of such issues is beyond the scope of this chapter. The experience of men of color has, most often, been quite different from the experience of most middle-class, English-speaking, Caucasian men (Appleby, 2001; Beam, 1986; Boykin, 1996; Chung & Szymanski, 2000, 2001; Hemphill & Beam, 1991; hooks, 2001; King, 2004; Longres, 1996; Nelson, 1993; Ritter & Terndrup, 2002; Roscoe, 1988, 1995, 1998; Smith, 1983; Thompson, 1987; Williams, 1986; Wright et al., 2001). Different ethnic groups have different values and norms for sexual identity development within their communities (Appleby, 2001; Chung & Szymanski, 2000, 2001; King, 2004; Roscoe, 1988, 1995, 1998; Sears, 1994; Smith, 1983; Thompson, 1987). Additionally, men of faith (de la Huerta, 1999; Fortunato, 1982, 1987; Lowenthal, 1997) may have unique experiences as they learn to integrate an understanding of sexual orientation into self-definitions that include membership in organized religious structures.

HIV/AIDS

A counselor cannot effectively work with gay men without having some understanding of the impact of HIV/AIDS on the gay population. For over 20 years, HIV has been a reality in the gay community. At times, it has been devastating, and men have had to confront issues of grief and loss as they have confronted their own mortality and have witnessed the loss of lovers, friends, and family members. At other times, it has hidden quietly, though formidably, in the background. For the past several years, there has been a powerful resurgence, particularly in the African American community and in the community of younger men, as men have become less vigilant in practicing healthy sexual behavior and in the presence of symptom-reducing medications for those men and boys who have sero-converted. Whereas AIDS was once seen as a death sentence, it is now often perceived as a controllable chronic disease except in those communities that do not have the fiscal and medical resources to provide comprehensive medical, social, and psychological services. In a politically hostile community, resources are increasingly less available. The perception that HIV-related illness has become less severe is being challenged daily in many communities, and advocates work diligently to educate at-risk groups, community members, decision makers, social service agencies, and others. Resources for counselors about what is happening in the HIV community include www.gaymenshealthsummit@yahoogroups.com.

Aging

In contemporary society, much emphasis is placed on youth. In gay society, this emphasis is even stronger. Many young gay men experience discrimination and antigay bias in school, at work, in their churches, and from friends and family. In the adolescent community, suicide risk is higher in young men struggling with sexual identity than it is in the community at large (Remafedi, 1994). In many areas within the young gay community, substance abuse and isolation are prevalent (Kus, 1990; Siegel & Lowe, 1994; Signoreli, 1997). In this youth-oriented culture, counselors may wish to explore ways to appropriately address changing cultural norms with clients and with organizations within the community at large.

A growing number of men are confronting the dynamics of aging within the gay world. Single gay men report that they become "invisible" at earlier and earlier ages. Many single men report increased isolation and alienation. The emphasis on youth supports this perception of increasing invisibility. The aging process, then, has some unique dynamics within the gay world (Gooch, 1999; Isay, 1989, 1996; Jackson, 1991, 1993; Kooden & Flowers, 2000; Ritter & Terndrup, 2002; Siegel & Lowe, 1994). As medical resources become more difficult to access, isolation and anxiety/depression increase in the older gay male population.

Chemical Dependency and Substance Abuse

Historically, the center of the gay community has been gay bars. Although this may be changing in some communities, alcohol and the social scene surrounding "bar life" are still a reality for many gay men. Additionally, many younger men are part of the "circuit party" set. In these venues, alcohol and drugs are a significant part of life (Kominars & Kominars, 1996; Kus, 1990; Signoreli, 1997). Gay men often report depression, isolation, and alienation, which can temporarily be alleviated by drug and alcohol use. Additionally, many men report that the incidences of at-risk sexual behavior increase when they are under the influence of drugs and alcohol.

Technology

An increasingly important factor in the gay community and in the community at large is the role of the Internet. Since the mid-1990s, more and more men have been making connections with other men through the Internet, chat rooms, Web sites, and other World Wide Web vehicles. Gay resources such as *The Advocate* have established Web sites (www.advocate.com). Additional resources that are available to gay men and those who work with them include www.planetout.com and www.gay.com. These and other resources open the world for many men who had previously been isolated from other gay men and the greater gay world. For some emerging gay men, the Internet has opened a new world within which they have begun to make connections with similarly searching men. For others, the Internet has helped to perpetuate isolation and alienation, as they become more reclusive and live more "virtual lives." Many lonely and isolated men are in danger of compulsive or addictive use of the Internet (Chaney & Dew, 2003; Dew & Chaney, 2004). Counselors need to see the dangers, as well as the resources, in this emerging culture.

Identity and Family

Within the gay community, ongoing discussions occur concerning acculturation, the loss of gay identity, and the importance of maintaining a unique community identity (Browning, 1994, 1998; Harris, 1997; Kooden & Flowers, 2000; Lowenthal, 1997; Siegel & Lowe, 1994; Signoreli, 1997). Appleby (2001) saw this discussion as that of primarily a White, middle-class population, with members of other groups being more concerned with issues of marginalization and daily living. Some activists and other members of the gay community believe that as gay men, members of the gay community should not aspire to the norms of a White, middle-class, heterosexual, and heterosexist society, whereas others work diligently for gay men to have domestic partner benefits, to have relationships recognized, to be able to adopt children, and to have the same access to power that White heterosexual men have.

Additionally, debate occurs within elements of the gay community focusing on the nature of relationships. Are there healthy alternatives to being either single or in a committed monogamous relationship with one other man? What is the nature of "family," and can "family of origin" be supplemented with, replaced by, or integrated with a "family of choice"? Should men be allowed to form legal contracts acknowledging their relationships? How can men work together and with the community at large to address discrimination in housing, employment, medical services, and other areas? How can a man ensure that he has hospital privileges when another man with whom he has shared his life is dying? What happens when a lover dies and there is a legal battle with members of the deceased lover's family of origin for the remains of a shared life? As gay men sort through such questions, counselors need to be asking about their beliefs and practices in these arenas. Additionally, counselors may need to advocate for legal and social inclusion.

Spirituality

With the maturing of the HIV epidemic, there is a growing interest in gay spirituality (de la Huerta, 1999; Johnson, 2000; Kooden & Flowers, 2000; Roscoe, 1995; Stowe, 1999; Thompson, 1987, 1990, 1997). Some of the interest is woven into the relationships with some organized religious structures concerning the acceptability of homosexual behavior and the meaning of homosexuality. Many gay men choose to remain in the religious tradition in which they were raised and attempt to blend into such religious groups and behave as if the issues do not exist for them. Others choose to remain in such structures and work to bring about change in doctrine and practice. As some traditional religious structures confront sexual crises, they can become unsafe communities for many emerging gay men. At times, such crises open the wounds of sexual trauma and abuse. Many gay men choose to look elsewhere for spiritual support. For many of these men, the decision to move away from the religious structures within which they were raised has led to an exploration of spirituality that is not grounded in historical religious structures or that is grounded in non-Judeo-Christian tradition. The role of spirituality is becoming increasingly important in the gay community, and many clients who come to counseling are exploring nontraditional expressions of spiritual growth.

Cass's (1979) Model of Homosexual Identity Formation

What follows is an exploration of some of the aforementioned dynamics in an attempt to further understanding of gay male identity development. The developmental stages of Cass's (1979) model of homosexual identity formation are presented through case studies with a variety of intervention possibilities and several different ways of addressing the client and his issue. As with any developmental model, the stages are described as separate and well-defined. The reality of such development is that the stages are often much less clear and more ambiguous. Counselors must be cognizant of such lack of clarity and see the model as a framework from which to explore, rather than as a box within which to fit individuals and communities.

In exploring the individual developmental stages, it can be conjectured that there are developmental stages through which a community at large moves as well. In referring to the community at large, it may include simple organizations, professional associations, social groups, local municipalities, state or regional coalitions, or the nation as a whole. As American society examines ways to integrate sexuality, the complex issues of sexual orientation are a critical part of the examination and exploration of the evolution of the identity of a gay man. For this reason, the evolution of a community is examined in each case study.

Stage 1: Identity Confusion

The initial stage of the model, which Cass (1979) labeled *Identity Confusion*, is marked by denial and confusion about sexual behavior, feelings of attraction, and sense of self. At this stage of development, the individual may focus on sexual behavior and not make a distinction between sexual behavior and sexual orientation.

The Center for Substance Abuse Treatment (2001) defined sexual orientation as

> the erotic and affectional (or loving) attraction to another person, including erotic fantasy, erotic activity or behavior, and affectional needs . . . [and indicated that] sexual behavior, or sexual activity, differs from sexual orientation and alone does not define someone as a (gay) individual. Any person may be capable of sexual behavior with the same or opposite sex, but an individual knows his . . . longings—erotic and affectional—and which sex is likely to satisfy those needs. (pp. 4–5)

In the Identity Confusion stage, the individual does not distinguish among the physical, erotic, emotional, and psychological aspects of sexuality and sexual orientation. He does recognize that information about homosexuality is somehow personally relevant and that the attraction cannot be ignored or denied completely. He experiences a sense of inconsistency and dissonance in his sense of self. He may privately begin to suspect that his thoughts, behaviors, or feelings could possibly be homosexual. He may appear to be heterosexual, or at least believes that he does, and believes that others perceive him as heterosexual as well. Fear about homosexuality is a strong component of this emerging man, though he may deny any fear. Often, when explored, fear of any kind of sexuality is even more fundamental than fear of being attracted to someone of the same sex.

According to Cass (1979), the individual does not find the definition of himself as homosexual to be desirable or acceptable. He may restrict getting information about homosexuality, may inhibit his sexual behavior, may deny any relevance of information about homosexuality, may actively engage in heterosexual behavior, may become asexual, may seek to be "cured," and/or may become an antigay crusader.

On many levels, the individual disowns feelings, thoughts, and actions that could be associated with same-sex attraction. When he "falls," he may define his actions and rationalize his behavior (e.g., "I was just experimenting," "I was drunk," "It was an accident," or "I just did it for the money"). For many men, this kind of behavior may continue, and they may not move beyond this stage.

Other men recognize that the information they are receiving does have meaning for them, and they begin to gather more information about same-sex attraction. In past generations, boys and men attempted to gather information (often furtively) from libraries, books, magazines, and others in whom they could trust. In contemporary society, men are using the Internet to gather information. Much of the information available is healthy and helpful. Other information may be confusing and may focus more on behavior or "acting out" rather than on integration of all aspects of sexuality (Chaney & Dew, 2003; Dew & Chaney, 2004).

Many segments of the community at large may exhibit a corresponding set of norms for addressing homosexuality. In such communities, sexuality is understood as behavior, and there is little or no understanding of the more integrated nature of sexuality. Fear of sexuality may be prevalent, and the community may not even acknowledge that homosexuality could be a part of the community. Such communities may, at times, be labeled as homophobic. In actuality, the underlying fear may be of any kind of sexual expression. If the community does look at the possibility that homosexuality can exist within its structure, it may focus on behavior and label such behavior as "sinful," "immoral," "unnatural," or "sick" and then develop ways to ostracize or punish individuals who engage in homosexual behavior. Such fear-based community norms can reinforce the individual man's struggle within himself.

For the emerging man, this stage of development can be tumultuous. He may seek counseling, reporting that he is depressed or anxious. Often, he does not seek counseling of his own volition. He may be immersed in a culture that does not value counseling and may not seek assistance for many different reasons. At times, younger men may seek assistance after having acted out, having been involved with drug-related activity, or feeling alienated and depressed and after "testing" begin to self-disclose issues related to sexual identity. Older men may act out and come into counseling when other parts of their lives begin to become problematic. Alcohol and other chemical dependency issues may precipitate interventions or counseling. At times, men are referred after legal difficulties. Even in such circumstances, there may be a very high level of denial based on fears of others discovering their behavior and fear of sanctions.

Case Study: Tyrone

Tyrone is a 30-year-old African American man who is a captain in the U.S. Army, stationed in rural Arizona. He was referred for counseling by his civilian attorney after charges were filed against him for attempted sodomy, indecent exposure, and driving while intoxicated.

Tyrone had regularly been chatting online with gay men in a local Internet chat room. One night, after he had been drinking at a local bar with fellow officers, he stopped at a rest area on the interstate and connected with an attractive man in the parking lot. He invited the man back to his apartment; and the man returned home with him. When they entered Tyrone's apartment, he reports that the man made sexual advances toward him, and he responded. At that point, the man identified himself as an undercover local police officer and arrested Tyrone.

Tyrone was charged with sexual offenses, and the information was forwarded to his commanding officer. The U.S. Army is investigating the incident to determine whether Tyrone should be separated from military service.

Tyrone does not identify as a gay man. He reports that if forced to identify a sexual orientation, he "might call myself bisexual." He reports that he has not had sexual contact with a woman in "about 10 years" and that his only sexual contact with men has been when he has been drinking heavily or, occasionally, when he has been using cocaine.

He reports that he does spend from 2 to 4 hours daily in Internet gay chat rooms and that "once in a while" will go online when he is in his office. He reports that he has made sexual contact "a few times" with the men with whom he has chatted online.

In sharing his sexual history, Tyrone acknowledges that he was introduced to being sexual by his football coach when he was 14. He reports that he felt ashamed of this contact, which lasted for several years, and that he would "get drunk" in order "to hide what was happening."

Throughout the first few counseling sessions, Tyrone maintained that he was not homosexual, that his behavior occurs only when he is under the influence of drugs or alcohol, that his drinking "could possibly be a problem," and that he was "trapped" by the police officer.

When Tyrone's case was brought before the local judge, according to Tyrone, the judge reported that he wanted to "send a message to men like you" and wanted "to make sure the community is safe." His attorney had referred Tyrone to counseling in order to demonstrate to the court that Tyrone was remorseful for his actions and that he was seeking help. His military attorney told him that "the best you can hope for is a General Discharge."

Discussion

In this case, the counselor can work with Tyrone in several areas. Initially, it is important for Tyrone to see that his behavior is problematic. It may be important to suspend any labels about sexuality and sexual orientation, to explore the loneliness and isolation he has experienced, and to look at the thinking, feeling, and behaving that led to his being in his current situation.

Much of the counseling at this point may involve providing information and teaching Tyrone some decision-making skills. The counselor may be called on to provide information about Tyrone's behavior and mental health in the court hearings. The initial sessions may need to focus on the immediacy of the court hearings and the military decisions. If Tyrone is placed on probation, he will need support and connections within the community. If he is to be separated from military service, he will need assistance in many areas of his life.

It is important to look at the role that alcohol and drugs play in his life and how his decision making is affected by such use. In one session, Tyrone acknowledged that in his loneliness, and under the influence of drugs and alcohol, he has engaged in unsafe sexual practices. He has refused to be tested for HIV, reporting that he does not want to know his HIV status. At some point, it is important to explore this decision and its implications.

According to Appleby (2001), it may be important to explore Tyrone's introduction to sexuality and the effects of that introduction. If Tyrone had been introduced to sexuality by his football coach, it is important to explore the effects of sexual abuse on his sexual identity development. It is also possible that his coach is still in a position in which he can have contact with young men. If this is the case, the counselor may need to explore reporting the coach's behavior.

Tyrone grew up in a working-class African American family and community. He reports that his mother was the head of the household and that church has been and continues to be an important part of the family's life. He reports that there is no acceptance of homosexuality in his family or church community. He has not yet told his family of his situation and may need to explore ways of doing that. He may find out that there are resources within his church community.

Tyrone's use of Internet chat rooms may come from his loneliness and isolation and/or may be compulsive behavior. It may be important to explore the dynamics underlying the behavior. While living in a rural community, he may find that the Internet is the most reasonable way to meet other men. However, it has many dangers, and Tyrone may need to explore these dangers.

The community in which Tyrone lives and the U.S. Army base on which he works are not rich sources of support and, as can be witnessed by the judge's statements, may be quite hostile. It may be helpful for the counselor to develop a coalition of helping professionals who can provide education about sexual identity development for local organizations and leadership. Additionally, it may be helpful to seek assistance from national organizations that address issues of discrimination based on sexual orientation. All such activity would need to be sensitive to Tyrone and the situation in which he finds himself.

Stage 2: Identity Comparison

When a man begins to ask the question "Am I homosexual?" he has begun exploring in the Identity Comparison stage. This stage occurs when the emerging man accepts that he may be homosexual. In the Identity Confusion stage, the person struggles with self-alienation. In this stage, the focus is on exploring the social alienation that comes from feeling different from family, peers, and society at large.

During this stage, the individual becomes aware that many of the social expectations that have been a part of his culture no longer apply to him. He begins to realize that traditional life structures do not apply to him and may experience a sense of loss and grief. Expressing this sense of loss in a healthy manner may help him to develop the resources to move through his life and integrate his sexual identity. When the opportunity to work through grief is not present, isolation, withdrawal, and/or acting out with "at-risk" behaviors can become factors in his development.

Historically, certain conditions have increased the sense of isolation for the emerging gay man. Geographic isolation has meant lack of access to information and other men who are exploring their emerging sexual identity. With the advent of the Internet, many men are learning to explore resources and make connections that were unavailable in the not-too-distant past. Often, if the individual is from a deeply religious background in which he has learned that homosexuality is sinful, he will find the alienation even more devastating.

During this stage, the individual may accept the possibility of being different, though not exploring this fully in his behavior. He may begin to grieve the loss of heterosexual expectations and ways of being in the world. Some men will accept being different and may creatively work through the feelings, thoughts, and behaviors of being different.

Others may attempt to "pass" as heterosexual. They may have women with whom they show up at social events or with whom they spend a great deal of time, though nothing romantic develops. At times, they may shun any social events that require heterosexuality. A man may become acutely aware of his wardrobe and work to make certain that he doesn't "look gay"; he may further avoid any behavior that might be interpreted as gay. During this stage, a man may actively cultivate a masculine image. In some cultures, this is even more highly valued, and an exaggerated sense of masculinity may be rewarded.

A man may recognize that he is attracted to other men at this stage and may seek ways to be connected with attractive men in ways that do not appear to be sexual. He may value a "best friend" and even fantasize about this man but never allow himself to fully accept the attraction. He develops such phrases as "If it weren't for this person, I wouldn't be gay"; "I refuse to categorize myself; gender doesn't matter to me"; "I could be heterosexual at any time"; or "It's nobody's business what I do in bed."

This can be a time of great anxiety and preoccupation with sexuality. There is a high risk for alcohol and drug abuse during this stage of development and a growing conflict about social situations. Younger men may be more willing to explore during this stage, reporting that it is "fashionable" to be undefined. For older men, this can be more nonfactual. Men may remain married during this stage but have sexual liaisons outside of the marriage, justifying such encounters as not being unfaithful to their primary relationships because they are not socially and emotionally connected to the men with whom they are having contact.

Men at this stage of development may not seek counseling unless something happens in their lives to upset the carefully developed equilibrium. In communities that are in a comparable stage of development, it is not safe to acknowledge homosexuality. Again, homosexuality in such communities may be understood in terms of acting out sexual behavior that may be labeled as "unnatural," "sinful," or "sick." These communities may continue to deny that homosexuality exists within the community. However, the community differs from the earlier stage in that it is not likely to go "witch-hunting" in search of "deviants." Although there continue to be fear and shame around misunderstood sexuality, the same level of hostility may not be present. In this climate, it may still not be safe to discuss sexuality or sexual orientation. Persons living in such communities need to get their information from resources outside of the main community support systems. If the counselor is a member of the community, it may be very important for the counselor to begin gathering support to provide education for the community at large about sexuality and sexual orientation. Again, in the age of Internet access, resources are more readily available.

Case Study: Henry

Henry is a 21-year-old male from the Navajo nation who is working as an apprentice silversmith in a small town in southern New Mexico. He grew up on the reservation in northern New Mexico until he graduated from high school, when he moved south to work with an artist who knows his family and who has always shown an interest in Henry. The artist is 15 years older than Henry, and according to Henry, they have been lovers for 3 years.

Henry is not certain that he is gay because, he reports, he does not know what being gay means. He does know that he and his partner use drugs and alcohol and that, at times, they have gotten violent with each other. He and his partner have been arrested for domestic violence. Henry recently discovered that his partner is HIV-positive. In fear, Henry was tested and discovered that he, too, is HIV-positive, although he is asymptomatic.

Henry was referred for counseling by the county public health department when he was given his test results. He reports that he does not want to talk about his situation and that, although he does not want to come to counseling, he does not know what else to do. During the session, Henry is very quiet, and there are long periods of silence. His appointment was scheduled as the last appointment of the day, and the counselor allowed the session to extend well beyond a 50-minute hour.

In the initial session, Henry was invited to share how he would address the situation if he were on the reservation. He smiled and reported that he would probably get drunk. When asked to explore other options, he thought for a long time. When he spoke, he reported that he would probably get up very early in the morning and walk eastward to meet the sun; he would dance with the men in his village; he would draw his story and incorporate it in his silver work; and, finally, he would go to his grandmother, tell her his story, and listen to her advice. He also reported that he would read stories about being a gay man and that he would get more information about HIV/AIDS.

With assistance from the counselor, Henry found a local group of Navajo men who danced together regularly and who, Henry discovered, were related to him. Additionally, he found an area along the Rio Grande River basin where he could run in the morning and pray. Henry agreed to create stories in pictures and share the stories with the counselor and with other men from his dance group, some of whom he suspected of being gay. Henry agreed to read *Living the Spirit: A Gay American Indian Anthology* (Roscoe, 1988) and *Queer Spirits: A Gay Men's Myth Book* (Roscoe, 1995) and to create some of his own drawings and paintings telling his stories.

Henry was referred to a physician who integrates Western medicine and traditional Navajo healing methods and who can work with him in developing a holistic health plan. Henry also agreed to see the counselor on a monthly basis to explore the role that substance abuse and domestic violence have played in his life.

Discussion

The initial contact with Henry established the scope of some of his concerns. He has questions about sexual orientation, but seeing a counselor and discussing issues of sexuality are not congruent with his cultural problem-solving style. He has sought a counselor because he does not know what else to do. There appear to be problems of substance abuse, depression, violence, and spiritual connectedness. Additionally, Henry's HIV status is of significant concern.

Henry can use information about what it means to be a gay man. He does not identify with the mainstream gay society and does not appear to have much, if any, information about sexual orientation in Native American communities. Henry has had a connection to the spiritual healing traditions of the Navajo nation while living on the reservation. Reconnecting with a Navajo community seems to be an important part of his growth. Additionally, it may be very important for Henry to discover men from his own nation who understand issues of sexuality.

The referral to a physician who integrates different healing approaches is important. It speaks to the need for counselors to have knowledge about all aspects of the communities in which they live. There are different responses to homosexuality and HIV in different Native American communities, and Henry can benefit from connectedness with his own culture as he attempts to integrate his sexual identity into his greater identity.

Stage 3: Identity Tolerance

The Identity Tolerance stage occurs when the emerging man comes to accept the possibility that he may be homosexual and recognizes the sexual/social/emotional needs that go with being homosexual. He moves beyond the confusion and turmoil of earlier stages and has the energy to begin exploring what may be available in a community. He begins to see greater differences between himself and heterosexual peers and begins seeking out a gay subculture. As he does this, he begins to decrease his social isolation, looking for others who are "more like me." The move toward a gay community helps him move toward a more positive gay identity. He may begin to find a more supportive and understanding support system, which increases his potential for meeting a potential partner or partners. He may have greater access to positive role models and may have greater opportunity to practice being more at ease as a gay man.

If his contacts with the gay community are positive, he is likely to develop a more positive sense of himself. If they are more negative, his entry into the community may be more difficult, and he may choose to remain outside of the community.

Historically, the center of gay life has been the "bar scene." A man who is not comfortable in such a scene may have found entry into the community to be very difficult. If he is a member of other marginalized communities, the entry is even more difficult. If and when men of color and other ethnic and language groups attempt to enter mainstream gay culture, they may encounter racism and other forms of discrimination. As society changes, more options are open for the emerging gay man. In many communities, gyms and fitness centers are replacing bars as places for men to meet. In communities that are emerging as more gay friendly, there are community centers; interest-based associations (hiking clubs, bowling leagues, photography clubs, theatre groups, softball leagues, ski clubs, bridge clubs, discussion groups, 12-step meetings, dinner clubs, etc.); local publications; political organizations; HIV service organizations; religious groups; groups based on racial, language, and ethnic identities; and business and professional associations on local, state, regional, and national levels. Many corporations have gay, lesbian, bisexual, and transgendered organizations within their companies and among their respective professions.

For some men, there can be an emerging sense of spiritual dissonance during this stage of development. Many gay men have explored relationships with God through organized religious structures. During this stage of development, they may begin to explore more openly their relationship with organized religious thought or practice. If they become aware of religion-based, gay-supportive groups, they may seek support through these groups. In later stages, spirituality may take on different forms.

As a man enters the gay community, he has much from which to choose. However, many of these communities reflect histories of fear, shame, discrimination, and oppression. If the individual has poor social skills, as is often the case, or low self-esteem or has a strong fear of exposure or fear of the unknown, he may find entry into the community more difficult. Often, the communities themselves are characterized by members who have the same concerns, issues, or characteristics. Additionally, if he is already a member of a marginalized community, he may choose an option other than assimilation into a gay community.

If he encounters members of the greater gay community who, themselves, are struggling with early stage concerns, he may have more difficulty. If he encounters men who are open and willing to invite his participation into the community, his chances of integrating into the community are greater.

At this stage of a man's development, it is important for him to find a community. However, for the gay community, it now becomes more important for the community at large to be more gay friendly. As communities enter a comparable stage of development, the community begins to acknowledge gay members. Members of the community may speak about the need for community support for diverse populations, including diversity based on sexual orientation. The fear that characterizes communities in earlier stages is lessened, although it often is still present. The denial about sexual orientation that was pervasive in previous developmental stages is not so pervasive here. Community members acknowledge that sexuality is about more than behavior, and the community begins to acknowledge the complexity of sexuality. In such emerging communities, there is an increased awareness of the effects of discrimination and oppression. The emerging gay man may or may not recognize the inclusiveness of some of these communities. However, as he becomes more involved in a gay culture, he will begin to be more aware of access to power and issues of social oppression.

At this point in his development, the emerging gay man begins to recognize that more of his support system is gay-identified. If this is a positive experience for him, he may move on to the next stage. If it is negative, he may experience greater difficulty.

Case Study: Chuck

Chuck is a 52-year-old White male who works as a dispatcher for a large trucking company. He was referred for counseling by his employer because he was beginning to miss work on a regular basis, and when he was at work, he appeared isolated and withdrawn.

In the initial session, Chuck admitted that he is an alcoholic in recovery and that he has remained sober by attending 12-step meetings and talking with his sponsor. He has not attended a meeting in "more than 3 months" and has not spoken to his sponsor in "more than a month." He believes that he is in danger of relapse.

Chuck grew up in Oklahoma and married at age 19. He married his high school sweetheart, and they had two children, a son, Tim, and a daughter, Carol, by the time Chuck was 22 years old. He reports that he and his exwife did not have much of a social life and that, during his wife's second pregnancy, he began having anonymous sexual encounters with other young men.

Chuck was trained as a long-distance trucker and began driving cross-country in his mid-20s. At this time, he began to increase his drinking and began having "regular" men in different cities along his trucking route. He became "serious" about one man who told Chuck that he was "in love with me." When Chuck attempted to break off the relationship, the man contacted Chuck's wife and employer. Through a series of "rough times," Chuck was divorced, lost his job, and was denied custody of his children.

When he was 30, Chuck moved to Dallas, got sporadic employment, and began drinking and "partying" heavily. By the time he was 32, he had become a regular in the Dallas bar scene. He proudly reports that "even when things were at their worst, I talked with my kids every week and never forgot their birthdays."

At age 33, Chuck met Tom, the manager of a trucking company, at a gay pride event in Dallas. They became lovers and moved in together. As their life developed together, they acknowledged that they "had drinking problems" and decided to "get sober together." They began attending 12-step meetings, and Chuck began working for Tom in his company. When he "got sober," Chuck was tested for HIV and discovered that he was HIV-positive. He became frightened, angry, and depressed. Tom was tested and was found to be HIV-negative. Chuck was suspicious of the local AIDS service organization but agreed to get help. He has had several bouts with pneumocystis pneumonia but is currently in good health and takes an "AIDS cocktail" several times a day.

While Chuck was "trying to get healthy," his son was beginning to get into trouble. Chuck's former wife called him when Tim was 14 years old and asked if he would take over parenting Tim. He agreed to do that, and Tim came to live with Chuck and Tom. For the next several years, Chuck and Tom raised Tim until he graduated from high school. Chuck reports that, though things were tough during these times, he was very happy, and life was going well. Chuck and Tom had, what Chuck calls, a "pretty good" relationship when they were raising Tim. There was some difficulty within the gay community until they found some other gay parents, and the school sometimes asked questions about their "family," which they chose to quietly avoid as best they could.

Chuck reports that "just when things were finally going smoothly," Tom came home and said that he had met a younger man and wanted to end his relationship with Chuck. Chuck was angry, hurt, and depressed when Tom left. They fought about possessions, and Chuck changed jobs, going to work for a competitor. Chuck was successful at using his "12-step family" to get through this time.

As a single man, Chuck has discovered that he "hates dating" and that he has become "invisible" in the gay community. His old friends are no longer around, and he is not interested in the bar scene. He tends to be attracted to men his own age, and they tend to be attracted to much younger men. He began "surfing the Web" to meet men and discovered that he was able to meet "cyber friends" online through local chat rooms. He had recently begun dating a man he met online and believed that things were "going o.k." and that there was some possibility for the relationship.

About 3 months ago, he discovered that the man was dating other men. Chuck ended the relationship and has been feeling lonely, depressed, and angry since the breakup. He believes that he could easily return to drinking to "numb the pain." He agreed to come for counseling when his boss explained that he was in danger of losing his job and when his sponsor called him and told him that he had better do something soon.

Discussion

Chuck is facing a number of issues. As a man in his 50s, he has become "invisible" in a youth-oriented gay community. His strengths are that he has a supportive 12-step family and he lives in a city that has many resources for gay men. Chuck has a relationship with his son and, apparently, with his boss and sponsor. Chuck is not likely to become voluntarily involved in insight-oriented psychotherapy, but he is likely to respond to action-oriented, practical interventions. He has some contact with the gay community and can begin to make use of that social community.

He describes himself as "interested in" church activities and is "willing to check out" some of the other non-bar-related social resources. He is also willing to do some volunteer work at the gay/lesbian/bisexual/transgendered community center. He is currently asymptomatic in terms of his HIV status. He manages his health through a medical regime, diet and nutrition, and "almost compulsive" working out. Although he has participated in "some HIV support groups," he reports that "they're too depressing and 12-step groups are more helpful."

Chuck is willing to explore other kinds of community involvement. He reports that he "doesn't care who knows I'm gay." Though he is more private about his HIV status, he reports that he is "no activist" and "doesn't expect anyone else to help me work out my problems." He laughs and reports, "That's probably the addict in me." He is willing to explore ways to get support from the gay 12-step community.

If Chuck was in a community with fewer resources, he acknowledges that he could find 12-step meetings online, but those would not be as helpful and he could "get in trouble online." He also acknowledges that he can get support from the gay Christian community in Dallas and that such support would be difficult to get "back in Oklahoma." He reports that he "would never go back" to a community where he would need to hide his sexual orientation, "even though it is nobody else's business."

Stage 4: Identity Acceptance

According to Cass (1979), Identity Acceptance occurs when the person accepts, rather than tolerates, a homosexual self-image and there is increasing contact with a gay culture. The individual now has a positive identification with other gay people, and his worldview may very much be formed by the views of those around him. If they compartmentalize their sexual orientation, he may choose to do so as well. To reduce stress, he has less and less contact with a more overtly homophobic world, choosing to spend more of his time and energy with newly found gay friends. He does not escape the effects of homophobia, but homophobia takes different forms. He may be selective about sharing his life with nongay associates and seeks to control personal information as much as possible. In many ways, his life is about fitting in and not making waves.

If his new associates are celebratory about their gay identities, he may easily accept that perception. Doing so may move him further from society at large but bring him closer to aspects of gay society. He begins to experience homophobic attitudes, his own and those of others, as offensive. He may continue in his own personal growth and become angrier at the inequities of society. If he is a man from other marginalized groups, he may already be in touch with this anger about inequity and may have some cultural norms for addressing his anger. For men from other marginalized groups, there is the multiple task of integrating different identities. For some, such integration becomes easier, depending on their development. For others, this multiple integration is considerably more stressful. With the increase in anger at injustice, the individual man may move to the next stage of development.

Some communities at large are emerging into an acceptance stage. Community leaders and others may see that there are members of the community who make significant contributions and that these members are gay. They may be willing to discuss issues of sexuality, ways to integrate gay members into the community, and ways to address discrimination based on sexual orientation. Community members are cognizant of their own homophobia and are willing to explore its effects. Attempts may be made, and, at times, may succeed, to have antidiscrimination measures passed and enforced. In such communities, there may be ordinances that prohibit discrimination in housing, employment, and other arenas. Although there may be "official" changes in policy, there may still be incidences of individual discrimination. These communities may, at times, be more inclusive in language and practice than the greater communities of which they are a part. Such communities may also explore how other forms of discrimination and oppression exist and are manifested in their culture. Although there may continue to be some misunderstanding about the nature of sexuality and sexual orientation, the community feels safe enough to explore issues and develop problem-solving strategies.

Case Study: Ben

Ben is a 50-year-old professional consultant who has lived in New York City for the past 20 years. Ben is Chinese American and has been closely connected to his family all of his life. His family has lived in California and Washington for most of Ben's adult life.

Since acknowledging his homosexuality as a young man, Ben has lived in large metropolitan areas that are far from his family. As a result, he has never discussed his homosexuality with his family. Ben has had a "boyfriend" for over 15 years. They do not live together and are not monogamous in their relationship. They do, however, describe their relationship as "primary" and report that they truly love each other. Ben's boyfriend is 20 years older than he is.

Ben has been active in the gay community in Chelsea, a New York City neighborhood. He has been involved in the gay/lesbian/bisexual/transgendered community center, having served on its board and on multiple committees. He is on the board of an AIDS service organization and is active in the gay/lesbian/bisexual/transgendered organization in his company. He is also active in Asians and Friends, an organization for Asian gay men and the men attracted to them.

Ben has entered counseling because he is experiencing dissonance in his life related to keeping secrets from his family. He reports feeling isolated and alienated. He reports that there is little tolerance for homosexuality in his family and in the Chinese American community in which he grew up. Although he has friends in the gay community at large, he reports that others do not fully understand the experiences of Asian gay men. He is angry about the racism in the gay community and about the homophobia in the Chinese community. He has considered moving to San Francisco, where, he believes, there is a more supportive, openly gay community. To do so would mean ending his long-term relationship with John, an Irish American, and leaving a career that is rewarding and nurturing for him. Additionally, he would be living in a city where he has siblings. Such a move would mean coming out to family members, and he believes that he is not ready to disclose his sexual orientation to his family at this time.

Ben initially sought counseling for depression through the company employee assistance program. He reported feeling frustrated and misunderstood and requested that he be referred to a gay-identified counselor who saw clients individually and in a group setting. Ben is currently in a counseling group with seven other men from diverse backgrounds. They are able to discuss concerns about marginalization, cultural expectations, and problem solving. The group focuses on coming to a greater understanding of the diversity of life experiences and worldviews. As a result of his participation in the group, Ben reports that his communication with his boyfriend, John, is improving. They are beginning to discuss the option of living together and the implications for their sexual lives if they make that move. He has spoken with his older sister about his relationship with John, only to find out that the family has known of the relationship for most of the time the men have been together. They have laughed about Ben's homophobia and have become closer as a result. They are discussing ways that Ben can share the information with other family members.

Ben has agreed to be a participant in an open discussion of racism at the gay/lesbian/bisexual/transgendered community center and is exploring ways to mentor young, gay Chinese American men through the community center. He acknowledges that his counseling group is a significant support for him and that he needs to find other sources of support within the community. Although he does not see himself "becoming an activist," he does acknowledge the need to channel his anger about homophobia and racism into avenues that can bring about some change.

Discussion

In this case, Ben has begun exploring his gay identity in the gay community. He works in a gay-supportive, primarily heterosexual world and is exploring ways to bridge the gap between several identities. As a professional man, he has a commitment to a career. As a Chinese American man, he has been integrating his identity in a Euro-centered, English-speaking world. As a gay-identified man, he is working to integrate his ethnic identity with his sexual identity. He is acutely aware of the racism in the gay community and, with support, sees that he has the skills to address some of the issues. He is less certain about his ability to address the homophobia in the Chinese American community. With the assistance of the group, he shared some of his life with his sister and discovered that his homophobia was at play in relationships within his family.

Ben is experiencing some of the anger encountered when individuals and groups are the target of oppression and discrimination. He has begun looking to the gay community for support and understanding. He voiced his lack of support with his initial counselor and was referred to a gay-identified counselor. At this point in his development, it may be critically important to work with a gay-identified professional. Whereas this may not be an issue in earlier stages of development, it is important at this stage.

Ben is exploring some of his racial/cultural identity. He is confronting some of the issues of Chinese American gay men. As he uses the group to clarify some of the issues, he is making a commitment to use his skills as a more mature man to mentor younger Chinese American men within the gay community. He is also addressing the issues of racism by participating in the panel at the cultural center.

Ben is addressing issues of growing older in the gay community. He has a vigorous workout program and brings up issues in his counseling group. He is also renegotiating his relationship with John. Issues of maintaining a primary relationship are discussed in the group, and Ben is looking at different ways of participating in his primary relationship.

As a result of his work in the group, Ben is continuing to take actions that are consistent with his sense of who he is and who he is becoming. He lives in a community that is large enough and sophisticated enough to provide support for his exploration. He acknowledges that he would have more difficulty finding support in a less cosmopolitan community.

Stage 5: Identity Pride

The next stage, Identity Pride, occurs when accepting the philosophy of full legitimatization, the person becomes immersed in the gay subculture and has less and less to do with heterosexual others. The individual now divides his world into those who are gay and those who are not. As he becomes more identified with the gay community, he feels greater pride in its accomplishments. In his daily living, he may still encounter the heterosexual world and homophobic responses, and these encounters can produce feelings of frustration and alienation. The combination of pride and anger may energize the individual, and with encouragement from peers, he may become an activist, speaking out to address issues of inequity in a public forum.

If the emerging man chooses to confront the heterosexual establishment, he moves more and more into public view and abandons attempts to conceal his sexual orientation. As a result, he continues his coming-out process. If he encounters resistance from heterosexual colleagues, he is confirmed in his beliefs in a "we/they" framework. When his colleagues are supportive of his emerging self, he may be encouraged to move to the final stage of development.

Some communities at large are also moving into a comparable stage of development. In such communities, sexual identity is supported and celebrated. Community leaders and supporters work for equity in all arenas of social development. There is a growing awareness of sexual and spiritual issues and a greater acceptance of diverse sexual and spiritual worldviews. When communities are in this stage of development, they may become increasingly aware of many different forms of discrimination and oppression and are increasingly aware of how they perpetuate such discrimination and oppression, thereby taking on the willingness to look within and create change in their own systems. In many gay-identified communities, discrimination based on age, physical attractiveness, race, sex, gender, ethnicity, language, and other criteria exists. In this stage of development, communities are willing to explore how this discrimination and oppression inhibit the growth of all individuals and of the community at large. The anger about all forms of discrimination becomes increasingly evident, and individuals and community leaders become increasingly socially active. At times, the dissonance in such communities is palpable as the communities struggle to develop coalition-building and collaboration skills.

Case Study: Javier

Javier is a 38-year-old Mexican American male graduate student who was referred for counseling after having been arrested for his participation in a demonstration after a friend had been assaulted and beaten outside of a gay bar. Javier is active in his gay/lesbian/bisexual/transgendered community center and was instrumental in organizing a meeting with the local police department after an investigation of how the police department handled this "hate crime" was resolved in a manner that was not satisfactory to leaders of the gay/lesbian/bisexual/transgendered community.

Javier acknowledges that he is very angry about the way that gays in his community are treated. He believes that the problem was not resolved satisfactorily because the man assaulted was not only gay but also Mexican American.

Javier reports that his anger may be disproportionate to the specific incident, but he acknowledges that he carries with him a growing, chronic anger at the injustices experienced by the Mexican American community in his city. Additionally, he is angry about the homophobia he experiences as a gay man in the Mexican American community and in the larger society.

He reports that he has been "openly gay" since he was in high school and that he had his first sexual experiences with his college roommate during his freshman year at the university. He reports that he has had several relationships, none lasting more than 2 years. He believes that he will eventually be involved in a monogamous relationship and that "when I am ready Mr. Right will come into my life."

He reports that when he "came out" to his family in high school at age 17, his mother said that she had always known that he was gay, and his father "said nothing." He has since spoken openly with his father about his attraction to men, and though his father "doesn't understand," he is supportive and proud of Javier, and they have a closer relationship now than they have ever had. He believes that this is the case because he has always been respectful of his father and that is what is most important. He has a less open relationship with his brothers, whom he describes as "being caught up in being 'macho'."

Javier does not believe that his counseling needs to focus on issues of sexual identity but rather on his anger and the injustice experienced by gay and Mexican American men. What he would like most from his counseling sessions is assistance and direction from the counselor as he develops the skills to creatively use his anger to address issues of social justice.

Discussion

In this case, Javier has identified the need to address his anger in a productive manner and to find ways to direct his experiences of injustice in a way that can bring about a change in his community. He can clearly see the injustice and understands that his anger about discrimination and oppression is appropriate. He does not like the way he expresses his anger, nor does he like the consequences of his behavior. At no time does he not accept responsibility for his anger. He does believe that the way he expresses his anger does not serve him or his community well.

He is in a position as a graduate student to have an impact on his community and to use resources to bring about greater awareness of oppression. Additionally, he can work with other activists in his community to build coalitions to address issues of injustice.

Javier's family is supportive of him, and as he describes the dynamics, if he is respectful and engaged in the family, they will continue to be supportive. He is the first family member to go to school beyond high school, and the family is proud of his accomplishments. He reports that he learned much of his commitment to social action from his father, who has been an activist for Mexican American migrant workers, and from his mother, who has been a union organizer.

The counselor in this case can support Javier in channeling his anger in ways that are life-enhancing for him and the community in which he lives. The counselor can help Javier to develop decision-making, problem-solving, and coalition-building skills. It is important, at this stage of Javier's development, to have a counselor who is familiar with the pride stage of development and aware of and sensitive to issues of discrimination within the community in which Javier lives. It is also helpful for the counselor to be familiar with social justice groups in the community with which Javier can be connected.

Stage 6: Identity Synthesis

A final stage, Identity Synthesis, occurs when a person develops awareness that the "them and us" philosophy, in which all heterosexuals are viewed negatively and all homosexuals positively, no longer holds true. The emerging man recognizes and accepts that there are non-gay people who can be active allies, who will support his developing gay identity, and who will work collaboratively to address issues of discrimination and oppression based on sexual orientation. The anger that the individual has experienced in previous stages does not cease to exist, but the intensity decreases, and the anger may be used to enhance his developing sense of self rather than inhibit it. Heterosexuals are not viewed in as hostile a manner, and he becomes increasingly aware of coalition-building and ally relationships with people in the community at large. As a result, he begins to regain trust in selected segments of the community at large, and it is no longer necessary to see the world from an "us/them" framework. With the decrease in the need to dichotomize, the emerging man can now integrate his sexual identity with all other aspects of himself.

With the emergence of Identity Synthesis, spirituality can become an ever-increasing aspect of the man's life. He may continue to seek spiritual integration and sees his sexual self as deeply woven together with his spiritual self. He may work to integrate a spiritual tradition that reflects his earlier religious upbringing, or he may seek out alternative spiritual modalities. Whatever the case, he continues to see the integration of spirituality and sexuality as essential in his life.

In communities that are moving into the synthesis stage, community members and leaders are aware of the sexual diversity within the community and are willing to openly discuss such diversity. The fear of differences is less pronounced, and different sexual identities are not seen as a danger to the community. When discrimination based on sexual orientation exists, it can be brought to the table for discussion and resolved. Such communities may advocate for community initiatives to acknowledge, legalize, celebrate, and support gay relationships and individual rights. In such communities, discrimination based on sexual orientation is not tolerated. At times, the community experiences the stress and dissonance of working through diverse issues. However, the community is not afraid to take on such issues because there is a respect for diversity, even when there may not be the understanding of all dynamics and the identified skills for resolving conflict. Other forms of discrimination and oppression may also exist within the community, and when recognized, such discrimination and oppression are openly brought to the table and resolved. Members of the community feel safe enough to address the issues and comfortable enough to celebrate the diversity. The need for all members of the community to share the same worldview is not present, and community members and leaders invite strength through diversity. There is an underlying sense of spiritual, social, emotional, and psychological harmony and safety that is characteristic of the community and its members.

Case Study: Patrick

Patrick is a 45-year-old Irish American man who grew up in a traditional Roman Catholic family. He graduated from Catholic schools and a Jesuit university. While in college, he met a Catholic priest, Sean, and they became lovers. Eventually, Sean left the priesthood, and they remained partners for 15 years. During that time, Patrick was actively involved in Dignity, an organization for gay Catholics.

Patrick and Sean separated after 15 years when Sean's alcoholism became serious and Patrick was no longer willing to support Sean's alcohol use and the resulting dissonance in their relationship. After the separation, Patrick moved to San Francisco and became actively involved in the gay community in the city.

For a while, Patrick became involved in the "party scene," taking designer drugs and exploring many forms of sexuality. During this time, many of his friends and acquaintances were diagnosed with HIV and died from HIV-related illnesses. Patrick reports that "it is a miracle that I have not sero-converted." In fear, Patrick decided not to have any sexual contact and remained celibate for 3 years.

Patrick has a wide circle of friends, professionally and personally. He is not currently in a long-term relationship and reports that he believes that a relationship will happen when he is ready for it to happen.

Patrick has entered counseling because he is feeling the "loss of a spiritual life." He no longer feels connected to Roman Catholicism and has attended services at other Christian denominations, reporting that he feels "disconnected" in these services. He reports that the churches "accept my homosexuality, but they don't really seem to understand it." He reports that he seeks balance in his life and that he works out physically, eats a healthy diet, enjoys physical activities, has a well-rounded circle of friends, is involved in the community, regularly attends cultural events, likes his job, and sees opportunities for career advancement.

After several individual counseling sessions, Patrick was referred to a group for gay men. The men in the group meet weekly to discuss issues related to gay spirituality. They frequently read excerpts from such books as *Coming Out Spiritually: The Next Step* (de la Huerta, 1999) and *Gay Soul: Finding the Heart of Gay Spirit and Nature* (Thompson, 1990). Several of the men have attended retreats sponsored by Spirit Journeys (www.spiritjourneys@worldnet.att.net), and the group facilitator has been trained in Jungian psychology. All of the men in the group are interested in exploring the spiritual dynamics related to sexual orientation, and they come from diverse backgrounds racially, ethnically, and spiritually. Patrick seems to have found an arena for his exploration. Along with the group, Patrick marched in the gay pride parade and is working with his peers to develop a series of retreats for younger gay men who have been diagnosed HIV-positive.

Discussion

In this case, Patrick has moved into the gay community and into the community at large. As a younger man, he was involved in a religious tradition that was important to him. In his relationship with Sean, Patrick was able to continue his religious/spiritual exploration. When the relationship ended, Patrick was able to move on in many aspects of his life. He acknowledges that his spiritual growth "got lost" as he attended to other aspects of his life. He further acknowledges that he was not able to find a spiritual connection but continued to explore. As a result of his involvement with the counseling group, Patrick connected with other men from a variety of spiritual traditions. He became involved in a variety of experiences and has decided to share his experiences with others as part of his spiritual growth. He is also living in a community that supports, encourages, and celebrates the kind of growth that Patrick seeks.

Conclusion

In counseling gay men, the counselor must be prepared to meet the man where he is in his own development. This means that the counselor must be aware of the individual's personal growth, his connection to his family, and the family's approach to sexual identity development. Often, family-of-origin dynamics have a strong influence on the developing gay man's sense of who he is and who he wishes to become. Additionally, it is important to have a working understanding of the culture within which the emerging man lives. At times, his culture will be supportive of his emerging self. More often, cultural dynamics may impede development.

If the counselor is to be most helpful to the emerging gay man, the counselor must be familiar with community resources. As the client evolves, he will need increased involvement in the gay community. For many emerging gay men, the only community with which they are familiar is the "bar community." In contemporary American society, many other options exist. The counselor must know his or her community and must be able to provide appropriate referrals for the emerging gay man. In some communities, this means that counselors may be on community boards, be active in providing services to many different community members, run for elected office in order to encourage legislative change, or serve in other capacities in their communities.

Often, the emerging gay man may need allies as he confronts community discrimination. Counselors may need to be prepared to become involved in "fighting oppression" workshops or other activities that help to bring about social change. As Appleby (2001) identified, counselors must be prepared to address the concerns of the emerging gay man in his emerging community on the historical, environmental–structural, cultural, familial, and individual levels. For many counselors, this becomes an opportunity for personal growth and development.

References

Appleby, G. (Ed.). (2001). *Working class gay and bisexual men*. New York: Harrington Park Press.

Beam, J. (Ed.). (1986). *In the life: A Black gay anthology*. Boston: Alyson.

Boykin, K. (1996). *One more river to cross: Black and gay in America*. New York: Anchor Books.

Browning, F. (1994). *The culture of desire: Paradox and perversity in gay lives today*. New York: Vintage Books.

Browning, F. (1998). *A queer geography: Journeys toward a sexual self*. New York: Noonday Press.

Cass, V. C. (1979). Homosexual identity formation: A theoretical model. *Journal of Homosexuality, 4,* 219–234.

Center for Substance Abuse Treatment. (2001). *A provider's introduction to substance abuse treatment for lesbian, gay, bisexual, and transgender individuals*. Rockville, MD: U.S. Department of Health and Human Services, Substance Abuse and Mental Health Services Administration.

Chaney, M. P., & Dew, B. J. (2003). Online experiences of sexually compulsive men who have sex with men. *Sexual Addiction and Compulsivity, 10,* 259–274.

Chung, Y. B., & Szymanski, D. M. (2000, August). *Multiple identities of Asian American gay men: A qualitative study*. Paper presented at the 108th Annual Convention of the American Psychological Association, Washington, DC.

Chung, Y. B., & Szymanski, D. (2001). *Ethnic and sexual identity attitudes in Asian American gay men*. Unpublished manuscript.

Coleman, E. (1982). Developmental stages of the coming out process. *Journal of Homosexuality, 7*(2–3), 31–43.

de la Huerta, C. (1999). *Coming out spiritually: The next step*. New York: Tarcher/Putnam.

Dew, B. J., & Chaney, M. P. (2004). Sexual addiction and the Internet: Implications for gay men. *Journal of Addictions & Offender Counseling, 24,* 101–114.

Fortunato, J. (1982). *Embracing the exile: Healing journeys of gay Christians*. San Francisco: Harper & Row.

Fortunato, J. (1987). *AIDS: The spiritual dilemma*. San Francisco: Harper & Row.

Gooch, B. (1999). *Finding the boyfriend within: A practical guide for tapping into your own source of love, happiness, and respect*. New York: Simon & Schuster.

Harris, D. (1997). *The rise and fall of gay culture*. New York: Hyperion.

Hemphill, E., & Beam, J. (1991). *Brother to brother: New writings by Black gay men*. Boston: Alyson.

hooks, b. (2001). *Salvation: Black people and love*. New York: Morrow.

Isay, R. (1989). *Being homosexual: Gay men and their development*. New York: Farrar, Straus, Giroux.

Isay, R. (1996). *Becoming gay: The journey to self-acceptance*. New York: Holt.

Jackson, G. (1991). *Patterns of male intimacy: Book 1. The secret lore of gardening*. Toronto, Ontario, Canada: Inner City Books.

Jackson, G. (1993). *Patterns of male intimacy: Book 2. The living room mysteries*. Toronto, Ontario, Canada: Inner City Books.

Johnson, T. (2000). *Gay spirituality: The role of gay identity in the transformation of human consciousness*. Los Angeles: Alyson Books.

King, J. L. (2004). *On the down low: A journey into the lives of "straight" Black men who sleep with men*. New York: Broadway Books.

Kominars, S., & Kominars, K. (1996). *Accepting ourselves and others: A journey into recovery from addiction and compulsive behaviors for gays, lesbians, and bisexuals*. Center City, MN: Hazelden.

Kooden, H., & Flowers, C. (2000). *Golden men: The power of gay midlife.* New York: Avon Books.

Kus, R. (1990). *Keys to caring: Assisting your gay and lesbian clients.* Boston: Alyson.

Longres, J. (Ed.). (1996). *Men of color: A context for service to homosexually active men.* New York: Harrington Park Press.

Lowenthal, M. (Ed.). (1997). *Gay men at the millennium: Sex, spirit, community.* New York: Tarcher/Putnam.

Nelson, E. (Ed.). (1993). *Critical essays: Gay and lesbian writers of color.* New York: Harrington Park Press.

Remafedi, G. (Ed.). (1994). *Death by denial: Studies of suicide in gay and lesbian teenagers.* Boston: Alyson.

Ritter, K. Y., & Terndrup, A. I. (2002). *Handbook of affirmative psychotherapy with lesbians and gay men.* New York: Guilford Press.

Roscoe, W. (Ed.). (1988). *Living the spirit: A gay American Indian anthology.* New York: St. Martin's Press.

Roscoe, W. (1995). *Queer spirits: A gay men's myth book.* Boston: Beacon Press.

Roscoe, W. (1998). *Changing ones: Third and fourth genders in Native North America.* New York: St. Martin's Press.

Sears, J. (Ed.). (1994). *Bound by diversity: Unity emerges from a chorus of voices. Contributions by members of the lesbian, gay, bisexual, and transgender communities.* Columbia, SC: Sebastian Press.

Siegel, S., & Lowe, E. (1994). *Uncharted lives: Understanding the life passages of gay men.* New York: Dutton.

Signoreli, M. (1997). *Life outside: The Signoreli report on gay men: Sex, drugs, muscles, and the passages of life.* New York: HarperCollins.

Smith, M. (Ed.). (1983). *Black men/White men.* San Francisco: Gay Sunshine Press.

Stowe, J. (1999). *Gay spirit warrior: An empowerment workbook for men who love men.* Tallahassee, FL: Findhorn Press.

Thompson, M. (Ed.). (1987). *Gay spirit: Myth and meaning.* New York: St. Martin's Press.

Thompson, M. (Ed.). (1990). *Gay soul: Finding the heart of gay spirit and nature.* San Francisco: HarperCollins.

Thompson, M. (1997). *Gay body: A journey through shadow to self.* New York: St. Martin's Press.

Tobias, A. (1998). *The best little boy in the world grows up.* New York: Ballentine.

Troiden, R. R. (1979). Becoming homosexual: A model for gay identity acquisition. *Psychiatry, 42,* 362–373.

Troiden, R. R. (1989). The formation of homosexual identities. *Journal of Homosexuality, 17*(1–2), 43–73.

Williams, W. (1986). *The spirit and the flesh: Sexual diversity in American Indian culture.* Boston: Beacon Press.

Wright, E. M., Sholton, C., Browning, M., Orduna, J. M. G., Martinez, V., & Wong, F. Y. (2001). *Cultural issues in working with lesbian, gay, bisexual, and transgender individuals: A provider's introduction to substance abuse treatment for lesbian, gay, bisexual, and transgender individuals.* Rockville, MD: U.S. Department of Health and Human Services, Substance Abuse and Mental Health Services Administration.

Chapter

Counseling Lesbian Clients

Colleen R. Logan

Well, that was an interesting session to say the least, Beatrice mused to herself. And I thought I'd encountered everything over the last few years in my private practice. This case really has me stumped. An attractive, feminine, 38-year-old woman who after 8 years of marriage has decided she's a lesbian. It seems unbelievable to me. I mean, she doesn't even look like a lesbian, let alone act like one. How could she all of a sudden decide she's a lesbian? She just must be unhappy in her marriage. Surely, she doesn't hate men. Anyway, how does she know she's a lesbian if she's never even kissed a woman? Maybe I can convince her that she's just going through a phase. Oh boy, I sure have more questions than I do answers. I wish I'd learned about this in graduate school, but homosexuality was barely even mentioned in my classes. Maybe I'll call my colleague Jennifer. I think she's a lesbian. Maybe she'll know how to approach this client.

Unfortunately, even in the age of political correctness and an overall greater awareness of the issues facing gay and lesbian clients, Beatrice's experience is not an isolated one. The mere mention of the word *lesbian* still elicits strong reactions ranging from disgust, to tawdry titillation and voyeuristic excitement, to complete dismissal of the existence or validity of the concept. And, needless to say, mental health professionals are not immune. In a recent review of the literature, Barrett and McWhirter (2002) reported that sexual minority clients continue to experience significant barriers to affirmative and effective therapy in spite of the fact that it has been more than 30 years since the American Psychiatric Association removed homosexuality from the *Diagnostic and Statistical Manual of Mental Disorders* in 1973. Numerous studies indicate that gay and lesbian clients frequently encounter bias, stereotyping, disapproval, stigmatization, and even complete ignorance about the challenges they face on a daily basis (Fassinger, 1991; Garnets, Hancock, Cochran, Goodchilds, & Peplau, 1991). What is even more frightening about these data is that sexual minority clients seek counseling at a rate 2 to 4 times higher than their heterosexual counterparts (Elliott, 1993). So, how can counselors overcome prejudice, ignorance, and bias and provide affirmative therapy to their lesbian clients?

The purpose of this chapter is to provide mental health professionals with a better understanding of the myriad issues associated with providing effective and affirmative therapy to lesbian clients. Interwoven throughout the chapter are case examples that are derived from numerous years of clinical work. The cases are not based on any one lesbian client but rather a composite of the many lesbian clients I have been honored to work with over the years. Both the information and the case examples are intended to provide counseling professionals with greater insight about and appreciation of the experiences of lesbian individuals and their significant others.

The bottom line is that the visceral discomfort that many people feel when they hear the word *lesbian* stems from the overwhelming effects of societal homoprejudice (Logan, 1996). All of us, including counselors, are taught from an early age that lesbians are immoral and disgusting and an abomination, completely inferior to "normal" heterosexual people. To overcome this onslaught of negativity and prejudice requires constant self-monitoring and analysis along with a steadfast commitment to refute the constant barrage of cultural stereotypes and negativity toward lesbians. This enormous task is particularly critical for mental health practitioners because they are likely to encounter lesbians who are seeking not only effective counseling services but also practitioners who are affirming and accepting of a nonheterosexual identity and relationship. To begin the process of understanding this often maligned and often ignored population, it is important to define the term *lesbian* and what constitutes a lesbian identity.

What Is a Lesbian?

Who are lesbians? What images come to mind when you hear the word *lesbian* or picture yourself in a counseling relationship with a lesbian? Cultural lore and stereotypical notions depict lesbians as anything from mysterious witches, to emasculating bullies or male wannabes, to dykes on bikes and ultrafeminine lesbian chic. Truth be known, all of these images fit to some degree, and yet lesbians represent so much more. Lesbians are chefs, business executives, professors, separatists, earth mothers, plumbers, women of color, old, young, and disabled. Lesbians play sports, wear makeup and skirts, have long hair and short hair, cut the lawn, and lead Fortune 500 companies. They typically aren't men haters and didn't become lesbians overnight because they couldn't get a man. As a couple, one doesn't necessarily "play" the husband to the other's role as the "wife," and they don't all secretly aspire to be men. In fact, the stereotypical notions of masculinity and femininity in the lesbian community, sometimes referred to as "butch" and "femme" respectively, primarily reflect lesbian choices to expand restrictive gender boundaries as opposed to assigned roles in a relationship.

For the purposes of this chapter, a lesbian is defined as a woman who self-identifies as a lesbian and is sexually, emotionally, and spiritually attracted to other women.

Use of Language

The challenges and choices associated with how to label oneself can vary among lesbians. This decision is often a product of how comfortable she is with her sexual orientation as well as other factors such as age, cultural background, geographical location, and so forth. Some women really don't like the "L" word and prefer to call themselves "queer" or "dyke." Some women may refuse to adopt any type of label because doing so would be seen as a form of submission to male-dominated societal norms (Clunis & Green, 2000). Older women may prefer to identify as "gay" or use code words such as "this is my friend or roommate." Younger women are typically more comfortable with the term *lesbian* or even terms such as *queer* or *dyke* (Clunis & Green, 2000). In contrast, women of color who are juggling multiple minority memberships may steer away from any type of self-identification as a lesbian because one more minority moniker may feel like too much to overcome.

For example, Mary, who is still in the early stages of coming to terms with her lesbian identity, refers to herself as a gay woman. For Mary, the "L" word or lesbian feels too dramatic. She's not ready to make such a strong self-statement; all she knows is that she loves Jane. Her partner, Jane, who's known she was a lesbian since she was 8 years old, is much more comfortable with her identity and energetically refers to herself as a "big ol' dyke."

Given the varying ways lesbians self-identify or don't self-identify, it is absolutely essential that counselors actively listen to their clients and avoid prematurely or carelessly imposing labels on their female clients. Be prepared to educate yourself as well as your clients about the different terms of identification and encourage your client to label herself in a way that is comfortable yet congruent with her sexual orientation. Listen carefully to how the client self-identifies and affirm her own experience, encouraging the evolution of her own unique story and coming-out process.

Lesbian Identity Development

Separating lesbian identity development from gay male development is a relatively new concept because lesbians have been typically subsumed under the general category of gays and not seen as a unique entity. Existing identity development models have been criticized for being stage sequential and linear in progression and based primarily on the retrospective accounts of White middle-age males, failing to recognize the more fluid and relationship-oriented aspects of lesbian identity development. According to McCarn and Fassinger (1996), these models also fail to recognize the effects of multiple minority statuses and multiple oppressive environments. In response, the authors proposed a dual lesbian identity developmental model that on the one hand tracks individual or personal identity development and on the other hand tracks relationship identity development or how one relates to the lesbian community. For example, a lesbian couple may live in a rural environment and have little or no contact with the lesbian community yet still feel positive and healthy as lesbians. Alternatively, a woman may have a strong affiliation with the women's community, be aware and accepting of lesbians, and yet remain uncomfortable with her emerging erotic feelings toward another woman.

This model is useful for mental health practitioners as they help facilitate the coming-out process of lesbian women. Clearly, lesbians can simultaneously be in different phases of the identity development process, making the coming-out process that much more difficult and stressful.

For example, Jenny described her recent discovery of her lesbian identity as an epiphany. Since divorcing her husband 5 years ago, she had become involved in the women's movement and had even encountered a number of lesbian women, but it had never crossed her mind that she was a lesbian. One day, she began to realize that she was having strong feelings for a female coworker. This had never happened to her before, and she found herself in turmoil. She immediately sought therapy because she thought she was going "crazy—turning into a bitter man-hater." Her therapist felt very comfortable supporting Jenny as she struggled to come to terms with her feelings. She didn't push Jenny to label her feelings as lesbian; instead, she provided a safe and supportive environment where Jenny could talk about her feelings and sort them out at her own pace.

Ann and Rachel are experiencing a different struggle. Rachel has self-identified as a lesbian for as long as she can remember. Ann, in contrast, has only recently come out to herself and a few trusted others. Rachel is angry with Ann because she won't come out to her parents. Holidays are spent apart, and Ann commonly refers to Rachel as her roommate. Clearly, they are at very different stages of the development process. Rachel may need to be more patient with Ann's reluctance to come out to her parents and recognize the steps she has already taken toward coming out. Ann may need to do some individual work around being a lesbian and process the internalized guilt and shame related to not meeting her family's expectations of heterosexuality. Together, they may need to devise alternative ways to celebrate the holidays alone together until Ann feels more comfortable bringing Rachel home and establishing their status as a couple.

Cultural Differences and the Coming-Out Process

Lesbian women of color are uniquely challenged by the tasks of managing multiple oppressions or "triple jeopardy," the combined effects of racism, sexism, and homoprejudice (Greene, 1994). As an effective and sensitive counselor, it is important to apply the templates of culture and ethnicity when working with lesbian clients. Be willing to explore the ethnic and cultural backgrounds of your lesbian clients, taking into account the importance of procreation; the nature and impact of traditional gender-role stereotypes; the importance of family and community; the nature, degree, and intensity of religious values; and, of course, the beliefs and attitudes toward women who have relationships with other women (Greene, 1997). At the same time, it is important to avoid generalizations and remember that there is great diversity within groups from different cultures and races.

The coming-out process may take a different turn for lesbians dealing with triple minority status. For example, it is very common for lesbians of color to struggle with and resist the idea of coming out to their families and cultural community. Many feel a strong sense of safety in the cultural group and live in fear of being labeled a lesbian and perhaps losing such an important source of identity and emotional support (Smith, 1997)—a sense of identity that has heretofore served them so well in the face of discrimination and prejudice from the White dominant culture. In fact, some lesbian clients of color may choose to remain closeted rather than risk further disenfranchisement and prejudice.

For example, Diane, an African American woman, has self-identified as a lesbian since she was 13 years old. Growing up, she was a star athlete; therefore, her tomboy behavior and lack of interest in boys were overlooked. As soon as possible, she moved away from her hometown so that she could have relationships with women without risking complete rejection from her family. She would bring her partner home for the holidays but never questioned her family's insistence on referring to her girlfriend as a "friend." At work, she keeps her personal life to herself. As a female and as an ethnic minority, she knows what it's like to face discrimination on a daily basis, and she's not about to add her lesbian identity as yet another reason that she might not be promoted or treated with respect. Counselors need to understand and affirm clients who feel caught between the need to maintain a strong cultural identity and a lesbian identity. It is important to recognize that this struggle is not necessarily indicative of a thwarted developmental process or a denial of one's lesbianism. In this case, pushing Diane to come out to family and friends may do more harm than good to her and the therapeutic relationship. What's more important, perhaps, in this case is an understanding of Diane's own personal sense of self-esteem and self-worth as a lesbian rather than her level of "outness."

Tragically, however, many women of color who do risk coming out are faced with discrimination from within the gay and lesbian community. They, in turn, feel marginalized by both communities, never truly part of any group, alone and isolated. Accordingly, counselors who are sensitive to this issue will validate their feelings and refer clients to various support groups specifically designed for lesbian groups of color, many of which are available in larger communities and through the Internet.

Lesbian Relationships

As stated earlier, lesbians are different from their gay male counterparts in that they are more likely to come out as a lesbian in the context of a relationship; therefore, it is highly likely that counselors either will work with lesbian clients struggling with sexual identity issues who are in a relationship or perhaps will even have the opportunity to work with the couple itself. The old joke about lesbians bringing a U-Haul on the second date actually rings true more often than not. This intense meshing together can often invoke what is fondly referred to within the lesbian community as "Dyke-U-Drama," a term that describes the emotionally intense, roller coaster, high-drama coupling and uncoupling of lesbian women. Many women find themselves intensely involved with another woman or living with a partner before they have had the chance to come to terms with the myriad issues associated with coming out to self and others. Often this abrupt coupling can wreak havoc on a relationship, whereas the opposite is also true in that issues related to creating a relationship can thwart and stifle individual growth. This tendency to become involved quickly has both positive and negative ramifications. Counselors who are sensitive to this tendency of lesbians to quickly couple will encourage clients to move slowly and date rather than immediately settle down in a committed relationship. This may literally mean teaching lesbian clients how to date. For example, have clients list characteristics of potential partners, have them role-play asking a woman out on a date, and encourage them to talk to other lesbians who are in long-term relationships in order to discover the joys and challenges associated with settling down with a partner. On a positive note, coupling quickly can help emerging lesbians have positive experiences with same-sex relationships and therefore provide a new and positive context that actively contradicts societal taboos and stereotypes. In fact, positive and meaningful same-sex relationships may actually contribute significantly to individual growth and healthy development in closeted or geographically isolated couples (Slater, 1995).

Fusion

As noted earlier, relationships between women tend to be emotionally intense and tightly entwined. This type of relationship could be described as fused, a term that has traditionally been used to signify an unhealthy relationship, one that it is overburdened with emotion and lacking clear boundaries (Nichols & Schwartz, 1998). Moving away from the traditional pejorative viewpoints of fusion, Ossana (2000) defined fusion as a relationship in which the boundaries between female partners may be blurred while a premium is placed on emotional intimacy, equality, and togetherness. As noted earlier, emotional intimacy and togetherness between two women can be a source of strength because it fosters deep trust and a sense of safety and allows the couple to bond together and meet the challenge of ongoing homoprejudice and oppression. A culturally informed counselor recognizes that lesbian relationships are unique and that high levels of shared activities are common. Too much togetherness or fusion should be determined by the individuals not by the therapist (Biaggio, Coan, & Adams, 2002).

Too much togetherness or fusion occurs when the individual begins to lose a sense of her separate self and partners become merged to the point where they may even begin to limit contact with the outside world. It is at this point that even sexual intimacy and physical connection can become much too threatening because all other aspects of life are merged. Remember Ann and Rachel? Ann had begun to feel overwhelmed by the relationship. She felt pressured by Rachel's demands for her to come out to her family. She felt she had lost herself, and in her opinion, the only way to find herself again was to end the relationship. She started to distance herself from Rachel, especially in the bedroom. In fact, she found herself questioning whether she was even a lesbian. Rachel was angry and heartbroken at the same time. She interpreted Ann's distance as disloyalty and abandonment. She also was ready to end the relationship. Fortunately, the women sought help from a therapist who had experience in working with lesbian couples. She helped the women address the issue of fusion by working with Rachel individually and helping her to understand and resolve her fears of abandonment. By doing so, she helped Rachel feel less threatened by Ann's request for space and alone time. She also helped Ann constructively ask for what she needed rather than trying to reclaim her autonomy by being destructive—starting fights, withholding sex, shutting down, or even breaking up. She worked with Ann individually to help her come to terms with her lesbian identity as well as to face her internalized shame and guilt about being different and not meeting her family's expectations of heterosexuality. She encouraged the women to spend time together as well as time apart. She also encouraged them to seek out other lesbian couples who may be facing similar issues.

Sexual Intimacy

One of the most common challenges faced by lesbian clients is learning how to remain sexual within the context of a relationship. In a review of the available literature, Schreurs (1993) found that, in general, lesbians meet the cultural stereotypes for all women in that they are indeed more interested in the romance and the emotional relationship. Lesbians seem to be more similar to heterosexual women than gay men in terms of their preferences for emotional intimacy and monogamy. And just like heterosexual couples, lack of communication, conflicts about sex, and an unequal power balance lead to dissatisfaction with the relationship. Techniques and strategies to address these issues that are effective with heterosexual women are likely to be useful with lesbian couples. These issues might include learning how to communicate with a partner, conflict resolution, and learning how to recognize and articulate needs and desires.

That said, most lesbians report that sex between two women is highly satisfying, usually orgasmic, emotionally fulfilling, and gratifying. This is in spite of the popular notion that lesbians have low sexual desire and female couples are destined to experience the dreaded "lesbian bed death." Studies indicate that lesbians may indeed have sex less frequently than heterosexual couples or gay male couples; however, they seem to spend much more time in each sexual encounter (Ossana, 2000). Lesbians seem to spend more time cuddling, passionately kissing, and holding each other. In truth, this notion of lesbian bed death or lack of sexual interest may actually be mitigated by society, in that deep emotional bonds with other women are socially sanctioned as long as they are nonsexual (Berzon, 1997). Lesbian couples are doubly constrained in that women are taught to repress sexual desire and sexual relationships between women are forbidden. Lesbian bed death or lack of sexual intimacy may simply be the result of programmed reluctance to initiate sex in case of appearing sexually aggressive or immoral. Or, as discussed previously, partners may withhold sex as a means to gain independence and escape merger. In any case, sensitive counselors can facilitate frank discussions about sexuality and the effects of sexism and homoprejudice and therefore provide the framework for renewed and improved sexual intimacy.

When working with issues related to intimacy and sexuality, one cannot overestimate the impact of homoprejudice. Adopting a positive lesbian self-identity in the face of society's onslaught of negativity and oppression is daunting and likely to have a profound effect on one's ability to be sexual and intimate with another woman. Given the pervasiveness of societal oppression, issues of comfort with sexual orientation and level of visibility or degree of "outness" are important to consider when working with lesbian clients who are struggling with sexual intimacy issues. Lacking even the minor privileges that heterosexual couples usually take for granted, such as the ability to be intimate in public or to have a legally sanctioned relationship, can have a profound effect on intimacy and sexual expression. For example, public displays of affection between lesbian partners are generally looked on with disdain, and couples either are forced into unnatural contact-free public situations or resort to furtive hand-holding and signs of affection when seemingly no one is looking. This cultural mandate to hide one's affection for one's same-sex partner surely and insidiously seeps into the bedroom, as it is difficult to switch back and forth between silence and shame and unfettered sexual celebration. As counselors, it is important to be proactive about affirming gay and lesbian relationships. All too often in society, sexual minorities are unnaturally forced to avoid physical contact and intimacy, and the counselor's office can be at least one place where they can be free and open about who they are and whom they love.

In recent years, there has been a shift in the lesbian community toward a more open sexual scene more akin to the gay men's culture (Esterberg, 1996). Women-made pornography, magazines, go-go clubs, and other more frank expressions of sexuality have challenged the previously held myths about the nature of lesbian sexuality. Younger lesbians seem to be much more comfortable with their sexuality and more open with public displays of affection and other types of intimacy.

Mental health practitioners working with lesbian clients must be willing to address issues related to sex and sexuality. Not doing so is a disservice to your client and probably indicative of your own internalized homoprejudice. Frank discussions about sexual practices may be uncomfortable for both you and your client, but they are important discussions to have nonetheless. Be aware of your comfort level with issues related to sex and assess and address any biases you may have toward lesbian sexuality.

For example, Cheryl liked to be vaginally penetrated but was afraid to admit it to her partner because she didn't want to be disloyal or hurtful, afraid that her partner would think she wanted a man. Filled with fear and shame, Cheryl reluctantly talked about this issue with her therapist. Fortunately, her therapist was comfortable with her own sexuality and not at all uncomfortable when clients talked about sex during counseling sessions. First, she normalized Cheryl's desire to be penetrated and role-played with her talking to her partner about her feelings. Her therapist also referred her to a feminist-owned sex-toy store and encouraged Cheryl to explore the possibilities of incorporating nonrepresentational dildos into their lovemaking.

Increasing Sexual Intimacy

When working with clients who are struggling with issues related to intimacy, it is useful to teach women how to give and receive sensual and sexual pleasure and learn how to say what feels good and what doesn't. Open communication is absolutely essential and may require practice and coaching from the counselor. Remember, for some women, open communication about sex will be completely foreign, and it may take time for her to understand and articulate her sexual needs. Take time to explore the effects of internalized homoprejudice as well the additional effects of sexism and heterosexism. Have the clients write down negative sexual messages and refute them with positive counterstatements. Help your clients to recognize and avoid getting stuck in roles in which someone is always the initiator and the other is always passive—take turns initiating. Encourage your clients to explore feelings and attitudes toward being the "sexual aggressor"—address negative self-talk and societal prohibitions. Also, encourage your clients to avoid saying "no" for unimportant reasons. If they don't have time or energy for a long, languorous session, teach them how to compromise or meet their lover halfway or discover ways to satisfy their partner when they're not as interested as she is. Challenge clients to avoid using sex to punish or hurt their partners. If they're hurt or angry, risk talking about it and working it out. Above all, teach and encourage your lesbian clients to explore and have fun in the bedroom (Tessina, 2000).

Sexual Abuse

The high incidence of sexual trauma and incest against women can also serve as an obstruction to sex and intimacy. According to a survey conducted by Loulan (1987), 38% of lesbians have experienced sexual abuse by a family member or stranger before the age of 18. And although this high percentage is similar to the rates of sexual abuse in heterosexual women, therefore disputing the notion that women become lesbian as a result of sexual abuse or sexual assault, there is a high probability in lesbian couples that not just one partner but both partners have experienced sexual abuse (Brown, 1995).

For example, Beth was very comfortable with her sexual orientation and knew that her history of sexual abuse did not make her choose to be a lesbian; however, to have a successful relationship with another woman, Beth knew she had to work through the issues related to her past. Wisely, her counselor understood that sexual abuse did not cause Beth to be lesbian, and he was able to validate and support her through the recovery process. In a relationship, the impact of issues related to sexual abuse can have a devastating effect on intimacy and sexuality. For example, each partner may be at different stages of recovery or have different needs. One or both may experience flashbacks of the abuse during sex or avoid sex altogether, which may anger or frustrate or even trigger a flashback for her partner (Browning, Reynolds, & Dworkin, 1991). Mental health practitioners need to be prepared to address the myriad effects of sexual abuse and assist perhaps both partners as they begin to negotiate the lifelong process of recovery.

Lesbians as Parents

More and more lesbian couples are choosing to have children. Heretofore, most lesbian couples had children while living in heterosexual marriages (Barret & Logan, 2000). Today, lesbian couples are choosing a variety of ways to have children, including adoption; donor insemination; coparenting with a gay man or a gay couple; and even comaternity, wherein one partner donates an egg that is inseminated and then implanted in the uterus of the other, making one partner the biological mother and the other the genetic partner (Barret & Logan, 2000). Heidi and Nancy have been together for 3 years and have just begun to start planning for their first child. They have already decided to coparent with a gay male friend, and now the only decision they need to make is whether to do it on their own at home or enlist the service of a fertility specialist. They sought therapy in order to better prepare for coparenting with each other as well as with a third person. Both acknowledge profound family-of-origin issues such as sexual abuse and alcoholism. They've had introductory talks about discipline and values, but these discussions usually ended with both partners in tears. It is more and more common for counselors to encounter lesbians either singly or in a couple who want to become parents. Therefore, it is paramount that counselors explore their own attitudes and internalized messages about lesbian parents. It is equally important for counselors to be aware of the current legal issues affecting lesbians who want to become parents. And although the issues that lesbians face as they think about parenthood are similar to those of heterosexual couples, again, one can never underestimate the impact of societal homoprejudice. The idea of lesbian parenting is certainly more palatable to the general public these days, but there are still many myths and stereotypes associated with lesbians who choose to parent. For example, lesbian parents are thought to create gay children, or lesbian parents are thought to be more likely to sexually abuse their children, and so forth. Counselors must be ready to counteract these stereotypes and support lesbian clients and couples as they pursue their choice to have a family.

Lesbians in Recovery

Research has indicated that lesbians tend to drink more heavily than heterosexual women (Bux, 1996). This higher incidence is probably the result of the devastating effects of homoprejudice, the challenge of managing multiple minority identities, and the overall tendency of lesbians to socialize in bars or club settings. Many lesbians find themselves heavily abusing drugs or alcohol as ways to numb the feelings of guilt and shame associated with being lesbian or being different from the heterosexual majority.

Pat, for example, never had a problem with alcohol until her mother passed away 3 years ago. In her family, her mother was the only one who had accepted her unconditionally when she came out as a lesbian 15 years ago. Now she was left with a father who rejected her and brothers who shunned her completely. Ever since her mother passed away, she found herself drinking more and more heavily. She knew she needed to stop drinking, but she wasn't willing to sober up and face the pain of her family's rejection. Moreover, she wasn't willing to enter into a treatment facility that would further ostracize her because she was lesbian. Sensitive counselors understand that treatment facilities can be fraught with homoprejudice and hostility. However, remaining hidden and closeted fuels the shame and guilt that are often at the root of chemical dependency. Be aware that there are a number of treatment facilities available locally and nationwide designed to meet the specific needs of lesbians in recovery. A second consideration is the extent to which a lesbian's partner or social support system will be involved in her recovery process. Given how relationship-oriented lesbians tend to be, partner and peer support may be critical to their success (Browning et al., 1991). Finally, lesbians who decide to use Alcoholics Anonymous as a path to recovery may have trouble with the traditional male-dominated approach. Sensitive counselors will assist lesbian clients in finding women-only or gay friendly meetings.

Lesbians and Domestic Violence

Traditionally, there has been a sense of reluctance to even admit that domestic violence between lesbians occurs. It somehow goes against how we perceive women and how we perceive lesbian relationships as happy, healthy, and violence-free (Coleman, 1996). Studies indicate that the prevalence and severity of domestic violence between women are comparable to those of heterosexual relationships. However, it is rarely talked about or even reported, and therefore, it is still not taken very seriously by mental health practitioners. Domestic violence between women, just like violence between men and women, is characterized by the need to dominate and control and likely develops from an overall sense of powerlessness fueled by homoprejudice, sexism, social isolation, and low self-esteem.

When seeking help, lesbians may encounter at least four significant challenges (Browning et al., 1991). The first and perhaps the most formidable challenge is the overall culturally pervasive denial that domestic violence occurs between women. Second, the lesbian victim may have trouble identifying physical battering as abuse because she may have reacted violently in self-defense, and therefore, she may inaccurately perceive violence as mutual aggression. The third reason is the resistance to report incidents of domestic violence because of lack of sensitivity and understanding by law enforcement professionals, and the fourth and final reason is the resistance of women's shelters to openly and sensitively deal with domestic violence between women.

Clearly, both education and sensitivity are sorely needed. Counselors need to understand that domestic violence between women does indeed occur, and they need to be prepared to address all aspects of the situation, including finding appropriate and affirming safe spaces for the victims and lesbian friendly treatment options for the perpetrators.

Conclusion: General Tips for Practitioners

1. Explore and challenge your own homoprejudice.
2. Understand and appreciate how difficult it is to come out and accept one's lesbian identity.
3. Be culturally sensitive to the realities of multiple oppressions.
4. Be prepared to help lesbian clients to develop healthy relationships with one another. Be willing to empathically address issues of fusion and avoid prejudging close lesbian relationships as unhealthy.
5. Be able to talk about sex and sexuality and become familiar and comfortable with lesbian sexuality and its expression.
6. Be prepared to work with lesbians who are struggling with chemical dependency and be aware of lesbian-friendly Alcoholics Anonymous programs and treatment facilities.
7. Be prepared to recognize that domestic violence does occur in lesbian relationships.

References

American Psychiatric Association. (1973). *Diagnostic and statistical manual of mental disorders*. Washington, DC: American Psychiatric Press.

Barret, B., & Logan, C. (2000). *Counseling gay men and lesbians: A practice primer*. Pacific Grove, CA: Brooks/Cole.

Barrett, K. A., & McWhirter, B. T. (2002). Counseling trainees' perceptions of clients based on sexual orientation. *Counselor Education and Supervision, 41*, 219–232.

Berzon, B. (1997). *The intimacy dance: A guide to long-term success in gay and lesbian relationships*. New York: Plume.

Biaggio, M., Coan, S., & Adams, W. (2002). Couples therapy for lesbians: Understanding merger and the impact of homophobia. *Journal of Lesbian Studies, 6*, 129–138.

Brown, L. S. (1995). Therapy with same-sex couples: An introduction. In N. S. Jacobson & A. S. Gurman (Eds.), *Clinical handbook of couples therapy* (pp. 274–291). New York: Guilford Press.

Browning, C., Reynolds, A. L., & Dworkin, S. H. (1991). Affirmative psychotherapy for lesbian women. *The Counseling Psychologist, 19*, 177–196.

Bux, D. A. (1996). The epidemiology of problem drinking in gay men and lesbians: A critical review. *Clinical Psychology Review, 16*, 277–298.

Clunis, D. M., & Green, G. (2000). *Lesbian couples: A guide to creating healthy relationships*. Seattle, WA: Seal Press.

Coleman, V. E. (1996). Lesbian battering: The relationship between personality and the perpetration of violence. In L. K. Hamberger & C. Renzetti (Eds.), *Domestic partner abuse* (pp. 77–102). New York: Springer.

Elliott, J. E. (1993). Career development with lesbian and gay clients. *The Career Development Quarterly, 41*, 210–226.

Esterberg, K. G. (1996). Gay cultures, gay communities: The social organization of lesbians, gay men, and bisexuals. In R. C. Williams & K. M. Cohen (Eds.), *The lives of lesbians, gays, and bisexuals: Children to adults* (pp. 377–393). Fort Worth, TX: Harcourt Brace.

Fassinger, R. E. (1991). The hidden minority: Issues and challenges in working with lesbian women and gay men. *Counseling Psychologist, 19*, 151–176.

Garnets, L., Hancock, K. A., Cochran, S. D., Goodchilds, J., & Peplau, L. A. (1991). Issues in psychotherapy with lesbians and gay men: A survey of psychologists. *American Psychologist, 46*, 964–972.

Greene, B. (1994). Lesbian women of color: Triple jeopardy. In L. Comas-Diaz & B. Greene (Eds.), *Women of color: Integrating ethnic and gender identities in psychotherapy* (pp. 389–427). New York: Guilford Press.

Greene, B. (1997). Ethnic minority lesbians and gay men: Mental health and treatment issues. In B. Greene (Ed.), *Ethnic and cultural diversity among lesbians and gay men* (pp. 216–227). New York: Guilford Press.

Logan, C. R. (1996). Homophobia? No, homoprejudice. *Journal of Homosexuality, 31,* 31–53.

Loulan, J. (1987). *Lesbian passion: Loving ourselves and each other.* San Francisco: Spinster Press.

McCarn, S. R., & Fassinger, R. E. (1996). Revisioning sexual minority identity formation: A new model of lesbian identity and its implications for counseling and research. *The Counseling Psychologist, 24,* 508–534.

Nichols, M. P., & Schwartz, R. C. (1998). *Family therapy: Concepts and methods.* Needham Heights, MA: Allyn & Bacon.

Ossana, S. M. (2000). Relationship and couples counseling. In R. M. Perez, K. A. Debord, & K. J. Bieschke (Eds.), *Handbook of counseling and therapy with lesbians, gays, and bisexuals* (pp. 275–302). Washington, DC: American Psychological Association.

Schreurs, K. M. G. (1993). Sexuality in lesbian couples: The importance of gender. *Annual Review of Sex Research, 4,* 49–66.

Slater, S. (1995). *The lesbian family life cycle.* New York: Free Press.

Smith, A. (1997). Cultural diversity and the coming-out process: Implications for clinical practice. In B. Greene (Ed.), *Ethnic and cultural diversity among lesbians and gay men* (pp. 279–300). New York: Guilford Press.

Tessina, T. B. (2000, January). Fanning the flames. *Girlfriends, 6*(7), 29.

Appendix

Additional Resources

American Counseling Association
www.counseling.org
Association for Gay, Lesbian, and Bisexual Issues in Counseling
www.aglbic.org
Human Rights Campaign
www.hrcusa.org
Lesbian Parenting
www.lesbian.org/lesbian-moms
www.familypride.org
Lesbian Health Issues
www.maunterproject.org
Parents and Friends of Gays
www.pflag.org

Affirmative Counseling With Transgendered Persons

Jeffrey Mostade

We all have, and express ourselves through, gender. As with race, culture, ability, class, age, and sexuality, gender is a dimension of humanity that varies along its continuum simultaneously with other human attributes. People whose socially sanctioned gender expression is congruent with their apparent sex are privileged not to feel ostracized for their gender expression. It is the unearned privilege of gender congruence. However, this congruence is often not the reality for scores of transgendered individuals. *Transgender* is an umbrella term used to describe people whose appearance or behavior does not conform to the cultural norm for their presumed sex/gender; it also includes intersexual people and cross-dressers.

Counseling work with transgendered clients must go beyond exploration and support. As clients look inward to discern their orientation and values, counselors must also help clients to challenge their acceptance of societal stigma placed on people whose gender expression varies from a narrow range of masculine and feminine. Much of the counseling process, therefore, should be focused on helping clients to form and maintain a healthy, functional adjustment to life in a society often hostile to them.

All individuals have lives as gendered cultural beings with the limitations or freedoms granted by our society to their culture, class, age, ability, and sexuality. We live in a society that expects people to exhibit the narrowly defined characteristics of a binary expression of gender—masculine or feminine. If one looks around, one will see a range of expression of masculinity and femininity among people, a diversity of gender that one perhaps has not begun to appreciate in its complexity.

This chapter begins with a discussion of the history and context of sex, sexuality, and gender from which an understanding of transgendered people must begin. Differences are then delineated among the four broad groups of people that comprise the transgendered spectrum: *intersexual people, people who cross-dress, transgenderist people,* and *transsexual people*. After a discussion of ethical issues and barriers to effective service with transgendered people, suggestions for affirmative counseling with this client group conclude the chapter.

Context: Sex, Sexuality, and Gender

Sex

Sex historically referred to the appearance of a person's external genitalia. With the advent of increasingly modern technologies, there are additional ways to assign sex: chromosomally, hormonally, and structurally—the presence, size, and appearance of both internal and external genitalia and gonadal tissues (Currah & Minter, 2000). Sex is more complex than a dichotomy. As in most things organic, sex occurs along a continuum—from relatively male through a number of variations to relatively female, moving through the presence of sexually ambiguous genitalia and the absence of external genitalia (Burke, 1997; Dreger, 2001; Fausto-Sterling, 1993; Feinberg, 1996). Along this continuum occurs a normal distribution of sizes, shapes, and configurations of external and internal genitalia (Burke, 1997). In Figure 21.1, the concepts of sex, sexuality, and gender are presented in a circular fashion, rather than as linear dichotomies. It is important to remember that there is more variety in real life than traditional concepts allow; much of what is ascribed as male or female is culturally bound in definitions. How a society deals with children and adults who do not conform to these inelastic concepts is also culturally bound. Currently, in North America, as many as five children per day experience medically recommended "normalizing" surgeries (Dreger, 2001). These children and adults are known as *intersexual people*. This grouping of people exists because our concepts of male and female sex are more simplistic than the reality of nature.

Sexuality

The expectation that a gay or lesbian sexual orientation automatically accompanies gender nonconformity is a rigid and unconstructive stereotype. Some people expect that gender nonconformists are gay and that gay men are slightly effeminate and gay women slightly masculine. Early mental health taxonomists, such as the German sexologist Magnus Hirschfeld, who coined the term *transvestite* in 1910 (Bullough & Bullough, 1993), utilized obviously gender-variant people as the sampling for their studies of homosexuals, or "inverts." This fusion of sexuality with gender identity and gender expression persists to this day in both the professional and lay communities.

Gay and lesbian people who express gender in a fluid manner are susceptible to gender oppression and discrimination, whereas heterosexually oriented transgendered people can become targets for homophobia. What about advocacy and support of the lesbian, gay, bisexual, and transgendered (LGBT) community, you may ask? This "community" is more of an identity-based political construction and may be said to comprise all nonexclusively heterosexual people (Hawley & Mostade, 1998) and gender nonconformists. This is an enormously rich, complex, and varied community of diverse culture, ethnicity, gender, sex, age, ability, religion, class, and national origin not easily reduced to brief generalizations and therapeutic heuristics. This diverse group of individuals has banded together as an identity-based community to engage in American style pluralism as a defensive political necessity (Browning, 1998; D'Emilio, 1996). Political acknowledgment of the rigid "identity," much of it based on cultural and institutionalized gender discrimination and oppression, unfortunately, merely reinforces the concept (Wilchins, 1997).

Although it is often assumed that people who are transgendered are gay or lesbian, this is not the case. Many transgendered people are heterosexual; others are gay, bisexual, or asexual. Cross-dressing is almost exclusively the domain of heterosexually oriented men, by diagnosis (American Psychiatric Association, 1994). Sexual orientation is a separate issue from gender identity. Important issues in any gender-focused counseling are to differentiate feelings, beliefs, and behaviors in gender, sex, and sexuality.

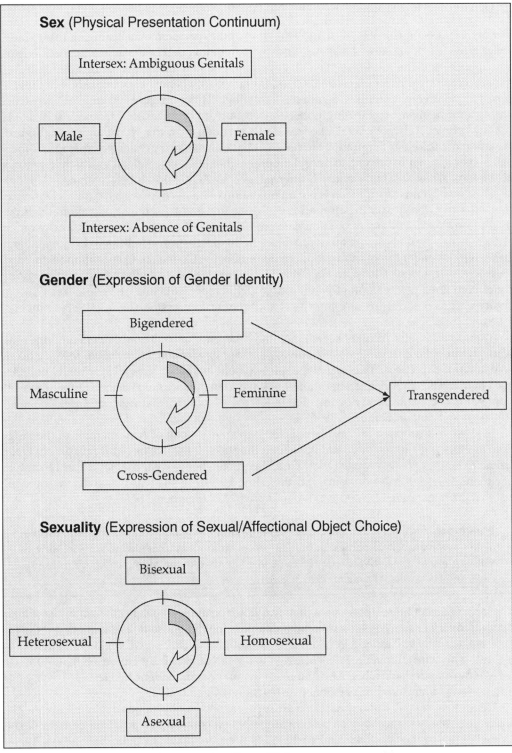

Figure 21.1
Nonlinear Representations of the Concepts of Sex, Gender, and Sexuality

Gender Expression

Gender expression consists of many behaviors and expressions, including clothing, hairstyles, presence or absence of makeup, body gestures and other body language, mannerisms and speech, and the roles one plays in society. These may be conscious or accidental behaviors (Phillips, 1997; Walworth, 2001). Gender identity is how people conceive of themselves as relatively masculine, feminine, or neither. This represents an internal construct and cannot be measured through observation but can be measured through self-report (Phillips, 1997; Walworth, 2001). For example, a young man may have an internal representation of himself as feminine, or female, yet have an exterior gender expression as a football player in order to pretend to himself or others that he has a gender identity that matches his biological sex. Gender identity is internal; gender expression is behavioral.

Fluidity of gender expression is not an invention of modern American culture. Dionysus (Bacchus in Greek) was the Roman cross-dressing god of wine and seasonal rebirth (Hamilton, 1942). Followers of Dionysus cross-dressed during celebrations, and women known as ithyphalloi carried huge phalluses in the processions (Bullfinch, 1983; Feinberg, 1996). Nor is gender oppression a modern invention; the Council of Constantinople forbade cross-dressing among Christians in 691 A.D. (Evans, 1988). Aside from Christian religious codes contained in the book of Deuteronomy, this represents one of the earliest written, civilly enforced codes proscribing dress and gender expression (Evans, 1988; Feinberg, 1996).

There is a long tradition of acceptance and reverence of multiple genders among some Native American cultures, most involving gender expression in vocation, role, or dress (Williams, 1986). These "two-spirit" people are honored as sacred and spiritually enlightened in many North American traditions but have been the focus of Western/Euro-American oppression and eradication documented in Roscoe's *Living the Spirit: A Gay American Indian Anthology* (as cited in Feinberg, 1996).

In Western European history, there is the narrative of Joan of Arc, liberator of the kingdom of France at the age of 17 and burned at the stake at the age of 19 for refusing to wear women's clothes. Joan of Arc felt that "God" instructed her to wear the clothes and hairstyle of a man. Although cross-dressing was the crime for which she was put to death, some insist that cross-gendered behavior is what doomed her (Feinberg, 1996).

> Trans expression emerged in culture throughout Europe in holiday celebrations, rituals, carnival days, masquerade parties, theater, literature, and opera. That's why cross-dressing is still part of holiday festivals today in the United States like the Mummer's Parade, Mardi Gras, and Halloween. (Feinberg, 1996, p. 80).

The jazz musician Billy Tipton, who died in 1989 of a ruptured ulcer rather than risk a hospital discovery of her gender variance, was a person who chose to live in a gender different from her natal sex. Indeed, very few people thought him to be anything other than a man, including his wife (Feinberg, 1996). Married to a woman, was Billy Tipton a female-to-male (FTM) transgenderist in a heterosexual relationship or a male-identified lesbian? These are not hardened identities but personal constructions of gender.

Gender expression fluidity has been an apparent and public hallmark of the lesbian–gay subculture almost since its first self-awareness as a community in urban centers of the United States in the late 1940s and early 1950s (Berube, 1989; D'Emilio, 1996; Katz, 1976). African American and Latina drag queens and transsexuals led the Stonewall Rebellion of July 17, 1969, which is often referred to as the beginning of modern gay liberation (Feinberg, 1996; Katz, 1976).

Intersexual People

An archaic clinical term for people with ambiguous external genitals is *hermaphrodite*. This term was coined from *Hermaphroditus*, the name of an offspring of the Greek god Hermes and the goddess Aphrodite who partook of the physical presentation of both sexes (Kerenyi, 1987). People who have these relatively common presentations along the continuum of sex are now known as intersexuals. Although this occurs in an estimated 1 in 2,000 births (Burke, 1997), how one determines this population varies by definition: Many scholars include hyperspadias (a urethral opening other than at the end of the penis) or congenital absence of a vagina (1 in 5,000 female births) as well as hormonal conditions that do not always manifest themselves until puberty (Burke, 1997; Walworth, 2001). Fausto-Sterling (1993) stated that between 1930 and 1960, there were many case histories of persons who made functional social adjustments to their intersexuality without surgery and without the "social emergency" (Burke, 1997, p. 221) that the birth of an intersexual child is likely to cause today.

Intersexual children are generally diagnosed at birth, and the medical community often recommends immediate surgical intervention to "normalize" the appearance of the genitals. The child is then raised in the gender that matches the chosen sex, very often female (Dreger, 2000; Fausto-Sterling, 1993). Recently, a political awareness and consciousness raising around the issues and lives of intersexual people has emerged.

"I am horrified by what has been done to me and by the conspiracy of silence and lies. I am filled with grief and rage, but also relief finally to believe that maybe I am not the only one. My doctor told me more than once that I wasn't the only one, but I never got to meet any of them," states Angela Moreno, a 24-year-old intersexual person writing about her feelings about surgeries to remove her "oversized" clitoris as a child, without her consent (Moreno, 1997).

Many intersexual adults resent the arbitrary and emergency surgeries deemed necessary by physicians and hospitals to bring their genitals and bodies into a societal standard of conformity. As the brochure of the Intersex Society of North America (2000) states,

> Our culture conceives of sex anatomy as a dichotomy: humans come in two sexes, conceived of as so different as to be nearly different species. However, developmental embryology, as well as the existence of intersexuals, proves this to be a cultural construction. Anatomic sex differentiation occurs on a male/female continuum, and there are several dimensions.

As in all multicultural counseling, it is imperative to remember that intersex issues make up only a portion of the humanity and concerns of any person.

People Who Cross-Dress

It is estimated that there may be as many as 10 people who cross-dress for every gender-variant person who wants to pursue hormonal or surgical intervention (Walworth, 2001). This is a quite common behavior, yet there is a lot of myth and misinformation surrounding it. Although neither women who wear pants nor people who cross-dress to entertain (drag queens or drag kings) are diagnosed for their behavior, cross-dressing among heterosexual males is diagnosable as a paraphilia (American Psychiatric Association, 1994). Cross-dressers may come into contact with a counselor after discovery by a spouse or partner or if they are unable to reduce the tension between their needs to express both their masculine and their feminine identities. Results from a survey of cross-dressers who socialize together indicated that 30% to 50% of those men had sought counseling (Bullough & Bullough, 1993).

Individuals who cross-dress, from the wearing of solitary feminine undergarments to full cross-dressing and social roles, might not identify with the transgender or the LGBT communities. These men are often married, with a heterosexual orientation, and may have little contact with or understanding about gay or lesbian people. Cross-dressers will likely have experienced this as a lifelong phenomenon: occurring early in youth, repeated to the point of habituation, possibly sexualizing this behavior during adolescence, and thus establishing an enduring pattern.

With people who cross-dress, there exists the need to express twin gender roles, usually combined with a heterosexual orientation (Bullough & Bullough, 1993). These people may be said to be *bigendered* (see Figure 21.1) in that they have the urge to express both genders and gender roles. They maintain their heterosexuality and outward show of masculine gendered behavior and may resolve their needs through wearing of cross-gendered undergarments or dressing in role with partner's support or possibly in social situations with the support of other cross-dressers and/or spouses (see TRI-ESS in the Appendix). Although the most common coping mechanism has been to keep the cross-dressing a secret (Bullough & Bullough, 1993), this coping mechanism is no longer effective when the client is discovered. Cross-dressing clients tend to present with one of three issues: (a) They want to save their marriage or relationship, (b) they want to feel better about themselves, or (c) they feel that cross-dressing has become compulsive, and they want to control it (Bullough & Bullough, 1993, p. 350). Integration of these disparate needs of gender expression and resolution of relationship tensions are the primary foci of clinical intervention.

Transgenderists and Transsexuals

Transgender is a term originally developed to express the experience of those people who identified neither as cross-dressers nor as transsexuals seeking genital reassignment surgery (Israel & Tarver, 1997)—people now sometimes known as transgenderists. The term *transgender* has since expanded to encompass a mythical, identity-based, political "community" of people who are seen to be transgressively gendered, that is, pre- and postoperative transsexuals, male-to-female (MTF) transsexuals, FTM transsexuals, transsexuals, transgenderists, intersexuals, cross-dressers, and individuals who find gender roles and expectations so repressive that they have chosen to discard or re-create these roles into self-defined identities such as boy-identified women, boyz, diesel dykes, androgynous people, he-shes, butches, bulldaggers, drag kings, bigenders, drag queens, androgynes, gender benders, gender blenders, male-identified women, and lesbian-identified men (Bornstein, 1994; Currah & Minter, 2000; Feinberg, 1996).

The transgenderist or transsexual possesses a gender identity that is at odds with his or her physical manifestation of sex. MTF transgender people are born with a male physical presentation but experience their lives gendered primarily as females; FTM transgender people are born with a female presentation yet experience their lives gendered primarily as male. Transsexual people pursue hormonal and/or surgical interventions to ameliorate the painful incongruence involved in the disparity between their apparent sex and their gender identity. Transgender people may resolve their gender presentation in other ways. Some dress part-time in the opposite gender; some may adopt a unisex or androgynous presentation (Phillips, 1997).

Ethical Issues

The most significant ethical issue to present itself repeatedly to the professional counselor engaged in clinical work with transsexual individuals is the gatekeeping role required with respect to the client's access to hormonal and surgical interventions. This can often be an emotionally charged issue between the client and the counselor as both struggle with the differences between eligibility and readiness. Individuals vary in their life experiences, coping skills, financial resources, emotional support, and life goals. The goals of any counseling with a transgendered person are to provide psychoeducation and support around options available to the individual (Meyer et al., 2001). Counseling must work to achieve mitigation of the effects of previous cultural oppression and augment existing coping skills while the individual works to achieve a healthy, realistic balance between achievable occupational and relational goals while transitioning or finding a useful gender expression.

There is tension between the medical model pathologizing of the diagnosis of gender dysphoria and its location of etiology within the client and the counselor's understanding of the contextual aspects of growing up within an oppressive culture. Ivey and Ivey (1998) pointed out that "there is no necessary conflict between a developmental and pathological view" (p. 334) and that the tension must be resolved through synthesis. The medical model locates the pathology in the individual, and the developmental synthesis locates the issue in the individual/family/cultural context (Ivey & Ivey, 1998, p. 355). In the medical model, the helper is in a hierarchical relationship to the client, and in the developmental synthesis, the helper is in a collaborative relationship to the client.

With this in mind, the counselor may want to approach both diagnosis and the tension concerning gatekeeping by acknowledging any discomfort with the process and the inequity in power. It is important to remind the client that both counselor and client will need to renegotiate the tension in the relationship over time. This models a coconstructive, nonhierarchical approach to problem solving while allowing an opportunity to discuss cultural transphobia, the medical model, and possible future advocacy actions on the part of the client.

Cultural and clinical competence is another issue for counselors to confront as they encounter transgender people. This chapter merely grazes the surface of the considerations, knowledge, awareness, and skill development that are required to provide ethical service to transgender people. Clinical competence is an important ethical issue, as are an awareness of barriers to services and the effect of diversity on understanding transgender people.

Barriers to Effective Counseling With Transgendered Persons

There are barriers to effective mental health and other health service delivery to transgendered people on many levels: cultural, organizational, interpersonal, and intrapersonal. On cultural and organizational levels, there is a lack of legal support for the rights of transgendered people. Employment discrimination, immigration status discrimination, denial of housing, denial of medical treatment, and risk of public humiliation, ridicule, or violence (Currah & Minter, 2000) are other examples of the barriers faced by transgendered people. Cross-dressing in public is illegal, for men, in many states, and people are often terminated from their employment if "off-time" personal cross-dressing behavior is revealed (Phillips, 1997; Stringer, 1990).

Interpersonal barriers may consist of genderism and transphobia on the part of the counselor/helper that prevent the helper from understanding the concrete issues and interfere with unconditional positive regard. This expression of an interpersonal barrier on the part of the counselor may activate and engage an intrapersonal barrier for the client: internalized genderism and transphobia. Other intrapersonal issues for clients may include shame, fear about disclosure and personal safety, adapting to social pressure and stigma, fear of or loss of relationships, and "self-imposed limitations of expression or aspirations" (Currah & Minter, 2000, p. 9).

An unwillingness to look at the unearned privilege of gender congruence is a significant intrapersonal barrier for a counselor to consider. Examining the feelings associated with unearned privilege may cause some emotional dissonance, but this is an essential step for a professional counselor who wants to work successfully with people examining gender issues.

Affirmative Counseling With Transgendered People: How Does One Actually Work in a Counseling Session With a Person Who Is Transgendered or Confronting Gender Issues?

A counselor must first look inward at his or her own gender, gendered upbringing, and feelings about mannish women, effeminate men, and transsexual people. This self-examination constitutes the beginning of a counselor's gender awareness work. The next steps are to gain knowledge and skill and involve a counselor's own real-life experience.

One way that a counselor can begin to gather experience in gender issues and working with people of variant gender is to cofacilitate an ongoing group working with transgendered people or their families. Moderate- to large-sized cities often house a counseling or other mental health practice that maintains an outreach or a specialty with transgendered people. Contact them and ask to work as a cofacilitator and begin to gather supervised experience. Another option is to locate and contact a local LGBT community center or an affirming and welcoming religious congregation. They may maintain a support group for transgendered or transitioning adults or their families. Seek out good, experienced supervision by a professional with experience with sex education, transitioning people, and other specialized areas of interest.

Negotiating healthy gender awareness involves effort on the part of the client and intense focus and metaprocessing on the part of the counselor. It is important not only to reflect and show compassion but also to reframe and challenge self-defeating beliefs on the part of the client. This is an emotionally profound process with those clients seeking hormonal or surgical intervention (Stringer, 1990). This process involves validation, cognitive restructuring, decision making, and social and behavioral adjustments to living in the world of another gender. These clients must learn a new language of expressions, spatial awareness, dress, mannerisms, gesture, and carriage that may involve many highs and lows during the journey for the client as well as the counselor. In an essay, hooks (1994) described a similar transformation of pain to wholeness:

> It's like having a sickness in your body that gets more fierce as it is passing to wellness. We don't have to view that period of intense sickness as an invitation to despair, but as a sign of transformation in the very depths of whatever pain it is we are experiencing. (p. 242)

Counselors must never overlook the stigma management resources of a person who has successfully negotiated a lifetime of marginalization and stigmatization (Hawley & Mostade, 1998). Goffman (1963) defined *stigma* as "the discrediting discrepancy between a person's public image and their [sic] private self" (as quoted in Bullough & Bullough, 1993, p. 341). If the client accepts the stigma, the person often develops loneliness or shame. Stigma management resources are the successful coping strategies developed by marginalized people to function in a society in which one is discriminated against and oppressed. We know, for instance, that older gay men and lesbian women have often developed healthy stigma management techniques that they later generalize to cope with their experiences of ageism as that occurs (Friend, 1990).

It is important to maintain collegial or other supervisory relationships in transgender work. Maintaining a relationship with another practice or mental health professional provides assessment referral options for clients when they are seeking a second confirmation for surgery. If the opportunity is available, it is helpful to use a team approach in assessments, which provides an opportunity for team interviews and confirmation for hormonal and surgical referrals. Recommending that clients attend a clinical counseling group for MTF and FTM transitioning adults at other clinical settings also provides more clinical and social input. Maintaining clinical supervisory relationships helps ensure ethical care as well as provides opportunities for confirmation of clinical diagnoses and interventions.

Counseling Intersexual Clients

The counseling needs of the intersexual person can overlap with issues of gender, and they can also be very different from other members of the transgender community. There are needs to address adjustment to issues of sex, gender, and gender presentation. Some individuals choose to explore another gender as they mature; others are happy with their sense of congruence. If these clients have experienced normalizing surgeries as children, they may well have issues of loss, violation, and anger at their circumstance, their families, and the medical establishment. Counselors can also work to help their intersexual clients become advocates for their own health care. Intersexual people involved in the Intersex Society of North America have addressed their hurt, loss, and anger through advocacy efforts to bring awareness of this medical and ethical issue to the larger community (see Intersex Society of North America in the Appendix).

The following points are important when counseling intersexual clients:

1. Encourage clinician and client education regarding the facts and current ethical debates surrounding common normalizing surgeries.
2. Normalize an awareness that adjustment to intersexuality during childhood and adolescence can be difficult, shaming, or arduous but that many people make quite healthy and satisfactory lives, careers, and relationships.
3. Encourage the client to connect with others who have had similar or congruent experiences (see the Appendix).
4. Encourage the concept of growth through grief, recognizing that the experience of unwanted normalizing surgeries can lead to posttraumatic syndromelike behaviors.
5. Be curious, congruent, and compassionate. Open yourself to empathy. Even if you are an LGBT person, consider that you know little or nothing of the experience of an intersexual person (Intersex Society of North America, 2000).

Counseling Cross-Dressing Clients

The counseling needs of cross-dressing clients vary by circumstance and their comfort level with their behaviors. A wife or romantic/affectional partner will pressure some clients into visiting a counselor after discovery. In these cases, it is most likely crisis counseling for the relationship while feelings, behaviors, and values are sorted out.

Clients may initiate counseling as they grow increasingly uncomfortable with their behavior, lacking an understanding or even a label for their behavior. Clients will approach a counselor and ask for help with sexual orientation issues, and it will be gradually revealed (perhaps to the clients) that their cross-gender dressing and impulses do not change their sexuality. As with other transgendered people, the issues vary, but the counseling work often focuses on sorting out issues of sex, sexuality, and gender.

When counseling cross-dressing clients, the following points should be considered:

1. Urge the client to define concrete patterns of behavior that are causing inter- or intrapersonal distress.
2. Encourage involvement of the client's partner or spouse, if there is one.
3. The counselor should work to understand the complex needs to express two differently gendered (bigendered) expressions of the client's personality, behavior, and appearance.
4. Normalize this behavior for client partners, help them understand that this behavior will probably continue, and assist in establishing acceptable compromises for the couple.
5. Encourage exploration on the part of an emerging transsexual person. Delay foreclosure on gender exploration so as not to confuse experimentation with crossdressing.

Counseling Clients Seeking Hormonal and/or Surgical Intervention

The standard course of treatment for a transitioning individual is called triadic therapy, which consists of the real-life test, hormonal treatment, and surgical treatment (Levine et al., 1998). As a counselor, one's involvement starts with a sensitive history, diagnosis, and treatment planning. It depends on at what point in transition the clients are located. If they are unaware that they are transgendered, this treatment will take longer than when clients have entered counseling because they want hormonal or surgical endorsement. Often, when clients enter counseling, they feel that the process is a hurdle that must be jumped to obtain the interventions that they desire. The relationship often grows to a much deeper and more meaningful interaction.

Interventions with transsexual or transgenderist persons may be easier to identify than in working with cross-dressers, as the ultimate goal is generally a consistent gender identity and expression. The five elements of clinical work with clients expressing gender identity dysphoria may involve "diagnostic assessment, psychotherapy, real-life-experience, hormone therapy, and surgical therapy" (Meyer et al., 2001, p. 3). Although counselors may be clinically involved with the provision of clinical expertise in the first three interventions, they stand as "gatekeepers" to access to the hormonal and surgical interventions. Each level of treatment has its own standards of readiness and eligibility recommended in the standards of care document. Recommendation for hormones (Levine et al., 1998; Meyer et al., 2001) requires one signature by at least a master's-level clinician responsible for the counseling and contact with the client. Access to surgical intervention requires two signatures, at least one of which must be at the level of a PhD clinician.

The Standards of Care for Gender Identity Disorders (Levine et al., 1998) has offered the only commonly accepted standards of care for work with people experiencing gender identity disorders (Israel & Tarver, 1997; Kirk & Rothblatt, 1995). The newest version—the 6th version (Meyer et al., 2001)—is flexible and recognizes that people enter their awareness of their personal work with gender and possible transition at different points in their own lives. It acknowledges that all people have their own cultural history and coping resources that they bring to their work.

In the 6th version of *The Standards of Care for Gender Identity Disorders*, 10 tasks of the mental health professional working with such a client are listed (Meyer et al., 2001):

1. To accurately diagnose the individual's gender disorder;
2. To accurately diagnose any comorbid psychiatric conditions and see to their appropriate treatment;
3. To counsel the individual about the range of treatment options and their implications;

4. To engage in psychotherapy;
5. To ascertain eligibility and readiness for hormone and surgical therapy;
6. To make formal recommendations to medical and surgical colleagues;
7. To document their patient's relevant history in a letter of recommendation;
8. To be a colleague on a team of professionals with an interest in the gender identity disorders;
9. To educate family members, employers, and institutions about gender identity disorders; and
10. To be available for follow-up of previously seen gender patients.

Another resource for the mental health clinician working with clients with gender issues is *Transgender Care: Recommended Guidelines, Practical Information, and Personal Accounts* (Israel & Tarver, 1997). This resource offered an approach to working with clients with gender issues that was more amenable to a developmentalist perspective until the recent publication of the 6th version of the standards of care (Meyer et al., 2001). Israel and Tarver made it clear that people are diagnosable only when their gender confusion is causing them pain or emotional, relational, or vocational difficulties. They further recognized that "thousands of transgender individuals lead well-adjusted lives as productive and law abiding participants in society" (Israel & Tarver, 1997, p. 54).

Some of the mechanics of working with transitioning individuals involve writing hormone treatment and surgical endorsement letters, writing letters to police officers and other officials explaining that these people are cross-dressing as part of a course of mental health treatment, and that the clients deserve to be treated as members of the sex to which they are transitioning. Significant milestones for clients may include legal name changes, change of other documentation (Social Security card, driver's license, etc.), beginning hormone treatments, and genital reassignment surgery.

There are both FTM and MTF transgenderists and transsexuals who choose not to surgically alter their genitals. They may bind or pad their breasts, have them removed or augmented, dress in the clothing of the opposite sex, and/or have masculinizing or feminizing implants placed. They may or may not pursue hormonal intervention, the results of which may include for FTM individuals facial hair growth, receding hairlines, male pattern baldness, coarsening of the skin, lowering of the voice, muscular development, enlargement of the clitoris, and cessation of menses (Kirk & Rothblatt, 1995). Similarly, natal male transgenderists and transsexuals (MTF) may choose among hormonal interventions that result in the following changes: refining of skin texture, swelling and growing of breast tissues, shrinkage of the penis and prostate, redistribution of fat in the body that yields a more feminine contour, and a lowering of serum cholesterol (Kirk & Rothblatt, 1995, p. 22). There are also complications that may occur as a result of hormonal therapy for both FTM and MTF individuals. Weight gain, hypertension, and liver changes are all potential complications for the transitioning individual (Kirk & Rothblatt, 1995). Professional counselors should make themselves aware of these complications and health risks, as they should be part of the psychoeducation of new clients.

Group Counseling

Some form of consistent group counseling or support group participation is vital for transsexual or transgenderist clients pursuing transition. Depending on the point in their transition when they pursue counseling, all clients should have some individual counseling sessions prior to participating in a group. It is very important for a facilitator to have gained quite a bit of experience before facilitating a gender transition group alone. Repeated experience as a facilitator reduces the anxiety attendant to novel or socially threatening groups. As shown by Duncan and Brown (1996), anxiety reduces the cognitive complexity of the counselor's response, but cognitive complexity in intervention design increases with experience. Additionally, "conceptually complex individuals are better able to attend simultaneously to their clients and their own internal states" (Duncan & Brown, 1996, p. 260). Gaining knowledge, awareness, and practice opportunities increases one's skill in handling group facilitation.

Reframing is a very useful aid in the group process that can be modeled initially by a facilitator. Inasmuch as gender itself is a social and cultural construct, the diverse backgrounds of clients coming together in transition work encourage "enriched reframes and transcend . . . the experience of any single person" (Clark, 1998, p. 69). This technique works well when one client cannot get past an issue and is able to solicit new information from the group.

Group work also offers an opportunity for clients to engage each other in issues of race, culture, age, ability, religion, natal sex, and sexuality concerns, especially as these relate to their gender journey. Although each person is in transition from the gender associated with his or her natal sex to a gender expression that reduces his or her pain and increases opportunities to interact successfully in society, each person comes from a different background and internal self-awareness. Working with such existing cultural differences in the group membership, scapegoating, splitting, and dysfunctional beliefs are highlighted within the group. As client members begin to "own" their projected prejudices or powerlessness as transgendered people, group participants can benefit from "ego strengthening . . . [and] lowered prejudicial attitudes and feelings, resulting in a building of community through an experience of universality" (Cheng, Chae, & Gunn, 1998, p. 375).

Conclusion

All clients possess multiple and complex identities, but it is only when one or more of these identities is nonnormative that the attributes of that identity usurp the individual. This is evident for clients who present with issues related to gender. These clients come with belief and value systems that were learned within their families or through the settings in which they were raised. Although various cultures seem to differ in their approach to gender variance, very few cultures cherish those members of their community who are transgendered.

Counselors have the opportunity to confront and interrupt genderism and transphobia not only with their clients but also in the larger world. As "there is no hierarchy of oppressions" (Lorde, 1993, p. 17), working with individuals who are addressing issues of gender is a rare privilege. This chapter has offered the most brief and cursory glance at a clinically complex issue. Clinical service to this population can be enhanced only when an individual counselor pursues training and supervision in the area of gender and transgender issues.

References

American Psychiatric Association. (1994). *Diagnostic and statistical manual of mental disorders* (4th ed.). Washington, DC: Author.

Berube, A. (1989). Marching to a different drummer: Lesbian and gay GIs in World War II. In M. Duberman, M. Vicinus, & G. Chauncey (Eds.), *Hidden from history: Reclaiming the gay and lesbian past* (pp. 383–384). New York: New American Library.

Bornstein, K. (1994). *Gender outlaw: On men, women, and the rest of us.* New York: Routledge.

Browning, F. (1998). *A queer geography: Journeys toward a sexual self* (Rev. ed.). New York: Farrer, Straus & Giroux.

Bullfinch, T. (1983). *Myths of Greece and Rome.* New York: Viking Penguin.

Bullough, V. L., & Bullough, B. (1993). *Cross-dressing, sex, and gender*. Philadelphia: University of Pennsylvania Press.

Burke, P. (1997). *Gender shock: Exploding the myths of male and female*. New York: Anchor Books.

Cheng, W. D., Chae, M., & Gunn, R. W. (1998). Splitting and projective identification in multicultural group counseling. *Journal for Specialists in Group Work, 23*(4), 372–387.

Clark, A. (1998). Reframing: A therapeutic technique in group counseling. *Journal for Specialists in Group Work, 23*(1), 66–73.

Currah, P., & Minter, S. (2000). *Transgender equality: A handbook for activists and policy makers*. Washington, DC: National Gay and Lesbian Task Force.

D'Emilio, J. (1996). Capitalism and gay identity. In D. Moron (Ed.), *The material queer: A lesbigay cultural studies reader* (pp. 263–271). Boulder, CO: Westview Press.

Dreger, A. D. (2000). *Hermaphrodites and the medical invention of sex*. Boston: Harvard University Press.

Dreger, A. D. (2001, February). Top 10 myths about intersex. *Intersex Society of North America Newsletter*. Retrieved March 30, 2005, from http://www.isna.org/files/hwa/feb2001.pdf

Duncan, D., & Brown, B. (1996). Anxiety and development of conceptual complexity. *Journal for Specialists in Group Work, 21*(4), 252–261.

Evans, A. (1988). *The god of ecstasy: Sex roles and the madness of Dionysus*. New York: St. Martin's Press.

Fausto-Sterling, A. (1993, March 12). How many sexes are there? *New York Times*, p. A29.

Feinberg, L. (1996). *Transgender warriors: Making history from Joan of Arc to Dennis Rodman*. Boston: Beacon Hill Press.

Friend, R. A. (1990). Older lesbian and gay people: A theory of successful aging. *Journal of Homosexuality, 20*, 99–118.

Hamilton, E. (1942). *Mythology*. Boston: Little, Brown.

Hawley, L. D., & Mostade, J. (1998). Transcending the culture of prejudice to a culture of pride as a counselor. In J. McFadden (Ed.), *Transcultural counseling* (2nd ed., pp. 317–339). Alexandria, VA: American Counseling Association.

hooks, b. (1994). *Outlaw culture: Resisting representations*. New York: Routledge.

Intersex Society of North America. (2000). *What is intersex?* [Brochure]. Petaluma, CA: Author.

Israel, G. I., & Tarver, D. E. (1997). *Transgender care: Recommended guidelines, practical information, and personal accounts*. Philadelphia: Temple University Press.

Ivey, A. E., & Ivey, M. B. (1998). Reframing *DSM–IV*: Positive strategies from developmental counseling and therapy. *Journal of Counseling & Development, 76*, 334–350.

Katz, J. (1976). *Gay American history: Lesbians and gay men in the USA*. New York: Avon Books.

Kerenyi, K. (1987). *Hermes, guide of souls: The mythologem of the masculine source of life*. Dallas, TX: Spring.

Kirk, S., & Rothblatt, M. (1995). *Medical, legal, and workplace issues for the transsexual: A guide for successful transformation*. Blawnox, PA: Together Lifeworks.

Levine, S. B. (Chair), Brown, G., Coleman, E., Cohen-Kettenis, P., Hage, J. J., Van Maasdamm, J., et al. (1998). *The standards of care for gender identity disorders* (5th version). Minneapolis, MN: Harry Benjamin International Gender Dysphoria Association. Retrieved March 31, 2005, from http://www.hbigda.org/pdf/soc5.pdf

Lorde, A. (1993). There is no hierarchy of oppressions. In R. Cleaver & P. Myers (Eds.), *Certain terror: Heterosexism, militarism, violence, and change* (pp. 17–18). Chicago: American Friends Service Committee.

Meyer, W. (Chair), Bockting, W., Cohen-Kettenis, P., Coleman, E., DiCeglie, D., Devor, H., et al. (2001). *The standards of care for gender identity disorders* (6th version). Düsseldorf, Germany: Harry Benjamin International Gender Dysphoria Association. Retrieved March 31, 2005, from http://www.hbigda.org/socv6.cfm

Moreno, A. (1997). In Amerika they call us hermaphrodites. *Chrysalis: Special Issue on Inter-sexuality.* Retrieved March 31, 2005, from http://www.libidomag.com/nakedbrunch/archive/hermaphrodites.html

Phillips, M. A. (1997). *Everything you ever wanted to know about sex change: But were afraid to ask.* Burbank, CA: Heart Corps.

Stringer, J. A. (1990). *The transsexual's survival guide to transition and beyond.* King of Prussia, PA: Creative Design Services.

Walworth, J. (2001). Transgendered workers in the organization. In L. Winfield (Ed.), *Training tough topics* (pp. 361–396). New York: American Management Association Amacom.

Wilchins, R. A. (1997). *Read my lips: Sexual subversion and the end of gender.* Ithaca, NY: Firebrand Books.

Williams, W. (1986). *Spirit and the flesh: Sexual diversity in American Indian culture.* New York: Random House.

Appendix

Professional, Web, and Other Resources

Cross-Dressing

Society for the Second Self, Inc. (TRI-ESS)
8880 Bellaire Boulevard, B2, PMB 104
Houston, TX 77036–4621
713–349–8969
http://www.tri-ess.net/

Intersex

Androgen Insensitivity Syndrome (AIS) Support Group
AISSG USA
191 University Boulevard, #507
Denver, CO 80206–4613
E-mail: sgroveman@aol.com
Web site (includes other branches): http://www.medhelp.org/www/ais

Intersex Society of North America (ISNA)
Cheryl Chase
P.O. Box 301
Petaluma, CA 94953–0301
www.isna.org

Klinefelter Syndrome Association of America
P.O. Box 93
Pine River, WI 54965
http://www.klinefeltersyndrome.org/index.html

Turner Syndrome Society
14450 TC Jester, Suite 260
Houston, TX 77014
800–365–9944
http://www.turner-syndrome-us.org/

Transgender

FTM International
5337 College Avenue, #142
Oakland, CA 94618
510–287–2646
www.ftm-intl.org

Gender Advocacy Web site
www.gender.org

Gender Public Advocacy Coalition (GenderPAC)
1638 R Street, NW, Suite 100
Washington, DC 10009–6446
202–462–6610
www.gpac.org

Harry Benjamin International Gender Dysphoria Association, Inc. (HBIGDA)
Bean Robinson, PhD, Executive Director
1300 South Second Street, Suite 180
Minneapolis, MN 55454
612–625–1500
www.hbigda.org

International Foundation for Gender Education (IFGE)
P.O. Box 540229
Waltham, MA 02454
www.ifge.org

National Transgender Advocacy Coalition (NTAC)
P.O. Box 123
Free Union, VA 22940
www.ntac.org

Parents & Friends of Lesbians & Gays (PFLAG)
1726 M Street, NW, Suite 400
Washington, DC 20036
202–467–8180
www.pflag.org

Renaissance Education Association
987 Old Eagle School Road, Suite 719
Wayne, PA 19087
610–975–9119
www.ren.org

Transgender Aging Network
49 Canterbury Circle
Vallejo, CA 94591
LoreeCD@aol.com

The Experience of People With Disabilities

People with disabilities constitute the largest minority group in the United States. The unique concerns and experiences of people with disabilities are often not considered in a cross-cultural context. Disability has been understood by many people as mobility impairment. Although mobility impairments are among the most immediately visible disabilities, not all functional impairments result in disability. Also, the majority of people with disabilities do not have mobility impairments. In recent years, people with disabilities have become more vocal in their efforts to be recognized and make the community at large aware of their issues. This effort has culminated in the Americans With Disabilities Act of the 1990s, which prohibits discrimination against people with disabilities in employment, transportation, public accommodation, communications, and activities of state and local government.

Counseling People With Disabilities: A Sociocultural Minority Group Perspective

William F. Hanjorgiris and John H. O'Neill

People with disabilities (PWD) constitute the largest minority group in the United States. Of the 276 million people living in America, it is estimated that 125 million Americans—nearly half of the population—are living with chronic disease (ranging from allergies to heart disease) or intellectual, physical, psychiatric, or sensory disability. According to the Partnership for Solutions (2001), this figure is expected to increase to 157 million by the year 2020. It is reasonable to believe that mental health professionals will increasingly be called on to provide counseling and/or mental health services for people with chronic illness or disability.

Like other minority group members, PWD are a highly diverse group of individuals who often do not resemble the young, attractive, verbal, intelligent, successful client described in the counseling literature. In addition, PWD do not often adhere to the accepted definition of an ethnic minority group described by Uswatte and Elliott (1997) and others (e.g., sharing a common country of origin, traditions, language, values, cuisine, family structure). Consequently, PWD, similar to lesbian, gay, bisexual, and transgendered community members, are excluded from the multicultural/minority group discourse and research occurring in graduate training programs. As Kemp and Mallinckrodt (1996) noted, professional training programs do not adequately prepare students to provide effective mental health services to PWD. Reeve (2000), Olkin (1999), and Deegan (2000) also considered the issue of training and stated that inadequately trained counselors may actually hurt rather than help clients with disabilities. These authors have noted that graduate psychology/counseling texts and courses fail to include a detailed discussion of the unique challenges confronted by PWD. When the challenges, concerns, and needs of PWD are mentioned, these issues are usually given cursory attention under the heading of "special populations." As a result, most counselors are unfamiliar with the discrimination, oppression, and stigma PWD routinely experience or the success, achievements, and advances made by the disability rights community. Given this fact, most mental health professionals are not equipped with the attitudes, knowledge, and skills needed to adequately conceptualize and address the concerns presented. Fortunately, disability scholars (e.g., Linton, 1998), members of the disability rights community, and others have made their voices heard, and circumstances have slowly begun to change for many PWD.

In this chapter, the two predominant approaches to understanding disability—the social constructivist and essentialist approaches—are compared and contrasted. However, the sociocultural aspects of the social constructivist approach are emphasized. The social constructivist approach recognizes that (a) questions asked and answers given about disability are always embedded in a sociohistorical context and (b) the language used to describe and discuss disability both shapes and reveals the underlying assumptions related to disability. In contrast, the essentialist approach primarily identifies disability as an inherent aspect of the individual that is ahistorical, unrelated to context, and universal. In the essentialist tradition, the problem or disability resides in the individual, and it is the individual who needs to change or adapt to the prevailing culture.

For social constructivists, limitations related to disability are seen as located in the surroundings that people encounter rather than within individuals. Thus, the limitations that PWD experience are not primarily due to their physical, mental, or emotional characteristics but to the social reactions of the surrounding dominant culture and the sociopolitical structure of society. The sociocultural, social constructivist perspective recognizes the minority group status of PWD, similar to other minority groups (e.g., African Americans, Latina/Latino Americans), and explicitly attends to the discrimination and oppression that PWD encounter as members of a devalued minority group. According to Dworkin and Dworkin (1976), a minority group can be identified by virtue of exhibiting a particular characteristic, having diminished socioeconomic and political influence, receiving pejorative treatment, and having a group awareness.

It is important for counselors to identify their personal understanding of disability and determine whether it is consistent with the social constructivist or the essentialist perspective. The choice of approach—whether made implicitly or explicitly—influences how the presenting problem is understood and conceptualized and determines the selection of goals and strategies used to reach them. Throughout this chapter, the reader is introduced to disability scholarship and the emerging field of disability studies. Parallels between the experiences of ethnic/racial/cultural minority groups and the disability community (disabled minority group) are drawn. The reader also is introduced to the knowledge, attitudes, and skills required to competently provide mental health services to PWD and people with chronic illness. In addition, the reader is challenged to consider the impact of belonging to more than one minority group (e.g., a gay Caucasian man in a wheelchair)—a situation that can lead to a compounding of problems that may overwhelm an individual's ability to cope.

Defining the Population

Who is considered disabled or not, independent of impairment or chronic illness, depends greatly on the context. The Americans With Disabilities Act of 1990 (ADA; Public Law 101-336) recognizes this contextuality, and under the ADA, a person may be considered to have a disability if he or she has an impairment that creates a functional limitation in a major life activity (e.g., reading, learning, working, traveling, walking). The functional limitations definition is common across many disability service contexts, and it is important to recognize that this definition stems from the essentialist tradition (i.e., it supports the assumption that the disability resides within the person). However, the congressional drafters of the ADA recognized that disability and its associated discrimination are often "in the eye of the beholder." As a result, people with a history of a disability (e.g., cancer, substance abuse) or people perceived to have a disability (e.g., facial scarring from burns, obesity) are also covered by the ADA. The ADA even recognizes that discrimination related to a disability can spread to those around the PWD. Consequently, those who are associated with a PWD (e.g., the life partner of an individual with HIV/AIDS or the mother of a child with mental retardation) are also protected against discrimination by the ADA.

As mentioned previously, PWD constitute the single largest minority group in the United States. For many people, the term *disability* brings to mind a person in a wheelchair (O'Keefe, 1993). This may be due, in part, to the international symbol for disability (i.e., a figure in a wheelchair). Although mobility impairments are among the most immediately visible disabilities, not all functional impairments result in disability. Also, the majority of PWD do not have mobility impairments.

Disability in its broadest sense identifies a variety of individuals who may or may not use that specific term to describe themselves or their experiences (Rauscher & McClintock, 1997). The term *disability* includes people whose disabilities are (a) perceptual (e.g., visual and hearing impairments, learning disabilities), (b) illness-related (e.g., cancer, AIDS), (c) physical (e.g., cerebral palsy, multiple sclerosis), (d) developmental (e.g., Down's syndrome), (e) psychiatric (e.g., bipolar disorder, major depression), (f) mobility-related (e.g., quadriplegia, paraplegia), and (g) environmental (e.g., asthma, allergies, environmental toxins).

The Disability Statistics Center (LaPlante, 1996) reported that approximately 38 million Americans with disabilities reported a total of 61 million disabling conditions. Many individuals identified as disabled had more than one impairment. A disabling condition was defined as any chronic health disorder, injury, or impairment that contributes to a person being limited in social or other activities. This 61 million figure comprises 42 million chronic conditions classified as physical health disorders, 16 million as impairments (e.g., orthopedic and sensory impairments, paralysis, learning disabilities, mental retardation), 2 million as mental health disorders, and about 1 million injuries not classified as impairments. Henderson and Bryan (1997) reported that most chronic disabilities are found in nine categories: (a) arthritis and rheumatism, (b) heart conditions, (c) hypertension, (d) impaired back or spine, (e) impaired lower extremities, (f) visual impairments, (g) hearing impairments, (h) diabetes, and (i) asthma. The short discussion above serves to highlight the diversity that exists in terms of who is considered to have a disability. In addition, it draws attention to the inconsistent use of terminology, groupings, and conceptualizations that exist across various scholars, authors, and researchers. The unintended consequences of these inconsistencies are that study findings cannot be compared; the emerging knowledge base becomes confusing; and research data, conclusions, recommendations, and so forth cannot be readily generalized to the larger community of PWD.

Morbidity and mortality actuarial data suggest that patterns of disability vary by gender and among racial and ethnic groups. For example, women have a higher rate of disability in general when compared with men in the general population, irrespective of racial/ethnic group membership (LaPlante, 1996). AIDS and perinatal conditions are among the top 10 killers of Hispanics but not of non-Hispanic Whites. The highest prevalence of cancer is found among Native Americans, closely followed by Blacks, and then drops considerably for Whites, Hispanics, and Asian/Pacific Islanders (Johnson et al., 1995). Patterns of illness and disability, and the reactions to illness and disability, differ across minority groups and within the dominant culture. Minority group members who also have a disability often experience a compounding of stress that is greater than the stress of managing a single devalued "difference." The multiple sources of discrimination, prejudice, stigma, and oppression that target the various sources of devalued difference within the individual can easily overwhelm the ability to cope. In addition, individuals with multiple sources of difference risk losing the support of their reference community that previously shared and celebrated the identified difference (e.g., skin color) because of the additional difference (e.g., a Black man with asthma who publicly identifies as gay). In this case, each identified difference creates a doubling or tripling of "jeopardy" or risk for the individual. However, the relative salience of any one difference or minority group identity varies from person to person and from time to time depending on context.

History of Disability

The history of PWD in Western cultures has been defined, for the most part, by the able-bodied majority and thus is the history of ableism (Griffin & McClintock, 1997). Although this history includes the influences of nondisabled reformers, supporters, and advocates who worked hard for better and more humane treatment for PWD, socially privileged individuals with disabilities who made significant contributions to society, and most recently, a powerful coalition of people who identify as disabled pushing for, or otherwise demanding, inclusion and civil rights, the primary force driving this history has been oppression. The various forms of oppression include discrimination, isolation, segregation, mistreatment, and even annihilation.

Reviewing the devalued roles that PWD have been assigned over time is an instructive methodology for obtaining an overview of the history of PWD in Western cultures (Wolfensberger, 1972). During the 13th through the 18th centuries, (1200s to 1700s) people who would be identified as having a psychiatric disability today were viewed as being possessed by the devil or evil spirits and were routinely tortured or executed. It is estimated that 100,000 people with some form of disability or mental illness were executed as witches from 1400 to 1700.

There was a brief period of enlightenment during the 18th and 19th centuries in which nondisabled reformers advocated for the educability of various disabled populations—deaf, blind, and those with mental retardation or psychiatric disabilities. These reformers were successful in establishing asylums or safe places to live and learn. However, this period was foreshortened as science replaced religion as the main source of authority in society. The new science of genetics created the eugenics scare, which continued well into the 20th century, and PWD were seen as menaces or objects of dread. It was believed that PWD threatened the contamination of the human species with bad genes, thus weakening the race (Hubbard, 1992; Huxley, 1941). As a result of this scare, (a) asylums became warehouses to segregate PWD from the nondisabled population, (b) most states and many European countries passed compulsory sterilization laws directed at PWD, and (c) Nazi Germany exterminated thousands of PWD.

Two prominent roles that PWD were likely to assume were burden of charity and object of pity. These roles have existed at least since the English Poor Laws (1598–1601) resulted in PWD being thrown out of hospitals and shelters for the poor and required to beg for survival. The object-of-pity role is still prominent today in the endless telethons that depict PWD, usually children, sympathetically in order to raise money. The burden-of-charity role is currently evident in the welfare and Social Security reform legislation that is requiring or encouraging PWD, as well as many nondisabled individuals, to go to work to relieve the taxpayers' burden.

From the mid-19th to the mid-20th centuries, PWD were often treated as objects of ridicule as they joined the amusement industry and were displayed as "freaks" or "human curiosities" in circuses and side shows.

The medicalization of disability is a relatively recent phenomenon that has led to PWD being cast into the roles of patient or client and placed under the care of health or allied health professionals. These professionals have often displayed strong paternalistic attitudes expecting PWD to yield to the advice and instruction given by the professionals. Also, within this context, disability status is equated with health status; thus, the well-being of PWD is addressed primarily in medical care, rehabilitation, and long-term health care settings. Four main misconceptions emerge from this contextual approach: (a) All PWD automatically have poor health, (b) public health should focus only on preventing disabling conditions, (c) a standard definition of disability or PWD is not needed for public health purposes, and (d) the environment plays no role in the disabling process. These misconceptions, according to *Healthy People 2010* (U.S. Department of Health and Human Services, 2000), have led to an underemphasis on health promotion and disease prevention for PWD and an increase in the occurrence of conditions secondary to the disability (medical, social, emotional, family, or community problems).

The latter part of the past century witnessed PWD taking up their status as a minority group and advocating for equal rights and control over their lives. This is best exemplified by the grassroots independent living movement that challenged the long-established paternalistic relationship between professionals and PWD. In addition, the deinstitutionalization movement fostered the dismantlement of large, dehumanizing state-run facilities for PWD and the creation of community-based services. Finally, many pieces of legislation have been passed to ensure the civil rights of PWD. The legislation culminated in the passage of the ADA in 1990.

Semantics of Disability

As the current paradigm of disability evolves from a medical model to a minority group model, the language used to describe disability changes. The new language departs from the essentialist approach and conveys different meanings by shifting the metacommunication into the social–political realm of social justice (Linton, Mello, & O'Neill, 1996). Consistent with the social constructivists' viewpoint, this section attempts to show how language shapes and reveals both underlying assumptions and overt behavior related to disability.

Much of the old language of disability is considered ableist, similar to historical terminology that is now understood to be racist or sexist. Some of the ableist language infers that PWD are more childlike, dependent, passive, miserable, and incompetent than people without disabilities. Conversely, ableist language can attribute unusual sensitivity, courage, or ability to people just because they are living with a disability.

There is an important distinction between disability and handicap even though the two terms are often used synonymously. *Disability* is a functional limitation, condition, or physical anomaly that is evident in the way a person looks, perceives the world, feels, moves, communicates, sees, hears, or processes information. The disability can be visible or invisible and exists as a relatively permanent characteristic of the individual that does not vary from one context to another. *Handicap* is the limitation experienced by an individual in certain activities or environments, and the degree of handicap is relative to the situation. Handicap emerges as the PWD interacts within environments that do not accommodate that characteristic of the person.

Distinguishing between disability and handicap emphasizes that a disability is not equally limiting in all situations and that society determines the degree of limitation imposed. Thus, a handicap is not a characteristic of the individual but of the environment, and the term *handicap* should be used when referring to the environment. For example, people who use wheelchairs are not handicapped; instead, it is inaccessible buildings that handicap people who use wheelchairs. In a similar vein, it is important to use *disability* as a noun (person with a disability) not as an adjective (disabled person) to emphasize disability as one of many characteristics of the individual instead of the defining factor in a person's identity.

Terms like *physically challenged* and *handicapable* may be well-meaning efforts to raise the perceived value of PWD, but their tone is euphemistically similar to the phrase "overcoming a disability." This phrase implies that an individual's disability no longer limits him or her because of his or her superior strength and willpower. In other words, the individual has overcome or risen above society's expectations for that PWD. Although intended to be a compliment, the implied message is that the larger group of PWD is inferior.

The use of the term *normal,* and always by implication *abnormal,* takes the communication to a level of abstraction allowing for vagueness and ambiguity, and there is seldom any opportunity to discuss the concrete, specific ways that individuals or groups differ. In such interactions, there is an assumed agreement between speaker and audience regarding what is normal that creates a sense of empathy. According to Freilich, Raybeck, and Savishinsky (1991, p. 22), this process "enhances social unity among those who feel they are normal" and excludes the "other" or abnormal. It is more precise and meaningful to discuss specific differences between people, instead of evaluating whether those differences are normal or abnormal.

PWD have not had opportunities to actively participate in society, and many social forces have undermined their capacity for self-determination. Furthermore, media portrayals of PWD routinely reinforce the stereotypes (see Norden, 1994). Consequently, it is not surprising that much of the language surrounding disability conveys passivity and victimization. The language used to depict PWD connects the lack of control to perceived incapacities and infers that sadness and misery are the by-products of the disability. Using phrases like "the person is a victim of muscular dystrophy" gives the disability life, power, and intention and disempowers the person with muscular dystrophy, leaving him or her passive and helpless. Similarly, "wheelchair bound" or "confined to a wheelchair" reinforces the stereotype of passivity, implying that the wheelchair somehow restricts the individual or holds the person prisoner. Alternative phrases like "wheelchair user" or "uses a wheelchair" are more accurate in that they imply that the user is an active person who uses the wheelchair for mobility and that the person gets in and out of the wheelchair for activities (e.g., swimming, driving a car, playing basketball, going to bed).

Finally, when a person is described as "suffering from" or "afflicted with" a certain condition, it suggests that he or she is in a perpetual state of misery without any moments of pleasure or satisfaction. It is more accurate to say that a person "has" a disability or is "living with a disability" and, if required, to describe the nature and extent of the difficulty.

Accommodation, Adjustment, and Disability Identity Development

Much of the research on adjustment to disability, particularly disability acquired later in life, has assumed that the adjustment process involves a number of distinct reaction phases—shock, anxiety, denial, depression, internalized anger, externalized hostility, acknowledgment, and final adjustment (Livneh & Antonak, 1997)—that are traversed, with the final outcome being that the person has a cohesive sense of self and is fully prepared to engage with the outside world. Following this, much current treatment provided to PWD is based on the concept of "normal" as established by the nondisabled majority. The cultural norms—and, by extension, valued goals—for functioning include good hearing and vision, physical independence and mobility, mental alertness, physical attractiveness, and the ability to communicate primarily through the written and spoken word. Deviations from these norms too often result in a loss of access to power, voice, or opportunity. Although stage models offer a useful heuristic, it is not reasonable to assume that these reaction phases must invariably occur, if they occur at all, in a fixed and orderly fashion. Phases can be reversed, omitted, or revisited as the person passes through the developmental process. Also, there is not a universal requirement that one grieve the losses associated with acquired disability. For example, people with congenital and developmental disabilities may not experience the phases of shock, anxiety, and depression because their developmental trajectories do not, per se, include a loss.

One of the most influential perspectives on adjustment to disability begins with the common assumption that disability is a misfortune that can lead to an underestimation of existing capacities or, at its most extreme, a devaluation of the whole person (Dembo, Leviton, & Wright, 1956/1975). Adjustment to or acceptance of disability within this framework requires a modification of one's values so that the real or perceived losses due to disability do not negatively affect the value placed on existing abilities. Wright (1983) proposed four changes in a person's value system that could obviate devaluation: (a) expand one's values to include events, abilities, and goals that are not in conflict with the disability; (b) deemphasize those values that are associated with physical beauty and ability relative to other values; (c) contain the spread of the disability to other aspects of identity such that it does not become the main focus of identity; and (d) use intrinsic standards to value oneself and avoid comparing oneself with others.

Vash (1981) referred to disability as a growth experience and presented disability as a three-stage route to higher consciousness. In Stage 1, there is recognition of the facts. Disability is seen as a tragedy and has negative valence. During Stage 2, acceptance of the implications of disability occurs, and it is viewed as an inconvenience that can be mastered. In Stage 3, the disability is embraced. It is seen as a gift that has contributed to the individual's growth as a person.

The three aforementioned perspectives on accommodation/adjustment to disability are primarily essentialist in their approach. They assume that disability resides within the person and that the primary locus for change is the individual. In contrast, Gill's (1997) work places heavy emphasis on environments in which people live when explaining the development of a disability identity. Gill, writing from the perspective of a psychotherapist with a disability who sees many PWD in her practice, discussed the process of achieving a sound disability identity. She claimed that this process has much in common with the path that other minority group members (e.g., African Americans, gay men, lesbians) experience as they strive to obtain a positive identity. Gill delineated four types of integration leading to a sound disability identity. The first is the desire to be part of the community through asserting one's rights to be included in all aspects of society. The second type of integration focuses on PWD connecting with each other and developing a sense of acceptance, community, culture, or coming home. The third challenge is to integrate that part of oneself that is defined by dominant culture as defective into one's identity in a positive way. The message has often been for PWD to forget or ignore the disabled parts of themselves and seek value in those parts that remain unimpaired. This leads to an incomplete self-image in which the self is split into good parts and bad parts. To reclaim their identities, PWD have had to separate from the larger culture that devalues disability while simultaneously maintaining links with the parent culture of the nondisabled.

On the basis of the minority identity developmental model of Atkinson, Morten, and Sue (1993), Grant (1996) developed and validated the Disability Identity Attitude Scale. Grant's research began to verify the theoretical musings of Gill (1997) and Vash (1981) regarding the development of a disability identity. The Disability Identity Attitude Scale documents the existence of four distinct phases of disability identity: dissociation, diffusion/dysphoria, immersion/solidarity, and introspective acceptance. During the dissociative phase, PWD protect their self-identity by not associating with others who have disabilities. The avoidance may be based on negative attitudes toward the disabled population in general, discomfort regarding these negative thoughts, or negative contact with others regarding disability issues. In the second phase of diffusion/dysphoria, PWD can experience considerable emotional distress and maintain self-identity by using certain defense mechanisms like projection, denial, displacement, and identification with the oppressor. In the third phase, immersion/solidarity, PWD begin to resolve their identity conflict by (a) trying to understand and bond with the disability community/culture and (b) distancing themselves from the dominant nondisabled community. Individuals with disabilities in the fourth phase, introspective acceptance, can integrate positive and negative experiences with both the disabled and nondisabled communities and make reality-based judgments regarding their relationships with others in the disabled and nondisabled communities.

The identity strivings of PWD have been impeded by the nagging details of oppressions. Social values that deem disability a fate worse than death discourage people from identifying as disabled individuals or seeking the company of stigmatized peers. The learned rejections of the disabled self can leave the individual in a painful state of disintegration. Inaccessible environments and transportation systems are barriers to community organizing. Poverty keeps resources beyond reach. Categorization by medicine and social services systems perpetuates the separation of PWD from each other.

Despite these difficulties, many PWD have taken the journey. It starts with the desire for social integration within the mainstream, then moves through a distancing of oneself from the nondisabled dominant culture while positively integrating the disabled self within one's identity. Finally, it involves being able to relate to the dominant society while having a sense of certainty about oneself. The disability pride and culture movements are culminating examples of the identity development process.

Best Practices

Kemp (as cited in Kemp & Mallinckrodt, 1996) stated that the minimum components of training on disability issues should include the following: education on the cultural history of PWD, including ongoing stereotypes and biases; education on related potential mental health issues, such as alienation, discrimination experiences, and relationship issues; and training in effective counseling strategies to avoid disruptions in the therapeutic alliance that result from inappropriate practitioner behaviors. The recent writings of disability scholars and the scholarly work created within the discipline of multicultural counseling can be used to assist counselors in modifying extant theories and counseling approaches when working with PWD.

O'Connor (1993) recognized the importance of not stereotyping PWD. O'Connor asserted that the possibility of stereotyping emerges anytime characteristics are aggregated and categories established to explain differences. It is incumbent on professional counselors to recognize that PWD are not a homogeneous and monolithic group but are a group populated by individuals who may share a common characteristic. In other words, generalizations made about any group should not be misunderstood as stereotypes. Many PWD have been affected by prejudice, discrimination, negative bias, and oppression, often related to lookism, ableism, paternalism, infantilization, marginalization, institutionalization, and so forth; however, each person's response may differ on the basis of a myriad of additional factors (e.g., socioeconomic status). One generalization that is likely to be true for most PWD was asserted by Longmore (1995): Unlike racial/ethnic minority groups, PWD rarely have disabled family members, neighbors, or important figures in the community who can validate their experiences, offer advice, or serve as role models. Longmore stated,

> Not having a similarly identified family to belong to, it is difficult to develop a shared experience with family and community members. Common cultural experiences bind persons in each of society's minorities. When we are with disabled peers and share our stories, a common thread of survival, restricted choices, enforced poverty, and benign oppression is found in all of them. Consequently, there is power in difference and strength within the stories. (p. 11)

Fancher (1995) examined the cultural underpinnings of the major schools of psychotherapy and treatment (i.e., psychoanalysis, behaviorism, cognitive therapy, and biological psychiatry) and determined that the four major theories of counseling are not value neutral but are derived from a Westernized perspective. Although the characteristics of autonomy, individuality, and independence are celebrated in many European American cultures, they are not as highly regarded among non-Westernized American cultures.

The current multicultural competencies for developing culturally competent skills can also serve to assist counselors in providing competent counseling services with PWD. According to the multicultural competencies, counselors must (a) develop awareness of their own assumptions, values, and biases; (b) develop an understanding of the worldview of the culturally different client; and (c) develop appropriate intervention strategies and techniques (Sue, Arrendondo, & McDavis, 1992). These competencies provide a framework for the following sections.

Counselors' Awareness of Their Own Assumptions, Values, and Biases Concerning Disability

Harper (1999) reported that children are rarely taught explicitly about liking or disliking particular physical disabilities. The process of acquiring values and attitudes toward physical disabilities occurs as part of the developmental–socialization process. Reportedly, children respond to the acculturation process by developing an increasingly complex set of expectations about people's physical appearance, dress, manners, movement, and behavior—a normative framework of historically based expectations. Children's responses to a particular disability were found to be determined by a "violation of expectations." That is, children learned a culturally informed way of responding to difference. Research by Williams, Hershenson, and Fabian (2000) revealed that all cultural groups have concepts for disability. Concepts are the mental categories that people use to classify and organize events, objects, situations, behaviors, characteristics, attributes, and so forth into meaningful and understandable events. Williams et al.'s review of the literature identified a combination of three perceived causal factors related to disability: (a) fate or predestination, (b) natural or medical causes, and (c) barriers imposed by society. Each of these causal factors can be understood, respectively, as being derived from a spiritual, essentialist, or social constructivist position.

Fine and Asch (1988) outlined a set of common assumptions that currently inform American society's perspective on disability. First, it is often assumed that disability is located solely in biology and thus disability is accepted uncritically as an independent variable. Second, when a disabled person faces problems, it is assumed that the impairment causes the problems. Third, it is assumed that the disabled person is a victim and that disability is central to the disabled person's self-concept, self-definition, social comparison, and reference groups. Finally, it is assumed that having a disability is synonymous with needing help and social support.

Linton (1998) described the evolution of social treatment of PWD throughout European and American history. Linton discussed six social orientations that influence attitudes and behaviors toward PWD. The six social orientations are as follows:

1. *Pariahs.* PWD determined by others to be pariahs become subjected to the withholding of societal resources (e.g., protection and care).
2. *Economic and Social Liability.* This orientation regarded PWD as draining precious resources and impairing the economic well-being of a society.

3. *Tolerant.* This utilization orientation permits limited participation in society to the extent that PWD assume roles for which they are suited (e.g., employing deaf workers on a noisy assembly line).

4. *Limited.* This orientation permits participation by PWD as long as they are able to adhere to the norms imposed by the nondisabled population.

5. *Laissez-Faire.* There is not explicit discrimination against PWD; however, society does not work toward accommodation, social justice, or equality. The societal attitude is to let the person do what he or she can do without any additional support.

6. *Participation and Accommodation.* This stance advocates equitable participation by all members of society. The social treatment of PWD is predicated on one of four prevailing social views of disability. According to Linton (1998), these views can be referred to as the burdensome, charitable, egalitarian, and advocacy views. Each view of PWD is linked to a particular perspective on acceptable treatment of PWD, and examples of each perspective can be easily recognized to this day (e.g., the philosophy underlying the eugenics movement and the evolution of the subspecialty of genetic counseling, special education that often results in limited education).

Reeve (2000), a counselor with a disability and a former counseling client, suggested that counselors are subject to the same negative images and stereotypes of PWD as the rest of society. Reeve stated, "The assumption that becoming disabled is psychologically devastating also implies that all disabled people will therefore need counseling to come to terms with their losses" (p. 670). Reeve believed that counselors who maintain this kind of misperception can become part of the oppressive culture that exists within and outside of the counseling room. Countertransference reactions and counselor bias present serious impediments to accurate case conceptualization and treatment planning for PWD.

Kemp and Mallinckrodt (1996) reported that one type of conceptualization error frequently occurs when counselors fail to ask about critical aspects of the client's life because the presence of a disability leads them to assume the issue is unimportant for the client when, in fact, it is crucial. This type of error is an error of omission. Conversely, errors of commission occur when counselors assume without justification that an issue should be important for a client because of a disability when, in fact, it is not. Counselors who are aware of their personal beliefs and assumptions regarding PWD and have spent the time and energy to gain the knowledge necessary to change misperceptions have taken a giant step toward gaining the skills and competence necessary for providing quality mental health services for PWD.

Understanding the Worldview of the Client With a Disability

PWD, like other minority individuals, must be able to function within two or more cultures—the majority and minority cultures. Kluckhohn and Murray (as cited in Aponte, Rivers, & Wohl, 1995) stated that bicultural adaptation, when applied to PWD, means gaining bicultural competence and developing the ability to switch between cultures when necessary.

The U.S. Department of Health and Human Services (2000) stated that disability, like race, ethnicity, and culture is a term whose definitions are culturally derived. Disability categories are primarily defined according to middle-class developmental norms. Professions come to believe that the definitions of disability deriving from the technological culture of the U.S. in fact represent universal truths. Cultures are constantly evolving in response to changes in the environment. Moreover, because culture is a learned phenomenon individuals and groups can and do change their ethnic or cultural identities and interests through such processes as migration, conversion, and assimilation or through exposure to modifying influences. Sometimes the interaction between cultures acts as a modifying factor. Life events, psychological characteristics, and other factors also can mediate cultural influences. (p. 3)

Vash (1981) stated that "being different and devalued, knowing extreme loss and pain, facing poverty and even death, force one to adopt new perspectives that might otherwise never have been tried; and each new vantage point enhances growth and knowledge" (p. 133). Vash also stated, "It is neither necessary nor desirable to accept such handicapping sequelae as no job, no friends, no sex life, no fun, and most importantly, no job!" (p. 131). Nevertheless, pervasive systems of discrimination and oppression prevent many PWD from experiencing fun, sex, and occupational fulfillment. Common barriers experienced by PWD are related to architectural, economic, social, educational, and occupational factors. Among the issues commonly faced by PWD are discrimination, alienation, and barriers to independence that affect development of coping skills and the creation of a positive self-concept. Ableism is one system of discrimination that is internalized by many PWD. Caron (1996), speaking as a member of the Barbwire Collective, stated,

All people have some sort of disability, but some know their disability and how best to live with it, while others don't. Therefore, PWD cannot be lumped together and treated homogeneously. We need first to see the person, and not the disability, and hear the person as she is able to name her own needs. (p. 22)

Caron further stated, "Little of the social and physical construction of North American society is encouraging to people who live with disabilities" (p. 23). Caron suggested that PWD and people with chronic illnesses who have internalized an ableist perspective need permission to feel anger and grief and to have safe spaces to explore and express that wide range of feelings that dwell inside. Caron also acknowledged the real threat of violence that exists for PWD. A crime that would be damaging to an able-bodied person is frequently a devastating blow to a PWD.

Tyiska (1998) reported that many PWD who have been victimized by crime have never participated in the criminal justice process, not even those who have been repeatedly and brutally victimized. According to Tyiska, persons with developmental disabilities have a 4 to 10 times higher risk of becoming crime victims than persons without a disability. Petersilia (as cited in Tyiska, 1998) reported that children with any kind of disability are more than twice as likely as nondisabled children to be physically abused and almost twice as likely to be sexually abused. Obstacles unique to the disability community that prevent involvement with the criminal justice system were found by Tyiska (1998) to include the following: (a) isolation—PWD are often segregated through institutionalization; (b) limited access—attitudinal, architectural, and transportation barriers mean PWD cannot visit criminal justice agencies and programs; (c) underreporting of crimes—this occurs because of mobility or communication barriers, the social or physical isolation of the victim, a victim's normal feelings of shame and self-blame, ignorance of the justice system, or the perpetrator is a family member or primary caregiver; (d) limited advocacy—by agencies outside of their community; (e) mythology—myths that describe PWD as "suffering," in need of "charity," and lacking the ability to make choices or determine for themselves what is personally best in all spheres of life (political, physical, mental, emotional, spiritual, sexual, financial) and worries that misfortunes of PWD are contagious; and (f) background—problems (e.g., poverty) resulting from lack of access to basic social services are compounded when PWD attempt to access the criminal justice system and may result in the victimized individual not reporting the victimization.

Employment and satisfying participation in the labor market by PWD continue to be dismal despite the lowest unemployment rates in a generation. The National Organization on Disability (NOD), founded in 1982 to promote full and equal participation of PWD in all aspects of life, has tracked the progress of PWD in employment and 9 other key quality-of-life areas. The findings of the NOD surveys—conducted during 1986, 1994, 1998, 2000, and 2004—have consistently found that PWD are at a critical disadvantage compared with other Americans on the 10 key areas of life. With respect to employment, the 1998 NOD (2004) survey of PWD found that for people between the ages of 18 and 64, 29% were employed full- or part-time. By the year 2000 survey, this had not changed. Only 29% of persons with mild/moderate disabilities were working full-time, and only 6% of people with severe disabilities were employed full-time (NOD, 2004). A recent press release (June 24, 2004) from NOD stated that the total number of PWD currently employed—full- or part-time—is at 35%. (In 1986, 33% of PWD were employed.) This number compares unfavorably with the finding that 78% of persons without disabilities are working. LaPlante (1996) reviewed data from the 1995 Bureau of the Census Current Population Survey. LaPlante reported that 67.9% of people with a work disability (11.4 million people) did not participate in the labor force. This meant they were neither working nor actively seeking work. An additional 723,000 people with work disabilities reported that they were seeking employment. When all people with work disabilities were considered, the unemployment rate for those seeking jobs was 13.4%. During the same year, the comparable unemployment rate for people without disabilities was 5.6%. The 2000 survey done by NOD also reported an unemployment rate of 13%. This survey included a randomly drawn sample of persons without disabilities. Fifty-two percent of the nondisabled group were employed full-time, and only 4% could be classified as unemployed. Thus, the unemployment and employment rates for PWD have remained persistently constant in spite of greater social awareness and legislative directives that have resulted since the passage of the ADA and in spite of a decade of high employment for every group except PWD.

French (2000) discussed the roots of denial and her personal reasons for hiding a disability while growing up. According to French, the social forces that caused her to hide her disability were (a) to avoid other people's anxiety and distress, (b) to avoid other people's disappointment and frustration, (c) to avoid other people's disbelief, (d) to avoid other people's disapproval, (e) to live up to other people's ideas of normality, (f) to avoid spoiling other people's fun, and (g) to collude with other people's pretenses. French insightfully described her desire to fit in by adapting to the norms and values of the majority culture.

Goffman's (1963) concept of stigmatized individuals helps to explain the negative reaction encountered by PWD. Goffman's concept of stigma reportedly applies to any group or individual who differs from the cultural norm (e.g., ethnic/racial minorities; gays, lesbians, bisexuals). According to Goffman (as quoted in Henderson & Bryan, 1997),

> the stigmatized individual finds himself in an arena of detailed argument and discussion concerning what he ought to think of himself. To his other troubles he must add that of being simultaneously pushed in several directions by professionals who tell him what he should do and feel about what he is and isn't. (p. 137)

For many PWD, their identities become "discredited" because their impairment is readily apparent. For others with less visible disabilities that can be hidden, their identity becomes discreditable. That is, as long as the stigma can be hidden, they may not have to endure the demeaning effects of ableism, lookism, and other prejudices, whereas those who are discredited must daily decide whether the world is responding to them or their stigma. The discreditable can engage in "passing" but with a cost. Considerable effort needs to be exerted on impression management, and once the stigma is discovered, relationships with others frequently change.

Stigma has been described as being a cognitive categorization process. Citing Jones et al., Harper (1999) reported that six dimensions have a significant influence on whether and how a perceived difference may affect the perceiver and lead to stigma. The factors contributing to stigma listed by Jones et al. included (a) concealability—Is the condition hidden or obvious? To what extent is its visibility controllable? (b) course—What pattern of change over time is shown by the condition? What is the ultimate outcome or outcomes? (c) disruptiveness—Does it block or hamper interaction and communication? (d) aesthetic qualities—To what extent does the mark make the possessor repugnant, ugly, or upsetting? and e) origin—Under what circumstances did the condition originate? Was anybody responsible for it? What was the person doing or trying to do when it occurred?

O'Connor (1993) and Edman and Kameoka (1997) recognized that disability is constructed (made meaningful) within a specific culture's illness schemas (schemas can be viewed as mental representations of the illness concept). According to schema theory, individuals process illness information in a top-down or theory-driven manner. Information is not processed objectively; instead, it is interpreted through assumptions and expectations about the illness experience. Illness schemas consist of several major components, including illness identity, time line, consequences, cause, and cure. Patients' illness concepts have been found to be related to a variety of illness behaviors among individuals with a variety of chronic illnesses (e.g., cancer, heart disease, respiratory problems, hypertension). Formal education and higher socioeconomic status may modify indigenous beliefs but may not eliminate spiritual aspects from the illness schema (Edman & Kameoka, 1997; O'Connor, 1993). Whyte and Ingstad (1998) also noted the importance of understanding the significance that people attach to various kinds of disability and the expectations they have about prognosis. Knowledge of sickness, death, and so forth is colored by perceptions of the body and how it functions. Cultural explanations (e.g., witches, spirits, pollution) resulting from improper behavior may be regarded as the causes of mental and physical impairment. In this way, cultural explanations place disability in context and make sense of it in relation to social conflicts, moral lapses, and the influence of unseen powers. They help people to understand an individual's condition in terms of the whole life situation. Causes can often focus attention on family relationships, and therefore, they have implications for the family as well as the impaired individual. Galanti (2000) emphasized the primacy of family relationships with respect to discussing patients' right to know in medical settings. Galanti reported that the custom in many cultures (e.g., Mexican, Filipino, Chinese, and Iranian) is for a patient's family to be the first to hear news about a prognosis, after which the family decides whether and how much to tell the patient. Zea, Quezada, and Belgrave (1994) reported that Latino cultural values of interdependence and strong commitment to family result in generally supportive attitudes toward PWD. However, these authors also noted that overprotectiveness on the part of family members may hinder movement toward rehabilitation and recovery.

Alberts, Sanderman, Gerstenbluth, and van den Heuvel (1998) stated that social and cultural background not only determines the choice of illness behavior (e.g., a given symptom may be perceived, evaluated, and acted on in different ways by different kinds of people) but already asserts its influence in the first phase of recognition and identification of symptoms. Anthropological and cross-cultural studies show that cultural beliefs about the nature of mental illness influence the community's view of its course and treatment. These views may affect, in turn, the actual duration of the illness. For example, Mexican Americans reportedly view people with symptoms of schizophrenia as vulnerable and ill, but they explain those symptoms as resulting from "nerves" and from being "sensitive." Complete recovery is assumed to be possible. In contrast, the majority American culture is more likely to categorize the same people as "crazy" with little or no hope of recovery. Research has illuminated the ways in which different cultures experience and express symptoms of mental illness. Because most psychiatric diagnoses are based on symptoms, those symptoms that are unique to certain cultures or subcultures (e.g., believing in devils, hearing voices of the dead, describing physical sensations in vivid metaphors not used in English) may lead clinicians unaware of this cultural characteristic to misunderstand and misdiagnose individuals from cultures different from their own. Also, many cultures tend to interpret certain bodily changes with somatic explanations, such as fatigue, muscle tension, and headache, whereas Westerners tend to focus more on psychological states. This predisposition may lead people to perceive and communicate certain classes of bodily sensations while ignoring or de-emphasizing others (Castillo, 1997). Preventive medical care is not a priority for Asian immigrants. Confucian teaching in Asian culture demands the upholding of a scrupulous public facade at all times. The cultural proscription against public admission of emotional problems is unequivocal. Seeking help would be evidence of personal weakness and suggestive of "bad blood" in the family lineage. This would bring disgrace on both seekers of help and their families. Asian Americans (e.g., Chinese, Japanese) believe that the avoidance of morbid thoughts is a way of gaining mental health. This belief system strenuously discourages many Asians and Asian Americans from participating in the Western tradition of disclosing morbid thoughts to therapists and others. Narikiyo and Kameoka (1992) reported that Japanese American cultural values also regard the use of mental health services as shameful. Among Asian people, the causes of mental illness are to be associated with organic factors, a lack of willpower, and morbid thinking. Consequently, many Asian clients will rely initially on herbalists, acupuncturists, and traditional Asian pharmacies for varying ailments and will seek Western medical/psychological help only as a last resort.

As the examples above illustrate, being ill is both an individual and a social experience. During serious illness, investigating the choices and decisions made by clients will reveal the underlying process of culture and worldview. Matsumoto (1996) stated,

> In many societies of the world, imbalance causes illness; harmony must be maintained to avoid disease and misfortune. The list of social relations that must be kept in balance includes close family, extended kin, neighbors, persons in high social status, and those in the spiritual realm. If obligations go unfulfilled, the result may be an illness or injury. The illness may be described as an infection or cancer, but the explanation for why this person at this time was susceptible to the infection includes knowledge of that unmet family obligation. It follows that for cure to be effective, both the infection must be treated, or the cancer eliminated, and the ancestor satisfied. Learning how meaning is assigned allows the clinician to place illness in the larger context of the person's life. (p. 112)

Aponte et al. (1995) discussed the broad similarities among ethnomedical (i.e., folk healing) practices. Aponte et al. asserted that all healing systems can be considered ethnomedical because they are shaped by the values, world, and self-views of the cultures in which they develop and are utilized. According to Aponte et al., ethnomedical systems share the following features: (a) There is a widespread belief that the cause of illness and misfortune has a locus external to the individual and is mostly spiritual or spiritual combined with physical aspects; (b) frequent group participation in healing rituals is often preferred to individual sessions; (c) the individual as sufferer is most often treated as if within a family or community; (d) morality, as both cause of illness and condition of recovery, is integral to healing; and (e) the healing process depends largely on nonverbal and symbolic interactions. The mind–body distinction is ignored. Themes of harmony and balance are found across ethnomedical systems of care. For example, a Navajo Indian may avoid eye contact to avoid "soul loss or theft." For orthodox Jews, hands-on care by outsiders is prohibited and can lead to illness. The practice of "coining" and "cupping," believed to draw illness out of the body, is frequently interpreted as evidence of abuse by American health professionals because the procedure raises red welts on the patient's body. In Chinese, the number four is perceived as being an ominous omen. The Chinese character for the number four is pronounced the same as the character for death. For many Asians, being assigned to a hospital or consulting room identified with a number four could lead to avoidance of services or unintended consequences for treatment (Aponte et al., 1995).

It is clear from the examples above that an understanding of cultural context, ethnicity, and worldview is important to the understanding of how illness or disability is interpreted by the client and suggests appropriate problem conceptualization and intervention strategies for the clinician.

Developing Appropriate Intervention Strategies and Techniques for PWD

Culturally responsive counseling for PWD can be considered within a number of important multicultural contexts. For example, Patterson, McKenzie, and Jenkins (1995) suggested several ways to enhance interactions with PWD. These authors recommended that counselors do the following: (a) Remember that individuals with disabilities are people, first and foremost, and that it is appropriate to acknowledge that a disability exists; (b) speak directly to the person with a disability, even when a third party (attendant, relative, interpreter) is present; (c) use common words such as *look* or *see* for individuals with visual impairments, as well as *run* or *walk* with people who use wheelchairs; and (d) offer assistance to a PWD, but one should wait until it is accepted before providing the assistance.

Similarly, the Public Interest Directorate of the American Psychological Association (APA; 1999) has produced an online document (www.apa.org) entitled *Enhancing Your Interactions With People With Disabilities*. The APA's recommendations included (a) using person-first language (e.g., woman with a disability rather than disabled woman); (b) avoiding language that sensationalizes a disability by attributing "superhuman" or "extraordinary" characteristics to the PWD or that catastrophizes the situation (e.g., struck by, afflicted with) ; (c) avoiding focusing on the disability, similar to gender, race, and so forth, unless it is relevant to the concern being addressed; (d) avoiding using verbs that suggest passivity (e.g., he's in a wheelchair); (e) maintaining the disability–disease distinction (i.e., disability is not always the result of a disease process); and (f) avoiding using euphemisms (e.g., physically challenged).

Paniagua's (1994) recommendations for beginning assessment and conducting a first session with African American clients can offer guidance, after minor modifications, to counselors providing services to a PWD. Paniagua's modified 11 points for providing service in a cross-cultural dyad are as follows:

1. Discuss apparent differences (disabled vs. nondisabled).
2. Explore the level of acculturation and level of disability identity development.
3. Avoid causal explanations of problems (recognize the impact of a disabling environment).
4. Include the church in the assessment and therapy process (include spirituality and religion).
5. Define the role of those accompanying the client (family members, significant others, personal care attendants, interpreters, etc.).
6. Begin counseling using a present-time focus.

7. Screen carefully for depression and determine whether etiology is endogenous or exogenous.
8. Avoid misdiagnosing (by failing to recognize cultural contributions to illness schemas).
9. Handle family secrets with care (and provide a safe and trusting environment for services).
10. Do not try "hard" to understand (rather, be willing to listen and learn from the PWD).
11. Emphasize strengths, not deficits.

Henderson and Bryan (1997) asserted that the principles adopted by APA's Division of Counseling Psychology for counseling women in 1979 can also provide guidelines for working with PWD. According to these APA guidelines:

1. Professional helpers must be knowledgeable about ethnic minorities and physical differences, particularly with regard to historical, psychological, and social issues.
2. Professional helpers must be aware that assumptions and precepts of theories relevant to their practice may apply differently to ethnic minorities and PWD. Professional helpers must be aware of the theories that prescribe or limit the potential of ethnic minorities and PWD.
3. After formal training, professional helpers must continue throughout their professional careers to explore and learn of issues related to ethnic minorities and PWD.
4. Professional helpers must recognize and be aware of various forms of oppression and how these interact with racism and handicapism.
5. Professional helpers must be knowledgeable and aware of verbal and nonverbal process variables (particularly with regard to power in the helping relationship) as these affect ethnic minorities and PWD in the helping relationship, so that helper–client interactions are not adversely affected. The need for shared responsibility between clients and helpers must be acknowledged and implemented.
6. Professional helpers must be capable of utilizing skills that are particularly facilitative to ethnic minorities and PWD in general and to specific clients in particular.
7. Professional helpers must ascribe to no preconceived limitations on the direction or nature of the life goals of ethnic minorities and PWD.
8. Professional helpers must be sensitive to circumstances in which it is more desirable for an ethnic minority or a PWD to be seen by a helper who is an ethnic minority or a PWD.
9. Professional helpers must use nonracist, nonablist, and other nondemeaning language in counseling/therapy, supervision, teaching, and publications.
10. Professional helpers must not engage in sexual activity with their clients.
11. Professional helpers must be aware of and continually review their own values and biases and the effect of these on their clients.
12. Professional helpers must be aware of how their personal functioning may influence their effectiveness in working with ethnic minorities and PWD. They must monitor their functioning through consultation, supervision, or therapy so that it does not adversely alter their work with ethnic minorities and PWD.
13. Professional helpers must report the presence of racism and handicapism within institutions and individuals.

Danek's (as cited in Brodwin, 1997) five recommendations to assist counselors in empowering women with disabilities are also instructive. Danek reported that counselors should strive to do the following:

1. Counter deficit thinking. Focus on what is present in a person, not on the limitation.
2. Teach self-management skills, including personal control and self-efficacy.
3. Emphasize individual choice when deciding on vocational goals. Look at productive and meaningful goals.
4. Develop strategies to overcome social isolation, such as women's support.
5. Focus on system change strategies, such as changing negative societal attitudes and beliefs toward women as well as toward PWD.

However, the best recommendation for working with PWD is offered by O'Connor (1993). O'Connor stressed the need to create partnerships with PWD and reminded counselors that PWD themselves are best equipped to offer insight into how to move forward in therapeutic partnerships. A counselor's willingness to listen and provide the client an opportunity to have a voice and exercise power and control during sessions will go a long way toward establishing an effective therapeutic alliance with clients. It will also enhance a client's quality of life by treating the client with dignity and respect

Case Study

Colin was referred for counseling services because he had become increasingly depressed, withdrawn, and isolated at age 44 after becoming paralyzed by a stroke secondary to diabetes. He arrived at the intake appointment alone via motorized wheelchair. Upon intake, Colin stated that he was "talked into" seeing a therapist by his medical doctor and physical therapist but did not believe he was having any problems that needed psychological intervention. He identified as being a male of Irish and Italian heritage who was a devout Catholic and closeted gay man. He shared that he was reluctant to leave his apartment, despite living on the first floor, because the entryway to his building was not wheelchair accessible, and he had to ask for assistance with placing a ramp over the entryway when he exited and returned to his apartment. This was offered as a partial explanation for his isolating behavior. When asked if he planned to ask the building management to erect a permanent ramp to accommodate his disability, he stated, "Why should the building have to pay for my problems?"

Colin shared that he was employed as a shift supervisor for a major construction company before having a stroke and was currently receiving a pension and disability benefits. He reported that being unemployed was not "such a big deal" because he had a source of income. He also reported that he missed the camaraderie of his coworkers and the physical demands of the job; he lamented the loss of his "buff" body. Although he learned to ambulate with a motorized wheelchair the year before, he rarely left his apartment. Contact with family and friends was limited to the telephone and Internet, and he refused to entertain visitors in his home (with the exception of visiting nurse services who were treating him for pain and management of diabetes). The majority of his day was reportedly spent watching television or sleeping. He stated, "I'm embarrassed for people to see me this way." During the intake interview, he reported that he has never been involved in a long-term intimate relationship with another man, was not sure he wanted to, and did not have much contact with the organized gay community. He shared that whenever he felt lonely, he would "hook up" with a man over the Internet or at a bar. He denied using any illicit drugs but reported daily use of alcohol. He shared that he was the youngest of three children growing up in an emotionally chaotic, alcoholic household and was frequently embarrassed by his parents' behavior in public. He stated that he worked diligently from an early age to become self-sufficient and to maintain the appearance of "normalcy" in the community. He revealed that he stopped attending Catholic mass when he began identifying as gay during his early 20s. He reported that he kept his sexual orientation a secret over the past 20 years so as not to upset his family or friends. He also feared he would be ostracized by his limited sources of social support. Colin openly worried that the "rugged" persona he actively cultivated over his lifetime would be compromised and people would regard him as an "invalid." He also feared that he would never have a satisfying sexual relationship again. Lastly, he was unable to imagine himself finding any type of satisfying employment in his future.

Case Analysis

Colin's disclosures during the initial and subsequent meetings revealed many significant concerns, with adjustment to disability being one among many. Salient concerns were revealed in comments such as "What's the use? Who would want me now anyway? I don't have a job, I've lost my body, and I'm in a wheelchair"; "I've made my bed and now I have to lie in it"; and "I'm not a man anymore. I think God has punished me and made it so I can't ever have sex again."

During the first few weeks of therapy, it became increasingly apparent that many issues, unrelated to disability but overlapping with his self-esteem, self-image, and self-concept, needed to be resolved before Colin could begin addressing lifestyle planning (Steere, Gregory, Heiny, & Butterworth, 1998) and productive, independent living (Nosek & Fuhrer, 1998) as a PWD. The approach to counseling was grounded in theoretical eclecticism. The following issues emerged as needing examination and working through: (a) coming out and developing a positive gay identity; (b) ameliorating internalized homophobia, shame, and guilt; (c) overcoming the internalized prejudice and discrimination inherent in the "ableist" mind-set (e.g., reconceptualizing notions of masculinity, normalcy, personal value); (d) resolving body-image concerns; (e) developing a satisfying spiritual connection with the Catholic church; (f) learning the skills and attitudes necessary to develop satisfying sexual and intimate relationships; (g) creating a self-concept that includes a positive masculine identity; (h) learning to identify and overcome obstacles that result in disability; (i) learning to access community resources (gay and nongay) that advocate for him and permit him to function autonomously as a gay man with a disability; and (j) establish realistic hope and faith that his life in the future will be satisfying and fulfilling. As this chapter goes to press, Colin has been in counseling for 2 years and has made considerable progress toward his goals. Initially, his concept of disability was grounded in an essentialist and spiritual mind-set. Consequently, he was unwilling to access support services or entitlements. After establishing support networks within the gay and disability communities, he's embraced a social constructivist belief system and situates his disability in the environment. He has come out to some of his family and friends and self-identifies as a gay man with a disability. However, he is reluctant to date or establish a romantic relationship because he fears rejection. He is currently seeking part-time employment and is contemplating enrolling in a local community college. Concerns that he continues to grapple with are related to fitting in, finding employment, coping with discrimination and body-image concerns, overcoming barriers (i.e., environmental, social, financial, institutional, emotional, and psychological) from within and without, waxing and waning self-esteem, and the existential meaning of life. Although Colin has made considerable progress toward his goals of finding a satisfying existence, he recognizes that there is much work remaining to be done and is fond of saying, "Doc, I'm going to take this thing one step at a time."

Summary and Conclusion

PWD often report that routine exposure to discrimination and environmental barriers is much more difficult to manage than the actual disability itself. Inaccessible and rejecting environments, limited employment opportunities, limited or no transportation options, limited opportunities to develop satisfying social contacts with other PWD and the larger disability community, societal expectations of celibacy or minimal interest in sex, a presumed lack of interest in or need for physical activity or recreation, social role assignments at odds with skills, experience, and abilities, stigmatization, discrimination, discredited identities, forced isolation, and second-class citizen status among other factors severely limit the opportunity that PWD have to create a satisfying existence. Accordingly, it is reasonable to anticipate that some PWD might seek out the services of mental health professionals outside of traditional rehabilitation centers to address concerns unrelated to acceptance of disability. Mental health practitioners are frequently called on to assist PWD in confronting and resolving the many societal impositions and obstacles encountered. Unfortunately, most training programs have yet to include disability-related topics in their curricula. Not surprisingly, graduates of these programs lack the requisite knowledge, skills, and attitudes necessary to render competent counseling services to PWD. However, the lack of disability-related topics or supervised experiences in professional training curricula does not mean the situation is bleak. Many clinicians who provide services to PWD have begun to form working collaborations with the disability community and are learning from the disability experts, PWD themselves. Others, prompted by the writings of disability scholars, the expressed needs and concerns of individual clients with disabilities, the demand for competent services by the emerging disability rights community, the revision of professional ethics codes that now hold clinicians to a minimum standard of care similar to working with other identified minority groups (e.g., older people), legislative actions such as the ADA and the personal desire on the part of individual practitioners to assist clients in the best, most informed way possible, have led to the emergence of disability studies and a disability-specific literature base. Nevertheless, much work remains to be done. Mental health practitioners who wish to work clinically with PWD must familiarize themselves with the specific concerns with which PWD often present in counseling (e.g., issues related to sexuality and sexual expression; marriage and dating; raising children; creating a healthy disability identity; disclosure of disability to others [i.e., "coming out"]; accessing entitlements and community supports; addressing barriers to personal happiness; developing assertiveness and the ability to advocate for self and others in the disability community). How well these and other issues are processed and resolved depends on the theoretical foundation, problem conceptualization, and choice of interventions utilized by each practicing clinician. With this in mind, it is important for each clinician to identify whether his or her views on disability are consistent with the essentialist or the social constructivist philosophy. In addition, research is needed to shed light on the utility of extant disability concepts, theories, and clinical lore. General guidelines delineating approaches to best practice have yet to be established. The dynamics and outcomes of various counselor–client dyadic interactions have yet to be investigated. For example, it has yet to be determined whether therapy outcomes are related to phase or level of disability identity development and the counselor's disability status. Investigations that focus on the interrelationship between the areas of race and disability, gender and disability, sexual orientation and disability, and class and disability have remained virtually untouched. Thus, the psychological impact of having dual or multiple stigmatized identities is not yet determined. For example, is an "out and proud" lesbian woman who has learned to manage routine exposure to prejudice and discrimination better able to adjust to the advent of a disabling condition than someone who is part of the mainstream and naive to prejudice and discrimination? If so, what factors account for this ability? These and many other questions remain unanswered. Yet, the prognosis is hopeful. Since the passage of the ADA, the disability community, disability scholars, social activists, and ethical, competent, and caring professionals, among others, have advocated for social justice for PWD. Among mental health practitioners, it is now understood that clinicians must gain the requisite knowledge and develop suitable skills and attitudes before providing clinical services to minority groups members, including PWD. To do otherwise would be unethical and very likely harmful to clients and the profession.

References

Alberts, J. F., Sanderman, R., Gerstenbluth, I., & van den Heuvel, W. J. A. (1998). Sociocultural variations in health-seeking behavior for everyday symptoms and chronic disorders. *Health Policy, 44,* 57–72.

American Psychological Association, Public Interest Directorate. (1999). *Enhancing your interactions with people with disabilities.* Washington, DC: Author.

Americans With Disabilities Act of 1990, Pub. L. No. 101-336, § 2, 104 Stat. 328 (1991).

Aponte, J. F., Rivers, R. Y., & Wohl, J. (1995). *Psychological interventions and cultural diversity.* Needham Heights, MA: Allyn & Bacon.

Atkinson, D. R., Morten, G., & Sue, D. W. (Eds.). (1993). *Counseling American minorities: A cross-cultural perspective* (4th ed.). Dubuque, IA: Brown.

Brodwin, M. G. (1997). Barriers to multicultural understanding: Improving university rehabilitation counselor education programs. *Disability and Diversity: New Leadership for a New Era.* Monograph retrieved March 31, 2004, from http://www.dinf.ne.jp/doc/english/US_EU/ada_e/pres_com/pres-dd/brodwin.htm

Caron, C. (1996). Making meaning out of the experiences of our lives. *Contemporary Women's Issues Database, 12,* 22–25.

Castillo, R. J. (1997). *Culture and mental illness: A client-centered approach.* New York: Brooks/Cole.

Deegan, P. E. (2000). Spirit breaking: When the helping professions hurt. *Humanistic Psychologist, 28*(1–3), 194–209.

Dembo, T., Leviton, G. L., & Wright, B. A. (1975). Adjustment to misfortune: A problem of social–psychological rehabilitation. *Rehabilitation Psychology, 22,* 1–100. (Reprinted from *Artificial Limbs,* 1956, 3, 4–62)

Dworkin, A. G., & Dworkin, R. J. (1976). *The minority report.* New York: Praeger.

Edman, J. L., & Kameoka, V. A. (1997). Cultural differences in illness schemas: An analysis of Filipino and American illness attribution. *Journal of Cross-Cultural Psychology, 28,* 252–265.

Fancher, R. T. (1995). *Cultures of healing: Correcting the image of American mental health care.* New York: Freeman.

Fine, M., & Asch, A. (1988). Disability beyond stigma: Social interaction, discrimination, and activism. *Journal of Social Issues, 44*(1), 3–21.

Freilich, M., Raybeck, D., & Savishinsky, J. (1991). *Deviance: Anthropological perspectives.* New York: Bergin & Garvey.

French, S. (2000). Can you see the rainbow? The roots of denial. In K. E. Rosenblum & T. C. Travis (Eds.), *The meaning of difference: American construction of race, sex and gender, social class and sexual orientation: A text-reader* (2nd ed., pp. 194–201). Boston: McGraw-Hill.

Galanti, G. A. (2000, May). An introduction to cultural differences. *Western Journal of Medicine, 172*(5), 335–336.

Gill, C. J. (1997). Four types of integration in disability identity development. *Journal of Vocational Rehabilitation, 9,* 39–46.

Goffman, E. (1963). *Stigma: Notes on the management of spoiled identity.* Englewood Cliffs, NJ: Prentice Hall.

Grant, S. K. (1996). Disability identity development: An exploratory investigation. *Dissertation Abstracts International, 57,* 5918. (UMI No. 9704201)

Griffin, P., & McClintock, M. (1997). Appendix 10C: History of ableism in Europe and the United States—Selected time line. In M. Adams, L. A. Bell, & P. Griffin (Eds.), *Teaching for diversity and social justice* (pp. 219–227). New York: Routledge.

Harper, D. C. (1999). Social psychology of difference: Stigma, spread, and stereotypes in childhood. *Rehabilitation Psychology, 44,* 131–144.

Henderson, G., & Bryan, W. V. (1997). *Psychosocial aspects of disability* (2nd ed.). Springfield, IL: Charles C Thomas.

Hubbard, R. (1992). Who should and who should not inhabit the earth. In R. Hubbard (Ed.), *The politics of women's biology* (pp. 179–198). New Brunswick, NJ: Rutgers University Press.

Huxley, J. (1941, August). The vital importance of eugenics. *Harpers Monthly Magazine, 163,* 324–331.

Johnson, K. W., Anderson, N. B., Bastida, E., Kramer, B. J., Williams, D., & Wong, M. (1995). Panel II: Macrosocial and environmental influences on minority health. *Health Psychology, 14,* 601–612.

Kemp, N. T., & Mallinckrodt, B. (1996). Impact of professional training on case conceptualization of clients with a disability. *Professional Psychology: Research and Practice, 27,* 378–385.

LaPlante, M. P. (1996). *Health conditions and impairments causing disability.* Retrieved March 31, 2004, from University of California, San Francisco Web site: http://www.ucsf.edu/main.php

Linton, S. (1998). *Claiming disability.* New York: New York University Press.

Linton, S., Mello, S., & O'Neill, J. (1996). *Expanding the parameters of diversity: Disability studies in the Hunter College curriculum.* New York: Hunter College, Disabilities Studies Project.

Livneh, H., & Antonak, R. F. (1997). *Psychosocial adaptation to chronic illness and disability.* Gaithersburg, MD: Aspen.

Longmore, P. K. (1995, September/October). The second phase: From disability rights to disability culture. *The Disability Rag and Resource, 16,* 4–11.

Matsumoto, D. (1996). *Culture and psychology.* Pacific Grove, CA: Brooks/Cole.

Narikiyo, T. A., & Kameoka, V. A. (1992). Attributions of mental illness and judgments about help seeking among Japanese American and White American students. *Journal of Counseling Psychology, 39,* 363–369.

National Organization on Disability. (2004). *2004 N.O.D./Harris survey document trends impacting 54 million Americans.* Retrieved April 1, 2004, from http://www.NOD.org/index.cfm:fuseaction=page.viewPage+pageID=31

Norden, M. F. (1994). *The cinema of isolation: A history of physical disability in the movies.* New Brunswick, NJ: Rutgers University Press.

Nosek, M. A., & Fuhrer, M. J. (1998). Independence among people with disabilities: A heuristic model. In D. R. Atkinson & G. Hackett (Eds.), *Counseling diverse populations* (2nd ed., pp. 141–170). New York: McGraw-Hill.

O'Connor, S. (1993). *Disability and the multicultural dialogue.* Retrieved April 1, 2004, from Syracuse University, Center on Human Policy Web site: http://thechp.syr.edu/multovw1.htm

O'Keefe, J. (1993). Disability, discrimination, and the Americans With Disabilities Act. *Consulting Psychology Journal, 45*(3), 3–9.

Olkin, R. (1999). *What psychotherapists should know about disability.* New York: Guilford Press.

Paniagua, F. A. (1994). *Assessing and treating culturally diverse clients: A practical guide.* Thousand Oaks, CA: Sage.

Partnership for Solutions. (2001). *Statistics and research prevalence: Rapid growth expected in number of Americans who have chronic conditions.* Retrieved March 31, 2004, from http://www.chronicnet.org/statistics/prevalence.htm

Patterson, J. B., McKenzie, B., & Jenkins, J. (1995). Creating accessible groups for individuals with disabilities. *Journal for Specialists in Group Work, 20,* 76–82.

Rauscher, L., & McClintock, M. (1997). Ableism curriculum design. In M. Adams, L. A. Bell, & P. Griffin (Eds.), *Teaching for diversity and social justice* (pp. 198–230). New York: Routledge.

Reeve, D. (2000). Oppression within the counseling room. *Disability and Society, 15,* 669–682.

Steere, D. E., Gregory, S. P., Heiny, R. W., & Butterworth, J. (1998). Lifestyle planning: Considerations for use with people with disabilities. In D. R. Atkinson & G. Hackett (Eds.), *Counseling diverse populations* (2nd ed., pp. 155–170). New York: McGraw-Hill.

Sue, D. W., Arrendondo, P., & McDavis, R. J. (1992). Multicultural counseling competencies and standards: A call to the profession. *Journal of Counseling & Development, 70,* 477–486.

Tyiska, C. G. (1998). *Working with victims of crime with disabilities.* Washington, DC: U.S. Department of Justice, Office for Victims of Crime.

U.S. Department of Health and Human Services. (2000, November). *Healthy People 2010: With understanding and improving health and objectives for improving health* (2 vols., 2nd ed.). Washington, DC: U.S. Government Printing Office.

Uswatte, G., & Elliott, T. R. (1997). Ethnic and minority issues in rehabilitation psychology. *Rehabilitation Psychology, 42,* 61–71.

Vash, C. L. (1981). *Springer series on rehabilitation: Vol. 1. The psychology of disability.* New York: Springer.

Whyte, S. R., & Ingstad, B. (1998). Help for people with disabilities: Do cultural differences matter? *World Health Forum, 19,* 42–46.

Williams, D. T., Hershenson, D. B., & Fabian, E. S. (2000). Causal attributions of disabilities and choice of rehabilitation approach. *Rehabilitation Counseling Bulletin, 43*(2), 106–112.

Wolfensberger, W. (1972). *The principle of normalization in human services.* Toronto, Ontario, Canada: National Institute on Mental Retardation.

Wright, B. A. (1983). *Physical disability: A psychosocial approach* (2nd ed.). New York: Harper & Row.

Zea, M. C., Quezada, T., & Belgrave, F. Z. (1994). Latino cultural values: Their role in adjustment to disability. *Journal of Social Behavior and Personality, 9*(5), 185–200.

The Experience of Socioeconomic Disadvantage

Socioeconomic disadvantage, more commonly known as poverty, transcends ethnicity, gender, religion, and ability status, affecting people from all cultural backgrounds. According to the 2000 U.S. Census, the number of people classified in "severe poverty" represented 40.7% of this population. The culture of poverty is characterized by low wages, underemployment, unemployment, little property ownership, lack of savings, and lack of food reserves. Individuals from economically disadvantaged backgrounds encounter poor or no housing, inadequate schooling, increased exposure to crime, and low-quality health care that negatively affect human development. Often isolated from mainstream society, people in the culture of poverty experience feelings of helplessness, dependence, powerlessness, and inferiority.

The Culture of Socioeconomic Disadvantage: Practical Approaches to Counseling

Claire Bienvenu and Cara J. Ramsey

Socioeconomic disadvantage, more commonly known as poverty, transcends ethnicity, gender, religion, and ability status, affecting the mental health of people from all backgrounds with specific and limiting realities. Census data indicate that 12.1% of the U.S. population was living below the official poverty thresholds in 2002 (Proctor & Dalaker, 2003). The number of people classified in "severe poverty" represented 40.7% of this population. In 1999, although the child poverty rate dropped to the lowest rate in 20 years, it was still significantly high, with 1 in 6 children living in poverty (U.S. Census Bureau, 2001). The rates of socioeconomically disadvantaged people disaggregated by race in 2002 were 8% for non-Hispanic Whites, approximately 10% for Asians, approximately 24% for Blacks, and approximately 22% for Hispanics (Proctor & Dalaker, 2003). Other demographics included a rise in families in poverty between 2001 and 2002, including married-couple families and female householder families. In fact, in 2002, half of all families in poverty were composed of a female householder and no husband present. Thus, the poverty experience varies on a number of dimensions; including age group, race/ethnicity, and family type (U.S. Census Bureau, 2001).

For counselors, who generally come from or have achieved middle- to upper-class status, it is often difficult to relate to the cultural phenomenon of poverty, the specific factors that affect the poor, and the effects of poverty on the individual. The purpose of this chapter is to look at socioeconomic disadvantage from a cross-cultural perspective. The culture of poverty and its effect on psychosocial development are examined first. Next, important issues for counseling across the socioeconomic divide are considered.

Important Characteristics of the Culture of Poverty

Lewis (1966) first discussed the need to regard poverty as a culture. According to Lewis, for the impoverished individual, life is characterized by low wages, underemployment, unemployment, little property ownership, lack of savings, and a lack of food reserves. Meeting the most basic needs of hunger and shelter are everyday concerns. Individuals from economically disadvantaged backgrounds readily encounter poor or no housing, inadequate schooling, increased exposure to crime, and low-quality health care that negatively affect psychosocial development. Often isolated from mainstream society, many poor people experience feelings of helplessness, dependence, powerlessness, and inferiority.

Psychological Dynamics of Poverty

Sarbin (1970) concluded that the following psychological outcomes are associated with poverty: present-time perspective, undifferentiated linguistic code, and external locus of control. Individuals from poor backgrounds, due to the struggle to meet everyday basic needs, experience limited practice with delay of gratification. An absence of clear-cut future-time perspective limits choice behavior for economically disadvantaged individuals.

Locus of control, a concept introduced by Rotter (1966), refers to internal values and beliefs. Individuals in the culture of poverty are more inclined to have an external locus of control, that is, to believe that external forces—luck, superstition, fate, agencies—exclusively control the rewards they receive and that their own effort and skill have little impact on rewards received (Hunt, 1970).

An external locus of control coupled with the stereotype that the poor are lazy, naturally inept, and irresponsible contribute to a sense of learned helplessness. Seligman (1975) described learned helplessness as the inability to achieve based on the expectation that events are independent of one's own responses and efforts. Low self-esteem on an individual's part or continually facing situations that are greatly beyond, or independent of, an individual's coping resources can be seen as predisposing an individual to learning helplessness as a way of maintaining self (Seligman, 1975). Individuals from low-income backgrounds may believe that others will handle difficult situations for them.

According to the 4th edition of the *Diagnostic and Statistical Manual of Mental Disorders* (American Psychiatric Association, 1994), some disorders are more prevalent among individuals from lower socioeconomic backgrounds. Alcohol and substance disorders are more commonly reported in individuals from poor backgrounds. Furthermore, Wilson (1978) maintained that the negative stresses associated with poverty are related to mental illness.

Significantly, mental retardation due to etiological factors is linked to lower socioeconomic status. Additionally, conduct disorder and antisocial personality disorder are more common among the poor. As a result of exposure to high levels of violence and gang activity, particularly in low-income inner-city areas, posttraumatic stress disorder is also prevalent in this population.

Educational Dynamics of Poverty

Poor school conditions and achievement are a common occurrence in socioeconomically disadvantaged communities. Many economically disadvantaged children attend schools of inferior quality (Education Trust, 2000). Low-income children encounter academic difficulties early in their school careers, leading to stratification at the elementary level. Initial placement filters poor students into continued stratification throughout their K–12 education. Unequal access to meaningful academic curricula results in children of the poor being underprepared for postsecondary education. Segregation ensures that these students are less likely to experience the college preparatory track associated with course work of extensive science, advanced math, foreign language, and technology (Education Trust, 2000).

In many educational settings, poor children are often the victims of a self-fulfilling prophecy. Rather than all students receiving equal treatment, studies have shown that teacher expectations for low-income students are that they will not succeed. Teachers perceive poor children as deficient in classroom behaviors known to foster learning and generally expect them to get low grades. As a result, low-income children's behavior often reflects this negative teacher expectation, resulting in poor academic achievement (Education Trust, 2000; Entwisle, Alexander, & Olson, 2000).

Within the context of the educational dynamics of poverty, it is important to note that one quarter of all children under the age of 4 years live in poverty (Children's Defense Fund, 1997). The official poverty rate for young children in the United States is 23% (National Center for Children in Poverty, 1998). This rate is the worst for all industrialized nations (Children's Defense Fund, 1997). Double jeopardy exists for poor children who, first, are exposed to more frequent family stress and other negative life conditions at home and, second, experience more serious consequences from these risks, particularly if poverty is long term (Parker, Greer, & Zuckerman, 1988). These children start at a disadvantage due to the dietary deficiencies and emotional stress of mothers in poverty before conception and during pregnancy, which can in turn hamper the fetal development of poor infants (Hunt, 1970). Many poor families are single-parent households headed by women. As a result, the children are often affected by maternal stress.

Due to the struggle to meet even the most basic needs of the family, parents of disadvantaged backgrounds often cannot provide the interactions that will assist their children in developing basic skills. A home life of extreme poverty contributes to children facing hunger, lack of sleep, and overcrowding on an ongoing basis. Obviously, these are not the optimal conditions for fostering early childhood development and learning.

Social Dynamics of Poverty

Segregation by class or income level seems to have risen over the past few decades, even while racial segregation has been declining (Jargowsky, 1996). Furthermore, the existence of community effects on education and employment outcomes has been empirically documented (Brooks-Gunn, Duncan, & Aber, 1998). Characteristics of poor communities include weaker schools, mentioned previously, and more incidents of violence, crime, drug use, gang activity, and teen pregnancy. Residential segregation has been found to be detrimental to those living in poor areas due to "spatial mismatch." Holzer (2000) argued that jobs are increasingly located in outlying suburban areas, which contributes to transportation issues and limited knowledge of employment opportunities among low-income people.

Counseling Across the Socioeconomic Divide

The psychological, educational, and social dynamics associated with economic disadvantage support the case for approaching this client group from a multicultural perspective. Counselors must adopt a culturally responsive approach to working with those living in the culture of poverty. "Research documentation concerning the inferior and biased quality of treatment to lower-class clients is historically legend" (Sue & Sue, 1990, p. 44). Members of low-income backgrounds are more frequently and more severely diagnosed, are prescribed differing treatments based solely on the class demographic, and are more often automatically placed in less demanding and noncollege preparatory tracking in education. Counselors must be aware of these tendencies and make concerted efforts to avoid attributing characteristics to the individual that instead may be characteristics of the culture of poverty.

Counseling for Empowerment

Counseling across the socioeconomic divide must be approached from an empowerment perspective. Counselors must have individual and group counseling skills that are grounded in the concept of empowerment. Empowerment is a developmental process in which people who are powerless or marginalized in some fashion become aware of how power affects their lives. They then develop the skills for gaining reasonable control over their lives that they use to help themselves and others in their community (McWhirter, 1994).

Given the personal and structural challenges that often confront economically disadvantaged people, counselors should be able to move beyond traditional counseling practice when promoting academic, career, and personal–social development. They should have the skills to engage in programmed intervention that facilitates a process in which low-income people become empowered to proactively address social and economic challenges that impede their overall development and well-being.

Adopting a Systemic Perspective

Counselors working with socioeconomically disadvantaged clients must adopt a systemic perspective with respect to their helping roles and functions. Rather than focus exclusively on the etiology of problems originating with low-income clients, the social systems in which people must develop and function must also become a center of attention for programmed intervention (Lee & Walz, 1998). Adopting a systemic perspective demands that counselors develop an understanding of important social and economic systems and how they interact to affect human development. These include the educational system, the family system, the political system, the criminal justice system, and the social welfare system.

Developing Advocacy Skills

Adopting a systemic perspective suggests advocacy. Counselors must be advocates for their low-income clients. In this role, counselors intervene in social systems on behalf of clients in ways designed to eliminate barriers to success and well-being (Lee, 1998). As advocates, counselors are systemic change agents, working to affect social systems in ways that will ultimately benefit the socioeconomically disadvantaged clients with whom they work.

Collaboration

Counselors must be able to collaborate with key stakeholders to promote the development of low-income clients. They should be able to collaborate, for example, with poor families to help them become empowered as a proactive force in the educational success of children. Such collaboration should be based on important considerations about the family life of socioeconomically disadvantaged individuals. Counselors must be sensitive to the economic and social realities of many low-income families and meet them where they are with respect to such things as language proficiency, cultural customs, and the need to meet basic needs on a daily basis.

In addition, counselors must collaborate with community stakeholders to advance the interests of socioeconomically disadvantaged clients. Counselors should be able to form alliances within the educational, business, religious, and political sectors of communities to promote client development. They should be able to broker such alliances so that they result in community resources being channeled into supporting counseling initiatives that focus on helping to empower low-income clients.

Leadership

Counselors helping to empower socioeconomically disadvantaged clients must be politically and socially active leaders in the community at large. They should seek leadership positions within strategic community organizations and institutions that affect the quality of life for young people and their families. They should be in a position to directly influence important community political decisions and policy initiatives that have a connection to the quality of education for students as well as the welfare of their families.

Darlene

Darlene, a 15-year-old from a low-income family, attends an inner-city school in a large, urban area. The oldest of five children raised by a single mother on governmental support, Darlene is meeting with the school counselor because she is considering dropping out of school when she turns 16.

"School has been real hard ever since kindergarten. I remember, some of the kids could count and say their alphabets, and knew all their colors and how to write their names on the first day! I didn't know any of that. My mama just told me to mind my teacher and to do what she told me. Boy, I was afraid my teacher would be mean like Joe, my mom's boyfriend at the time. But my teacher wasn't mean at all. She was always worrying over me and asking what was wrong. She learned that my stomachache was from being hungry, and after that she would come and meet me at the bus every day to make sure I went to the cafeteria to eat breakfast. I liked her class a lot and even got better at school after my stomach stopped hurting me. You know, I got an award for being the best dancer in the class.

I wanted to stay in her class another year. She told my mom that I needed more time to learn the basics and wanted me to go to school in the summer for a program that she said would help me. She really wanted me to learn more before first grade. We would have gone on trips and played sports and other cool stuff.

But my mom wanted me to go to second grade. I wish I would've done that program and kindergarten again. That would have been better than being in the pull out program in the first grade, repeating the second grade, and being referred to special education classes. I really dread school now because I feel stupid a lot and can't get things like math. I'm afraid I might flunk out.

So, I think I will leave school instead. My mom wants me to so I can get a job and help with the kids. My ma dropped out of high school after I was born and never went back. You know she was pregnant with my third brother when I was in kindergarten. She was and still is always worrying about money and getting food and where we going to live and what to do if we get sick. She's always waiting around to see agents for governmental assistance to help us out.

I know I don't want a baby now and have to struggle like my mom. But I hate school, so I thought that maybe if I can get a good job it will be better than school. Trouble is, I been having a hard time getting any job. A lot of jobs want you to graduate from high school."

Counseling to Help Empower Darlene

In the case of Darlene, the school counselor can help to empower her to overcome the obstacles and barriers impeding her ability to be successful in school and in life. Darlene's feelings of helplessness and failure in school, compounded by the additional stresses of poverty and responsibilities at home, limit her ability to feel empowered to achieve academically. The school counselor, therefore, must work from a systemic perspective to address not only the individual but also the institutional barriers impeding Darlene's academic, social–personal, and career development.

Building on Darlene's strengths, the counselor can help her begin to change her self-image, feel empowered, and develop the self-confidence necessary to overcome her current challenges. Exploring her interests, values, and abilities can help Darlene and the counselor to identify her strengths.

■ 349

Darlene's present-time perspective as she worries about the daily pressures of life and inability to be successful in school can be refocused as the counselor assists her in considering various options for the future. The counselor can help Darlene navigate through the decision-making process and consider the possible consequences for each potential choice she has the power to make. For example, the counselor may educate Darlene about the benefits of both a high school diploma and a postsecondary education. The counselor should also assist Darlene in exploring a variety of options and setting realistic goals while reinforcing high expectations for Darlene. Once Darlene has obtained a new perspective of herself as an individual capable of success, with an array of options, the counselor should provide her with support, encouragement, and the resources necessary to be successful in accomplishing her goals.

Advocating for Darlene and her family, the counselor can have an influence over the multiple systems affecting them. By collaborating with resources in the school and community, the counselor can link Darlene and her family with systemic supports in order to overcome the barriers associated with poverty. For example, Darlene could benefit from tutoring through the school or a local, nonprofit community agency in order to gain academic support. In addition, job skills training, apprenticeships, or internships through a school-to-work program could give Darlene additional skills that could better prepare her for the world of work. Directing Darlene into academic courses that reflect her interests and abilities, receiving support from a tutor to promote academic achievement, and developing work skills in preparation for the future can help her be successful in high school, develop an internal locus of control, feel empowered to work toward future goals, and develop interests and skills that she can use in postsecondary education or the workforce.

In addition, working as an agent of systemic change, the counselor can build partnerships with community agencies and stakeholders to provide mentors for Darlene and other economically disadvantaged students. A mentor can act as both a role model and a support system for Darlene as she sets and accomplishes future goals.

That notwithstanding, it is important to consider additional systems that affect Darlene's ability to be successful in school, such as the educational, family, and social welfare systems. Referring Darlene's mother to community resources and advocating on behalf of the family, the counselor can help to relieve some of the daily stresses of life that are influencing Darlene to consider dropping out of school. For example, Darlene's mother might benefit from a nonprofit community agency that teaches professional skills to individuals living on government support so they can be more competitive candidates on the job market. The counselor might also refer Darlene's mother to child care agencies or educational programs for her children, including free prekindergarten academic enrichment programs or after-school programs for older children. Finally, the counselor could collaborate with community partnerships or agencies in order to educate Darlene and her mother about funding postsecondary education if Darlene chooses to graduate from high school and continue her education. Presently, Darlene has considered limited options in life; however, with additional support and knowledge, Darlene can become aware of and consider other opportunities that can help her reach her full potential.

In summary, the counselor can promote Darlene's empowerment by building on her strengths, assisting her in exploring her interests and abilities, reinforcing high expectations, helping her to consider an array of life options, and assisting her in setting goals for the future. In the school setting, professional school counselors work with students from a systemic perspective in order to eliminate the multiple barriers that impede students' academic success. In Darlene's case, the counselor can not only work to assist Darlene in overcoming the personal challenges that she faces but also to advocate for Darlene in the multiple systems that affect her life. By addressing the needs of the client from a systemic perspective and linking Darlene to appropriate school and community resources, Darlene can become empowered to be successful in life and have a new outlook for the future.

Kathleen

Kathleen is a 30-year-old woman who lives in a socioeconomically disadvantaged area of Appalachia. She is unemployed and has two small children. Kathleen is separated from her husband and attempting to divorce him. She and her children are currently on welfare to meet their daily needs, as she receives no financial support from her husband, who is an unemployed steel worker.

Kathleen left her husband because he was physically and mentally abusive toward her. Her welfare caseworker has mandated that she seek counseling. Her presenting issues are that she is experiencing anxiety over ongoing threats from her husband related to her attempts to divorce him. She also seems to be in denial about the threats. In addition, she professes strong fundamentalist religious beliefs that seem to play a role in her view of the situation. She believes that her situation is God's way of punishing her for her sins. Kathleen is also concerned about her lack of education (she dropped out of high school after the tenth grade) and limited employment experience (she was a waitress for 2 years at a truck stop) and how this will affect her job opportunities as she struggles to get off welfare.

Counseling to Help Empower Kathleen

In the case of Kathleen, the counselor can use his or her skills in counseling, advocacy, and collaboration to help Kathleen develop a sense of empowerment and overcome the present challenges in her life. By counseling the individual client, advocating on her behalf, and brokering community services that offer additional support, the counselor can intervene within the various social systems affecting Kathleen's current situation.

First, considering that Kathleen is mandated to seek counseling by her welfare caseworker, it is important that the counselor develop rapport with her in order to establish a trusting, supportive relationship. This can be done by adopting an interpersonal counseling style that emphasizes a genuine, open mode of communication and honesty. The counselor should take the time to really listen to Kathleen's story and attempt to forge a solid interpersonal bond with her. The counselor can then use counseling skills from an empowerment perspective to help Kathleen gain control over her life.

The counselor should start by assessing the issues that are impeding Kathleen's sense of self-efficacy. It is evident that Kathleen is experiencing anxiety and denial with respect to her current marital situation. It is also apparent that she has an external locus of control with respect to her religious beliefs about her life situation. Compounding these issues is the fact that she has a lack of education and limited employment experience. All of this is underscored by the issues related to caring for two young children while coping with the pressures of welfare. Exploring her feelings of stress, denial, helplessness, and loss of control can help Kathleen understand her current situation and make the first steps toward change. Furthermore, by assessing and building on her strengths and assisting her in goal setting, Kathleen can gain a new perspective on her life and begin the process of empowerment.

In addition to a focus on individual counseling with Kathleen, it is incumbent on the counselor to intervene in the various social systems affecting her present situation. The aim of this systemic intervention should be to further promote Kathleen's sense of empowerment. Collaborating with community support systems is a way that the counselor can advocate on Kathleen's behalf. In doing so, she should receive the support necessary to overcome the multiple barriers that her socioeconomic status and limited life options present.

The Appalachian culture in which Kathleen resides generally offers a strong system of community support. The support often offered by family, friends, neighbors, and the community at large may be valuable resources for Kathleen to utilize during this challenging period in her life. For example, child mentor programs, such as Big Brothers/Big Sisters, and local food banks could offer support to the family. The counselor could also help Kathleen arrange legal assistance so she is safe from threats from her husband and is able to terminate the abusive relationship. Moreover, through legal assistance, Kathleen could obtain the child support entitled to her children so her family can live a more economically secure existence. In addition to helping Kathleen receive support from her local community, the counselor could also help Kathleen access government programs for support with finances, food, housing, and heath care.

Furthermore, the counselor could present Kathleen with educational options, such as a general equivalency diploma, that would advance her education. She could also be directed to agencies that specialize in job skills development. Both of these counseling strategies would be aimed at helping Kathleen become financially stable to more effectively meet her needs on a daily basis. If school and work are to be viable options, then child care for her two young children will need to be arranged. This could be done through family, friends, or community resources.

Finally, the counselor may need to ensure that Kathleen is in contact with a religious community congruent with her belief system. The religious community can serve as an important aspect of support for Kathleen. It might be beneficial for the counselor to find a way to consult with a religious leader with respect to additional pastoral counseling for Kathleen's issues, given her strong beliefs.

Conclusion

Knowledge of practical approaches to counseling individuals from socioeconomically disadvantaged backgrounds is vital in the realm of multicultural issues. Socioeconomic disadvantage, more commonly known as poverty, affects the mental health of people from all backgrounds. Counselors are urged to gain familiarity with the statistics and characteristics of the culture of poverty as well as the psychological, educational, and social dynamics involved and the consequences of these dynamics on development.

Strategies for working with those from impoverished backgrounds include counseling for empowerment, adopting a systemic perspective, developing advocacy skills, using collaboration, and taking a leadership role. These strategies, along with specific examples, are illustrated through the two case studies provided. As illustrated, in order for clients to move beyond the constraints that exist with poverty, counselors need to understand the cultural aspects of the socioeconomically disadvantaged as well as possess the willingness to expand the traditional approaches to counseling interventions.

References

American Psychiatric Association. (1994). *Diagnostic and statistical manual of mental disorders* (4th ed.). Washington, DC: Author.

Brooks-Gunn, J., Duncan, G. J., & Aber, L. (1998). *Neighborhood poverty*. New York: Russell Sage Foundation.

Children's Defense Fund. (1997). *The state of America's children*. Washington, DC: Author.

Education Trust. (2000). *National initiative for transforming school counseling summer academy for counselor educators proceedings*. Washington, DC: Author.

Entwisle, D. R., Alexander, K. L., & Olson, L. S. (2000). Summer learning and home environment. In R. D. Kahlenberg (Ed.), *A nation at risk* (pp. 9–30). New York: Century Foundation Press.

Holzer, H. J. (2000). *Career advancement prospects and strategies for low-wage minority workers.* Washington, DC: Urban Institute. Retrieved March 27, 2001, from http://www.urban.org/url.cfm?ID=410403

Hunt, J. M. (1970). Poverty versus equality of opportunity. In V. L. Allen (Ed.), *Psychological factors in poverty* (pp. 47–64). Chicago: Markham.

Jargowsky, P. (1996). *Poverty and place.* New York: Russell Sage Foundation.

Lee, C. C. (1998). Counselors as agents of social change. In C. C. Lee & G. R. Walz (Eds.), *Social action: A mandate for counselors* (pp. 3–14). Alexandria, VA: American Counseling Association.

Lee, C. C., & Walz, G. R. (Eds.). (1998). *Social action: A mandate for counselors.* Alexandria, VA: American Counseling Association.

Lewis, O. (1966). *La vida: A Puerto Rican family in the context of poverty—San Juan and New York.* New York: Random House.

McWhirter, E. H. (1994). *Counseling for empowerment.* Alexandria, VA: American Counseling Association.

National Center for Children in Poverty. (1998, Spring). Child poverty rates remain high despite booming U.S. economy. *News and Issues, 8,* 3.

Parker, S., Greer, S., & Zuckerman, B. (1988). Double jeopardy: The impact of poverty on children's development. *Pediatric Clinic of North America, 35,* 1227–1240.

Proctor, B. D., & Dalaker, J. (2003). *Poverty in the United States: 2002* (Current Population Reports, P60-222). Washington, DC: U.S. Government Printing Office.

Rotter, J. B. (1966). Generalized expectancies for internal versus external control of reinforcement. *Psychological Monographs: General and Applied, 80*(Whole No. 609).

Sarbin, T. R. (1970). The culture of poverty, social identity, and cognitive outcomes. In V. L. Allen (Ed.), *Psychological factors in poverty* (pp. 29–47). Chicago: Markham.

Seligman, M. E. P. (1975). *Helplessness.* San Francisco: Freeman.

Sue, D. W., & Sue, D. (1990). *Counseling the culturally different* (2nd ed.). New York: Wiley.

U.S. Census Bureau. (2001). *Population profile of the United States: 1999* (Current Population Reports, P23-205). Washington, DC: U.S. Government Printing Office.

Wilson, W. (1978). *The declining significance of race.* Chicago: University of Chicago Press.

Professional Issues in Multicultural Counseling

Part

III

Ethical Issues in Multicultural Counseling

24

Beth A. Durodoye

E thics in counseling in the United States have been nurtured from a Western philosophical perspective. Changing demographics have mandated that both counseling and its ensuing ethical processes be expanded to consider people and situations that have not been fully addressed in traditional formats. This chapter frames ethical issues in a multicultural context and examines strategies relevant to ethical practice with culturally diverse client populations.

For the purposes of this chapter, counseling ethnic groups of color is emphasized. Importantly, these groups do not have a monopoly on prejudice, discrimination, and oppression. Although the depth and degree may vary, negatively influenced attitudes and behaviors are experienced by women; gay, lesbian, bisexual, and transgendered persons; individuals with disabilities; poor individuals; and numerous other disenfranchised populations as well. However, it is the struggles experienced by ethnic groups of color that have historically acted as a bellwether for other marginalized groups in the United States. Additionally, multicultural counseling is defined as the therapeutic process that takes into account ethnic differences between helper and helpee in the counselor–client relationship.

The Nature of Ethics: Principle and Virtue Ethics

Ethics refers to the philosophy of morals and moral choices made by an individual within the context of his or her interactions with others. Issues involving behavior that is good or bad, right or wrong, play a part in how ethics are viewed (Remley & Herlihy, 2001). In relating this philosophy to the counseling arena, Remley and Herlihy framed it as those postures judged as good or correct that guide members of the counseling profession. Ethics in the counseling context then speaks to one's professional conduct and interactions.

There are two important principles believed to be fundamental to the moral philosophy. First, counseling as a profession has generally aligned itself with principle ethics, which is the model of ethics emphasized in medicine and bioethics (Cottone & Tarvydas, 1998). Principle ethics focuses on the application of the rules and directives that guide one's acts and choices in a given situation (Freeman, 2000). Five duties associated with principle ethics have been identified by Kitchener (1984) as follows:

1. *Autonomy.* This principle addresses one's right to self-determination. This right is also accorded to others. Counselors encourage clients to direct their own beliefs and personal courses of action.
2. *Nonmaleficence.* This concept entails doing no harm to others. The counselor shuns behaviors that intentionally hurt clients. Counselors also avoid behaviors that risk the infliction of harm on others.
3. *Beneficence.* Beneficence refers to the quality of charitableness. Counselors are obligated to contribute to the well-being of clients through good and helpful service.
4. *Justice.* Justice is associated with the idea of fairness. The counselor treats clients in an appropriate manner, all the while weighing equal versus fair versus different treatment.
5. *Fidelity.* Fidelity involves ideas surrounding faithfulness, commitment, and loyalty. The counselor respects his or her therapeutic obligations and fulfills these obligations in a trustworthy manner.

Remley and Herlihy (2001) added a sixth moral principle that has also been commonly cited in professional counseling literature, veracity, which refers to the quality of truthfulness. Counselors are expected to interface with clients in an honest and factual capacity.

Sole focus on a principle ethics perspective within a multicultural counseling context has been roundly criticized for its lack of cultural foresight. The Western views that permeate principalism are in some cases antithetical to non-Western views. Traditionally, ethnic groups of color have stressed group cooperativeness, rather than individual feats. Intuitiveness may be valued over rationality. Religion and spirituality may not be considered distinct from the self but an everyday and holistic part of the self. Meara, Schmidt, and Day (1996) related that principalism emphasizes autonomy and self-determinism over communal issues. Its rational framework de-emphasizes emotionalism. Secularism competes with spiritual wisdom. In essence, it promotes myopic ethical objectives.

The second moral principle, virtue ethics, incorporates a more global view in its vision. Virtue ethics promotes the idea that ethics are more than just the sum of moral actions. Emphasis is placed on the examination of those personal qualities that will lead one to become a better individual and a productive citizen. It is complementary, albeit totally different from a principle ethics stance (Meara et al., 1996). Virtue ethics considers counselor traits and characteristics integral to responsible practice, whereas principle ethics emphasizes the tangible, concrete, and cognitive aspects of the process (Tarvydas, 1998); virtue ethics embraces the ideals to which counselors aspire, whereas principle ethics are bound by prima facie obligations (Meara et al., 1996); virtue ethics ponders on the Aristotelian question "Who shall I be?" rather than on the question "What shall I do?" (Vasquez, 1996, p. 98).

Meara et al. (1996) delineated five characteristics of virtuous agents as well as virtues considered germane to mental health professionals. A virtuous individual (a) is motivated to do good, (b) is clear-sighted, (c) understands how affect influences the assessment of appropriate conduct, (d) is highly self-aware, and (e) is involved in the community and understands the interface between the community and political, economic, and social forces.

The four virtues are based on those believed by Meara et al. (1996) to contribute to the betterment of ethical decisions and policies and to the improvement of the character of mental health professionals.

1. *Prudence.* This is a multidimensional concept that uses planfulness, cautiousness, foresight, and good judgment. The counselor is motivated to do what is good on the basis of sound goals and the deliberate planning it takes to accomplish them.

2. *Integrity.* This virtue involves upholding one's beliefs and integrating them into judgment and action. The counselor has the ability to articulate to others his or her view of and adherence to moral values.
3. *Respectfulness.* This virtue addresses the respect accorded to another individual on the shared basis of humanness. The counselor believes in the worthiness of others yet is receptive to others' personal views on the meaning of respect and how others might wish to be respected.
4. *Benevolence.* Benevolence means wanting to do good. Counselors protect the welfare of others and contribute to the common good of society.

Meara et al. (1996) indicated that increased focus on virtues may be a reaction to what some consider the extremes of individual rights. As far as multicultural contributions are concerned, Meara et al. believed that a virtue ethics approach emphasizes self- and other awareness, focuses on similarities and differences of cultural groups, promotes the evaluation and development of virtues appropriate to the profession, and considers the inclusion of ideals as assurance that ethical behaviors take place in professional multicultural interactions. Kitchener (1996) stated that too much reliance on community-specific virtues promotes ethnocentrism. She wisely cautioned that "neither principles nor virtues are absolute guarantees of ethical responses to others" (Kitchener, 1996, p. 95).

A philosophical debate concerning the appropriateness of principle or virtue ethics in multicultural counseling can be widened to include both perspectives. One has to be right in order to act right and live right (virtue ethics). To "do the right thing," however, is not enough. Standards (principle ethics) that help to guide one on the path to good are necessary. A complementary, rather than a dichotomous, view of these approaches "provides concrete direction to virtuous traits and prudence to principles and rules" (Freeman, 2000, p. 97).

Principle and Virtue Ethics in Action

Case Study

Early one morning two counselors, one male and one female, were walking down the hallway of the local middle school where they worked. At this time of the day, the halls were usually empty of students. If students were in the halls at this time, it was at a teacher's discretion as to whether their excuse was OK.

On this particular morning, two students were coming toward both counselors from the opposite end of the hall, one after the other. The first student, a White female dressed in a cheerleader outfit, passed the counselors, who said nothing. The second student who walked by was a Latino male dressed in baggy jeans and a black T-shirt. The first counselor stopped the male student and asked him where he was going. The student said he was on his way to see a teacher about a make-up class assignment. The first counselor stepped up to the student and told him he was not allowed to be in the hallway. The student said to the counselor, "You didn't say anything to that girl when she passed by." The counselor then started to yell at the student and told him to "get some respect" and not talk back. The student became angry but said nothing while looking down at the floor. The first counselor then became upset that the student did not look at him while he was yelling. The second counselor watched the entire episode but did not say or do anything. The first counselor immediately went to the principal to report the male student's "acting out behavior." Later that day, the second counselor went alone to the principal to report her perception of the incident. She stated that she thought the behavior of the first counselor was wrong, but she was pulled to support her fellow counselor and did not want to dispute his judgment in front of the student.

Multicultural Analysis and Synthesis

The first counselor's reaction to the student is indicative of discrimination. He practiced differential and unequal treatment in terms of letting one student pass in the hall and holding the other student for further questioning. Although it is not entirely clear as to whether his motives were based on gender, ethnicity, or both, his allusions and later commentary surrounding the Latino male appeared to be biased. In addition, the first counselor automatically assumed that the boy was disrespecting him because the boy did not look directly at him when he spoke. This could or could not be the case, as traditional Latino children are taught that looking down in the face of authority is respectful and nondefying. At the very least, the principle of justice is not being served in this case.

The first counselor's report to an administrator, minus student and witness accounts, appeared self-serving. The principles of nonmaleficence and beneficence seem to have been violated as a result. A case might also be made for the first counselor's lack of veracity, as he was not truthful to himself or the student regarding his reasons, cultural or otherwise, for preventing the student from proceeding in the hall. The first counselor appeared to violate the virtue of prudence, due to his lack of good judgment in this situation. Respect was also an issue, in that the counselor appeared to work hard at intimidating the student. The first counselor's verbal interaction with the administrator seemed one-sided, which does not appear to be a benevolent act.

The second counselor in this case stood silently by while the incident took place, which is why the same principle ethics presented above could also be applied to her for the same reasons. As for virtues, the second counselor did not demonstrate prudence, respectfulness, benevolence, or integrity while "in the moment." Ironically, these same virtues seemed to propel her to constructive action following this episode.

It is important to note that although each counselor has voiced his or her story, the student's story has yet to be heard. It seems that rectification of this issue would entail a change in ineffective behaviors promoted by principle ethics. Both counselors would benefit from personal awareness and knowledge of other cultures per virtue ethics. Involving the community even on a small scale (i.e., both counselors, student, and principal) allows all voices to be heard for this one incident.

The Nature of Ethical Guidelines

A code of ethics is a written document of ethical standards and guidelines meant for particular professionals. For professional counselors, this is the American Counseling Association's *Code of Ethics and Standards of Practice* (1995). Ethical codes serve to

- Educate members of the profession about what constitutes sound, ethical conduct.
- Provide a means to ensure accountability by enforcing the standards.
- Serve as a catalyst for improving practice.
- Protect the profession from government, allowing the profession to regulate itself and function more autonomously.
- Help control internal disagreement, thus promoting stability within the profession.
- Protect practitioners—if professionals behave according to established guidelines, their behavior is more likely to be judged in compliance with accepted standards in a malpractice suit or licensing board complaint. (Remley & Herlihy, 2001, p. 9)

Ethical Guidelines and Multicultural Counseling

A counselor is first and foremost called on to protect and foster the welfare of his or her client. From a multicultural standpoint, the ACA *Code of Ethics and Standards of Practice* make it clear from inception that the issue of inclusiveness is integral to the functioning of effective counselors. The *Code's* preamble states, "Association members recognize diversity in our society and embrace a cross-cultural approach in support of the worth, dignity, potential, and uniqueness of each individual." Age, color, culture, disability, ethnic group, gender, race, religion, sexual orientation, marital status, and socioeconomic status all envelop the definition of diversity in the *Code* and are addressed in theoretical, practice, training, and research capacities (Corey, Corey, & Callanan, 1998). Subsumed within the above items are issues relating to interethnic boundaries, assessment, and training.

Select Practice Issues in Multicultural Counseling

The Counseling Relationship

The ACA *Code of Ethics* has been periodically brought to task for multicultural transgressions. References to an agenda centered on individuality and Western ideas (Burn, 1992; Corey et al., 1998; Ibrahim, 1996; Ponterotto & Casas, 1991) have been most pronounced. One such area is dual relationships. Section A.6.a. states in part,

> Counselors are aware of their influential positions with respect to clients, and they avoid exploiting the trust and dependency of clients. Counselors make every effort to avoid dual relationships with clients that could impair professional judgment or increase the risk of harm to clients. . . . When a dual relationship cannot be avoided, counselors take appropriate professional precautions such as informed consent, consultation, supervision, and documentation to ensure that judgment is not impaired and no exploitation occurs. (ACA, 1995)

Referring to the considerations of race, culture, and multiple relationships, for example, Helms and Cook (1999) stated that although they adamantly endorse the principle of doing no harm to clients, they do believe "relationships outside of the therapy room per se need not harm the client. Rather, we view such interactions, when handled properly, as extensions of the therapeutic relationship" (p. 196). Parham (1997) noted how the areas of multiple roles and dual relationships in the African American community may run counter to professional association ethical standards.

Ideas of collectiveness and interconnectedness are central to the African worldview. The ethics that guide this thinking are concerned with proper ways of being, rather than with Western principles that seek to control behavior. Traditionally, the expectation for African Americans is that they will help others. This might involve multiple roles, such as supporter, adviser, protector, and instructor. As persons interact with one another in these capacities, the positive intent of the helper is stressed over the possibility of exploitation. There is the likelihood then that a counselor would be expected to participate in multiple roles, especially if both the counselor and the client believed the relationship to be in the best interest of the client.

Parham (1997) asked the reader to contemplate a situation involving the sole African American counselor in an agency setting who, because of his or her prominence in the community, agrees to teach a multicultural class, is asked to lead a group, is mentoring African American students, and has been assigned a caseload of 12 clients (of whom several are African American). What if, in a situation that is not out of the ordinary, there is a Black student in the counselor's multicultural class who may also want to see an African American clinician and who also would like to connect with an African American mentor? Parham reminded us that a denial of any of the above services because of dual-relationship concerns may be ethically responsible according to the professional association codes while at the same time violating the standards of persons whose culture emphasizes helping others in the way that he or she knows how to do.

Evaluation, Assessment, and Interpretation

Cayleff (1986) cogently pointed out that professionals who have the power to define health and illness play an integral role in the manner in which physical and mental capabilities are perceived and how socially acceptable client roles are defined. Biased themes in mental health have witnessed ethnic minorities being psychiatrically mislabeled and treated on the basis of mainstream definitions of what is normal. An Asian American woman who resides at home with her parents is not necessarily displaying enmeshed tendencies. This may be a result of a gender role expectation in her family, of which she approves. A male international student from Nigeria who complains of being possessed by ghosts is not necessarily schizophrenic. This would ring true as well for a Mexican American individual who hears the voice of a very close but recently deceased relative. These may be self-expressive states that are condoned in these respective cultures during trying life events. All traditional Sioux folk healers should not be dismissed as "quacks." These professionals may be part of the client's support system and act as a point of therapeutic intervention in conjunction with the work of the therapist. A 7-year-old African American male who is active and disruptive in school should not automatically be classified with conduct disorder, particularly given the disparities that can exist between parents, teachers, and counselors as to the nature of the behavior.

Sue and Sue (1999) noted that in addition to differential diagnoses, ethnic minorities have tended to receive less favored treatment modalities. The ACA *Code of Ethics* speaks to the culturally sensitive and proper diagnosis of mental disorders in Section E.5.b. by stating, "Counselors recognize that culture affects the manner in which clients' problems are defined. Clients' socioeconomic and cultural experience is considered when diagnosing mental disorders" (ACA, 1995).

In 1979, a decision was rendered in California in the case of *Larry P. v. Witness for the Defense*. Litigation was focused on the disproportionate representation of minority children in educably mentally retarded special education classes (Lambert, 1981). The use of IQ tests for placement of children in these classes was ruled unconstitutional if the use of the tests resulted in the disproportionate placement of African American children. This case is a classic example of how sectors of ethnic minority populations can be tested and subsequently labeled on the basis of mainstream normative measures. Section E.6.b. of the *Code of Ethics* addresses culturally diverse populations and states, "Counselors are cautious when selecting tests for culturally diverse populations to avoid inappropriateness of testing that may be outside of socialized behavioral and cognitive patterns" (ACA, 1995). Section E.8. addresses diversity in testing and states the following:

> Counselors are cautious in using assessment techniques, making evaluations, and interpreting the performance of populations not represented in the norm group on which an instrument was standardized. They recognize the effects of age, color, culture, disability, ethnic group, gender, race, religion, sexual orientation, and socioeconomic status on test administration and interpretation and place test results in proper perspective with other relevant factors. (ACA, 1995)

It is necessary for the counselor to understand that some clients may not be familiar with the process of counseling as practiced in the United States. The counselor cannot assume that the client has been informed about his or her qualifications to work with ethnic minorities, the goals and procedures of the process, or treatment outcomes. LaFromboise, Foster, and James (1996) stated that counselors disrespect client rights if they do not fully inform clients of these and other processes.

Teaching, Training, and Supervision

A multicultural supervisory process focuses on multicultural factors among and between supervisees and their clients. Section F.1.f. of the ACA *Code of Ethics* states in part, "Counselors who offer clinical supervision services are adequately prepared in supervision methods and techniques." It must be remembered that an important part of this preparation is the ability of the supervisor to examine his or her own ethnic background and its impact on supervision interaction.

It is ironic to note that although the supervisor's multicultural awareness, knowledge, and skills have a direct influence on the awareness, knowledge, and skills of the supervisee, there is a blatant omission of attention given specifically to the counselor educator's awareness of his or her own prejudices (Brown & Landrum-Brown, 1995; Midgette & Meggert, 1991). This may be attributed to supervisors who have not had vast opportunities for comprehensive training in this area, because multiculturalism is relatively recent to the profession. Much of the literature in multicultural counseling focuses on counselor training. Midgette and Meggert stated that little is known about counselor education faculty's attitudes pertaining to multicultural concerns.

A lack of insight in this area directly violates Section A.2.b., Respecting Differences, of the ACA *Code of Ethics*, which includes but does not exhaust "learning how the counselor's own cultural/ethnic/racial identity impacts her/his values and beliefs about the counseling process." Implications for professional responsibility are also present in Section C.2.b., New Specialty Areas of Practice:

> Counselors practice in specialty areas new to them only after appropriate education, training, and supervised experience. While developing skills in new specialty areas, counselors take steps to ensure the competence of their work and to protect others from possible harm. (ACA, 1995)

Multicultural counseling is a legitimate enterprise. This means that training involves more than one class, workshop, or in-service program to be fully competent. The counselor who works behind this facade of multicultural competency is committing academic fraud. Sue and Sue (1999) reminded counseling professionals that the courage to acknowledge one's own multicultural liabilities is a strength and an ethical responsibility.

Research and Publication

McCormick (1998) raised as an ethical issue whether or not research supports counseling approaches used with First Nations (i.e., Native American) populations. He noted that counseling literature offers advice to counselors on how to work with this population but stops short of providing actual evidence that gives credence to the advice. Unless and until the counselor is familiar with the intricacies of this culture, he or she will diminish his or her effectiveness in the provision of mental health services to this population. McCormick went on to say that counselors need to be familiar with what facilitates healing for this population. Is the counselor alert and knowledgeable as to alternative intervention methods (i.e., folk healers)? Has the counselor studied the psychology of the people? Can the counselor work within a theoretical framework that interfaces a First Nations value system with research-based recommendations? Failure to speak to the idea of appreciation of the client's belief system violates the ethical principle of beneficence, as discussed earlier (Cayleff, 1986).

Ethical Decision Making

In the face of an ethical quandary, ethical codes can seem daunting. Tarvydas (1998) reframed this situation by stating that "ethical dilemmas are not so much a failure of ethical codes as a natural and appropriate juncture of recognizing the importance of professional judgment" (p. 145). The juncture that Tarvydas mentioned comprises the process of ethical decision making. It is a process that links the use of teaching and learning skills to the counselor's own intuitive inferences.

Numerous counseling and psychology models are available to guide counselors in their determination of appropriate courses of action in the wake of ethical dilemmas (Cottone & Claus, 2000). These models represent theoretical, practice-based, and specialty practice conceptualizations (Corey et al., 1998; Cottone & Claus, 2000; Gottlieb, 1993; Kitchener, 1984; Woody, 1990). In their look toward future directions for multicultural ethics, LaFromboise et al. (1996) called for the resolution of ethical problems through new or different approaches that consider culturally astute moral reasoning within social environments such as the workplace, professional organizations, and the broader community.

A seeming answer to this call lies in the emergence of postmodernism in counseling. One psychological construct borne out of this trend is social constructivism. It is a psychological idea that contends that reality is construed from the conversations of people (Nystul, 1999). Nystul (1999) noted that the theory suggests that "human experience is a highly individualized process based contextually on the interactions of cognition, social–cultural forces, language, and narratives. Knowledge and the concept of 'truth' are therefore subjective and generate the possibility of multiple realities" (p. 69). The counseling process in this context focuses on an exploration of personal narratives to elicit insights that generate new personal perspectives. The ready acknowledgment of culture and language as components to this conceptual rubric is a promising trend in the multicultural counseling arena.

A Postmodern Ethical Decision-Making Approach

Postmodernist thinking is central to Cottone's (2001) proposal of a social constructivist approach to the ethical decision-making process. Cottone (2001) noted that several decision-making models are construed as autonomous. The counselor is viewed as "a psychological 'entity' making the decision alone or within some social context" (Cottone, 2001, p. 40). An abundance of attention is paid to individual, intrapsychic, and intuitive processes, thereby de-emphasizing an interpersonal process. This is a reflection of the Western worldview that permeates the counseling process and that is in some cases antithetical to non-Western views.

The social constructivist position to ethical decision making assumes a relational emphasis that stresses group and cooperative work values that bespeak orientations integral to traditional ethnic groups of color. This position maintains that there is no absolute reality; there are several ways in which the world can be understood (e.g., the reality of the African American experience differs from that of Asians). Reality is considered to be the outcome of the interaction and construction of a people's understanding of the world; the overt racialist ideas that served to exclude people of color from counseling in the past are now considered politically incorrect, for instance. Social constructivism asserts that certain understandings prevail in a given field because they serve a function. Three highly influential forces of counseling should be considered here: psychodynamic, behavioral, and humanistic–

existential (Axelson, 1993; Goble, 1970; Pedersen, 1990). These forces dominated the counseling scene in turn, until the arrival of a fourth—multiculturalism (Essandoh, 1996; Pedersen, 1990). The focus then turned to the need for cross-cultural perspectives in counseling. Lastly, social constructivism dictates that one's understanding of the world has direct implications for one's perceptions of and responses to the environment. This may be exemplified by stating that the ethical beliefs that I hold about myself and the world are closely tied to my behavior (Gergen, 1985).

Following this mode of thought, Cottone and Claus (2000) indicated that "the social constructivism perspective of the ethical decision making takes the decision out of the 'head,' so to speak, and places it in the interactive process between people" (p. 277). It is a model that incorporates social and cultural elements into the definition of good ethical procedure. To this end, Cottone (2001) proposed an ethical decision-making model composed of five steps: (a) gathering information from each party, (b) assessing the nature of current relationships, (c) consulting professional peers and experts (this includes ethical standards and other pertinent literature), (d) negotiating when disagreement exists, and (e) responding in a consensual fashion about continued negotiation. A lack of consensus would entail continued negotiation, consensus, or possible arbitration. These steps are illuminated in the discussion following the scenario presented below.

Postmodern Ethical Decision-Making Model in Action

Case Study

A Middle Eastern graduate student went to a White counselor education faculty member for academic advising. He was interested in finding out what he would need to do in his efforts to get into the doctoral program, as his current GRE score was not high enough for admission. The student stated that he did plan to take the GRE again.

After listening to the student's story, the faculty member told him that he should look into other programs if he planned to continue in his graduate studies. The student was also told that he would not make a good counselor in the United States because he was not an American and did not speak English well enough. The student then left the office. He received a letter from the faculty member 2 weeks later informing him that his scores were such that he would not be considered for doctoral study in the program. The student later heard through some friends who were aware of his circumstances that there were some other students admitted into the doctoral program without GRE scores and that they had been told they could submit scores by the end of their first semester. The student then went to the chair of the program to report the faculty member for unethical behavior based on ACA Code of Ethics Sections A.2.a. (nondiscrimination in the counseling relationship), C.5.a. (nondiscrimination in professional responsibility), and F.2.i. (diversity in programs as related to counselor education and training programs).

Multicultural Analysis and Synthesis

For those who are uncomfortable dealing with ethnically charged subject matter, it may be easier to deal with this situation in extremes. The cultural aspect of this situation could be ignored or downplayed as simply an extraneous variable to the core issues involved. One could also focus solely on the cultural variable presented to the detriment of the entire scenario. A program chair handling this incident from a social constructivist decision model perspective, however, understands that many steps need to be taken to resolve this situation in a collective and culturally sensitive manner.

After meeting with the student, the chair would also need to meet with the professor to get her interpretation of events (gathering of information from those involved) to inform her of the situation and the contents of the student's letter. If the professor does not deny that she made statements regarding the student's citizenship status and English language proficiency (assessing nature of relationship), the chair can proceed to the next phase. If, however, there is a difference of opinion, the chair can approach a colleague with expertise in this area to get an opinion on this case, which should be presented anonymously (consulting colleagues). The chair would also need to closely reread the ethical standards cited by the student in the ACA *Code of Ethics* (consulting the ethical standards). Should the chair conclude that ethnic bias was present on the part of the professor, the chair would again meet with the faculty member to discuss this as well as the issue of the faculty member going beyond the program's boundaries as she sought to work as the sole gatekeeper of the program. The chair would point out that although the faculty member had a right to her views, these same views acted as a barrier to the provision of equitable access to the admission process for the student. The faculty member would need to be reprimanded for sending a rejection letter to the student that did not follow program protocol. The faculty member would be assigned to meet with a representative of the university's office of equity and diversity for detailed information on the do's and don'ts of the admissions process. She would also need to be reminded to work within the confines of the program's admissions committee.

Another meeting would also need to be scheduled with the student, at which he would be told that he was well within his rights to retake the GRE and apply to the program. The chair would be unable to speak to the issue of students being admitted to the program without their GRE scores, as this would be considered hearsay at this point (negotiation). It would be important to acknowledge the student for sharing his experiences with the professor and his astuteness in the use of the ethical codes to support his story. The chair would also inform the student that issues of equity and diversity raised by the cited standards were being actively addressed with the professor. Should both the professor and the student be satisfied with this intervention, the case would close, although follow-up with both parties would be encouraged. If at any point in the process there was disagreement on either side, continued negotiation and even mediation would be warranted (negotiation, consentualizing).

Clearly, this and like episodes do not have to be "swept under the rug," placated, or dealt with intrapsychically. The resolution of this case has witnessed privacy that has been maintained and a consensus drawn, all in the midst of a highly social, interactive, and culturally astute process.

Conclusion

Responsible ethical practice demands a responsible multicultural sensibility. How well do the ethical codes and the premises on which they are based fit the multicultural counseling sphere? Because ethics in multicultural counseling is a complex, challenging, and ever-changing subject, this question and its many answers will continue to reverberate throughout the profession. A given, however, is the necessity for the counselor to thread self-awareness, client awareness, awareness of the mainstream and specific population trends, and awareness of appropriate counseling procedure throughout the ethical process (Axelson, 1999). This will take time, effort, examination, follow-up, and, due to the counselor's position in the counselor–client relationship, much responsibility. Counselors who are versed in these fundamentals prepare themselves to take on ethical issues in multicultural counseling, regardless of what form they take. This is the essence of a positive contribution to the well-being of clients and society.

References

American Counseling Association. (1995). *Code of ethics and standards of practice*. Alexandria, VA: Author.

Axelson, J. A. (1993). *Counseling and development in a multicultural society* (2nd ed.). Pacific Grove, CA: Brooks/Cole.

Axelson, J. A. (1999). *Counseling and development in a multicultural society* (3rd ed.). Pacific Grove, CA: Brooks/Cole.

Brown, M. T., & Landrum-Brown, J. (1995). Counselor supervision. In J. G. Ponterotto, J. M. Casas, L. A. Suzuki, & C. M. Alexander (Eds.), *Handbook of multicultural counseling* (pp. 263–285). Thousand Oaks, CA: Sage.

Burn, D. (1992). Ethical implications in cross-cultural counseling and training. *Journal of Counseling & Development, 70*, 578–583.

Cayleff, S. E. (1986). Ethical issues in counseling gender, race, and culturally distinct groups. *Journal of Counseling & Development, 64*, 345–347.

Corey, G., Corey, M. S., & Callanan, P. (1998). *Issues and ethics in the helping professions* (5th ed.). Pacific Grove, CA: Brooks/Cole.

Cottone, R. R. (2001). A social constructivism model of ethical decision making in counseling. *Journal of Counseling & Development, 79*, 39–45.

Cottone, R. R., & Claus, R. E. (2000). Ethical decision-making models: A review of the literature. *Journal of Counseling & Development, 78*, 275–283.

Cottone, R. R., & Tarvydas, V. M. (Eds.). (1998). *Ethical and professional issues in counseling*. Upper Saddle River, NJ: Prentice Hall.

Essandoh, P. K. (1996). Multicultural counseling as the "fourth force": A call to arms. *The Counseling Psychologist, 24*, 126–137.

Freeman, S. J. (2000). *Ethics: An introduction to philosophy and practice*. Belmont, CA: Wadsworth.

Gergen, K. J. (1985). The social constructionist movement in modern psychology. *American Psychologist, 40*, 266–275.

Goble, F. (1970). *The third force*. New York: Grossman.

Gottlieb, M. C. (1993). Avoiding exploitative relationships: A decision-making model. *Psychotherapy, 30*, 41–48.

Helms, J. E., & Cook, D. A. (1999). *Using race and culture in counseling and psychotherapy: Theory and process*. Boston: Allyn & Bacon.

Ibrahim, F. A. (1996). A multicultural perspective on principle and virtue ethics. *The Counseling Psychologist, 24*, 78–85.

Kitchener, K. S. (1984). Intuition, critical evaluation, and ethical principles: The foundation for ethical decisions in counseling psychology. *The Counseling Psychologist, 12*, 43–55.

Kitchener, K. S. (1996). There is more to ethics than principles. *The Counseling Psychologist, 24*, 92–97.

LaFromboise, T. D., Foster, S., & James, A. (1996). Ethics in multicultural counseling. In P. B. Pedersen, J. G. Draguns, W. J. Lonner, & J. E. Trimble (Eds.), *Counseling across cultures* (4th ed., pp. 47–72). Thousand Oaks, CA: Sage.

Lambert, N. M. (1981). Psychological evidence in *Larry P. v. Wilson Riles*: An evaluation by a witness for the defense. *American Psychologist, 36*, 937–952.

McCormick, R. M. (1998). Ethical considerations in First Nations counselling and research. *Canadian Journal of Counselling, 32*, 284–297.

Meara, N. M., Schmidt, L. D., & Day, J. K. (1996). Principles and virtues: A foundation for ethical decisions, policies, and character. *The Counseling Psychologist, 24*, 4–77.

Midgette, T. E., & Meggert, S. S. (1991). Multicultural counseling instructions: A challenge for faculties in the 21st century. *Journal of Counseling & Development, 70*, 136–141.

Nystul, M. S. (1999). *Introduction to counseling: An art and science perspective.* New York: Allyn & Bacon.

Parham, T. A. (1997). An African-centered view of dual relationships. In B. Herlihy & G. Corey (Eds.), *Boundary issues in counseling* (pp. 109–112). Alexandria, VA: American Counseling Association.

Pedersen, P. (1990). The multicultural perspective as a forth force in counseling. *Journal of Mental Health Counseling, 12,* 93–95.

Ponterotto, J. G., & Casas, J. M. (1991). *Handbook of racial/ethnic minority counseling research.* Springfield, IL: Charles C Thomas.

Remley, T. P., & Herlihy, B. (2001). *Ethical, legal, and professional issues in counseling.* Upper Saddle River, NJ: Prentice Hall.

Sue, D. W., & Sue, D. (1999). *Counseling the culturally different: Theory and practice* (3rd ed.). New York: Wiley.

Tarvydas, V. M. (1998). Ethical decision-making processes. In R. R. Cottone & V. M. Tarvydas (Eds.), *Ethical and professional issues in counseling* (pp. 144–155). Upper Saddle River, NJ: Prentice Hall.

Vasquez, M. J. T. (1996). Will virtue ethics improve ethical conduct in multicultural settings and interactions? *The Counseling Psychologist, 24,* 98–104.

Woody, J. D. (1990). Resolving ethical concerns in clinical practice: Toward a pragmatic model. *Journal of Marriage and Family Therapy, 2,* 133–150.

Research in Multicultural Counseling: Client Needs and Counselor Competencies

Gargi Roysircar

Multicultural counseling is based on the assumptions that cultural heritage influences the worldviews of clients and counselors; that race relations, prejudice, stereotyping, and discrimination account for substantial stress in racial and ethnic minority clients; and that the exploration of racial and cultural issues is relevant to treatment. Multicultural counseling is not restricted to doing psychotherapy. It includes advocacy services, such as mentoring, tutoring, life skills coaching, empowering clients to retain their cultural identifications, psychoeducation, guidance with adaptation and daily life skills, social justice advocacy, and affirmation of biculturalism (Huynh & Roysircar, 2005; Roysircar, Gard, Hubbell, & Ortega, 2005). Along these same lines, Atkinson, Thompson, and Grant (1993) provided eight possible roles of the counselor: adviser, consultant, advocate, change agent, facilitator of indigenous support systems, facilitator of indigenous healing methods, counselor, and psychotherapist. So the expectation is that in multicultural counseling, counselors are able to help with societal problems (e.g., unemployment) as well as assist with psychological problems.

Applied within the framework of primary prevention and promotion of multicultural assets, interventions include building racial–ethnic pride, teaching social skills, and being supportive when clients refer to experiences of oppression and marginalization, wars in their country of origin, or family interactions that are different from societal expectations in the United States. Socially supportive work with clients has been shown to be effective in my own research on trainees' self-reports on their multicultural counseling competencies (Roysircar, 2003a, 2003b, 2004c; Roysircar, Webster, et al., 2003); observers' ratings of trainees' reflections on their assumptions, values, and biases (Roysircar et al., 2005); and clients' evaluations of effective counselor interactions and working alliances (Roysircar, 2004a; Roysircar et al., 2001; Sweet & Estey, 2003; Wilczak, 2003).

By definition, multicultural counseling competence (Arredondo et al., 1996; Roysircar, Arredondo, Fuertes, Ponterotto, & Toporek, 2003; Roysircar, Sandhu, & Bibbins, 2003; Sue, Arredondo, & McDavis, 1992) pertains to the effective delivery of counseling service that includes a broad constellation of awareness of counselor attitudes and values, knowledge, and skills. Chief among its components are the following:

- having good self-awareness of the attitudes or worldviews into which the counselor has been socialized;
- recognizing and being sensitive to the client's worldviews and attitudes;
- having knowledge of the cultural groups with which one works;
- understanding the effects of racial identity, acculturation, ethnic identity, minority stress, and coping with minority status on the individual;
- understanding the impact of sociopolitical influences on minority persons;
- possessing proficiencies, such as bilingualism, to work with culturally different groups; and
- having the ability to be culturally responsive and to translate mainstream interventions into multiculturally sensitive strategies, skills, and interactional proficiencies.

Thus, multicultural competence is a standard that counselors should be able to work effectively with culturally diverse clients (Coleman, 2003; Fuertes & Ponterotto, 2003; Toporek, 2003). The focus is on the counselor's actual clinical interactions, relationships, skills, and ultimately outcome.

The first section of this chapter discusses research concerning the impact of the counselor on the minority client in terms of the counselor's cultural and racial awareness, counselor's application of cultural knowledge, counselor's recognition of client–counselor racial dynamics, and counselor's interface with minority client mistrust. The second section addresses related research on multicultural counseling competencies and its future directions.

Counselors' Cultural Sensitivity to Minority Clients

Several studies since the 1990s have investigated the counseling process when counselors have used culturally responsive approaches. These are as follows.

Cultural and Racial Awareness

In a study that interviewed White American therapists of African American clients, representing nine dyads, therapists' awareness of the privilege associated with being White in the United States, the historical legacy of White oppression of others, and the historical and contemporary existence of racism was significant (Fuertes, Mueller, Chauhan, Walker, & Ladany, 2002). Skills that seemed to be used by the therapists were also ones of awareness—of having been oppressed in some way themselves, of having been oppressors, of having a one-up position with their clients, and of recognizing that the reality of racism and tension between White Americans and African Americans is reflected in the counseling hour. Specifically, skills included being direct but sensitive to issues pertaining to race, conveying a sense of openness, and showing acceptance of the historic effects of racism. Therapists had knowledge of racial identity and its central role in their clients' lives, and they were aware of and able to make statements about their clients' racial identity. Therapists approached in a sensitive way other variables salient to the clients' identity, such as gender, socioeconomic status, physical disability, and sexual orientation. All nine therapists reported appreciable gains for their clients, including lifts in depression, reduced anxiety, and decrease in panic attacks. They reported in clients an increase in insight and racial identity awareness and a better sense of direction. Therapists reported better rapport, increased intimacy, increased disclosure on the part of their clients, some risk-taking with respect to the clients' disclosure of aspects of their lives never before discussed, and overall improved client participation and involvement in therapy. It is important to note that the therapists did not develop tunnel vision by focusing exclusively on the race of the clients or by overestimating its relevance to the exclusion of other factors. In fact, therapists described their clients' interpersonal concerns as deeply intertwined with factors such as sexism, homophobia, and poverty. Whereas Fuertes et al. (2002) indicated the significance of therapists' awareness of their own White racial identity in their interface with their African American clients, Holcomb-McCoy and Meyers (1999) found in their survey study that professional counselors of the American Counseling Association had self-reported low awareness of racial identity issues.

Whereas Fuertes et al.'s (2002) study gave therapists' perspectives about their racial sensitivity when counseling, another interview study (Pope-Davis et al., 2002) provided clients' ($N = 10$) perceptions of their experiences in multicultural counseling. Each client identified multicultural counseling competence as critical; however, in situations in which the clients felt that other needs were more significant, they forgave their counselors for a lack of cultural knowledge or sensitivity. These clients worked to adapt to their counselors' abilities and approaches, limiting the amount of material that they were willing to discuss with their counselors. The study highlighted the integral role that clients may play in determining how, what, and when cultural issues might be explored in therapy. A key finding was that clients whose counselors lacked in cultural understanding blamed themselves, and thus, they may have accumulated additional psychological baggage from therapy. An important implication was that counselors could have benefited from feedback from their clients regarding their effectiveness. The types of cultural knowledge that clients identified as important included culturally specific knowledge of family relationships and expectations, racism and discrimination, acculturation, sexism and gender role issues, communication styles, cultural beliefs about counseling, cultural issues related to sexual orientation, ethnic and cultural identity, and norms for behavior (Pope-Davis et al., 2002). The significance of these topics to minority clients was also found in client feedback included in recently published case studies (DeFrino, 2003; Roysircar, 2004a; Spanakis, 2004; Sweet & Estey, 2003; Wilczak, 2003).

Cultural responsiveness results from shared attitudes between the counselor and the client. Counselor trainees' 8th session, out of 10 counseling sessions with language minority (English as a second language [ESL]) middle school students, was randomly chosen for taping; these tapes were qualitatively analyzed (Roysircar et al., 2001). Analyses completed consensually by a team indicated that as counselors guided the ESL students through a structured drawing exercise and made probing remarks and reflections that were affirmative of the students' thoughts and behaviors, the students made many self-disclosures, some of which were intimate. At termination, the students gave positive evaluations on satisfaction, perceived effectiveness, well-being, and help-seeking attitudes. Similarly, in another study (Pomales, Claiborn, & LaFromboise, 1986), African American college students rated racially sensitive counselors higher on credibility. Racial sensitivity meant that the counselor discussed racial aspects of the client's problem.

Wade and Bernstein (1991) investigated African American female clients' perceptions of experienced African American counselors and White counselors who either received cultural sensitivity training or did not receive this type of training. Training in cultural sensitivity included a summary of concerns that might be presented by culturally diverse clients, discussion on counselor self-awareness and minority clients, and discussion on the acquisition of skills through experiential training. After three sessions, client ratings of counselors who had received cultural sensitivity training were significantly higher for credibility, empathy, unconditional regard, and client satisfaction compared with client ratings of counselors who had not received such training. Even though half of the counselors were White and half Black, positive client ratings were not affected by counselor race but rather by sensitivity. However, it is to be noted that more clients returned to see African American counselors than

White counselors, supporting what has been demonstrated by the empirical literature that many African Americans prefer African American counselors.

Cultural Knowledge Tailored to the Individual

Counselors must have some knowledge of the clients' culture and its history, which, however, was found to be lacking in professional counselors of the American Counseling Association in a survey study (Holcomb-McCoy & Meyers, 1999). Nonetheless, culture-specific knowledge about ethnic minority groups must not be uncritically applied to a client who comes from an ethnic minority or culturally diverse group (for counselor overgeneralizations, see DeFrino, 2003; Roysircar et al., 2005; Uchison, 2003; Wilczak, 2003). Constantine and Ladany (2001) have added understanding unique client variables as a multicultural counseling competency. In my own clinical writings (Roysircar, 2003a, 2004b), I have said that the multiculturally competent counselor does not resolve the client's identity problems but explores, processes, and holds the paradox between a person's individual identity and multiple reference-group identifications (ethnic; first language; lesbian, gay, bisexual, or transgender; gender role; class) and contexts.

Cultural Stereotypes

An example of cultural stereotyping is the tendency to see Asians as collectivistic in their thoughts and attitudes. In reality, with regard to coping responses, collectivistic coping and individualistic coping might be dependent on Chinese immigrants' level of acculturation, generation status, length of stay in the United States, English language proficiency, and availability of social resources (Kuo & Roysircar, 2004; Kuo, Roysircar, & Newby-Clark, 2004). Similarly, in another study, Hong Kong college students were both individualistic and collectivistic. They made internal (self-referenced) and external (other-referenced) attributions about causes of mental health problems, although they mostly used internal attributions (self-responsibility) for curing the problems, which might also involve using interpersonal resources (Luk & Bond, 1992).

Likewise, although Japanese Americans were more likely than White Americans to view mental illness as having social causes, they wanted to resolve the problems on their own, possibly with help from family and friends (Narikiyo & Kameoka, 1992). Both Anglo-American and Japanese subjects (Kawanishi, 1995) agreed that successful coping depends mostly on one's own effort. However, Japanese subjects also agreed much more strongly than White Americans with the statements that successful coping depends mostly on luck and stressful events are brought on by bad luck. Thus, internal attributions were not exclusive of external attributions and vice versa. Research is needed to study complex interactions of individualism and collectivism with various cultural and individual variables, such that the application of cultural knowledge in counseling Asian Americans is not stereotypic.

Cultural Knowledge Translated Into Strategies

Sodowsky (1991) tested whether applications of cultural understanding would affect Asian Indian international students' perception of counselor credibility. In one tape, a White counselor tailored his case conceptualization, treatment methods, and goals to the family values of an Asian Indian male international student client. The client presented himself as a responsible person but expressed hesitation in changing his major from computer science to the social sciences. The client referred to family expectations back in India and to his U.S. relatives' support while he attended college in the United States. In a second tape, the same counselor used a practice based on Western values about personal needs and choice with regard to vocational interests. Asian Indian international students, South Korean international students, and White American students were randomly assigned to watch one of the two tapes. Asian Indian students rated the counselor using culturally sensitive strategies as significantly more expert and trustworthy than the culturally discrepant counselor. White Americans rated the counselor using mainstream methods as significantly more expert and trustworthy. There was an interaction effect, with Asian Indian scores being higher than White American scores for the culturally sensitive counselor. Koreans did not react as Asian Indians, suggesting that Asian international student groups might hold some distinct values that are different from each other's as well as from those of the host society.

LaFromboise (1992) developed five vignettes of American Indian families with few lines of initial dialogue between a client and a counselor. Subsequently, the counselor made three sets of responses: affinity attempts, clarifications, and helpfulness. Affinity attempts include the counselor disclosing personal information to establish a connection with the client. The intention of such an affinity response is to be submissive and friendly. Clarifications establish exactly what is being said and felt for both the client and the counselor. The intention of clarification is to be friendly and submissive. Helpfulness refers to making suggestions or offering advice. The intention of helpfulness is to be dominant and friendly. American Indians rated on various scales the impressions that the three sets of responses made on them. Affinity responses clustered around affiliation, agreeableness, and nurturance domains. Affinity statements were seen as submissive, with counselors remaining affiliated with clients (when differences would yield confrontation). Clarification responses clustered on agreeableness and nurturance domains and were seen as friendly and submissive counselor intentions. Helpful responses clustered around competitive, mistrusting, and hostile domains and were seen as a negative counselor intention. The findings agreed with earlier studies in the 1980s that American Indians pay more attention to potential indicators of insincerity in a counselor. The helpful response, although intending to show friendly dominance, was perceived negatively. The implication is that a counselor who makes suggestions is perceived as hostile, manipulative, and competitive by a person who comes from an oppressed group that has been deceived by people in power.

Trimble, Fleming, Beauvais, and Jumper-Thurman (1996) stated that knowledge and awareness of American Indian cultural legacy and historical and present-day influences on Indian life are essential to counseling effectiveness. Such knowledge is translated into competent counseling strategies. For example, the therapist develops comfort with silence, as silence often represents the client's acknowledgment that what the therapist has said requires considered thought and reflection. It is seen as a gesture of respect and careful listening and not as classic "resistance."

Counselors must have knowledge about the cultures with which they work. They cannot expect their clients to educate them when, in fact, the clients have come to them for help. Counselors could consult with professionals who have expertise in specific cultures. Other than counselors and psychologists, the experts could include anthropologists, historians, political scientists, people in international industry and businesses, and well-traveled individuals. However, asking clients to share their understanding of their cultural beliefs, religion, and practices may translate into client empowerment as well as into the counselor's understanding of the clients' worldview. Engaging the client to describe cultural issues of significance to him or her also helps in the assessment of the client's unique characteristics interfacing with multiple cultural contexts and identifications.

Racial Dynamics of the Client and the Counselor

Richardson and Helms (1994) examined the perceptions that Black men have of parallel dyads involving a Black male client and a White male counselor. Parallel dyads are defined as involving a client and a counselor who share similar racial identity attitudes relative to Blacks and Whites as reference groups. In this case, the White counselor had autonomy attitudes, and the Black client had internalization attitudes. These two sets are parallel attitudes; they are positive racial attitudes and are at the most advanced developmental level. In one audiotaped dyad, the client reported a problem with coworkers' insensitivity to cultural differences; in the other dyad, the client reported being cut from the university basketball team because of the client's race. Black undergraduate students in a predominantly White university were shown the tapes in a counterbalanced order, in which half of the participants heard each of the tapes first. Participants' racial identity attitudes predicted their reactions to the counseling session. Higher levels of participant encounter attitudes, which were developmentally less mature than the attitudes of the counselor and the client indicated in the tape, were predictive of negative reactions to the counseling, that is, the higher the participants' encounter attitudes, the more anxious the participants felt. Richardson and Helms stated that participants may have responded to the counselor in a negative manner when their encounter attitudes were high because the counselor's balanced, integrated manner of addressing race-related concerns did not focus on issues of confusion associated with the encounter stage.

Helms's (1995) model of Black–White counseling interactions proposes that it is the interface of the counselor's and the client's racial identity attitudes rather than application of cultural knowledge or multicultural skills that influences client perceptions of the counseling process. The implication is that counselors, first, must understand not only how racial identity attitudes affect the Black client but also how their own White racial identity influences counseling dynamics. Second, counselors must be able to accurately assess racial identity variables that influence the counseling relationship. Third, counselors need to use interventions that are sensitive to the racial identity development process while addressing race-related concerns of Black clients.

Client Mistrust

Watkins and Terrel (1988) showed that Black people who scored high on the Cultural Mistrust Inventory expected less from counseling regardless of counselor race. In the 1990s, client mistrust became a salient variable of interest because of research interest in client self-disclosure and premature termination.

Thompson, Worthington, and Atkinson (1994) studied the interactions of counselor race-based versus universal statements, counselor race (Black or White), and client mistrust. Although Black clients found counselors in both statement conditions equally credible, they were more willing to self-refer and to disclose more intimately when the counselor responded with racial content than were clients who were exposed to universal content. Low levels of mistrust were associated with a greater number of disclosing statements to Black counselors, whereas high levels of mistrust were associated with a lesser number of disclosing statements to White counselors. It is important to note the interaction among mistrust, the race of the counselor, and the race of the client.

Because interpersonal trust is a constant concern in the client–counselor multicultural relationship, LaFromboise and Dixon (1981) specified seven negative counselor responses that create an atmosphere of distrust for American Indians: (a) an abrupt shift in topic, (b) purposeful inaccurate paraphrasing, (c) mood and interest change, (d) a break in confidentiality, (e) exposure of a hidden agenda, (f) a stereotyping statement, and (g) a broken promise. The antithetical trustworthy responses included being attentive, structured, directive (mainstream responses), and respectful of cultural identity (culture-specific response). American Indian students (LaFromboise & Dixon, 1981) clearly gave more positive ratings to both the American Indian counselor and the White counselor who demonstrated trust-worthy behaviors. However, generalization from this study is cautioned regarding the importance or nonimportance of ethnic similarity between the counselor and the client because the stimulus sample of counselors was limited to one non-Indian and one Indian counselor.

It is suggested that both Black and White counselors have to contend with the mistrust factor of Black clients, with high levels of mistrust being related to superficial exploration and potential early termination. This suggestion is in line with the writings of authors who propose an emic or culture-specific approach to counseling. In particular, Black psychologists have advocated this approach to assist troubled Black clients in the context of a deracinated social climate, a climate that minimizes or even questions the significance of the Black experience as a positive or growth-promoting aspect of their psyche. Also from the emic framework, it can be argued that studying perceived counselor credibility may be limited in explaining the multicultural client–counselor process. For example, Black clients may perceive highly skilled counselors, trained in conventional relationship skills, as credible. However, these same counselors may not elicit deep disclosure for meaningful work with Blacks because they are not racially sensitive, such as addressing issues of race.

Implications

In the studies reviewed to this point, counselors were culturally or racially responsive to client concerns, such as the importance of client–counselor shared attitudes, counselor cultural sensitivity, counselor respect for the individuality and complexity of the minority client, counselor application of cultural knowledge, counselor–client racial dynamics, and counselor awareness of client racial mistrust. Cultural and racial responsiveness obviously improves client perceptions of the counselor. It increases client willingness to return for counseling, satisfaction, disclosure, and depth of disclosure. Although the studies mentioned earlier were very informative, additional research is needed to determine whether including cultural or racial contents in counseling and observing a facilitative interactional process produce a positive effect for minority clients. I have provided a model on how trainees can (a) use cultural content in counseling and (b) observe a facilitative interactional process with their clients (Roysircar, 2004b, 2004c; Roysircar et al., 2005). Information is also needed on how clients are affected by the use of cultural content and process (e.g., Pope Davis et al., 2002).

Managed Care Issues

The question for culture-specific services is whether they will encourage segregation. Will the mental health system use the above type of research findings and justify the segregation of ethnic minority mental health services to separate and, consequently, unequal clinics? How will managed care respond to culturally responsive care leading to longer treatment? Likewise, will managed care use these data to argue against culturally responsive treatment to reduce cost? These are the dilemmas of multicultural counseling research. The history of race relations in the United States makes ethnic minority research volatile. The complexity of issues in multicultural counseling research must be recognized, and the potential side effects of such research must be anticipated.

Assessment of Multicultural Counseling Competencies

The multicultural counseling research reviewed to this point has focused more on the client and less on the counselor. Research in multicultural counseling competency focuses specifically on counselors (for more explanation, see Daniel, Roysircar, Abeles, & Boyd, 2004), with suggested proficiencies resulting in a positive counseling relationship.

Since the 1980s, multicultural counseling competence has received growing interest. It represents a philosophical shift in defining ethnic and race relations, traditionally seen as involving a conflict between assimilation and separatism and later seen as a melting pot where racial and cultural differences blend in. In the shift to multiculturalism, the belief in the inferiority of minority groups to European Americans is questioned, which is accompanied with a requirement for respectful and equitable interactions. The philosophical shift means that cultural differences are recognized in research to affect the validity of diagnosis and assessment, the counselor–client alliance, and treatment effectiveness (Roysircar, 2005; Roysircar-Sodowsky & Kuo, 2001).

The inadequacy of mainstream counseling, as evidenced by underutilization, biased assessment, and early termination, became the impetus for the multicultural competency effort in the 1980s (Sue et al., 1982) and early 1990s (Sue et al., 1992). Multicultural counseling competency constructs presented by Sue et al., beliefs/attitudes, knowledge, and skills, were operationalized in a number of instruments applied in counselor training programs for evaluation of training. These measures are the Multicultural Counseling Inventory (MCI; Sodowsky, 1996; Sodowsky, Taffe, Gutkin, & Wise, 1994), Multicultural Awareness Knowledge Skills Survey (MAKSS; D'Andrea, Daniels, & Heck, 1991), Cross-Cultural Counseling Inventory–Revised (CCCI-R; LaFromboise, Coleman, & Hernandez, 1991), Multicultural Counseling Awareness Scale (Ponterotto, Gretchen, Utsey, Rieger, & Austin, 2002), Multicultural Counseling Competence and Training Survey (Holcomb-McCoy & Meyers, 1999), and the California Brief Multicultural Competence Scale (Gamst et al., 2004). Multicultural competence training gradually incorporated these instruments in a context of trainee or counselor assessment issues as well as advocacy for research designed to increase multicultural competence.

Chief among the multicultural competency elements are the following: The counselor has a good understanding of his or her own worldviews and attitudes in which one is socialized, so that the counselor approaches the minority client with cultural self-awareness; the counselor has a good understanding of a client's worldviews and attitudes; the counselor has specific knowledge of the cultural groups with which he or she works; the counselor knows about individual differences in racial identity, acculturation, ethnic identity, minority stress, and coping; the counselor has an understanding of sociopolitical influences; the counselor possesses specific skills in working with culturally diverse individuals; and the counselor has the ability to use culturally based interventions and to translate mainstream interventions into culturally consistent strategies. To illustrate specifics, Table 25.1 summarizes the competencies articulated by Sue et al. (1992), and Table 25.2 summarizes the item contents of the MCI (Sodowsky et al., 1994), a self-report measure of multicultural counseling competencies. Sue et al.'s (1992) proposed competencies of beliefs, knowledge, and skills are identifiable in each counselor practice: counselor awareness of own assumptions, values, and biases; understanding the worldview of the culturally different client; and developing appropriate interventions, strategies, and techniques.

Self-Reported Multicultural Competency's Relationship With Racial Identity and Training

When studying counselor characteristics, Sodowsky, Kuo-Jackson, Richardson, and Corey (1998) considered it important to first control for the contributions of counselor race and multicultural social desirability. The effect of race needed attention because of repeated evidence, as indicated by this review, about the effects of race and ethnicity on the attitudes of people in the United States. The authors also intended to show that multicultural counseling competence can hold its own outside multicultural social desirability, or what is

Table 25.1

Table 25.1
A Summary of Sue, Arredondo, and McDavis's (1992) Expanded Construct of
Multicultural Counseling Competencies

	Counselor's Awareness of Own Assumptions, Values, and Bias	Understanding the Worldview of the Culturally Different Client	Developing Appropriate Counselor Interventions, Strategies, and Techniques	Total
Beliefs	1. Has cultural awareness and sensitivity 2. Understands influence of culture on experiences 3. Recognizes limitations 4. Comfortable with differences	1. Aware of negative emotional reactions to client 2. Aware of stereotypes and preconceptions	1. Respects diverse religious or spiritual beliefs and values 2. Respects indigenous helping practices and networks 3. Values bilingualism	9
Knowledge	1. Aware that cultural heritage affects definition of normality 2. Acknowledges racist attitudes, beliefs, and feelings 3. Knows about variations in communication styles	1. Has specific knowledge of particular group one is working with 2. Understands impact of culture on personality and preferences (e.g., vocation, counseling style) 3. Understands sociopolitical influences	1. Sensitive to conflicts between counseling and cultural values 2. Understands institutional barriers 3. Aware of bias in assessment 4. Understands family structure, hierarchies, values, and beliefs 5. Knows discriminatory practices in society / community	11
Skills	1. Seeks out educational, consultative, and training experiences; recognizes limits of competencies 2. Actively propagates nonracist identity	1. Familiar with relevant research and findings 2. Pursues nonprofessional social involvement with minority individuals	1. Conveys accurate and appropriate nonverbal messages 2. Intervenes institutionally 3. Consults with traditional healers and spiritual leaders 4. Interacts in client's language 5. Appropriately uses traditional assessment with diverse clients 6. Works to eliminate bias, prejudice, and discrimination 7. Educates and informs clients	11
Total	9	7	15	31

Note: Current discussions on multicultural competencies for organizational, social policy, and social justice changes have not been included (see Toporek, Gerstein, Fouad, Roysircar, & Israel, 2005). This table is limited to counselor personal interactional proficiencies with minority clients

Table 25.2
Multicultural Counseling Competencies

Multicultural Counseling Skills	Multicultural Awareness	Multicultural Counseling Relationship	Multicultural Counseling Knowledge
Possesses general counseling skills and proficiencies	Embraces life experiences and professional interactions of a multicultural nature	Comfortable with minority client's differences	Possesses a pluralistic worldview
Utilizes multiple methods of assessment	Enjoys multicultural interactions	Confident in facing personal limitations	Examines own cultural biases
Able to differentiate between needs for structured vs. unstructured therapies	Advocates against barriers to mental health services	Sensitive to client mistrust	Self-monitors and self-corrects
Understands own philosophical preferences/worldview	Has an awareness and understanding of diverse racial, cultural, and ethnic minority groups	Understands countertransference and/or defensive reactions with minority clients	Uses innovative approaches and methods
Able to retain minority clients	Is aware of legalities regarding visa, passport, green card, and naturalization	Sensitive to difficulties based on cognitive style	Familiar with current trends and practices
	Has knowledge of and tolerance for nonstandard English	Strives to avoid stereotyped and biased case conceptualization	Understands impact of acculturation
	Draws on multicultural consultation and training resources	Understands minority client–majority group comparisons	Utilizes research on minority client preferences
	Problem solves in unfamiliar settings	Knows how differences in worldviews affect counseling	Sensitive to withingroup differences
	Has increasing multicultural caseload		Minority identity development considered in referrals or consultation
			Includes demographic variables in cultural understanding
			Integrates sociopolitical history into client conceptualizations

Note: Adapted From Sodowsky, Taffe, Gutkin, & Wise, 1994.

popularly called "political correctness." *Multicultural social desirability* is defined as a preference to make a good impression on others by self-reporting that one is very responsive and attentive in all personal and social interactions with racial and ethnic minorities and that one always favors institutional policies for diversity. Constantine and Ladany (2000) and Ponterotto et al. (1996) recommended that self-report multicultural competency measures be accompanied by measures of social desirability.

After the significant contributions of counselor race and multicultural social desirability were partialed out, counselor attitudes (racial ideology and social self-esteem) and training were shown to be significant predictors of self-reported multicultural competence ($R^2 = .34$ for the full model), as measured by Sodowsky et al.'s (1994) MCI measure. Counselor racial ideology is a belief system about personal versus external control of race relations in the United States. For example, it includes racist attributions, such as "African Americans can overcome racism by working harder." Racial ideology was a significant negative predictor of multicultural competence. Social inadequacy is the opposite of social self-esteem, indicating a lack of openness to social influences and to feedback on social behaviors. Social inadequacy was a significant negative predictor of multicultural competence. Racial and ethnic minority counselors had lower scores than White counselors in racial ideology and social inadequacy. Counselors who perceived themselves as multiculturally competent indicated a preference for externality (with regard to racial ideology) and collectivism (with regard to social self-esteem) as opposed to internality and individualism. All minority counselors scored higher than White counselors in multicultural awareness. African Americans had the highest multicultural relationship score, and Whites had the lowest. Hispanics/Latinos and Asians had the highest scores in multicultural knowledge. Counselors' clinical work and research with minority populations were significant predictors of increasing multicultural competence.

Ongoing examination of multicultural community services provided by counselor trainees has enabled the identification of normative multicultural social desirability scores as well as normative self-reported multicultural counseling competence scores (Roysircar et al., 2005; Roysircar, Webster, et al., 2003; Sodowsky et al., 1998). A benchmark social desirability score enables the identification of invalid self-reported multicultural competence. Similarly, benchmarks for high and low self-reported multicultural competence indicate the professional level to which less competent counselors need to aspire.

Trainee Reflections on Multicultural Awareness

Themes derived from counselor trainees' process notes about barriers to and connections with their middle school ESL clients were significantly related to self-reported multicultural counseling competence (Roysircar et al., 2005 [$N = 67$]; Roysircar, Webster, et al., 2003 [$N = 16$]). Those who were categorized as low scorers on the MCI (Roysircar, Webster, et al., 2003) endorsed more frequently the themes of barriers, frustrations with barriers, preoccupation with cultural similarities–differences, and anxiety about progress than did those who were categorized as higher scorers. Overall, these negative themes (labeled *multicultural disconnection/distance* in Roysircar et al., 2005) showed the highest number of significant negative correlations with multicultural skills and multicultural relationship. Those trainees who were categorized as high scorers on the MCI endorsed more frequently the themes of other-awareness and reflection, self-awareness and reflection, empathy and self-disclosure, treatment planning and implementation, analyses of counselor biases, and intentional exchange of cultural information. Overall, these positive themes (labeled *multicultural connection/closeness* in Roysircar et al., 2005) had the highest number of significant positive correlations with multicultural relationship and multicultural awareness. Thus, training experience with minority clients involved trainees in the process of the multicultural relationship-building competency, in addition to working on multicultural skills and awareness (Roysircar, Webster, et al., 2003). In a subsequent study (Roysircar et al., 2005), multicultural connection/closeness of trainees ($N = 67$) had significant positive correlations with self-reported multicultural competence (MCI) and higher level White racial identity attitudes (i.e., pseudoindependence and autonomy subscales in the White Racial Identity Attitudes Scale; Helms, 1995) and showed no relationship with multicultural social desirability. Multicultural disconnection/distance did not relate to the MCI and pseudoindependence and autonomy. Additionally, *t* tests of these counselors' ESL clients showed significantly stronger Help-Seeking Attitudes, Well-Being, Satisfaction, and Effectiveness scores for 32 clients whose counselors had significantly higher MCI scores than other counselors (Roysircar et al., 2001). This study indicated that when studying self-reported increased multicultural competence over time (i.e., 10 sessions), counselor self-evaluations on the MCI could be corroborated by external sources: their minority clients and other counselor observers.

In another study that also investigated the relationship of White racial identity attitudes and multicultural counseling competence (Ladany, Inman, Constantine, & Hofheinz, 1997), White supervisees who had high pseudoindependence were likely to report high multicultural competence. High levels of dissonance and awareness in White supervises were also related to high self-reported multicultural competence. However, there seemed to be a more direct translation between racial identity and self-reported multicultural competence for supervisees of color, who were assessed on their persons of color racial identity statuses, than for White supervisees. Self-reported multicultural competence, however, was not related to multicultural case conceptualization ability. Ladany et al. (1997) implied that the supervisees may have been overconfident of their multicultural competence. In addition, some of the respondents who were instructed to include racial factors in their conceptualizations noted that although the supervisor instructed them to include racial factors, these issues were not relevant to the case conceptualization, and they thus chose not to include them. Therefore, Ladany et al. stated that a supervisor's interventions may prove ineffective unless a supervisee believes cultural differences are important to therapy.

Studies (e.g., Constantine & Yeh, 2001; D'Andrea et al., 1991; Pope-Davis & Ottavi, 1994; Roysircar et al., 2001; Sodowsky et al., 1998) have shown that greater exposure to multicultural training that includes classroom didactics, experiential training, and practicum increases self-reported multicultural competencies. A one-semester multicultural counseling course taught at three predominantly White state universities in the Midwest and on the East Coast and the West Coast (Neville et al., 1996) was related to White counseling students' adoption of more positive White racial identity attitudes. Pseudoindependence and autonomy racial identity attitudes were associated with stronger endorsement of multicultural competency, as measured by D'Andrea et al.'s (1991) MAKSS measure. Higher levels of contact and disintegration of racial identity attitudes were related to lower levels of reported multicultural competency. Changes in racial identity attitudes were sustained over a 1-year period. Qualitative analyses underscored the importance of ethnically diverse speakers and panels in promoting multicultural competence.

Studies reviewed here (Fuertes et al., 2002; Ladany et al., 1997; Neville et al., 1996; Roysircar et al., 2005; Richardson & Helms, 1994) have indicated that a counselor's racial identity is an empirical correlate of multicultural competence. This predictive relationship between a counselor's self-reported competence and his or her racial identity has shown up in a different form in a multicultural competence scale: Knowledge of Racial Identity is a subscale in the Multicultural Counseling Competence and Training Survey (Holcomb-McCoy & Meyers, 1999). As stated by Parker, Moore, and Neimeyer (1998), "One assumption in the literature is that White therapists can better understand others when they can understand their own racial identity attitudes and development" (p. 302). Thus, effective multicultural training requires that a White trainee work through various levels of White racial identity development, such as obliviousness about race relations in the United States (called contact). In addition, McIntosh's (2001) article on White privilege and male privilege enables many trainees to understand the "invisible package of unearned assets that [White people] can count on cashing in each day" (p. 95).

Observed Multicultural Competence

Constantine (2001) has shown that increased multicultural training and counselor race or ethnicity were significant predictors of observer-rated multicultural counselor competencies, as measured by an observer rating adaptation of LaFromboise et al.'s (1991) CCCI-R. In another study, Constantine (2002) found that client attitudes about counseling, client ratings of perceived counselor credibility, and client ratings of multicultural competencies (use of an adapted CCCI-R measure) accounted for significant variance ($R^2 = .58$) on a measure of client satisfaction. Client ratings of multicultural competence specifically contributed significant variance (R^2 change $= .07$) over and above perceived counselor credibility. Similar to Constantine (2002), Fuertes and Brobst (2002) have shown that White counselors' multicultural competence on an adapted CCCI-R measure, as assessed by counseling psychology students who reported being recipients of therapy, accounted for significant variance in client satisfaction. Counselor multicultural competence was not a significant contributor to client satisfaction of the White American sample, but it was significant for the minority sample, offering support for multicultural counseling's perspective that minority clients seek multicultural competencies in their counselors.

Worthington, Mobley, Franks, and Tan (2000) found that after taking social desirability into account, observer-rated therapist multicultural competence, as measured by the CCCI-R, was significantly correlated with the therapist being able to conceptualize client distress as symptomatic of external/systemic sources such as sociopolitical forces (e.g., racism), to attribute the locus of cause of client distress outside of the client, and to verbalize multicultural issues in session. In addition, these authors found that therapist self-reported multicultural counseling knowledge, as measured by a subscale of the MCI, was significantly predictive ($R^2 = .20$) of observer-rated scores on the CCCI-R, even after social desirability had been controlled. The perceived importance of the counselor's multicultural knowledge was also identified by Holcomb-McCoy and Meyers (1999) in their study of the multicultural competencies of professional counselors.

Self-report ratings and observer report ratings in multicultural counseling competencies are relevant, depending on the purpose of the evaluation. Counselor self-report of multicultural competencies is methodologically appropriate and distinct, capturing a phenomenon that is not identified by observer-rated checklists of behavior. Counselor self-reports are used to study change scores in self-efficacy and self-beliefs over time and training. Although observer ratings can provide a checklist of counselor behaviors, these cannot gauge counselors' intrapersonal processes. Similarly, client evaluations of counselors are methodologically appropriate and distinct. It should be noted that a qualitative study (Pope-Davis et al., 2002) on client experiences has suggested that clients do not conceptualize multicultural competency in the same ways that clinicians and researchers do. Counselors, like clients, know best their experiences and issues on which supervisors can provide feedback.

Experiential Multicultural Training

Multicultural courses include an experiential component to personalize didactics, research, and discussions. Vasquez and Vasquez (2003) advocated a nontraditional multicultural course in which trainees begin a self-reflective process and move toward understanding the alternative worldviews of clients and their families. For this learning to occur, the multicultural curriculum must be experientially based and process oriented. Other trainers also support this view (Faubert & Locke, 2003; Heppner & O'Brien, 1994; Kim & Lyons, 2003; Manese, Wu, & Nepomuceno, 2001; Sandhu & Looby, 2003; Santiago-Rivera & Moody, 2003). I have written on trainees' practice of the self-reflexive process in experiential, community-based activities for their development of multicultural competence (Roysircar, 2003a, 2003b, 2004c; Roysircar, Webster, et al., 2003). Trainees write these self-reflections in their weekly process notes for 10 sessions and include the most transformative self-reflections in their written case conceptualizations (e.g., Spanakis, 2004). I have provided thick descriptions of trainees' reflections on critical incidents with clients that resulted in trainees' "increased understanding of self and others, and a greater appreciation and respect for differences" (Roysircar, 2003a, p. 34) as well as in an increased ability to "'retell' the story, incorporating the client's worldview and correcting one's assumptions, values, and biases" (Roysircar, 2004c, p. 18).

Multicultural Counseling Relationship

The research on multicultural competence has provided considerable information on multicultural awareness, knowledge, and skills but not on the counseling relationship or bond/working alliance with the minority client. It is my hypothesis that the multicultural competencies that focus on the professional persona of the counselor together lead to the development of a positive counselor–client relationship. Sodowsky (Roysircar, 2003a, 2004c; Roysircar et al., 2005; Roysircar, Webster, et al., 2003; Sodowsky, 1996; Sodowsky et al., 1994) has considered the multicultural counseling relationship to be the human element in counselor–client interactions, which she has described as "ethnotherapeutic empathy," entailing the integration of "cultural knowledge with a dynamic experience of the client's subjective culture" (Sodowsky et al., 1998, p. 262). Her trainees' reflections on bonding with their ESL clients were related to their self-reported multicultural competence (Roysircar et al., 2005). Her research on the multicultural counseling relationship is finding concurrent validity in recent studies, as described below.

In interviews (Fuertes et al., 2002), White Americans reporting on their work with African American clients described using core relationship-building skills, such as listening, attending, paraphrasing, asking open-ended questions, and conveying open and accepting nonverbal cues to engage the client in therapy. In addition, a communication of empathy from the therapists seemed to strengthen rapport and deepen the level of affect and work from the client. All of the therapists mentioned the importance of collaboratively setting goals to engage and empower the client. In another interview study, in this case with clients (Pope-Davis et al., 2002), it was found that clients' interpersonal process with the counselor and the client–counselor relationship was an active process in which the clients were engaged. These studies lend empirical support to including the counseling relationship in the conceptualization of multicultural counseling competencies. It is to be noted that Constantine and Ladany (2001) expanded the multicultural counseling competency model to add two additional factors: counselors' understanding of unique client variables and establishment of an effective working alliance. Fuertes and Ponterotto (2003) stated the following about the working alliance with culturally diverse individuals:

> They are able to establish core conditions in counseling, regardless of their preferred theoretical and technical conditions in counseling. They are able to establish rapport and working alliances with their clients; they can heal ruptures in the alliance; they are open to criticism from or to being tested by the client; and they can establish goals and formulate tasks with the client. They are able to communicate openness to and are able to discuss issues associated with gender, race, ethnicity, culture, socioeconomic background, sexual orientation, and other human diversity factors with their clients. They can sensitively process differences in race and culture. They are able to name or identify for their clients experiences that may be of a racist or oppressive nature. They are able and willing to modify their theoretical and technical styles and/or interventions to meet the client psychologically, including knowing when not to discuss race or salient cultural differences with their clients. And they are able to continually evaluate the process of counseling, the progress being made on mutually agreed upon goals, and the quality of the relationship with their clients. (pp. 55–56)

McRae and Johnson (1991) said, "Aside from understanding one's self as a racial–ethnic cultural being, it is important for counselors to examine the counselor–client relationship"

(p. 131), which is characterized "with similar and different cultural values, racial identity attitudes, [and] issues of power, control, and oppression" (p. 135). In Martinez and Holloway's (1997) supervision model for multicultural counseling, power is viewed as a vehicle for the counselor to construct a mutually empowering relationship, indicating a shift from a perspective of "power over" to one of "power with." As the counselor commits to the process of multicultural self-awareness, power becomes a shared property of the multicultural relationship and not of one individual. In addition to shared power, involvement is an affiliative dimension that is integral to the relationship, carrying the meaning of forming intentional attachments as each member uses the other as a source of self-affirmation, relating freely as individuals rather than in stereotyped roles (Martinez & Holloway, 1997).

Multicultural competency training and evaluation using competency instruments and other measures of racial–ethnic-specific elements have enabled cultural issues to become the central core of the counseling profession's identity. Nonetheless, there is still a dearth of specialized multicultural training necessary for mental health diagnosis, assessment, and services for racial and ethnic minorities, now including more than one third of all mental health clients.

References

Arredondo, P., Toporek, R., Brown, S. P., Jones, J., Locke, D. C., Sanchez, J., et al. (1996). Operationalization of the multicultural counseling competencies. *Journal of Multicultural Counseling and Development, 24,* 42–78.

Atkinson, D. R., Thompson, C. E., & Grant, S. (1993). A three-dimensional model for counseling racial/ethnic minority clients. *The Counseling Psychologist, 21,* 257–277.

Coleman, H. L. K. (2003). Culturally relevant empirically supported treatment. In G. Roysircar, P. Arredondo, J. N. Fuertes, J. G. Ponterotto, & R. L. Toporek (Eds.), *Multicultural counseling competencies 2003: Association for Multicultural Counseling and Development* (pp. 79–86). Alexandria, VA: Association for Multicultural Counseling and Development.

Constantine, M. G. (2001). Predictors of observer ratings of multicultural counseling competence in trainees. *Journal of Counseling Psychology, 48,* 456–462.

Constantine, M. G. (2002). Predictors of satisfaction with counseling: Racial and ethnic minority clients' attitudes toward counseling and ratings of their therapists' general and multicultural counseling competence. *Journal of Counseling Psychology, 49,* 255–263.

Constantine, M. G., & Ladany, N. (2000). Self-report multicultural counseling competence scales: Their relation to social desirability attitudes and multicultural case conceptualization ability. *Journal of Counseling Psychology, 47,* 155–164.

Constantine, M. G., & Ladany, N. (2001). New visions for defining and assessing multicultural counseling competence. In J. G. Ponterotto, J. M. Casas, L. A. Suzuki, & C. M. Alexander (Eds.), *Handbook of multicultural counseling* (2nd ed., pp. 482–498). Thousand Oaks, CA: Sage.

Constantine, M. G., & Yeh, C. J. (2001). Multicultural training, self-construals, and multicultural competence of school counselors. *Professional School Counseling, 4,* 202–207.

D'Andrea, M., Daniels, J., & Heck, R. (1991). Evaluating the impact of multicultural counseling training. *Journal of Counseling & Development, 70,* 143–150.

Daniel, J. H., Roysircar, G., Abeles, N., & Boyd, C. (2004). Individual and cultural diversity competence: Focus on the therapist. *Journal of Clinical Psychology, 25,* 255–267.

DeFrino, B. (2003). Multicultural interactions with Jewish American adolescents. In G. Roysircar, P. Arredondo, J. N. Fuertes, J. G. Ponterotto, & R. L. Toporek (Eds.), *Multicultural counseling competencies 2003: Association for Multicultural Counseling and Development* (pp. 121–130). Alexandria, VA: Association for Multicultural Counseling and Development.

Faubert, M., & Locke, D. C. (2003). Cultural considerations in counselor training and supervision. In G. Roysircar, D. S. Sandhu, & V. E. Bibbins, Sr. (Eds.), *Multicultural competencies: A guidebook of practices* (pp. 51–63). Alexandria, VA: American Counseling Association.

Fuertes, J. N., & Brobst, K. (2002). Clients' perspectives of therapist multicultural competence. *Cultural Diversity and Ethnic Minority Psychology, 8,* 214–223.

Fuertes, J. N., Mueller, L. N., Chauhan, R. V., Walker, J. A., & Ladany, N. (2002). An investigation of Euro-American therapists' approach to counseling African American clients. *The Counseling Psychologist, 30,* 763–789.

Fuertes, J. N., & Ponterotto, J. G. (2003). Culturally appropriate intervention strategies. In G. Roysircar, P. Arredondo, J. N. Fuertes, J. G. Ponterotto, & R. L. Toporek (Eds.), *Multicultural counseling competencies 2003: Association for Multicultural Counseling and Development* (pp. 51–58). Alexandria, VA: Association for Multicultural Counseling and Development.

Gamst, G., Dana, R. H., Der-Karabetian, A., Aragon, M., Arellano, L., Morrow, G., et al. (2004). Cultural competency revised: The California Brief Multicultural Competence Scale. *Measurement and Evaluation in Counseling and Development, 37,* 163–183.

Helms, J. E. (1995). An update of Helms's White and people of color racial identity models. In J. G. Ponterotto, J. M. Casas, L. A. Suzuki, & C. M. Alexander (Eds.), *Handbook of multicultural counseling* (pp. 181–198). Thousand Oaks, CA: Sage.

Heppner, M. J., & O'Brien, K. M. (1994). Multicultural counseling training: Students' perceptions of helpful and hindering events. *Counselor Education and Supervision, 34,* 4–18.

Holcomb-McCoy, C., & Meyers, J. E. (1999). Multicultural competence and counselor training: A national survey. *Journal of Counseling & Development, 77,* 294–302.

Huynh, U., & Roysircar, G. (in press). Community health promotion curriculum: A case study on Vietnamese and Cambodian refugees. In R. L. Toporek, L. H. Gerstein, N. A. Fouad, G. Roysircar, & T. Israel (Eds.), *Handbook for social justice in counseling psychology: Leadership, vision, and action.* Thousand Oaks, CA: Sage.

Kawanishi, Y. (1995). The effects of culture on beliefs about stress and coping: Causal attribution of Anglo-American and Japanese persons. *Journal of Contemporary Psychotherapy, 25,* 49–60.

Kim, B. S. K., & Lyons, H. Z. (2003). Experiential activities and multicultural counseling competency training. *Journal of Counseling & Development, 81,* 400–408.

Kuo, B. C. H., & Roysircar, G. (2004). Predictors of acculturation for Chinese adolescents in Canada: Age of arrival, length of stay, social class, and English reading ability. *Journal of Multicultural Counseling and Development, 32,* 143–154.

Kuo, B. C. H., Roysircar, G., & Newby-Clark, I. R. (2004). *Development of the Cross-Cultural Coping Scale: Collective, avoidance, and engagement coping.* Manuscript submitted for publication.

Ladany, N., Inman, A. G., Constantine, M. G., & Hofheinz, E. W. (1997). Supervisee multicultural case conceptualization ability and self-reported multicultural competence as functions of supervisee racial identity and supervisor focus. *Journal of Counseling Psychology, 44,* 284–293.

LaFromboise, T. D. (1992). An interpersonal analysis of affinity, clarification, and helping responses with American Indians. *Professional Psychology: Research and Practice, 23,* 281–286.

LaFromboise, T. D., Coleman, H. L., & Hernandez, A. (1991). Development and factor structure of the Cross-Cultural Counseling Inventory—Revised. *Professional Psychology: Research and Practice, 22,* 380–388.

LaFromboise, T. D., & Dixon, D. N. (1981). American Indian perception of trustworthiness in a counseling review. *Journal of Counseling Psychology, 28,* 135–139.

Luk, C. L., & Bond, M. H. (1992). Chinese lay beliefs about the causes and cures of psychological problems. *Journal of Social and Clinical Psychology, 11,* 140–157.

Manese, J. E., Wu, J. T., & Nepomuceno, C. A. (2001). The effect of training on multicultural counseling competencies: An exploratory study over a 10-year period. *Journal of Multicultural Counseling and Development, 29,* 31–40.

Martinez, R. P., & Holloway, E. L. (1997). The supervision relationship in multicultural training. In D. B. Pope-Davis & H. L. K. Coleman (Eds.), *Multicultural counseling competencies: Assessment, education and training, and supervision* (pp. 325–349). Thousand Oaks, CA: Sage.

McIntosh, P. (2001). White privilege and male privilege: A personal account of coming to see correspondences through work in women's studies. In M. L. Andersen & P. H. Collins (Eds.), *Race, class, and gender* (4th ed., pp. 95–105). Belmont, CA: Wadsworth.

McRae, M. B., & Johnson, S. D. (1991). Toward training for competence in multicultural counselor education. *Journal of Counseling & Development, 70,* 131–135.

Narikiyo, T. A., & Kameoka, V. A. (1992). Attributions of mental illness and judgments about help seeking among Japanese American and White American students. *Journal of Counseling Psychology, 39,* 363–369.

Neville, H. A., Heppner, M. J., Louie, C. E., Thompson, C. E., Brooks, L., & Baker, C. E. (1996). The impact of multicultural training on White racial identity attitudes and therapy competencies. *Professional Psychology: Research and Practice, 27,* 83–89.

Parker, W. M., Moore, M. A., & Neimeyer, G. J. (1998). Altering White racial identity and interracial comfort through multicultural training. *Journal of Counseling & Development, 76,* 302–310.

Pomales, J., Claiborn, C. D., & LaFromboise, T. D. (1986). Effects of Black students' racial identity on perceptions of White therapists varying in cultural sensitivity. *Journal of Counseling Psychology, 33,* 57–61.

Ponterotto, J. G., Gretchen, D., Utsey, S. O., Rieger, B. P., & Austin, R. (2002). A revision of the Multicultural Counseling Awareness Scale. *Journal of Multicultural Counseling and Development, 30,* 153–180.

Pope-Davis, D. B., & Ottavi, T. M. (1994). Examining the association between self-reported multicultural counseling competencies and demographic and educational variables among therapists. *Journal of Counseling & Development, 72,* 651–654.

Pope-Davis, D. B., Toporek, R. L., Ortega-Villalobos, L. D., Ligiero, D., Brittan-Powell, C. S., Liu, W. M., et al. (2002). Client perspectives of multicultural counseling competence: A qualitative examination. *The Counseling Psychologist, 30,* 355–393.

Richardson, T. Q., & Helms, J. E. (1994). The relationship of the racial identity attitudes of Black men to perceptions of "parallel" counseling dyads. *Journal of Counseling & Development, 73,* 172–177.

Roysircar, G. (2003a). Counselor awareness of own assumptions, values, and biases. In G. Roysircar, P. Arredondo, J. N. Fuertes, J. G. Ponterotto, & R. L. Toporek (Eds.), *Multicultural counseling competencies 2003: Association for Multicultural Counseling and Development* (pp. 17–38). Alexandria, VA: Association for Multicultural Counseling and Development.

Roysircar, G. (2003b). Religious differences: Psychological and sociopolitical aspects of counseling. *International Journal for the Advancement of Counseling, 25,* 255–267.

Roysircar, G. (2004a). Child survivor of war: A case study. *Journal of Multicultural Counseling and Development, 32,* 168–180.

Roysircar, G. (2004b). Counseling and psychotherapy for acculturation and ethnic identity concerns with immigrants and international student clients. In T. B. Smith (Ed.), *Practicing multiculturalism: Affirming diversity in counseling and psychology* (pp. 248–268). Boston: Allyn & Bacon.

Roysircar, G. (2004c). Cultural self-awareness assessment: Practice examples from psychology training. *Professional Psychology: Research and Practice, 35,* 658–666.

Roysircar, G. (2005). Culturally sensitive assessment, diagnosis, and guidelines. In M. G. Constantine & D. W. Sue (Eds.), *Strategies for building multicultural competence in mental health and educational settings* (pp. 19–38). Hoboken, NJ: Wiley.

Roysircar, G., Arredondo, P., Fuertes, J. N., Ponterotto, J. G., & Toporek, R. L. (Eds.). (2003). *Multicultural counseling competencies 2003: Association for Multicultural Counseling and Development.* Alexandria, VA: Association for Multicultural Counseling and Development.

Roysircar, G., Gard, G., Hubbell, R., & Ortega, M. (2005). Development of counseling trainees' multicultural awareness through mentoring ESL students. *Journal of Multicultural Counseling and Development, 33,* 17–36.

Roysircar, G., Gard, G., Taliouridis, C., Potter, B., Huynh, U. K., Utsch, H., et al. (2001, August). *Multicultural counseling competencies: An outcome evaluation study.* Paper presented at the 109th Annual Convention of the American Psychological Association, San Francisco.

Roysircar, G., Sandhu, D. S., & Bibbins, V. E., Sr. (Eds.). (2003). *Multicultural competencies: A guidebook of practices.* Alexandria, VA: American Counseling Association.

Roysircar, G., Webster, D. R., Germer, J., Palensky, J. J., Lynne, E., Campbell, G. R., et al. (2003). Experiential training in multicultural counseling: Implementation and evaluation. In G. Roysircar, D. S. Sandhu, & V. E. Bibbins Sr. (Eds.), *Multicultural competencies: A guidebook of practices* (pp. 3–15). Alexandria, VA: American Counseling Association.

Roysircar-Sodowsky, G., & Kuo, P. Y. (2001). Determining cultural validity of personality assessment: Some guidelines. In D. Pope-Davis & H. Coleman (Eds.), *The intersection of race, class, and gender: Implications for multicultural counseling* (pp. 213–239). Thousand Oaks, CA: Sage.

Sandhu, D. S., & Looby, E. J. (2003). Multicultural competency interventions for building positive White racial identity in White counselor trainees. In G. Roysircar, D. S. Sandhu, & V. E. Bibbins, Sr. (Eds.), *Multicultural competencies: A guidebook of practices* (pp. 17–37). Alexandria, VA: American Counseling Association.

Santiago-Rivera, A. L., & Moody, M. (2003). Engaging students in the quest for competence in multiculturalism: An expanded view of mentoring. In G. Roysircar, D. S. Sandhu, & V. E. Bibbins, Sr. (Eds.), *Multicultural competencies: A guidebook of practices* (pp. 39–50). Alexandria, VA: American Counseling Association.

Sodowsky, G. R. (1991). Effects of culturally consistent counseling tasks on American and international student observers' perception of therapist credibility. *Journal of Counseling & Development, 69,* 253–256.

Sodowsky, G. R. (1996). The Multicultural Counseling Inventory: Validity and applications in multicultural training. In G. R. Sodowsky & J. C. Impara (Eds.), *Multicultural assessment in counseling and clinical psychology* (pp. 283–324). Lincoln, NE: Buros Institute of Mental Measurements.

Sodowsky, G. R., Kuo-Jackson, P. Y., Richardson, M. F., & Corey, A. T. (1998). Correlates of self-reported multicultural competencies: Therapist multicultural social desirability, race, social inadequacy, locus of control, racial ideology, and multicultural training. *Journal of Counseling Psychology, 45,* 256–264.

Sodowsky, G. R., Taffe, R. C., Gutkin, T. B., & Wise, S. L. (1994). Development of the Multicultural Counseling Inventory: A self-report measure of multicultural competencies. *Journal of Counseling Psychology, 41,* 137–148.

Spanakis, N. C. (2004). Difficult dialogues: Interviewer, White inner voice, and Latina interviewee. *Journal of Multicultural Counseling and Development, 32,* 249–254.

Sue, D. W., Arredondo, P., & McDavis, R. J. (1992). Multicultural counseling competencies and standards: A call to the profession. *Journal of Multicultural Counseling and Development, 20,* 64–68.

Sue, D. W., Bernier, J. E., Durran, A., Feinberg, L., Pedersen, P., Smith, E. J., et al. (1982). Position paper: Cross-cultural counseling competencies. *The Counseling Psychologist, 10,* 64–68.

Sweet, S. G., & Estey, M. (2003). A step toward multicultural competencies: Listening to individuals with multiple sclerosis and cerebral palsy. In G. Roysircar, P. Arredondo, J. N. Fuertes, J. G. Ponterotto, & R. L. Toporek (Eds.), *Multicultural counseling competencies 2003: Association for Multicultural Counseling and Development* (pp. 103–120). Alexandria, VA: Association for Multicultural Counseling and Development.

Thompson, C. E., Worthington, R., & Atkinson, D. R. (1994). Therapist content, orientation, therapist race, and Black women's cultural mistrust and self-disclosure. *Journal of Counseling Psychology, 41,* 155–161.

Toporek, R. L. (2003). Counselor awareness of client's worldview. In G. Roysircar, P. Arredondo, J. N. Fuertes, J. G. Ponterotto, & R. L. Toporek (Eds.), *Multicultural counseling competencies 2003: Association for Multicultural Counseling and Development* (pp. 39–50). Alexandria, VA: Association for Multicultural Counseling and Development.

Toporek, R. L., Gerstein, L. H., Fouad, N. A., Roysircar, G., & Israel, T. (Eds.). (2005). *Handbook for social justice in counseling psychology.* Thousand Oaks, CA: Sage.

Trimble, J. E., Fleming, C. M., Beauvais, F., & Jumper-Thurman, P. (1996). Essential cultural and social strategies for counseling Native American Indians. In P. Pedersen, J. G. Draguns, W. J. Lonner, & J. E. Trimble (Eds.), *Counseling across cultures* (pp. 177–209). Thousand Oaks, CA: Sage.

Uchison, J. (2003). Multiculturalism and immigrants. In G. Roysircar, D. S. Sandhu, & V. E. Bibbins, Sr. (Eds.), *Multicultural competencies: A guidebook of practices* (pp. 129–138). Alexandria, VA: American Counseling Association.

Vasquez, L. A., & Vasquez, E. G. (2003). Teaching multicultural competence in counseling curriculum. In W. M. Liu, R. L. Toporek, H. L. K. Coleman, & D. B. Pope-Davis (Eds.), *Handbook of multicultural competency in counseling and psychology* (pp. 546–561). Thousand Oaks, CA: Sage.

Wade, P., & Bernstein, B. L. (1991). Culture sensitivity training and therapist's race: Effects on Black female clients' perceptions and attrition. *Journal of Counseling Psychology, 38,* 9–15.

Watkins, C. E., & Terrel, F. (1988). Mistrust level and its effects on counseling expectations in Black–White therapist relationships: An analogue study. *Journal of Counseling Psychology, 35,* 194–197.

Wilczak, C. (2003). A counselor trainee's conversations with a Colombian immigrant woman. In G. Roysircar, P. Arredondo, J. N. Fuertes, J. G. Ponterotto, & R. L. Toporek (Eds.), *Multicultural counseling competencies 2003: Association for Multicultural Counseling and Development* (pp. 89–101). Alexandria, VA: Association for Multicultural Counseling and Development.

Worthington, R. L., Mobley, M., Franks, R. P., & Tan, J. A. (2000). Multicultural counseling competencies: Verbal content, counselor attributions, and social desirability. *Journal of Counseling Psychology, 47,* 460–468.

Index

A

ableism, and cross-cultural counseling, 13, 17
acculturation
  in Chinese American values and culture, 128
  Japanese Americans, 141–42
  Korean Americans, 173–74, 175
  among Mexican American college students, 208–9
  in Native American values and culture, 26, 30–33, 43–44
  Southeast Asian refugees and acculturative stress, 153
achievement ideology, high-achieving Blacks and, 70–71
Adam! Where Are You? (Kunjufu), 121–22
adolescents and children
  African American, 72–74, 81–82, 85–89, 93, 95–100
  Arab American children, 238
  child-rearing practices, 129–30, 155
  children's responses to disability, 329
  counseling multiracial, 257–58
  intersexual children, 304, 307
  Korean children, 172, 173, 175
  Latino children, 207
  lesbian, gay, and transgender (LGT) youth, 4
  lesbians as parents, 298
  multiracial, 253–54, 257–58
  socioeconomically disadvantaged children, 346–47
  in Southeast Asian refugee population, 157
  transracial adoption, 251, 261–64
  See also education
adoption. *See* transracial adoption
adults, multiracial, 254–55
  counseling, 258–60
Advocate, The (gay resource), 271

African American church, 113–14, 122–23
  guidelines for working within a church context, 119–22
  intervention strategies using the resources of the, 117–19
  need for partnership with clergy, 116–17
  psychosocial support and the Black church, 59
  and its role in mental health, 114–16
  role of African American clergy, 116
  seven denominations, 113, 120–21
  See also spirituality
African American male youth and men, counseling, 93–94, 109
  case study, 105–9
  crucial stages in a counseling process with African American males, 103–4
  framework for counseling with African American male youth, 98–100
  framework for counseling with African American men, 103
  historical and cultural perspectives, 94–95
  issues to consider in counseling African American male youth, 95–97
  issues to consider in counseling African American men, 100–102
  Project: Gentlemen on the Move, 99–100
African American women and girls, counseling, 79
  culturally responsive counseling strategies, 82–89
  environmental and cultural influences, 80
  group approach, 83–89
  strengths and effective coping methods, 82
  transmission of cultural values, 81–82
African Americans, counseling high-achieving, 63, 76–77
  achievement ideology, 70–71

African Americans, counseling—*(continued)*
allegiance issues, 69–70
case study, 72, 73–74
concept of high achievement, 63–64
counseling interventions, 74–76
double standards, 65
exclusion and isolation, 65–66
factors affecting mental health, 64–67
identity conflicts, 67–69
limited access and glass ceilings, 64–65
pigeonholing, 67
potential barriers, 71–72
powerlessness, 66
second guessing, 66–67
survival guilt, 70
token status, 66
voicelessness and invisibility, 66
within-group competition, 71
African Americans, cultural framework for
counseling, 57–60
Afrocentric: Self Inventory and Discovery Workbook
(Perkins), 89
Afrocentricity
defined, 57–59
implications for counseling, 59–60
and mental health, 59
aggression and control, and counseling African
American men, 101
aging
ageism in multicultural counseling
paradigm, 7
in gay male society, 271
AIDS
AIDS-related deaths among Latinos, 212
in the gay community, 270–71
Ain't No Makin' It (MacLeod), 65
Alberts, J. F., 333
allegiance issues/peer pressures, high-achieving
Blacks and, 69–70
Allen, Paula Gunn, 25
alocentrismo, 190
American Counseling Association (ACA)
Code of Ethics and Standards of Practice,
360–61, 362, 363, 366
and religious issues in counseling, 122
American Indian Religious Freedom Act, 28
American Psychiatric Association, 291
American Psychological Association, 122
*Enhancing Your Interactions With People
With Disabilities,* 335

guidelines for working with people with
disabilities, 336
Americans With Disabilities Act of 1990 (ADA),
322–23, 332
animism, 158
anthropology, psychological, 230
antisocial personality disorder, poverty and, 346
Aphrodite, 307
Aponte, J. F., 334
Appleby, G., 269, 275, 287
*Arab America Today: A Demographic Profile of Arab
Americans* (Zogby), 235
Arab Americans, counseling, 235–36, 246
Arab American culture, 236–38
Arab Americans' mental health, 239–43
barriers to successful counseling, 240–41
case study, 243–45
diversity of Arab Americans, 236
family, 238
intervention techniques and strategies,
241–43
racial-religious-ethnic identification issues,
238–39
religion, 237–38
Arredondo, P., 196, 376, 377
Asch, A., 329
"Asian Americans: Are They Making the
Grade?" (article), 127
Asians
cultural stereotyping of, 372
with disabilities, 334, 335
See also Chinese Americans; Korean
Americans; Southeast Asian descent,
Americans of
assertiveness training, for Chinese Americans,
134, 135–36
assimilated Native Americans, 30
Association for Multicultural Counseling and
Development, 82–83
at-risk groups, Southeast Asian refugee
population, 156–57
Atkinson, D. R., 71, 215–18, 327, 369, 374
attitudes, parallel, 374
autonomy, in principle ethics, 358

B

Bacchus, 306
Bae, H., 175
Banks, J. A., 74

Barón, A., Jr., 213–14
Barrett, K. A., 291
Basic Principles of Biblical Counseling (Crabb), 121
Bean, R. A., 196, 204
beauty, feminine, 80, 82, 88
Beauvais, F., 373
Beiser, M., 156, 162
Belgrave, F. Z., 333
Belleroe, Eddie, 35
Bemak, F., 153, 154, 155, 162, 166
beneficence, in principle ethics, 358
benevolence, in virtue ethics, 359
Bergin, A. E., 122
Bernstein, B. L., 371
Biblical counseling, 121–22
Biblical Counseling With African Americans (Walker), 121
bicultural competence, in Native Americans, 33, 42
bicultural Native Americans, 30, 32
bicultural stress, 69
bigendered persons, 305, 308
bilingual/bicultural mental health profession-als, 159–60
biracial identity, 16
Black Church in the African American Experience, The (Lincoln and Mamiya), 121, 122
"Black Expressiveness" phenomenon, 59
Black Family: Past, Present, and Future, The (June), 121
Black Rage (Grier and Cobbs), 143
Bock, P. K., 230
Bonilla, F., 224
Bowen, M., 130
Boyd-Franklin, N., 114–15, 117, 118
Brendtro, L. K., 33
Brief Strategic Family Therapy model, 196
Brobst, K., 381
Brokenleg, M., 33
Brown, B., 314
Bryan, W. V., 323, 336
Buddhism, 140, 158, 162
Bureau of Indian Affairs, U.S., 27
Bureau of the Census, U.S., 27, 189, 235, 332

C

California Brief Multicultural Competence Scale, 376
Campbell, S. M., 182
Caron, C., 331

Casas, J. M., 213
Cass, V. C., model of homosexual identity formation, 269, 272–87
Castillo, R. J., 191, 192
Cayleff, S. E., 362
Center for Substance Abuse Treatment, 273
Chatters, L. M., 114
chemical dependency
    in the gay male community, 271
    lesbians in recovery, 299
Chen, C., 128, 174, 176
Chicago Tribune, 69
Chicano and Chicana, use of terms, 209
Chief Joseph, 28
child-rearing practices
    Chinese American parents, 129–30
    Southeast Asian, 155
children. *See* adolescents and children
Chinese Americans, counseling strategies for, 127–28
    academic and career orientation, 132–33
    assertiveness training for Chinese Americans, 135–36
    case study, 133–35
    Chinese American cultural values and their impact, 128–31
    control over strong emotions, 130–31
    family therapy based on Chinese values, 131–33
    filial piety, 128–29
    guidelines for assertiveness training, 135–36
    personality tests and assertiveness, 134–35
    roles and status, 129–30
    somatization vs. psychologization, 130
    stress on family bonds and unity, 129
Chips, Godfrey, 42
Christian and Biblical counseling, 121–22
Christian Counseling: A Comprehensive Guide (Colins), 121
Christian Counselor's Manuel, The (Adams), 121
Chung, R. C.-Y., 154, 155, 156, 159, 163
Citizenship Act of 1924 (Native Americans), 28
Civil Liberties Act of 1988, 139
civil rights movement, 118
classism, and cross-cultural counseling, 17
Claus, R. E., 365
client mistrust, 374–75
Cobbs, P. M., 143
Code of Ethics and Standards of Practice (ACA), 360–61, 362, 363, 366

cognitive-behavioral interventions, with Southeast Asian refugees, 162
cognitive-behavioral theory, 5
colectivismo, 190
collective unconscious, among African peoples, 57
color, counseling clients of, 6
Comas-Diaz, L., 209
coming-out process, lesbian, 294
communication
    among Chinese Americans, 129
    and counseling Arab Americans, 240
    and counseling Korean Americans, 178
    and counseling Native Americans, 46–47
    Korean values and high context, 173
Competent to Counsel (Adams), 121
Condie, H., 182
conduct disorder, poverty and, 346
Coner-Edwards, A. F., 70
confianza, 212, 214
Confucianism, 129, 140, 158, 172, 173, 175, 334
Congress, E. P., 178, 180
Constantine, M. G., 214, 372, 378, 380–81, 382
Cook, D. A., 115, 120, 121, 122, 361
Corey, A. T., 376, 378
Cose, E., 65, 69, 74
Cottone, R. R., 364, 365
Counseling in African American Communities (June, Black, and Richardson), 121
Counseling Refugees: A Psychosocial Approach to Innovative Multicultural Interventions (Bemak et al.), 166
counselor knowledge, in cross-cultural zone, 15–17
counselor self-awareness, in cross-cultural zone, 15
counselor skills, in cross-cultural zone, 17
Crittenden, K., 175
Cross-Cultural Counseling Inventory-Revised, 376, 380–81
cross-cultural zone, counseling in, 13–14
    best practice framework in, 14–15
    counselor knowledge in, 15–17
    counselor self-awareness in, 15
    counselor skills in, 17
cross-dressing, 304, 306, 307–8
    counseling cross-dressing clients, 311–12
cross-racial adoptions, 251, 262
Cross, W. E., Jr., racial identity model, 68–69, 71
Crumbley, J., 262

Cuban Americans, counseling, 140, 195–96
    culturally competent practice with Hispanic families, 196–97
    Framework for Embracing Cultural Diversity, 197–204
culturagrams, 178–79, 180
cultural alienation/disconnection, and counseling African American men, 101
cultural background, of lesbian clients, ethnic and, 294
cultural conflicts, Korean American acculturation process and, 173, 175
cultural continuum, 260
cultural diversity
    Framework for Embracing Cultural Diversity, 195, 197–204
    in generic theory of multiculturalism, 5
cultural empowerment, and Southeast Asian refugees, 162–63
cultural identity
    of Arab Americans, 239
    cultural identity development and cross-cultural counseling, 15–16
    of Native Americans, 28, 33, 42
cultural mapping, 196
Cultural Mistrust Inventory, 374
cultural privilege, 16
cultural values
    African Americans, 81–82, 94–95
    Arab Americans, 236–38
    Chinese Americans, 128–31
    Korean Americans, 172–73
    Latinas and their, 189–91
    Southeast Asians cultural belief systems, 157–59
    traditional Japanese values and norms, 140–41
culturally competent counselors, emergence and need for, 7–8
culturally competent practice, with Hispanic families, 196–97
culturally responsive counseling strategies
    for African American women and girls, 82–89
    client mistrust, 374–75
    cultural and racial awareness, 370–72
    cultural knowledge tailored to the individual, 372
    cultural knowledge translated into strategies, 372–73

emergence and need for culturally responsive counselors, 7–8
implications of, 375
racial dynamics of the client and the counselor, 373–74
culture, defined, 5, 197–98

D̄

D'Andrea, M., 380
Day, J. K., 358
De Silva, P., 162
decision making, ethical, 364–66
Deegan, P.E., 321
defense mechanisms, 72
demographic considerations, in diversity, 3–5
denial, 72
dependency issues, in counseling African American men, 102
depression
in Korean immigrants, 174–75
in Southeast Asian refugee population, 156, 157
developmental tasks, completion of, African American male youth and, 96–97
Diagnostic and Statistical Manual of Mental Disorders (DSM-IV-TR), 187, 191, 291, 346
diagnostic ethnocentrism, 192
dignidad, 214
Dionysus, 306
disabilities, counseling people with, 321–22, 338–40
accommodation, adjustment, and disability identity development, 326–28
assumptions, values, and biases concerning disability, 329–30
best practices, 328–37
case study, 337–38
defining the population, 322–24
developing appropriate intervention strategies and techniques, 335–37
disability vs. handicap, 325
disabled children and adults in U.S. population, 4
history of disability, 324–25
semantics of disability, 325–26
understanding the worldview, 330–35
disability identity, 16
Disability Identity Attitude Scale, 327–28
Disability Statistics Center, 323

discrimination
against high-achieving Blacks, 65
quadripartite, 81–82
diversity, within the gay male community, 270
Dixon, D. N., 374
domestic violence, lesbians and, 299
DuBois, W. E. B., 69, 114
DuBray, W. H., 37
Dudley, R. G., Jr., 72
Duncan, D., 314
Dworkin, A. G., 322
Dworkin, R. J., 322
dyads, parallel, 373–74
Dyke-U-Drama, 295

Ē

Echevarria–Doan, Silvia, 203
ecomap, 260
Edman, J. L., 333
education
academic success of Chinese Americans, 127, 129, 132–33
educational attainment of African American male youth, 95, 96, 97
educational dynamics of poverty, 346–47
Korean American college students, 175
and Korean Americans, 173, 175–76
and Native Americans, 26, 27–28, 29, 32
and Southeast Asian refugees, 155
See also Mexican American college students
Edwards, J., 70
Effective Biblical Counseling (Crabb), 121
Elliott, T. R., 321
Ellis, Albert, 6
employment
downward occupational mobility of Korean immigrants, 175
and people with disabilities, 332
Southeast Asian refugees and lack of, 154
Employment Assistance Program, for relocated Native Americans, 28
empowerment
in counseling Latinas, 193–94
cultural empowerment and Southeast Asian refugees, 162–63
the socioeconomic divide and counseling for, 347–48, 349–52
enculturation, 32
English as a second language (ESL), 154, 371

English language skills, in refugees' adjustment process, 154, 155
English Poor Laws (1598–1601), 324
Enhancing Your Interactions With People Disabilities (American Psychological Association), 335
environmental and cultural experiences, affecting African American women females, 80
environmental stressors, negative, affecting African American male youth, 95–96, 97
Epp, L. R., 187
Erikson, E. H., 74
essentialism, 208
Eth, S., 162
ethical issues, for transgendered people, 308–9
ethical issues in multicultural counseling, 303, 357, 366
    the counseling relationship, 361–62
    ethical decision making, 364–66
    evaluation, assessment, and interpretation, 362–63
    nature of ethical guidelines, 360–61
    principle and virtue ethics, 357–60
    research and publication, 363–64
    teaching, training, and supervision, 363
ethnicity
    ethnic and cultural backgrounds of lesbian clients, 294
    ethnic identity of Arab Americans, 238–39
    ethnic identity of Mexican American college students, 209
    ethnic identity of Puerto Ricans, 225–29
    Korean Americans and ethnic attachment, 174
    Korean Americans and ethnic identity development, 173–74
    and race in U.S. population, 4
ethnomedical systems of care, 334–35
ethnotherapeutic empathy, 382
Eugene, T. M., 82
existential-humanistic theory, 5
external locus of control, 346
Exum, H. A., 75–76

F

Fabian, E. S., 329
Falicov, C. J., 196, 204
families
    African American, 58–59, 98

Arab American, 238
changing family dynamics for Southeast Asian refugees, 154–55
Chinese American, 129, 130
Cuban American, 196–97
gay men and family relationships, 272
Japanese American, 140, 141
Korean American, 172, 175
lesbians as parents, 298
Mexican American college students and family and familial roles, 210–11
Native American, 34, 37–38
Puerto Rican, 224, 225
socioeconomically disadvantaged, 346–47
See also multiracial individuals and families
familismo, 189–90, 210–11, 214
family counseling/therapy
    for Chinese Americans, 130, 131–33
    for high-achieving Blacks, 75–76
    for Southeast Asian refugees, 162
Fancher, R. T., 329
Fassinger, R. E., 293
fatalismo, 190
Fausto-Sterling, A., 307
female-to-male (FTM) transgenderists, 306, 308, 313
female-to-male (FTM) transsexuals, 308, 313
feminist and womanist identity, 16
fidelity, in principle ethics, 358
filial piety, 128–29, 172, 174
finances, Mexican American students, 211
Fine, M., 329
Fleming, C. M., 373
Ford, D. Y., 71
Fordham, S., 71
formalismo, 190
Foster, S., 363
400 Years Without a Comb (film), 88
Framework for Cultural Awareness, 195–96
Framework for Embracing Cultural Diversity, 195, 197–200
    personal journey using, 203–4
    use with students and supervisees, 200–203
Frankenberg, R., 252
Franks, R. P., 381
Free African Society, 113
Freeman, E. M., 260
Freilich, M., 326
French, S., 332
Friedman, M., 162

From Holy Power to Holy Profits (Malone), 121
Fuertes, J. N., 371, 381, 382
Fugita, S., 175
fusion, in lesbian relationships, 295–96

G

Gade, E., 32
Galanti, G. A., 333
Gallup, G., Jr., 114
Garcia-Prieto, N., 193
Gardner, H., 64
gay, lesbian, and bisexual (GLB) communities
    Mexican American college students, 212
    transracial adoptions in, 264
    See also transgendered persons
gay liberation, beginning of modern, 306
gay men, counseling, 269–70, 287
    aging, 271
    Cass's model of homosexual identity
        formation, 272–87
    chemical dependency and substance abuse,
        271
    diversity, 270
    HIV/AIDS, 270–71
    identity and family, 272
    spirituality, 272
    technology, 271
gender development, of African American
    women, 81
gender expression, transgendered persons and,
    306
gender identity. *See* transgendered persons
gender roles, in Mexican American culture,
    210
generational status, of Mexican American
    college students, 208–9
genogram, 260
Gerstenbluth, I., 333
Gibbs, J. T., 104, 258, 261
Gill, C. J., 327
Giovanni, Nikki, 87
glass ceilings, 64–65
Gloria, A. M., 214–16
Goffman, E., 332
Good Tracks, J. G., 39
Grant, S. K., 369
    Disability Attitude Scale, 327–28
    three-dimemsional model of counseling
        racial and ethnic minorities, 215–18

grief and bereavement, rituals in Southeast
    Asian refugee population, 158–59
Grier, W. H., 143
group assertiveness training, for Chinese
    Americans, 135–36
group counseling
    for African American females, 83–89
    for high-achieving Blacks, 75
    for Southeast Asian refugees, 162
    for transgendered persons, 313–14
guilt
    guilt by association threat to high-achieving
        Blacks, 67
    Korean concepts of shame and, 172
    survival guilt and high-achieving Blacks,
        70
    survivor's guilt and Southeast Asian
        refugees, 154

H

Hall, C. C. I., 255
Hallenberg, K., 141, 143
Handbook of Psychotherapy and Religious Diversity
    (Richards and Bergin), 121, 122
handicap vs. disability, 325
harmony ethic, among Native Americans, 38
Harper, D. C., 329, 333
healing methods, Western and traditional,
    Southeast Asian refugees and, 163
health. *See* mental health
Healthy People 2010 (U.S. Dept. of Health and
    Human Services), 325
Helms, J. E., 361, 373–74
help-seeking attitudes and behaviors, and
    counseling African American men, 102
hembrismo, 210
Henderson, G., 323, 336
Herlihy, B., 358
hermaphrodites, 307
Hermes, 307
Herring, R. D., 257
Hershemson, D. B., 329
Herstory: Black Female Rites of Passage (Lewis),
    87
Hirschfeld, Magnus, 304
Hispanics
    use of term, 189
    See also Cuban Americans; Latinas; Mexican
        American college students; Puerto Ricans

HIV/AIDS
    AIDS-related deaths among Latinos, 212
    in the gay community, 270–71
Ho, M. K., 130
Holcomb-McCoy, C., 371, 381
holism, among African people, 59
Holloway, E. L., 383
Holzer, H. J., 347
homophobia
    and cross-cultural counseling, 13, 17
    in multicultural counseling paradigm, 7
homosexual/gay/lesbian/bisexual identity, 16
    See also gay men; lesbian clients;
        transgendered persons
homosexual identity formation model, Cass's,
    269, 272–73
    Stage 1: Identity Confusion, 273–76
    Stage 2: Identity Comparison, 276–78
    Stage 3: Identity Tolerance, 278–81
    Stage 4: Identity Acceptance, 281–83
    Stage 5: Identity Pride, 283–85
    Stage 6: Identity Synthesis, 285–87
Hong, J., 174
hooks, b., 82, 83, 310
"Hoop Dancer" (Allen), 25
hormonal intervention, for transgendered
    persons, 312–13
How to Equip the African American Family
    (Abatso and Abatso), 121
Hsu, F. L. K., 128–29
Hulburt, G., 32
human relations, African-oriented view of, 58
Hunt, P., 119
Hurh, W. M., 174
hwa-byung, 176
hyperspadias, 307
Hyun, K. J., 174, 175

I

Ibrahim, F. A., 256, 261
identity, within the gay community, 272
identity conflicts, high-achieving Blacks and,
    67–69
identity development
    of African American women, 81
    disability, 327–28
    lesbian, 293–94
    racial identity development and high-
        achieving African Americans, 74
    See also cultural identity

illness schemas, 333
immigrant vs. refugee status, 151
immigration, Korean, 171–72
Immigration and Naturalization Law of 1965,
    171
Indian Child Welfare Act, 1978, 262
Indian Religious Crimes Code, 28
individualismo, 190
Ingstad, B., 333
Integrating Spirituality Into Treatment: Resources
    for Practitioners (Miller), 122
Integration of Psychology and Theology, The
    (Carter and Narramore), 121
integrity, in virtue ethics, 359
intermarriage, 252
Internet access, in the gale male community, 271
internment camps, Japanese, 139–40, 141, 143, 147
interracial couples
    counseling, 255–57
    defined, 251
    issues and concerns of, 252
Intersex Society of North America, 307, 311
intersexual people, 304, 305, 307, 308
    counseling intersexual clients, 311
intervention strategies
    for African Americans, 74–76, 83–85, 117–19
    for Arab Americans, 241–43
    for Japanese Americans, 143–47
    for people with disabilities, 335–37
introspection counseling process, with African
    American men, 103
Ishii-Kuntz, M., 172
Islam, 120, 121, 237–38, 241
Israel, G. I., 313
issei (first generation Japanese), 141, 142
Ivey, A. E., 42, 309
Ivey, M. B., 309

J

Jackson, Andrew, 28–29
James, A., 363
Japanese American Redress Bill, 139
Japanese Americans, counseling, 139–40
    the acculturation variable, 141–42
    internment camps, 139–40, 141, 143, 147
    intervention strategies, 143–47
    mental illness and, 372
    the presenting problem, 143
    traditional Japanese values and norms,
        140–41

Jaranson, J., 162
Jenkins, J., 335
Jennings, R. G., 71
Joan of Arc, 306
Johnson, J. A., 187
Johnson, S. D., 382–83
Jones, T., 114
Jordan, J. M., 83–85
Jumper-Thurman, P., 373
June, L. N., 113
Jung, C., 57
justice, in principle ethics, 358

K

Kagawa-Singer, M., 154, 156
Kameoka, V. A., 333, 334
Karenga, M. Ron, 89
Kemp, N. T., 321, 328, 330
Kenney, K., 261
Khoun, F., 152
Kim, K. C., 174
Kim, S., 174
King, Martin Luther, Jr., 118
Kinzie, J. D., 162
Kitano, H. H. L., 174
Kitchener, K. S., 357–58, 359
knowledge, counselor, in cross-cultural zone, 15–17
Knox, D. H., 115
Kochman, T., 74
Korean Americans, counseling, 171
    acculturation and ethnic identity, 173–74
    barriers to mental health services, 176–77
    cases study, 179–80
    counseling strategies, 177–79
    immigration history, 171–72
    mental health issues, 174–76
    traditional Korean values, 172–73
Kroeker, R., 32
Kuo-Jackson, P. Y., 376, 378
Kuo, W. H., 174
Kurpius, Gloria and Robinson, 208
Kwanzaa, celebration of, 89

L

Ladany, N., 372, 378, 380, 382
LaFromboise, T. D., 33, 363, 364, 373, 374, 380
Lame Deer, Archie Fire, 41
Lamug, C., 175

language
    English as a second language (ESL), 154, 371
    and identification of lesbian clients, 292–93
    Mexican American college students and English language fluency, 209–10
    semantics of disability, 325–26
language barriers
    and Korean immigrants, 175
    and Southeast Asian refugee population, 155, 159–60
LaPlante, M. P., 332
Larry P. v. Witness for the Defense, 362
Latinas, counseling interventions with, 187
    case studies and interventions, 188–89, 192–94
    clinical considerations, 191–92
    Latinas and their cultural values, 189–91
Latinos: A Biography of the People (Shorris), 203
Lavelle, J., 152
learned helplessness, 346
Lee, C. C., 98
Lee, E., 252
Leong, F. T. L., 173
lesbian clients, counseling, 291–92, 300
    cultural differences and the coming-out process, 294
    fusion, 295–96
    lesbian identity development, 293–94
    lesbian relationships, 294–95
    lesbians and domestic violence, 299
    lesbians as parents, 298
    lesbians in recovery, 299
    sexual abuse, 298
    sexual intimacy, 296–97
    use of language in, 292–93
    what is a lesbian?, 292
lesbian, gay, bisexual, and transgendered (LGBT) community, 4, 304, 308, 310
    See also transgendered persons
Levine, S. B., 312–13
Lewis, M. C., 87
Lewis, O., 345
Lin, C., 175
Lin, K. M., 154, 159, 163, 174
Lincoln, C. E., 113, 114, 121, 122
Lindsay, D. M., 114
Linton, S., 329–30
Liongson, L., 71
Little Soldier, L., 31
Liu, J. H., 182

Living the Spirit: A Gay American Indian Anthology (Roscoe), 306
locus of control, 346
Locust, C., 40–42
Logan, S. L., 260
Longmore, P. K., 328
"loss of face," Korean concept of, 172
Loulan, J., 298
Lovinger, R. J., 115

M

machismo, 210, 229
machista, 210
MacLeod, J., 65
male-to-female (MTF) transgenderists, 308, 313
male-to-female (MTF) transsexuals, 308, 313
Mallinckrodt, B., 321, 330
Malone, W., Jr., 114
Mamiya, L. H., 113, 114, 121, 122
managed care issues, 375
marginal Native Americans, 30, 31–32
marianismo, 191, 210, 229
marianista, 210
Marin, B. V., 190
Marin, G., 190
Marquez, Martha Gonzalez, 195–96
Martinez, R., 226, 228, 383
Masuda, M., 154
Matsumoto, D., 334
Mbiti, J. S., 118
McCarn, S. R., 293
McClain, Leanita, 69
McCormick, R. M., 363
McDavis, R. J., 196, 376, 377
McFadden, J., 253
McGoldrick, M., 142, 197
McIntosh, P., 380
McKenzie, B., 335
McRae, M. B., 382–83
McRoy, R. G., 260
McWhirter, B. T., 291
Meara, N. M., 358–59
Meggert, S. S., 363
melting-pot ideology, 227
Men to Men (June and Parker), 121
mental health
    African American church and its role in, 114–16
    of African Americans and Afrocentricity, 59

    and first-generation Japanese Americans, 141
    issues for Arab Americans, 239–43
    issues for high-achieving African Americans, 64–67
    issues for Korean Americans, 174–77
    Japanese Americans and mental illness, 372
    poverty and mental illness, 346
    of Southeast Asian refugee population, 157–58, 159
mentors, for high-achieving Blacks, 75
Mexican American college students, counseling, 207–8, 218
    acculturation and generational status, 208–9
    counseling frameworks for addressing the psychological issues of, 213–15
    ethnic identity, 209
    family and familial roles, 210–11
    finances and socioeconomic status, 211
    gender roles, 210
    language, 209–10
    possible roles of counselors, 215–18
    salient cultural considerations in, 208–13
    sexual orientation, 212
    spirituality and religion, 212–13
Meyers, J. E., 371, 381
"Middle Class Black's Burden, The" (McClain), 69
Middle East. *See* Arab Americans
Midgette, T. E., 363
migration narrative, 204
Mikulas, W., 162
Min, P. G., 174
missionaries, 28
mistrust, client, 374–75
mistrust of counselors, 239–40
Mobley, M., 381
model minority myth, 175–76
Mollica, R. F., 152
monocultural Native Americans, 33
Moore, M. A., 380
Morales, E. S., 212
Moreno, Angela, 307
Morten, G., 327
Moskowitz-Sweet, G., 258, 261
Multicultural Awareness Knowledge Skills Survey, 376
multicultural counseling, 3, 9
    changing demographics in, 3–5

defined, 5–6

new paradigm of, 6

pitfalls of, 8–9

promise of a new paradigm of, 7–8

Multicultural Counseling Awareness Scale, 376

Multicultural Counseling Awareness Scale and Training Survey, 376

multicultural counseling competence

client needs and counselor competencies, 369–83

defined, 369–70

expanded construct of counseling competencies, 376, 377

Multicultural Counseling Competence and Training Survey, 380

Multicultural Counseling Inventory, 376, 378, 379, 381

Multicultural Ecosystem Comparative Approach (MECA), 196

multicultural social desirability, 378

multicultural theory, 5

multiculturalism, generic theory of, 5

Multiethnic Placement Act, 1994, 261, 262

Multilevel Model (MLM), approach to psychotherapy with refugees, 161–65

multiracial individuals and families, counseling, 261, 264

counseling a transracial adoptee and family, 262–64

counseling interracial couples, 255–57

counseling multiracial adolescents, 258

counseling multiracial adults, 258–60

counseling multiracial children, 257

definitions, 251

issues and concerns of interracial couples, 252

issues and concerns of multiracial individuals, 253

multiracial adolescents, 254

multiracial adults, 254–55

multiracial children, 253–54

transracial adoption, 261–62

Muslims. *See* Arab Americans

─
N
─

Narikiyo, T. A., 334

National Association of Black Social Workers (NABSW), 261–62

National Biblical Counseling Association, 122

National Organization on Disability (NOD), 332

Native Americans, 23, 25–27

acculturation, 30–33, 43–44

adoption of Native American children, 262

comparison of cultural values and expectations, 31

counseling strategies and knowledge of cultural legacy of, 373

ethical counseling approaches with First Nations, 363–64

gender expression in Native American culture, 306

generosity among, 36

harmony ethic among, 38

historical context of Native and White relations, 27–30, 43

humility among, 35–36

implications for counseling, 42–49

Indian elders as "Keepers of the Wisdom," 34–35

and meaning of family, 37–38

Medicine persons, 41–42, 45

the "Medicine Way," 36, 39

Native American defined, 27

Native traditions/values, 34–40

noninterference, culture of, 38–40

patience among, 36, 40

sense of "being" among, 36

spirituality and wellness, 40–42, 45

time, observance of, 36

the tribe/nation, 34

Native Americans, counseling

communication, 46–47

counseling recommendations, 47–49

historical context, 43

identity issues, 42–43

Native American Acculturation Scale: Informal Assessment/Interview, 43–44

native values and worldview, 44–45

spiritual ways, 45

Native people, defined, 27

Neimeyer, G. J., 380

Ng, F., 174

Nguzo Saba, principles of, 89

Nigrescence, psychology of (racial identity model), 68–69, 71

nisei (second generation Japanese), 141–42

Nobles, W. W., 59, 118

nonmaleficence, in principle ethics, 358

Nydell, M., 237–38
Nystul, M. S., 364

O

O'Connor, S., 328, 333, 337
Okun, B. F., 257, 262, 264
Olkin, R., 321
oppression
    African American males and, 94
    and counseling Native people, 29
Orfalea, G., 236
Oriental Exclusion Act of 1924, 141
Ossana, S. M., 295
Oswalt, W. H., 27
out-of-country transracial adoptions, 262

P

pacing the counseling process, in counseling
    African American men, 103
Padilla, E., 225
Paniagua, F. A., 190, 335–36
pantraditional Native Americans, 30
parallel attitudes, 374
parallel dyads, 373–74
paranorm concept, 143
Parham, T. A., 72, 361
Parker, W. M., 380
Partnership for Solutions, 321
Pasteur, A. B., 59
Pastoral Care in the Black Church (Wimberly), 121
Patterson, J. B., 335
Patton, J. M., 96
perception of reality, African, 58
perceptual dissonance, 226
Perkins, Useni, 89
Perls, Fritz, 6
personalismo, 190, 214
personality tests, for Chinese Americans, 134–35
Philadelphia Negro, The (DuBois), 114
Piorkowski, G. K., 70
Pok, T., 153
political correctness, 378
Ponterotto, J. G., 378, 382
post-traumatic stress disorder
    poverty and, 346
    in Southeast Asian refugee population, 156
poverty (socioeconomic disadvantage), 5, 345–46
    educational dynamics of poverty, 346–47

psychological dynamics of poverty, 346
    social dynamics of poverty, 347
pre- and postoperative transsexuals, 308
premigration trauma, in Southeast Asian
    refugee population, 152–53, 154, 156, 157
principle and virtue ethics, 357–59
    in action, 359–60
Project: Gentlemen on the Move (GOTM),
    99–100
Project: Gentlemen on the Move Race Against
    Drugs, 100
Project: Gentlemen on the Move Summer
    Academy, 100
Promise Keepers (religious group), 93
prudence, in virtue ethics, 358
psychodynamic theory, 5
psychoeducational counseling, with African
    American men, 103
psychological anthropology, 230
psychological distress, in Southeast Asian
    refugee population, 156, 157–58
psychological issues, in counseling Mexican
    American college students, 213–15
Psychology of Counseling, The (Narramore), 121
Puerto Ricans in the counseling process, 223–24,
    229–30
    case study, 227–29
    racial/ethnic identity, 225–26
    socioeconomics, 224–25
Pynoos, R., 162

Q

quadripartite discrimination, 81–82
Quezada, T., 333

R

race and ethnicity, in U.S. population, 4
racial and ethnic minorities, three-dimensional
    model of counseling, 215–18
racial/ethnic identity, 16
    Puerto Rican, 225–29
racial identity
    African Americans and, 67–69, 72, 74
    racial identity development, 74
    racial identity model, Cross's (psychology
        of Nigrescence), 68–69, 71
    racial-religious-ethnic identification issues
        of Arab Americans, 238–39

and self-report multicultural competency, 376, 378

racial socialization, of Black females, 81

racism
and counseling African American men, 94, 101
and cross-cultural counseling, 13, 17
in multicultural counseling paradigm, 7
and nonassertiveness of Chinese Americans, 135
towards Native Americans, 29–30, 33
towards Vietnamese Amerasian refugees, 153

racism-sensitive counseling, with African American men, 103

Rage of a Privileged Class, The (Cose), 69

rapport, developing, in counseling African American men, 103

Raybeck, D., 326

reality, African perception of, 58

Red Horse, J. G., 35

Reeve, D., 321, 330

reframing
and family therapy for Chinese Americans, 132
in group counseling, 314

refugees
counseling Southeast Asian, 159–65
refugee vs. immigrant status, 151
Southeast Asian, 151–58

relationships, lesbian, 294–95

religion
of Arab Americans, 237–38
gay men of faith, 270
Korean church, 174, 177
in Mexican American life, 212–13
Native American traditions and Christianity, 28
outlawing of Native religions, 28
religious and spiritual counseling, 121–22
religious beliefs among Southeast Asian refugee groups, 158
See also African American church; spirituality

Religion and the Clinical Practice of Psychology (Shafranske), 122

religious groups, Promise Keepers, 93

Remley, T. P., 358

research in multicultural counseling, 369–70
assessment of multicultural counseling competencies, 375–83

cultural sensitivity to minority clients, 370–75

resettlement, of Southeast Asian refugees, 152–54

respectfulness, in virtue ethics, 359

respeto, 190, 214

Richards, P. S., 122

Richardson, M. F., 376, 378

Richardson, T. Q., 373–74

Rodriguez, C. E., 225, 226, 228, 229

Rodriguez, E. R., 214–15

Rogers, Carl, 6

role models
African American male youth and lack of, 97
for high-achieving Blacks, 75

Roosevelt, Franklin D., 139

Root, M. P. P., 254–55, 259–60

Rotter, J. B., 346

Ruiz, R. A., 213

S̄

Sanchez, Sonia, 87

Sanderman, R., 333

Sanders, Bradley and Lipford, 94

sansei (third generation Japanese), 141, 142

Sarbin, T. R., 346

Savishinsky, J., 326

schema theory, 333

Schmidt, L. D., 358

Schreurs, K. M. G., 296

Schroeder, D. G., 256

self-awareness, counselor, in cross-cultural zone, 15

self-disclosure, counselor, in counseling African American men, 103

self-esteem
African American men and, 102
Chinese Americans and low, 127
learned helplessness and low, 346
and multiracial adults, 255

Seligman, M. E. P., 346

sex, sexuality, and gender, concepts of, 304–5

sexism
and cross-cultural counseling, 13, 17
in multicultural counseling paradigm, 7

sexual abuse, lesbian, 298

sexual identity development, 269

sexual intimacy, in lesbian relationships, 296–97

sexual orientation
    defined, 273
    of Mexican American college students, 212
    in U.S. population, 4
    See also gay men; lesbian clients;
      transgendered persons
shame and guilt, Korean concepts of, 172, 173, 178
Shin, K. R., 174–75
Shorris, E., 203
silence
    and Japanese internment experience, 143
    Korean values and importance of, 173, 178
simpatia, 190, 214
sister-friend counseling intervention, 83–85
situational assertiveness, 135
skills, counselor, in cross-cultural zone, 17
slavery, cultural contraints of, African
    Americans and, 80, 94, 113
Smith, A., 113, 115
Smith, E. M. J., 70
social constructivism, ethical decision-making
    and, 364–65
social dynamics, of poverty, 347
socialization, of Black children, 81
socioeconomic disadvantage, the culture of, 345,
    352
    characteristics of the culture of poverty,
      345–47
    counseling across the socioeconomic divide,
      347–52
socioeconomic status (SES)
    lower SES African Americans, 63
    of Mexican American college students, 211
    of Puerto Ricans, 224–25
Sodowsky, G. R., 372, 376, 378, 382
Solomon, B. B., 120
Solsberry, P. W., 252
Soo-Hoo, T., 131–32
Southeast Asian descent, counseling Americans
    of, 151–52, 165–66
    barriers to mainstream mental health
      services and use of traditional methods,
      159
    case study, 163–65
    counseling refugees, 159–65
    cultural belief systems, 157–59
    psychological distress, 156–57
    psychosocial adjustment and adaptation,
      152–55

Spiritual Strategy for Counseling and Psychotherapy,
    A (Richards and Bergin), 122
spirituality
    in African American life, 58, 59, 82, 93, 103
    in the gay community, 272
    in Mexican American life, 212–13
    Native American, 28, 40–42, 45
    religious and spiritual counseling, 121–22
    See also African American church; religion
Standards of Care for Gender Identity Disorders,
    The (Levine et al.), 312–13
Steele, C. M., 67
stereotypes
    concept of stereotype threat, 67
    cultural, 372
    "mammy" stereotype, 80
Sternberg, R. J., 64
stigma
    defined, 310
    Goffman's concept of, 332
    and people with disabilities, 332–33
Stolley, K. S., 251
Stonewall Rebellion of July 17, 1969, 306
stress
    acculturative, 153
    bicultural, 69
    Chinese Americans and stress on family
      bonds and unity, 129
    Korean Americans and family stresses, 175,
      176
    negative environmental stressors and
      African American male youth,
      95–96, 97
    post-traumatic stress disorder, 156, 346
    social sources of stress on African
      Americans, 67–71
Structural Ecosystem Theory, 196
substance abuse
    in the gay male community, 271
    lesbians in recovery, 299
    poverty and, 346
Sue, D., 52, 362, 363
Sue, D. W., 52, 196, 327, 362, 363, 376, 377
Sue, S., 132–33
surgical intervention, for transgendered
    persons, 312–13
survival guilt/survivor's guilt
    high-achieving Blacks, 70
    Southeast Asian refugees, 154

Switzer, D. K., 116
Szapocznik, J., 196

T

Tan, J. A., 381
Taoism, 158
Tarver, D. E., 313
Tarvydas, V. M., 364
Tayabas, T., 153
Taylor, R. L., 114
Tazuma, L., 154
Terrel, F., 374
Thompson, C. E., 215–18, 369, 374
Thornton, M. C., 114
three-dimensional model of counseling racial
    and ethnic minorities, 215–18
time
    African concept of, 58
    Native American observance of, 36
Timm, J., 162
Tipton, Billy, 306
"To America With Skills" (article), 127
Toldson, I. L., 59
traditional Native Americans, 30–31
training, multicultural competency, 369–83
Transgender Care: Recommended Guidelines,
    Practical Information, and Personal Accounts
    (Israel and Tarver), 313
transgendered persons, affirmative counseling
    with, 303, 310–11, 314
    barriers to effective counseling, 309–10
    counseling clients seeking hormonal
        and/or surgical intervention, 312–13
    counseling cross-dressing clients, 311–12
    counseling intersexual clients, 311
    ethical issues, 308–9
    group counseling, 313–14
    intersexual people, 307
    people who cross-dress, 307–8
    sex, sexuality, and gender, 304–6
    transgender constituency, 307–8
    transgenderists and transsexuals, 308
transgenderists, 306, 308
translators and interpreters, using trained,
    160
transracial adoption
    counseling a transracial adoptee and
        family, 262–64

defined, 251
    issues of, 261–62
transsexuals, 308
transvestites, 304
trauma, premigration, in Southeast Asian
    refugee population, 152–53, 154, 156
triadic therapy, 312
Triandis, H. C., 190
Trimble, J. E., 373
Turner, C. W., 83
Tyiska, C. G., 331

U

United Nations High Commissioner for
    Refugees, 156
Uswatte, G., 321

V

Van Bockern, S., 33
van den Heuvel, W. J. A., 333
Vandiver, B. J., 69
Vash, C. L., 327, 331
Vasquez, E. G., 381
Vasquez, L. A., 381
Vasquez, M. J., 192, 193
veracity, in principle ethics, 358
Vietnamese. *See* Southeast Asian descent
violence
    lesbians and domestic violence, 299
    people with disabilities as crime victims,
        331
virtue ethics, 358–59
    in action, 359–60
Voluntary Relocation Program, Native
    American, 28
Vontress, C. E., 187
vortex of psychological Nigrescence, 68

W

Wade, P., 371
Wardle, F., 253, 254
Watkins, C. E., 374
Wehrly, B., 257
White Racial Identity Attitudes Scale, 379
Whyte, S. R., 333
Wiley, C. Y., 115, 120, 121

Williams, D. T., 329
Williams, R. A., 196
Wilson, W., 346
Wimberly, Edward, 121
within-group conflict, high-achieving Blacks, 71
women
    Arab American, 238
    Korean American, 174–75
    Mexican American females, 210, 211
    multiracial, 255
    Southeast Asian, 156–57
    See also African American women and girls;
      Latinas
Women to Women (N. Carter and Parker), 121

World Health Organization, 163
World War II, 139–40
Worthington, R. L., 374, 381
Wright, B. A., 327

Y

Yalom, I. D., 72
Yang, D., 128

Z

Zane, N. W. S., 132–33
Zea, M. C., 333
Zogby, John, 235